.50

MICROPROCESS
& MICROCOMPUTERS
MICROPROCESSORS
& MICROCOMPUTERS

SELECTED REPRINTS ON
MICROPROCESSORS
& MICROCOMPUTERS

Selected reprints from COMPUTER and IEEE MICRO

(3rd Edition)

Edited by J . T. Cain

IEEE COMPUTER SOCIETY

1884 · 1984

INSTITUTE OF ELECTRICAL AND ELECTRONICS ENGINEERS

IEEE Catalog Number EHO214-7
Library of Congress Number 84-80986
IEEE Computer Society Order Number 585
ISBN 0-8186-0585-5

Published by IEEE Computer Society Press
1109 Spring Street
Suite 300
Silver Spring, MD 20910

IEEE Catalog Number EH0214-7
Library of Congress Number 84-80986
IEEE Computer Society Order Number 585
ISBN 0-8186-0585-5 (Paper)
ISBN 0-8186-4585-7 (Microfiche)

Order from: IEEE Computer Society   IEEE Service Center
Post Office Box 80452   445 Hoes Lane
Worldway Postal Center   Piscataway, NJ 08854
Los Angeles, CA 90080

 The Institute of Electrical and Electronics Engineers, Inc.

Introduction

We are now into the second decade of the "microprocessor revolution," a revolution that shows no sign of abatement. The technological developments that created and have fueled this revolution continue at the same frenetic pace. From the introduction of the first microprocessor in 1971 to today there has been a threefold increase in microprocessor performance together with a correspondingly significant decrease in price. Similar price-performance improvements have occurred in the memory and other peripheral chip areas.

This document is a collection of papers from two Computer Society publications, *COMPUTER* and *IEEE MICRO*. The papers in the collection have been selected to provide an overview of fundamentals and a snapshot of the status of this revolution.

The first section contains two papers that provide an historical perspective of the field as measured by microprocessor developments at Intel Corporation from late 1971 through late 1980. Even the casual observer or neophite is aware that other corporations have provided parallel technological developments that have also significantly impacted developments in this field. However, these two articles put into perspective all developments in the field.

The second section, 16- or 32-Bit Microprocessors, consists of a set of papers that describe the architectures and design constraints of a representative sample of current 16- and 32-bit microprocessors. These include Motorola's 68000 family, Intel's 8086, Zilog's Z8000 family, TI's 9900 family, and National's 16000 family. Also included are several papers that present the results of comparative performance studies conducted on subsets of these processors. Only the 8086, Z8000, MC68000, 16032, Bellmac 32, HP 32-bit processor, and iAPX 432 are compared, but the papers illustrate some of the parameters and techniques that can form the basis for any comparison.

In the past several years, several novel microprocessor architectures have been proposed and are now in various stages of development and evaluation. The five papers in this next section present some of these novel architectures and some of the evaluative studies. Projects such as these may have a significant impact on future microprocessor developments.

Even after tremendous increases in device densities, no single-chip microprocessor has been produced that implements a floating-point arithmetic unit as an integral portion of the chip circuitry. The approach taken has been to design and implement floating-point arithmetic units as part of arithmetic coprocessors and/or peripheral processors. The first paper in the section on Peripheral Processors describes a Motorola-designed chip that will function as a closely coupled coprocessor to the MC68020 and as a peripheral processor to the other members of the 68000 family. Microcomputer architecture has followed the historic developmental trends of the mainframes and minis in the I/O subsystem area. Intelligent I/O processors implemented as separate chips are now available for many of the latest microprocessors. The second paper in this section discusses the 8089 I/O processor designed by Intel.

There is a plethora of microprocessors available on the market, each with unique pinouts and signal definitions. There is also a natural desire on the part of system designers to shorten design time and facilitate incremental system expansion utilizing multivendor subsystems. This, in part, has led to efforts to define standard bus structures. The three papers in this section on Bus Structures address some of the general issues and problems in this area. The first paper also presents an excellent overview of the various levels of bus structures.

Software has become the most costly aspect of microprocessor- or microcomputer-based systems. The papers included in this section present a small sample of the issues in this area. The first article presents a methodology for selecting a programming language, compiler, and real-time support environment. This methodology is contrasted to the unfortunately common practice in which a language, etc., is chosen in a hasty, unscientific manner. The second article presents a systematic technique for microcomputer system software development. The development of applicable software standards is one hope to reduce the cost of software development. The last two papers are draft standards that give an indication of some of the standard efforts to increase portability and utility.

The real effect of the "microprocessor revolution" is in the area of applications. The small size and low cost of the initial microprocessors opened up a vast array of new applications. As the computational power and available memory capacity have increased, so has the range of applications. Society will be impacted by the relatively cheap processing power of home and personal computers. The productivity of professionals will be significantly impacted by present and future "workstations." Microprocessors imbedded in systems/products, however, will have a more pervasive, yet subtler impact. As an example, automobiles in the late 1980s will have multiple onboard processors utilizing close to 100k bytes of program. The four articles in the Applications section present a small sample of this range of imbedded applications.

The "microprocessor revolution" will continue into the foreseeable future. After reading the papers in this collection, you will gain an appreciation of the field and establish a foundation for future work and study.

J.T. Cain
University of Pittsburgh

Table of Contents

MICROPROCESSORS & MICROCOMPUTERS

MICROPROCESSORS & MICROCOMPUTERS

SELECTED REPRINTS ON MICROPROCESSORS & MICROCOMPUTERS

SECTION 1
HISTORICAL PERSPECTIVES

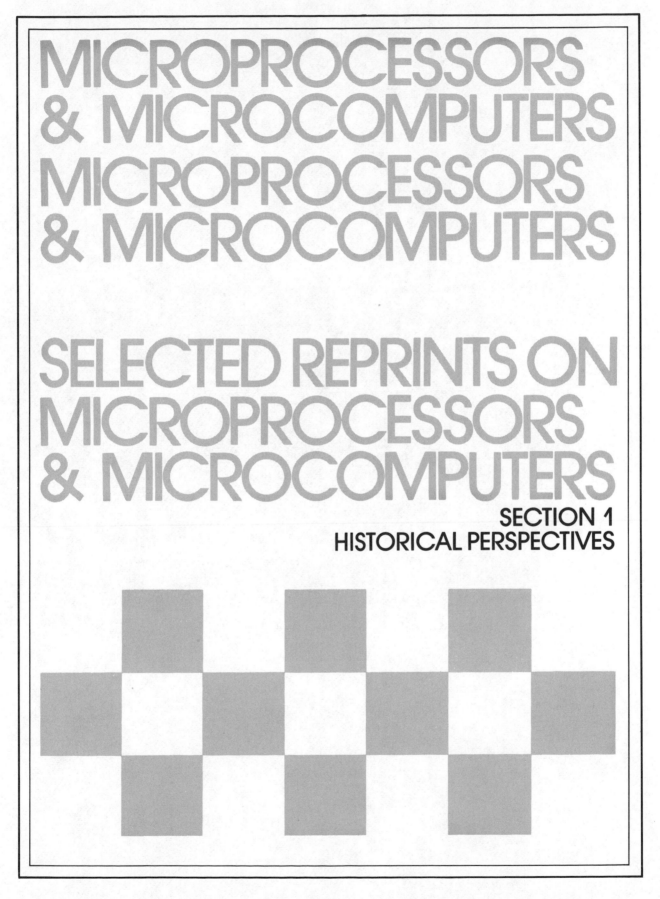

In its first decade, the "computer on a chip" has achieved power, applicability,

and pervasiveness unimagined even by its developers.

A History of Microprocessor Development at Intel

Robert N. Noyce and Marcian E. Hoff, Jr.

Intel Corporation

Few advertisements have proved to be as prophetic as one that appeared in the November 15, 1971, issue of *Electronic News*. It was placed by Intel Corporation, at that time a three-year-old manufacturer of MOS and bipolar RAMs with annual sales of $9 million and about 500 employees. The ad announced nothing less than "a new era of integrated electronics," a phrase suggested by Gordon Moore, cofounder and now chairman of Intel. Available from Intel, according to the ad, was a "micro-programmable computer on a chip" composed of an "integrated CPU complete with a four-bit parallel adder, 16 four-bit registers, an accumulator and a push-down stack on one chip." This 4004 CPU joined with ROM, RAM, and shift register chips to make up the MCS-4 microcomputer system. Also noted in the ad was another interesting new invention, the 1701 "erasable and re-programmable ROM," for customers "who require rapid turn-around or need only a few systems."

The ad's claim of a new era has stood up remarkably well. By 1979, manufacturers were selling 75 million of those "micro-programmable computers on a chip" annually, according to an estimate by Dataquest, a California market research firm.[1] (The term "microprocessor," first came into use at Intel in 1972.)

The microprocessor has indeed brought electronics into a new era. In 10 years the device has made a far deeper penetration into society than mainframes did in their first 20 years. Moreover, it has caused components manufacturers, OEMs, and end users to rethink the role of the computer. What was once a giant machine attended by specialists in a room of its own is now a tiny device, conveniently transparent to users of automobiles, games, instruments, office equipment, and a large array of other products. As *Fortune* magazine noted in 1975,[2] the microprocessor is one of those rare innovations that simultaneously cuts manufacturing costs and adds to the value and capabilities of the product. As a result, the microprocessor has invaded a host of existing products and has created new products, such as electronic games and home computers, that were never before possible.

The impact of the microprocessor, however, goes far deeper than new and improved products. It is altering the structure of our society by changing how we gather and use information, how we communicate with one another, and how and where we work. The changes are just beginning and it will take decades to assess fully the microprocessor's impact on society. It is certain, though, that a world with hundreds of millions of computers will be different from the world we have known.

A necessary invention

If we look back on the electronics industry environment that preceded the microprocessor revolution, we can see that the microprocessor was a very necessary invention—and that its rapid acceptance was in many ways predetermined.

By the late 1960's, the semiconductor industry was becoming aware of a serious design problem. The complexity of random logic designs was increasing steadily. If this continued, the number of circuits needed would proliferate beyond the available supply of circuit designers. At the same time, the relative usage of each circuit would fall. IC cost effectiveness would suffer; increased design cost and diminished usage would prevent manufacturers from amortizing costs over a large user population and would cut off the advantages of the learning curve.

Computer-aided design was seen as one solution, and large investments were made to automate IC design and testing. Another possible solution was the use of discretionary wiring or master slice approaches, in which a basic circuit module is combined with a final custom layer of interconnects to produce a variety of designs.

Viewed from today's vantage point, many developments were leading to the microprocessor. (At the time preceding the development of LSI computers, the term "microprocessor" was used to refer to the processor of a microprogrammed computer. Today the term refers to an LSI single-chip processor and is so used throughout this article.) A number of LSI chip sets capable of significant computation had already been produced or were in design. For example, development programs sponsored by the US military services were leading toward LSI com-

3

puters. General Microelectronics had been pioneering in LSI for calculators, but by the late sixties the technology was not ready. Several manufacturers, such as Viatron and Four-Phase Systems, were working on intelligent terminal chip sets. Most of these approaches, however, were for multichip sets, and most of the developers were aiming those chip sets at particular system problems, not at general logic replacement.

Electronics, then, was at a turning point. Intel was a fertile environment for an innovation as bold as the microprocessor. The small company was technology-driven, and it had no stake in random logic markets.

From calculator to computer

The genesis of the microprocessor was sparked by an assignment from Busicom, a now defunct Japanese manufacturer of calculators. In the summer of 1969, Busicom asked Intel to produce a chip set for a planned family of high-performance, programmable calculators. The 12 chips specified by Busicom were intended to realize designs for printing and display models, among others. ROM chips would be used to customize the basic design for the various models.

By that time the use of MOS circuitry in calculator designs was well established. The calculators in pro-

duction typically required half a dozen chips, each chip having 600 to 1000 MOS transistors. Intel believed its recently developed silicon gate technology could achieve reasonable yields at a complexity of perhaps 2000 transistors per chip. This confidence led the company to examine Busicom's needs with an eye toward a more aggressive design solution.

Marcian E. "Ted" Hoff, Jr., a young engineer from Stanford who had joined Intel in 1968 as the twelfth employee of the fledgling company, was assigned to the Busicom project because of his systems and application experience. He looked at the design being developed by a team of Busicom designers, who had come to Intel from Japan, and concluded it was too complex to be cost effective. It required 3000-5000 transistors per chip and packages with 36 to 40 leads—package types not then in use at Intel. Hoff identified three major sources of complexity in the Busicom design:

(1) Most of the control logic for peripherals such as the keyboard, displays, and printers was done by separate structures.
(2) The shift register memory required fairly complex timing.
(3) The elemental instructions were quite intricate. Many corresponded to one or more passes through a register, involving alteration of both mantissa

The first advertisement for a microprocessor ran in *Electronic News,* **November 15; 1971. The ad's bold announcement of "a new era of integrated electronics" has proved very accurate.**

and exponents of a floating-point number. Even though some of the logic had been implemented by ROM, a major portion was still done by random logic circuits.

Hoff had been working with a Digital Equipment Corporation PDP-8 and was struck by the contrast between that machine's lean architecture and the complexity of the Busicom design. The PDP-8 had a primitive instruction set but could perform highly complex control and arithmetic functions because of its fairly large program memory. Intel had begun making some significant headway in delivering relatively dense, low-cost MOS memories; Hoff reasoned it would be cost effective to reduce random logic in the Busicom design by raising memory requirements.

Reducing complexity of the elemental instructions could also make the resultant processor a more general-purpose machine. In the calculator, a program stored in ROM could utilize sequences of more general instructions not only for arithmetic, but for keyboard scan and debounce, display maintenance, and other functions as well. With this flexibility, Hoff thought, a more general-purpose processor might find applications quite apart from calculators.

He proposed that Intel begin a program to define such a processor. Intel's executive staff endorsed the idea enthusiastically and the effort began. Meanwhile, Busicom's design team from Japan continued work at Intel on the original approach to the calculator family. The team was convinced it could reduce the number of transistors by redesigning some of the control logic.

The calculator design specifications provided the starting point for the Intel team's search for a simpler processor. A four-bit data quantity seemed natural for BCD arithmetic. With four-bit binary and separate instructions to convert the result back to BCD, addressing of up to 16 digit positions could be retained. Members of the calculator family would vary both in function and the number of registers required. To meet this need for flexibility, the Intel team decided on a three-chip design: a CPU, a ROM for program memory, and a RAM for data memory. (A simple shift register chip for output expansion was added later.) The number of ROM and RAM chips would vary with different calculator models.

Other decisions included use of a three-step approach to execute each instruction, a parallel, four-bit-wide, bi-directional data bus, and multiplexing via an eight-step, fixed-length instruction cycle and a 12-bit instruction address space.

The use of RAM for data memory offered higher density than the shift registers of the original design and also simplified timing logic. Addressing the RAM, however, presented a problem. The eight-step cycle did not leave

When work on the first microprocessor was under way at Intel in 1970, the company had fewer than 200 employees. Intel had already acquired a reputation for innovation in memories with the introduction of the 3101 64-bit bipolar RAM, the 1101 256-bit MOS RAM, and the 1103 1K MOS RAM. Intel was also developing the first EPROM at the time this photo was taken.

Masatoshi Shima, designer of the Intel 8080 and the Zilog Z80 and Z8000. Shima now heads Intel's design center in Japan.

enough time to transmit an address, read the memory content, and return or write a data value. The problem was solved by separating RAM address transmission from RAM read/write operations.

Tests of the proposed processor's architecture indicated the machine would meet the needs of the planned calculator family. The next critical hurdle was to determine if the design could be manufactured cost effectively. Les Vadasz, head of Intel's MOS design team, provided valuable assistance to Hoff and Stan Mazor, who had joined Hoff's project and had contributed several architectural improvements to the processor design. The team produced an initial estimate of 1900 transistors, a number that justified continuing with the design. (In final form, the 4004 CPU had about 2300 transistors.) Meanwhile, the Busicom team had simplified the original design, but it still required 12 chips, averaging over 2000 transistors each, and still required 36 to 40-pin packages.

In late fall 1969, Busicom's executives came to Intel to make their decision. They chose the Intel design for its simplicity and range of applications. Then the work of taking the design from the architectural concept to finished silicon was begun. Because of Intel's small design staff and active development programs in memory products, however, little progress was made until Federico Faggin joined Intel in the spring of 1970.

Faggin (later founder and president of Zilog) came to Intel from Fairchild, where he had worked in process development. He quickly grasped the concept of the new processor and began optimizing it for MOS implementation. He worked closely with the Busicom engineering team that was developing the programs for the first

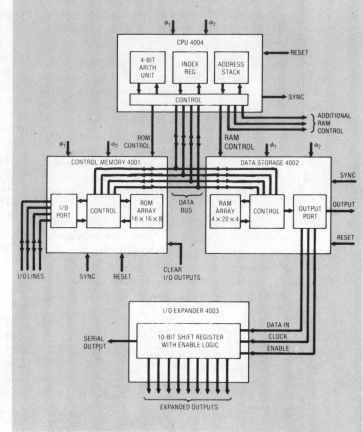

MCS-4 interconnections.

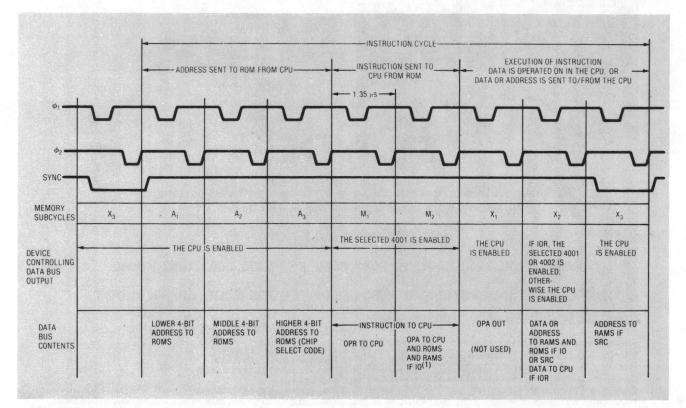

MCS-4 instruction cycle.

calculator. One member of that team was Masatoshi Shima, a young engineer who would later go on to be the lead designer of the Intel 8080 and, during a four-year stint with Zilog, the Z80 and Z8000. With these credits, it seems fair to say Shima probably has been the most influential microprocessor designer. He now heads Intel's design center in Japan.

Faggin worked at a furious pace and in only nine months produced working samples of the four chips that would become the MCS-4.

When completed, the new chip set could be sold only to Busicom due to contractual restrictions. But by the summer of 1971, the calculator business had become more competitive, and Busicom asked Intel to reduce prices for the calculator components. Through negotiation, Intel gained the right to sell the chip set to other customers for non-calculator applications.

There was debate, though, as to whether Intel should exercise its new option. Some members of the board of directors were not certain the company should venture into the systems business. In the end, the view of Arthur Rock, chairman of the board, prevailed and the board endorsed the venture.

The marketing department was also concerned. First, it felt the potential market for the MCS-4 was at best a 10 percent slice of the minicomputer market. Since that market totaled only 20,000 units per year at the time, the marketing department could see little reason to proceed. That objection was overcome when Ed Gelbach, now a senior vice-president of Intel, joined the company from Texas Instruments as marketing director. He realized the microcomputer's potential was not as a replacement for minicomputers but as a way to insert intelligence into many products for the first time.

A second and very legitimate marketing concern was that Intel could offer little in software and development tools to support this entirely new class of product. It was nearly impossible to get computer programmers to consider joining a semiconductor company, especially to work on such a contemptible little toy as the microprocessor. That was the era of large computers and many programmers felt they would lose prestige if they worked on anything less than a mainframe. Intel would be able to provide some assistance to major customers, but had to warn many others they would have to develop their own design aids. Some customers fortunately realized that if the MCS-4 were considered a replacement for complex random logic in high-volume applications, the design effort might be no greater than for the logic replaced.

The quandary over whether to announce the MCS-4 continued through the summer and early fall of 1971. Intel's management group ultimately decided to proceed and the first advertisement appeared in mid-November. There was considerable interest in the product at that year's Fall Joint Computer Conference in Las Vegas, and by February 1972 Intel had sold a modest but promising $85,000 worth of MCS-4 chip sets.

The microprocessor happened at Intel because of a confluence of good people, support from a management group comfortable with technological experimentation, and, not to be forgotten, the concurrent invention of the EPROM by Dov Frohman. By giving designers a flexible,

nonvolatile memory, the EPROM made the microprocessor practical and far easier to use. Frohman is now head of Intel's design center in Israel.

Into the eight-bit dimension

While Intel was working on the MCS-4, a parallel development project was under way; it would lead to the introduction of the first eight-bit microprocessor, the 8008.

Computer Terminals Corporation (now Datapoint) contacted Intel in late 1969, shortly after the 4004 instruction set had been defined. CTC wanted Intel to develop LSI for the registers of a new intelligent terminal, the Datapoint 2200. Mazor and Hoff of Intel felt it would be possible to put the complete processor on a chip and proposed this idea to CTC. An eight-bit processor was defined and the chip design was assigned to Hal Feeney. In the meantime, CTC took the specifications to Texas Instruments, which developed a 212 × 224-mil eight-bit chip for the 2200 terminal. The chip was demonstrated to CTC in March 1971. Gary Boone of TI later received a patent for this architecture, but the TI device was never incorporated into the 2200; CTC brought its terminal to market with TTL and shift register memory.

Although the work for CTC had ended, Feeney continued on the 8008 project with the assistance of Mazor and Hoff. Several enhancements were made to the instruction set, particularly improved loop control via increment register commands.

The 8008 was introduced in April 1972 as an eight-bit parallel CPU with 45 instructions oriented toward character string handling. It had a 30-μs average instruction execution time and offered six eight-bit general-purpose registers. It was packaged in an 18-pin DIP and was executed in silicon gate PMOS technology. Requiring a minimum of 20 TTL packages for memory and I/O interface, the 8008 could address 16K bytes of memory.

Missionary work

In 1972, a customer base began developing as venturesome OEMs realized the potential of the 4004 and 8008 for logic replacement. Still, there was widespread skepticism in the industry about the promise of the microprocessor. Many saw it as too slow and limited to be of much use. Others couldn't envision the breadth of potential applications waiting to absorb the millions of computers per year possible through LSI.

To spread the word about the microcomputer, Intel began an ambitious program of seminars, customer training, and promotion. The company was seeking to replace hard-wired logic rather than computer systems. Hardware circuit designers thus had to become convinced it was worthwhile to switch to software-based solutions and had to become comfortable working with this less familiar tool. Intel's customer training program, a rudimentary list of courses in 1973, has since grown to become a broad-based international operation. The com-

7

pany's Insite User's Program Library, begun in 1972, now numbers several hundred titles.

An increasing number of orders and letters of inquiry from electronics professionals around the world gave evidence that Intel was beginning to succeed in its efforts to draw attention to the microprocessor. One letter, for example, came in late 1972 from a Dutch engineer who had been isolated for the previous year teaching mathematics in rural Kenya. In just 12 months, he noted with some amazement, the microprocessor had changed electronics unalterably.

Early design aids and software

In 1972, Intel moved quickly to begin offering design aids to assist customers in product development. The first were the SIM4-01 and SIM4-02 prototyping boards introduced in May 1972. They incorporated a 4004 CPU, two-phase clock generator, test and reset generators, an interface for ASR-33 teletypewriters, and PROM and RAM sockets. The 4-01 had four PROM and RAM sockets while the 4-02 had 16 each.

Intel introduced its first software product in June 1972, an assembler and simulator written in Fortran IV on punched cards or paper tape for use on mainframes and minis. It was available by license but was offered free to customers whose annual orders exceeded $20,000.

Also in 1972, the company brought out assembler PROMs for the 4004 and 8008 and the SIM8-01 prototyping boards for the 8008. The Intellec 4 and Intellec 8 Development Systems were offered in 1973, complete with cross assemblers and simulators. The Intellec 8 also had a cross compiler.

These tools had a strong lever effect on Intel's business. They generated revenue on their own, helped sell microprocessor components, and stimulated sales of memory devices needed in microcomputers. It would be some time before component sales exceeded the revenues generated by these early design aids.

PL/M, a macroassembler language based on IBM's PL/1, was introduced by Intel in 1973. It was originally offered in cross-compiler form but in 1974 became resident in the Intellec Development System. For the first time, microprocessor designers could do modular software design through generation of linkable, relocatable object code modules, producing more reliable, better-documented code in significantly less time than with assembly language.

ISIS and ICE modules were two more important developments, both introduced in 1975. ISIS—Intel Systems Implementation Supervisor—incorporated modular programming resources such as a macroassembler, linker, locater, Library Manager software, and text editor. ICE (in-circuit emulation) units replaced needed simulators with cross compilers and enabled designers to debug hardware and software concurrently.

The software and development tools introduced in the first five years after the microprocessor's invention made possible an order-of-magnitude increase in programmer productivity. While the rapid advance in processor architecture tends to get more attention, it is obvious that without corresponding progress in design aids, the microprocessor would be much less pervasive than it is today.

The proliferation of devices

From 1972 to 1976 many manufacturers introduced microprocessor components, boards, and systems in an effort to gain a niche in the rapidly developing market. As of July 1974, 19 microprocessors were either available or announced, according to Microcomputer Techniques' "Microprocessor Scorecard."[3] One year later, the number had grown to 40, and by 1976 it had risen to 54.

Shortly after the introduction of the 4004 microprocessor, Intel began offering design aids to help customers develop 4004-based products. Shown here, the MCB 410 connector board with the SIM4-01 prototyping board and the MP7-02 PROM programming board mounted.

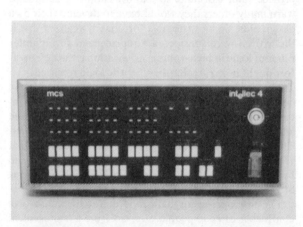

In 1973 Intel introduced the Intellec 4 Development System, a programming package including cross assemblers and simulators.

Intel had the market to itself until late 1972. Then Rockwell entered with its PPS-4, a four-bit parallel processor executed in PMOS. It offered a 50-instruction set and an instruction cycle time of five μs. Clock speed was 200 kHz.

Fairchild, National, Signetics, Toshiba, and AMI were among the companies that introduced processors in 1973 and 1974. Devices ranged from calculator-oriented four-bit processors to National's IMP-16, a five-chip, bit-slice 16-bit CPU, and RCA's 1802, the first CMOS processor, introduced in 1974. It was clearly a time of wide-ranging experimentation in architectures, processes, and packaging. Teledyne Systems, for example, brought out its TDY-52A microcomputer in a unique package: instead of DIPs on PC boards, Teledyne mounted the Intel 4004 and other IC dice on a ceramic substrate, cutting system size significantly. The result was a complete microcomputer in a two-by-two-inch package.

Texas Instruments introduced its TMS-1000 four-bit PMOS processor line in 1974. Over the years TI has become the leading manufacturer of four-bit processors, used by the millions in games, toys, and other low-end controller applications.

Micro minis

A breakthrough of sorts occurred in March 1974 when Digital Equipment Corporation announced it would offer MPS, a series of microprocessor modules built around the Intel 8008. Such recognition from the leading manufacturer of minicomputers was to some extent a coming of age for the microprocessor.

But DEC was not the first minicomputer manufacturer to offer a microprocessor-based board. General Automation introduced its LSI-16 microcomputer in December 1973. It was a functional equivalent of the company's SPC-16, but at half the cost. Using custom silicon-on-sapphire chips, it produced speeds comparable to conventional bipolar minis.

The second generation

With the introduction of the Intel 8080 in April 1974, microprocessors took a major step forward. The 8080 was the first device with the speed and power to make the microprocessor an important tool for the designer. It quickly became accepted as the standard eight-bit machine and was widely second-sourced.

The 8080 emerged from Intel's experience with its first-generation 4004 and 8008. However trend-setting they had been, they had definite shortcomings. The 8008, for example, had only a rudimentary interrupt and did not have adequate facilities for status saving upon interrupt. It required too many external TTL circuits and it was not much faster than the 4004.

Federico Faggin proposed development of a new and upgraded eight-bit processor that would be executed in the high-performance, N-channel process Intel was developing. It was at this time that Intel began its policy of upward compatibility, an idea that has been integral to the company's operations ever since. The instruction set for the 8080, worked out by Faggin, Mazor, and Hoff, incorporated the 8008 instruction set while also correcting the earlier processor's limitations. (As noted previously, Masatoshi Shima directed the design of the 8080.)

With a two-μs instruction cycle and 30 more instructions, the 8080 offered a tenfold increase in throughput over the 8008. It could directly address 64K bytes of memory versus the 8008's 16K. The stack had been removed from the chip and put into memory. Restrictions on subroutine nesting were thus removed and stack operations were expanded to include status and register saving. Input and output ports were increased from eight and 24, respectively, in the 8008, to 256 each in the 8080. Able to execute decimal and BCD arithmetic, the 8080 offered better operand addressing, better interrupt processing, and a 16-bit address bus. Only six peripheral ICs were needed, versus the 8008's 20. The 8080 was executed in only 5000 transistors, a highly efficient design. Package size moved up to a 40-pin DIP from the 18-pin 8008.

The 8080 was the first Intel microprocessor announced before it was actually available. The 8080 represented such an improvement over existing designs that the company wanted to give customers adequate lead time to design the part into new products.

The rapid acceptance of and high demand for the 8080 spawned two eight-bit competitors, the Motorola 6800 and the Zilog Z80. The 6800, introduced in mid-1974, was the first +5-volt single-power-supply microprocessor. Elimination of the need for multiple power supplies lowered product cost and made the 6800 a popular processor. Motorola also introduced a development system and four peripheral chips mated to the 6800.

Motorola's systems-oriented approach influenced the industry; henceforth CPUs would be introduced with full support available rather than on a trailing schedule. Peripheral processors replaced the significant amount of TTL necessary with first-generation microprocessors and gave designers useful building blocks to execute functions such as CRT and floppy disk control. Over the past six years, Intel and other manufacturers have introduced a broad range of peripherals to support CPUs.

Zilog's Z80, unveiled in 1976, reflected improvements in architectures made in the two years since the 8080's introduction. Also designed by Shima, one of its important features was that it incorporated the 8080's instruction set and OP codes within its 158 instructions. Thus, the Z80 was entirely compatible with the numerous programs that had been written by that time for the 8080.

The Zilog Z80 offered definite performance enhancements over early eight-bit processors, as did the Intel 8085, designed by Roger Swanson, Peter Stoll, and Andrew Volk. Introduced in 1976, the 8085 was a single-power-supply +5-volt device that required fewer peripherals than the 8080 and offered features such as vectored interrupts and a serial I/O port.

Another eight-bit advance was the arrival late in the decade of processors such as Texas Instruments' 9980, Intel's 8088 (iAPX 88), and Motorola's 6809. These devices offered eight-bit external buses but processed data internally in 16 bit words. This approach permits full compatibility with eight-bit hardware, while also providing faster processing and a smooth transition to 16-bit processors if program complexity warrants it.

With the emergence of the 8080, 6800, and Z80, N-channel MOS became the dominant mode for general-purpose microprocessors. Bipolar offered speed, CMOS offered low power, but NMOS offered density and enough speed to make it the preferred technology for general-purpose applications.

The use of the 8080 in personal computers and small business computers was initiated in 1975 by MITS's Altair microcomputer. A kit selling for $395 enabled many individuals to have computers in their own homes. This movement was greatly assisted by the availability of a capable operating system, CP/M, written by Gary Kildall of Digital Research. For a cost of $70, not only a disk operating system, but an assembler, a dynamic debugger, and an editor were provided. The bus structure used in the Altair became widely adopted and known as the S-100 bus. Recently, this bus has been augmented, extended to 16 bits, and standardized by a working group of the IEEE Computer Society; it will be known as the IEEE 696 bus.

The microcontroller arrives

As early as 1971, Gary Boone and Michael Cochran of Texas Instruments had demonstrated the feasibility of putting all the essential circuitry of a microcomputer on a single chip. They received a patent in 1978. This work evolved into the TMS-1000 family of four-bit microcomputer chips. The Fairchild F8 eight-bit two-chip microcomputer provided an early minimum chip device for many applications and was followed by the highly successful 3870 introduced by Mostek.

The first eight-bit single-chip microcomputer was Intel's 8048, introduced in 1976. It was made possible by the progress in device density that enabled the company to put a CPU, I/O, RAM, and ROM on one die. This migration of peripherals onto one chip produced a highly versatile device that could be designed easily into a whole new range of products from automobiles to appliances to games. Also introduced was the 8748, identical to the 8048 except that it had an on-board EPROM for easy program revision by the user. Motorola, Rockwell, and others soon followed with their own devices and many manufacturers second-sourced the 8048.

The microprocessor tree branched again in 1979 with the introduction of the Intel 2920 Analog Signal Processor. Developed by Ted Hoff and Matt Townsend, the 2920 performs real-time digital processing of analog signals. Its special instruction set for signal processing and its 25-bit ALU enable implementation of very complex subsystems. Digital circuitry includes an EPROM for program storage, a RAM scratch pad, clock and timing circuitry, a binary scaler, and the ALU. Analog circuitry consists of four analog inputs, input and output multiplexing, input sample-and-hold, A/D and D/A converters, eight analog outputs, and buffered output sample-and-holds. In short, it provides fully integrated, high-speed digital processing in analog environments.

The move to board level

Intel's SIM4-01 design aid, introduced in 1972, qualifies as the first board-level microcomputer. Multiboard, packaged microcomputers were also available quite early from Micral, Pro-Log, and other manufacturers. Digital Equipment Corporation's LSI-11 series gave OEMs full compatibility with the vast amount of software already generated for the company's PDP-11 microcomputers. Data General countered with its Micronova and General Automation with its GA-16/110. All were designed to reach the smaller OEMs seeking a

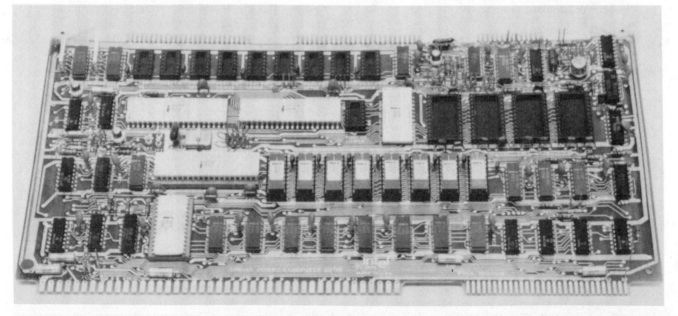

The first product in Intel's single-board computer line was the iSBC 80/10, introduced in February 1976. The 8080-based board included one KB of static RAM, four KB of ROM or EPROM, and 48 I/O lines.

10

premounted, fully debugged microcomputer that needed few special features.

Intel entered the market in February 1976 with its low-priced ($295) 80/10 Single Board Computer. It offered programmable parallel and serial I/O to permit users to shift easily from one application to another. Based on the 8080, it included one kilobyte of static RAM, four kilobytes of ROM or EPROM, and 48 I/O lines. Later that year, Intel brought out a more powerful version, the 80/20, and introduced the Multibus system architecture. Up to 16 80/20s could be linked by this new approach. The 80/20 also offered eight-level programmable interrupt control, additional peripheral controllers to offload the CPU, and twice as much RAM as the 80/10. The Multibus has been extended to 16-bit processors and is currently undergoing standardization as the IEEE 796 bus.

Rising demand

Component shortages began occurring in early 1974 as the number of products designed with microprocessors started escalating rapidly. The 1974-75 recession slowed demand, but this downturn proved to be merely a minor interruption in the growth curve.

The microprocessor was becoming ubiquitous. It had taken minicomputers seven years to exceed the mainframe population; it took only three years for microprocessors to exceed the population of both mainframes and minicomputers. The market grew from a standing start to $37.7 million in 1974. Meanwhile, performance was escalating rapidly and prices were being driven down by the expanding market and learning-curve process. In his 1977 *Microcomputer Handbook,*[4] Charles J. Sippl mentioned that one OEM was asking when price/performance would settle down. From our 1981 perspective, we can provide only an interim answer: "Not yet."

The 16-bit era

In 1975 the industry's R&D labs were at work on the next generation of microprocessors. These high-performance, 16-bit machines (and the eight-bit machines discussed already) would offer significant improvements on the second-generation eight-bit processors introduced in 1974, just as that generation had made major strides over the first microprocessors.

The first 16-bit, single-chip microprocessor was introduced as early as 1974, when National Semiconductor offered its Pace unit, a one-chip version of the IMP-16, a bit slice processor dating to 1973. Pace was a P-channel machine with a 10-μs instruction time, packaged in a 40-pin DIP. National followed with Super-Pace, a 16-bit bipolar processor that was considerably faster than the original Pace unit. Other early entrants in the 16-bit race were Texas Instruments' first 9900 machine and General Instruments' CP1600.

In 1978 Intel introduced its high-performance, 16-bit MOS processor, the 8086 (now called the iAPX 86). The 8086 was designed by Stephen Morse, Bruce Ravenel, James McKevitt, and John Bayliss, all working under William Pohlman. The processor they produced offered power, speed, and features far beyond the second-generation machines of the mid-70's. Throughput increased an order of magnitude over the 8080, memory space was 16 times greater (one megabyte versus 64 bytes), and the number of I/O ports grew from 256 each in the 8080 to 64K each in the 8086. Other features included efficient high-level language addressing, interruptible string manipulation, and full decimal arthimetic—all executed in 29K transistors on a die only 27 percent larger than the 8080.

The speed and density of the 8086 were made possible through the application of HMOS, a technology developed by Intel's Dick Pashley in 1977. The tighter geometries of HMOS circuits yield smaller dice, lower power requirements, and faster processing times.

The 8086 was followed by Motorola's 68000, Zilog's Z8000, National's 16000 series, and other 16-bit processors.

The industry today

Worldwide MOS microprocessor shipments totaled 75 million units in 1979, up 193 percent over the previous year. From 1975 through 1979, microprocessor sales grew at an average annual compounded rate of 188 percent. Microprocessors are being designed into a steadily lengthening list of products and the scenario of electronic pervasiveness laid out by Patrick Haggerty of Texas Instruments in 1964[5] is well on its way to becoming reality. While microelectronics was still in its infancy, Haggerty predicted that electronic techniques would continue to displace other modes of control and would reach into nearly all aspects of our lives. The industry's ability to deliver steadily greater functionality at ever lower costs has brought about the displacement Haggerty foresaw.

The effect on some industries has been very significant. Two especially good examples, discussed in a 1979 *Business Week* special report,[6] are instrumentation and the toy/game market. Microprocessors have made possible a new generation of intelligent, friendly instruments with capabilities unavailable 10 years ago. Analytical instrument sales, for instance, are growing at an 18 percent annual rate, and sales of field servicing equipment are expected to expand from $27 million in 1978 to $250 million in 1982. The microprocessor has made instruments more accurate, more reliable, and easier to use. Self-diagnostic instruments are on the market now and self-repairing units are a distinct possibility for the future.

In terms of unit volume, electronic games and toys are the single largest market for microprocessors. Fully half the games sold in the United States are electronic, and researchers at Arthur D. Little[7] expect the market to increase sixfold by 1987. It is fair to say the microprocessor has completely transformed what was until recently a mature and rather predictable industry.

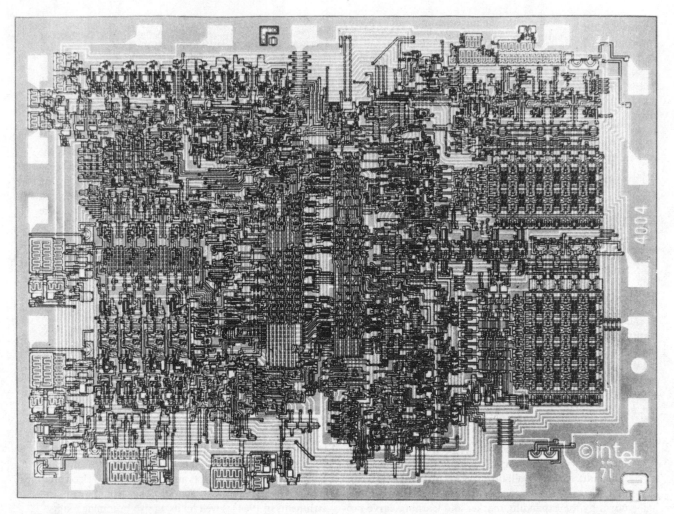

Intel's 4004, the first microprocessor, was introduced in November 1971. Chip design integrated 2300 transistors. The 4004 had a four-bit parallel adder, 16 four-bit registers, an accumulator, and a push-down stack, and it was executed in silicon gate P-channel technology.

The developing impasse. The VLSI age is here and with it comes both the opportunity for further improvements in technology and the challenge of dealing with two fundamental problems. First, manufacturers must make some rapid progress in improving the productivity of their product development programs. The complexity of new device designs is driving the cost of these programs into untenable ranges. The 4004 microprocessor was designed by one man in nine months. Intel's new iAPX 432, by contrast, has required 100 man-years of engineering time. To date, Intel has spent over $100 million to design its next generation of processors.

Progress is being made in developing computer-aided design techniques that can help contain costs by making each designer more effective. Much more will have to be done. Failure to achieve such advances will impede the rate of technological progress, dissuade the start-up ventures that have made the industry vital, and drive undercapitalized companies toward steadily smaller market shares.

The second problem is the much-publicized software "crunch" faced by designers of microprocessor-based products. The quantity and complexity of applications are growing rapidly; the human resources needed to develop these applications are not. Unless this impasse is resolved, microelectronics will see its growth limited by the supply of available programmers. The solution to this problem is to use the power of microtechnology to enable programmers to do more by doing less. The industry has successfully integrated simple hardware functionality into silicon; now we must do the same at the system level. Intel is approaching this task in two ways: first by introducing coprocessors for more efficient handling of routines such as I/O and arithmetic, and then by integrating operating systems and high-level language functionality into hardware. The goal is a tenfold reduction in the amount of code that must be written for complex applications.

Beginning the fourth generation. In 1975 Intel established its Special Systems Operation in a corner of a building in Santa Clara, California. Others at Intel were designing the company's high-performance 16-bit processor, the 8086, for a 1978 introduction. SSO's goal was

By 1978, microprocessor chip complexity had increased an order of magnitude over the first four-bit processors. Intel's 8086 16-bit processor, shown here, integrates 29,000 transistors, over 12 times as many as the original Intel 4004.

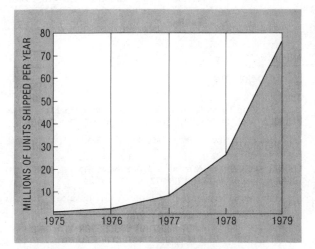

Estimated worldwide microprocessor shipments.
(Source: Dataquest, Inc.)

longer range: a microsystem with the power of a mainframe computer.

Establishment of the SSO reflected management's view that there were limits to the usefulness of the architectures the industry was then pursuing. It would be necessary to rethink those architectures in order to develop the powerful—and different—processors that would be needed in the 1980's. With that in mind, SSO set to work. It was necessarily a secret operation and Intel soon found Silicon Valley was not a good place to keep a secret. So in 1977 SSO migrated to Oregon to continue its work.

The company is currently introducing the result of that project, the 32-bit iAPX 432, which can be characterized as the first of the fourth-generation microprocessors. Its 32-bit architecture is oriented toward efficient development and execution of applications requiring complex parallel interaction of software subsystems.

The iAPX 432, integrating about 200,000 transistors, has a 16-megabyte physical address space and a virtual ad-

Table.
Trend-setting microprocessors.

NAME	MANUFACTURER	DISTINCTION
4004	INTEL	THE FIRST MICROPROCESSOR (1971)
8008	INTEL	FIRST EIGHT-BIT MICROPROCESSOR (1972)
8080	INTEL	FIRST N-CHANNEL, SECOND GENERATION EIGHT-BIT MICROPROCESSOR (1974)
6800	MOTOROLA	FIRST +5-VOLT-ONLY MICROPROCESSOR (1974)
TMS 1000	TEXAS INSTRUMENTS	LARGEST SELLING FOUR-BIT MICROCONTROLLER (1974)
PACE	NATIONAL SEMICONDUCTOR	FIRST 16-BIT SINGLE-CHIP MICROPROCESSOR (1974)
1802	RCA	FIRST CMOS MICROPROCESSOR (1974)
8048	INTEL	FIRST EIGHT-BIT, SINGLE-CHIP MICROCOMPUTER (1976)
8088	INTEL	FIRST EIGHT-BIT PROCESSOR WITH 16-BIT INTERNAL ARCHITECTURE (1979)
2920	INTEL	FIRST ANALOG SIGNAL PROCESSOR (1979)
iAPX 432	INTEL	FIRST 32-BIT MICROPROCESSOR

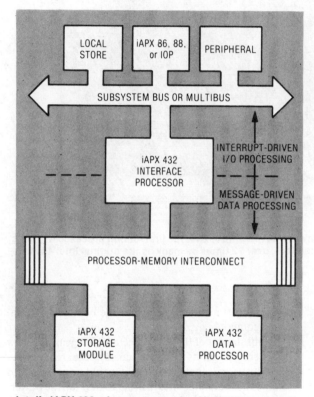

Intel's iAPX 432 microsystem, using VLSI technology, integrates high-level language and operating system functionality into silicon.

dress space of one trillion bytes. It executes two million instructions per second when multiple processors are used, a rate comparable to an IBM 370/158. Components are a two-chip CPU (instruction decode and execution units) and I/O processor for subsystem interface.

The object-oriented architecture of the iAPX 432 permits programmers to treat stacks and other data structures as entities. As a result, unnecessary hardware details are hidden and productivity can be increased. The silicon operating system is built into the processor's high-level language instruction set.

The iAPX 432 will be useful in on-line critical resource management and control systems, such as data bases, networks, and switching systems. Typically, these are large-scale software applications requiring the ability to adapt to a wide range of operating factors, such as system load, lifetime application growth, on-line system updating, and fault conditions.

This new microsystem was created by a multidisciplinary team of hardware and software architects directed by William Lattin and, in the latter stages of the project, Jean-Claude Cornet.

We have evolved in one decade from the simplicity of the 4004 to the complexity of the iAPX 432. The progress has been enormous and the pace of innovation shows no sign of slowing. It seems likely, then, that we can look forward to a second decade every bit as exciting as the first. ■

Acknowledgment

The authors wish to acknowledge the assistance of James Jarrett, who organized the material and located many of the relevant historical articles and documents.

References

1. Daniel L. Klesken and Lane Mason, "MOS Microprocessor Shipments," *Dataquest Research Newsletter,* Feb. 29, 1980, p. 1.

2. G. Bylinsky, "Here Comes the Second Computer Revolution," *Fortune,* Vol. 92, No. 5,Nov. 1975, p. 135.

3. Edward A. Torrero, "Focus on Microprocessors," *Electronic Design,* Vol. 22, No. 18, Sept. 1, 1974, p. 57.

4. Charles J. Sippl, *Microcomputer Handbook,* Petrocelli/Charter, New York, 1977, p. 158.

5. Patrick Haggerty, "Integrated Electronics, a Perspective," *Proc. IEEE,* Vol. 52, No. 12, Dec. 1964, pp. 1400-1405.

6. "The Microprocessor: A Revolution for Growth," *Business Week,* No. 2577, Mar. 19, 1979, pp. 42B-42X.

7. Ibid., p. 42J.

Bibliography

"CPU Chip Turns Terminal into Stand-Alone Machine," *Electronics,* Vol. 44, No. 12, June 7, 1971, pp. 36-37.

"The Digital Age," *Electronics,* Vol. 53, No. 9, Apr. 17, 1980, pp. 373-414.

"Microcomputers Aim at a Huge New Market," *Business Week,* No. 2279, May 12, 1973, pp. 180-182.

"Microcomputers Throw the Industry Off Balance," *Business Week,* No. 2322, Mar. 16, 1974, pp. 56-57.

"Microsystem 80 Advance Information," Intel Corporation, 1980.

Morse, Stephen P., Bruce W. Ravenel, Stanley Mazor, and William B. Pohlman, "Intel Microprocessors—8008 to 8086," *Computer,* Vol. 13, No. 10, Oct. 1980, pp. 42-60.

Noyce, Robert N., "The Microprocessor Revolution," speech to Dataquest Semiconductor Industry Seminar, Oct. 22, 1975.

Sippl, Charles J., *Microcomputer Handbook,* Petrocelli/Charter, New York, 1977.

Streitmatter, Gene A., and Vito Fiore, *Microprocessors: Theory and Applications,* Reston Publishing Co., Reston, Va., 1979.

Torrero, Edward A., "Focus on Microprocessors," *Electronic Design,* Vol. 22, No. 18, Sept. 1, 1974, pp. 52-68.

Welty, John, "The Pervasive Microprocessor," speech to Dataquest Semiconductor Industry Seminar, Oct. 13, 1976.

Robert N. Noyce is cofounder and vice-chairman of the board of directors of Intel Corporation, Santa Clara, California. He previously served as president and chairman of the company. He was also co-founder of Fairchild Semiconductor Corporation in 1957 and was vice-president of Fairchild Camera and Instrument Company in 1968 when he left to start Intel.

Co-inventor of the integrated circuit, Noyce has received numerous awards for his contributions to electronics and holds 16 patents for semiconductor devices, methods, and structures.

Noyce received a BA (Phi Beta Kappa) from Grinnell College in 1949 and a PhD in physical electronics from Massachusetts Institute of Technology in 1953. He is a Fellow of the IEEE, a member of the National Academy of Science, the National Academy of Engineering, and the American Academy of Arts and Sciences. In 1978 he received the IEEE Medal of Honor and, in 1979, the National Medal of Science and the I.E.E. Faraday Medal.

Marcian E. Hoff, Jr., is manager of applications research at Intel Corporation, which he joined in 1968. He has worked on memory circuits, MOS and bipolar microcomputer architectures, microcomputer support software, circuit modeling programs, and techniques for redundancy and very large scale integration. Since 1974 he has been active in Intel's telecommunications product development.

Hoff received the BEE degree from Rensselaer Polytechnic Institute in 1958, and the MS and PhD degrees from Stanford University in 1959 and 1962. He remained at Stanford for six years as a research associate, working on adaptive systems.

The inventor or co-inventor on 10 US patents, Hoff is a member of the IEEE, Eta Kappa Nu, Tau Beta Pi, and Sigma Xi. He is also a recipient of the IEEE's Cledo Brunetti Award and the Franklin Institute's Stuart Ballantine Medal.

15

*A mere six years of microprocessor evolution have yielded a
three-orders-of-magnitude performance improvement.*

Intel Microprocessors — 8008 to 8086

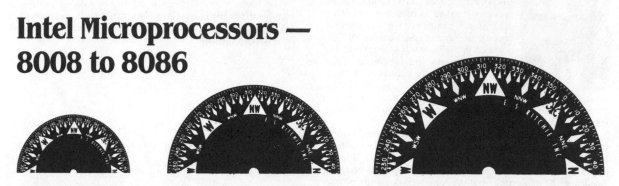

Stephen P. Morse, * **Bruce W. Ravenel,** * **Stanley Mazor, and William B. Pohlman**
Intel Corporation

Intel introduced its first microprocessor in November 1971 with the advertisement, "Announcing a New Era in Integrated Electronics." The fulfillment of this prophecy has already occurred with the delivery of the 8008 in 1972, the 8080 in 1974, the 8085 in 1976, and the 8086 in 1978. During this time, throughput has improved one-hundred-fold, the price of a CPU chip has declined from $300 to $3, and microcomputers have revolutionized design concepts in countless applications. They are now entering our homes and cars.

Each successive product implementation depended on fabrication innovations, improved architecture, better circuit design, and more sophisticated software, and throughout this development, upward compatibility not envisioned by the first designers was maintained. Here, we will try to provide an insight into the evolutionary process that transformed the 8008 into the 8086 and give descriptions of the various processors, emphasizing the 8086.

Historical setting. In the late 1960's it became clear that the practical use of LSI circuits depended on defining chips having

- a high gate-to-pin ratio,
- a regular cell structure, and
- a large standard part market.

In 1968, Intel Corporation was founded to exploit the semiconductor memory market, which uniquely fulfilled these criteria. Early semiconductor RAMs, ROMs, and shift registers were welcomed wherever small memories were needed, especially in calculators and CRT terminals.

In 1969, Intel engineers began to study ways of integrating and partitioning the control logic functions of these systems into LSI chips.

At this time, other companies (notably Texas Instruments) were exploring ways to reduce the time needed to develop custom integrated circuits. Computer-aided design of custom ICs was a hot issue then. Custom ICs are making a comeback today, this time, in the high-volume applications that typify the low end of the microprocessor market.

An alternate approach was to think of a customer's application as a computer system requiring a control program, I/O monitoring, and arithmetic routines, rather than as a collection of special-purpose logic chips. Drawing on its strength in memory, Intel partitioned systems into RAM, ROM, and single controller chips, i.e., CPUs.

Intel embarked on the design of two customer-sponsored microprocessors—the 4004 for a calculator and the 8008 for a CRT terminal. The 4004 replaced what otherwise would have been six customized chips usable by only one customer. Because the first microcomputer applications were known and easy to understand, instruction sets and architectures were defined in a matter of weeks. As programmable computers, their uses could be extended indefinitely.

Both microprocessors were complete CPUs on a chip and had similar characteristics. But because the 4004 was designed for serial BCD arithmetic and the 8008 for 8-bit character handling, their instruction sets differed.

The succeeding years saw the evolution that eventually led to the 8086. Table 1 summarizes the progression of features that took place during these years.

*Currently with Language Resources, Sunnyvale, California.

16

EHO214-7/84/0000/0016$01.00©1980 IEEE

The 8008

Late in 1969, Computer Terminal Corporation (today called Datapoint) contracted Intel to do a pushdown stack chip for a processor to be used in a CRT terminal. Datapoint had intended to build a bit-serial processor in TTL logic, using shift register memory. Intel counterproposed that the entire processor be implemented on one chip. This processor was to become the 8008 and, along with the 4004, was to be fabricated using PMOS, the then-current memory fabrication technology. Due to the long lead time required by Intel, Datapoint proceeded to market the serial processor, and thus compatibility constraints were imposed on the 8008.

Most of the instruction set and register organization were specified by Datapoint. Intel modified the instruction set so the processor would fit on one chip and added instructions to make it more general-purpose. For although Intel was developing the 8008 for a specific customer, they wanted to have the option of selling it to others. And since Intel was using only 16- and 18-pin packages in those days, they chose to use 18 pins for the 8008 rather than design a new package for what was believed to be a low-volume chip.

8008 instruction set processor. The 8008 processor architecture is quite simple compared to that of today's microprocessors. The data handling facilities provide for byte data only. The memory space is limited to 16K bytes, and the stack is on the chip and limited to a depth of eight. The instruction set is small but symmetrical, with only a few operand addressing modes available. An interrupt mechanism is provided, but there is no way to disable interrupts.

Memory and I/O structure. The 8008 addressable memory space consists of 16K bytes. That seemed like a lot back in 1970 when memories were expensive and LSI devices were slow. It was inconceivable in those days that anybody would want to put more than 16K of this precious resource on anything as slow as a microprocessor.

The memory size limitation was imposed by the lack of available pins. Addresses are sent out in two consecutive clock cycles over an 8-bit address bus. Two control signals, which would have been on dedicated pins if such were available, are sent out with every address instead, thereby limiting addresses to 14 bits.

The 8008 supports eight 8-bit input ports and 24 8-bit output ports. Each port is directly addressable by the in-

Table 1.
Feature comparison—Intel microprocessors, 1972-1978.

	8008	8080	8085	8086
INTRODUCTION DATE	1972	1974	1976	1978
NUMBER OF INSTRUCTIONS	66	111	113	133
NUMBER OF FLAGS	4	5	5	9
MAXIMUM MEMORY SIZE	16K BYTES	64K BYTES	64K BYTES	1M BYTES
I/O PORTS	8 INPUT 24 OUTPUT	256 INPUT 256 OUTPUT	256 INPUT 256 OUTPUT	64K INPUT 64K OUTPUT
NUMBER OF PINS	16	40	40	40
ADDRESS BUS WIDTH	8*	16	16	20*
DATA BUS WIDTH	8*	8	8	16*
DATA TYPES	8-BIT UNSIGNED	8-BIT UNSIGNED 16-BIT UNSIGNED (LIMITED) PACKED BCD (LIMITED)	8-BIT UNSIGNED 16-BIT UNSIGNED (LIMITED) PACKED BCD (LIMITED)	8-BIT UNSIGNED 8-BIT SIGNED 16-BIT UNSIGNED 16-BIT SIGNED PACKED BCD UNPACKED BCD
ADDRESSING MODES	REGISTER IMMEDIATE**	MEMORY DIRECT (LIMITED) MEMORY INDIRECT (LIMITED) REGISTER IMMEDIATE**	MEMORY DIRECT (LIMITED) MEMORY INDIRECT (LIMITED) REGISTER IMMEDIATE**	MEMORY DIRECT MEMORY INDIRECT REGISTER IMMEDIATE INDEXING

*ADDRESS AND DATA BUS MULTIPLEXED.
**MEMORY CAN BE ADDRESSED AS A SPECIAL CASE BY USING REGISTER M.

17

struction set. The chip's designers felt that output ports were more important than input ports because input ports can always be multiplexed by external hardware under control of additional output ports.

One of the interesting things about that era was that, for the first time, users were given access to the memory bus and could define their own memory structure; they were not confined to what the vendors offered, as they had been with minicomputers. The user had the option, for example, of putting I/O ports inside the memory address space instead of in a separate I/O space.

Register structure. The 8008 processor contains two register files and four 1-bit flags. The register files are the scratchpad and the address stack.

Scratchpad. The scratchpad file contains an 8-bit accumulator called A and six additional 8-bit registers called B, C, D, E, H, and L. All arithmetic operations use the accumulator as one of the operands and store the result back in the accumulator. All seven registers can be used interchangeably for on-chip temporary storage.

There is one pseudoregister, M, which can be used interchangeably with the scratchpad registers. M is, in ef-

---

Saving and restoring flags in the 8008

Interrupt routines must leave all processor flags and registers unaltered so as not to contaminate the processing that was interrupted. This is most simply done by having the interrupt routine save all flags and registers on entry and restore them prior to exiting. The 8008, unlike its successors, has no instruction for directly saving or restoring flags. Thus, 8008 interrupt routines that alter flags (practically every routine does) must conditionally test each flag to obtain its value and must then save that value. Since there are no instructions for directly setting or clearing flags, the flag values must be restored by executing code that will put the flags in the saved state.

The 8008 flags can be restored very efficiently if they are saved in a byte in memory in the following format:

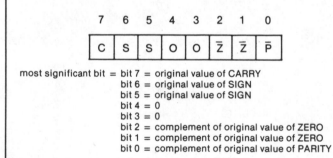

```
      7   6   5   4   3   2   1   0
    ┌───┬───┬───┬───┬───┬───┬───┬───┐
    │ C │ S │ S │ O │ O │ Z̄ │ Z̄ │ P̄ │
    └───┴───┴───┴───┴───┴───┴───┴───┘
```

most significant bit = bit 7 = original value of CARRY
                       bit 6 = original value of SIGN
                       bit 5 = original value of SIGN
                       bit 4 = 0
                       bit 3 = 0
                       bit 2 = complement of original value of ZERO
                       bit 1 = complement of original value of ZERO
                       bit 0 = complement of original value of PARITY

With the formatted information saved in a byte called FLAGS, the following two instructions will restore all the saved flag values:

```
LDA FLAGS    ; load saved flags into accumulator
ADD A        ; add the accumulator to itself
```

This instruction sequence loads the saved flags into the accumulator and then doubles the value, thereby moving each bit one position to the left. This causes each flag to be set to its original value for the following reasons:

- The original value of the CARRY flag, in the leftmost bit, will be moved out of the accumulator and wind up in the CARRY flag.
- The original value of the SIGN flag, in bit 6, will wind up in bit 7 and will become the sign of the result. The new value of the SIGN flag will reflect this sign.
- The complement of the original value of the PARITY flag will wind up in bit 1, and it alone will determine the parity of the result (all other bits in the result are paired up and have no

net effect on parity). The new setting of the PARITY flag will be the complement of this bit (flag denotes even parity) and therefore will take on the original value of the PARITY flag.

- Whenever the ZERO flag is 1, the SIGN flag must be 0 (zero is a positive 2's-complement number) and the PARITY flag must be 1 (zero has even parity). Thus, an original ZERO flag value of 1 will cause all bits of FLAGS, with the possible exception of bit 7, to be 0. After the execution of the ADD instruction, all bits of the result will be 0 and the new value of the ZERO flag will therefore be 1.
- An original ZERO flag value of 0 will cause two bits in FLAGS to be 1 and will wind up in the result as well. The new value of the ZERO flag will therefore be 0.

The above algorithm relies on consistent flag values; i.e., the SIGN flag cannot be a 1 when the ZERO flag is a 1. This is always true in the 8008, since the flags come up in a consistent state whenever the processor is reset and since flags can be modified only by instructions which always leave the flags in a consistent state. The 8080 and its derivatives allow the programmer to arbitrarily modify the flags by popping a value of his choice off the stack and into the flags. Thus, the above algorithm will not work on those processors.

A code sequence for saving the flags in the required format is as follows:

```
    MVI  A,0      ; move zero in accumulator
    JNC  L1       ; jump if CARRY not set
    ORA  80H      ; OR accumulator with 80H hex
                    (set bit 7)
L1: JZ   L3       ; jump if ZERO set (and SIGN
                    not set and PARITY set)
    ORA  06H      ; OR accumulator with 03 hex
                    (set bits 1 and 2)
    JM   L2       ; jump if negative (SIGN set)
    ORA  60H      ; OR accumulator with 60 hex
                    (set bits 5 and 6)
L2: JPE  L3       ; jump if parity even (PARITY set)
    ORA  01H      ; OR accumulator with 01 hex
                    (set bit 0)
L3: STA  FLAGS    ; store accumulator in FLAGS
```

---

fect, that particular byte in memory whose address is currently contained in H and L (L contains the eight low-order bits of the address and H contains the six high-order bits). Thus, M is a byte in memory and not a register; although instructions address M as if it were a register, accesses to M actually involve memory references. The M register is the only mechanism by which data in memory can be accessed.

Address stack. The address stack contains a 3-bit stack pointer and eight 14-bit address registers providing storage for eight addresses. The programmer cannot directly access these registers; instead, he manipulates them with control-transfer instructions.

Any one of the eight address registers in the address stack can serve as the program counter; the current program counter is specified by the stack pointer. The other seven address registers permit storage for nesting of subroutines up to seven levels deep. The execution of a call instruction causes the next address register to become the current program counter, and the return instruction causes the address register that last served as the program counter to again become the program counter. The stack will wrap around if subroutines are nested more than seven levels deep.

Flags. The four flags in the 8008 are CARRY, ZERO, SIGN, and PARITY. They reflect the status of the latest arithmetic or logical operation. Any flag can be used to alter program flow through the use of the conditional jump, call, or return instructions. There is no direct mechanism for saving or restoring flags, which places a severe burden on interrupt processing (see box at left for details).

The CARRY flag indicates if a carry-out or borrow-in was generated, thereby providing a multiple-precision binary arithmetic capability.

The ZERO flag indicates whether or not the result is zero. This provides the ability to compare two values for equality.

The SIGN flag reflects the setting of the leftmost bit of the result. The presence of this flag creates the illusion that the 8008 is able to handle signed numbers. However, there is no facility for detecting signed overflow on additions and subtractions. Furthermore, comparing signed numbers by subtracting them and then testing the SIGN flag will not give the correct result if the subtraction resulted in signed overflow. This oversight was not corrected until the 8086.

The PARITY flag indicates whether the result is of even or odd parity. This permits testing for transmission errors, an obviously useful function for a CRT terminal.

Instruction set. The 8008 instructions are designed for moving or modifying 8-bit operands. Operands are contained in the instruction itself (immediate operand), in a scratchpad register (register operand), or in the M register (memory operand). Since the M registers can be used interchangeably with the scratchpad registers, there are only two distinct operand addressing modes—immediate and register. Typical instruction formats for these modes are shown in Figure 1.

The instruction set consists of scratchpad-register instructions, accumulator-specific instructions, transfer-of-control instructions, input/output instructions, and processor-control instructions.

The scratchpad-register instructions modify the contents of the M register or any scratchpad register. This can

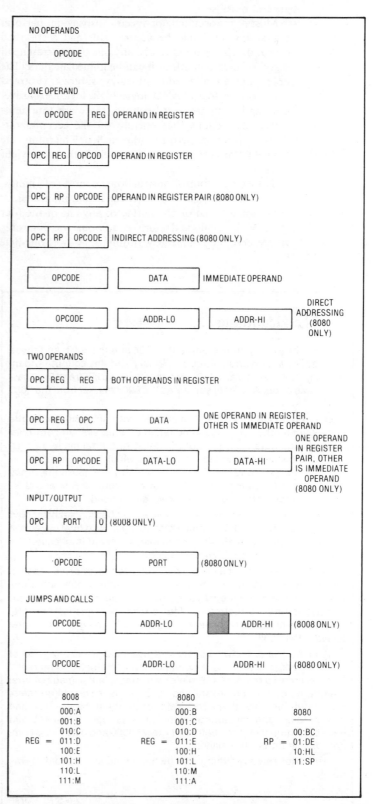

Figure 1. Typical 8008 and 8080 instruction formats.

19

involve moving data between any two registers, moving immediate data into a register, or incrementing or decrementing the contents of a register. The incrementing and decrementing instructions were not in Datapoint's specified instruction set; they were added by Intel to provide for loop control, thereby making the processor more general-purpose.

Most of the accumulator-specific instructions perform operations involving the accumulator and a specified operand. The operand can be any one of the scratchpad registers, including M, or it can be immediate data. The operations are add, add-with-carry, subtract, subtract-with-borrow, logical AND, logical OR, logical exclusive-OR, and compare. Furthermore, there are four unit-rotate instructions that operate on the accumulator. These instructions perform either an 8- or 9-bit rotate (the CARRY flag acts as a ninth bit) in either the left or right direction.

Transfer-of-control instructions consist of jumps, calls, and returns. Any transfer can be unconditional, or conditional based on the setting of any one of the four flags. Making calls and returns conditional was done only to preserve the symmetry with jumps. A short one-byte

form of call—which will be discussed with interrupts—is also provided.

Each jump and call instruction (with the exception of the one-byte call) specifies an absolute code address in the second and third byte of the instruction. The second byte contains the six high-order bits of the address and the third byte the eight low-order bits. This inverted storage, which was to haunt all processors evolved from the 8008, was a result of a need for compatibility with the Datapoint bit-serial processor, which processes addresses from low bit to high bit. This inverted storage did have a virtue in those early days when 256 x 8 memory chips were popular: It allowed all memory chips to select a byte and latch it for output while waiting for the six high-order bits which selected the chip. This speeded up memory access.

There are eight input and 24 output instructions using up 32 opcodes. Each I/O instruction transfers a byte of data between the accumulator and a designated I/O port.

The processor-control instructions are halt and no-op. Halt puts the processor into a waiting state. The processor remains in that state until an interrupt occurs. No-op is actually one of the move instructions; specifically, it moves the contents of the accumulator into the accumulator, thereby having no net effect (move instructions do not alter flag settings).

Interrupts. Interrupt processing was not a requirement for the 8008. Hence, only the most primitive mechanism conceivable—not incrementing the program counter—was provided. Such a mechanism permits an interrupting device to jam an instruction into the processor's instruction stream. This is accomplished by having the interrupting device, instead of memory, respond to the instruction fetch; since the program counter isn't incremented, the instruction in memory that didn't get fetched won't be skipped. The instruction typically supplied by the interrupting device is a call, so that an interrupt service routine can be entered and then the main program can be resumed after interrupt processing is complete (a jump instruction would result in the loss of the main program return address). To simplify the interrupting device's task of generating an instruction, the 8008 instruction set provides eight one-byte subroutine calls, each to a fixed location in memory.

There are no instructions for disabling the interrupt mechanism; thus, this function must be realized with external hardware. More important, there are no instructions for conveniently saving the registers and flags when an interrupt occurs.

The 8080

By 1973, memory fabrication technology had advanced from PMOS to NMOS. As an engineering exercise, Intel decided to use the 8008 layout masks with the NMOS process to obtain a faster 8008. After a short study, the company determined that a new layout was required. It therefore decided to enhance the processor at the same time and to utilize the new 40-pin package made practical by high-volume calculator chips. The result was the 8080 processor.

In The Beginning . . .

In the beginning Intel created the 4004 and the 8008. And these processors were without enough memory and throughput. And Intel said, "Let there be an 8080," and there was an 8080 and Intel saw that it was good. And Intel separated the 8008 market from the 8080 market.

And Intel said, "Let there be an 8085 with an oscillator on the same chip as the processor, and let an on-chip system controller separate the data from the control lines. And Intel made a firmament and divided the added instructions which were under the firmament from the added instructions which were above the firmament. And Intel called the first set of instructions RIM and SIM. And the other instructions Intel never announced.

And Intel said, "Let the market below the 8085 market be served with a processor and let on-chip ROM appear." And Intel called the new processor the 8048. And the market it served Intel called the low end. And Intel saw that it was good.

And Intel said, "Let a new-generation processor serve the mid-range market. And let there be true 16-bit facilities in the mid-range. And let there be one megabyte of memory and efficient interruptible byte-string instructions and full decimal arithmetic." And Intel saw the collection of all these things, that it was good, and Intel called it the 8086.

And Intel said, "Now let us make a processor in our image, after our likeness, and let it have dominion over the high-end market." So Intel created the APX 432 in his own image, in the image of Intel created he it, data processor and I/O processor created he them. And Intel blessed them and said unto them be fruitful and multiprocess and revolutionize the microprocessor market and have dominion over the Z8000 and the M68000 and over every competitor that enters the market.

And Intel saw everything that he had made and, behold, it was good.

—S.P. Morse

The 8080 was the first processor designed specifically for the microprocessor market. It was constrained to include all the 8008 instructions, but not necessarily with the same encodings. This meant that a user's software would be portable, but that the actual ROM chips containing the programs would have to be replaced. The main objective of the 8080 was to obtain a ten-to-one improvement in throughput, eliminate many of the 8008 shortcomings that had by then become apparent, and provide new processing capabilities not found in the 8008. The latter included handling of 16-bit data types (mainly for address computations), BCD arithmetic, enhanced operand addressing modes, and improved interrupt processing. Memory costs had come down and processing speed was approaching TTL, so larger memory spaces seemed more practical. Hence, another goal was direct addressing of more than 16K bytes. Symmetry was not a goal because the benefits to be gained from making the extensions symmetric would not have justified the resulting increase in chip size and opcode space.

The 8080 instruction set processor. The 8080 architecture is an unsymmetrical extension of the 8008. The byte handling facilities are augmented with a limited number of 16-bit facilities. The memory space is 64K bytes and the stack is virtually unlimited.

Various alternatives for the 8080 were considered. The simplest involved merely adding a memory stack and stack instructions to the 8008. An intermediate strategy was to augment the above with 16-bit arithmetic facilities that could be used for explicit address manipulation as well as for 16-bit data manipulation. The most difficult alternative involved a symmetric extension which replaced the one-byte M-register instructions with three-byte generalized memory access instructions. The last two bytes of these instructions contained two address mode bits specifying indirect addressing and indexing (using HL as an index register) and a 14-bit displacement. Although this would have been a more versatile addressing mechanism, it would have resulted in significant code expansion on existing 8008 programs. Furthermore, the logic needed to implement this solution would have precluded 16-bit arithmetic; such arithmetic would not have been needed for address manipulations under this enhanced addressing facility, but would still have been desirable for data manipulations. For these reasons, the intermediate approach was finally taken.

Memory and I/O structure. The 8080 can address up to 64K bytes of memory, a four-fold increase over the 8008 (the 14-bit address stack of the 8008 was eliminated). The address bus of the 8080 is 16 bits wide (in contrast to eight bits for the 8008), so an entire address can be sent down the bus in one memory cycle. Although the data handling facilities of the 8080 are primarily byte-oriented (the 8008 was exclusively byte-oriented), certain operations permit two consecutive bytes of memory to be treated as a single data item. The two bytes are called a word. The data bus of the 8080 is only eight bits wide, and hence, word accesses require an extra memory cycle.

The most significant eight bits of a word arc located at the higher memory address. This results in the same kind of inverted storage already noted in the transfer instructions of the 8008.

The 8080 extends the 32-port capacity of the 8008 to 256 input ports and 256 output ports. Here, the 8080 is actually more symmetrical than the 8008. Like the 8008, the 8080 instruction set can directly address all the ports.

Register structure. The 8080 processor contains a file of seven 8-bit general registers, a 16-bit program counter (PC) and stack pointer (SP), and five 1-bit flags. A comparison between the 8008 and 8080 register sets is shown in Figure 2.

General registers. The 8080 registers are the same seven 8-bit registers that were in the 8008 scratchpad—namely, A,B,C,D,E,H, and L. In order to incorporate 16-bit data

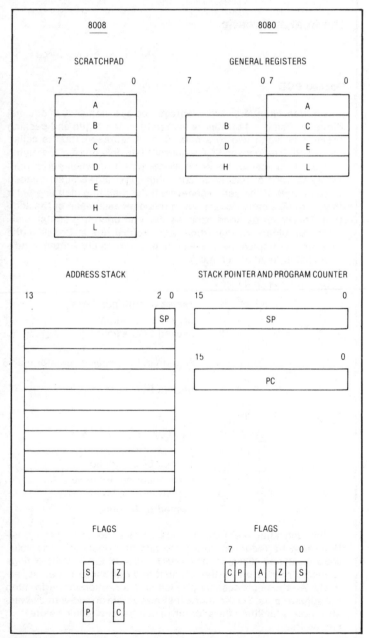

Figure 2. 8008 and 8080 registers.

facilities in the 8080, certain instructions operate on the register pairs BC, DE, and HL.

The seven registers can be used interchangeably for on-chip temporary storage. The three register pairs are used for address manipulations, but their roles are not interchangeable; there is an 8080 instruction that allows operations on DE and not BC, and there are address modes that access memory indirectly through BC or DE but not through HL.

As in the 8008, the A register has a unique role in arithmetic and logical operations: It serves as one of the operands and is the receptacle for the result. The HL register again has its special role of pointing to the pseudoregister M.

Stack pointer and program counter. The 8080 has a single program counter instead of the floating program counter of the 8008. The program counter is 16 bits (two bits more than the 8008's program counter), thereby permitting an address space of 64K.

The stack is contained in memory instead of on the chip, a strategy which removes the restriction of only seven levels of nested subroutines. The entries on the stack are 16 bits wide. The 16-bit stack pointer is used to locate the stack in memory. The execution of a call instruction causes the contents of the program counter to be pushed onto the stack, and the return instruction causes the last stack entry to be popped into the program counter. The stack pointer was chosen to run "downhill"

Decimal arithmetic

Packed BCD

Addition. Numbers can be represented as a sequence of decimal digits by using a 4-bit binary encoding of the digits and packing these encodings two to a byte. Such a representation is called packed BCD (unpacked BCD would contain only one digit per byte). In order to preserve this decimal interpretation when performing binary addition on packed BCD numbers, the value 6 must be added to each digit of the sum whenever (1) the resulting digit is greater than 9, or (2) a carry occurs out of this digit as a result of the addition. This must be done because the 4-bit encoding contains six more combinations than there are decimal digits. Consider the following examples (for convenience, numbers are written in hexadecimal instead of in binary):

Example 1: 81 + 52

	d2	d1	d0	names of digit positions
		8	1	packed BCD augend
+		5	2	packed BCD addend
		D	3	
+		6		adjustment because d1 greater than 9
	1	3	3	packed BCD sum

Example 2: 28 + 19

	d2	d1	d0	names of digit positions
		2	8	packed BCD augend
+		1	9	packed BCD addend
		4	1	carry occurred out of d0
+			6	adjustment for above carry
		4	7	packed BCD sum

For such adjustments to be made, carries out of either digit position must be recorded during the addition operation. The 4004, 8080, 8085, and 8086 use the CARRY and AUXILIARY CARRY flags to record carries out of the leftmost and rightmost digits, respectively. All these processors provide an instruction for performing the adjustments. Furthermore, they all contain an add-with-carry instruction to facilitate the addition of numbers containing more than two digits.

Subtraction. Subtraction of packed BCD numbers is performed in a similar manner. However, none of the Intel processors prior to the 8086 provides an instruction for performing decimal adjustment following a subtraction (Zilog's Z-80, introduced two years before the 8086, has such an instruction). On processors without the subtract adjustment instruction, subtraction of packed BCD numbers is accomplished by generating the 10's complement of the subtrahend and adding.

Multiplication. Multiplication of packed BCD numbers can also be adjusted to give the correct decimal result if the out-of-digit carries occurring during the multiplication are recorded. The result of multiplying two one-byte operands is two bytes long (four digits); out-of-digit carries can occur on any of the three low-order digits, all of which must be recorded. Furthermore, the carries out of any digit are no longer restricted to unity, so counters rather than flags are required to record the carries. This is illustrated in the following example (again, numbers are written in hexadecimal instead of in binary):

Example 3: 94 * 63

	d3	d2	d1	d0	names of digit positions
			9	4	packed BCD multiplicand
*			6	3	packed BCD multiplier
		1	B	C	carry occurred out of d1
	3	7	8		carry occurred out of d1, three out of d2
	3	9	3	C	carry occurred out of d1
+		6	6		adjustment for . . .
+		6	6		. . . above six . . .
+			6	6	. . . carries
	4	C	5	C	carry occurred out of d1 and out of d2
+		6	6		adjustment for above two carries
	5	2	B	C	carry occurred out of d2
+		6			adjustment for above carry
	5	8	B	C	
+				6	adjustment because d0 is greater than 9
	5	8	C	2	

(with the stack advancing toward lower memory) to simplify both indexing into the stack from the user's program (positive indexing) and displaying the contents of the stack from a front panel.

The programmer can directly access the stack pointer in the 8080, unlike that in the 8008. Furthermore, the stack itself is directly accessible, and instructions are provided that permit the programmer to push and pop his own 16-bit items onto the stack.

Flags. A fifth flag, AUXILIARY CARRY, augments the 8008 flag set. AUXILIARY CARRY indicates whether a carry was generated out of the four low-order bits. This flag, in conjunction with a decimal-adjust instruction, makes possible packed BCD addition (see box below for details). This facility can be traced back to the 4004 processor. AUXILIARY CARRY has no purpose other than BCD arithmetic, and hence the conditional transfer instructions were not expanded to include tests on the AUXILIARY CARRY flag.

It was proposed too late in the design that the PARITY flag double as an OVERFLOW flag. Although this feature didn't make it into the 8080, it did show up two years later in Zilog's Z-80.

Instruction set. The 8080 includes the entire 8008 instruction set as a subset. The added instructions provide some new operand addressing modes and some 16-bit data manipulation facilities. These extensions have in-

---

```
   +      6         adjustment because d1 is
                    greater than 9
   ___ ___ ___ ___
    5  9  2  2      packed BCD product
```

This example illustrates two facts. First, packed BCD multiplication adjustments are possible if the necessary out-of-digit carry information is recorded by the multiply instruction. Second, the facilities the processor needs to record this information and apply the correction are nontrivial.

Another approach to determining the out-of-digit carries is to analyze the multiplication process on a digit-by-digit basis:

let $x1$ and $x2$ be packed BCD digits in multiplicand
let $y1$ and $y2$ be packed BCD digits in multiplier

binary value of multiplicand = $16*x1 + x2$
binary value of multiplier = $16*y1 + y2$

binary value of product = $256*x1*y1 + 16*(x1*y2 + x2*y1) + y1*y2$
= $x1*y1$ in most significant byte,
$y1*y2$ in least significant byte,
$(x1*y2 + x2*y1)$ straddling both bytes

If there were no cross terms (i.e., $x1$ or $y2$ is zero and $x2$ or $y1$ is zero), the number of out-of-digit carries generated by the $x1*y1$ term is simply the most significant digit in the most significant byte of the product. Similarly, the number of out-of-digit carries generated by the $y1*y2$ term is simply the most significant digit in the least significant byte of the product. This is illustrated in the following example:

Example 4: 90 * 20

```
   d3 d2 d1 d0       names of digit positions
   ___ ___ ___ ___
       9  0          packed BCD multiplicand
*      2  0          packed BCD multiplier
   ___ ___ ___ ___
       0  0  0
    1  2  0
   ___ ___ ___ ___
    1  2  0  0
    \  /  \  /
    9*2    0*0
```

The most significant digit of the most significant byte is 1, indicating that there was one out-of-digit carry from the low-order digit when the 9*2 term was formed. The adjustment is to add 6 to that digit.

```
    1  2  0  0
  +    6
   ___ ___ ___ ___       adjustment
    1  8  0  0           packed BCD product
```

So, in the absence of cross terms, the number of out-of-digit carries occurring during a multiplication can be determined by examining the binary product. The cross terms, when present, overshadow the out-of-digit carry information in the product, thereby making some other carry-recording mechanism essential. None of the Intel processors incorporate such a mechanism. (Prior to the 8086, multiplication itself was not even supported.) Having decided not to support packed BCD multiplication in the processors, Intel designers made no attempt to analyze packed BCD division.

Unpacked BCD

Unpacked BCD representation of numbers consists of storing the encoded digits in the low-order four bits of consecutive bytes. An ASCII string of digits is a special case of unpacked BCD, with the high-order four bits of each byte containing 0110.

Arithmetic operations on numbers represented as unpacked BCD digit strings can be formulated in terms of more primitive BCD operations on single digit (dividends and products are two digits) unpacked BCD numbers.

Addition and subtraction. Primitive unpacked additions and subtractions follow the same adjustment procedures as packed additions and subtractions.

Multiplication. Primitive unpacked multiplication involves multiplying a one-digit (one-byte) unpacked multiplicand by a one-digit (one-byte) unpacked multiplier to yield a two-digit (two-byte) unpacked product. If the high-order four bits of the multiplicand and multiplier are zero (instead of don't cares), the multiplicand as well as the multiplier represent the same value interpreted as a binary number or as a BCD number. A binary multiplication yields a two-byte product, with the high-order byte being zero. The low-order byte of this product has the correct value when interpreted as a binary number; that byte can be adjusted to a two-byte BCD number as follows:

high-order byte = binary product / 10
low-order byte = binary product modulo 10

Continued on overleaf

23

troduced a good deal of asymmetry. Typical instruction formats are shown in Figure 1.

The 8080 can access operands in memory only via the M register. The 8080 has certain instructions that access memory by specifying the memory address (direct addressing) and also certain instructions that access memory by specifying a pair of general registers in which the memory address is contained (indirect addressing). In addition, the 8080 includes the register and immediate operand addressing modes of the 8008. A 16-bit immediate mode is also included.

The added instructions can be classified as load/store instructions, register-pair instructions, HL-specific instructions, accumulator-adjust instructions, carry instructions, expanded I/O instructions, and interrupt instructions.

The load/store instructions load and store the accumulator register and the HL register pair, using the direct and indirect addressing mode. Both modes can be used for the accumulator but, due to chip size constraints, only the direct mode was implemented for HL.

The register-pair instructions provide for the manipulation of 16-bit data items. Specifically, register pairs can be loaded with 16-bit immediate data and incremented, decremented, added to HL, pushed on the stack, or popped off the stack. Furthermore, the flag settings themselves can be pushed and popped, thereby

---

This is illustrated by the following:

Example 5: 7 * 5

d1	d0	names of digit positions
0	7	unpacked BCD multiplicand
0	5	unpacked BCD multiplier
2	3	binary product
2	3	binary product
0	A	adjustment for high-order byte (/10)
0	3	unpacked BCD product (higher-order byte)
2	3	binary product
modulo 0	A	adjustment for low-order byte (modulo 10)
0	5	unpacked BCD product (low-order byte)

Division. Primitive unpacked division involves dividing a two-digit (two-byte) unpacked dividend by a one-digit (one-byte) unpacked divisor to yield a one-digit (one-byte) unpacked quotient and a one-digit (one-byte) unpacked remainder. If the high-order four bits in each byte of the dividend are zeroes (instead of don't cares), the dividend can be adjusted to a one-byte binary number:

binary dividend = 10 * high-order byte + low-order byte

If the high-order four bits of the divisor are zero, the divisor represents the same value interpreted as a binary number or as a BCD number. A binary division of the adjusted (binary) dividend and BCD divisor yields a one-byte quotient and a one-byte remainder, each representing the same value interpreted as a binary number or as a BCD number. This is illustrated by the following:

Example 6: 45 / 6

d1	d0	names of digit positions
0	4	unpacked BCD dividend (high-order byte)
0	5	unpacked BCD dividend (low-order byte)
2	D	adjusted dividend (4*10 + 5)
0	6	unpacked BCD divisor

| 0 | 7 | unpacked BCD quotient |
| 0 | 3 | unpacked BCD remainder |

Adjustment instructions. The 8086 processor provides four adjustment instructions for performing primitive unpacked BCD arithmetic—one for addition, one for subtraction, one for multiplication, and one for division.

The addition and subtraction adjustments are performed on a binary sum or difference assumed to be left in the one-byte AL register. Whenever AL is altered by the addition or subtraction adjustments, the adjustments will also do the following to facilitate multidigit arithmetic:

- set the CARRY flag (this facilitates multidigit unpacked additions and subtractions) and

- consider the one-byte AH register to contain the next most significant digit, and increment or decrement it as appropriate (this permits the addition adjustment to be used in a multidigit unpacked multiplication).

The multiplication adjustment assumes that AL contains a binary product and places the two-digit unpacked BCD equivalent in AH and AL. The division adjustment assumes that AH and AL contain a two-digit unpacked BCD dividend and places the binary equivalent in AH and AL.

The following algorithms show how the adjustment instructions can be used to perform multidigit unpacked arithmetic.

ADDITION

```
let augend  =  a[N] a[N – 1] . . . a[2] a[1]
let addend  =  b[N] b[N – 1] . . . b[2] b[1]
let sum     =  c[N] c[N – 1] . . . c[2] c[1]

0 –> (CARRY)
DO i = 1 to N
    (a[i]) –> (AL)
    (AL) + (b[i]) –> (AL)
        where " + " denotes add-with-carry
    add-adjust (AL) –> (AX)
    (AL) –> (c[i])
```

simplifying saving the environment when interrupts occur (this was not possible in the 8008).

The HL-specific instructions include facilities for transferring HL to the program counter or to the stack pointer, and for exchanging HL with DE or with the top entry on the stack. The last of these instructions was included to provide a mechanism for (1) removing a subroutine return address from the stack so that passed parameters can be discarded, or (2) burying a result-to-be returned under the return address. This became the longest instruction in the 8080 (five memory cycles); its implementation precluded the inclusion of several other instructions already proposed for the processor.

SUBTRACTION

let minuend   = a[N] a[N − 1] . . . a[2] a[1]
let subtrahend = b[N] b[N − 1] . . . b[2] b[1]
let difference = c[N] c[N − 1] . . . c[2] c[1]

0 − > (CARRY)
DO i = 1 to N
   (a[i]) − > (AL)
   (AL) − (b[i]) − > (AL)
      where " − " denotes subtract-with-borrow
   subtract-adjust (AL) − > (AX)
   (AL) − > (c[i])

MULTIPLICATION

let multiplicand = a[N] a[N − 1] . . . a[2] a[1]
let multiplier   = b
let product   = c[N + 1] c[N] . . . c[2] c[1]

(b) AND OFH − > (b)
0 − > (c[1])
DO i = 1 to N
   (a[i]) AND OFH − > (AL)
   (AL) * (b) − > (AX)
   multiply-adjust (AL) − > (AX)
   (AL) + (c[i]) − > (AL)
   add-adjust (AL) − > (AX)
   (AL) − > (c[i])
   (AH) − > (c[i + 1])

DIVISION

let dividend = a[N] a[N − 1] . . . a[2] a[1]
let divisor = b
let quotient = c[N] c[N − 1] . . . c[2] c[1]

(b) and OFH − > (b)
0 − > (AH)
DO i = N to 1
   (a[i]) AND OFH − > (AL)
   divide-adjust (AX) − > (AL)
   (AL) / (b) − > (AL)
      with remainder going into (AH)
   (AL) − > (c[i])

Two accumulator-adjust instructions are provided. One complements each bit in the accumulator, and the other modifies the accumulator so that it contains the correct decimal result after a packed BCD addition is performed.

The carry instructions provide for setting or complementing the CARRY flag. No instruction is provided for clearing the CARRY flag. Because of the way the CARRY flag semantics are defined, the CARRY flag can be cleared simply by ORing and ANDing the accumulator with itself.

The expanded I/O instructions permit the contents of any one of 256 8-bit ports to be transferred either to or from the accumulator. The port number is explicitly stated in the instructions; hence, the instruction is two bytes long. The equivalent 8008 instruction is only one byte long. This is the only instance in which an 8080 instruction requires a different number of bytes than its 8008 counterpart. The 8080's designers did this more to free up 32 opcodes than to increase the number of I/O ports.

The 8080 has an interrupt mechanism identical to that of the 8008 but includes instructions for enabling or disabling the mechanism. This feature, along with the ability to push and pop the processor flags, makes the interrupt mechanism practical.

The 8085

In 1976 advances in technology allowed Intel to consider enhancing the 8080. The objective was a processor set utilizing a single power supply and requiring fewer chips (the 8080 required both an oscillator chip and a system controller chip). The new processor, called the 8085, was constrained to be compatible with the 8080 at the machine-code level. This meant that extensions to the instruction set could use only the 12 unused opcodes of the 8080.

Architecturally, the 8085 turned out to be not much more than a repackaging of the 8080. The major differences were added features such as an on-chip oscillator, power-on reset, vectored interrupts, decoded control lines, a serial I/O port, and a single power supply. Two new instructions, RIM and SIM, were added to handle the serial port and the interrupt mask. Several other instructions that had been included were never announced because of their ramifications on the 8085 support software and because of the compatibility constraints they would have placed on the forthcoming 8086.

The 8086

The 8086 was designed to provide an order-of-magnitude increase in processing throughput over the 8080. The processor was to be compatible with the 8080 at the assembly language level, so that existing 8080 software could be reassembled and correctly executed on the 8086. To allow for this, the 8080 register and instruction sets were to appear as logical subsets of the 8086 registers and instructions. By utilizing a general-register structure, In-

25

tel could capitalize on its experience with the 8080 to obtain a processor with a higher degree of sophistication. Strict 8080 compatibility, however, was not attempted, especially in areas where it would have compromised the final design.

The goals of the 8086 architecture were the symmetric extension of existing 8080 features and the addition of processing capabilities not found in the 8080. New features and capabilities included 16-bit arithmetic, signed 8- and 16-bit arithmetic (including multiply and divide), efficient interruptible byte-string operations, improved bit-manipulation facilities, and mechanisms to provide for re-entrant code, position-independent code, and dynamically relocatable programs.

By now memory had become inexpensive and microprocessors were being used in applications requiring large amounts of code and data. Thus, another design goal was direct addressing of more than 64K bytes and support of multiprocessor configurations.

The 8086 instruction set processor. The 8086 processor architecture comprises a memory structure, a register structure, an instruction set, and an external interface. The 8086 can access up to one million bytes of memory and up to 64K input/output ports. The 8086 has three files of registers. One file contains general registers that hold intermediate results; the second contains pointer and index registers used to locate information within specified portions of memory; the third contains segment registers used to specify these portions of memory. The 8086 has nine flags that are used to record the state of the processor and to control its operations.

The 8086 instruction set and addressing modes are richer and more symmetric than the 8080. And the 8086 external interface, consisting of such things as interrupts, multiprocessor synchronization, and resource sharing, goes way beyond the facilities provided in the 8080.

Memory structure. The input/output space and the memory space of the 8086 are treated in a parallel fashion and are collectively called the memory structure. Code and data reside in the memory space whereas (non-memory-mapped) peripheral devices reside in the I/O space.

Memory space. The memory in an 8086 system is a sequence of up to one million bytes (a 64-fold increase over the 8080). An 8086 word is any two consecutive bytes in memory. Like the 8080, words are stored in memory with the most significant byte at the higher memory address. The data bus of the 8086 is 16 bits wide, so, unlike the 8080, a word can be accessed in one memory cycle (however, words starting at odd byte addresses still require two memory cycles).

Since the 8086 can address up to one megabyte of memory, it would seem that, within the 8086 processor, byte and word addresses must be represented as 20-bit quantities. But the 8086 was designed to perform 16-bit arithmetic, and thus the address objects it manipulates can only be 16 bits in length. An additional mechanism is therefore required to build addresses. The one-megabyte memory can be conceived of as an arbitrary number of segments, each containing at most 64K bytes. The starting address of each segment is evenly divisible by 16. In other words, the four least significant bits of each segment's starting address are 0. At any moment, the program can immediately access the contents of four such segments—the current code segment, the current data segment, the current stack segment, and the current extra segment. Each of these segments can be identified by placing the 16 most significant bits of the segment starting address into one of the four 16-bit segment registers. By contrast, the 8080 memory structure is simply the 8086 memory structure with all four of the current segments starting at 0.

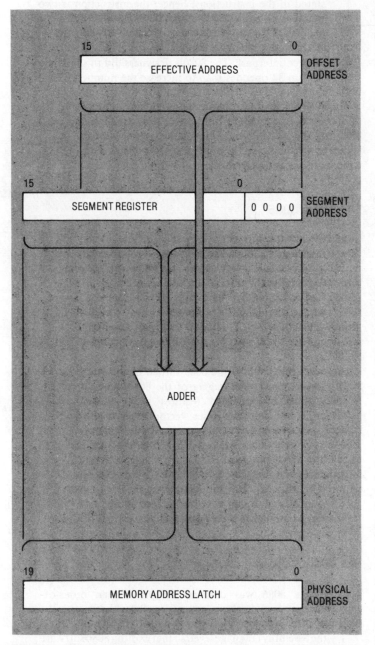

Figure 3. Addressing one million bytes requires a 20-bit memory address. This 20-bit address is constructed by offsetting the effective address four bits to the right of the segment address, filling in the four low-order bits of the segment address with zeroes, and then adding the two.

An 8086 instruction can refer to bytes or words within a segment by using a 16-bit offset address within a 64K-byte segment. The processor constructs the 20-bit byte or word address by adding the 16-bit offset address to the contents of a 16-bit segment register, with four low-order zeroes appended (Figure 3).

Various alternatives for extending the 8080 address space were considered. One such alternative consisted of appending eight rather than four low-order zero bits to the contents of a segment register, thereby providing a 24-bit physical address capable of addressing up to 16 megabytes of memory. This was rejected because

- segments would be forced to start on 256-byte boundaries, resulting in excessive memory fragmentation,
- the four additional pins that would be required were not available, and
- the designers felt that a one megabyte address space was sufficient.

Input/output space. The 8086 I/O space consists of 64K ports (a 256-fold increase over the 8080). Ports are addressed in the same manner that memory bytes or words are addressed, except that there are no port segment registers. In other words, all ports are considered to be in one segment. Like memory, ports may be 8 or 16 bits in size.

The first 256 ports are directly addressable (address in the instruction), whereas all 64K ports are indirectly addressable (address in a register). Such indirect addressing permits consecutive ports to be accessed in a program loop.

Register structure. The 8086 processor contains a total of thirteen 16-bit registers and nine 1-bit flags. For descriptive purposes, the registers are subdivided into three files of four registers each. The thirteenth register, namely the instruction pointer (called the program counter in the earlier processors), is not directly accessible to the programmer; it is manipulated with control-transfer instructions. The 8080 register set is a subset of the 8086 register set (Figures 4 and 5). In order to unify the

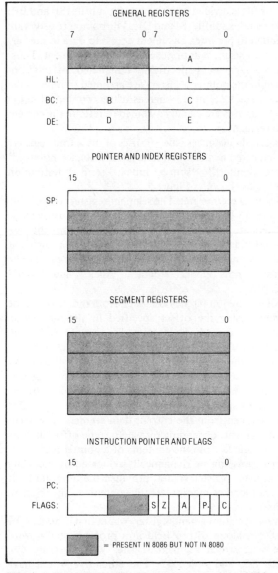
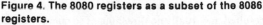

Figure 4. The 8080 registers as a subset of the 8086 registers.

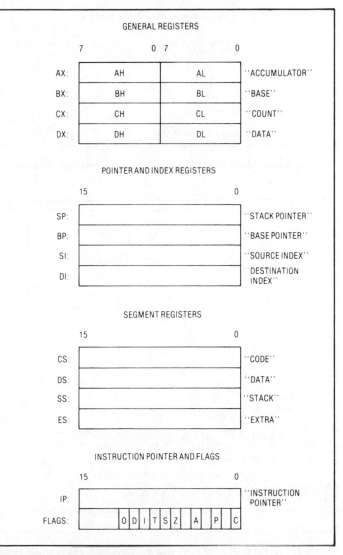

Figure 5. The 8086 register structure.

8086 register names, corresponding registers in the 8080 and 8086 do not necessarily have the same names.

General register file. The general register file comprises the seven 8-bit registers of the 8080, with an eighth register added so that the registers can be paired up to form four 16-bit registers. The general registers can be addressed as either 8- or 16-bit registers, whereas the registers in the next two files can be addressed only as 16-bit registers. The dual nature of these registers permits them to handle both byte and word quantities with equal ease. The 16-bit registers are named AX, BX, CX, and DX; when considered as 8-bit registers, they are named AL, AH, BL,

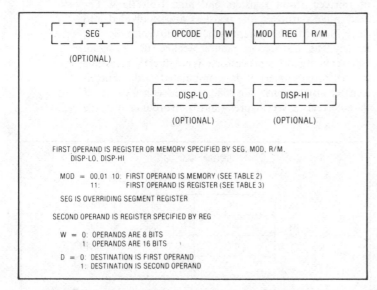

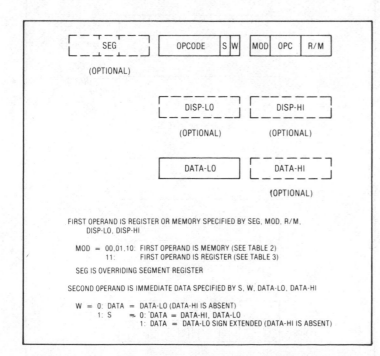

Figure 6. Typical format of 8086 two-operand operation, when second operand is register.

Figure 7. Typical format of 8086 two-operand operation, when second operand is a constant (immediate data).

BH, CL, CH, DL, and DH (the L or H suffix designates high-order or low-order byte).

For the most part, contents of the general registers can participate interchangeably in the arithmetic and logical operations of the 8086. However, there are a few instructions (e.g., string instructions) that dedicate certain general registers to specific uses. These uses are indicated by the mnemonic phrases "accumulator," "base," "count," and "data" in Figure 5.

Pointer and index register file. The pointer and index registers of the 8086 consist of the 16-bit registers SP, BP, SI, and DI. These registers usually contain offset addresses for addressing within a segment. They reduce the size of programs by not requiring each instruction to specify frequently used addresses. But they serve another (and perhaps more important) function; they provide for dynamic effective-address computations as described in the section on operand addressing below. In order to accomplish this, the 8086 permits the pointer and index registers to participate in arithmetic and logical operations along with the 16-bit general registers.

This file is divided into the pointer subfile (SP and BP) and the index subfile (SI and DI). The pointer registers are intended to provide convenient access to data in the current stack segment as opposed to the data segment. Thus, unless a segment is specifically designated, offsets contained in the pointer registers are assumed to refer to the current stack segment, whereas offsets contained in the index registers are usually assumed to refer to the current data segment.

In certain instances, specific uses of these four registers are indicated by the mnemonic phrases "stack pointer," "base pointer," "source index," and "destination index," as shown in Figure 5.

Segment register file. The segment registers of the 8086 are the 16-bit registers CS, DS, SS, and ES. These registers are used to identify the four segments that are currently addressable. Each register identifies a particular current segment and hence has an associated mnemonic phrase such as "code," "data," "stack," and "extra" (Figure 5).

All instruction fetches are taken from the current code segment using the offset specified in the instruction pointer (IP) register. The segment for operand fetches can usually be designated by appending a special one-byte prefix to the instruction. This prefix, as well as other prefixes described later, has a unique encoding that permits it to be distinguished from the opcodes. In the absence of such a prefix (the usual case), the operand is usually taken from the current data segment or current stack segment, depending on whether the offset address was calculated from the contents of a pointer register.

Programs can be dynamically relocated by changing the segment register values, provided the program itself does not load or manipulate the contents of the segment registers.

A set of eight segment registers was at first proposed for the 8086, along with a field in a program status word specifying which segment register was currently CS, which DS, and which SS. The other five would have served as extra segment registers. Such a scheme would have resulted in virtually no thrashing of segment register contents; start addresses of all needed segments would have been loaded initially into one of the eight segment registers and the roles of the various segment registers would have varied dynamically during program execution. However, concern over the size of the resulting processor chip forced the number of segment registers to be reduced to the minimum number necessary, namely four. With this minimum number, each segment register can be dedicated to a segment type (code, data, stack, and extra) and the specifying fields in the program status word are no longer needed.

Flag register file. Six flags record processor status information. Five are the 8080 flags and usually reflect the status of the latest arithmetic or logical operation. The sixth, an OVERFLOW flag, reflects a signed overflow condition.

The 8086 also contains three flags that control processor operations. These are the DIRECTION flag, which controls the direction of the string manipulations (auto-increment or auto-decrement); the INTERRUPT flag, which enables or disables external interrupts; and the TRAP flag, which puts the processor into a single-step mode for program debugging.

Instruction set. The 8086 instruction set is not a superset of the 8080 instruction set. Although most of the 8080 instructions are included in the 8086, some of the infrequently used ones (e.g., conditional calls and returns) are not. The operand addressing modes of the 8080 have been greatly enhanced.

Operand addressing. Instructions in the 8086 usually perform operations on one or two source operands, with the result overwriting one of the operands. The first operand of a two-operand instruction can be usually either a register or a memory location; the second operand can be either a register or a constant within the instruction. (The terms first and second operand are used to distinguish the operands only—their use does not imply any directionality for data transfers.) Typical formats for two-operand instructions are shown in Figure 6 (second operand is a register) and Figure 7 (second operand is a constant). Single-operand instructions generally allow either a register or a memory location to serve as the operand. Figure 8 shows a typical one-operand format. Virtually all 8086 operators may specify 8- or 16-bit operands.

Memory operands. An instruction may address an operand residing in memory in one of the following ways, as determined by the "mod" and "r/m" fields in the instruction (see Table 2):

- direct (16-bit offset address), or
- indirect (optionally with an 8- or 16-bit displacement)
  —through a base register (BP or BX),
  —through an index register (SI or DI),
  —through the sum of a base register and an index register.

Auto-incrementing and auto-decrementing address modes are not included, in general, since their use is mainly oriented toward string processing. These modes are included on the string primitive instructions.

Register operands. An instruction may address an operand residing in one of the general registers or in one of the pointer or index registers. Table 3 shows the register selection as determined by the "r/m" field (first operand) or the "res" field (second operand) in the instruction.

Immediate operands. In general, one of the two operands of a two-operand instruction can be immediate data appearing within the instruction. These operands are represented in 2's-complement form and may be abbreviated to 8 bits (instead of the usual 16) if the high-order byte is the sign extension of the low-order byte.

Addressing mode usage. The addressing modes were designed to permit efficient implementation of high-level language features. For example, a simple variable is

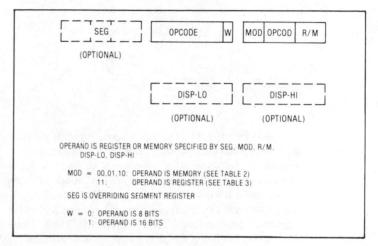

Figure 8. Typical format of 8086 one-operand operation.

Table 2.
Determining 8086 offset address of a memory operand.

MOD SPECIFIES HOW DISP-LO AND DISP-HI ARE USED TO DEFINE A DISPLACEMENT AS FOLLOWS:

MOD =
00: DISP = 0 (DISP-LO AND DISP-HI ARE ABSENT)
01: DISP = DISP-LO SIGN EXTENDED (DISP-HI IS ABSENT)
10: DISP = DISP-HI, DISP-LO

R/M SPECIFIES WHICH BASE AND INDEX REGISTER CONTENTS ARE TO BE ADDED TO THE DISPLACEMENT TO FORM THE OPERAND OFFSET ADDRESS AS FOLLOWS:

R/M =
000: OFFSET = (BX) + (SI) + DISP
001: OFFSET = (BX) + (DI) + DISP
010: OFFSET = (BP) + (SI) + DISP   } INDIRECT
011: OFFSET = (BP) + (DI) + DISP   } ADDRESS
100: OFFSET =   (SI) + DISP   } MODE
101: OFFSET =   (DI) + DISP
110: OFFSET = (BP)   + DISP
111: OFFSET = (BX)   + DISP

( ) MEANS "CONTENTS OF"

THE FOLLOWING SPECIAL CASE IS AN EXCEPTION TO THE ABOVE RULES:

IF
MOD = 00
AND   } DIRECT
R/M = 100   } ADDRESS
                   } MODE
THEN OFFSET = DISP-HI, DISP-LO

USE THIS TABLE WHEN MOD ≠ 11; OTHERWISE USE TABLE 3.
THIS TABLE APPLIES TO THE FIRST OPERAND ONLY; THE SECOND OPERAND CAN NEVER BE A MEMORY OPERAND.

Table 3.
Determining 8086 register operand.

FIRST OPERAND

R/M	8-BIT	16-BIT
000:	AL	AX
001:	CL	CX
010:	DL	DX
011:	BL	BX
100:	AH	SP
101:	CH	BP
110:	DH	SI
111:	BH	DI

SECOND OPERAND

REG	8-BIT	16-BIT
000:	AL	AX
001:	CL	CX
010:	DL	DX
011:	BL	BX
100:	AH	SP
101:	CH	BP
110:	DH	SI
111:	BH	DI

USE THIS TABLE WHEN MOD = 11; OTHERWISE USE TABLE 2.

accessed with the direct mode, whereas an array element in a based record (record located at a memory address pointed at by some other variable) is accessed with the indirect-through-BX-plus-SI-plus-offset mode (where base register BX contains a pointer to start-of-record, offset is the start of the array within the record, and index register SI contains the index into the array). The addressing modes involving BP as the base register provide for accessing data in the stack segment instead of in the data segment. Data is frequently stored in (activation records in) the stack segment when recursive procedures and block-structured languages are implemented. Addressing modes used for accessing various data elements are shown in Table 4.

Data transfers. The 8086 has four classes of data transfer instructions: general-purpose, accumulator-specific, address-object, and flag.

Three of the general-purpose transfers—move, push, and pop—are derived from the 8080. The 8086 also has an exchange instruction, which was not present in the 8080.

The accumulator-specific transfers are input, output, and translate. The input and output instructions provide direct access to the first 256 ports, just as in the 8080.

Table 4.
Addressing modes for accessing data elements.

	NOT BASED	BASED	ACTIVATION RECORD
SIMPLE VARIABLE:	DIRECT	BX	BP + OFFSET
ARRAYS:	SI + OFFSET	BX + SI	BP + SI + OFFSET
	DI + OFFSET	BX + DI	BP + DI + OFFSET
RECORDS:	DIRECT	BX + OFFSET	BP + OFFSET
ARRAYS OF RECORDS:	SI + OFFSET	BX + SI + OFFSET	BP + SI + OFFSET
	DI + OFFSET	BX + DI + OFFSET	BP + DI + OFFSET

These instructions also provide indirect access to any of the 64K ports, a facility not found in the 8080. Furthermore, the 8086 I/O instructions provide access to 8- or 16-bit-wide ports, whereas the 8080 I/O instructions provide access to 8-bit-wide ports only. The translate instruction performs a table-lookup byte translation, which is useful when combined with string operations. Neither the translate instruction nor the string operations are present in the 8080.

Address-object transfers represent another facility not found in the 8080. These instructions—load effective address (provide access to the offset address of an operand as opposed to the value of the operand itself) and load pointer (provide means of loading a segment start address into a segment register and an offset address into a general or pointer register in a single instruction)—provide the programmer with some control over the 8086 addressing mechanism.

The 8080 treats the collection of all its flags as a single data item that can be pushed on or popped off the stack. The 8086's flag transfer instructions permit the collection of all the flags to be loaded or stored as well. However, these load and store operations involve only those flags that already exist in the 8080. This is a concession to compatibility (without these operations, it would take nine 8086 bytes of code to perform an 8080 PUSH PSW or POP PSW instruction).

Arithmetics. The only arithmetic instructions in the 8080 are addition and subtraction of 8-bit unsigned numbers and addition of 16-bit unsigned numbers. The 8086, on the other hand, provides for all combinations of addition, subtraction, multiplication, and division on 8-bit and 16-bit signed and unsigned numbers. Signed-number facilities for addition and subtraction consist of sufficient conditional transfers to allow for signed comparisons and an OVERFLOW flag to detect signed overflow (two features missing in the 8080).

The designers considered providing separate operations for signed addition and subtraction which would automatically trap on signed overflow (signed overflow is an exception condition, whereas unsigned overflow is not). However, lack of room in the opcode space prohibited this. As a compromise, a one-byte trap-on-overflow instruction was included to make testing for signed overflow less painful.

The 8080's only binary-coded decimal arithmetic instruction is for addition of packed BCD numbers. This takes the form of an adjustment instruction that is applied after the numbers are added in the normal way. The 8086 provides adjustment instructions for performing both addition and subtraction of packed BCD numbers. Packed multiply and divide adjustments are not provided because the cross terms generated make it impossible to recover the decimal result without additional processor facilities (see box on page 48 for details).

The 8086 also provides adjustment instructions for performing arithmetic operations on unpacked BCD numbers. Since ASCII-encoded numbers are a special case of unpacked BCD numbers, this facility permits ASCII-encoded numbers to be operated on directly. Unpacked BCD multiplication does not generate cross terms, so multiplication and division adjustments, as well as addition and subtraction adjustments, are provided for unpacked BCD. The multiply adjustment consists of converting an 8-bit binary number into two 4-bit BCD digits; the divide adjustment does the reverse. Adjustment for division is made before the execution of the divide instruction, whereas addition, subtraction, and multiplication adjustments are made after the execution of the corresponding arithmetic instruction. In other words, the addition, subtraction, and multiplication adjustments correct a bad (i.e., non-BCD) result, whereas the division adjustment prevents a bad result from occurring. See, again, the box on page 48 for more details on unpacked BCD adjustments.

Logicals. The 8086 processor contains the 8080's logical AND, OR, XOR, and NOT instructions as well as a logical TEST (testing for specific bits) instruction not found in the 8080. TEST sets the processor's flags exactly as an AND would but, unlike the AND, does not store the result. Thus, both source operands are intact after execution of a TEST instruction, whereas one of them would have been overwritten if an AND instruction had been executed instead.

The 8080 contains four unit-rotate instructions. The 8086 augments this with four unit-shift instructions and with multibit shift and rotate instructions. The multibit shift and rotate instructions permit the number of bits over which to shift or rotate to be computed at run time.

String manipulation. A string is simply a sequence of bytes or words in memory. A string operation is an operation that is performed on each item in a string. Since string operations usually involve repetitions, they may take a long time to execute. The 8086 has a set of instructions that decrease the time required to perform string operations by (1) having a powerful set of primitive instructions so that the time taken to process each item in the string is reduced, and (2) eliminating the bookkeeping and overhead that is usually performed between the processing of successive items. The 8080 does not provide any string manipulation facilities.

Transfer of control. Transfer-of-control instructions (jumps, calls, returns) are of two basic varieties: intrasegment transfers, which transfer control within the current code segment by specifying a new value for IP; and intersegment transfers, which transfer control to an arbitrary code segment by specifying a new value for both CS and IP. Transfers can be either direct or indirect. Direct transfers specify the destination of the transfer (new value of IP and possibly CS) in the instruction; indirect transfers use the standard addressing modes, as described previously, to locate an operand specifying the destination of the transfer. The 8086 has all four combinations of transfers, whereas the 8080 has direct, intrasegment transfers only.

The 8080 jump and call instructions specify an absolute destination address; the corresponding 8086 transfers specify a self-relative destination address. This provides for code compaction (a shortened jump instruction is available for close jumps) as well as for position-independent code.

The 8086 return instruction may adjust the SP register

so that stacked parameters are discarded, thereby making parameter passing more efficient. This is a better solution to the problem than the 8080 instruction, which exchanges the contents of HL with the top of the stack.

The conditional jump instructions in the 8080 are useful for determining relations among unsigned numbers only. The 8086 provides conditional jump instructions that determine relations among both signed and unsigned numbers. Table 5 shows the conditional jumps as functions of flag settings.

The 8080 provides conditional call and return instructions merely as accidents of implementation. In order to free up valuable opcodes, these seldom-used instructions have not been incorporated in the 8086.

Interrupts. The 8080 interrupt mechanism is general enough to permit the interrupting device to supply any operation for out-of-sequence execution. However, the only operation that has any utility for interrupt processing is the one-byte subroutine call. This byte comprises five bits of opcode and three bits that identify one of eight interrupt subroutines residing at eight fixed locations in memory. If the unnecessary generalization is removed, the interrupting device does not have to provide the opcode, and all eight bits can be used to identify the interrupt subroutine. Furthermore, if the eight bits are used to index a table of subroutine addresses, the actual subroutine can reside anywhere in memory. The 8086 interrupt mechanism reflects this line of thinking.

The six years of evolution traced here encompass many advances in technology and performance (Figure 9, Tables 6 and 7). During this period, computing costs declined by over three orders of magnitude. By removing a hurdle that had inhibited the computer industry—the need to conserve expensive processors—the new era has freed system designers to concentrate on the applications themselves. ∎

Table 5.
8086 conditional jumps as functions of flag settings.

JUMP ON	FLAG SETTINGS
EQUAL	ZF = 1
NOT EQUAL	ZF = 0
LESS THAN	(SF XOR OF) = 1
GREATER THAN	((SF XOR OF) OR ZF) = 0
LESS THAN OR EQUAL	((SF XOR OF) OR ZF) = 1
GREATER THAN OR EQUAL	(SF XOR OF) = 0
BELOW	CF = 1
ABOVE	(CF OR ZF) = 0
BELOW OR EQUAL	(CF OR ZF) = 1
ABOVE OR EQUAL	CF = 0
PARITY EVEN	PF = 1
PARITY ODD	PF = 0
OVERFLOW	OF = 1
NO OVERFLOW	OF = 0
SIGN	SF = 1
NO SIGN	SF = 0

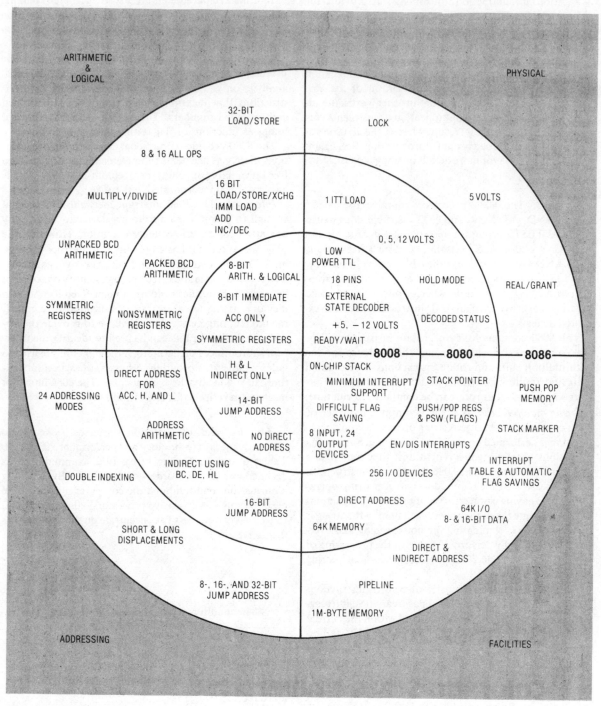

Figure 9. 8008-8086 evolution.

Table 6.
Performance comparison.

	8008 (1972)	8080 (2 MHZ) (1974)	8086 (8 MHZ) (1978)
REGISTER-REGISTER TRANSFER	12.5	2	0.25
JUMP	25	5	0.875
REGISTER-IMMEDIATE OPERATION	20	3.5	0.5
SUBROUTINE CALL	28	9	2.5
INCREMENT (16-BIT)	50	2.5	0.25
ADDITION (16-BIT)	75	5	0.375
TRANSFERS (16-BIT)	25	2	0.25

ALL TIMES ARE IN MICROSECONDS.

Table 7.
Technology comparison.

	8008 (1972)	8080 (1974)	8085 (1976)	8086 (1978)
SILICON GATE TECHNOLOGY	P-CHANNEL ENHANCEMENT LOAD DEVICE	N-CHANNEL ENHANCEMENT LOAD DEVICE	N-CHANNEL DEPLETION LOAD DEVICE	SCALED N-CHANNEL (HMOS) DEPLETION LOAD DEVICE
CLOCK RATE	0.5-0.8 MHz	2-3 MHz	3-5 MHz	5-8 MHz
MIN. GATE DELAY[1] FO = FI = 1	30 NS[2]	15 NS[2]	5 NS	3 NS
TYPICAL SPEED POWER PRODUCT	100 PJ	40 PJ	10 PJ	2 PJ
APPROXIMATE NUMBER OF TRANSISTORS[3]	2000	4500	6500	20,000[4]
AVERAGE TRANSISTOR DENSITY (MIL-SQRD PER TRANSISTOR)	8.4	7.5	5.7	2.5

NOTES:

1. FASTEST INVERTER FUNCTION AVAILABLE WITH WORST CASE PROCESSING.
2. LINEAR MODE ENHANCEMENT LOAD.
3. GATE EQUIVALENT CAN BE ESTIMATED BY DIVIDING BY THREE.
4. THIS IS 29,000 TRANSISTORS, IF ALL ROM AND PLA PLACEMENT SITES AVAILABLE ARE COUNTED.

Acknowledgments

Many people played significant roles in the development of these processors. Hence, it is not possible to single out a few for all the credit. However, if forced to choose those people who played the most significant roles on each chip, we can name the following: M. E. (Ted) Hoff was the architect and Federico Faggin the chip designer of the 4004. Stanley Mazor contributed to the 4004 architecture as well as to the architectures of the 8008 and 8080. Hoff and Hal Feeney were the major contributors to the 8008 development. Faggin managed the development of the 8080 and participated in defining its architecture, with Masatoshi Shima doing the logic and circuit design. Roger Swanson defined the new instructions for the 8085, while Peter Stoll and Andrew Volk performed the 8085 logic and circuit design. The 8086 architecture was defined by Stephen Morse and refined by Bruce Ravenel, with James McKevitt and John Bayliss responsible for the logic and circuit design. William Pohlman managed both the 8085 and 8086 activities.

The authors thank Stephen Hanna for reviewing this material and providing many helpful suggestions and comments.

Bibliography

Bylinsky, G., "Here Comes the Second Computer Revolution," *Fortune*, Nov. 1975.

Faggin, F., et al., "The MCS-4—An LSI Microcomputer System," *IEEE 1972 Region Six Conf.*, 1972, pp. 8-11.

Hoff, M. E., Jr., "The New LSI Components," *Digest of Papers—COMPCON 72*, IEEE Computer Society, pp. 141-143.

Intel MCS-8 User's Manual, Apr. 1975.

Intel MCS-40 User's Manual, third ed., Mar. 1976.

Intel MCS-85 User's Manual, Mar. 1977.

Intel MCS-86 User's Manual, July 1978.

Intel 8080 Microcomputer Systems User's Manual, Sept. 1975.

Morse, S. P., *The 8086 Primer*, Hayden Book Company, New York, 1980.

Morse, S. P., W. B. Pohlman, and B. W. Ravenel, "The Intel 8086 Microprocessor: A 16-Bit Evolution of the 8080," *Computer*, Vol. 11, No. 6, June 1978, pp. 18-27.

Shima, M., F. Faggin, and S. Mazor, "An N-Channel 8-Bit Single Chip Microprocessor," *IEEE Int'l Solid-State Circuits Conf.*, Feb. 1974, pp. 56-57.

Vadasz, L. L., et al., "Silicon Gate Technology," *IEEE Spectrum*, Oct. 1969, pp. 27-35.

Stephen P. Morse is currently on the staff of Language Resources, a software firm involved in the development of Pascal compilers for microprocessors. Previously he was with Intel Corp., where he was responsible for the architectural definition of the 8086 and served in an advisory staff position in the high-level language area.

Morse has delivered numerous guest lectures on the 8086 (including one in Taiwan) and has recently written a textbook describing the 8086. He has published numerous technical articles on microprocessors, language and compiler design, and computer graphics.

Morse received a BEE degree from the City University of New York in 1962 and an MS and PhD in electrical engineering from the Polytechnic Institute of New York in 1963 and 1967, respectively. He is a member of the ACM.

Stanley Mazor is with Intel Corp., where he has participated in the designs of the MCS-4, MCS-8, 8080, and several other microcomputers. Prior to joining Intel in 1969, he was assistant manager of the computer center at San Francisco State College and a principal designer of the Symbol computer at Fairchild.

Mazor has published 25 articles and papers on microcomputers and shares patents on the 8080 and MCS-4. He is a member of the IEEE.

Bruce W. Ravenel is president of Language Resources. Previously at Intel Corporation, he was coarchitect of the 8086 microprocessor, architect of the 8087 numeric processor, and designer of the PL/M-86 programming language. Before joining Intel in 1976, Ravenel earned a BA in economics at the University of Colorado, Boulder; his computer science graduate studies at Boulder focused on software portability and compiler construction.

Ravenel is cochairman of the Joint ANSI/X3J9—IEEE Pascal Standards Committee. He is a member of the IEEE and of the IEEE Computer Society.

William B. Pohlman was program manager for mid-range microprocessors at Intel Corporation. His technical interests include computer architecture, VLSI structures and implementation techniques, and multimicroprocessor systems. Before joining Intel in 1975, he was responsible for the LSI-11 chip set development at Western Digital Corporation.

Pohlman received his BSEE from California State University at Northridge in 1966, and his MSEE from the University of Southern California in 1969. He is a member of the ACM and the IEEE.

COMPUTER

MICROPROCESSORS & MICROCOMPUTERS
MICROPROCESSORS & MICROCOMPUTERS

SELECTED REPRINTS ON MICROPROCESSORS & MICROCOMPUTERS

SECTION 2
16-32 BIT MICROPROCESSORS

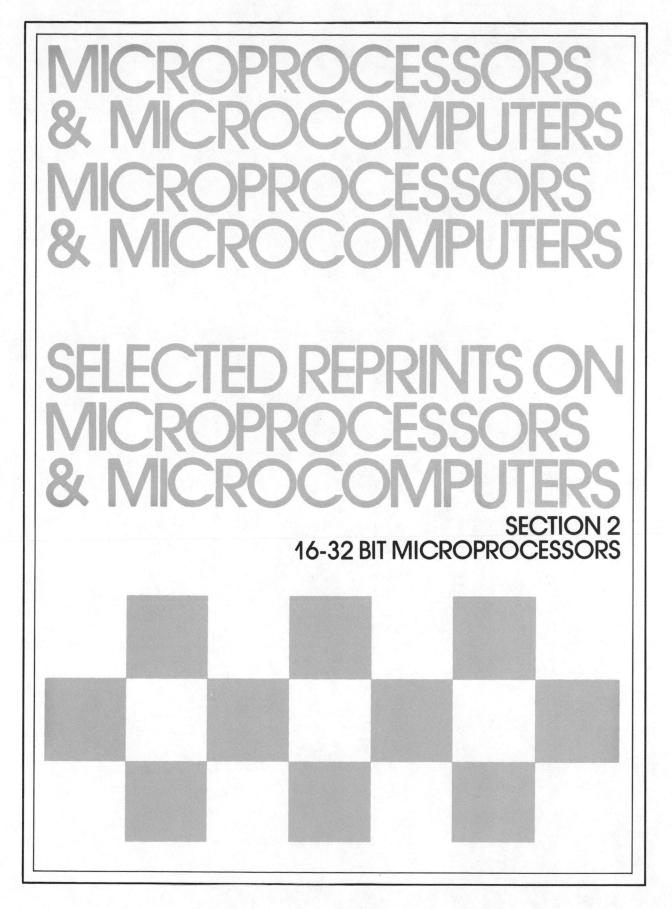

Reprinted from *Computer*, February 1979, pages 43-52. Copyright © 1979 by
The Institute of Electrical and Electronics Engineers, Inc.

MICROSYSTEMS

*The first implementation of a new microprocessor architecture
promises to narrow the gap between the power
of very small and very large computers.*

A Microprocessor Architecture for a Changing World: The Motorola 68000

Edward Stritter
Tom Gunter
Motorola Semiconductor

Microprocessor technology is entering a new and especially challenging era. While technology constraints have not completely disappeared, we are nearly to the point where the limiting factor in microprocessor design is not how much function can be included, but how imaginative and creative the designer can be.[1] As a result, several companies have introduced new-generation microprocessors. We describe how one of them, the Motorola 6800, responds to these unique conditions.

Motivations for a new microprocessor architecture

Previous generations of microprocessors were limited by the available technology. Brooks, in an overview article,[2] discusses how the technology constraints and the perceived microprocessor market motivated early microprocessor architecture. Microprocessors were limited in number of registers, data-path width, and instruction-set power primarily because technology could not support more features on a single chip. Other limitations of microprocessors, such as having too small an address space[3] and awkwardness of address computation,[4] may be attributed as much to prevailing perceptions of the potential market as to technology constraints.[5] Whatever the former sources of restraint, however, we are now in a period of technical innovation and spirited competition.

Technological advances. The basic microprocessor technology, MOS, has been steadily advanced in the last few years. The most noticeable improvement has been circuit density (Figure 1), which translates directly into the amount of capability that can be put on a single-chip microprocessor. Whereas earlier microprocessors contained from 5000 to 10,000 transistors per chip, current processors have from 25,000 to 70,000 transistors, which is less than an order of magnitude away from the number in many of the largest maxi-computers. Circuit density is not the only technology advance that has been made: corresponding improvements have been achieved in circuit speed and power dissipation.

Advances in technology have been more evolutionary than revolutionary. The major advance, increased circuit density, is the result of gradual improvements in processing techniques that permit smaller circuit dimensions. Density improvements are expected to continue, since they depend not on overcoming fundamental limitations but only on further evolutionary improvement of existing processes. New microprocessor architectures must be devised to take advantage of this future advancement.

Market demands. The demand for microprocessors in applications not foreseen just a few years ago is providing new opportunities for microprocessor manufacturers. Just as the original microprocessor designers could not predict the many uses that would be found for their devices, today's designers cannot hope to envision more than a few of the eventual applications of new microprocessors. The implication for the designer is that new designs must be flexible and general if they are to be useful in a large number of potential applications.

High software costs. The problem of software costs is even worse in microprocessor applications than it is with computers generally. Decreasing memory costs,

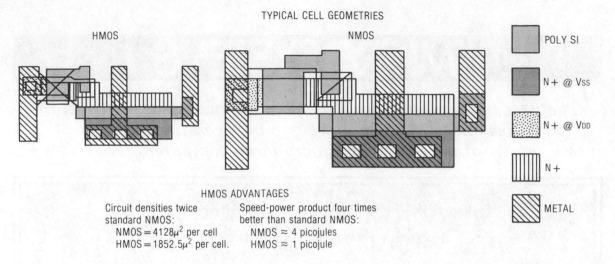

TYPICAL CELL GEOMETRIES

HMOS

NMOS

POLY SI

N+ @ Vss

N+ @ Vdd

N+

METAL

HMOS ADVANTAGES

Circuit densities twice
standard NMOS:
    $NMOS = 4128\mu^2$ per cell
    $HMOS = 1852.5\mu^2$ per cell.

Speed-power product four times
better than standard NMOS:
    $NMOS \approx 4$ picojules
    $HMOS \approx 1$ picojule

Figure 1. Comparisons of HMOS and NMOS technologies. The HMOS technology used for the MC68000 results in significant improvements to circuit densities and speed-power products.

increasing processor functionality, and more complex applications are combining to increase the size and complexity of microprocessor programs. Software costs of $100,000 or more are clearly incompatible with hardware costs of hundreds of dollars. This cost disparity may be unimportant in large-volume applications, where software costs can be amortized over thousands of hardware units, but it often precludes the use of microprocessors in applications characterized by complex programs but low volume. To help reduce the high cost of software, microprocessor designers must make a strong commitment to supporting high-level languages and disciplined programming practices.

High design costs. The cost of designing and implementing a new device with tens of thousands of transistors is high. Computer design aids are indispensible, but they are also expensive. Designers must attack this design-cost problem in several ways. First, straightforward designs, using regular structures, are easier to implement, test, and correct, and are therefore less expensive than exotic designs. Second, each new architecture must be planned to last for as long as possible and must be easy to expand in the future. Manufacturers can no longer afford to produce new architectures every few years. Experience with trying to extend and improve the original 8-bit microprocessor architectures demonstrates the need for planned expansion. Designers must be careful to include as few limitations to future expansion as possible. The most common mistakes in the past have been limiting address size and not providing unused operation codes for future new instructions.

Design goals for the 68000. Motorola's 68000 microprocessor architecture has been designed to meet the requirements outlined above. (The MC68000's characteristics are summarized in Table 1.)

Architectural family. The 68000 design specifies a computer architecture of which a number of different versions or "implementations" will be produced.[6] The first version, the MC68000, implements only the subset of the complete 68000 architecture allowed by current technology constraints.

Flexibility and usefulness. The 68000 design ensures that the processor is easy to program. As much as possible, there are no unnatural limitations, artifacts, special cases, or other awkward features in the architecture.

Marketability. The 68000 is a general-purpose architecture, reflecting the increasing market acceptance of general-purpose microprocessors for diverse applications.

Expandability. The 68000 design specifies several features, such as floating-point and string operations, that are not implemented in the first version but have been specified now to guarantee future consistency. In addition, unused space has been left in the architecture to accommodate new features that future advances in technology will make possible.

Support of high-level languages. The 68000 architecture contains features for implementing high-level languages, and Morotola is commited to supplying software support for program development in well-known high-level languages.

**Table 1.
Motorola MC68000 characteristics.**

INTEGER SIZES	8, 16, and 32 bits
ADDRESSING CAPABILITY	16,777,216 bytes
INPUT/OUTPUT	memory-mapped
TECHNOLOGY	HMOS
INTERNAL CYCLE	250 nsec
MEMORY ACCESS	500 nsec
RELATIVE PERFORMANCE	10 to 25 times 6800
PINS	64
POWER	+5V

Resources. The 68000 design provides an address space of 2^{32} bytes (limited to 2^{24} bytes in the initial implementation). Memory is byte addressable, with individual-bit addressing provided for bit-manipulation instructions. Memory may be accessed in units of 1, 8, 16, or 32 bits. CPU resources include sixteen 32-bit registers, a 32-bit program counter (24 bits in the initial implementation), and a 16-bit status register.

The registers (Figure 2) are divided into two classes. The eight data registers are used primarily for data manipulation; they may be operand sources or destinations for all operations but are used in addressing only as index registers. The eight remaining (address) registers are used primarily for addressing. The stack pointer is one of the address registers. The program counter and status word are separate registers.

Addressing. Memory is logically addressed in 8-bit bytes, 16-bit words, or 32-bit long words. The current implementation requires that word and long-word

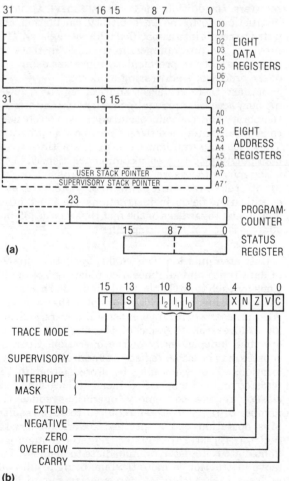

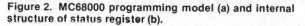

(a)

(b)

Figure 2. MC68000 programming model (a) and internal structure of status register (b).

Table 2.
MC68000 addressing modes.

REGISTER DIRECT ADDRESSING:

data register direct	EA	= Dn
address register direct	EA	= An
status register direct	EA	= SR

REGISTER DEFERRED ADDRESSING:

register deferred	EA	= (An)
register deferred post-increment	EA	= (An); An <− An + N
register deferred pre-decrement	An <− An − N; EA	= (An)
base relative	EA	= (An) + d16
indexed	EA	= (An) + (Xn) + d8

PROGRAM COUNTER RELATIVE:

relative with offset	EA	= (PC) + d16
relative indexed	EA	= (PC) + (Xn) + d8
short PC relative branch	EA	= (PC) + d8
long PC relative branch	EA	= (PC) + d16

ABSOLUTE ADDRESSING:

absolute short	EA	= (next instruction word)
absolute long	EA	= (next two instruction words)

IMMEDIATE DATA ADDRESSING:

immediate	DATA	= next instruction word(s)
quick immediate	DATA	= subfield of instruction (4 bits)

DEFINITIONS:

EA	=	effective address
An	=	address register
Dn	=	data register
Xn	=	address or data register used as index register
SR	=	status register
PC	=	program counter
d8	=	8-bit displacement
d16	=	16-bit displacement
N	=	1 for byte, 2 for word, and 4 for long word operands
( )	=	contents of
<−	=	replaces

data be word aligned. Bits are individually addressable in the bit-manipulation instructions.

The architecture specifies an optimal memory-management scheme that implements and enforces variable-length segmentation of the address space with access rights specifiable for individual segments. The processor can be used with or without memory management.

Address calculations (Table 2) are specified by 6-bit fields of the instruction. The addressing specification is orthogonal to the operation specification of the instruction; that is, any addressing mode can be used in any instruction that uses addressing.

Addresses are 32-bit quantities (24 bits in the current implementation). The architecture efficiently supports small systems (those with fewer than 2^{16} addressable bytes) by allowing 16-bit address quantities to be specified, moved, or calculated in almost every addressing situation. For example, an absolute address carried in an instruction can use 16 or 32 bits, or an index calculation can use 16 bits (sign extended to 24 bits) or 32 bits of a register as input. This feature allows the architecture to support very large addresses without penalizing the efficiency of programs that require only small addresses. The address size (16 or 32 bits) is individually specified for each use, so that large and small addresses can be intermixed arbitrarily in a program.

39

A variety of addressing modes are available:

Register direct. The data or address register contains the operand.

Address register deferred. The operand address is in the specified address register.

Address register deferred post-increment. The operand address is in the specified address register. After the operand is accessed, the address in the register is incremented by the operand size (1, 2, or 4).

Address register deferred pre-decrement. The operand address is in the specified address register. Before the operand is accessed, the address register is decremented by the operand size.

Base relative. The operand address is the contents of the specified address register plus a 16-bit signed displacement in the instruction.

Program counter relative. The operand address is the current program counter value plus a 16-bit signed displacement in the instruction.

Indexed. The operand address is the contents of the specified address register plus the contents of an additional (data or address) register specified plus an 8-bit signed displacement in the instruction.

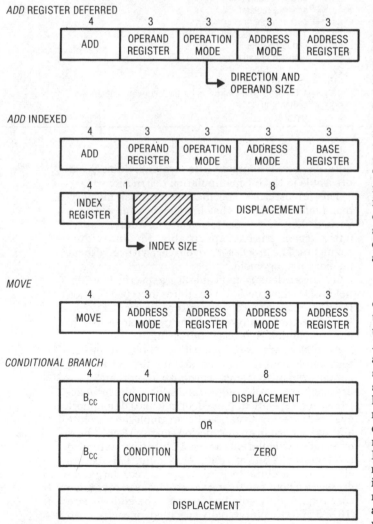

Figure 3. Typical MC68000 instruction formats.

Program counter indexed. The operand address is the current value of the program counter, plus the contents of the specified data or address register, plus an 8-bit signed displacement in the instruction.

Absolute. The operand address is in the instruction.

Immediate. The operand is in the instruction.

Bit addressing. A complete set of bit-manipulation instructions (SET, CLEAR, CHANGE, and TEST) is provided. For these instructions, an individual memory word is addressed using one of the above addressing modes. The individual bit to be manipulated is addressed by its bit number in that word. The bit specification is contained in the instruction or previously calculated in a data register. This mechanism allows bits to be addressed simply, without requiring the use of logical instructions and masks. For registers, all 32 bits are individually addressable.

In all cases, the addresses specified by the program can span the entire address space. No arbitrary segment sizes are imposed, and no separate segment numbers need be manipulated.

Address, like integer, is a fully supported data type. A complete set of address-manipulation operations (MOVE, COMPARE, INCREMENT, DECREMENT, ADD TO, SUBTRACT FROM) is implemented on the address registers. In addition, the LOAD EFFECTIVE ADDRESS instruction performs an arbitrary calculation and puts the result into a specified address register. This provides the programmer, in a single instruction, with the ability to precalculate addresses using any of the processor's addressing modes.

Because there are eight address registers, fewer memory accesses are required for loading and storing temporary address values, and addresses rarely need to be recalculated in different parts of the program. These features minimize the program time spent manipulating addresses, a common bottleneck in existing microprocessors. They also establish a degree of address-size independence;[7] the address-specification fields in instructions are most often only 6 bits, regardless of the fact that a large (32-bit) address is actually being specified.

Data manipulation. The 68000 supports a number of data types and supplies a complete set of operations for each type (Table 3 and Figure 3). In general, the addressing mode is independent of the data type. Also, in cases where it makes sense (integers, logicals, and addresses), the size of the operand may be specified independently of the operation. Operand sources may be either registers or addressed memory locations. The result may be stored either in the register or in the specified memory location. This class of "register-to-memory" operations reduces the number of register stores required to save results. Most operations can be specified to work memory-to-register, register-to-register, register-to-memory, immediate-to-register, or immediate-to-memory. The move instruction is more flexible, being a full two-address instruction. It can specify memory-to-memory move operations as well as the options listed above.

The 68000 data types and the operations that support them are:

Integer. The operations are ADD, SUBTRACT, MULTIPLY, DIVIDE, NEGATE, COMPARE, and ARITHMETIC SHIFT. Integers may be 1, 2, or 4 bytes. Shifts are multiple-bit shifts, either left or right, with shift count specified in the instruction or previously calculated in a data register, and indicate overflow as appropriate.

Multiprecision integer. ADD WITH EXTEND, SUBTRACT WITH EXTEND, NEGATE WITH EXTEND, UNSIGNED MULTIPLY, and UNSIGNED DIVIDE are the primitives supplied for easily implementing multiprecision integer arithmetic. Operands may be 1, 2, or 4 bytes, except for multiply and divide, which operate only on 2-byte quantities.

Logical. The operations are AND, OR, EXCLUSIVE OR, COMPLEMENT, COMPARE, SHIFT, and ROTATE (which allow multiple-position shifts and rotates, left or right, with or without extend bit). Logicals may be 1, 2, or 4 bytes.

Boolean. AND, OR, EXCLUSIVE OR, COMPLEMENT, IMPLICATION, and SET ACCORDING TO CONDITION CODES are provided. (SET ACCORDING TO CONDITION CODES is used to retrieve the logical value of any of the conditional tests that are available to the CONDITIONAL BRANCH instruction.) Boolean data are one-byte quantities.

Bit. The operations are SET, CLEAR, CHANGE, and TEST. Bits are individually addressable.

Decimal. ADD, SUBTRACT, NEGATE, and COMPARE are decimal operations. The decimal (BCD) instructions work on operands in memory (memory-to-memory) two digits (one byte) at a time. Combined with a looping instruction, the decimal instructions implement variable-length memory-to-memory decimal operations.

Character. Character instructions, MOVE and COMPARE, work on operands in memory (memory-to-memory).

Address. Address operations include INCREMENT (by 1, 2, or 4), DECREMENT (by 1, 2, or 4), ADD INTEGER, SUBTRACT INTEGER, COMPARE, and LOAD EFFECTIVE ADDRESS.

Real. Floating-point ADD, SUBTRACT, MULTIPLY, and DIVIDE are specified but not implemented in the first version.

String. STRING MOVE, STRING SEARCH, and TRANSLATE are specified but not implemented in the first version.

Program control. Program-control instructions include CONDITIONAL BRANCH (program counter relative), JUMP, JUMP TO SUBROUTINE, RETURN FROM SUBROUTINE, and RETURN FROM INTERRUPT, all of which are traditional instructions. Sixteen separate operating-system calls are specifiable with the TRAP instruction. Conditional traps, looping, and subroutine control are discussed below. The STOP instruction halts the processor, the RESET instruction reinitializes the system environment, and the MOVE instruction can manipulate the processor status word.

Privilege states. The 68000 processor can operate in user or supervisor state. In supervisor state, the entire instruction set is available. Indication of the current state is given to the external world so that, for instance, address translation can be inhibited when the processor is in supervisor state. In user state, certain instructions, such as STOP, RESET, and those that modify the status word, are not allowed; they cause a

**Table 3.
MC6800 instruction set.**

MNEMONIC	DESCRIPTION
ABCD	Add decimal with extend
ADD	Add
ADDX	Add with extend
AND	Logical and
ASL	Arithmetic shift left
ASR	Arithmetic shift right
BCC	Branch conditionally
BCHG	Bit test and change
BCLR	Bit test and clear
BRA	Branch always
BSET	Bit test and set
BSR	Branch to subroutine
BTST	Bit test
CHK	Check register against bounds
CLR	Clear operand
CMP	Arithmetic compare
DCNT	Decrement and branch non-zero
DIVS	Signed divide
DIVU	Unsigned divide
EOR	Exclusive or
EXG	Exchange registers
EXT	Signed extend
JMP	Jump
JSR	Jump to subroutine
LDM	Load multiple registers
LDQ	Load register quick
LEA	Load effective address
LINK	Link stack
LSL	Logical shift left
LSR	Logical shift right
MOVE	Move
MULS	Signed multiply
MULU	Unsigned multiply
NBCD	Negate decimal with extend
NEG	Two's complement
NEGX	Two's complement with extend
NOP	No operation
NOT	One's complement
OR	Logical or
PEA	Push effective address
RESET	Reset external devices
ROTL	Rotate left without extend
ROTR	Rotate right without extend
ROTXL	Rotate left with extend
ROTXR	Rotate right with extend
RTR	Return and restore
RTS	Return from subroutine
SBCD	Subtract decimal from extend
SCC	Set conditionally
STM	Store multiple registers
STOP	Stop
SUB	Subtract
SUBX	Subtract with extend
SWAP	Swap data register halves
TAS	Test and set operand
TRAP	Trap
TRAPV	Trap on overflow
TST	Test
UNLK	Unlink stack

41

```
SAMPLE PROGRAM:

 PROGRAM EXAMPLE;
 VAR PARAM1, PARAM2: INTEGER;
 PROCEDURE PROC (X: INTEGER; VAR Y: INTEGER);
   VAR A, B: INTEGER;
   BEGIN
     <procedure body>
   END;
 BEGIN
   PROC (PARAM1, PARAM2)
 END.

PROGRAM BODY:

 MOVE      PARAM1 TO −SP@         "push first parameter"
 PEA       PARAM2                 "push address of 2nd parameter"
 JSR       PROC                   "call the procedure"
 ADD       #6 TO SP               "pop parameters from the stack"

PROCEDURE BODY:

 LINK      FP, 4                  "link and allocate three local
                                    variables"
 MOVEM     <registerlist> TO −SP@ "push some register contents"
 <procedure body>
 MOVEM     <registerlist> FROM SP@ + "restore registers"
 UNLK      FP                     "restore stack"
 RETURN                           "return to calling procedure"
```

Figure 4. Sample Pascal program and equivalent 68000 code.

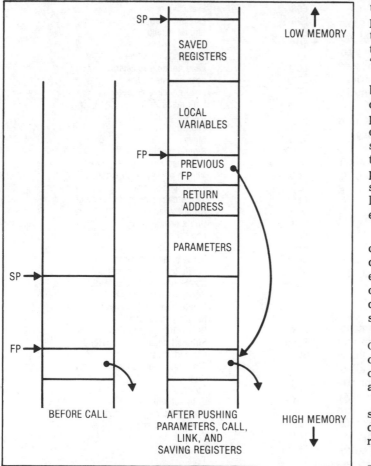

Figure 5. Stack activity on procedure call.

trap to supervisor state (by stacking the current program and status word and loading a new context from a pre-assigned trap vector). Illegal instructions, unimplemented instructions, interrupts, and traps (operating as system calls) all cause the processor to trap and switch to supervisor state. To ensure proper operation when returning to supervisor state, regardless of user-state activity, there are two stack-pointer registers—one active in user state, one in supervisor state. The user stack-pointer contents are available, by special instructions, to the supervisor-state program.

The 68000's user/system state distinction will allow a small operating-system kernel to provide fully protected virtual address spaces to any number of independent tasks or users.

Trapping on illegal and unimplemented instructions allows the operating system to provide a more functional virtual machine to user-state tasks. For instance, the operating system can transparently provide software implementation of any currently unimplemented instructions (such as floating-point or string manipulation) executed by a user-state task.

High-level-language support. A recent paper by Allison[8] suggests ways in which microprocessor architecture should be designed to support high-level languages. This method, followed by the 68000 designers, is to "examine...the runtime representation required for the class of languages to be implemented" and to "provide adequate instructions...to support the required runtime representation" and transformations on that representation "without extensive in-line computation."

The 68000 design supports high-level languages, at both compilation time and execution time, with a clean, consistent instruction set; with hardware implementation of commonly used functions (multiply, divide, and address calculation); and with a set of special-purpose instructions designed to manipulate the runtime environment of a high-level-language program. The language constructs aided by these special-purpose instructions include array accessing, limited-precision arithmetic, looping, Boolean-expression evaluation, and procedure calls.

Array accessing. The BOUNDS CHECK instruction compares a previously calculated array index (in a data register) against zero and a limit value addressed by the instruction. A trap occurs if the index is out of bounds for that array. This replaces a common sequence of instructions (at least four) with a single instruction.

Limited-precision arithmetic. The TRAP ON OVERFLOW instruction causes a trap if the preceding operation resulted in overflow. This allows efficient overflow testing to encourage proper checking of arithmetic results.

Looping. A restricted form of the FOR-loop construct is implemented in a single instruction that decrements a count and branches backward if the result is nonzero.

Boolean-expression evaluation. The CONDITIONAL SET instructions assign a true or false value to a Boolean variable on the same conditions that are used by the CONDITIONAL BRANCH instructions. These instructions help implement Boolean-expression evaluation by avoiding extra conditional branches, especially in the case (as with Pascal) where "short-circuited" evaluation may be undesirable because of possible side effects.

Procedure calls. The 68000 uses a stack—pointed to by one of the address registers, called the stack pointer—to build the nested environments of called procedures. Three instructions (plus an additional one for each parameter) implement a high-level-language procedure call (Figure 4). The entire call mechanism uses only the stack and is completely reentrant (Figure 5). These instructions are described in more detail below.

Push parameter values or addresses onto the stack. The MOVE instruction pushes a value onto the stack, and the PUSH EFFECTIVE ADDRESS (see LOAD EFFECTIVE ADDRESS explained earlier) pushes the result of an artitrary address calculation onto the stack for call by reference.

Call procedure. The JUMP TO SUBROUTINE instruction pushes the return address on the stack and jumps to the procedure entry point.

Establish new local environment. The LINK instruction does all of the following: saves the old contents of the frame pointer (an arbitrary address register) on the stack, points the frame pointer to the new top of stack, and subtracts the number of bytes of local storage required by the procedure from the stack pointer. This establishes local storage for the called procedure and a frame pointer (address register) for index addressing of local variables and parameters.

Save an arbitrary subset of the registers on the stack. The MOVE MULTIPLE REGISTERS instruction saves an arbitrary subset of the registers on the stack (or anywhere in memory) in a single instruction. The registers to be saved are indicated by setting the corresponding bits in a 16-bit field of the instruction.

A set of at most four instructions reverses the process for procedure return:

Reload saved registers. The MOVE MULTIPLE REGISTERS instruction is used here also.

Reestablish previous environment. The UNLINK instruction undoes the work of the LINK instruction.

Return from procedure. The RETURN instruction pops the return address from the stack and returns to the calling procedure.

Pop parameters from the stack. The ADD IMMEDIATE instruction used on the stack pointer pops any number of values off the stack.

The 68000 system architecture

A computer architecture specifies interactions between the processor and its environment by defining such things as interrupt structure, memory segmentation, bus interfaces, and input/output structure. The 68000 system architecture is designed to be as flexible as possible. For instance, I/O device registers are addressed as memory locations (memory-mapped I/O), as on other Motorola microprocessors. Memory-mapped I/O gives the programmer the flexibility and power of the entire instruction set for manipulating device-control and data registers. Since no additional instructions are required for I/O, the processor is simpler, and the instruction set is easier to remember. The I/O space is protected by the same memory-management facilities that are used to protect critical areas of memory.

The 68000 bus structure is also designed for simplicity, speed, and flexibilty. The address and data lines are separate; no multiplexing is needed. This avoids the need for any separate devices for demultiplexing, ensuring maximum performance for systems in which speed is important. The bus is asynchronous; transfers on the bus are controlled by accompanying handshake signals, so that no assumptions need be made about timing or system synchrony. The use of handshake signals allows devices and memories with large variations in response time to be used on the same processor bus. The processor waits an arbitrary amount of time until the accessed device or memory signals that the transfer is occurring.

A simple bus request/grant protocol is implemented on-chip so that processors and direct-memory-access devices can cooperatively share the system bus with no extra arbitration logic. Also, the chip has a bus-fault input pin that causes instruction execution to be terminated at any point and a trap to be taken if an illegal or faulty memory access is made. This facilitates memory protection.

The 68000 interrupt structure is like that of most minicomputers. Eight priority levels are implemented. Interrrupts are vectored so that software has full control over the placement and execution of interrupt-handling routines. The current priority level of the processor is kept in its status word. Interrupts at or below the current priority are inhibited. Interrupts at higher levels may occur, so interrupt handling may be nested. When an enabled interrupt occurs, the processor sends an acknowledge signal. The interrupting device responds with a vector number. The vector number is used by the processor

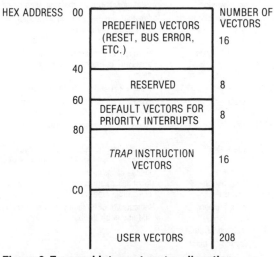

Figure 6. Trap and interrupt vector allocation.

43

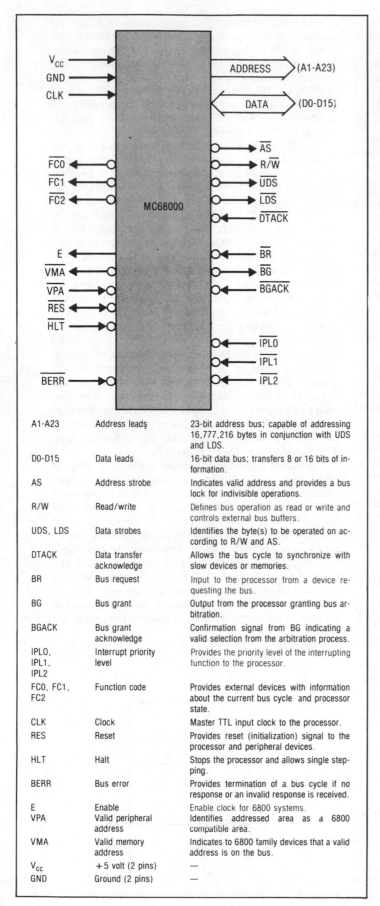

A1-A23	Address leads	23-bit address bus; capable of addressing 16,777,216 bytes in conjunction with UDS and LDS.
D0-D15	Data leads	16-bit data bus; transfers 8 or 16 bits of information.
AS	Address strobe	Indicates valid address and provides a bus lock for indivisible operations.
R/W	Read/write	Defines bus operation as read or write and controls external bus buffers.
UDS, LDS	Data strobes	Identifies the byte(s) to be operated on according to R/W and AS.
DTACK	Data transfer acknowledge	Allows the bus cycle to synchronize with slow devices or memories.
BR	Bus request	Input to the processor from a device requesting the bus.
BG	Bus grant	Output from the processor granting bus arbitration.
BGACK	Bus grant acknowledge	Confirmation signal from BG indicating a valid selection from the arbitration process.
IPL0, IPL1, IPL2	Interrupt priority level	Provides the priority level of the interrupting function to the processor.
FC0, FC1, FC2	Function code	Provides external devices with information about the current bus cycle and processor state.
CLK	Clock	Master TTL input clock to the processor.
RES	Reset	Provides reset (initialization) signal to the processor and peripheral devices.
HLT	Halt	Stops the processor and allows single stepping.
BERR	Bus error	Provides termination of a bus cycle if no response or an invalid response is received.
E	Enable	Enable clock for 6800 systems.
VPA	Valid peripheral address	Identifies addressed area as a 6800 compatible area.
VMA	Valid memory address	Indicates to 6800 family devices that a valid address is on the bus.
V_{cc}	+5 volt (2 pins)	—
GND	Ground (2 pins)	—

to index into a table of interrupt vectors in low memory to find the appropriate entry point to the interrupt handler; there are 256 such vectors (Figure 6). Individual devices on the same priority level can be distinguished by different vector numbers, so no device polling is required. Software traps and exception conditions in the processor also transfer through the vector table; in these cases the vector numbers are assigned by the processor. The vector table is in main memory and therefore can be manipulated by the operating system as necessary. The processor implements a set of default vectors (one for each priority level) so that existing peripheral devices, not equipped to respond with vector numbers, can be used.

68000 systems can be configured with a processor directly connected to memory; the addresses generated by the program are then for the physical memory. This will suffice for many applications. More complex applications, especially those with multiple tasks or even multiple users, will require more sophisticated memory management. A separate single-chip device will be available to provide memory segmentation, address translation, and memory protection.

68000 design and implementation

The single-chip MC68000 microprocessor (Figure 7) is a partial implementation of the 68000 architecture. It implements as large a subset of the complete architecture as current technologies will allow. The relevant technological constraints are limitations on the number of pins and on circuit density. Addresses are limited to 24 bits by present-day packaging technology, which restricts the number of pins per package to 64. Similarly the data path to memory is only 16 bits wide. This is not an architectural limitation, but it does require that two memory accesses be made for each 32-bit datum.

Circuit density limits the number of instructions that can be implemented. One-eighth of the operation-code map is currently unimplemented. Some of this space is allocated in the architecture—for example, for floating-point and string operations. Some of the free space is currently unspecified and will be allocated for future architectural enhancement. All unimplemented instructions cause traps, so that software emulation is possible.

Future implementations of the architecture may expand upwards or shrink downwards in performance and functional capability. Technological advances will soon allow the full architecture to be implemented. As circuit densities improve further, new versions will be faster and smaller (and thus less expensive) and will consume less power. Increased circuit density will also allow the inclusion of on-chip memory and sophisticated speed-up techniques.

Today's state of the art in MOS LSI technology permits approximately one transistor per square mil

Figure 7. MC8000 pin identifications and definitions. The microprocessor is housed in a 64-pin package that allows the use of separate (non-multiplexed) address and data buses.

44

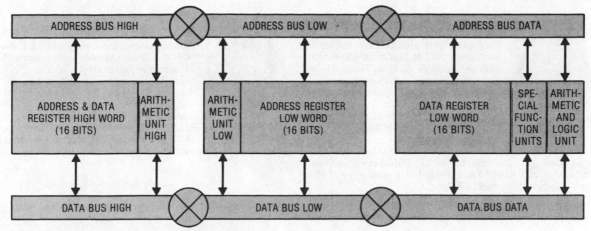

Figure 8. MC68000 execution unit configuration.

of circuit area and permits logic gates to be designed with a speed-to-power product of one picojoule. An advanced high-density *n*-channel silicon-gate MOS technology was selected for the design of the 68000. This technology supports three-micron device geometries and provides the designer with multiple MOS transistor threshold voltages. The technology allows the circuit designer to develop high-performance logic gates using minimum-size devices and to develop internal buffer circuits requiring little power.

The execution unit is a dual-bus structure that performs both address and data processing (Figure 8). The two buses are 16 bits wide, and each can be dynamically reconfigured into three independent sections as required by the microcode. Three independent arithmetic units are available to perform these calculations; also, special logic functions are provided to execute long shifts, priority encoding, and bit manipulation. Each of these units is connected to two internal buses and receives both input operands simultaneously from the registers. Each bus contains both the true and the complement logic values so that differential circuit design can be used for higher-speed operation. The execution unit directly interfaces to the external bus logic and buffers, but its operation is independent of the external timing requirements of the bus.

The control of the 68000 is implemented by microcode. The actual structure of the microprogrammed control structure is discussed in detail in another paper.[9] The microcontrol is implemented as a two-level structure. The first level contains sequences of microinstructions with short "vertical" format and complex branching capabilities. Microinstructions contain the addresses of nanoinstructions, wide "horizontal" control words, stored in the second level. The nanoinstructions directly control the execution unit. The use of microcode is motivated by the high design cost of new VLSI chips. The microcode's regularity of structure compared to combinatorial logic significantly decreases the design complexity. Microcode also permits some engineering decisions—for instance, details of specific instructions—to be delayed. In other words, once the micromachine architecture is determined, hardware implementation (circuit design) and firmware implementation (microprogramming) can be done in parallel.

Conclusion

The Motorola 68000 architecture combines advanced technology improvements with a better understanding of the architectural needs of microprocessor users and microprocessor applications. The 68000 is a step into an area previously occupied only by high-end minicomputers. It is a 32-bit architecture that supports many data types and data sizes. The advantages of the 68000 include a flexible addressing mechanism, a simple and effective instruction set that can be used to easily build complex operations, a multilevel vectored interrupt structure, and a fast, asynchronous, nonmultiplexed bus architecture. The 68000 architecture describes a family of microprocessors designed for the expanding high-end microcomputer market. ■

References

1. J. R. Rattner, "Microprocessor Architecture—Where Do We Go From Here," *COMPCON Spring 1977 Digest of Papers*, pp. 223-224.

2. F. P. Brooks, "An Overview of Microcomputer Architecture and Software," *Proc. EUROMICRO 1976*, North Holland, pp. 1-6.

3. C. G. Bell and W. D. Strecker, "Computer Structures: What Have We Learned From the PDP-11?," *Proc. 3rd Symposium on Computer Architecture*, 1976, pp. 1-14.

4. L. A. Levanthal and W. C. Walsh, "Addressing Considerations in Microprocessor Design," *COMPCON Spring 1977 Digest of Papers*, pp. 225-229.

5. B. L. Peuto and L. J. Shustek, "Current Issues in the Architecture of Microprocessors," *Computer*, Vol. 10, No. 2, Feb. 1977, pp. 20-25.

6. S. A. Ward, "Toward the Renaissance Computer Architecture," *MIDCON 1977 Preprints*, pp. 1-6.

7. P. E. Stanley, "Address Size Independence in a 16-bit Minicomputer," *Proc. 5th Symposium on Computer Architecture*, 1978, pp. 152-157.

8. D. R. Allison, "A Design Philosophy for Microcomputer Architectures," *Computer*, Vol. 10, No. 2, Feb. 1977, pp. 35-41.

9. E. P. Stritter and H. L. Tredennick, "Microprogrammed Implementation of a Single Chip Microprocessor," *Proc. 11th Annual Microprogramming Workshop*, Nov. 1978, pp. 8-16.

Edward Stritter has been working on microprocessor architecture and software since 1977 at Motorola's Semiconductor Group in Austin, Texas. He is also a visiting assistant professor in the Computer Science Department of the University of Texas at Austin. Previously, he was a member of the technical staff at Bell Telephone Labs in Holmdel, New Jersey.

Stritter received a BA degree in mathematics from Dartmouth College in 1968 and MS and PhD degrees from Stanford University in 1969 and 1976. He is a member of Phi Beta Kappa, ACM, and IEEE.

Tom Gunter is design manager of advanced microcomputer systems for the NMOS Microcomponent Operations of Motorola's Integrated Circuits Division. He is currently designing and developing the 68000 family of microcomputer microcomponents. A member of IEEE and ACM, he received his BSEE from Texas A&M University in 1969 and has done graduate work at Arizona State University and the University of Texas.

Reprinted from *Computer,* February 1979, pages 10-21. Copyright ©
1979 by The Institute of Electrical and Electronics Engineers, Inc.

Architecture of a New Microprocessor

Bernard L. Peuto
Zilog, Inc.

*Increased capabilities,
architectural compatibility, and
clearly defined interfaces were
the chief architectural goals of
Zilog's new Z8000 microprocessor
family. Here is an account
of how those goals were met
for two members of that family—
the Z8000 CPU and the MMU.*

The Z8000 family is a new set of microprocessor
components (CPU, CPU support chips, peripherals,
and memories) which supports the Z8000 architecture. The account of how architectural goals were
selected and achieved for two key members of this
family—the Z8000 CPU and the memory management unit—illustrates how much of a challenge
microprocessor architecture represents to the semiconductor industry. MOS technology shows enormous potential, but it is still difficult to use because
of limitations on pin count, power dissipation, speed,
and complexity.[1]

Since this discussion is restricted to technical
issues, we will not allude to the many additional factors (marketing considerations, human considerations, self-imposed restrictions, etc.) which make architecture such a fascinating and difficult discipline.
Furthermore, no attempt has been made to ex-
haustively describe the Z8000 architecture and components. Interested readers should consult the
specific manuals for a more complete description.[2,3]

The goals of the Z8000 architecture:
increased capabilities, architectural
compatibility, increased clarity

The primary reason for introducing a new system
architecture is to significantly improve the control
and processing capabilities of microprocessors while
maintaining their price/performance advantages.
Technical advances have permitted the implementation of substantially increased processor power, but
the most significant motivation for a new component
family is generality. Only through such a family
could we provide for architecturally compatible
growth over a wide range of processing power requirements.

Our approach was a staged system architecture
which attempts to provide new components, enhanced features, and new functions, while protecting the
user's investment in hardware and software. The
Z8000 family supports a single unified architecture
for all small, medium, and high-end user applications
which are implemented using a mix of components
within the same family.

The goals of the Z8000 architecture can be grouped
into three categories: increased capabilities, architectural compatibility over a wide range of processing
powers, and increased clarity. In all these cases the
resulting architectural features apply either to the
basic architecture (that seen by an applications programmer) or to system architecture (that seen by a
system designer or an operating system programmer).

Increased capabilities. All existing 8-bit microprocessors and many 16-bit minicomputers suffer
from having a small address space. So, one of our
goals was to provide access to a large address space
(8M bytes). A second goal was to provide more resources in terms of registers (16 general-purpose
16-bit registers), in terms of data types (from bits to
32 bits), and in terms of additional instructions compared to existing microprocessors (multiply and
divide, multiple register saving instructions,
specialized instructions for compiler support etc.).

To facilitate complex applications it was important
to support multiprogramming with good hardware
support of task switching, interrupts, traps, and two
execution modes. Operating systems also required a
good hardware protection system.

Finally, we wanted to increase overall system performance. This resulted in the choice of an implementation using a 16-bit-wide data path to memory.

47

Architectural compatibility. One of the important lessons learned from previous computer system designs is that the design of a new family architecture is a rare occurrence. One way to apply this lesson is to design a unified architecture compatible over a wide range of processing powers. If we anticipate user growth from small to large systems within a family architecture, then such an approach can significantly increase its life.

The two versions of the Z8000 (a 40-pin unsegmented and a 48-pin segmented version) are designed to achieve this goal, but many other features contribute indirectly to the family compatibility. For small aplications an unsegmented Z8000 with one or more 64K-byte address spaces can be used. For medium applications, a segmented Z8000 and one memory management unit allows direct access to 4M bytes of address space. For large applications a segmented Z8000 and multiple pairs of MMUs allow the use of several 8M-byte address spaces.

Since the segmented Z8000 can run in an unsegmented mode, both systems are compatible. Finally, to achieve even larger processing power through hardware replication, the architecture provides basic mechanisms for both multiprocessing and distributed processing.

Clarity. Clarity in an architecture is a measure of how well key interfaces are defined and specified. This is an elusive but important goal in a family where new and unforeseen components will be added during the life of its architecture.

We felt bus protocols were so important that we developed an independent specification for the Z-bus along with the individual device manuals.

Clarity in terms of the basic architecture means regularity and extendability of the instruction set, as well as the general and simple handling of the operating system interfaces. Clarity in terms of the system architecture means a well-defined method of communication between the various components. The key link between these components is the Z-bus, which is a shared system bus. In the section on communication with other devices, we describe some of the various types of bus protocols. At Zilog we felt this was so important that we developed an independent specification for the Z-bus along with the individual device manuals.[4]

Comparison with other system architectures

We are convinced that the differences between microprocessor system architecture and large computer system architecture are not sufficient to re-

quire a different design approach, although they certainly influence the details of design compromises. The last section of this paper deals with implementation tradeoffs and illustrates some particular compromises. (In a few places we mix implementation considerations with descriptions of architectural tradeoffs. Despite the importance of separating an architecture from its implementation, we found that this separation is often absent during the actual creation of a new architecture.)

Two differences between conventional computer systems and microprocessor systems have the greatest impact: price structure and component boundary differences. For high-end LSI systems, it makes sense to have one unified architecture, but unlike their computer family counterparts (IBM 360/370, PDP-11) different implementations cannot be justified on a price/performance basis. Speed and performance are mainly dependent on the state of technology, and therefore, for a given application, a user will waste the speed willingly since another slower implementation would cost the same. This does not exclude different versions of one implementation, which reflect only different test and production criteria such as package type, functional temperature range, and even speed range.

Most computer systems have both external and internal interfaces. External interfaces which define system boundaries are often standardized (e.g., the IBM channel interface or the DEC unibus). The internal interfaces of most mini or large computer systems are essentially hidden. In contrast, the component boundaries of a microprocessor-based system represent actual interfaces, and most users must be familiar with them as well as with external interfaces. Because the component interfaces are more visible and often must be more general, the microprocessor-oriented system bus emerges as a key standardization link to allow a wider mix of components and designs.

The basic architecture

Address space considerations. It is advantageous to have more than one address space, with each address space as large as possible. In the Z8000, memory references and I/O references are viewed as references to different address spaces. The I/O space is discussed in the section below on communication with other devices. Memory references may be instructions or data and stack accesses, with each type of access possible in either system or normal modes. The Z8000 distinguishes between each of these reference possibilities by using different combinations of its status lines. Separating the various address spaces can be used to increase the total number of addressable bytes and to achieve protection. The size of each address space depends on the versions of the Z8000 used. The 40-pin package version allows each address space to be at most 64K bytes, the 48-pin package version allows each address space to be at most 8000K bytes.

48

The 40-pin version is intended for systems, often used as dedicated systems, where the program and data spaces are small. In this case, relocation is not usually important. Using the different address spaces, one has a simple way to address in practice up to 4 x 64K bytes (with a maximum of 6 x 64K bytes). Some simple protection is achieved by separating these spaces in hardware.

The 48-pin version with one or more MMUs is intended for the medium to large applications where relocation and better memory protection are important.[3] In these cases, status information can also be used to separate between address spaces by using multiple MMUs. But it is also essential to achieve the detailed memory protection required. (It is possible to use the 48-pin version without an MMU.) For these high-end applications, the address spaces are so large that one is unlikely to exhaust them. Experience with large computers shows that 8M bytes is probably adequate. The current implementation of the Z8000 uses 8M-byte address spaces, but the architecture provides for 31-bit address (2147M bytes).

In both versions, the Z8000 allows direct access to each address space. Direct access means that the addresses used in instructions or registers have as many bits as the address space size requires. In other schemes the effective address is a combination of a shorter field in the instruction and other extension bits often found in an implied register. Despite the shorter address fields, we believe this "indirect access" does not save bytes, because extra instructions must be used to load and save the implied registers, which are typically in short supply.

Registers. The Z8000 is primarily a memory-to-register architecture. This characteristic does not entirely exclude other organizations, and mechanisms exist in the Z8000 to support them. For example, memory-to-memory operations are supported for strings, whereas stack operations are supported for procedure and process changes. This choice provides upward compatibility with the Z80. A register architecture also results in good performance, since register accesses are made at a greater speed than memory accesses in the current implementation.

Experience with register-oriented machines seems to confirm that four general-purpose registers are not enough and that a "proper" number is between eight and 32.[5] The Z8000 supports bytes, words (16-bit), and long words (32-bit), and a few instructions even use quadruple-word (64-bit) data elements. If we choose 16, 16-bit registers allow eight 32-bit registers as well as four 64-bit registers (Figure 1). Since addresses are 32 bits, the necessity of at least eight 32-bit registers was obvious. The impact of the 4-bit register field on the instruction format depends also on the number of address modes and operands. Sixteen registers allowed a reasonable tradeoff, whereas 32 registers would have resulted in too few one-word instructions.

With one minor restriction any register can be used by any instruction as an accumulator, source operand, index, or memory pointer. This regularity of

the structure is so important that it is worthwhile to sacrifice any possible encoding improvements in instruction formats which could result from dedicating registers to special functions. Encoding improvements based on instruction frequency, so that frequent instructions use one word, are more effective in saving space without having a negative effect on the architecture.

Why not have specialized registers? The difficulty lies in the fact that the restrictions caused by dedication are inconsistent with one another.

Most applications dedicate the available registers to specific functions. For example, most high-level languages require a stack pointer and a stack frame pointer. Then why not, one might argue, have specialized registers? The difficulty lies in the fact that the restrictions caused by dedication are inconsistent with one another. If the architecture supplies only general-purpose registers, the user is free to dedicate them to specific usages for his application without restrictions. This is important in the context of microprocessors where user applications are not well known and where high-level languages are still used infrequently.

For example, the Z8000 allows software stacks to be implemented with any register. There are also two hardware supported stacks, but the registers used are still general-purpose and can participate in any operation. There is no allocated stack frame pointer, since any register can be used by means of the proper combination of addressing modes. The savings realized by register specialization are unattractive when the given function can still be performed simply. The loss that would result from restricting the applications would be too great. In contrast, significant savings result from excluding R0 from use as an index or memory pointer. This exclusion allows one to distinguish between the indexed and direct addressing modes which use the same combination of the instruction address mode field. The price is small, since R0 still can be an accumulator or source register and 15 others accumulator, index, and/or memory pointers are available. In this case the restriction made sense.

Another decision to be made about registers is their size. Since the architecture handles multiple data types we must have multiple data register sizes, which can hold each data type. The solution of the problem is implemented in the architecture by pairing registers, two 1-byte registers make a word register, two word registers make a long word register, etc.

Data types. Users would like to have as many directly implemented data types as possible. A data type is supported when it has a hardware representa-

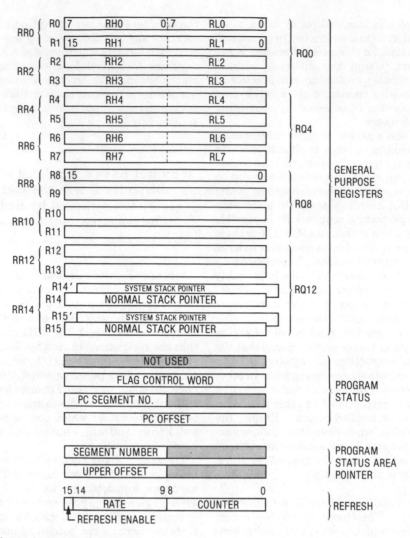

Figure 1. CPU registers (segmented version).

tion and instructions which directly apply to it. New data types can always be simulated in terms of basic data types, but hardware support provides faster and more convenient operations. At the same time, a proliferation of fully supported data types complicates the architecture and the implementations.

The Z8000 supports several primitive types in the architecture and provides expansion mechanisms. The basic data types are obviously the ones expected to be used most frequently. The extended data types are built using existing data types and manipulated using existing instructions.

The basic data type is the byte, which is also the basic addressable element. All other data types are referenced using their first byte address and their length in bytes. The architecture also supports the following data types: bytes (8 bits), words (16 bits), long words (32 bits), bytes, and word strings. In addition, bits are fully supported and addressed by number within a byte or word. BCD digits are supported and represented as two 4-bit digits in 1 byte. One consequence of this data type organization is that byte, word, and long-word registers are needed

to support them. The Z8000 even provides quadruple register—another extension—used in long-word manipulation.

Other data types are supported by using one of the preceding data types; for example, addresses are manipulated as long words, and each element (segment number or offset) can be manipulated as a byte or a word. Instructions are one to five-word strings, the program status is four words, etc.

As the family grows, support for new data types will be added. The architecture will need to support them in its registers or in memory if they do not fit in registers (as strings are implemented today). But most important, the architecture will have to support the addition of new instructions to its repertoire.

Instructions. In designing an instruction format the architect must decide how to allocate a limited number of bits to the opcode field, address mode field, and other operand subfields. Instruction usage statistics are the best source of data to influence decisions about instruction set format.[1, 6, 7] Behind their usage lies a strong technical position: we do not

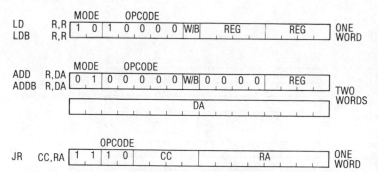

Figure 2. Examples of instruction formats (nonsegmented version).

believe that any one of the various instruction set structures—register oriented, memory oriented, stack oriented, symmetrical, or asymmetrical, etc.—are always better when used exclusively. Thus the task of the architect is to decide what his most important goals are, and for each of them adapt the best features of the various structures so that on the average, and for his set of goals, an optimum solution can be found. We do not believe that the optimum will be very sharp; it will be more like a range of applications for which the resulting composite structure works well. We decided to use a register structure for compatibility, multiple word instructions for speed, memory-to-memory instructions for strings, stack structure for process control and procedure support, "short" instruction for byte density improvement, etc.

Instruction format consideration. The Z8000 has over 110 distinct instruction types; several instruction formats are illustrated in Figure 2. The opcode field specifies the type of instruction (for example, ADD and LD). The mode field indicates the addressing modes (for example, Register (R), Direct Address (DA). The data element type (W/B) and register designator fields complete the basic instruction fields. Long word instructions use a different opcode value from their byte or word counterpart. Frequent instructions are encoded in a single word, and less frequent instructions which use more than two operands use two words. There are often additional fields for special elements such as immediate values or condition code descriptors (CC). Instructions can designate one, two, or three operands explicitly. The instruction TRANSLATE AND TEST is the only one with four operands and is also the only one with an implied register operand.

Several restraints can guide the proper choice of an instruction format. A large number of opcodes (used or reserved) is very important: having a given instruction implemented in hardware saves bytes and improves speed. But one usually needs to concentrate more on the completeness of the operations available on a particular data type rather than on adding more and more esoteric instructions which, if used frequently, will not significantly affect performance. Great care must be given to the problem of expanding the instruction set so, for example, new data types can be added.

Addressing modes. The Z8000 has eight addressing modes: *register* (R), *indirect register* (IR), *direct address* (DA), *indexed* (X), *immediate* (IM), *base address* (BA), *base indexed* (BX), and *relative address* (RA). Several other addressing modes are implied by specific instructions such as autoincrement or autodecrement.

Although a very large number of addressing modes is beneficial, usage statistics demonstrate that not all combinations of operands, address modes, and operators are meaningful.[6] The five basic addressing modes of R, IR, DA, X, and IM are the most frequently used and apply to most instructions with more than one address mode. For two-operand instructions, statistics show that most of the time the destination is a register. Other cases of addressing mode combinations and less basic addressing modes are associated with special instructions. Thus, the frequent combination of autodecrement for the destination operand with the five basic address modes for the source operand is provided by the PUSH instruction. The combination of autoincrement addressing modes for both source and destination operands is one of the block move instructions. In essence, the address mode field space has been traded for opcode field space. This allows more instructions and combinations while staying within a one-word format.

The price for this tradeoff is the infrequent occurrence of pairs or triples of instructions simulating a missing addressing mode. This situation occurs in most instruction sets in any case.

Code density. Because current microprocessors are restricted to primitive pipeline structures, their speed is largely dependent on the number of executed instruction words. Therefore, code density is not only important because of program size reduction but also because of speed improvement. One would like to encode in the smallest number of bits the most frequent instructions. The basic instruction size increment was chosen to be a word for reasons dealing with alignment, speed penalties, and hardware complexity. Thus the most frequent one and two-operand instructions take one word in their register or register-to-register forms. Less frequent instructions or instructions which use more than two operands use at least two words.

The Z8000 goes even further by selecting several special instructions as "short" instructions which take only one word, when normally they would take two words. These instructions, such as LOAD BYTE REGISTER IMMEDIATE and LOAD WORD REGISTER IMMEDIATE (for small immediate values), CALL RELATIVE, and JUMP RELATIVE, are so frequent statistically that they deserve such special treatment.

A one-word JUMP RELATIVE and DECREMENT AND JUMP ON NON-ZERO also have a very significant impact on speed. The short offset mechanism used by addresses (and described below) is also designed to allow one-word addresses. Compared to previous microprocessors, the largest reduction in size and increase in speed results from the Z8000's consistent and regular structure of the architecture and from its more powerful instruction set—which allows fewer instructions to accomplish a given task.

High-level language support. For microprocessor users, the transition from assembly language to high-level languages will allow greater freedom from architectural dependency and will improve ease of programming.[8] It is easy and tempting to adapt a computer architecture to execute a particular high-level language efficiently.[9] Most programming languages act as a filter and can be supported by a subset of available hardware with greater efficiency.[10] But efficiency for one particular high-level language is likely to lead to inefficiency for unrelated languages. The Z8000 will be used in a wide variety of applications, and we know that a large number of users will still be using assembly languages. Since the Z8000 is a general-purpose microprocessor, language support has been provided only through the inclusion of features designed to minimize typical compilation and code-generation problems. Among these is the regularity of the Z8000 addressing modes and data types. The addressing structure provided by segmentation should support procedures that result from structured programming. Access to parameters and local variables on the procedure stack is supported by index with short offset address mode as well as base address and base indexed address modes. In addition, address arithmetic is aided by the INCREMENT BY 1 TO 16 and DECREMENT BY 1 TO 16 instructions.

Testing of data, logical evaluation, initialization, and comparison of data are made possible by the instructions TEST, TEST CONDITION CODES, LOAD IMMEDIATE INTO MEMORY, and COMPARE IMMEDIATE WITH MEMORY. Compilers and assemblers manipulate character strings frequently, and the instructions TRANSLATE, TRANSLATE AND TEST, BLOCK COMPARE, and COMPARE STRING all result in dramatic speed improvements over software simulations of these important tasks, especially for certain types of languages. In addition, any register can be used as a stack pointer by the PUSH and POP instructions.

Segmentation. In order to provide for convenient code generation and data access, addresses must also be easy to manipulate. Architectures with direct access to memory typically use a linear address space, so that address arithmetic may be used on the entire address. In this case, addresses are manipulated as one of the data types of the same size. This removes the need to distinguish an address as a new data type. In contrast, the Z8000 has a non-linear address space. Addresses are made of two parts: a 7-bit segment number and a 16-bit offset. Only the offset participates in address arithmetic. The segment number is essentially a pointer to a part of the total address space, which can vary in size from 0 to 64K bytes. The hardware representation of a segmented address is a long word or a register pair (Figure 3), which allows the easy manipulation of each part of the address.

The segmented addresses are one of the key mechanisms used to support both large and small

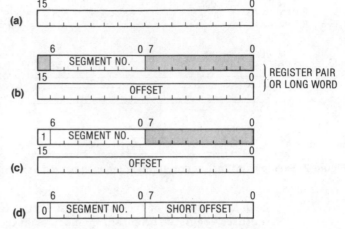

Figure 3. Hardware representation of segmented addresses. Any non-segmented address is one word, whether it is in a register, memory, or an instruction (Figure 3a). Segmented addresses are always two words in a register or memory (Figure 3b); however, instructions can have one of two forms. The usual case (long offset) requires two words (Figure 3c); however, there is also a short offset form that uses only one word (Figure 3d).

memory systems efficiently. The two versions of the Z8000 implementation, the 40-pin unsegmented and the 48-pin segmented, allow the maintenance of the architectural compatibility and ease the growth between these two application groups. The segmented address space guarantees that each 64K-byte address space of the 40-pin version becomes one of the segments of the 48-pin version. Each 40-pin version's 16-bit address becomes an offset within the segment, and a mode exists in the 48-pin package version in which 40-pin version code can be executed. Furthermore, compatibility with any current 8-bit microprocessor such as the Z80 is easy, and a new microcomputer such as the Z8 can address external data in a shared segment with the Z8000.

The hardware performance of the Z8000 is also improved by address segmentation. Since a segment number does not participate in arithmetic, it can be put on the bus before the result of an address computation is available. This feature allows the use of MMUs with essentially no impact on memory access time by allowing it to function in parallel with the CPU. Indexing operations are also faster because only a 16-bit addition must be performed. Because of the distinction between the segment number and its offset, one can use shorter addresses without software constraints. Short addresses can use a short offset (fewer than 256 bytes) and thereby reduce program size (Figure 3).

Finally, it is very easy to associate with each of the 128 segments of the address space the protection and dynamic relocation features desirable for larger systems. Relocation allows a user to write his application using logical addresses independent of any physical addresses. Relocation is essential, for example, in a disk-based general data processing system with several users. Relocation is not essential for dedicated applications with code typically residing in

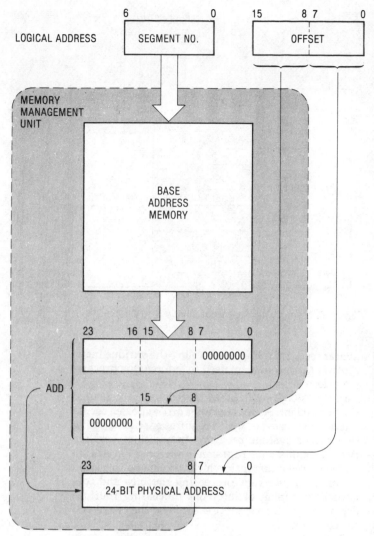

LOGICAL ADDRESS   SEGMENT NO.   OFFSET

6   0   15   8 7   0

MEMORY MANAGEMENT UNIT

BASE ADDRESS MEMORY

23   16 15   8 7   0

00000000

ADD

15   8

00000000

23   8 | 7   0

24-BIT PHYSICAL ADDRESS

Figure 4. Logical to physical address translation.

ROM. Users whose total memory needs are small are also unlikely to need relocation.

In summary, the choice of a segmented address space has provided—at low cost and with few practical limitations—a powerful solution to the problem of user growth, relocation, and protection as well as virtual memory implementation. We believe that a linear address space could have achieved these results but at a considerably higher price.

The system architecture

Protection facilities. The Z8000 protection facilities can be divided into system protection features and memory protection features. Experience with large computers has demonstrated the advantages of having at least two execution modes with different access rights to hardware facilities. The Z8000 provides the system and normal modes for this purpose. A simple protection system results from the presence of these two modes and their associated stacks. A special class of "privileged" instructions is defined, which deals with I/O, interrupts, traps, and mode changes. Programs in normal mode which attempt to execute a privileged instruction will cause a trap and a change to system mode. The switch from user to system mode can also be caused by the system call instruction. These mechanisms enforce protection and help in designing reliable and efficient operating systems with clean user interfaces. Several other traps are required to achieve a consistent system: segmentation trap, privileged instruction trap, and undefined instruction trap.

A desirable memory protection scheme is one for which protection information (read only, read write, execute only, system only, size of data or code, etc.) is easily associated with the data and code structures of a given application. It is also one for which a large number of different types of protection information can be verified.

The relocation and memory protection mechanisms described above are provided by an external device: the memory management unit.[3] To provide relocation and protection features directly on the Z8000 would have demanded too much simplification. The external MMU has the further advantage of providing for easier growth by the addition of components. The Z8000 40-pin package does not have to carry the burden of the unused advanced relocation and protection features, although some form of protection can be achieved by hardware separation of the different address spaces. With multiple MMUs, the 48-pin package user can control the relocation and protection complexity desired in his application.

The memory management unit. The MMU performs three functions: (1) address translation of logical address to physical address using dynamic relocation, (2) memory protection, and (3) segment management. The addresses manipulated by the programmer, used by the instructions, and output by the Z8000 are called logical addresses. The MMU uses these logical addresses, composed of a 7-bit segment number and 16-bit offset, and transforms them into a 24-bit physical address (Figure 4). A 24-bit origin or base is logically associated with each segment. To form a 24-bit physical address, the 16-bit offset is added to the base for the given segment. In effect, with the help of one memory management device, the Z8000 can address 8M bytes directly within a 16M-byte physical memory space. The reasons for the choice of a large physical address space include an expectation that large systems will want to use extra bits for complex resource management purposes.

Each segment is given a number of attributes when it is initially entered into the MMU. When a memory reference is made, the protection mechanism checks these attributes against the status information from the CPU. If a mismatch occurs, a trap is generated which interrupts the CPU. The CPU can then check the MMU status registers to determine the cause of the trap. Segment attributes include segment size and type (read only, system only, execute only, in-

53

valid DMA, invalid CPU, etc.) Other segment protection features include a write warning zone useful for stack operations.

When a memory protection violation is detected, a write inhibit line guarantees that memory will not be incorrectly changed. The invalid DMA and CPU bits indicate that the entry cannot be used by the DMA or CPU respectively, because either the segment number is illegal or the segment entry is not loaded. This fast feature, in conjunction with the segment history information (segment "changed" and segment "referenced" bits) and the segmentation trap mechanism, allows the implementation of a virtual segmented memory system.

The MMU comes in a 48-pin package (Figure 5). The chip inputs are the segment number, the upper 8 bits of the offset, and status information from the CPU. The outputs from the segment chip are the upper 16 bits of the 24-bit physical address and the segmentation trap line. Since the memory management device processes only the upper 8 bits of the offset, the lower 8 bits go directly to memory. This is equivalent to having zeros in the 8 lower bits of the 24-bit origin. Thus, the memory management device only needs to store the upper 16 bits of each base address. Segment limit protection is done in the memory management device, and thus segments can be protected in increments of 256 bytes.

Each MMU stores 64 segment entries that consist of the segment base address, its attributes, size, and status. A pair of MMUs support the 128 segments available in an address space. Additional MMUs can be used to accommodate multiple translation tables. Using the status information provided with each reference, pairs of MMUs can be enabled dynamically.

The memory management device functions constantly while memory references are made, but its translation and protection tables are loaded and unloaded as an I/O peripheral. To achieve this, the memory management device has chip select, address strobe, data strobe, and read/write lines. The Z8000 special byte I/O instructions that use the upper byte of the data bus can load or unload the memory management device.

Mode switching: interrupt and trap handling. From small users in dedicated process control applications to large users in general-purpose data processing applications, asynchronous events such as interrupts and synchronous events like traps must be handled. When these events occur, the state of any currently executing program must be saved during what is generally called a task switch or process switch. The users benefit from the availability of many interrupts and traps. They also benefit from a fast, easy, and uniform handling of process switching.

Peripherals using interrupts have widely varying constraints on interrupt processing time. To solve this problem, peripherals with the same characteristics are often associated with one of several interrupts. A priority enforced among the several interrupts allows the required processing time to be

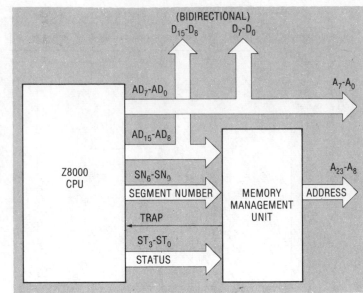

Figure 5. Memory management device with Z8000 CPU.

guaranteed. Enabling or disabling the various interrupts is the mechanism used to enforce this processing priority.

In the Z8000, we felt that three levels of interupts were sufficient. A *non-maskable interrupt* represents a catastrophic event which requires special handling to preserve system integrity. In addition there are two maskable interrupts: *non-vectored interrupts* and *vectored interrupts*, which correspond to a fixed mapping of interrupt processing routines and to a variable mapping of interrupt processing routines depending on the vector presented by the peripheral to the Z8000.

Both interrupts and traps result in similar process switches. Information related to the old process (its program status) is saved on a special system stack with a code describing the reason for the switch.. This allows recursive task switches to occur while leaving the normal stack undisturbed by system information. The state of the new process (its new program status) is loaded from a special area in memory—the program status area—designated by a pointer resident in the CPU (see Figure 6).

The use of the stack and of a pointer to the program status area are specific choices made to allow architectural compatibility if new interrupts or traps are added to the architecture. The choice of the two modes of execution has a strong impact on the design of clean user interfaces. Experience has shown that in large systems the normal mode instruction set and the user interfaces together constitute the most important element in achieving architectural compatibility.

Communication with other devices: the Z-bus. The Z-bus is the shared bus which links all the components of the Z8000 family.[4] The variety and performance requirements of the components are so different that in fact the Z-bus is composed of five buses:

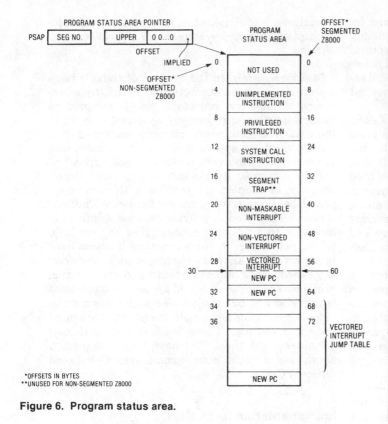

Figure 6. Program status area.

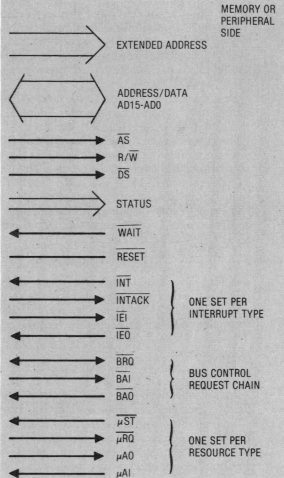

Figure 7. Z-bus signals.

a memory bus, an I/O bus, an interrupt bus, and two resource request buses (Figure 7).

The Z-bus is called a "shared" bus because several components can use it. A bus user is a CPU or a peripheral which can usually generate one or more bus transactions such as memory data request or an I/O request. Identical bus transactions cannot take place at the same time, but serialization mechanisms allow sequential use of the Z-bus. Architecturally, the buses can be grouped into two structures. The I/O structure uses the I/O bus and the interrupt bus. The memory structure uses the memory bus with or without address extensions. Both structures can use the resource request bus and the mastership request bus.

Each bus consists of a set of signals and the protocols which preside over the various types of transactions. Part of each protocol is the timing relationship between relevant signals. The Z8000 CPU provides most of these timing relations. The advantage of such a choice is the significant reduction in the number of components required to build such a system. One consequence is that bus transactions cannot be aborted or delayed freely since some devices, especially memory, have specific timing constraints. The most important consideration for the Z-bus is the need to interface to multiplexed address and data lines of the Z8000 CPU which must fit in 40- and 48-pin packages. The Z-bus maintains these multiplexed address and data lines. Very little speed could be gained by demultiplexing these lines for memory references since memories are themselves multiplexed. The most important advantage of a multiplexed Z-bus is the direct addressability of

peripheral internal registers. This feature allows the construction of complex peripherals which maintain a simple program interface.

The Z-bus is known as a transparent or asynchronous bus. Z8000 components do not require that their clocks be synchronized with the CPU clock. The signals used by each transaction provide all the necessary timing. This concept is important: it allows, for example, I/O references to be independent of the speed and clock frequencies required by other Z-bus transactions.

I/O bus versus memory bus. The I/O and memory buses are the most important. The Z8000 family architecture distinguishes between memory and I/O spaces and thus requires specific I/O instructions. This architectural separation allows better protection and has a nicer potential for extension. The I/O and memory buses use a 16-bit address/data bus, which allows 16-bit I/O addresses and 8- or 16-bit data elements. Memory addresses are 16 bits for the 40-pin package or extended to 23 bits using the segmented version. Thus, the memory bus is in fact a logical address bus. The increased speed requirements of future microprocessors is likely to be achieved by tailoring memory and I/O references to their respective characteristic reference patterns and by using simultaneous I/O and memory referencing. These future possibilities require an architectural separation today. Memory-mapped I/O is still possible, but we feel the loss of protection and potential expandability are too severe to justify memory-mapped I/O by itself.

Both the I/O and memory buses need address, data, and control signals. One important implementation decision was to overlap the signals used by the memory and I/O buses on the same Z8000 CPU pins, with the obvious exception of the status signals used to distinguish between the two types of bus requests. For the current Z8000 implementation the resulting reduction in number of pins is significant. In contrast the impossibility of doing concurrent memory and I/O referencing is not very significant since their speeds are essentially the same.

In addition, memories and peripherals both benefit from the availability of early status information defining the bus transaction type (I/O versus memory, read versus write) ahead of the actual transaction so that bidirectional drivers and other hardware elements can be enabled before the reference. The status lines of the Z8000 CPU provide this type of early status.

The I/O structure. Since many peripherals are connected with one CPU, the I/O bus is shared and serialization must be provided. One solution involves using a master/slave protocol. The CPU is a master which can initiate an I/O transation at any time. The peripherals are slaves which participate in a transaction only when requested by the master. In order to find out if a peripheral needs to be serviced the master can poll each in turn. The Z-bus also provides a faster way of getting the attention of a master: an interrupt bus. In contrast, with the I/O transaction data bus, each peripheral sharing the interrupt bus may "try" to use it simultaneously. The interrupt bus uses an interrupt line, interrupt acknowledge line, and two more lines used to form a daisy chain. The daisy chain is an implementation of a distributed arbitration policy between the requests. Priority of processing is determined by the position in the daisy chain, and peripherals can be preempted. Interrupt vectors are used to determine the identity of the peripherals requesting service via an interrupt.

Other buses. The two resource request buses are used to request the control of the Z-bus from the CPU and to request control of any generalized resource.

The Z8000 CPU or any Z-bus compatible CPU does not need to request the bus to access it as a master, and is, therefore, the default master. Other devices can request bus mastership, but they must go through a non-preemptive distributed arbitration using another daisy chain. The CPU always relinquishes the bus at the end of its current bus transaction.

The resource request chain is a generalization of that concept in which each resource requestor has equal importance and can use the resource in a non-preemptive manner. This mechanism in the Z8000 CPU permits one to implement in software the kind of exclusion and serialization mechanisms needed for multiple distributed systems with critical resource sharing.

Multiprocessing. In the context of today's large mainframe systems characterized by multiple processes sharing one processor, one is tempted to design distributed processing systems with many low-cost microprocessors running dedicated processes. Such an approach distributes intelligence towards the peripherals, results in modularization, and permits easier development and growth. Unfortunately, in the past, the problem with such an approach has been software and not hardware. Thus one cannot be expected to provide detailed solutions in hardware to a software problem that has not been solved yet. However, some basic mechanisms have been provided to allow the sharing of address spaces: large segmented address spaces and the external MMU make this possible, and a resource request bus is provided which in conjunction with software provides the exclusion and serialization control of shared critical resources. These mechanisms and new peripherals like the Z-FIO have been designed to allow easy asynchronous communication between different CPUs.

Implementation tradeoffs

The key family decision: producibility. Confronted with the problem of designing a new LSI-based system architecture, we could have ignored package size considerations by accepting packages with 64 or more pins, or we could have ignored mass production technology constraints by using die sizes larger than 260 mils square. Such solutions are often justified in the implementation of an existing computer system. The component boundaries, package limitations, and technological limitations are secondary to achieving the goal of exact membership in the computer family. But if one were to design a new system architecture with the same lack of constraints, the individual component would not be price-competitive—only the total system would be. A new system architecture based on this approach could only be used to design yet another traditional computer.

The Z8000 family provides basic, general-purpose blocks out of which a system solution to most problems can be implemented.

The Z8000 family market is intended to be much broader, and each component of the family must be economically viable. The staged introduction of components which are economically viable by themselves allows us to serve the market from very small configurations to very large configurations by using more components, in any combination. Not only do we believe that this approach does not restrict

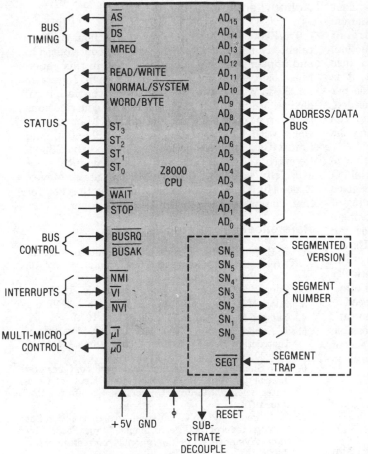

Figure 8. Z8000 pin functions.

The following labels appear in the figure:

BUS TIMING: $\overline{AS}$, $\overline{DS}$, $\overline{MREQ}$

STATUS: READ/$\overline{WRITE}$, NORMAL/$\overline{SYSTEM}$, WORD/$\overline{BYTE}$, ST_3, ST_2, ST_1, ST_0

$\overline{WAIT}$, $\overline{STOP}$

BUS CONTROL: $\overline{BUSRQ}$, BUSAK

INTERRUPTS: $\overline{NMI}$, $\overline{VI}$, $\overline{NVI}$

MULTI-MICRO CONTROL: $\overline{\mu I}$, μO

Z8000 CPU

ADDRESS/DATA BUS: AD_{15}, AD_{14}, AD_{13}, AD_{12}, AD_{11}, AD_{10}, AD_9, AD_8, AD_7, AD_6, AD_5, AD_4, AD_3, AD_2, AD_1, AD_0

SEGMENTED VERSION / SEGMENT NUMBER: SN_6, SN_5, SN_4, SN_3, SN_2, SN_1, SN_0

$\overline{SEGT}$ — SEGMENT TRAP

+5V, GND, ϕ, SUB-STRATE DECOUPLE, $\overline{RESET}$

ALU. These implementation decisions, which were guided by the technological and practical considerations, have a strong impact on performance.

To achieve good performance with the instruction format and data type envisioned for the Z8000, only a 16-bit bus seens adequate; a 32-bit bus would have necessitated using an unacceptable 56-pin or larger package. Optimal performace is obtained with this chosen bus width if the size of the frequently used register-to-register operations becomes one word. The choice of ALU and internal register widths is a tradeoff between speed of the most frequent operations and the chip area needed to implement a wider ALU or data path inside the CPU.

None of these implementation decisions should limit the architecture. Instructions are from one to five words long, and data types and addresses are not limited to 16 bits. For example, 32-bit words are one of the main data types of the machines, and addresses occupy two words. The *address* mechanism illustrates the strong distinction between an architecture and its implementation. The architectural address representation uses a 32-bit word of which 8 bits are reserved and 1 is a short format/long format descriptor. Thus, the Z8000 architecture provides up to 31-bit addresses, but only 23 are currently implemented and 23 pins of the current package are allocated to addresses.

MMU tradeoffs. The MMU and its relation to the Z8000 CPU illustrate tradeoffs that a microprocessor architect and designer team must make to ensure component manufacturability.

To achieve the goals of good architectural compatibility for high-end systems, it was necessry to include the protection and relocation mechanicms described above. But if all desired features were implemented as a one-chip CPU/MMU combination, it would have been too large and, therefore, uneconomical. And if a reduced set of features were implemented, it would have been architecturally too primitive. Thus, the choice was made to maintain all features and use two chips. This new organization has several significant advantages, such as a capability for multiple MMUs, and allows the access of a DMA device to the MMU.

Given the choice of an external MMU, the next set of decisions concerns package size and circuit speed. Having each relocated segment start on a word boundary would have required a 64-pin package and a very fast 24-bit adder (in fact, a 16-bit adder and 8 bits of carry propagation). In contrast, the decision to start segments on 256-byte boundaries allows the use of a 48-pin package, a fast 8-bit adder, and 8 bits of carry propagation. The latter solution is technically superior and places practically no restriction on the architecture. Segment granularity can be viewed as an implementation restriction and not as an architectural restriction.

Making the 8 low-order bits of the offset go directly to memory also significantly reduces memory access time. Since dynamic memories use these bits first, most of the MMU relocation time is hidden during a

system architectural possibilities, but we also believe that the family will be more effective because it will grow with its customer.

The Z8000 family does not always attempt to provide specific architectural solutions, often implemented in hardware, to all system architecture problems. Instead, it provides basic, general-purpose blocks out of which a system solution to most problems can be implemented. The multi-microprocessor and distributed system capabilities of the Z8000 family illustrate the use of open-ended mechanisms to solve a variety of architectural problems, while the memory management of address space illustrates a specific problem supported by a specific solution—the MMU. However, other solutions more appropriate to a particular problem can be used and an advance in the state of the art might be mapped into a new device for the family.

This vision of the family often results in components more powerful and complex than an application may require. The user should not take this as a cause for alarm, but rather as the reason his applications growth will be easier.

Basic CPU implementation decisions. The Z8000 currently uses a 16-bit data bus (Figure 8), an internal register array of 16-bit registers, and a 16-bit parallel

normal memory access. The availability of segment numbers earlier than the associated offset bits reinforces this advantage and allows the MMU to result in essentially no memory access speed reduction. Each MMU entry also requires 8 bits less for base and segment size value. This is important: it is desirable to pack as many entries as possible per MMU. With 64 entries a 2K-bit memory is needed, which is technologically difficult in view of the amount of logic surrounding this memory and the complexity of its organization.

The fact than an MMU is only connected to the upper byte of the data bus requires the use of special I/O instructions for its loading and obliges us to replace the possible use of an automatic demand loading of entries by explicit instruction loading. To compensate for the time penalty associated with the loading of potentially unused entries, multiple MMUs are used. They not only allow the implementation of 128 entries, but pairs of MMUs can be automatically enabled by the system and normal mode pins effecting a full environment switch at electronic speed.

We feel this example illustrates one important design approach: to compromise as little as possible on advanced architectural features but to accept compromises which result in implementation ease in order to achieve economical components.

Conclusion

The architectural sophistication of the new 16-bit microprocessors is rapidly approaching the level of the minicomputer and large computer. Problems such as component families, large address spaces, bus standards, I/O structures, software investments, and architectural compatibility are being directly addressed. Some of the solutions to these problems are known, and therefore the transition from 8-bit microprocessors was relatively easy. But the challenges ahead—networks, distributed processing, new applications—are much harder. The impact of microprocessors is already enormous, but we feel they will achieve the often-predicted computer revolution only after these new problems are solved. ∎

Acknowledgements

The Z8000 family would not exist without the very talented and dedicated designers who contributed to and implemented the ideas described in this paper: Masatoshi Shima for the Z8000, Hiroshi Yonezawa for the MMU, and Ross Freeman for the peripheral devices. Judy Estrin made invaluable contributions to the architecture of the Z8000 and Z8. Many discussions with Charlie Bass, Leonard Shustek, and Forest Baskett have greatly influenced the Z8000. Leonard's instruction set measurements were especially valuable. Dennis Allison, Steve Meyer, Bruce Hunt, and many others must be thanked for their comments on early drafts of this paper.

References

1. B. L. Peuto and L. J. Shustek, "Current Issues in the Architecture of Microprocessors," *Computer*, Vol. 10, No. 2, Feb. 1977, pp. 20-25.
2. Zilog, *Z8000 Technical Manual*, Zilog, Inc., 1979.
3. Zilog, *MMU Technical Manual*, Zilog, Inc., 1979.
4. Zilog, *Z-Bus Specification*, Zilog, Inc., 1979.
5. A. Lunde, "Empirical Evaluation of Some Features of Instruction Set Processor Architectures," *CACM*, Vol. 20, No. 3, Mar. 1977, pp. 143-152.
6. L. J. Shustek, *Analysis and Performance of Computer Instruction Sets*, PhD Dissertation, Dept. of Computer Science, Stanford University, Stanford, Calif., Jan. 1978.
7. B. L. Peuto and L. J. Shustek, "An Instruction Set Timing Model of CPU Performance," *Proc. Fourth Annual Symposium on Computer Architecture*, Mar. 23-25, 1977, pp. 165-178.
8. C. Bass, "PLZ: A Family of System Programming Languages for Microprocessors," *Computer*, Vol. 11, No. 3, Mar. 1978, pp. 34-39.
9. A. S. Tannenbaum, "Implications of Structured Programming for Machine Architecture," *CACM*, Vol. 21, No. 3, Mar. 1978, pp. 237-246.
10. N. G. Alexander and D. B. Wortman, "Static and Dynamic Characteristics of XPL Programs," *Computer*, Vol. 8, No. 11, Nov. 1975, pp. 41-46.

Bernard L. Peuto is one of the guest editors for this special section; his biography appears with the introduction on p. 9.

58

Reprinted from *IEEE Micro*, May 1981, pages 57-69. Copyright © 1981 by
The Institute of Electrical and Electronics Engineers, Inc.

By supporting modular programs and high-level languages, this microprocessor

architecture aids the implementation of complex software.

A VLSI Architecture for Software Structure: The Intel 8086

Alfred C. Hartmann

Scott Fehr

Intel Corporation

By the end of the last decade, the "software crisis" had struck the microcomputer industry just as it had the mainframe computer industry a decade earlier. No longer employed merely for simple logic replacement, microprocessors faced software challenges that saw the unit of program size grow from kilobyte to megabyte. In this decade, data-base applications and bubble memory systems will routinely employ gigabytes of system storage. The sheer magnitude of the software required by such systems has begun to force attention to the use of structuring mechanisms within microprocessor architectures. Tools of abstraction and logical decomposition are being applied to software and are being supported architecturally in computer designs.[2,3,4]

The Intel 8086 microprocessor[5] is designed to support the evolving requirements of structured software systems. It incorporates two architectural concepts that aid in the implementation of complex software: modular program support and high-level language orientation.

Figure 1 shows the growth of software complexity with the introduction of new architectural concepts. Small, single-module programs (Figure 1a) performing simple logic replacement functions are served appropriately by the current variety of eight-bit microprocessors. Assembly language provides the necessary level of detail for implementing logic functions, and the typical 4K-byte to 16K-byte program needs no abstraction. Such a program may be used in a control application,[6] where, for example, it can replace an analog mechanism that controls a single device parameter—such as fuel flow, fan speed, damper opening, or power consumption—in a heating or cooling unit.

Larger multimodule programs (Figure 1b) that perform intelligent control functions introduce the need for two architectural concepts not present in most eight-bit microprocessors. One is program modularity, which permits better management of the use and growth of larger

programs. The other is high-level language orientation, since modules in larger programs are typically implemented in high-level programming languages. Some of these[7,8] support both abstraction (the hiding of irrelevant or superfluous detail) and security (since assertions about programs may be proved). The 8086 partially addresses this level of complexity in software design. Continuing the previous example, intelligent device control would support operator-specified, feedback-driven control of multiple parameters within an individual heating or cooling unit. Fuel flow, power consumption, fan speed, and damper opening might all be coordinated with desired room temperature, outside air temperature, KWH-cost versus time-of-day, and the building workers' shift schedule.

Still larger systems (Figure 1c)—with multiple processes running on single processors—require the two previous concepts as well as higher performance, greater addressability, and, most important, operating system support. Operating systems manage the shared resources, provide common support functions, and enforce the separation, security, and communication of logically separate processes. The needs of this category are not entirely met by the 8086 microprocessor (since process security is not enforced), although the 8086's concepts of modular program support and language orientation are still required. Continuing the example, our application at this level now supports intelligent control of multiple heating and cooling units, each managed by its own process, with identical units sharing module code. An operator process communicates with the facilities engineer and allows heating or cooling units to be dynamically added or removed from operation, and parameters to be dynamically varied. The units are located near one another, and although this permits the use of a single processor for all, each probably has a simple, single-chip processor performing logic replacement for that unit.

59

EHO214-7/84/0000/0059$01.00©1981 IEEE

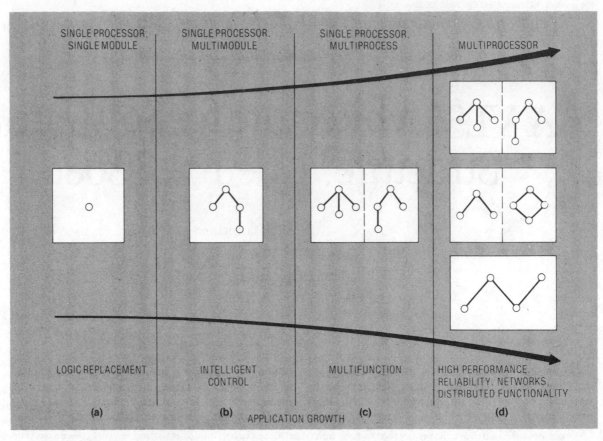

Figure 1. Evolving software complexity.

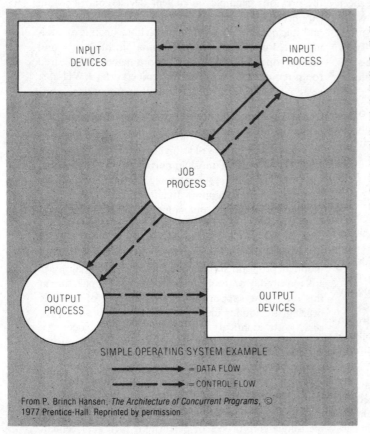

SIMPLE OPERATING SYSTEM EXAMPLE

→ = DATA FLOW
--→ = CONTROL FLOW

From P. Brinch Hansen, *The Architecture of Concurrent Programs,* ©
1977 Prentice-Hall. Reprinted by permission.

Figure 2. System structure—multiple processes.

Multiprocessor configurations (Figure 1d) supporting
reliable, distributed functions require all of the architectural concepts of the previous level, plus some unique
concepts of their own. The many forms and variations of
such configurations imply a need for multiprocessing and
interprocessor communication. Nonhierarchical, distributed, and secure sharing and control of information
lead to revolutionary changes in system and software
structure that are far beyond the design goals of traditional, multiprogrammed single-processor systems. At
least one microprocessor architecture supports multiprocessing,[9,10] as do several mainframe architectures.[11]
Our example now grows into a distributed energy
management system with intelligent control of individual
units through time-dependent power-cycling, shift
change control, alarm monitoring and control override,
overall circulation control, adaptive response to subsystem failure, energy consumption report generation,
maintenance reporting and scheduling, and self-
diagnosis.

If we take a higher-level view of Figure 1, we note that
the vertical lines separating each level of application are
significant—they represent growth thresholds. Crossing a
growth threshold can occur gradually, and if not accompanied by the new concepts can become a "growth crisis"
as the old solution is outgrown. A company employing
microprocessors for logic replacement may choose an appropriate architecture (8085, say) and language (assembler) for that level. Market pressures make a progression to intelligent control natural, though, and the

previous solution may become inadequate. If the company never planned for the incorporation of new concepts, it may find the consequences expensive—it will have to bear the cost of reengineering or risk the competitiveness of its product.

A previous article[12] described the 8086 features that supported growth from the old eight-bit environment to the then new 16-bit one. Our discussion again describes the 8086, but focuses on the two key concepts—modular program support and language orientation—that support growth to still more complex environments.

Modular program support

Higher-level applications demand systems consisting of one or more processors that execute multiple processes. Figure 2 shows a simple three-process system presented in a standard text on concurrent programs.[13] This system consists of a *job process* that performs some item of useful work (such as controlling a group of heating and cooling units, as in our examples), an *input process* that provides the necessary data to the job process (in our example, by sampling and queueing the outputs of various sensors in the units), and an *output process* that delivers the results of the computation to the output devices (which in our example involves dequeueing orders to the various units and controlling servo operations).

At the level of abstraction shown in the figure, it is irrelevant whether the processes execute on the same or on different processors—they operate in parallel to accomplish the desired objective of the system. At the next lower level of abstraction, Figure 3 shows a possible modular decomposition of the input process of Figure 2 for the energy system example. The *command module* accepts commands from the job process for execution. Commands to initialize or calibrate sensors are directed to the *sensor calibration module,* while commands for sensor data are directed to the *logical sensor module*. This module deals with sensors as though they provide final data in numeric representation and proper units on command. The logical sensor module obtains this data and the *command module* queues it for the job process. Of course, some sampling, conversion, or other computation on the raw data may be required from the sensor, and these operations are performed by the *physical sensor input module*. The sensor calibration module also has access to the physical sensor input module for calibration purposes.

The modular decomposition outlined above should result in a sound, structured design, with well-defined interfaces and appropriate functional partitioning. For example, we can term the interface between the logical sensor input module and the physical sensor input module the *logical sensor interface*. This interface is independent of the physical sampling, averaging, and conversion requirements of particular sensors.

The *physical sensor interface* lies between the physical sensor input module and the sensor itself; advances in sensor technology that change that interface should require changes *only* to the physical sensor input module. Alternatively, any new queueing discipline between the command module and the job process should not affect either the logical or the physical sensor input modules.

This partitioning of functions into modules and defining of module interfaces is part of what is commonly called structured design. It is usually done by chief system designers, with module specifications implemented in a given language by a programming team. Figure 4 illustrates this approach—the system is composed of processes, which are constructed from modules, which implement functions. A module is a collection of related functions and data whose internal structure need not be known by users of the module. Newer programming languages such as Ada,[8] Simula,[14] Alphard,[15] Clu,[16] and Mesa[17] strongly support this system model, while older

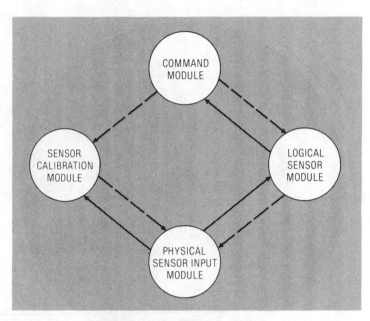

Figure 3. Process structure—multiple modules.

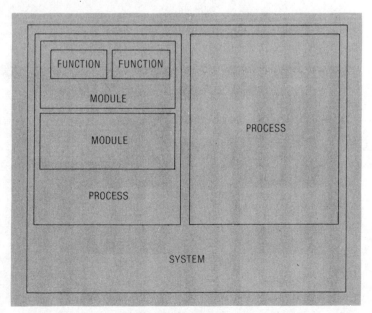

Figure 4. The system/process/module/function layers.

languages such as Fortran, Cobol, Pascal, C, and Basic require nonstandard language extensions to group functions and data into modules. Ada, for example, was specifically designed to solve Pascal's lack of support of modularity.

Continuing the three-process example of Figure 2, Figure 5 shows the system memory structure that results from the modular approach. This time, concentric rings illustrate the system/process/module layering. The innermost ring is the *system communication area,* where the three processes can send and receive messages that coordinate their activity and pass data and results. The next ring is divided into individual areas for each process, so that data can be private (local) to a single process. The

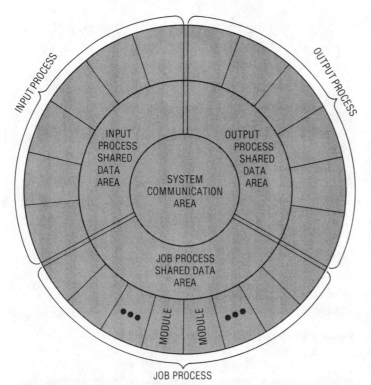

Figure 5. System memory structure.

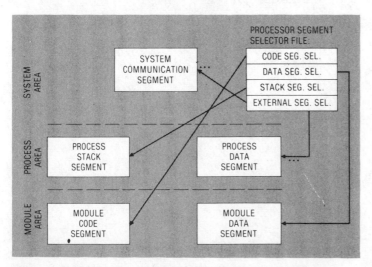

Figure 6. Decomposition of the memory areas into segments.

outer ring is divided into areas for each module; each area contains code and data that is private to its module. The area for a particular process is public, or global, to the modules in the process.

Each area has a certain set of modules or processes that may access it and, depending on the size of items stored in it, has its own particular length. The classical architectural realization of this structure is *segmentation.*[18] Through segmentation, memory areas of variable size can be efficiently and securely separated, accessed, and shared.[19,20] Without segmentation, all memory areas coexist in a flat, unstructured, linear array with no secure and efficient mechanism for dynamic sharing or position independence. The larger the address space, the more important is the ability to add structure and to control access. As a consequence of its original design goals, the 8086 does not yet enforce security (through limit checks), although it does benefit from the structuring advantages of segmentation.

Figure 6 shows the decomposition of the memory areas into segments. The *system area* is divided into system communication segments that may hold messages or data that is passed among processes. The *process area* contains a stack segment for the process and one or more data segments that are private to the process and global to its modules. The *module area* contains a code segment and a data segment for each module. The 8086 processor contains a four-element, segment selector file used to reference these segments, as shown in the figure. The current module code segment, module data segment, and process stack segment are implicitly selected via the code, data, and stack segment selectors, according to the type of access. Outside this immediate environment, access may be made to any process data segment or system communication segment via the explicit segment selector.

Context changes are efficiently performed in this environment. Intraprocess (intermodule) transfers are accomplished by changing the code and the data segment selectors. Interprocess transfers, in addition to altering the code and the data segment selectors, need only alter the stack segment selector to establish the new segment environment.

This scheme has a number of advantages. First, since it defaults to the localized references of modular programs, segments can be usually referenced implicitly, without adding a segment selector to each instruction. Second, it provides efficient context switching, as just described. Third, the short, four-element selector file can be implemented in the same VLSI package as the processor to avoid off-chip access delays or timing constraints. Fourth, the explicit contents of the segment selector can be readily changed to access as large a number of segments as necessary—i.e., there is no arbitrarily small limit of 8, 16, 48, 128, etc., segments. In addition to these advantages, segmentation itself provides an important benefit—efficient access management.

Language orientation

Language orientation is the second key concept implemented in the 8086 microprocessor. Having parti-

IEEE MICRO

tioned a system design into modules, the engineer faces the task of implementing the module specifications in a programming language. The processor architecture should provide a natural and efficient environment for the language chosen, which today is likely to be a high-level one rather than an assembler. The effect of language choice on the trade-offs involved in processor design requires more discussion.

All programming languages manipulate data. Stripped of all pretense, data exist as abstractions of the real world; greater complexity in the real world leads to greater structure in data. Scalar quantities become vectors, vectors become lists, and lists become list structures in order to represent and manipulate real world events.

Small, self-contained programs that manipulate simple data can be adequately implemented in assembly language. Data having simple structure can be stored directly in processor registers or referenced indirectly through the registers. Simple operations are generally provided as machine instructions, so that both data and operations are implemented within the processor. Assembly language is processor-oriented and hence is focused on processor resources, an approach entirely adequate for simple programs.

As an application widens its world, its representation of that world begins to outgrow the processor's narrow physical limits. The operations employed on larger and more structured data are probably no longer implemented as elementary machine operations such as add or subtract. Higher-level programming tools are needed, and the focus of attention shifts from processor resources to *system* resources.

Growth of processor resources from microprocessor generation to generation is constrained by several factors (e.g., double-register width or number, double opcodes), whereas growth in system resources can cover orders of magnitude (e.g., kilobyte to megabyte) and even include the introduction of totally new concepts. The most powerful processors are those that direct growth so as to maximize the utilization of system resources.

The register architecture of the 8086 is a realization of this approach. It views registers as tools to manipulate memory-resident data rather than as places to store data. The processor-oriented, assembly language approach maximizes the effectiveness of registers (a processor resource), while the system-oriented, high-level language approach maximizes the effectiveness of memory (a system resource). The trade-off will be made clear in the following sections.

The language orientation of the 8086 can be viewed in terms of

- a data reference model, and
- a data manipulation model.

The natural memory orientation of high-level language programs, combined with their slower access to memory (as compared to registers) means that performance is more a matter of reference efficiency than of manipulation efficiency.

The data reference model. The addressing needs of different programming languages vary, but Figure 7 shows a fragment of a Pascal program that exemplifies the major categories of need. Line 1 declares "PROG" as the name of the program module. The module has associated data, declared as variables "G1" and "G2" of type "TG" on line 2, that is global to the entire module. This data will be stored in the module data area referenced via the 8086's data segment selector. This segment selector permits the module data segment to be dynamically allocated to memory so that the module itself can be loaded anywhere in the memory space. Also, a single module can be shared by several programs if the data segment selector is altered while the code segment selector is left unchanged. These advantages of segmentation—position independence and transparent sharing—are common to the various segment types (code, data, stack, and external).

Lines 3 and 4 show declarations of parameters ("P1" and "P2" of type "TP") and local variables ("L1" and "L2" of type "TL") that are allocated on the process stack when the procedure is activated. They are referenced via the stack segment selector, and that value is offset by the current base of the procedure data area on the stack.

Line 5 shows reference to a dynamically allocated variable. The variable is referenced indirectly through a pointer variable—"PTR" in the example. Dynamically allocated variables and list structures can exist anywhere but will typically be allocated from a "heap" in the process or system data areas. These areas are referenced via the external segment selector that explicitly selects a segment outside the local module environment.

The type of data referenced is independent of the area that contains the data. For example, scalar data can exist in any of the data segments in the module, process, or system areas. So, in addition to a segment selector, other addressing components are required, depending on the data type "T." These additional components may be either static (consisting of a fixed displacement) or dynamic (consisting of a run-time base or index value), depending on factors such as language used, data type, reference form (direct or indirect), and compiler optimization strategy.

With segmentation, static address components can be used for dynamically allocated data segments, since the ordinary operand addressing mechanism is decoupled from the dynamic data segment creation, deletion, movement, or sharing within the system.

Representing a static component by "d" for displacement and a dynamic component by "B" for base or "I" for index, Table 1 shows the data types and addressing components required for access to them. A *static scalar*

```
LINE
1    PROGRAM PROG;
2       VAR G1, G2: TG;
3       PROCEDURE PROC (P1, P2: TP);
4          VAR I1, I2: TI;
5          ... PTR↑ ...
6       END PROC ;
7    END PROG
```

Figure 7. Programming language example.

reference uses a fixed displacement "d" from the base of the data segment, while a *dynamic scalar reference* uses a runtime base value "B." A *static vector reference* uses a fixed displacement "d" for the base of the array within the segment, and a runtime index value "I" for the array element selector. A *dynamic vector reference* uses a runtime array base value "B" as well as a runtime index value "I." A *static record reference* uses two fixed displacements—one from the base of the segment to the base of the record, the other from the base of the record to the desired field within the record. The compiler adds the displacements to obtain a single static component "d." *Dynamic record references* use a runtime base value "B" to locate the record within the segment, as well as a fixed displacement "d" to locate the desired field within the record.

Figure 8 shows the three most common varieties of data type references. From these, more complex forms can be constructed such as arrays of arrays (multidimensional arrays), arrays of records, or records of arrays. These more complex forms can be broken down into their component structures by successive applications of the elementary addressing forms shown in the figure.

The 8086 implementation of this addressing model is not ideal, but represents reasonable engineering trade-offs among VLSI technological limits, performance, simplicity, encoding efficiency, and intended application. The 8086 multicomponent addressing style is shown in Figure 8. Four independently selectable components, segment (S), base (B), index (I), and displacement (d) are provided. This orthogonality in component selection removes the usual restrictions on component combinations that typical prepackaged "addressing modes" imply. Since reasonable encoding efficiency requires holding the line on the number of component selection bits, this orthogonality was obtained at the expense of orthogonality in address register selection. Two base registers are provided—as well as two index registers—rather than the ability to select any of eight general registers for either purpose. This was a clear choice that favored system

memory utility (via orthogonal component selection) over processor register utility (via orthogonal register selection). For a fixed addressing-mode field, more flexibility in address construction was obtained, with less flexibility in address register selection. This choice matches the intended application of the 8086—i.e., its use as a vehicle for high-level language programs.

Amund Lunde's detailed study of compiler code[21] addresses the question of index registers. Although his data was not available to the 8086's designers, their decision to provide four base and index registers agrees well with Lunde's results. His analysis of 38 high-level language programs comprising about five million DEC-10 instructions indicated that 90 percent of the time a statistical average of 3.4 index registers is sufficient.

The four-component 8086 addressing style requires that the segment component always be present, accompanied by at least one other component. The choice of the other components can be made independently, with the sole exception that the (S, d) form must use a 16-bit displacement. Otherwise, the displacement length, like all other component choices, is independent of the other selections made, and the appropriate length can be used in each case.

One limitation of this implementation is that the address components are all referenced directly, and the appropriate registers must be explicitly loaded whenever indirect addressing is employed. This is characteristic of many register/memory architectures, but is not representative of the best that can be done as technological constraints are removed and indirect components supported.

Another limitation of this implementation is a maximum segment displacement of 16 bits, which restricts segment size to 64K bytes. For some applications (such as handling large matrices), this is unreasonably small. But here subsegmentation (essentially segment "column vectors") can be employed, albeit at some performance loss. However, this loss should be weighed against the performance loss involved in simulating segmentation in a linear addressing environment, where the concept of segmentation may be necessary for sharing, dynamic program management, or logical separation of memory areas. It is easier to subsegment in a segmented environment than it is to fabricate an entirely absent concept in a nonsegmented environment. The steady rise in processor addressing ranges makes segmentation an increasingly attractive strategy for avoiding the chaos of an unstructured gigabyte of memory. The 8086 is the first microprocessor with dynamic segmentation, but the pressure to deal intelligently with ever larger memories will eventually make dynamic segmentation a standard in all structured higher-end microprocessors.

Although the requirement for segment sizes larger than 64K bytes did not surface when the 8086 was designed (1977), providing for such sizes would have been beyond practical VLSI density achievements at the time, since it would have required the addition of paging to permit partial allocation of large (say megabyte) segments. The addition of Multics-like[3] paging underneath segmentation would have required the use of a cache to implement associative page translation, a capability that could not have been integrated onto a single chip.

[S]	= SEGMENT COMPONENT (CS, DS, SS, ES)
[B]	= BASE COMPONENT (NIL, BX, BP)
[I]	= INDEX COMPONENT (NIL, SI, DI)
[d]	= DISPLACEMENT COMPONENT (NIL, 8-, 16-BITS)

Figure 8. 8086 multicomponent addressing.

Table 1.
8086 data type address components.

| DATA TYPE | ADDRESS COMPONENTS | |
	STATIC FORM	DYNAMIC FORM
SCALAR	d	B
VECTOR	d,I	B,I
RECORD	d	B,d

d = STATIC DISPLACEMENT COMPONENT
B = DYNAMIC BASE COMPONENT
I = DYNAMIC INDEX COMPONENT

A separate off-chip memory management device would have degraded performance or constrained access times and was never seriously considered. Advances in VLSI technology are removing many such constraints, however, and will facilitate both evolution and revolution in the handling of system resources.

The data manipulation model. Sandwiched between the references to source operands and destination fields is the actual manipulation of data. Efficient manipulation of data exploits two notions—parallelism and specialization.[22] Assuming for the moment a *very* simple, totally uncoupled model with c processor categories, n_i processors in each category ($i = 1, 2, \ldots, c$), eff_i average processor instruction "effectiveness" (e.g., average ratio of source language operations to machine language instructions for a given function), and $rate_i$ average instruction execution rate, the total system processing power P is determined by

$$P = \sum_{i=1}^{c} n_i \; eff_i \; rate_i$$

Absolute physical limits (such as the speed of light) as well as economic realities obviously constrain the power that can be provided by any single processor. Parallelism increases the value of n_i, while specialization raises the value of both eff_i and $rate_i$ by tailoring the design of individual processor categories to particular functional needs. The effect of processor coupling is complex but, simply stated, makes $rate_i$ a function of the degree of coupling rather than a constant for a given processor category.

In pure symmetric multiprocessing, c is set to 1 and n_i is greater than 1. In simple functional partitioning, c is greater than 1 and n_i is equal to 1 for each functional category $i = 1, 2 \ldots, c$. The general case is a combination of the two, in which multiple categories each contain multiple processors.

The 8086 family implements three processors for the above model: general data processors (8086), numeric data processors (8087), and input/output processors (8089). Operations are partitioned among the three to take advantage of functional specialization and processor concurrency. A simple three-processor example is shown in Figure 9.

General data processors (such as the 8086 or 8088) provide general system control operations, logical operations, short or single-precision integer computation, and string processing. The 8087 numeric data processor provides accurate, anomaly-free, transparent, multiprecision floating-point or fixed-point computation in support of the proposed hardware-independent IEEE floating-point standard.[23] The 8089 I/O processor provides two channels of I/O processing with bit or byte manipulation, on-the-fly computation, and a block transfer rate of two megabytes per second, and supports two-bus (local processor and system I/O) configurations.

The 8086 general data processor and 8087 numeric data processor are tightly coupled (one-on-one), and the pair execute concurrently on a single instruction stream managed by the 8086, with a special synchronization instruction (WAIT) to coordinate their operation.

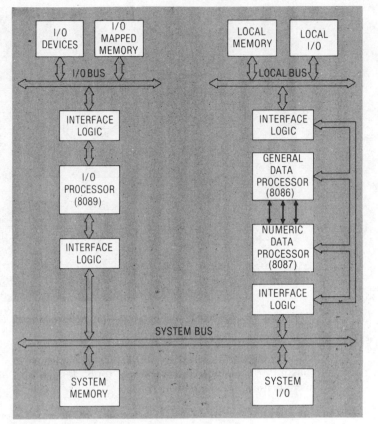

Figure 9. A three-processor system.

Parallelism provided by this family is implemented within the compiler and is transparent to the high-level language programmer, who is aware only of the apparent performance advantage. Figure 10 shows the cooperation of the two processors on a single instruction stream. In Figure 10(a), the two operate in nonoverlapped fashion, with the 8086 performing a WAIT operation after each numeric operation. In Figure 10(b), the two operate in overlapped fashion, with execution of the numeric instructions concurrent with execution of the nonnumeric instructions. This can boost performance by partially or wholly "hiding" the execution time of numeric operations.

The 8086 general data processor and the 8089 I/O processor are loosely coupled and operate on separate instruction streams. The system architecture is designed to support a fast processor bus and a standard system I/O bus. The 8089 supports the latter with two bus interfaces and so can reduce contention for bus availability. Figure 11 is a block diagram for a system with two general-processor/numeric-processor pairs and two I/O processors (providing four channels of I/O).

Functional specialization determines the register set characteristics in each processor category. Figure 12 shows the functionally partitioned register sets of the 8086 family. The general data processor provides segment, base, index, working, and status registers. The numeric data processor provides an eight-register-deep, 80-bit-wide evaluation stack for numeric computation, as well as control and status registers. The I/O processor provides a group of pointer and control registers, one group per

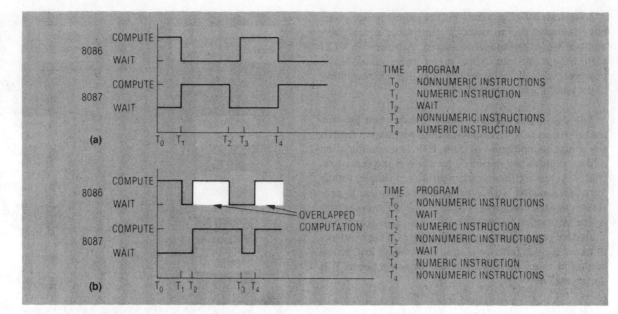

TIME	PROGRAM
T_0	NONNUMERIC INSTRUCTIONS
T_1	NUMERIC INSTRUCTION
T_2	WAIT
T_3	NONNUMERIC INSTRUCTIONS
T_4	NUMERIC INSTRUCTION

TIME	PROGRAM
T_0	NONNUMERIC INSTRUCTIONS
T_1	WAIT
T_2	NUMERIC INSTRUCTION
T_2	NONNUMERIC INSTRUCTIONS
T_3	WAIT
T_4	NUMERIC INSTRUCTION
T_4	NONNUMERIC INSTRUCTIONS

Figure 10. 8086/8087 cooperation—(a) nonoverlapped (sequential) operation; (b) overlapped (parallel) operation.

channel. Together, the register sets of the three processors constitute functionally specialized tools for data manipulation.

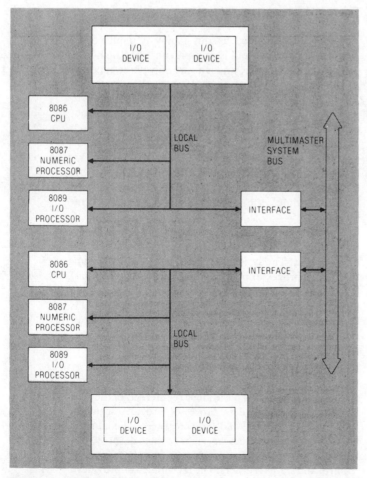

Figure 11. Multiprocessor system.

Instruction encoding

The usual objective of instruction set encoding is to minimize the average instruction length, where the average is weighted by frequency of usage. This reduces the overhead for both instruction reference and instruction storage.

Using a minimal encoding to reduce the overhead for instruction *reference* has two benefits. First, it reduces the additional memory bandwidth required for instruction fetch (as opposed to data fetch or store). This reduction in memory bus loading can yield higher performance as a result of less demanding memory access times. Second, the number of nonoverlapped instruction fetch cycles is reduced even in pipelined or cached environments. Control tranfers that cause instruction pipe breakage or instruction cache faults require less recovery time if the newly fetched instructions are shorter. These two benefits, then, mean that reduced instruction reference overhead raises performance and lowers cost.

Using a minimal encoding to reduce the overhead for instruction *storage* also has cost and performance advantages. Shorter programs certainly reduce the cost of program memory. In microprocessor applications, this cost may be measured not only in dollars, but also in physical size, power consumption, reliability, heat dissipation, and other metrics related to memory size. Shorter programs also have performance advantages, since they often can be stored in onboard memory that can be accessed with minimum delay. In larger, higher-performance systems, shorter programs mean less cache faulting, swapping, or overlaying—providing another speed advantage.

Given a knowledge of the frequency of instruction usage, the designer can use the decades-old Huffman encoding technique[24] to obtain a theoretical minimal encoding. Unfortunately, such an encoding, while minimal, consists of instructions of various bit lengths, whose handling can be more complicated than that of word-length instructions. At least two architectures[10,25] implement this approach.

Two recent architectures, by Tanenbaum[26] and by the Institute for Information Systems at the University of California, San Diego,[27] successfully use byte-aligned, frequency-based encodings. These encodings seem to achieve a compromise between the compactness of the Huffman method and the simplicity and low cost of word-oriented methods.

The 8086 employs just such a variable-length, byte-aligned instruction format. Not only does this achieve the performance and cost advantages associated with efficient encodings, but it indirectly supports program modularity and high-level languages.

Modular programs employ segmentation more efficiently, since optional one-byte segment selector prefixes can be used with any instruction. High-level-language programs can employ a memory-oriented, orthogonal addressing structure, since operand displacement lengths may be a variable number of bytes long. Block-structured, high-level languages (such as Pascal, PL/I, C, and Algol) that primarily reference local variables or parameters frequently use short (eight-bit) displacements into the local

data area on the stack. This means that a non-word-aligned, three-byte instruction (opcode, register/mode, displacement) is common. Packed (nonaligned) *data* in Pascal is also efficiently implemented with this design.

The byte-aligned instruction and data format is implemented in a 16-bit-word memory system by dividing the general data processor into two independent parallel processors in the same integrated circuit. The *bus interface unit* packs and unpacks data or instructions that fall on arbitrary byte boundaries within the memory. The *execution unit* interprets the instructions and executes the data operations from internal registers. Figure 13 illustrates this concurrency.

The bus interface unit fills an instruction prefetch queue with sequential instruction bytes that are then decoded by the execution unit. This causes instruction fetch to overlap instruction execution, and also buffers the byte-stream instruction decoder from a physically word-stream memory.

Variable, byte-length instructions mean that many short one-, two-, or three-byte instructions can be implemented and treated as instruction *fragments* from which more complex instructions can be composed. The traditional engineering trade-offs that apply to word-

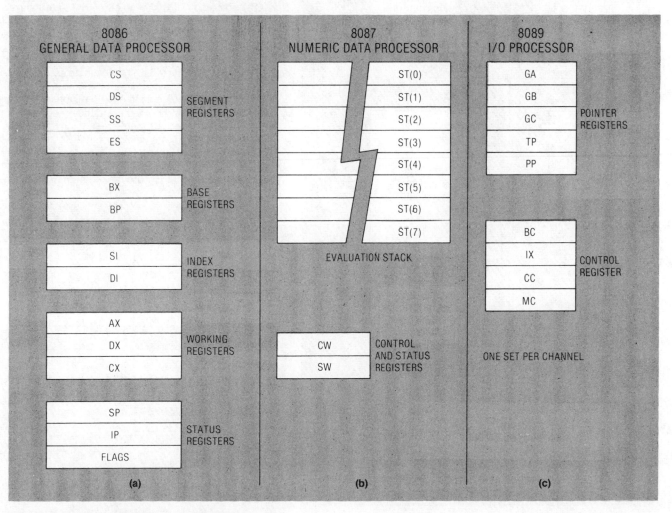

Figure 12. Functionally partitioned register set.

aligned processors are altered in this prefetched, byte-aligned design. No longer is it necessary to "do it in one instruction," since combined instruction fragments are only a little larger than equivalent single instructions, and the additional instruction fetch time is hidden by the sequential prefetch unit. For example, a memory-to-memory move instruction on the 8086 can be created from two three-byte, memory-to-register and register-to-memory move instructions. The resulting six-byte macro-instruction compares favorably with memory-to-memory instructions on forced word-alignment machines.

Any such minimal encoding faces a trade-off among the various opcodes, addressing modes, data types, registers, segment selectors, and segment offsets. The many value judgments involved make successful encodings an iterative and artistic endeavor. The general 8086 instruction format that emerged from this design process is described in the box below.

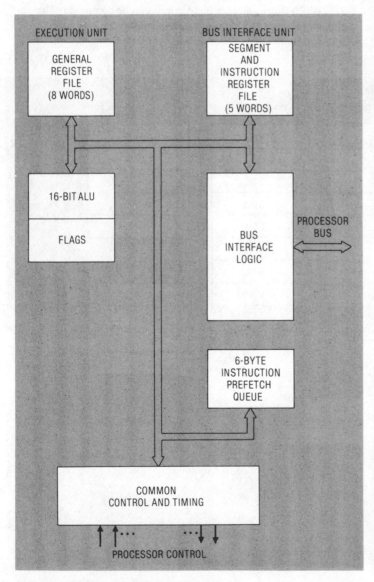

Figure 13. 8086 functional block diagram.

The 8086 instruction format

Figure 14 shows the general 8086 instruction format that emerged from the design process described in this article.

Since the 8086 general data processor handles system data, space need not be found in the opcode map for computational data types implemented in the numeric data processor, or for special I/O operations of the I/O processor. A six-bit opcode is sufficient for dyadic operations on byte- or word-length data, with one bit (W) specifying the data length. Monadic memory operations can use a longer opcode by consuming the unnecessary register (REG) field.

An architecture for high-level language support, with its natural memory orientation, would like to be able to specify a memory destination (as well as a register destination) for operation results. This is the function of the direction bit (D). Most studies show a predominance of short constants in high-level language programs,[26, 28, 29] so the sign-extension bit (S) can specify either sign-extension or zero-extension for short (eight-bit) constants used in 16-bit operations. This avoids the need for such architectural appendages as special short or "quick" immediate data instruction forms.

The end result of this is an eight-bit operation byte consisting of a six-bit opcode plus a destination (or sign-extension) bit and a data-width bit.

Figure 15 shows the compact matrix encoding employed for the already described addressing structure. A two-bit mode (MOD) field selects among zero-, eight-, or 16-bit displacements or the register file. A three-bit register/memory field (R/M) selects the appropriate combination of base and index registers for memory use, or the appropriate register in the register file. A three-bit register selector field (REG) chooses among eight 16-bit or eight 8-bit registers. These five bits of addressing mode selection and three bits of register selection constitute the register/ mode byte.

OPCODE	D OR S	W	MOD	REG (2-OP) OR OPCODE EXT	R/M

d_low (OPTIONAL)	d_high (OPTIONAL)

7 6 5 4 3 2 1 0   7 6 5 4 3 2 1 0

i_low (OPTIONAL)	i_high (OPTIONAL)

D = DIRECTION (REGISTER OR MEMORY DESTINATION) FOR NONIMMEDIATE OPERANDS
S = SIGN-EXTEND (FOR IMMEDIATE OPERANDS)
W = WIDTH (8- OR 16-BIT DATA)
MOD, R/M = ADDRESSING MODE FIELDS
REG = THE 8086 REGISTER, FOR TWO-OPERAND INSTRUCTIONS
OPCODE EXT = THE OPCODE EXTENSION FIELD, FOR ONE-OPERAND INSTRUCTIONS
d = OPERAND DISPLACEMENT WITHIN A SEGMENT
i = AN IMMEDIATE OPERAND

Figure 14. Instruction format for the 8086 general data processor.

IEEE MICRO

Following the operation and register/mode bytes are an optional one or two bytes of displacement and one or two bytes of immediate (constant) data.

Figure 16 shows the numeric data processor instruction format. The one-byte WAIT instruction (already discussed) permits overlap and synchronization of general-processor and numeric-processor operation. The five-bit escape (ESC) opcode instructs the general processor to ignore the instruction and place the effective address on the address bus for reference by the numeric processor. The numeric processor has its own six-bit opcode space (CP01 and CP02) that is distinct from the general processor opcode space, although the numeric processor "sees" the same addressing structure.

Figure 17 shows the instruction format used to replace the numeric data processor with a software simulator. The software trap instruction (INT) traps the unimplemented (in hardware) numeric processor instruction and simulates it in software. The real and the simulated instruction formats are the same length—only the WAIT/INT and ESC/TRAP fields differ in con-

tent. These fields can be filled in by a binder late in the program development process, to permit delayed binding of processor configuration information into the final program.

Figure 18 shows the I/O processor formats for source and object instructions. The operand field may contain no operands or one or more operands, as required by the instruction. When a source operand refers to an I/O device address, data is input from the device. Similarly, when a destination operand refers to an I/O device address, data is output to the device. An operand that refers to an I/O device always specifies one of four pointer registers, from which the base address of the device is taken. Any of the memory addressing modes (based, offset, indexed, indexed and auto-increment) may be used to modify the base address to produce the effective address of the device. A one-bit flag in the pointer register locates the device in the system space or the I/O space.■

	MOD			
R/M	00	01	10	11
000	BX + SI	BX + SI + d8	BX + SI + d16	AL/AX
001	BX + DI	BX + DI + d8	BX + DI + d16	CL/CX
010	BP + SI	BP + SI + d8	BP + SI + d16	DL/DX
011	BP + DI	BP + DI + d8	BP + DI + d16	BL/BX
100	SI	SI + d8	SI + d16	AH/SP
101	DI	DI + d8	DI + d16	CH/BP
110	d16	BP + d8	BP + d16	DH/SI
111	BX	BX + d8	BX + d16	BH/DI

Figure 15. 8086 addressing mode encoding.

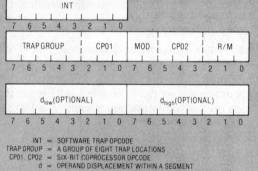

INT   =   SOFTWARE TRAP OPCODE
TRAP GROUP =   A GROUP OF EIGHT TRAP LOCATIONS
CP01, CP02 =   SIX-BIT COPROCESSOR OPCODE
d   =   OPERAND DISPLACEMENT WITHIN A SEGMENT

Figure 17. Instruction format for the simulated numeric data processor.

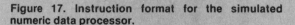

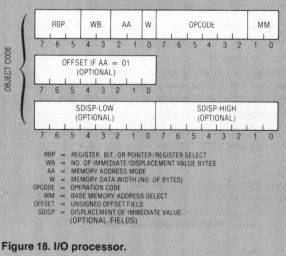

RBP   =   REGISTER, BIT, OR POINTER/REGISTER SELECT
WB   =   NO. OF IMMEDIATE/DISPLACEMENT VALUE BYTES
AA   =   MEMORY ADDRESS MODE
W   =   MEMORY DATA WIDTH (NO. OF BYTES)
OPCODE   =   OPERATION CODE
MM   =   BASE MEMORY ADDRESS SELECT
OFFSET   =   UNSIGNED OFFSET FIELD
SDISP   =   DISPLACEMENT OF IMMEDIATE VALUE
      (OPTIONAL FIELDS)

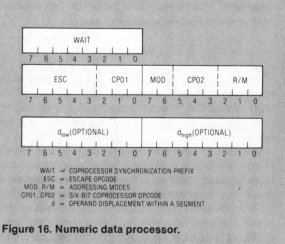

WAIT   =   COPROCESSOR SYNCHRONIZATION PREFIX
ESC   =   ESCAPE OPCODE
MOD, R/M =   ADDRESSING MODES
CP01, CP02 =   SIX-BIT COPROCESSOR OPCODE
d   =   OPERAND DISPLACEMENT WITHIN A SEGMENT

Figure 16. Numeric data processor.

Figure 18. I/O processor.

The Intel 8086 16-bit microprocessor is designed for the evolving requirements of structured software systems. It supports modular programs through dynamic segmentation and high-level languages through orthogonal, multicomponent data addressing over a spectrum of logical, computational, and hierarchical data types. A trio of processors—general, numeric, and I/O—implement parallel functional specialization in individual integrated circuit packages. These processors utilize a uniform, nonaligned, byte-addressable memory space for simple, compact instruction and data storage.

The 8086 does not directly implement operating system functions. It does provide a simple, dynamic, and elegant segmentation scheme drawn from an elementary module-addressing model. This model is readily integrated with the processor, avoiding access path delays or constraints. Dynamic forms of segmentation support the controlled growth and sharing of programs and data.

The 8086 operand-addressing mechanism reflects a programming language orientation toward memory-resident data structures. It makes the multiple address components of segment, base, index, and displacement orthogonal and provides a distinct set of address registers at each level. These selectable components perform static or dynamic addressing of scalar, vector, and record data types.

The 8086 data manipulation mechanism employs functionally partitioned parallel processors of general, numeric, and I/O processing form. The general and numeric processors are tightly coupled and overlap their execution on a single instruction stream. The I/O processors are loosely coupled, execute a distinct instruction stream, and support distributed bus architectures.

The 8086 instruction encoding results in a variable-length, byte-stream instruction flow that utilizes a two-in-one CPU for execution and bus interfacing. The bus-interface processor performs instruction prefetching, which can enhance the performance of macroinstructions composed of shorter one-to-three-byte instruction fragments. The bus-interface processor also provides a uniformly byte-addressable data space.

The 8086 microprocessor supports a broad yet reasonably constrained range of applications. Its concepts of modular program support, high-level-language orientation, functional partitioning, and uniform byte-addressability are relatively new to microprocessors.

Greater VLSI densities will probably result in more attractive trade-offs (yielding a larger segment size limit, more segment selectors, a higher degree of address indirection, greater exploitation of pipelining and registers, etc.). At the same time, the continuing collapse of traditional architectural styles will spur new solutions in operating systems, programming languages, and applications support. ■

References

1. O. J. Dahl, E. W. Dijkstra, and C.A.R. Hoare, *Structured Programming,* Academic Press, New York, 1972.

2. P. Brinch Hansen, *Concurrent Pascal Machine,* Information Science Report, California Institute of Technology, Pasadena, CA, Oct. 1975.

3. A. Bensoussan, C. T. Clingen, and R. C. Daley, "The Multics Virtual Memory: Concepts and Design," *Comm. ACM,* Vol. 15, No. 5, May 1972, pp. 308-318.

4. W. A. Wulf and C. G. Bell, "C.mmp—A Multi-Mini-Processor," *AFIPS Conf. Proc.,* Vol. 41, 1972 FJCC, pp. 765-777.

5. Intel Corp., *The 8086 Family User's Manual,* Form. No. 9800722, 1979.

6. M. J. Shah, "Automatic Programming for Energy Management Using Sensor Based Computers," *IBM Systems J.,* Vol. 18, No. 3, Mar. 1979, pp. 457-469.

7. K. Jensen and N. Wirth, *Pascal User Manual and Report,* Springer-Verlag, New York, 1974.

8. DOD Higher Order Language Working Group, "Preliminary Ada Reference Manual," *Sigplan Notices,* Vol. 14, No. 6, June 1979.

9. J. Rattner and W. Lattin, "Ada Determines Architecture of 32-Bit Microprocessor," *Electronics,* Vol. 54, No. 4, Feb. 24, 1981, pp. 119-126.

10. Intel Corp., *iAPX 432 GDP Architecture Reference Manual,* Form. No. 171860, 1981.

11. M. Satyanarayanan, "Commercial Multiprocessing Systems," *Computer,* Vol. 13, No. 5, May 1980, pp. 75-96.

12. S. P. Morse, "The Intel 8086 Microprocessor: A 16-Bit Evolution of the 8080," *Computer,* Vol. 11, No. 6, June 1978, pp. 18-27.

13. P. Brinch Hansen, *The Architecture of Concurrent Programs,* Prentice-Hall, Inc., Englewood Cliffs, NJ, 1977, pp. 69-147.

14. O. J. Dahl, B. Myhrhaug, and K. Nygaard, "The Simula 67 Common Base Language," Norwegian Computing Center, Oslo, Norway, 1968.

15. W. A. Wulf, "Alphard: Toward a Language to Support Structured Programs," Dept. of Computer Science Internal Report, Carnegie-Mellon Univ., Pittsburgh, PA, Apr. 1974.

16. B. Liskov and S. Zilles, "Programming with Abstract Data Types," *Sigplan Notices* (Proc. Symposium Very High Level Languages), Vol. 9, No. 4, Apr. 1974, pp. 50-59.

17. J. G. Mitchell, W. Maybury, and R. Surett, "Mesa Language Manual Version 5.0," Xerox Palo Alto Research Center, Palo Alto, CA, Apr. 1979.

18. P. Wegner, *Programming Languages, Information Structures, and Machine Organization,* McGraw-Hill Book Co., New York, 1968, pp. 80-94.

19. P. Brinch Hansen, *Operating System Principles,* Prentice-Hall, Inc., Englewood Cliffs, NJ, 1973, pp. 159-169.

20. J. J. Donovan, *Systems Programming,* McGraw-Hill Book Co., New York, 1972, pp. 424-430.

21. A. Lunde, "Empirical Evaluation of Some Features of In-

struction Set Processor Architectures," *Comm. ACM,* Vol. 20, No. 3, Mar. 1977, pp. 143-152.

22. J. E. Thorton, "Parallel Operations in the Control Data 6600," in C. G. Bell and A. Newell, *Computer Structures: Readings and Examples,* McGraw-Hill Book Co., New York, 1976.

23. "A Proposed Standard for Binary Floating-Point Arithmetic," *Computer,* Vol. 14, No. 3, Mar. 1981, pp. 51-62.

24. D. Huffman, "A Method for the Construction of Minimum Redundancy Codes," *Proc. IRE,* Vol. 40, Sept. 1952, pp. 1098-1101.

25. W. T. Wilner, "Design of the Burroughs B1700," *AFIPS Conf. Proc.,* Vol. 41, 1972 FJCC, pp. 489-497.

26. A. S. Tanenbaum, "Implications of Structured Programming for Machine Architecture," *Comm. ACM,* Vol. 21, No. 3, Mar. 1978, pp. 237-246.

27. Institute for Information Systems, "UCSD (Mini-Micro Computer) Pascal Release Version 1.4," Univ. of California, San Diego, La Jolla, CA, Jan. 1978, pp. 141-156.

28. D. E. Knuth, "An Empirical Study of FORTRAN Programs," *Software—Practice & Experience,* Vol. 1, 1971, pp. 105-133.

29. W. G. Alexander and D. B. Wortman, "Static and Dynamic Characteristics of XPL Programs," *Computer,* Vol. 8, No. 11, Nov. 1975, pp. 41-46.

Alfred C. Hartmann is a software engineering manager in the Development Systems Operation at Intel Corporation. He has been with Intel since 1976, working in the areas of compiler development, microprocessor architecture, and language-oriented programming systems. He also serves as an evening instructor in computer science engineering at San Jose State University. While in graduate studies at Caltech, he developed the compiler for Concurrent Pascal.

Hartmann received a BS in electrical engineering from Carnegie-Mellon University and an MS and PhD in information science from the California Institute of Technology.

E. Scott Fehr is a staff architect at Zilog, Inc., with responsibility for architecture in new product definition. His interests include architecture research and implementation, the relationship between high-level languages and architecture, and the development and integration of architectural tools into CAD methodology. He was previously with Intel Corp., Tektronix, and Texas Instruments.

Fehr received the BS degree in physics in 1971, and the MSEE in 1975, from the University of Texas at Austin. He is working toward the PhD in EECS/computer science at the University of California, Berkeley. He is a member of ACM and IEEE.

Alfred C. Hartmann's address is Mail Stop 6-216, Intel Corporation, 3065 Bowers Ave., Santa Clara, CA 95051.

An established microprocessor family—especially its newest member—offers speed,

compatibility with a large body of existing software, and multiprocessing capability.

An Overview of the 9900 Microprocessor Family

Richard V. Orlando

Thomas L. Anderson

American Microsystems, Inc.

A recent article in *IEEE Micro* (Toong and Gupta, May 1981[1]) discussed at some length the main features of several currently available 16-bit microprocessors. Although the authors made no pretense about covering all such processors, we feel they erred in omitting at least one machine, the 9900. As we will show, the 9900 microprocessor and its successor, the 9995, are powerful machines with architectural and performance characteristics rivalling those of the 8086, Z8000, and 68000. We will also discuss the recently disclosed 99000 family, a highly sophisticated, upward-compatible extension to the 9900 family.

Besides its power, the 9900 is notable for being the first commercially available 16-bit microprocessor—Texas Instruments first offered the TMS9900 in 1976 and it is still on the market. In addition, the 9900 is second-sourced by AMI as the S9900. We will briefly outline the salient features of this processor and its successors in a manner similar to that used by Toong and Gupta—by following the format of the original article, we hope to present a valid comparison to the machines discussed there.

General characteristics

Since the 9900 was the pioneering 16-bit microprocessor, it does not contain all the features found on later machines. However, it does provide 16-bit internal and external data buses, byte and word instructions, and most of the common addressing modes. The machine architecture provides 16 general-purpose registers, although these actually reside in main memory. This strategy achieves one of the benefits of register addressing: the coding efficiency gained by not having to specify full memory ad-

dresses. However, no increase in speed is attained by using register instead of memory instructions. The address space is 64K, with no internal provision for extension. The 9900 emphasizes the "family" approach to microprocessors, with several different software-compatible models available. The 9940 is a single-chip microcomputer with an enhanced 9900 as its CPU; the 9980 is an 8-bit data bus version of the 9900; the 9995 is a high-performance version of the 9980. We will examine the 9900 and the 9995, pointing out the differences between them where appropriate.

Architectural details

The basic structure of the 9900 is shown in Figure 1; its specifications are listed in Table 1 (along with those for the 9995). The operation of the processor is straightforward. There is no instruction prefetch or pipelining. The I/O interface is handled by a communications register unit, or CRU, which uses specific instructions to address external devices via the CRU lines and address bus. Most important, I/O bits can be addressed individually or in fields of 1 to 16 bits. The structure of the 9995 (Figure 2) is similar to that of the 9900, although it adds a single instruction prefetch, 256 bytes of internal RAM, and internal clock generation. To save pins and to allow the use of byte-wide memories, the 9995 provides only an eight-bit external data bus. However, the 16-bit-wide on-chip RAM prevents this from becoming a bottleneck.

Register organization. 9900 processors contain three primary internal registers: the program counter (PC), the status register, and the workspace pointer (WP). The

72

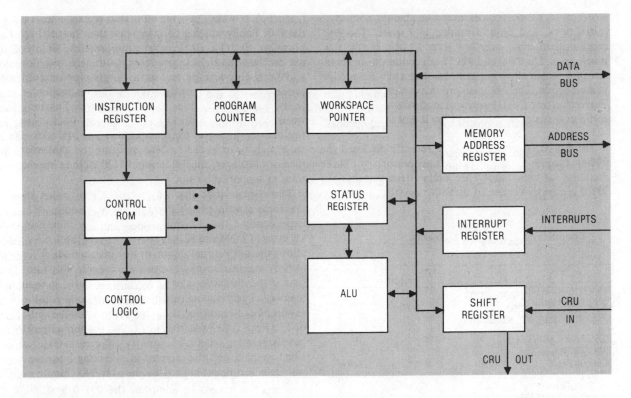

Figure 1. Basic structure of the 9900.

status register contains a four-bit interrupt mask and processor status bits (seven for the 9900 and eight for the 9995). The WP points to the starting location in memory of the 16 general-purpose "workspace" registers, which must be held in contiguous words. A "context switch" mechanism loads the WP with a new value, thus defining a new set of work-space registers in main memory. This multiple-register-set scheme allows the 9900 family to efficiently handle interrupt and subroutine calls without saving or stacking the contents of the workspace registers. In essence, the 9900 family uses a linked-list approach to program control linkage rather than the more traditional hardware stack. Since certain workspace locations are used to store processor status during subroutine calls, the "general-purpose" registers are not completely general. The 9995's 256 bytes of internal RAM are commonly used to store workspaces—this greatly improves the performance of register operations.

System structure. The microprocessor, memory, and I/O devices are interconnected by a local bus as defined by the processor pin-out. The data portion of this bus is used only for memory operations; I/O is handled by a separate serial interface (described in a later section). A microprocessor, memory, and I/O devices form a module which may be connected through bus control and arbiter modules to a global bus (see Hirschman, Ali, and Swan[5]).

Memory. The 9900 and 9995 use a straightforward 64K address space, which can be expanded only by external memory management. The 9900 always accesses an entire 16-bit word of memory at one time, although it has byte instructions to perform operations on either of the two bytes.

Stack organization. The 9900 and 9995 are not stack-oriented machines and provide no direct hardware support for stacks. For example, for a subroutine call or interrupt response, several of the work-space registers—rather than a stack—are used to save the processor state. However, it is a relatively straightforward matter to set up a stack of workspaces to permit recursive and multiple subroutine calls.

I/O mechanisms. Up to 4K bits each of input and output may be individually addressed by the CRU mechanism in the 9900, and up to 32K bits in the 9995. These bits may be addressed in fields of 1 to 16 bits, which allows single-operation flag testing or setting. Data transfer to and from I/O devices is handled serially through the CRUIN and CRUOUT lines. External decoding of the low-order address lines determines the actual number of I/O devices being addressed.

Software. Unlike other 16-bit microprocessors, the 9900 was designed to be software-compatible with a minicomputer family—the Texas Instruments 990 series—rather than with a microprocessor. Texas Instruments' philosophy of microprocessor design dictates that advances in minicomputer systems development be incorporated into new microprocessors as soon as improvements in VLSI technology permit it. The result is a parallel development of both a microprocessor and a minicomputer family, with software compatibility between families and among individual members of each family.

The 9900 family supports a full memory-to-memory architecture, although workspace registers are provided to reduce program size through encoding efficiency. The instruction set supports most addressing modes, some byte instructions, and bit-addressable I/O space. The 9995 contains arithmetic overflow traps to help handle runtime errors. The 9900 and 9995 both contain software interrupts, which allow a user to emulate a new instruction in macrocode. The 9995 also provides an unimplemented instruction trap (MID interrupt) to allow users to simulate complex instructions or to trap on illegal opcodes.

The 99000. Texas Instruments recently disclosed the 99000 family of 16-bit microprocessors.[6,7] Three members of this family are under development—the 99105 is a faster version of the 9900; the 99110 and 99120

Table 1.
Specifications for the 9900 family.

	9900	9995
YEAR OF COMMERCIAL INTRODUCTION	1976	1981
NO. OF BASIC INSTRUCTIONS	69	73
NO. OF GENERAL-PURPOSE REGISTERS	16	16
PIN COUNT	64	40
DIRECT ADDRESS RANGE (BYTES)	64K	64K
NUMBER OF ADDRESSING MODES	8	8
BASIC CLOCK FREQUENCY	3 MHz*	3 MHz
SYSTEM STRUCTURES		
UNIFORM ADDRESSABILITY		
MODULE MAP AND MODULES		
VIRTUAL		
PRIMITIVE DATA TYPES		
BITS	•	•
INTEGER BYTE OR WORD	•	•
INTEGER DOUBLE-WORD		
LOGICAL BYTE OR WORD	•	•
LOGICAL DOUBLE-WORD		
CHARACTER STRINGS		
(BYTE, WORD)	•	•
CHARACTER STRINGS		
(DOUBLE-WORD)		
BCD BYTE		
BCD WORD		
BCD DOUBLE-WORD		
FLOATING-POINT		
DATA STRUCTURES		
STACKS	•	•
ARRAYS	•	•
PACKED ARRAYS	•	•
RECORDS	•	•
PACKED RECORDS		
STRINGS		
PRIMITIVE CONTROL OPERATIONS		
CONDITION CODE PRIMITIVES	•	•
JUMP	•	•
CONDITIONAL BRANCH	•	•
SIMPLE ITERATIVE LOOP CONTROL	•	•
SUBROUTINE CALL	•	•
MULTIWAY BRANCH		
CONTROL STRUCTURE		
EXTERNAL PROCEDURE CALL		
SEMAPHORES		
TRAPS	•	•
INTERRUPTS	•	•
SUPERVISOR CALL	•	•
OTHERS		
USER MICROCODE		
DEBUG MODE		

*The 9900 clock frequency is 3.0 MHz, but since two clock cycles are required for each machine state, the effective clock frequency is actually only 1.5 MHz.

(Figure 3), however, provide numerous enhancements to the 9900 family which greatly increase their range of application. Each has single instruction prefetch, an internal oscillator and clock generator, arithmetic overflow and illegal opcode traps, and status output pins for multiprocessor and DMA configurations. The instruction set includes many extensions to the 9900, including longword arithmetic, support for user-defined stacks, and test-and-set primitives for semaphores. The 64K address space may be extended to 16M by using the TIM99610 memory manager; the 99110 and 99120 include instructions to support this chip.

These processors also include a feature called the macrostore, an internal high-speed memory addressed independently of main memory and currently comprising 1K bytes of ROM and 32 bytes of RAM. This fast memory allows the software emulation of new instructions or frequently executed routines to operate considerably faster than if the instructions or routines were stored in main memory. The 99110 will contain floating-point routines as part of its macrostore; the 99120 will contain the kernel of TI's Real-Time Executive, which will support a Pascal-based operating system. These new architectural features, when coupled with the increase in operating frequency, will yield significant improvements over 9900 family execution times. In addition, the 99110 and 99120 can operate in either user or supervisor (privileged) mode.

Microcomputers

There are several single-card microcomputers based on members of the 9900 family. Table 2 summarizes the characteristics of the Texas Instruments TM990/101 single-card microcomputer, which contains a 9900 as its CPU.

Multiprocessor capabilities

As already mentioned, the designer can configure 9900 family processors in a multiprocessor system by interconnecting them on a global bus. Although no *specific* multiprocessing features were incorporated into the design of the 9900 and 9995, the 99110 and 99120 provide several features designed specifically for multiprocessing environments. They send out bus status codes so that other modules in the system know exactly what phase of instruction execution they are in. Such status information is critical to efficient arbitration of system bus contention. They provide primitives for testing and setting semaphores, with external signals to lock out other processors during atomic operations.

Selection strategy

Technical issues. The machines of the 9900 family have both advantages and disadvantages when compared to the 8086, Z8000, 68000, and NS16000. Their direct address space, 64K, is the smallest of the group, although this address space is externally extensible. Their I/O facilities are addressed separately from memory, allowing implementation of useful features such as individual bit access.

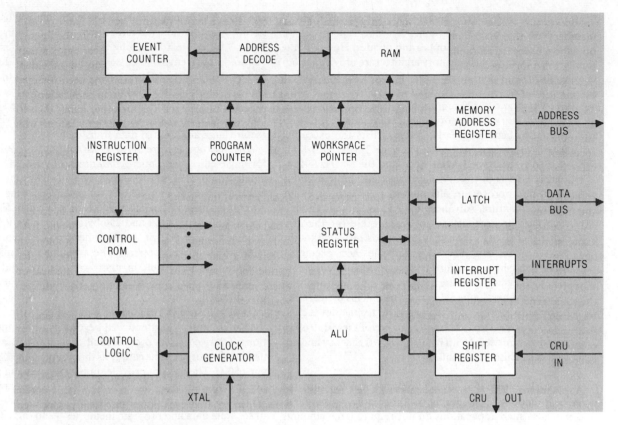

Figure 2. Basic structure of the 9995.

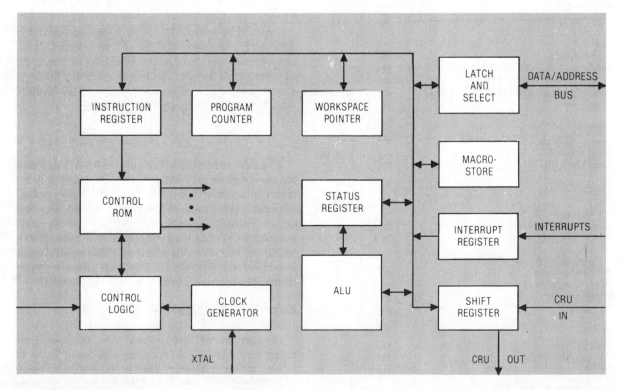

Figure 3. Basic structure of the 99110 and 99120.

75

Unlike the Z8000 and 68000, currently available members of the 9900 family do not support 32-bit operands, except in multiplies and divides. However, the family's memory-to-memory architecture provides an advantage not found in the other 16-bit micros by reducing the number of instructions required to access operands. The 99110 and 99120 support both long-word operations and a memory-to-memory architecture; hence, their performance benefits greatly. Table 3 lists the execution speeds of various instructions for the 3-MHz (1.5-MHz effective) 9900, the 3-MHz 9995, and the 6-MHz 99110.

The 9900 is obviously the slowest currently available 16-bit microprocessor, although it is the least expensive and most mature. Advances in VLSI technology and microprocessor architecture are responsible for the dramatic increases in the execution speeds provided by the newer processors. The 9900 and the 9995 exemplify this—they show great differences in performance even though they both operate at the same cycle time and with the same general internal architecture. This increase can be directly attributed to architectural techniques such as instruction prefetch. The performance of the 99110 is impressive, consistent with its high clock frequency and advanced architectural features.

Applications. The ideal "application niche" for the 9900 and 9995 is probably a control environment. Because such applications do not require large amounts of memory, the limited direct address space of the 9900

Table 2.
TM990/101 microcomputer characteristics.

GENERAL	
PROCESSOR USED	TMS9900
WORD SIZE (BITS)	16
ADDRESSING	
ADDRESS SIZE (BITS)	15
TOTAL MEMORY ADDRESSABLE (BYTES)	64K
AMT. OF RAM ON CARD (BYTES)	4K
AMT. OF ROM ON CARD (BYTES)	0-8K
DMA CAPABILITY	YES
FREQUENCY, ETC.	
CLOCK FREQUENCY (MHz)	3
SUPPLY VOLTAGES	+5, +12, −12
BOARD SIZE (INCHES)	7.5 × 11
I/O CAPABILITY	
BUS TYPE	SPECIAL
PARALLEL I/O LINES	16+
NUMBER OF I/O PORTS	2
MAX. I/O RATE (K BAUD)	38.4
ADDITIONAL HARDWARE DETAILS	
INTERRUPT PROVISIONS	YES
MULTIPROCESSING CAPABILITY	YES
NO. OF TIMERS	3
BITS PER TIMER	8-14
SOFTWARE	
OPERATING SYSTEM	YES
HIGH-LEVEL LANGUAGE(S)	YES
ASSEMBLER	YES
DEBUGGING AIDS	YES
APPLICATION PACKAGES	YES

and 9995 is not a major factor. The 9900 family's fast interrupt response time (as can be seen from the figures in Table 3 for context switching and restoring) is a useful feature in such environments. Its ability to individually address I/O bits and fields without the need for masks makes it particularly useful in bit-map applications such as terminals and printers. On the other hand, the serial I/O is not particularly well-suited for applications which require large amounts of data transfer.

An important feature of the 9900 family is its provision for single-chip, 16-bit micro*computers*. The 9940, for example, contains 2K of ROM, 128 bytes of RAM, internal clock generation, and 32 bits of general-purpose I/O ports in a single, 40-pin package. The 9995 includes internal clock generation and 256 bytes of on-chip RAM, making it somewhat of a hybrid between a microcomputer and a microprocessor. The availability of microcomputers is important in many control applications, where space and speed constraints do not permit use of board-level systems.

The 99110 and 99120 have enough enhancements that their usefulness will extend well beyond control applications. The two devices provide multiprocessor and multiuser support of the same caliber as that found in the Z8000 and 68000. They do not provide support for demand paging, which may limit their use in certain large applications. However, they do support functional paging—e.g., of separate data and program memories—and this can be useful in numerous applications.

There are many support chips for the 9900 family (Table 4). Although the 9900 does not have a set of peripheral chips from an eight-bit predecessor to fall back on, it has been around longer than the other 16-bit microprocessors discussed. Thus, there has been sufficient time to develop support chips for typical applications.

Commercial issues. The 9900 is second-sourced by AMI and, internationally, by ITT Intermettel. It is a mature product with the largest established software and hardware base in the 16-bit world. Both Texas Instruments and AMI will continue to support the family, as well as develop its future generations.

We have attempted to evaluate the 9900 family using the same metrics as those used by Toong and Gupta in their evaluation of 16-bit microprocessors. We conclude by presenting our own rating of the 9900, 9995, and 99000 family (Table 5) and include for comparison the ratings assigned by Toong and Gupta to the 8086, Z8000, MC68000, and NS16000. Our results show performance impressive enough to demand the 9900's inclusion in any treatment of currently available 16-bit machines. ∎

Acknowledgments

The assistance of Dave Laffitte, John Schabowski, and others in the 16-bit microprocessor group at Texas Instruments was invaluable. Their proofreading and assistance in obtaining 99000 information contributed greatly to this article.

OPERATION	DATA TYPE	9900	9995	99110
REGISTER-TO- REGISTER MOVE	BYTE/WORD DOUBLE-WORD	4.60 9.80	(1.30)* (2.60)	0.50 1.00
MEMORY-TO- REGISTER MOVE	BYTE WORD DOUBLE-WORD	7.30 7.30 14.60	(1.99) (2.33) (4.66)	0.83 0.67 1.33
MEMORY-TO- MEMORY MOVE	BYTE WORD DOUBLE-WORD	9.90 9.90 19.80	(1.30),2.60 (1.90),3.30 (3.90),6.60	1.00 0.83 1.67
ADD MEMORY TO REGISTER	BYTE/WORD DOUBLE-WORD	7.32 21.30	(2.60) (5.30)	0.83 2.00
COMPARE MEMORY TO MEMORY	BYTE/WORD DOUBLE-WORD	9.90 19.80	1.99 3.98	1.00 2.00
MULTIPLY MEMORY-TO- MEMORY	BYTE WORD DOUBLE-WORD	21.90 21.90 180.64	(7.90),8.60 (7.90),8.60 59.95	4.17 4.17 26.38
CONDITIONAL BRANCH	BRANCH TAKEN BRANCH NOT TAKEN	3.60 2.90	1.30 1.30	0.50 0.50
MODIFY INDEX BRANCH IF ZERO	BRANCH TAKEN	7.60	2.60	1.00
BRANCH TO SUBROUTINE		7.90	3.90	1.00
CONTEXT SWITCH		13.60	5.60	2.00
RETURN CONTEXT		5.90	2.30	1.00

*Times in parentheses are for references to internal RAM.

Table 4.
9900 family support chips.

MEMORY MANAGEMENT	TIM99610
BUS ARBITER	
FLOATING-POINT	
DMA CONTROLLER	TMS9911
INTERRUPT CONTROL UNIT	TMS9901
I/O PROCESSOR/INTERFACE	TMS9901
PERIPHERAL CONTROLLER	TMS9901
FLOPPY DISK CONTROLLER	TMS9909
CRT CONTROLLER	TMS9927
ARRAY PROCESSOR	
BUBBLE MEMORY CONTROLLER	

Table 5.
Ranking of 16-bit microprocessors.

	8086	Z8000	MC68000	NS16000	9900	9995	99000
SPEED	C	B	A	A	D	B	A
NUMBER OF REGISTERS	B	A	A	C	A	A	A
ADDRESS RANGE	D	A	A	B	D	D	D
COMPATIBILITY WITH EARLIER MICROPROCESSORS	A	B	B	B	NA	A	A
SUPPORT CHIPS	A	B	C	D	A	A	A
MULTIPROCESSING CAPABILITY	B	B	B	C	C	C	A
SECOND SOURCE	A	A	A	D	B	D	D

August 1981

References

1. Hoo-min D. Toong and Amar Gupta, "An Architectural Comparison of Contemporary 16-Bit Microprocessors," *IEEE Micro,* Vol. 1, No. 2, May 1981, pp. 26-37.

2. Henry A. Davis, "Comparing Architectures of Three 16-Bit Microprocessors," *Computer Design,* Vol. 18, No. 7, July 1979, pp. 91-100.

3. *9900 Family Systems Design and Data Book,* Texas Instruments, Inc., Houston, 1978.

4. *TMS 9995 Microcomputer Preliminary Data Manual,* Texas Instruments, Inc., Houston, 1981.

5. Alan D. Hirschman, Gamil Ali, and Richard Swan, "Standard Modules Offer Flexible Multiprocessor System Design," *Computer Design,* Vol. 18, No. 5, May 1979, pp. 181-189.

6. David S. Laffitte and Karl M. Guttag, "Fast On-Chip Memory Extends 16-Bit Family's Reach," *Electronics,* Vol. 54, No. 4, Feb. 24, 1981, pp. 157-161.

7. David Laffitte, "New-Generation 16-Bit Microprocessors—Fast and Function-Oriented," *Electronic Design,* Vol. 29, No. 4, Feb. 19, 1981, pp. 111-117.

Rick Orlando is manager of the Microprocessor/Microcomputer Applications Group at American Microsystems, Inc., of Santa Clara, California. His research interests include processor architecture, multiprocessing, networking, and computer graphics hardware development. A member of Tau Beta Pi, Eta Kappa Nu, the IEEE, and the IEEE Computer Society, Orlando received a BS in computer systems engineering from the University of Massachusetts at Amherst in 1980.

Thomas L. Anderson is employed for the summer of 1981 as an applications engineer for American Microsystems, Inc., of Santa Clara, California. Currently he is pursuing an SM in computer science and engineering at MIT, having received his BS in computer systems engineering from the University of Massachusetts at Amherst in 1980. His research interests include computer architecture, multiprocessor systems, and microprocessor applications. Anderson has previously worked for IBM and Digital Equipment Corporation and is a student member of Tau Beta Pi, Eta Kappa Nu, ACM, SIAM, and the IEEE.

The authors' address is American Microsystems, Inc., 3800 Homestead Road, Santa Clara, CA 95051.

Reprinted from *Computer*, June 1982, pages 58-68. Copyright © 1982 by The Institute of Electrical and Electronics Engineers, Inc.

With the aid of features such as 32-bit architecture and slave processors, this group of microprocessors addresses a wide range of system applications.

The NS16000 Family—Advances in Architecture and Hardware

Subhash Bal, Asher Kaminker, Yoav Lavi, Abraham Menachem, Zvi Soha

National Semiconductor

When LSI/MOS chips were first developed, it was possible for designers to place approximately 1000 active elements on a single chip. Now, ten years later, the number of active elements per chip has risen to over 100,000. As we enter the second decade of LSI/MOS technology, applications for its use are continually expanding as the computational power of newly developed 16- and 32-bit microprocessors approaches that of mainframe computers. In short, microprocessor designers have their work cut out for them.

Currently, software development efforts are becoming responsible for ever larger shares of product development costs. To offset these costs, microcomputer designers are shifting toward high-level language programming. Increasingly, users expect microprocessors to provide a cost-effective solution for HLL support with minimal degradation in overall system performance; this sets tougher requirements for microprocessor designers.

Sophisticated future systems will require a combination of capabilities. Anticipating these needs, National Semiconductor has developed the NS16000 microprocessor family to incorporate various architectural features into a new generation of devices. Utilizing National Semiconductor's XMOS technology, the design of the NS16000 family is implemented with 3.5-micron gate technology. This allows for a smaller die size, leading to a reduction in chip cost.

The design challenges in creating this new family were met only after thoroughly considering market requirements and LSI technology limitations. This article describes some of the capabilities provided by the NS16000 architecture.

Supporting system software

Operating system design can be simplified with built-in hardware features. The powerful NS16000 control in-

structions aid the implementation of efficient operating systems and of systems oriented to high-level languages. These NS16000 facilities include semaphores, traps, interrupts, supervisor calls, easy context switching, and procedure calls.

One feature of the NS16000 architecture is virtual memory support, which includes the instructions-abort facility. This facility allows an instruction to be reexecuted after it as been aborted due to an address fault (that is, virtual memory page fault).

With the increasing level of multiprocessor system complexity, we expect to see a concurrent increase in the number of users demanding some level of system protection. In the multitasking/multiuser system environment, absolute protection is desired. To achieve a high level of protection, we must assure total isolation of one user's environment from another and from system resources. Any attempt to violate this protection, either accidentally or maliciously, should result in a trap which will transfer control to a system supervisor.

The NS16032 MPU (microprocessing unit) and the NS16082 MMU (memory management unit) together provide a high level of system protection with a set of 11 privileged instructions supported by the NS16032 user and supervisor modes and stack pointers:

- Set and clear bit in the processor status register,
- Load and store processor register,
- Return from interrupts and traps,
- Four MMU instructions, and
- Set system configuration.

To reduce system development cost, the NS16032 was designed to utilize the debugging facilities implemented on the MMU (16082). The MMU has built-in debugging tools to support both high-level and assembly-level programming in a virtual machine environment and hardware debugging in an in-system emulation environment.

EHO214-7/84/0000/0079$01.00©1982 IEEE

Several MMU instructions are available to activate breakpoints and the memory access trace. Among other features used by the debugging software are memory protection and user/supervisor modes.

Managing large address space

The decreasing price of mass storage serial access devices now allows their use in microprocessor applications. Extended addressability is required for the ever-growing number of users expanding their system memory to sizes greater than 65K bytes. To manage large address space, microprocessor designers have adopted segmentation techniques previously used by minicomputers. To avoid the disadvantage associated with the minicomputer approach to segmentation, the NS16032 architecture has incorporated an important feature in its addressability: a large, uniform, unsegmented address space. This provides for a flexible memory management scheme without additional expense and simplifies the operating system and compilers. For example, if a user wants data handling in large address space but does not need sophisticated memory management, then there is no need to pay for it.

For more sophisticated memory management support, generally in multitasking environments, the NS16032 can be linked with the MMU to provide additional system capabilities: dynamic virtual-to-physical address translation, dynamic page table handling, and memory protection. The MMU can treat both main memory and a secondary mass storage as one large, uniform space completely transparent to the programmer, and special control instructions have been included in the architecture to support the MMU operations.

An on-chip cache memory enables the MMU to perform most mappings without actually referring to the translation tables in memory. The cache memory contains direct virtual-to-physical mapping of the presently used pages. With a hit-ratio of better than 95 percent, the overhead caused by translation is minimal.

When page swapping is required, the MMU aborts the execution on the MPU. A dedicated hardware mechanism, integrated within the CPU chip, guarantees graceful recovery from the abort function. This is an essential feature for virtual memory support. Unlike classic interrupt schemes, the abort cannot be suspended until the end of instruction execution. Also, the execution cannot be terminated since some of the operands are not in physical memory. While some processors supply an abort mechanism, they do not guarantee that an aborted instruction will yield correct results when retried.

The NS16032 CPU execution algorithms assure that whenever a processor register or a memory location is referenced, the access will not prevent reexecution. The CPU verifies either that the specific access allows graceful recovery or that no abort can possibly occur at this phase of the instruction execution (that is, there are no more memory accesses in the current instruction). If these conditions are not present, the CPU saves the old contents of the register in an on-chip back-up register, so that they can be recovered in case of abort.

NS16000 architecture

Register set. The architecture supports 16 registers forming two register files: eight dedicated registers and eight general-purpose registers (see Figure 1). The eight dedicated registers on the CPU are

• Program counter. The PC points to the first byte of the currently executing instruction.

• Static base register. The SB register points to a RAM data storage area for the currently running module. All references to the module's data are relative to this register, making them easily relocatable.

• Frame pointer. The FP points to the stack frame of the currently executing procedure. This is also referred to as the "activation record," containing the parameters for the currently executing subroutine and also the volatile (as opposed to static) local variables.

• User stack and interrupt stack pointers. Two stack pointers controlled by the U bit in the PSR: US is used as the stack pointer when $U = 0$, IS when $U = 1$. The U bit may be altered only in supervisor mode or by an interrupt.

• Interrupt base register. The INTBASE register points to an interrupt table for traps and interrupts.

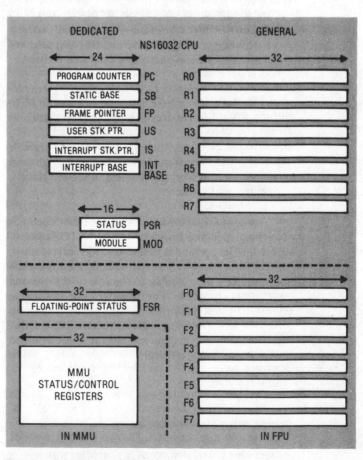

Figure 1. NS16000 register set.

• Processor status register. The PSR contains status information such as the arithmetic flags. It also contains supervisor state information for the operating system. This information is automatically saved on interrupt.

• Module register. The MOD register points to the appropriate area of the module map that indicates the module under current execution. The module map is a directory containing all the necessary address pointers for each module, which is applicable even to ROM-based codes.

The above are 24-bit registers, except for the 16-bit PSR and MOD registers. The eight general-purpose registers (R0-R7) are 32-bit registers.

Addressing modes

The NS16000 addressing modes, combined with the instruction set, contribute to efficient high-level language support. The basic instructions reference two operands, each of which is addressable by nine general addressing modes. The standard addressing modes, common to other processors, are:

• *Register addressing*—direct reference to a general purpose register,
• *Immediate addressing*—operand is provided as part of the instruction,
• *Absolute addressing*—absolute operand's address is specified, and
• *Register-relative addressing*—the operand's address is derived by adding a displacement to the contents of a specified general-purpose or dedicated register.

In addition to these four modes, the NS16000 architecture introduces five addressing modes oriented to high-level-languages and not usually found in other machines:

• *Memory-space addressing*. This allows relocatable reference to memory areas commonly used in high-level languages—specifically, the problem, static (or global), frame, and stack areas.

• *Top-of-stack addressing*. Any operand or operands of an instruction may be referred to by the TOS addressing mode. The operand is pushed into the current stack, popped from it, or referenced without modifying the stack pointer—all according to the role of the operand within the instruction. For example, the instruction SUBD TOS, TOS performs standard stack subtraction of two 32-bit operands in a single instruction. (Operands 1 and 2 are popped from the stack, and the result is pushed into the stack). Thus, efficient stack machine operation is achieved.

• *The memory-relative addressing mode*. This is a powerful addressing mode that is useful for handling address pointers and manipulating fields in a record. This mode uses two displacements. The first is added to one of the dedicated registers (static base register, stack pointer, or frame pointer), which is specified by the mode. The re-

sulting double-word intermediate address is added to the second displacement for the final address of the operand.

• *The scaled-index addressing mode*. This mode, one of the most powerful features of the machine, computes the effective address by adding the contents of any of the general-purpose registers, multiplied by 1, 2, 4, or 8, to the basic address, as defined by the basic addressing mode. The scaled index mode is quite useful for indexing into an array while the basic addressing mode points to the head of the array. The elements of the array can be bytes, words, double words, quad words, floating-point numbers, or long floating-point numbers. Any memory addressing mode has the option of being indexed.

• *The external addressing mode*. Unique to the 16000, this supports the modular software (described below) and allows modules to be relocated without linkage editing. This mode is used to reference operands external to the current executing module. Associated with each module is a linkage table containing the absolute addresses of external variables and relative addresses of operands to be accessed by other modules. The external addressing mode specifies two displacements: the ordinal number of the external variable (the linkage-table entry to be used) and an offset to a subfield of the referenced variable (a subfield of a Pascal record, say). Since code need not be edited for external reference or for relocation, it is completely relocatable even in ROM form. This addressing mode has the capability of going through the tables and accessing the external operands. (See the listing in the box starting at right for more details.)

Supporting high-level languages

The NS16000 architecture is designed to support high-level languages, such as Pascal, Ada, and Fortran. Its architectural features increase the efficiency of HLL compilers to generate compact code, and special emphasis has been put on modular programming. Its address pointers are large enough to address directly the entire addressing space. In the NS16032, address pointers are 24-bits wide and address 16M bytes of memory. Future CPUs can use a larger addressing space with complete software compatibility. This uniform, unsegmented addressing provides a flexible memory management scheme and allows upward compatibility with future CPUs. It also eliminates artificial limitation to segment size.

Instruction set. The NS16000 instruction set includes over 100 basic instruction types coded in variable-length machine codes. The basic instruction code is one byte to three bytes long. There are genuine two-operand instructions, supporting a variety of addressing modes for both operands. However, some instructions use up to five operands, with one to three displacements (of one to four bytes each).

The instruction codes were carefully assigned, so that frequently used instructions have very short codes while rarely used, yet extremely powerful instructions utilize longer opcodes.

Instruction set summary

The instruction column gives the instruction as coded in assembly language and the description column provides a short description of the function provided by that instruction.

NOTATIONS:

i = Integer length suffix: B = Byte
                               W = Word
                               D = Double word

f = Floating-point length suffix: F = Standard floating
                                         L = Long floating

gen = General operand. Any addressing mode can be specified.

short = A 4-bit value encoded within the basic instruction.

imm = Immediate operand. An 8-bit value appended after any addressing extensions.

disp = Displacement (addressing constant): 8, 16, or 32 bits. All three lengths legal.

reg = Any general-purpose register: R0-R7.

areg = Any dedicated/address register: SP, SB, FP, MOD, INTBASE, PSR, US (bottom 8 PSR bits).

mreg = Any memory management status/control register.

creg = A custom slave processor register (implementation dependent).

cond = Any condition code, encoded as a 4-bit field within the basic instruction.

MOVES

INSTRUCTION		DESCRIPTION
MOVi	gen,gen	Move a value
MOVQi	short,gen	Extend and move a 4-bit constant
MOVMi	gen,gen,disp	Move multiple:disp bytes
MOVZBW	gen,gen	Move with zero extension
MOVZiD	gen,gen	Move with zero extension
MOVXBW	gen,gen	Move with sign extension
MOVXiD	gen,gen	Move with sign extension
ADDR	gen,gen	Move effective address

INTEGER ARITHMETIC

INSTRUCTION		DESCRIPTION
ADDi	gen,gen	Add
ADDQi	short,gen	Add 4-bit constant
ADDCi	gen,gen	Add with carry
SUBi	gen,gen	Subtract
SUBCi	gen,gen	Subtract with carry (borrow)
NEGi	gen,gen	Negate (2's complement)
ABSi	gen,gen	Take absolute value
MULi	gen,gen	Multiply
QUOi	gen,gen	Divide, rounding toward zero
REMi	gen,gen	Remainder from QUO
DIVi	gen,gen	Divide, rounding down
MODi	gen,gen	Remainder from DIV (Modulus)
MEIi	gen,gen	Multiply to extended integer
DEIi	gen,gen	Divide extended integer

PACKED DECIMAL (BCD)

INSTRUCTION		DESCRIPTION
ADDPi	gen,gen	Add packed
SUBPi	gen,gen	Subtract packed

INTEGER COMPARISON

INSTRUCTION		DESCRIPTION
CMPi	gen,gen	Compare
CMPQi	short,gen	Compare to 4-bit constant
CMPMi	gen,gen,disp	Compare multiple:disp bytes

LOGICAL AND BOOLEAN

INSTRUCTION		DESCRIPTION
ANDi	gen,gen	Logical AND
ORi	gen,gen	Logical OR
BICi	gen,gen	Clear selected bits
XORi	gen,gen	Logical exclusive OR
COMi	gen,gen	Complement all bits
NOTi	gen,gen	Boolean complement:LSB only
Scondi	gen	Save condition code (cond) as a boolean variable of size i.

SHIFTS

INSTRUCTION		DESCRIPTION
LSHi	gen,gen	Logical shift, left or right
ASHi	gen,gen	Arithmetic shift, left or right
ROTi	gen,gen	Rotate, left or right

BITS

INSTRUCTION		DESCRIPTION
TBITi	gen,gen	Test bit
SBITi	gen,gen	Test and set bit
SBITIi	gen,gen	Test and set bit, interlocked
CBITi	gen,gen	Test and clear bit
CBITIi	gen,gen	Test and clear bit, interlocked
IBITi	gen,gen	Test and invert bit
FFSi	gen,gen	Find first set bit

BIT FIELDS

Bit fields are values in memory which are not aligned to byte boundaries. Examples are PACKED arrays and records used in Pascal. "Extract" instructions read and align a bit field. "Insert" instructions write a bit field from an aligned source.

INSTRUCTION		DESCRIPTION
EXTi	reg,gen,gen,disp	Extract bit field (array oriented)
INSi	reg,gen,gen,disp	Insert bit field (array oriented)
EXTSi	gen,gen,imm	Extract bit field (short form)
INSSi	gen,gen,imm	Insert bit field (short form)
CVTP	reg,gen,gen	Convert to bit field pointer

ARRAYS

INSTRUCTION		DESCRIPTION
CHECKi	reg,gen,gen	Index bounds check
INDEXi	reg,gen,gen	Recursive indexing step for multiple-dimensional arrays

STRINGS

String instructions assign specific functions to the general-purpose registers:

R4—Comparison value
R3—Translation table pointer
R2—String 2 pointer
R1—String 1 pointer
R0—Limit count

Options on all string instructions are

B(Backward):   Decrement string pointers after each step rather than incrementing
U(Until match):   End instruction if String 1 entry matches R4
W(While match):   End instruction if String 1 entry does not match R4

All string instructions end when R0 decrements to zero.

INSTRUCTION		DESCRIPTION
MOVSi	options	Move String 1 to String 2
MOVST	options	Move string, translating bytes
CMPSi	options	Compare String 1 to String 2
CMPST	options	Compare, translating String 1 bytes
SKPSi	options	Skip over String 1 entries
SKPST	options	Skip, translating bytes for Until/While

JUMPS AND LINKAGE

INSTRUCTION		DESCRIPTION
JUMP	gen	Jump
BR	disp	Branch (PC relative)

The data types in the instruction set include bytes, words, double words, and BCD operands as well as floating-point numbers (single and double precision), strings, bits, and bit-fields. These can be arranged in a variety of data structures.

In addition to conventional CPU instructions such as data movement, arithmetic/logic operations, and shifting (all with inherent memory-to-memory capability), the architecture includes advanced instructions that are very useful in an HLL environment. The CHECK instruction determines whether an array index is within bounds and adjusts it to a zero-based value. The INDEX instruction implements the recursive indexing step for multiple-dimensioned arrays. The STRING instructions manipulate data strings with optional translation, escape-characters test, and limit counting. The CXP instruction allows automatic calls of external routines by a simple "call external procedure" type of statement. ENTER and EXIT instructions minimize the overhead in procedure calls by managing the resources (registers and stack frame) allocated at the beginning of a procedure and reclaimed at the end. The INTERLOCKED instructions (test and set/clear) provide interlocked semaphore primitives for multitasking and multiprocessing coordination. And the FLOATING POINT instructions handle single precision (32-bit) and double precision (64-bit) arithmetic, move, and conversion operations.

Supporting modular programming

As we stated at the beginning of this article, modern high-level languages implement modular software techniques as a means of reducing development cost and increasing design flexibility. The NS16000 allows the creation of a library of independently developed software

Bcond	disp	Conditional branch
CASEi	gen	Multiway branch
ACBi	short,gen,disp	Add 4-bit constant and branch if non-zero
JSR	gen	Jump to subroutine
BSR	disp	Branch to subroutine
CXP	disp	Call external procedure
CXPD	gen	Call external procedure using descriptor
SVC		Supervisor call
FLAG		Flag trap
BPT		Breakpoint trap
ENTER	[reg list],disp	Save registers and allocate stack frame (enter procedure)
EXIT	[reg list]	Restore registers and reclaim stack frame (exit procedure)
RET	disp	Return from subroutine
RXP	disp	Return from external procedure call
RETT	disp	Return from trap (privileged)
RETI		Return from interrupt (privileged)

CPU REGISTER MANIPULATION

INSTRUCTION		DESCRIPTION
SAVE	[reg list]	Save general-purpose registers
RESTORE	[reg list]	Restore general-purpose registers
LPRi	areg,gen	Load dedicated register (privileged if PSR or INTBASE)
SPRi	areg,gen	Store dedicated register (privileged if PSR or INTBASE)
ADJSPi	gen	Adjust stack pointer
BISPSRi	gen	Set selected bits in PSR (privileged if not byte length)
BICPSRi	gen	Clear selected bits in PSR (privileged if not byte length)
SETCFG	[option list]	Set configuration register (privileged)

FLOATING POINT

INSTRUCTION		DESCRIPTION
MOVf	gen,gen	Move a floating-point value
MOVLF	gen,gen	Move and shorten a long value to standard
MOVFL	gen,gen	Move and lengthen a standard value to long
MOVif	gen,gen	Convert any integer to standard or long floating
ROUNDfi	gen,gen	Convert to integer by rounding
TRUNCfi	gen,gen	Convert to integer by truncating, toward zero
FLOORfi	gen,gen	Convert to largest integer less than or equal to value
ADDf	gen,gen	Add
SUBf	gen,gen	Subtract
MULf	gen,gen	Multiply
DIVf	gen,gen	Divide
CMPf	gen,gen	Compare
NEGf	gen,gen	Negate
ABSf	gen,gen	Take absolute value
LFSR	gen	Load FSR
SFSR	gen	Store FSR

MEMORY MANAGEMENT

INSTRUCTION		DESCRIPTION
LMR	mreg,gen	Load memory management register (privileged)
SMR	mreg,gen	Store memory management register (privileged)
RDVAL	gen	Validate address for reading (privileged)
WRVAL	gen	Validate address for writing (privileged)
MOVSUi	gen,gen	Move a value from supervisor space to user space (privileged)
MOVUSi	gen,gen	Move a value from user space to supervisor space (privileged)

MISCELLANEOUS

INSTRUCTION	DESCRIPTION
NOP	No operation
WAIT	Wait for interrupt
DIA	Diagnose. Single-byte "branch to self" for hardware breakpointing. Not for use in programming

CUSTOM SLAVE

INSTRUCTION		DESCRIPTION
CCAL0c	gen,gen	Custom calculate
CCAL1c	gen,gen	
CCAL2c	gen,gen	
CCAL3c	gen,gen	

modules to be linked at runtime. This feature provides totally relocatable code that can be stored in ROMs to suit various applications.

Each module consists of three components:

- a code component, which contains the code to be executed in a given module,
- a static data component, which contains the module's local variables and data, and
- a linkage component, which contains the information required to make link reference from one module to another.

In a typical system, the static data and linkage components would be in RAM and the code component would be in either RAM or ROM.

The MOD register contains the number of the currently executing module and points to the appropriate area of the module table, which in turn specifies the relevant component addresses of the module. The module table pointers are only used for external procedure calls. When referencing static data, the MPU uses the static base register, shown in Figure 2.

The external procedure call sequence is

CALL (external descriptor) =

push	MOD
push	PC of next instruction
MOD	= mod from the external-procedure descriptor in the link table
SB	= ((MOD))
PC	= ((MOD) + 8) + offset from descriptor

The procedure return sequence is

CMOV0c	gen,gen	Custom move				
CMOV1c	gen,gen					
CMOV2c	gen,gen					
CCMPc	gen,gen	Custom compare				
CCV0ci	gen,gen	Custom convert				
CCV1ci	gen,gen					
CCV2ci	gen,gen					
CCV3ci	gen,gen					
CCV4DQ	gen,gen					
CCV5QD	gen,gen					
LCSR	gen	Load custom status register				
SCSR	gen	Store custom status register				
CATST0	gen	Custom address test (privileged)				
CATST1	gen	(privileged)				
LCR	creg,gen	Load custom register (privileged)				
SCR	creg,gen	Store custom register (privileged)				

NS16032 addressing modes

ENCODING	MODE	ASSEMBLER SYNTAX	EFFECTIVE ADDRESS
REGISTER			
00000	Register 0	R0 or F0	None. Operand is in the register
00001	Register 1	R1 or F1	
00010	Register 2	R2 or F2	
00011	Register 3	R3 or F3	
00100	Register 4	R4 or F4	
00101	Register 5	R5 or F5	
00110	Register 6	R6 or F6	
00111	Register 7	R7 or F7	
REGISTER RELATIVE			
01000	Register 0 relative	disp(R0)	Disp + register
01001	Register 1 relative	disp(R1)	
01010	Register 2 relative	disp(R2)	
01011	Register 3 relative	disp(R3)	
01100	Register 4 relative	disp(R4)	
01101	Register 5 relative	disp(R5)	
01110	Register 6 relative	disp(R6)	
01111	Register 7 relative	disp(R7)	

MEMORY SPACE			
11000	Frame memory	disp(FP)	Disp + register; "SP" is either SP0 or SP1, as selected in PSR
11001	Stack memory	disp(SP)	
11010	Static memory	disp(SB)	
11011	Program memory	disp(PC)	
MEMORY RELATIVE			
10000	Frame memory relative	disp2 (disp1(FP))	Disp2 + Pointer; Pointer found at address Disp1 + register. "SP" is either SP0 or SP1, as selected in PSR
10001	Stack memory relative	disp2 (disp1(SP))	
10010	Static memory relative	disp2 (disp1(SB))	
IMMEDIATE			
10100	Immediate	value	None. Operand is input from instruction queue
ABSOLUTE			
10101	Absolute	@disp	Disp
EXTERNAL			
10110	External	EXTERNAL (disp1) + disp2	Disp2 + pointer; pointer is found at link table entry number disp1
TOP OF STACK			
10111	Top of stack	TOS	Top of current stack using either user or interrupt stack pointer as selected in PSR. Automatic push/pop included
SCALED INDEX			
11100	Index, bytes	mode[Rn:B]	Mode + Rn
11101	Index, words	mode[Rn:W]	Mode + 2 × Rn
11110	Index, double words	mode[Rn:D]	Mode + 4 × Rn
11111	Index, quad words	mode[Rn:Q]	Mode + 8 × Rn "Mode" and "n" are contained within the index byte
10011	(Reserved for future use)		

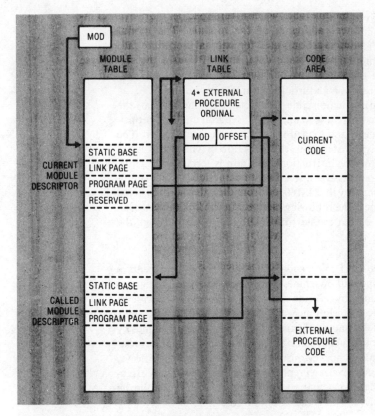

Figure 2. Module table and external procedure referencing.

RETURN =

pop	PC
pop	MOD
SB	= ((MOD))

As mentioned above, reference to external variables is done via the external addressing mode. In this case, no CPU registers are affected. The CPU indirectly references the external variable through the linkage table of the current module.

In short, NS16000 programs can consist solely of a library of ROM modules. As modules are loaded, the linking loader need only update the module table and fill the linkage table entries with the appropriate values.

Expandable architecture

As each "new generation" of microprocessors makes its predecessors obsolete, users are forced to reinvest in software development as they adopt these advanced microprocessor systems. National Semiconductor has attacked the future expansion problem by introducing the slave processor concept. Slave processor chips are defined as hardware extensions of the basic CPU chip. The slave processor "instructions" are an integral part of the instruction set. Presently, they are implemented by dedicated chips.

The communication protocol between the master CPU and the slave processors is transparent to the software. As technology advances, slave-processor hardware will be incorporated within the CPU chip. This means that no software modifications will be required and that the same programs will execute much faster. Moreover, if the present system requirements do not justify the inclusion of slave processors, the user can set up a "nonslave system" configuration. If a slave is not connected to the system and a slave instruction is encountered, the program traps to a software routine, emulating the nonexisting slave. In the future, slave processors or future "super CPUs" may be used without software modifications.

The NS16000 microprocessor family presently has two slave processors—the NS16081 floating-point unit and the NS16082 memory management unit. The slave instructions are executed by the slaves with complete software transparency. A fast, self-contained protocol is used for communicating between the master CPU and the slave processors. The fact that there are two or three different chips is transparent to the system designer.

Since the slave processor is designed as a subset of a "super CPU," it takes advantage of CPU functions already implemented on the master CPU chip such as effective address calculation, memory bus interface, etc. This results in low cost, high performance, and software symmetry. The user can treat floating-point numbers (both single and double precision) like any other NS16000 data types and may use any of the NS16000 addressing modes to reference them.

The slave processors and the CPU are tightly coupled by a well-defined, simple and yet effective, protocol. To the programmer, the CPU and the slaves present an integrated monolithic architecture, as shown in Figure 3. The slave processor instructions have a three-byte basic instruction field, consisting of an ID byte followed by a operation word. The ID byte has three functions:

- it identifies the instruction as being a slave processor instruction,
- it specifies which slave processor will execute it, and
- it determines the format of the following operation word of the instruction.

Upon receiving a slave processor instruction, the CPU initiates the sequence outlined below:

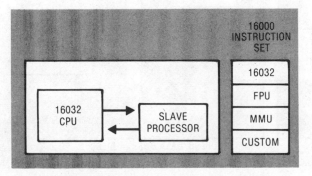

Figure 3. NS16000 CPU-slave architecture.

Step	Action
1	CPU sends ID byte
2	CPU sends operation word
3	CPU sends required operand
4	Slave starts execution. CPU ---
5	Slave sends termination indication at the end of operation
6	CPU reads status word (flags, etc.)
7	CPU reads results

The instruction set and the slave-processors' protocol provide support for additional future slave processors. Future technology will allow integration of the slave processor functions as part of the master CPU chip.

Internal description

The NS16032 chip design, shown in Figure 4, is tailored to support all of these features while achieving high performance. (For more details, see pages 61-63.) This requires the introduction of novel elements, not previously required in microprocessor implementations, as well as the use of current VLSI/MOS technology.

Pipelining. The powerful instruction set includes a variety of instructions with execution times ranging from 300 nanoseconds to tens of microseconds. The compact code yields instructions coded in one or two bytes versus instructions consuming up to 25 bytes of code (including associated displacements). An instruction look-ahead mechanism prefetches the instruction stream into an 8-byte on-chip queue. The NS16032 pipelined architecture ensures high throughput in this environment.

The instruction code is extracted from the queue by the loader where it is manipulated, separated into appropriate fields, and loaded into the instruction register. The code is transferred to the execution machine only when the previous instruction execution is terminated. Thus, three successive instructions can be processed simultaneously by the NS16032. While one instruction is being executed, the following one is loaded into the instruction register, and the next instruction is shifted through the queue.

Two-level microcode. The architecture represents a two-operand machine, with each operand being addressable by all the addressing modes. A two-level microcode technique was implemented, to allow the sharing of common, effective address calculation routines by all the instructions and to avoid time-consuming subroutine calls or space-consuming repeated microcode flows. The outer level is a preprocessor, which controls the effective address calculation and execution sequences while the inner level details the execution steps.

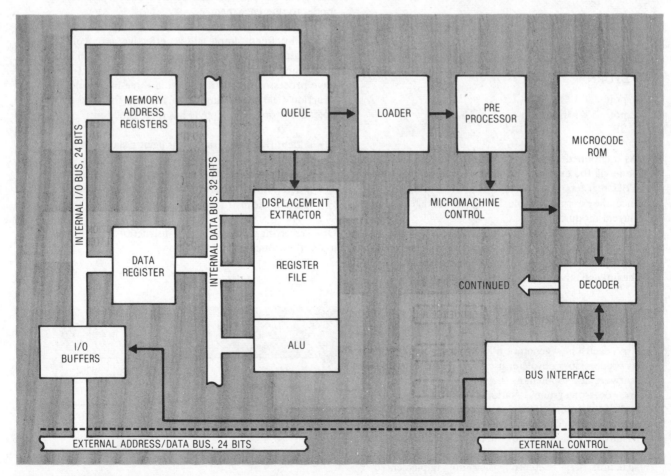

Figure 4. NS16032 block diagram.

The micromachine control unit controls the microcode execution and provides a flow control mechanism for microsubroutine calls, looping, and conditional branching. The microprogram counter is loaded with the sequence start address determined by the instruction opcode and the preprocessor. The microinstruction decoder decodes the microcode ROM outputs and controls the execution steps. A handshake protocol synchronizes the microcode execution to the bus interface unit whenever memory reference is required. The instruction execution flow is depicted in Figure 5.

Internal buses. Internally, the NS16032 is a parallel 32-bit machine and includes a 32-bit data bus, 32-bit registers, and a 32-bit arithmetic logic unit. The internal data bus allows the transfer of 32-bit data between bus elements—the NS16000 register set members, temporary registers, memory registers, the data register, and the ALU. The displacement extractor transfers displacements from the instruction stream via the queue, to any on-chip register.

Additionally, the internal I/O bus is used for external memory access. It communicates with the internal bus, the memory address registers (for address transfers), and the data registers (for memory data transfers).

32-bit ALU. The arithmetic and logic operations are carried out by a 32-bit ALU. The ALU is configured by the ALU control unit into one of 12 operating modes. Each ALU operation handles the accumulator and any register as operands, and can transfer the result to any NS16032 register. The ALU source and destination are specified by microcode. Certain ALU operations modify the NS16032 condition-code flags.

In addition to the standard arithmetic and logic operations (add, subtract, and, exclusive or, etc.), the ALU is capable of performing complex operations. Dedicated ALU operations support binary coded decimal addition and subtraction (8 digits at a time) and multiply/divide algorithms. As a result, the NS16032 performs multiplication and division of two 32-bit operands in 9.4 microseconds. Addition and subtraction of two 32-bit (8-BCD-digit) numbers is carried out in two microseconds.

Bus interface. The bus interface unit, or BIU, controls the communication between the CPU and the external

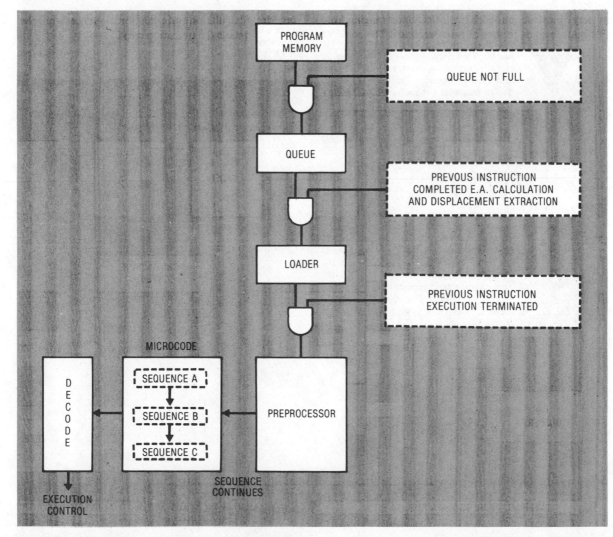

Figure 5. Processing of an instruction by the NS16032.

bus. It generates the various memory cycles and drives the status flags and external control signals. The bus interface unit controls memory data transfers through the internal I/O bus and initiates memory cycles upon requests from the execution machine's microcode. When no request is pending, instruction prefetch cycles are generated. The operand types with lengths of one to eight bytes (non-aligned to any memory location boundaries) are supported by the BIU, which determines the exact number of memory cycles required for each operand.

Summary

In summary, the NS16000 family addresses a wide range of system applications, including the development of modular software and the support of high-level language and operating systems through the use of its 32-bit architecture, powerful instruction set, uniform and unsegmented address space, and slave processors. ∎

Yoav Lavi is a project manager for National Semiconductor Ltd. in Israel, where he participated in the definition and design of the NS16000 family components. He has also worked for the Israeli Ministry of Defence (1972 to 1977) in digital systems design, and for Intel Israel Ltd. where he designed LSI microcomputer components. Lavi received a BSc degree in electrical engineering from the Technion, Haifa, in 1972.

Abraham Menachem joined National Semiconductor in 1978 and is currently a project manager responsible for the development of advanced microprocessor chips. Previously, he was a design engineer for Intel and a system engineer in the Israeli Defence Forces. Menachem received a BSc degree in electrical engineering from the Technion (Israel Institute of Technology) in Haifa in 1970.

Subhash Bal joined National Semiconductor in 1971 and is now program director for advanced microprocessor products. He has been a design engineer for all types of circuits, including memories, calculators, and microprocessors, and has served as design manager for each of these product lines. Bal holds a BS from ITT, Bombay, India; an MBA from the University of Santa Clara, California; and an MS in business administration from the Carnegie Mellon Institute in Pittsburgh, Pennsylvania.

Zvi Soha is currently managing director of National Semiconductor's LSI/MOS Design Center in Israel. The center, which he established, designs high-end and midrange microprocessors. Soha has also worked for National Semiconductor as an MOS engineering manager; for Intel as a project manager engaged in the development of the iAPX 432; for Western Digital as a project manager for the LSI-II chip set; and for NCR's data processing division, where he worked on advanced computer systems.

Soha received a BS and MS in electrical engineering from UCLA in 1967 and 1969, respectively.

Asher Kaminker is currently a project manager for National Semiconductor and is responsible for the development of advanced microprocessor chips. After working as a system engineer in the Israeli Defence Forces, Kaminker was a senior design engineer and project manager for Intel. He received the BSc in 1968 and MSc in 1976 in electrical engineering from the Technion.

88

Virtual Memory and the MC68010

Douglas MacGregor and David S. Mothersole

Motorola, Inc.

The designers of this microprocessor used the continuation method

to provide an elegant general solution to the

problem of virtual memory support.

Virtual Memory and the MC68010

Douglas MacGregor and David S. Mothersole

Motorola, Inc.

Just a few years ago, the introduction of 16-bit devices signalled a new generation of microprocessors. With them came powerful capabilities previously available only on minicomputers and mainframes. However, most of these microprocessors did not have the facilities to easily manage this new power. With the introduction of the MC68010, Motorola is providing support for virtual memory and virtual machine operation. In order to assist the reader in understanding how this was done, we will first briefly define the concepts of virtual memory. We will then compare two different methods of implementation from an architectural perspective. After providing this background, we will present the details of the actual implementation of the MC68010 and review its facilities.

The MC68010 16-bit microprocessor is an extension of the MC68000. It provides virtual memory capability, virtual machine support, and increased performance, while maintaining code compatibility with the M68000 architecture. One of the most important requirements of any new member of a processor family is that it not require major revisions of the software written for previous members of the family. For this reason we considered it essential that the MC68010 be code-compatible with the MC68000. Since the extensions provided by the MC68010 required changes in the processor interface to the operating system (i.e., exception processing, privileged instructions, and dispatching), the MC68010 was designed so that the required software modifications would be confined to the operating system.

Virtual memory

The most significant feature of the MC68010 is its ability to support virtual memory in a system by providing all of the mechanisms needed for its implementation. When the MC68000 was introduced, with its 32-bit addresses and its addressing range of 16 megabytes, it became clear that there was a need for mechanisms by which this large address space could be hierarchically maintained and accessed. The fundamental notion of a virtual memory system involves maintaining a large address space on a hierarchy of memory devices with different storage capacity, cost, and speed ratios.[1] A simple example of a system with three levels of hierarchically organized memory is shown in Figure 1.

The concept of using a paged memory with a backing store is not at all new; it was first introduced in the late 1950's when it was used in the ATLAS machine developed at Manchester University.[2] Although the virtual memory concept has been expanded in the last two and a half decades, the basic theory underlying it has changed little. What has changed is the size of the processors on which this support is provided; functionality that was previously only available on mainframes and high-end minicomputers is now available on microprocessors.

The need to organize memory heirarchically becomes all the more acute as the clock frequencies at which processors execute continue to increase. In the case of the MC68000, a physical memory design that could hold the entire 16-megabyte address space and provide no wait-state access would involve substantial expense.

Virtual memory concepts. Originally, the need to more efficiently utilize expensive memory provided the motivation for the development of virtual memory concepts. A virtual memory system allows the user to execute programs on a very large store of virtual address space without regard for its physical existence. A memory management system, which may comprise hardware and/or software, maps the virtual (or logical) address of the user into the smaller physical memory. Virtual and physical address spaces are divided into fixed-size pages to facilitate mapping. The user need not have any knowledge about the organization of the physical memory into which his program is mapped. If an access is attempted to an address on a page which is not resident in the physical memory, a page fault occurs, interrupting the processor and initiating exception processing. The virtual memory system can correct this fault by fetching the page from an element lower in the

hierarchy and substituting it for one of the pages in the physical store. While this replacement operation is occurring, the processor is free to service other users and thus support multiprogramming more efficiently. After correcting the fault, the processor is then permitted to resume execution of the faulted program.

This description is very general and in theory simple. Unfortunately, when it is necessary to implement virtual memory on a processor, some of the details of implementation create several difficult problems for either the group designing the processor or the end user.

MC68010 processor design goals. The goal adopted by the microprocessor design group at Motorola was to develop a processor capable of cleanly and elegantly supporting the fault detection/fault correction/program resumption process. To achieve this, the group needed to design a processor able to recognize a fault indication on any bus access attempted and, regardless of the instruction being executed at the time of the fault, able to carry out a simple recovery and resumption process.

Ironically, the reason that it is not possible to provide a complete recovery for 100 percent of fault conditions lies in one of the strongest aspects of the M68000 family architecture—its generality. The one situation from which the MC68010 cannot make a successful recovery is a fault on an access to the system stack pointer. The fundamental cause of this problem is the general nature of the M68000 stack pointer. Under almost all circumstances, it is desirable to treat the stack pointer as a general-purpose register. This generality, however, also implies that it is possible to load any address into the supervisor stack pointer without regard to the residency of that address in physical memory. If a fault occurs, the processor needs to save the internal state of the processor on the supervisor stack before it can proceed with handling the exception. Thus, if the supervisor stack is not resident in physical memory, the attempt by the processor to save the state of the faulted process results in yet another fault, a double bus fault, which overwhelms

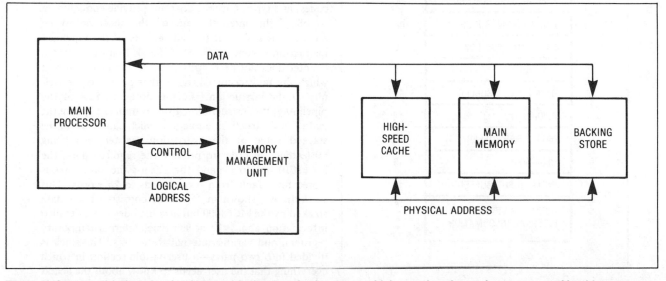

Figure 1. System with three levels of hierarchically organized memory—high-speed cache, main memory, and backing store.

the fault recovery hardware and forces the MC68010 into an unrecoverable situation. In order for the processor to provide *complete* protection, any address to be loaded into the supervisor stack pointer would first have to be checked to ensure its validity. However, such an activity would be inconsistent with the general stack-pointer register concept. Nevertheless, it is desirable to provide complete coverage. Another solution is available—keeping the supervisor stack resident in physical memory. This eliminates the need to check addresses to be loaded into the supervisor stack pointer. Thus, the general stack-pointer register concept is preserved and complete fault coverage is provided.

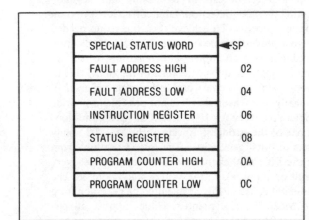

Figure 2. MC68000 address error/bus error stack.

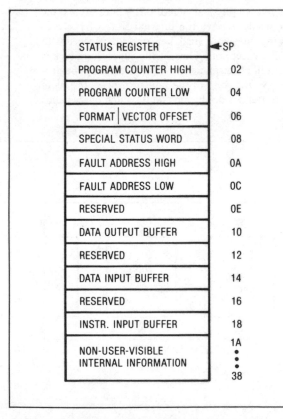

Figure 3. MC68010 address error/bus error stack.

.Basic virtual memory processor requirements. In order to provide virtual memory support, a processor must be able to perform three basic functions: recognizing a fault, saving any information needed to recover from the fault and executing the exception handler, and restoring the saved state and resuming normal processing. The MC68000 provides some of these functions, since it can recognize the unsuccessful termination of a bus cycle, save some state information, and execute the exception handler.[3] By expanding these capabilities to include a complete save of the internal state of the processor, and by providing the ability to restore the state of the machine and resume execution, the MC68010 provides all of the mechanisms needed to support virtual memory.

An essential element in providing virtual memory support is the ability to recognize an access fault when it occurs. The MC68000 can recognize these faults both internally and externally. When an access is made to a misaligned instruction or operand, an address error is internally detected, initiating the address error-fault handling routine. Externally, the bus error (BERR) pin provides the user with a method to signal that some aspect of the access has generated an error. In the context of virtual memory, a Motorola MC68451 memory management unit, or any other address translation device which can detect a fault situation, can signal a fault to the main processor via the BERR pin. BERR is shown in Figure 1 as a control signal. Although this fault recognition capability does not need to be enhanced to support virtual memory, some of the timings associated with it were made more liberal to provide support for error detection and correction hardware.

Once the processor has recognized an access fault, the next step is to save any state information that will be needed to reconstruct the state of the machine after the fault has been corrected. The MC68000 saves only enough internal state information (Figure 2) to provide the user with an approximate indication of the state of the processor when the fault occurred. This information, though providing the fault address, function codes, and type of access, does not provide enough data to allow the internal state of the machine to be reconstructed. One of the side effects of the pipelined instruction stream on the MC68000 is that the program counter does not necessarily point at the instruction in which the fault occurred, but rather points to the vicinity of the instruction.[4] Furthermore, because of the pipelining, the instruction register is updated before the end of an instruction, an action which can result in the stacked value of the instruction register also being misleading. In order to provide the required data, the MC68010 has to expand the size of the state that is stored on a fault from seven words to 26 words. This stack frame, shown in Figure 3, consists of the data stacked by the MC68000 but also includes more detailed information about the access type, internal temporary registers, and various internal status bits. The stack is divided into two parts—a user-visible section in which everything that the user needs to know about the access and its correction are provided, and a non-user-visible section in which the internal status and temporaries are stored. After the internal state has been saved, the processor returns control to the operating system by providing a vector to the address error or bus error exception-handler routine. The operating system is then responsible for reconfiguring the system to either successfully complete the access or abort the process. While this activity is taking place, a different program can be dispatched to the potentially idle processor in a multiprogrammed environment.

The last step is the most complex for the processor. After the operating system has made any repairs that are necessary, the state of the program suspended by the fault must be reloaded and the execution of that program resumed. If operating in a multiprocessor system, the suspended program can be dispatched to any processor throughout the system, which may or may not be the processor that was originally faulted. The processor must use the saved state information to reconstruct the internal state of the machine and must allow execution of the faulted program to resume. Reconstructing the internal state is composed of two steps: reading the internal state from memory and loading it into the machine, and evaluating this state to determine what actions are needed to restore the state of the machine to its prefault condition. In the MC68000, an address error or a bus error is considered to be exception from which no recovery can be made. Hence, it has no facilities to allow the machine to return from these exceptions. The mechanism described here is an addition made on the MC68010.

Processor instruction flow. In order to provide some framework for the topics to be discussed later, it will be advantageous to first study an example of a simple instruction and define the terms used in describing instruction flow.

Any instruction can be implemented internally as a series of microinstructions. A microinstruction is an integral unit of activity within a processor. Let us examine a simple move instruction. In a word-sized move-memory-to-memory instruction, in which both source and destination are addressed using the predecrement addressing mode [MOVE. W − (An), − (Am)], the following activities must take place. The address register An is decremented by two and the processor then uses that address to read the word-sized data. The data are then written to the memory location addressed by address register Am decremented by two. In each case, the decremented value is stored back into address registers An and Am, respectively. This instruction can be partitioned into three microinstructions, as shown in the flowchart in Figure 4.

There must be some way to synchronize the external world and the processor. This is done by allowing the internal sequencing of the machine to be effected by the bus controller. When an access is initiated in a microinstruction, that microinstruction is not considered complete until that access has been terminated. In reality, because the execution time of a microinstruction is half the time required to execute a bus cycle, there can be two microinstructions associated with one bus access. In this case, the first microinstruction initiates the bus access and the second microinstruction waits until the access is completed before releasing the machine to continue execution. If the access is completed successfully, then normal processing is allowed to continue. Figure 5 provides two examples of this synchronization, one without any memory delays, and the second with a one-clock wait state. In the first case, microinstruction E initiates the bus cycle and microinstruction F completes it. In the second case, microinstruction F is extended by one clock cycle to accommodate the memory delay. In the example provided in Figure 4, the processor is not allowed to begin execution of microinstruction C until the access in microinstruction B has been completed. This ordering is necessary because microinstruction C will use that data to write to memory and to set the condition codes. The processor, however, has completed all of the other activities associated with microinstruction B and is simply waiting for the access to be completed.

Virtual memory implementation methods

There are two basic methods of implementing virtual memory on a processor: instruction "restart" and instruction "continuation." Both methods have their

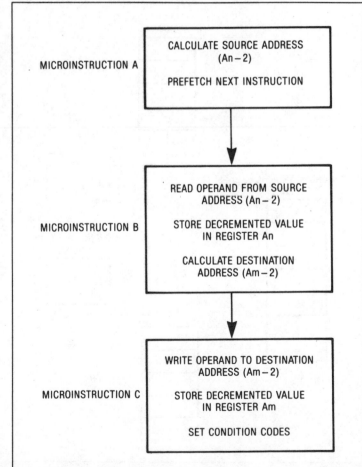

Figure 4. MOVE.W − (An), − (Am) microflow.

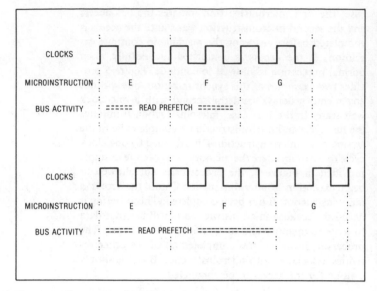

Figure 5. Bus controller/micromachine synchronization.

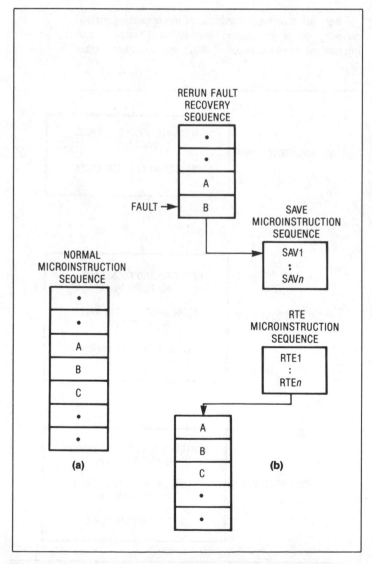

Figure 6. Restart method microflow—normal microinstruction sequence (a); rerun fault recovery sequence (b).

advantages and disadvantages. The MC68010 was implemented with the less commonly used of the two—the instruction continuation method—for reasons that we will explain later in this article.

Instruction restart method. The most commonly used method of virtual memory support is the restart method. In this method, the instruction in which the fault occurred is restarted from the beginning, after the exception handler has completed all activity associated with the correction of the fault. This is done regardless of the stage of the instruction the processor had reached when the fault was recognized. Figure 6 illustrates the flow of the microcode for a faulted routine with the restart method. Under normal conditions, microinstructions A, B, and C will execute consecutively (Figure 6a). If microinstruction B has a fault associated with it (Figure 6b), the processor will execute A and B but will then be interrupted by the save routine. It will then save the state and execute whatever handling routine is appropriate. This handling routine should conclude with a return from exception (RTE) instruction. This return will restore the state and then restart the faulted instruction over again at microinstruction A. Thus, in this scheme there will always be an A, B, C sequence of microinstruction flow.

The restart method implies that the processor is able to restore or reconstruct the state of the machine as it existed at the beginning of the instruction. When a user-visible resource is used as both a source and destination for data within one instruction, this method becomes quite complicated. One example of this problem occurs with extended precision arithmetic operations, another with autoincrement/autodecrement addressing modes. In an extended arithmetic operation, a bit of the status register indicates whether a previous carry or borrow should be considered in the current calculation. The instruction will in turn set that same bit to indicate whether there was a carry or a borrow result in the current calculation. If the processor is faulted after this bit of the status register is updated, the original value must be restored before the instruction can be restarted. This is evident in the sample instruction presented in Figure 4, where an autodecrement addressing mode is used. It is generally desirable to update the decremented address register while the operand fetch is taking place (as shown in the flowchart). Furthermore, if both source and destination addressing modes use the same address register, then the updated value of the register must be used in the address calculation of the destination address. If a fault is detected later in that instruction, the register must be restored to its original value before the instruction can be re-executed.

There are three methods commonly used to deal with this problem. First, the processor can prevent any user-visible resource from being altered until the instruction is completely executed, when it can be assured that no fault will occur. Second, the processor can maintain copies of resources as they are altered. These copies will contain the original value of the resource at the beginning of the instruction. If the instruction is faulted, the copies are used to restore the user state. Third, any updating of a user-visible resource can be tagged to indicate which resource was altered and how the original data can be restored.

The level of difficulty involved in implementing one of these methods depends on how complete the instruction set is and how orthogonal it and its addressing modes are. If the number of situations where resource conflicts can occur are limited, the complexity of providing a comprehensive solution is manageable. However, if a processor with a powerful instruction set is used, extensive resources could be required. Unfortunately, it is too often deemed acceptable in the microprocessor community to provide a limited solution to the problem either by identifying a limited set of instructions that can be provided to the user as virtual memory instructions, or by expecting the user to conduct all of the repairs needed to reconstruct the internal state of the machine. In the first case, one can define instructions in which there can be no resource conflicts and advise the user to employ them to ensure that the page to be accessed resides in physical memory. For instructions in which there *can* be resource conflicts, no reliable recovery can be made, and hence their use is somewhat limited. The second solution is also unattractive, since it requires the user to evaluate the saved state of the processor to determine if the faulted instruction presented a potential resource conflict and, if it did, to make the needed corrections. In either case the processor simply restores the state of the machine and executes the faulted instruction again, regardless of the validity of the restored state.

There is another class of problems associated with the restart method that, although very subtle and in some cases improbable, still presents situations from which the processor cannot be predictably recovered. The first situation involves an access made to an I/O device. It is felt that in most systems there are significant advantages to memory-mapped I/O, since any general instruction is capable of communicating with an I/O device. If, however, there is a fault of any kind after the access to the I/O device, and if there is successful restoration after the fault, the processor proceeds to refetch or rewrite data to or from the I/O device. This can be catastrophic, since the status of many I/O devices is altered as the result of the access. Thus, the second access to the device can result in incorrect data being transferred. Another problem can occur when an operand is transferred from memory to memory and the operands overlap. For example, if a long-word move from an address register indirect to an address register indirect [(MOVE.L (An), (Am)] is executed with address registers An and Am pointing as shown in Figure 7, the instruction moves the long word X:Y into location Y:Z. This is done by reading the words X and Y, then writing X to location Y and Y to location Z. However, when the write to location Z takes place, a fault can occur. In the restart method, when the processor executes the instruction the second time, it reads X from location X but also reads X from location Y, since location Y has been updated by the first partial execution of the instruction. Thus, the result of the instruction is that both locations Y and Z contain X.

Instruction continuation method. The second method of virtual memory implementation, the instruction continuation method, provides an attractive alternative to the restart method. In the continuation method, the entire non-user-visible state of the machine is saved when an access fault is detected. On completion of the fault handler routine, the processor is allowed to resume instruction processing at the same location within the instruction at which execution was suspended by the fault. This action occurs regardless of the location within the instruction at which the access fault occurs.

In the example given in Figure 8, activity within the processor is suspended in microinstruction B until the completion of the data access. If that access is terminated unsuccessfully, the processor saves the internal state of the machine and enters the exception handler routine. The operating system is free to make any repairs to the system that are necessary. After these repairs are complete, the operating system signals the processor to restore the state and resume normal execution. The state is reloaded into the machine and the access that caused the fault is repeated. When the access is successfully completed, the processor resumes execution with microinstruction C. Thus, the continuation method is analogous to an interrupt operation at the microinstruction level.

There are several problems associated with the continuation method of virtual memory support; they involve

- instructions that require execution without interruption,
- silicon resources that must be provided to support the saving and restoring of the internal state, and
- the time that is required for such saving and restoring.

Moreover, the greater complexity of the continuation method makes any virtual memory implementation that uses it more vulnerable to design errors.

In general, continuation provides a more natural method of virtual memory support. It is less disruptive

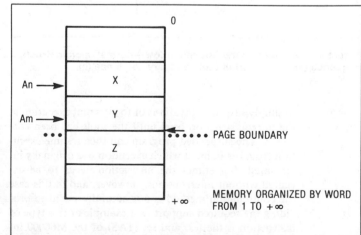

Figure 7. The operand overlap problem.

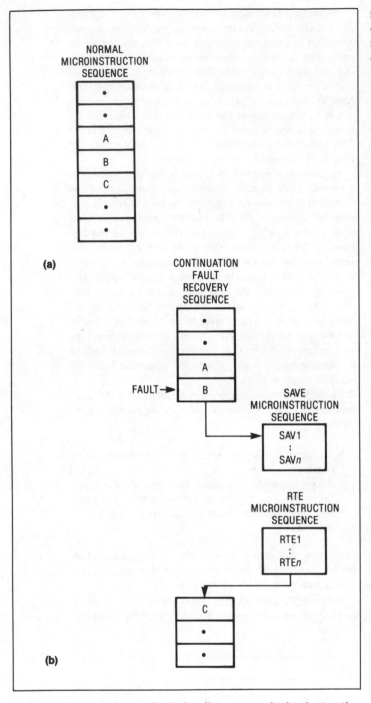

Figure 8. Continuation method microflow—normal microinstruction sequence (a); continuation fault recovery sequence (b).

to simply suspend operations or to interrupt execution at the microinstruction level until the fault has been corrected. The suspended program can then resume execution from the point at which execution was originally interrupted. Sometimes the instruction needs to be executed without interruptions, however, and in this case the continuation method is not naturally suited to providing the required support. An example of this type of instruction is the test and set (TAS) of the M68000 instruction set. The TAS instruction provides the user with a primitive operation which can be used to implement

resource protection mechanisms via semaphores or other means. For the TAS instruction, the processor must provide an uninterruptible read-modify-write sequence during which the bus cannot be arbitrated away. If a fault occurs on the write portion of the access, it is necessary to reinitiate the entire read-modify-write cycle rather than simply rerun the write portion of the cycle. In this case, there must be some mechanism to force the entire read-modify-write cycle to be reinitiated.

The continuation method as implemented on the MC68010 requires that the entire internal state of the processor be saved when an access fault occurs. Because of the complexity of the MC68010, this state comprises a large number of temporary execution-unit registers, sequencer state registers, and control latches. For the state to be saved, the information about it must be stored internally. In addition, there must be access paths from the state information, and there must be the control needed to access this information. Similarly, additional control logic is required to perform the reloading of the state. In terms of silicon area, the additional resources require a 22 percent increase over the MC68000 in total area. Figure 9 is a labelled die photograph of the MC68010; the crosshatched areas indicate the approximate increase in area due to virtual memory support. While 22 percent is a significant amount of growth, the most critical aspect of product design—development time—was greatly reduced, since most of the increase involved areas consisting of regular structures.[5,6]

Another expense associated with the larger stacked internal state is the additional time it takes to read and write the state during the save and restore operations. While the time required to execute the save and restore operations is shorter than the normal execution time for some instructions, any time required to perform these functions degrades overall performance. This is a particularly important concern because once the state has been saved in a multiprogrammed environment, a different program can be dispatched to the idle processor. This allows the time required for the page replacement and other system repairs to be available to the system for other processing tasks. Another problem associated with the save time is that it contributes directly to the interrupt latency. Because any instruction can cause a fault, the interrupt latency must be calculated by adding the time required to save the state to the time required to execute the longest instruction. In the MC68010, the interrupt latency could have increased by nearly 50 percent over the interrupt latency of the MC68000. This did not occur due to other optimizations made in the design. Specifically, the latency associated with normal instruction processing was reduced by 50 percent, from 284 clock cycles to 148. The resulting normal instruction latency is equivalent to the time required to save the state—132 clock cycles. Thus, we were able to avoid the latency problem inherent in saving the state. The MC68010 interrupt latency is essentially the same as that of the MC68000.

One of the most difficult problems associated with the continuation method is the increased vulnerability to microcode errors it causes. Since an access fault can occur at almost any point within the execution of an instruction, the processor must suspend and then resume execution from that point as if the fault had never occurred. This implies a much more detailed prediction of the state of the machine than that performed in the MC68000. In order to simplify the verification of correct execution, the microinstructions associated with an instruction can be categorized into general microinstruction routines. The categories, which are also present in the MC68000, are shown in Figure 10. All of the microinstructions are attributed to one of three categories—either they fetch an immediate operand, evaluate an effective address and fetch the operand, or do the operation fundamental to the instruction. These routines perform all or part of the activity associated with an instruction. A simple instruction may be composed of only one routine while a more complex instruction can be composed of several functional routines. Let us examine variations of the ADD instruction (Figure 10). Breaking instructions into these routines makes it possible to define a series of boundary conditions. These boundary conditions define the state of the machine at the beginning of the functional routine. With these simplified state definitions, the routines can be verified by confirming that the entrance boundary conditions are satisfied, the functionality of the routine is correct, and the exit boundary conditions are satisfied. Similarly, it is possible to verify the correctness of instructions by checking the functionality of the routines that compose the instruction and by verifying that the boundary conditions synchronize correctly. One of the difficulties implicit in the continuation method is that when the processor is suspended and then restored, its state must reflect the exact conditions that existed before the fault. In the continuation environment, the steps taken to verify the validity of operations must be more rigorous.

Figure 9. The MC68010—the crosshatched areas indicate circuitry added to support virtual memory.

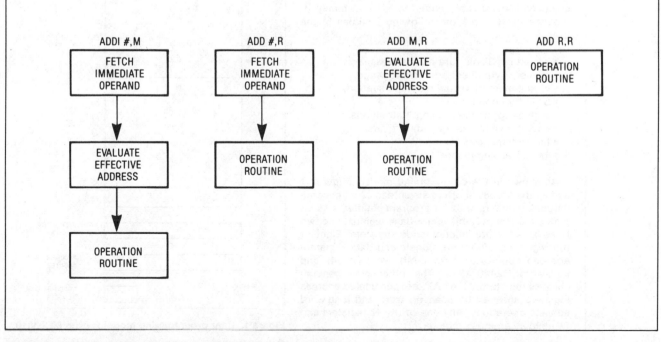

Figure 10. Decomposition of instructions into functional routines.

An example of this difficulty is an error that was found on one of the initial (preproduction) versions of the MC68010 processor. Figure 11 will be used to illustrate this problem. Figure 11a shows the normal processing of two instructions. These instructions are composed of microinstructions A, B, and C for one instruction and D, E, and F for the next. In Figure 11b, examples of the same two instructions are given, but this time with an interrupt being recognized during the first instruction. This interrupt is acted on at the boundary between the two instructions. At the conclusion of the first instruction (at microinstruction C), the interrupt microinstructions are executed if the interrupt has been recognized internally during microinstruction B. After all of the operations associated with the interrupt are completed, execution of the second instruction commences.

The problem was encountered when a fault occurred in microinstruction C after an interrupt had been recognized in microinstruction B. Figure 11c shows this situation as it should have been handled. Because of internal piping, the microinstruction sequencer must know the next microinstruction to be executed during the current microinstruction. This is state information which must be saved to allow the processor to return to the location from which activity was suspended. In this case, the next microinstruction that was scheduled when the fault occurred was the first microinstruction of the interrupt

routine. Unfortunately, the interrupt that caused the sequencer to select the interrupt handler had been resolved immediately after the save routine, so that when the interrupt handler was executed again, a superfluous interrupt-acknowledge cycle occurred. To solve the problem, the MC68010 had to internally recognize this situation during the return operation and take compensating actions. It should be clear, however, that totally protecting the user from inconsistencies requires strenuous efforts. In this case, the boundary conditions did not correctly mesh with the conditions for the beginning of a new instruction; that is, the boundary conditions were not properly defined to prevent this condition from occurring.

When examining the difficulties associated with the continuation method, one finds few situations in which the operation of the machine is altered at all. The difficulties are instead related to the resources required to implement the method, the execution time associated with a larger state, and the difficulty of verifying the correctness of the machine. If resources are available to solve the problems described above, one can make many simple enhancements to the continuation method that will provide services of practical value to the user. These will be described in detail later. In general, the continuation method is much more natural and less disruptive to the flow of the machine.

What is the MC68010?

The Motorola MC68010 is a 16-bit microprocessor with 32-bit registers, an expanded instruction set, and flexible addressing modes. The MC68010 is object-code-compatible with the M68000 family of processors. It offers the following facilities to the user:

- seventeen 32-bit data and address registers,
- 16-megabyte direct addressing range,
- virtual memory/virtual machine support,
- 57 instruction types,
- high-performance looping instructions,
- operations on five main data types,
- memory-mapped I/O, and
- 14 addressing modes.

As shown in the programming models (Figures 1 and 2), the MC68010 offers seventeen 32-bit general-purpose registers, a 32-bit program counter, a 16-bit status register, a 32-bit vector-base register, and two three-bit alternate-function-code registers. Eight of the registers, D0-D7, are considered data registers and can operate on byte (8-bit), word (16-bit), and long-word (32-bit) data. The other nine general-purpose registers, A0-A7,A7', are considered address registers and can be used on word and long-word address operations. Any one of the 17 registers can be used as an index register.

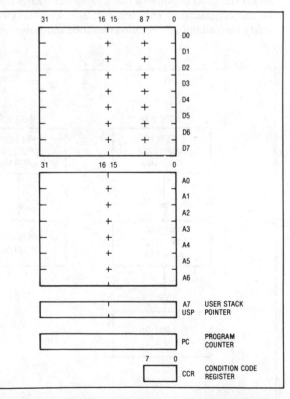

Figure 1. User programming model for the MC68010.

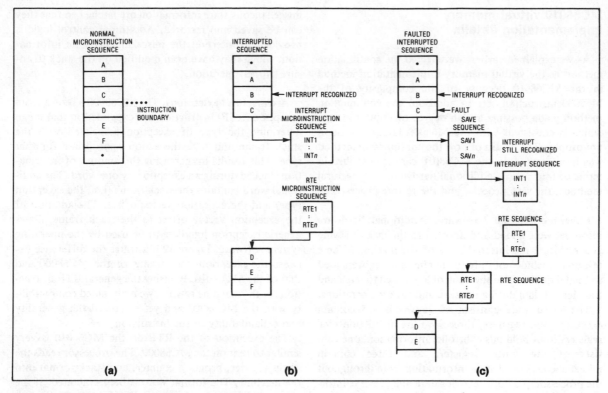

Figure 11. Interrupt processing on the MC68010—normal microinstruction sequence (a); interrupted sequence (b); faulted interrupted sequence (c).

The status register (Figure 3) contains the interrupt mask (eight levels available) as well as the condition codes: extend (X), negative (N), zero (Z), overflow (V), and carry (C). Additional status bits indicate whether the processor is in the trace (T) mode or the supervisor (S) state.

The vector-base register is used to determine the location of the exception vector table in memory. It supports multiple vector tables. The alternate-function-code registers allow the supervisor to access any of the eight address spaces.

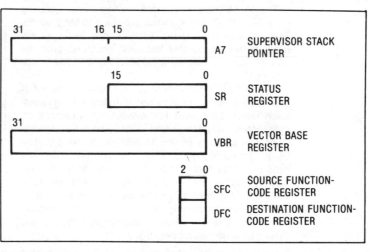

Figure 2. Supervisor programming model for the MC68010.

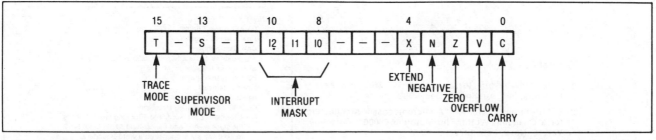

Figure 3. MC68010 status register.

MC68010 virtual memory implementation details

As we explained earlier, we selected the continuation method as the virtual memory implementation method in the MC68010 because of the complexity of the M68000 instruction set. In addition, the continuation method made possible a high degree of fault coverage, which is consistent with the M68000 family exception philosophy. The details of how the continuation method was implemented on the MC68010 can be described in terms of four areas—additional hardware, architectural methods, the save process, and the restore process.

Enhanced internal hardware. Additional hardware resources were added and devoted to the task of saving and restoring the internal state of the machine. These resources include not only the latches and registers used to hold data, but also the control logic used to latch and transfer the data during the save and restore operations.

The saved state consists of 26 words—15 contain execution-unit registers, three save the instruction pipe registers, four hold bus controller information, one consists of the status register, and three contain miscellaneous bits of state information from throughout the processor. To both save this data and preserve information relevant to the faulted access, additional registers are provided to store the address and data associated with the faulted access. The three words of

miscellaneous state information are latched so that they can be saved and restored. Additional control logic is provided to interpret the miscellaneous state information, which may have been modified on the stack to ensure proper operation.

Architectural extensions. The MC68000's return from exception (RTE) instruction was expanded so that it can determine the type of exception associated with the stack frame and take the action appropriate for that type. This results in increasing the amount of information stacked during an exception by one word. The additional word contains the stack frame (i.e., the exception type) and the exception vector offset. The addition of the exception vector offset to the stack frame allows generic exception handlers to be used by the operating system software. Figure 12 illustrates the difference between the exception stack frame of the MC68000 and that of the MC68010. By using the general RTE instruction for the machine restore, we maintained compatibility with the MC68000 and yet enhanced the generality and expandability of the instruction.

The execution of the RTE on the MC68010 is very similar to that on the MC68000. The processor reads the status register, program counter, and stack format into the machine. The format word is then evaluated. If the short stack format is present, then the information needed for the return is resident in the machine and normal processing resumes at the address indicated by the

---

The MC68010 can operate on five basic types of data: bits, BCD digits, bytes, words, and long words. The 14 address modes include six basic types: register direct, register indirect, absolute, program counter relative, immediate, and implied. These are shown in Table 1.

The MC68010 instruction set is shown in Table 2. It readily supports structured high-level languages. Each instruction, with few exceptions, operates on byte, word, and long-word data, and most instructions can use any of the 14 addressing modes. The basic instructions can be combined with the available data types and addressing modes to provide over 1000 total instructions. Furthermore, 33 of the basic instructions can be used in the loop mode with certain addressing modes and the DBcc instruction to provide 230 string, block manipulation, and extended arithmetic operations.

References

1. *MC68010—16-bit Virtual Memory Microprocessor*, Motorola, Inc., Austin, TX, Dec. 1982.

2. E. Stritter and T. Gunter, "A Microprocessor Architecture for a Changing World: The Motorola 68000," *Computer*, Vol. 12, No. 2, Feb. 1979, pp. 43-52.

**Table 1.
Addressing modes.**

Mode	Generation
Register Direct Addressing	
Data Register Direct	EA = Dn
Address Register Direct	EA = An
Absolute Data Addressing	
Absolute Short	EA = (Next Word)
Absolute Long	EA = (Next Two Words)
Program Counter Relative Addressing	
Relative with Offset	EA = (PC) + d_{16}
Relative with Index and Offset	EA = (PC) + (Xn) + d_8
Register Indirect Addressing	
Register Indirect	EA = (An)
Postincrement Register Indirect	EA = (An), An ← An + N
Predecrement Register Indirect	An ← An − N, EA = (An)
Register Indirect with Offset	EA = (An) + d_{16}
Indexed Register Indirect with Offset	EA = (An) + (Xn) + d_8
Immediate Data Addressing	
Immediate	DATA = Next Word(s)
Quick Immediate	Inherent Data
Implied Addressing	
Implied Register	EA = SR, USP, SSP, PC, VBR, SFC, DFC

NOTES:

EA = Effective Address
An = Address Register
Dn = Data Register
Xn = Address or Data Register used as Index Register
SR = Status Register
PC = Program Counter
( ) = Contents of
d_8 = 8-Bit Offset (Displacement)
d_{16} = 16-Bit Offset (Displacement)
N = 1 for byte, 2 for word, and 4 for long word. If An is the stack pointer and the operand size is byte, N = 2 to keep the stack pointer on a word boundary.
← = Replaces

restored program counter. If the long stack format is present, then the 26 words of state information must be read from the stack and restored to their appropriate location before execution can continue at the point of the exception.

In order to allow for expansion and for verification of the state information, we installed certain protection mechanisms into the restore process. Currently there are only two valid stack formats, $0 for the normal four-word format, and $8 for the long 29-word format. Any other formats are identified as illegal by the MC68010 and cause a "format error" exception.

Machine fault and state save process. The state save process begins when a bus fault is detected via assertion of the BERR pin or via a program-generated address error. A flowchart of the save operation is provided in Figure 13. The processor latches and holds information relevant to the faulted cycle, which includes the function code (address space), data access type (read/write), and various internal status information. The processor next saves information resident in the save process hardware by storing it in registers dedicated to this task. Examples of this information include the contents of the address output buffer register and data output buffer registers. This clears a path for external accesses to memory; this cleared path allows the remainder of the internal state to be saved on the stack. After the completion of the state save, exception processing continues, with vector generation followed by execution from the vector location. Detection of another bus fault during the state save process constitutes a double bus fault exception, which causes the processor to halt all processing pending assertion of the external reset pin.

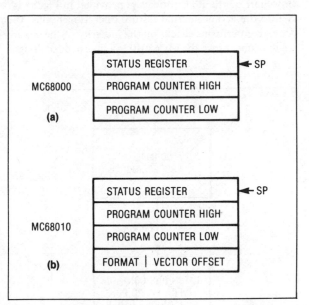

Figure 12. Exception stack frame of the MC68000 (a) and of the MC68010 (b).

Table 2.
Instruction set summary.

Mnemonic	Description	Mnemonic	Description
ABCD*	Add Decimal with Extend	MOVE*	Move Source to Destination
ADD*	Add	MULS	Signed Multiply
AND*	Logical And	MULU	Unsigned Multiply
ASL*	Arithmetic Shift Left	NBCD*	Negate Decimal with Extend
ASR*	Arithmetic Shift Right	NEG*	Negate
B$_{CC}$	Branch Conditionally	NOP	No Operation
BCHG	Bit Test and Change	NOT*	One's Complement
BCLR	Bit Test and Clear	OR*	Logical Or
BRA	Branch Always	PEA	Push Effective Address
BSET	Bit Test and Set	RESET	Reset External Devices
BSR	Branch to Subroutine	ROL*	Rotate Left without Extend
BTST	Bit Test	ROR*	Rotate Right without Extend
CHK	Check Register Against Bounds	ROXL*	Rotate Left with Extend
CLR*	Clear Operand	ROXR*	Rotate Right with Extend
CMP*	Compare	RTD	Return and Deallocate
DB$_{CC}$	Decrement and Branch Conditionally	RTE	Return from Exception
DIVS	Signed Divide	RTR	Return and Restore
DIVU	Unsigned Divide	RTS	Return from Subroutine
EOR*	Exclusive Or	SBCD*	Subtract Decimal with Extend
EXG	Exchange Registers	S$_{CC}$	Set Conditional
EXT	Sign Extend	STOP	Stop
JMP	Jump	SUB*	Subtract
JSR	Jump to Subroutine	SWAP	Swap Data Register Halves
LEA	Load Effective Address	TAS	Test and Set Operand
LINK	Link Stack	TRAP	Trap
LSL*	Logical Shift Left	TRAPV	Trap on Overflow
LSR*	Logical Shift Right	TST*	Test
		UNLK	Unlink

* Loopable Instructions

Machine restore and return process. After the exception handler has completed any corrections it deems necessary, the processor can be directed to reload its stacked state and resume execution at the point at which the fault occurred. This is initiated by the execution of the enhanced RTE instruction described previously. A flowchart of the RTE process is provided in Figure 14. Before the actual internal restore operation begins, the processor performs checks on the integrity of the restore stack frame. Since the MC68010 is a microcoded design, part of the state information includes the address of the next microinstruction to be executed. This makes necessary a mechanism by which the processor can check the validity of the microinstruction address associated with the bus fault. This mechanism detects the situation in which there are multiple processors with different versions of microcode in the same system. If this situation exists, it is possible for a process to be faulted while on one processor and then redispatched to a different processor with a different set of microcode.

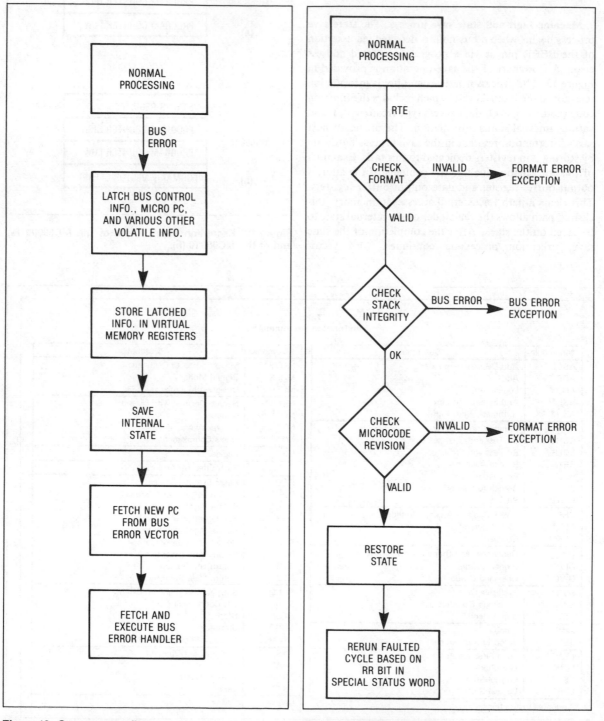

Figure 13. Save process flow.

Figure 14. RTE process flow.

Since the microcode is different, the pointer to the next microinstruction will not be valid, and a format error exception must be taken or erroneous execution may occur. The processor then performs a restore check which pertains to the supervisor stack, although in general the integrity of the supervisor stack pointer is the responsibility of the software. Because of the size of the stored machine state, we found it desirable to have the processor ensure that the entire stack frame is resident in physical memory before it is read in, while it is still possible to accept another fault. For this reason the length of the save stack frame is traversed and its residency assured before significant amounts of state information are loaded during the restore process. Once the validity of the stack is determined, the entire 26 words of machine state information are read into the machine and restored to their original locations. A bus fault during the loading of the machine results in a double bus fault, since during the loading the registers that are dedicated to saving the registers associated with the bus activity are not predictably loaded. However, it is possible to have a fault before the stack frame has been traversed, or upon the rerunning of the access that originally caused the fault, without precipitating a double bus fault. Only the faulted access must be completed before the processor is allowed to begin execution of the next microinstruction.

So that the user can handle a number of different situations, he has been given the power to determine how the access that caused the fault will be handled. Fault information is available to the supervisor fault handler in the special status word (Figure 15) that resides on the supervisor stack. This information allows the fault handler to determine the cause of the fault and to take the appropriate corrective and compensatory action. It also includes the nature of the fault, the fault address, and the prospective destinations for the data within the microinstruction. The fault handler also has the ability to signal the processor whether it will correct the faulted access or whether the processor should re-attempt it. This is done by means of the rerun bit of the special status word. Situations in which it may be desirable for the operating system to complete the access include operation with misaligned operands or data, operation with I/O faults, or virtual operations (i.e., when the accessed resource does not exist). All of these are readily supported by this mode. The meaning of a software rerun does not limit itself simply to transferring the appropriate data—when the exception handler signals the main processor that it has completed the access, the processor assumes that all aspects of the transfer have been accomplished. In the case of a TAS instruction with an uninterruptible read-modify-write cycle, a software rerun includes the setting of the condition code bits within the status register to reflect the data that were read. One of the limitations of the MC68000 is that it cannot support misaligned data or instructions (address error exception). However, if a misaligned program must be executed, then a software rerun must be performed. The only way in which an address error fault can be corrected on the MC68010 is through a software rerun or through a modification of the fault address on the stack. While it is certainly possible to alter the address that caused the fault, there are few situations in which this is appropriate. If a software rerun is not made, the processor restores the state and attempts to make the same access that previously caused the fault. The access will fault again with the same results.

Once the state of the machine is restored and the access is completed, either by the user or by the machine, the processor is permitted to continue execution at the microinstruction following the faulted microinstruction. Note that if the rerunning of the access is left to the processor, it is possible for that

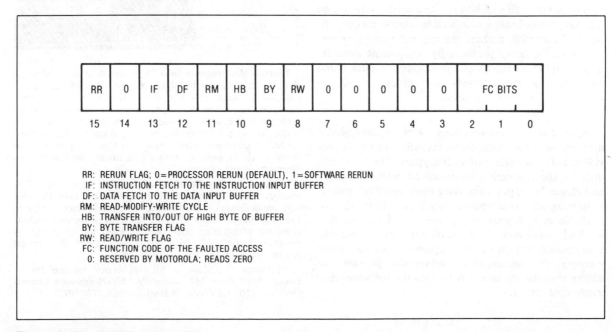

RR	0	IF	DF	RM	HB	BY	RW	0	0	0	0	0	FC BITS		
15	14	13	12	11	10	9	8	7	6	5	4	3	2	1	0

RR: RERUN FLAG; 0 = PROCESSOR RERUN (DEFAULT), 1 = SOFTWARE RERUN
IF: INSTRUCTION FETCH TO THE INSTRUCTION INPUT BUFFER
DF: DATA FETCH TO THE DATA INPUT BUFFER
RM: READ-MODIFY-WRITE CYCLE
HB: TRANSFER INTO/OUT OF HIGH BYTE OF BUFFER
BY: BYTE TRANSFER FLAG
RW: READ/WRITE FLAG
FC: FUNCTION CODE OF THE FAULTED ACCESS
0: RESERVED BY MOTOROLA; READS ZERO

Figure 15. The special status word.

access to cause another bus fault. Thus, if the problem that first caused the fault is not corrected, and the fault handler signals to the processor that the machine is to complete the access, a continuous fault-loop effect occurs. During this loop, the stack frame occupies the same location; thus, such a loop does not cause the stack to grow.

MC68010 facilities

Virtual machine operation. The MC68010 provides the mechanisms needed to implement a virtual machine environment in which any degree of emulation is supported. This is achieved in large part by the virtual memory mechanisms described above. Virtual I/O, for instance, is readily achieved by defining a memory area as an I/O device which is not physically resident. When an access is made to that address, an access fault occurs. The fault address can then be evaluated by the operating system to determine the activity that should take place. After the appropriate action has been taken, a software rerun can be signalled and the RTE executed. Indicating to the processor that the access has been completed makes it possible to provide virtual I/O transfers. This technique can of course be generalized to any other type of virtual activity that the processor requests the operating system to execute.

Performance enhancements. Since some new internal resources had to be added to the processor to support virtual operations, we wanted to apply these resources, whenever possible, to other instructions to improve their performance. The result of these efforts is a small performance improvement, which we have estimated to be about 15 percent for a typical instruction mix. A common criticism of the MC68000 is that it is not optimized for fast block operations. Instructions dedicated to handling block operations, however, carry with them some rather unattractive architectural consequences, as they tend not to fit well into the instruction map and do not have the full range of available address modes. The MC68010 provides perhaps the best solution to the performance/regularity problem by recognizing code sequences in which the block operations are defined and by executing these loops very quickly, with no superfluous instruction accesses.

Several new microprocessors which support virtual memory have been introduced recently, with each providing different degrees of such support. The MC68010, utilizing the instruction continuation method, cleanly and elegantly supports the fault detection/fault correction/program resumption process. The options available as a consequence of the use of continuation method—hardware and software rerun—provide powerful support for various implementations of virtual memory. The continuation method also provides the ability to make any access virtual via the software rerun method of return.

One of the most challenging aspects of any design is trying to provide an elegant general solution to a problem while at the same time ensuring that any exceptions to the general case are also handled appropriately. In the MC68010, this challenge has been met. ∎

References

1. Peter Denning, "Virtual Memory," *Computing Surveys,* Vol. 2, No. 3, Sept. 1970, pp. 153-189.

2. T. Kilburn, D. B. G. Edwards, M. J. Lanigan, and F. H. Sumner, "One-Level Storage System," *IRE Trans. Electronic Computers,* Vol. EC-11, No. 2, Apr. 1962, pp. 223-235.

3. J. Zolnowsky and N. Tredennick, "Design and Implementation of System Features for the MC68000," *Proc. Compcon Fall 79,* Sept. 1979, pp. 2-9.

4. *MC68000 16-bit Microprocessor User's Manual,* 3rd ed., Prentice-Hall, Englewood Cliffs, NJ, 1982, pp. 57-69.

5. Saburo Muroga, *VLSI System Design—When and How to Design Very-Large-Scale Integrated Circuits,* John Wiley and Sons, New York, 1982, pp. 417-421.

6. E. Stritter and N. Tredennick, "Microprogrammed Implementation of a Single-Chip Microprocessor," *Proc. 11th Ann. Workshop on Microprogramming* (Micro-11), Nov. 1978, pp. 8-16.

Douglas MacGregor defined the control structures and wrote the microcode for the MC68010 and the MC68020. He enjoys studying Japanese language and culture as well as reading Farley Mowat. He served six years in the Navy, obtaining some direction in life, while completing a BA in history and Asian studies at night. After evaluating the job market, he obtained an MS in computer science from the University of Illinois, from which he went to Motorola's Microprocessor Design Group in Austin, Texas.

David S. Mothersole is project manager of the MC68020 microprocessor systems design group. He has been involved with the definition of the M68000 architecture since coming to Motorola in November of 1978. His areas of research include computer architecture and microprocessor bus structures. A member of the IEEE, he holds a BS and MS in electrical engineering from the University of Texas.

The authors' address is Microprocessor Systems Design Group, Mail Drop M2, Motorola MOS Integrated Circuits Division, 3501 Ed Bluestein Blvd., Austin, TX 78721.

Today's microprocessors exhibit powerful computing capabilities. Their characteristic

differences favor each machine for a distinct portion of the applications spectrum.

An Architectural Comparison of Contemporary 16-Bit Microprocessors

Hoo-min D. Toong and Amar Gupta

Massachusetts Institute of Technology

The evolution of microprocessor architecture during the past decade has progressed at an incredible pace. From the primitive 4004, introduced in 1971, to the present spectrum of sophisticated microprocessors, the growth has been swift, dramatic, and almost revolutionary. Today's products possess astonishing computational capabilities and support primary memories of up to 64M bytes. They incorporate high-level languages and technical innovations only recently introduced on larger mainframes. Microprocessor-based systems now offer facilities for direct support of multiuser/multitask environments and sophisticated operating system implementations.

The current single-chip, 16-bit microprocessor market has three major contenders:

- the 8086 (iAPX 86): designed by Intel; second-sourced by Mostek in the US and by Siemens in Europe;
- the Z8000: designed by Zilog; second-sourced by AMD in the US, by SGS/ATES in Europe, and by Sharp in Asia;
- the MC68000: designed by Motorola; second-sourced by AMD and Rockwell in the US, by EFCIS in Europe, and by Hitachi in Asia.

Several of these devices are also being produced by major systems houses for internal use. In addition, National Semiconductor has recently announced the NS16000 microprocessor chip family, scheduled to be introduced during 1981. In the following paragraphs, we examine and compare the architectures of the three processors. A section is devoted to the preliminary data on the National 16000 series.

General characteristics

The characteristics of the microprocessors being discussed here are summarized in Table 1.

The 8086. Of the three processors, the Intel 8086 is the oldest and simplest. Basically, it is an improved, 16-bit version of the 8080; an 8080-type multiplexed bus is expanded to a 16-bit external bus. As in the 8080, the instructions are byte-oriented. One of the major enhancements is a six-byte instruction prefetch queue. This buffer feeds instructions to the execution unit in eight-bit segments. The queue decreases address bus/data bus idle times by prefetching data, thus increasing processor speed. The 8086 register structure is very similar to the 8080's. Registers in both machines are special-purpose. Rooted in a basic design philosophy requiring storage efficiency, special-purpose registers allow implied register addressing in most instructions and permit shortened instructions. Most addressing modes are the same in both machines. An address space of one megabyte is implemented in the 8086 through a memory segmentation scheme using 64K segments. Memory segments of up to 64K bytes can be placed on an eight-bit boundary, allowing a maximum of one megabyte to be addressed. By basing the segmentation and addressing mechanisms on 16 bits, Intel has preserved close compatibility between the 8086 and the 8080.

The 8086 has 95 basic instructions, of which a substantial number are only eight bits long. In the few 16-bit instructions, only the first eight bits are used for operation codes; the additional byte specifies data displacement. Instructions longer than two bytes use the remaining bytes for specifying data. The 8086 instruction set is an expanded version of the 8080 instruction set. Hence 8080 code can be converted easily to 8086 code. Many enhanced programming features are available in the 8086 instruction set. Base segment registers have been added to provide software support for certain operating system functions and for extended addressing range. Changing these segment registers allows the programmer to do process swaps with relative ease. Internally, the 8086 retains an eight-bit instruction path similar to the 8080's. The ALU is 16 bits wide, like the 8080's ALU. Thus, the 8086 is a widened 8080 with enhanced addressing and instruction prefetch. In all, 24 addressing modes are supported. With a clock frequency of 5 MHz, the fastest instruction time is 0.4 microseconds.

The Z8000. A register-rich 16-bit processor, the Z8000 is not an enhancement of Zilog's Z80 family and has a different internal structure. The Z8000 is based on a regular register use and a symmetric instruction set. Its operating system support is far more sophisticated than that available on eight-bit machines. An entire set of registers controls systems calls and manages process swaps. Internal registers allow 32-bit double-word operations. Traps of illegal addresses and illegal instructions serve as debugging tools through the use of an expanded flag register, also permitting software expansion of the instruction set. The Z8000 is a true 16-bit machine, as data and instruction paths are 16 bits wide.

Table 1.
Specifications of 16-bit microprocessors.

	8086	Z8000	68000	16008/16016	16032
YEAR OF COMMERCIAL INTRODUCTION	1978	1979	1980	1981	1981
NO. OF BASIC INSTRUCTIONS	95	110	61	100	100
NO. OF GENERAL-PURPOSE REGISTERS	14	16	16	8	8
PIN COUNT	40	48/40	64	40	48
DIRECT ADDRESS RANGE (BYTES)	1M	48M*	16M/64M	64K/16M	16M
NUMBER OF ADDRESSING MODES	24	6	14	9	9
BASIC CLOCK FREQUENCY	5MHz (4-8MHz)	2.5-3.9MHz	5-8MHz	10MHz	10MHz
SYSTEM STRUCTURES					
UNIFORM ADDRESSABILITY			•	•	•
MODULE MAP AND MODULES				•	•
VIRTUAL					•
PRIMITIVE DATA TYPES					
BITS		•	•	•	•
INTEGER BYTE OR WORD	•	•	•	•	•
INTEGER DOUBLE-WORD		•	•		•
LOGICAL BYTE OR WORD	•	•	•		•
LOGICAL DOUBLE-WORD					•
CHARACTER STRINGS (BYTE, WORD)	•	•	•	•	•
CHARACTER STRINGS (DOUBLE-WORD)					•
BCD BYTE	•	•	•	•	•
BCD WORD				•	•
BCD DOUBLE-WORD					•
FLOATING-POINT				•	•
DATA STRUCTURES					
STACKS	•	•	•	•	•
ARRAYS				•	•
PACKED ARRAYS				•	
RECORDS	•	•	•	•	•
PACKED RECORDS				•	
STRINGS	•	•	•	•	•
PRIMITIVE CONTROL OPERATIONS					
CONDITION CODE PRIMITIVES		•	•	•	•
JUMP	•	•	•	•	•
CONDITIONAL BRANCH	•	•	•	•	•
SIMPLE ITERATIVE LOOP CONTROL	•	•	•	•	•
SUBROUTINE CALL	•	•	•	•	•
MULTIWAY BRANCH				•	•
CONTROL STRUCTURE					
EXTERNAL PROCEDURE CALL				•	•
SEMAPHORES	•	•	•	•	•
TRAPS	•	•	•	•	•
INTERRUPTS	•	•	•	•	•
SUPERVISOR CALL		•	•		
OTHERS					
USER MICROCODE			•		
DEBUG MODE			•		

*6 SEGMENTS OF 8M EACH

May 1981

The machine's 110 basic instructions are either 16 or 32 bits long, and the instruction set is word-oriented with vector operations strongly represented. These instructions are the basis of the performance of the Z8000, as is most evident in the block operations. A single 32-bit instruction is used for set and move operations, while in the 8086, six single-byte instructions must be used. For future expansion, the designers of the Z8000 have left one register unused and unassigned. With the present 4-MHz clock speed, the fastest and the slowest instruction times are 0.75 microseconds and 90 microseconds, respectively. A 6-MHz version is being made available.

The MC68000. The designers of this microprogrammed machine have chosen to implement a very wide engine. The external 16-bit bus is multiplexed from the 32 bits inside the engine. A wide, 32-bit ALU has been coded as the user machine. Unlike the general-purpose registers of the Z8000, the 16- by 32-bit registers of the 68000 are partitioned into eight address registers and eight data registers. Motorola has made a great effort to design the engine with a very regular instruction set, making available several general addressing modes for most instructions. This design permits easy implementation of stacks and queues without special instructions. Two 32-bit stack pointers are provided for aiding in systems calls. A special flag register can be set to move the machine into a debugging, single-step mode for program development. Traps for illegal instructions can be used for software extension of the basic instruction set and for floating-point operations. Besides reducing software development problems, the traps allow software compatibility with future hardware improvements.

The MC68000 supports 56 basic instructions and 14 addressing modes. The total number of instructions is misleading, however, because many instructions perform triple functions and are encoded differently. The number 56 is an artifact of the assembler. Instruction sizes vary from one to five words. The address bus uses 23 bits for word addressing, providing an addressing capability of 16M bytes.

Architectural details

Basic principles of operation. The basic structure of the Intel 8086 is shown in Figure 1. The 8086 (and the 8088) CPU consists of two separate processing units, the execution unit, or EU, and the bus interface unit, or BIU, connected by a 16-bit ALU data bus and an eight-bit Q bus. The EU obtains instructions from the instruction prefetch queue, IQ, maintained by the BIU, and executes instructions using the 16-bit ALU. Execution of instructions involves maintenance of CPU status and control logic, manipulation of general registers and instruction operands, and manipulation of segment offset addresses within 16-bit limits. The EU accesses memory and peripheral devices through requests to the BIU, which is the second processing unit, performing all bus operations for the EU on a demand basis. This involves generating physical addresses from segment register and offset values, reading operands, and writing results. The BIU is also responsible for prefetching instructions from the IQ whenever possible, to keep the EU busy with prefetched instructions under normal conditions, and for resetting the IQ when the EU transfers control to another location. The execution unit and the bus interface unit operate independently of each other, enabling the 8086 to overlap instruction fetch and execution.

The Z8000 is a random-logic-based CPU; its basic structure is shown in Figure 2. The internal 16-bit data bus is used for internal addressing and data communication. The instructions are fetched through the Z-bus interface and executed by the instruction execute control unit. Throughput is enhanced through "limited" pipelining, which allows prefetching of the next single-word instruction (or the first word of the next multiword instruction) from the memory into the instruction buffer. This occurs only during execution of the current instruction, provided the current instruction does not require the bus to complete the execution cycle. No instruction prefetching occurs when the bus is assigned to another bus master. The 16-bit ALU manipulates data and generates logical offset addresses in the general-purpose register block in accordance with the instruction executed. The CPU status and control flags are maintained in the program status registers, and the CPU, which can operate in a system mode or normal mode, can execute privileged instructions only in the system mode. Interrupts and traps are handled by the exception-handling control unit, and there is provision for multiple interrupt tables. A refresh

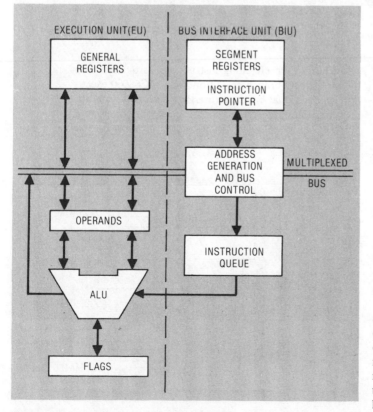

Figure 1. Basic structure of the Intel 8086.

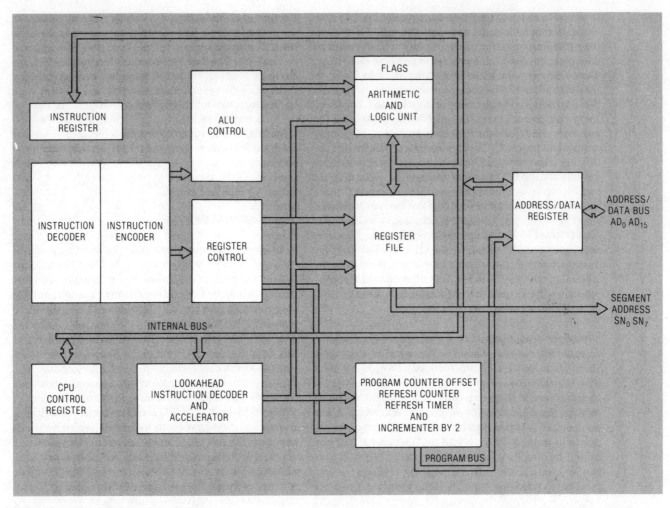

Figure 2. Basic structure of the Z8000.

counter provides the refresh control logic with timing information for CPU-driven memory refresh operation.

The MC68000 is architecturally quite distinct from the others. Its block structure is shown in Figure 3. The microcode-based CPU is centered around a microprogram-controlled execution unit. The control store area size is minimized through the use of a two-level control structure. At level one, the machine instructions are produced by sequences of micro-instructions in the micro-control store. These micro-instructions are actually pointers (addresses) to nano-instructions in the nanostore at level two. The nano-control store contains an arbitrarily ordered set of unduplicated machine-state control words, which control the execution unit. All information that is machine instruction static (timing-independent) bypasses the control store and is transmitted directly to the execution unit. In all, about 22.5K bits of control store is used, 50 percent less than the control store required for a single-level implementation. However, the two-level structure increases total access time. An attempt has been made to overcome this by means of a pipelined architecture, in which the instruction fetch, instruction decode, and instruction execute cycles are fully overlapped across every macro-instruction boundary. An attempt has also been made to minimize delays in looping

(branching) by prefetching instructions associated with the most likely branch condition. The MC68000 execution unit is a dual bus structure that performs both address and data processing. The CPU may run in either a

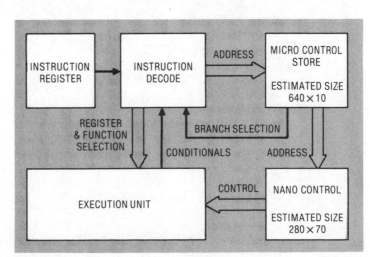

Figure 3. Basic structure of the MC68000.

supervisor mode with privileged instructions or in a user mode. Although internal data paths are all 32 bits wide, the packaging limitation on the number of pins constrains data paths to and from memory to be only 16 bits wide. The 64 pins are comprised of 23 pins for address bus, 16 for data bus, five for asynchronous bus control, three for bus arbitration control, three for interrupt control, three for system control, three for peripheral control, three for processor status, and the remaining five for power supply ground and for clock. The chip specifications provide for floating-point and string operations, but current versions do not have these features because of technological limitations on circuit density and size. At present, these unimplemented instructions cause traps for software emulation. Overall, the MC68000 CPU implements as large a subset of the complete 68000 system architecture as is feasible under current technology. It is expected that on-chip memory, faster clock speeds, custom microprogramming, and facilities for run-time changes in microprogram will be provided by Motorola during the lifetime of the 68000 architecture.

Register organization. The Intel 8086 execution unit contains four 16-bit pointer and index registers and four 16-bit data registers addressable on an individual byte basis. These eight registers are used implicitly by the instruction set, providing compact encoding at the cost of reduced flexibility. The BIU contains one 16-bit instruction pointer, which contains the offset of the next instruction to be fetched. This pointer is updated by the BIU but cannot be directly accessed by programs. The BIU also contains four 16-bit dedicated segment registers for segment base addressing, which enables programs to access up to four 64K-byte segments at a time. Finally, the EU contains six one-bit status flags and three one-bit control flags.

The Z8000 family is characterized by sixteen 16-bit general-purpose registers. All can be used as accumulators, and all but one can be used as index pointers or memory pointers. The one exception is an escape mechanism for address changes. The general register architecture avoids bottlenecks inherent in dedicated or implied registers. Register grouping and overlapping provide for byte, double-word, and 64-bit registers. Two registers are used as implied stack pointers for system mode and normal mode. All Z8000 family chips contain one 16-bit segment offset register, and the Z8001 also contains one 16-bit segment number register. The Z8001 also contains a 16-bit reserved register, two 16-bit program status area pointers, one 16-bit flag and control register, and one 16-bit refresh counter.

The MC68000 has eight 32-bit data registers, seven 32-bit address registers, and two implied 32-bit stack pointers. The data registers can be addressed as byte registers, word registers, or double-word registers. The address registers are used for 32-bit base addressing, 32-bit software stack operations, and word and long word address operations. The implied stack pointers are used for 32-bit base addressing and for word and long word address operations. The MC68000 also contains a 32-bit program counter and a 16-bit status register. The program counter addresses one large linear address space

from a full 32-bit address, but only 24 bits are available in the present version. There is no segmentation at the CPU level. The status register contains one user byte and one system byte. The user byte contains five control bits, including the extend bit for extended operations. The system byte contains a trade mode bit, a supervisor state bit, and a three-bit interrupt mask.

System structure. The 8086 utilizes two types of multi-master buses, the local bus and the system bus. Microprocessors are always connected to a local bus, and memory and I/O usually reside on a system bus. The two buses are linked by interface components, the number of which depends on the size and complexity of the system. On the local bus, the address and data lines are multiplexed to reduce the number of processor pins. Signals coordinate up to three processors with an implied priority structure. On-chip arbitration logic enables both independent processors and coprocessors to share the bus. The system bus is functionally and electrically compatible with the Intel Multibus and provides for interconnection of multiple processing modules. This bus is composed of address lines, data lines, control lines, interrupt lines, and arbitration lines. Because it is modular in design, only a subset may be implemented, according to the needs of the application. All memory and I/O modules on the system bus are accessible to all the processing modules.

The Z-bus interconnects Z8000 family components in a master/slave fashion. The CPUs obey the Z-bus protocol directly at the chip level, and no extra circuitry is needed to generate bus signals. Multiplexing of address and data minimizes pin count without significant performance loss in "read-oriented" applications. Demultiplexing is performed when necessary within the individual modules. The daisy chain serial priority philosophy resolves interrupts/traps, bus requests, and requests for shared resources. The Z-bus is always controlled by one of the devices, which, on request, grants control to legal bus masters for bus transactions. Multiple CPUs communicate on a bus-to-bus basis, using the FIFO input/output interface units, or FIOs. Multiple FIOs may be connected to one Z-bus.

The MC68000 family is supported by two different master/slave-based multimaster buses for interconnection of components—the local bus and the global bus. The local bus connects microprocessor, memory, and I/O devices to form individual microcomputer modules, and the global bus interfaces to various local buses through bus arbitration modules. In the minimum version, the local bus uses transmission and control lines as they appear directly at the CPU. The extended version of the local bus, the Versabus, designed to support all future versions of the 68000 family, utilizes additional control lines.

Memory. The one megabyte of real addressing space in the 8086 is treated as a group of segments, each segment 64K bytes in size. Four segments are addressable at one time, providing up to 64K bytes of code, 64K bytes for stack, and 128K bytes for data. The starting address is obtained through segment registers. Segmentation permits writing of position-independent programs. Two portions of the memory are dedicated and reserved. Physical addresses are generated by shifting the segment base value four bits to the left and adding the offset. In the case of programming code, the offset is obtained from the instruction pointer, and, in the case of operands, it is the result of calculation based on the addressing mode. This organization of memory does not provide easy management and protection.

On the Z8000 chips, addresses are always expressed in bytes. Single bytes can be read and written using the byte/word output line. The eight megabytes of directly addressable memory is split up as 128 segments, each of 64K bytes. The 23 address lines (on the Z8001) provide a seven-bit segment number and a 16-bit segment offset pointer. The two address parts can be manipulated separately or together by all the available word and long word operations. The CPU generates processor status information, which enables the address range to be increased beyond its nominal limits by physically separating code, data, and stack spaces in system and normal modes (6 × 8M bytes = 48M bytes). External logic is needed for this memory extension. The Z8010 memory management unit, or MMU, can be used with the Z8001 microprocessor to improve and expand memory addressing capabilities, randomly relocating all 128 segments in the six address spaces with translation tables for each space.

The MC68000 has 23 address lines, providing a 16M-byte addressing capability. The address space is linear with no internal segmentation. Although words are normally addressed, single bytes can be read or written using upper and lower data strobes. Instructions and multibyte data are always aligned on even byte boundaries. Similar to that of the Z8000, the processor status information separates address space into four areas: the supervisor program, the supervisor data, the user program, and the user data. The proposed memory management unit, MC68451, would support sophisticated management and protection of 32 variable-sized segments, ranging from 256 bytes to 16M bytes in increments of 256 bytes, and would allow trapping of unauthorized accesses. Without the MMU, it is possible to equip the MC68000 with a simple memory protection mechanism by separating user and supervisor space into high and low memory.

Stack organization. While Intel 8086 systems can have many stacks, each less than or equal to 64K bytes, only the current stack is directly addressable. Other stack pointers are located in memory and are implemented through the stack segment register, SS. Thus, multiple concurrent stacks are not feasible on Intel systems.

In contrast, the Z8000 can have multiple concurrent stacks; stacks can be located anywhere in memory and are addressed via stack pointer registers. Any register except RO can serve as a stack pointer by means of PUSH and POP. Call return, interrupts, and traps use implied stack. The system stack can be accessed only in system mode, whereas the normal stack can be accessed in both modes.

The MC68000 has two implied stack pointers for use in user mode and supervisor mode. Multiple concurrent user stacks and queues can be created and maintained by employing the address register indirectly with post-increment and predecrement addressing modes.

I/O mechanisms. The Intel 8086 has a 64K-byte (32K words) separate I/O space. A memory-mapped I/O capability that can respond like a memory device is available for linking I/O devices, but Intel does not recommend its use for the Multibus. Any memory reference instruction can be used to access an I/O device, providing additional programming flexibility. Word-based devices should use even addresses for maximum throughput. Intel has reserved eight locations for future products. High-speed I/O operations can be carried out with traditional DMA controllers. Intel also offers the 8089 IOP, an independent processor with two DMA channels and an instruction set tailored for I/O operations.

The Z8000 family CPUs support two different I/O address spaces of 64K bytes through special I/O instructions, which can be executed only in the system mode. Standard I/O instructions transfer data between the CPU and peripherals, and special I/O instructions transfer data to and from external CPU support chips. Processor status information enables separation of address spaces. The I/O addressing scheme is identical to the basic memory addressing scheme. For DMA operations, two signals, bus request and bus acknowledge, are available, Inhibited from controlling the bus during DMA operations, the CPU must wait for the bus to be given up by the DMA controller.

The MC68000 possesses no separate I/O space. All I/O is memory-mapped and all I/O protection must occur at the memory protection level. Three signals, bus request, bus grant, and bus grant acknowledge, allow master devices to get control of the bus for DMA operations. The three signals are used by potential bus masters to decide who will be the next bus master. The actual arbitration protocol handles overlapped arbitration and data transfer and resolves multiple simultaneous bus requests. The CPU has been designed to operate in conjunction with the MC68450, a direct memory access controller scheduled to be available during 1981, which will allow block transfer rates of up to four megabytes per second.

Software. As mentioned previously, the 8086 is an improved and expanded version of the 8080. The 8080's basic eight-bit instructions have been retained, and expanded with extended instruction lengths when necessary. For efficient code, the instructions most often executed are only a single byte long. Implied register addressing also reduces code size. To allow for expansion of the instruction set, an "escape" facility is available for transferring control to a coprocessor. The 8086 instruction set provides automatic repetition of many non-decision-making instructions, large I/O space with register indirect addressing, decimal operations, error traps, and software traps. The addressing highlights of the 8086 include the ability to finely segment memory, and the facilities for indexing with displacement and without displacement.

The Z8000 achieves high speeds through random logic encoding. Code is space-efficient because the instructions most often executed are shortest in length, and because it distinguishes between long branches and short branches. The Z8000 also has an expandable instruction set. Unlike the 8086, it does not use implied registers. Zilog provides

16 completely general registers and consciously avoids specialized ones. The instruction set facilitates multiprogramming through a context switching facility. Other instruction highlights include signed 32-bit multiply and divide, decimal operations, multiple load, vector-based instructions, and the test and set instruction, which is especially valuable in multiprocessor applications. Addressing schemes include indexing, with and without displacement, and multiple increment indexing. Multiple stacks, segmented memory, and the very large address space (48M bytes) ease programming effort. Finally, the user/supervisor stacks are all hardwired.

The MC68000 has a regular instruction set and provides multiuser support. It emphasizes space-efficient code through "quick" instructions and short jumps on loops. The MC68000 offers the advantage of excellent debug tools like single-step execution, traps on illegal instructions, and debug mode. The instruction set can be expanded by remasking the microcode or by traps. Context switching facilitates multiprogramming, and the test and set instruction aids in multiprocessor and data-base applications. Other advantages include complex push and pop capabilities, the 32-bit internal structure, and instructions for multiple load and signed multiply and divide. It is possible to address 16M bytes directly and 64M bytes through functional segmentation. Post/pre increment/decrement facilities are available for most instructions. Real-time control applications are aided by multilevel interrupt and seven auto-vector interrupt capabilities.

National 16000. National Semiconductor has announced a family of 16-bit microprocessors, and sample production is expected to begin in 1981. The 16000 series consists of the NS16008, NS16016, and NS16032 processors. Of these, the NS16008 and the NS16016 are very similar, each offering an internal data ALU bus 16 bits wide and a direct addressing range of 64K bytes. Further, either of these two chips can operate in two distinct modes:

(1) native mode, in which the two processors have 100 basic instructions and are directly compatible with the NS16032;

(2) 8080 compatibility mode, which permits direct emulation of the 8080, with a speed four times that of the 8080.

Transfer from one mode to another within a program is implemented with an ESCAPE instruction. No separate translator and assembly programs are needed.

The NS16008 and NS16016 processors are designed to bridge the gap between the 8080 and the high-end members of the NS16000 family. The NS16008 and 16016 have 16-bit address pointers that are upwardly compatible through software to the 16032 address space. The primary difference between them is that the NS16016 has a 16-bit data bus, whereas the NS16008 has only an eight-bit data bus and is primarily suitable for use in systems with eight-bit-wide memory and peripherals.

The NS16032 achieves an address range of 32M bytes by means of a memory management unit, or MMU. However, it does not have an 8080 compatibility mode. The NS16032 has an internal data ALU bus that is 32-bits wide and a direct address range of 16M bytes using 24-bit address pointers. Unlike the 16032, the 16008 cannot be supplemented with an MMU to increase the address space.

All the National microprocessors have eight general-purpose registers that can be used (without any restrictions) as base registers and index registers. Instructions are not register-specific and can make use of every relevant addressing mode, including scale index (powerful when using high-level languages), external address (used to construct modular software), and memory relative. Furthermore, the symmetry between registers and memory means that each memory location can serve as an accumulator or base register as needed. The NS16081 floating-point unit, or FPU, has an additional set of eight general-purpose registers, supplementing the GPRs on the master processor. The MMU, NS16082, can serve as a second slave processor.

The main CPU has eight dedicated registers: program counter register, processor status register, user stack pointer, interrupt stack pointer, frame pointer, static base register, mod register (for module map), and interrupt base register. The MMU provides eight dedicated registers, and the FPU provides one floating-point status register. The NS16000 family offers several symmetric addressing modes, including top of stack addressing, memory relative addressing, external addressing, and scaled indexing. National is unique in providing modular software capabilities for the new microprocessors, permitting a user to develop a software package independent of all other packages and without regard to individual addressing. This provides flexibility in system design and lower programming costs. The ROM code is totally relocatable and easy to access. Within the system, a module consists of three components: a code component (contains the code that the processor executes in a given module), a static data component (contains local variables and data for the particular module), and a linkage component (contains all information required to link references from one module to another).

National has attempted to provide as much compatibility as feasible. The floating-point unit, the NS16081, is compatible with the proposed IEEE floating-point formats by means of its hardware and software features. It can be driven not only by National microprocessors but also by any Microbus-compatible CPU.

Microcomputers

Several microcomputers configured around 16-bit microprocessors are now available. Intel Corporation offers the SDK-86 based on the 8086, Zilog offers the Z8000 Development Module based on the Z8002, and Motorola offers the MEX-68-KDM based on the MC68000. Several independent system houses offer equivalent systems. The broad features of various systems are summarized in Table 2.

Multiprocessor capabilities

To increase computational bandwidth and/or system resilience, integration of several microprocessors in a single system frequently becomes necessary. The overall throughput and efficiency of such systems is directly dependent on the hardware and software interconnection mechanisms supported by the basic microprocessor chips. Many different interconnection systems have evolved over the years, but the single timeshared bus offers distinct advantages as an interconnection mechanism for multimicroprocessor systems. Under such a scheme, different modules can share the bus resource equally on a time-multiplexed or demand-multiplexed basis. However, the internal design of the present 16-bit microprocessors does not facilitate efficient concurrent operation of a large number of processors on such a bus.

Intel 8086. The Multibus is the structure for interfacing Intel's 8080/85/86 products. It supports a one-megabyte address space. The 8289 bus arbiter controls Multibus accesses by multiple masters. The control lines are designed according to a master-slave concept: a master (processor) in the system takes control of the Multibus; then the slave device (I/O or memory), upon recognizing its address, acts upon the command provided by the master. An asynchronous handshaking protocol allows modules of different speeds to use the bus. Although the basic definition

in the bus standard specifies only two types of units—bus masters and bus slaves—the system also can include "intelligent" slaves, which cannot control the bus, but put more processing power into the bus slave. Multiple masters can be connected in either a daisy chain priority scheme or in a parallel priority scheme.

Coordination features of the 8086 multiprocessor include

- the 8289 bus arbiter, which decides which master may use the bus during the next cycle;
- the bus lock signal, activated on execution of lock prefix instructions, blocking interrupts and requests by other processors until the lock sequence is completed;
- semaphore using the lock prefix in conjunction with the XCHG instruction;
- synchronization to an external event using a WAIT instruction and the test input signal;
- escape instruction allowing other processors to obtain an instruction and/or a memory operand from the host;
- two bidirectional request/grant lines, used to share the local bus between one host and two other pro-

**Table 2.
Microcomputer characteristics.**

	ADVANCED MICRO COMPUTERS 96/4016	ADVANCED MICRO COMPUTERS 96/4116	INTEL ISBC 86/12A	INTEL SDK-86	MICRODA-SYS MD-68K	MOTOROLA MEX-68-KDM	ZILOG 05-6101-01
GENERAL							
PROCESSOR USED	AMZ8002	Z8000	8086	8086	68000	68000	Z8002
WORD SIZE (BITS)	16	16	16	16	16	16	16
ADDRESSING							
ADDRESS SIZE (BITS)	16	16	20	20	24	24	16
TOTAL MEMORY ADDRESSABLE (BYTES)	64K	160K	1M	1M	4M	16M	64K
AMT. OF RAM ON CARD (BYTES)	8K	32K	32-64K	2-4K	128K	32K	32-48K
AMT. OF ROM ON CARD (BYTES)	0-12K	0-8K	0-32K	8K	0-16K	8-64K	4-16K
DMA CAPABILITY	NO	YES	YES	YES	YES	NO	YES
FREQUENCY, ETC.							
CLOCK FREQUENCY (MHz)	4	4	5	2.5 or 5.0	?	8	2.5 or 3.9
SUPPLY VOLTAGES	+5, +12	+5, +12	+5, +12	+5	+5, +12	+5, +12	+5, +12
BOARD SIZE (IN)	6.75×12	6.75×12	6.75×12	12×13.5	12×15	9.75×14	11×14
I/O CAPABILITY							
BUS TYPE	SPECIAL	MULTIBUS	MULTIBUS	SPECIAL	SPECIAL	EXORCISER	SPECIAL
PARALLEL I/O LINES	24+	24+	24	48+	32+	32+	32+
NUMBER OF I/O PORTS	2	2	1	1	4	2	2
MAX I/O RATE (K BAUD)	38.4	19.2	38.4	4.8	300	9.6	19.2
ADDTL. H'WARE DETAILS							
INTERRUPT PROVISIONS	YES	YES	YES	YES	YES	YES	YES
MULTIPROCESSING CAPABILITY	NO	YES	YES	NO	YES	YES	NO
NO. OF TIMERS	3	5	2	?	4	3	5
BITS PER TIMER	16	16	16	?	16	16	8
SOFTWARE							
OPERATING SYSTEM	YES	YES	YES	YES	NO	YES	YES
HIGH-LEVEL LANGUAGE(S)	YES	YES	YES	YES	NO	YES	YES
ASSEMBLER	YES	YES	YES	YES	YES	YES	YES
DEBUGGING AIDS	YES	YES	YES	YES	YES	YES	YES
APPLICATION PACKAGES	NO	NO	YES	NO	NO	NO	YES

112

cessors via a handshake sequence—request, grant, release;
- the 8288 bus controller that outputs system bus signals compatible with Multibus.

Z8000. Two different multimicroprocessor mechanisms are possible on the Z8000. Zilog has designed a FIFO buffer communication module, which can run each processor as a separate system and pass messages back and forth through buffers to achieve total system communication. The processors are very loosely coupled, and any high-speed resource sharing is virtually impossible.

The second multiprocessor mechanism employs two signal pins called micro-in and micro-out (MI and MO) for implementation of a daisy-chained, software-controlled, global priority scheme. A processor examines the chain for busy condition (global resource allocation locked). If the bus is not busy, the processor places a request into the chain and then re-examines it after a settling delay (to prevent races). The result of the operation is reported with a flag handled in software. Thus, with an appropriate software driver, a single global locking scheme can be implemented. However, the time required to operate this locking mechanism rules out any high-speed communication.

Multimicroprocessor operation with the Z8000 is facilitated by the following features:

- four special, privileged "multimicro" instructions— MBIT, MREQ, MRES, and MSET;
- pins for bus request, bus acknowledge, multimicro in, multimicro out, and segment trap;
- test and set instructions, TSET and TSEB;
- special output instructions;
- bus arbitration mechanisms;
- normal and system modes;
- provision for asynchronous Z-bus to Z-bus communication using the Z8038 FIO;
- simple external SSI logic to establish actual daisy-chain;
- semaphore using TSET (test and set) to synchronize software processes that require exclusive access to certain data or instructions at one time;
- sharing of large memory by various processors under the memory management scheme.

On the Z8000, six op-codes have been reserved for extended instructions to be used in conjunction with extended processing units (coprocessors).

MC68000. In a Motorola environment, each processor has a local bus with local memory and peripherals. A global bus connects all local buses together through bus arbitration modules (BAMs). A processor is free to execute at full speed in its own bus space until it needs something from another processor's area, or until another device needs something from the former's domain. This is not a true multiprocessing system, but rather a connected group of individual microcomputer systems. Resources are not equally available to each processor. Any access involving the global bus takes longer than a simple local access. Access from the global bus back to a local bus is obtained through a DMA operation. There are

no strictly global, shared resources, and the mechanism is suitable only for low, nonlocal access rates. Also, there is nothing to prevent several processors from making continuous accesses into one processor, effectively stopping that processor entirely. With the priority on the global bus fixed, a processor with the lowest priority may never get a global transaction started or completed.

MC68000 multimicroprocessor operation is facilitated by

- bus arbitration modules (BAMs), which provide support in global bus multiprocessor design;
- the TAS (test and set) instruction;
- signals for bus request, bus grant, and bus grant acknowledge, which provide necessary input signals for arbitration purposes. Such arbitration requires some external hardware.

Interlocked multiprocessor communication is achieved through an indivisible read-modify-write cycle. For this purpose, the TAS instruction is used, and the address strobe is asserted throughout the cycle to inhibit other bus members from accessing the bus. The bus arbitration handles overlapped bus arbitration and transmission; however, it is not very powerful for multiple CPUs. The extended bus arbitration provided by Versabus is more powerful, but the inherent master/slave nature of its protocol presents a major bottleneck as the number of processors increases.

NS16000. The NS16000 series uses local buses and system buses. The local bus can connect the NS16032 CPU to the NS16081 floating-point unit, the NS16082 memory management unit, and the NS16203 DMA controller. The system bus is used for communications to other processors and global memory, and also to the bus arbiter and the interrupt control unit. The two buses communicate through "drivers" and "address latch" circuitry. It is too early to comment on specific system capabilities and potential bottlenecks of the National bus protocols.

Multiprocessing overview. In all the 16-bit chips, support for multiprocessing is rather primitive, and one must consciously avoid the various pitfalls mentioned above. National Semiconductor still has to make known the details of its more sophisticated mechanisms. Among the other multiprocessors, the amount of resource sharing in the 8086 Multibus design is more restricted than that in the MC68000 local/global bus structure. Although all resources on the system bus can be accessed by any master, local bus resources are directly accessible only by the resident 8086. A further constraint imposed by Multibus is the fixed master-slave relationship of devices on the system bus, limiting interprocessor communication to the level of mailbox messages via global memory. Multibus, like the MC68000 local/global structure, is subject to saturation by high-priority devices. Individual transactions on Multibus are much faster than those on the MC68000 bus for two reasons: fetches from MC68000 local memory involve contention with the local processor, while Multibus global memory fetches do not; MC68000 inter-BAM communication adds two additional steps to the global memory access procedure. The Z8000 offers special signal pins, MI and MO, and four special instructions to support multiprocessing.

Selection strategy

In selecting a microprocessor for a particular application, one must analyze a spectrum of issues, both technical and nontechnical. Let us consider the relevant technical issues first.

Technical issues. The operational speeds of all the 16-bit microprocessors have improved over the previous generation 8080, Z80, and MC6800 processors. The shortest execution (assuming sufficiently fast memory) is 400 ns for the 8086, 750 ns for the Z8000, and 500 ns for the MC68000. In all three microprocessors, extended address ranges allow large memory sizes to be directly accessed. The upper limit on directly addressable memory is one megabyte on the 8086, 48M bytes on the Z8000, and 64M bytes on the MC68000. Such large memory space requires some form of management. The internal segment registers of the 8086 provide internally controlled memory management via relocation. Both the Z8000 and the MC68000 are designed to be used with an external memory management chip, which allows increased function by increasing silicon area. These management units can relocate, check bounds, and check functions of all references to support very sophisticated memory mapping and protection facilities.

The 8086 and Z8000 have separate I/O addressing facilities, while the MC68000 uses memory-mapped I/O. Separate I/O space makes system memory design and management easier. Memory-mapped I/O allows all memory referencing instructions to also be I/O-referenced. This saves instructions, but the I/O cannot be protected at the instruction level; it can be protected only at the memory level.

A valuable feature of the Z8000 and MC68000 processors is the implementation of supervisor/user mode separations, allowing the protection of certain instructions and separate system/user stack pointers. The 8086 does not offer such facilities. Also, the Z8000 and the MC68000 can handle 32-bit operands.

The basic speed of instruction execution is an important selection criterion. Available independent benchmark studies do not cover the NS16000 series, which is not yet commercially available. Hence, we must use the figures published by National Semiconductor. The speed data, listed in Table 3 for the four microprocessors, must be interpreted with caution. Actual throughput is a function of the exact instruction sequence, displacements, data lengths, clock frequency, and other factors. Also, the numbers may represent a slight positive bias in favor of National. Overall, the MC68000 is the best on the various branch operations. For simple data transfer operations, the NS16032 and the MC68000 are superior to the 8086 and the Z8000.

The direct address sizes supported by the various microprocessors are considerably different, making the machines suitable for different application areas. Simple text editing, for example, generally requires less memory than data-base management, and memory requirements increase in direct proportion to the number of users simultaneously on-line. Thus, each processor has its own application niche (see Figure 4). The sophisticated addressing modes and segmentation schemes used in both the MC68000 and the Z8000 families simplify the implementation of large programs. Conversely, the small address space of the NS16008 and the NS16016 prevents their use for any large-scale programs.

Software is another factor determining application suitability of the various microprocessors. The Z8000 is

Table 3.
Execution speeds (in microseconds) of 16-bit microprocessors.

OPERATION	DATA TYPE	8086	Z8000	MC68000	NS16032
REGISTER-TO- REGISTER MOVE	BYTE/WORD DOUBLE-WORD	0.40 0.80	0.75 1.25	0.50 0.50	0.30 0.30
MEMORY-TO- REGISTER MOVE	BYTE/WORD DOUBLE-WORD	3.40 6.80	3.50 4.25	1.50 2.00	1.00 1.40
MEMORY-TO- MEMORY MOVE	BYTE/WORD DOUBLE-WORD	7.00 14.00	7.00 8.50	2.50 3.75	1.60 2.40
ADD MEMORY TO REGISTER	BYTE/WORD DOUBLE-WORD	3.60 7.20	3.75 5.25	1.50 2.25	1.10 1.50
COMPARE MEMORY TO MEMORY	BYTE/WORD DOUBLE-WORD	7.00 14.00	7.25 9.50	3.00 4.00	1.80 2.60
MULTIPLY MEMORY TO MEMORY	BYTE WORD DOUBLE-WORD	13.00 23.00 115.20	20.25 16.00 85.75	N/A 8.75 43.00	2.80 4.60 7.60
CONDITIONAL BRANCH	BRANCH TAKEN BRANCH NOT TAKEN	1.60 0.80	1.50 1.50	1.25 1.00	1.40 0.70
MODIFY INDEX BRANCH IF ZERO	BRANCH TAKEN	2.20	2.75	1.25	1.30
BRANCH TO SUBROUTINE		3.80	3.75	2.25	2.50

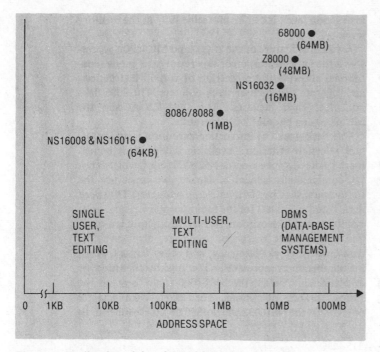

Figure 4. Application niches for 16-bit microprocessors.

best suited for word processing and text editing applications because of its sophisticated string instruction repertoire. On the other hand, the MC68000 lacks this capability but offers excellent support for handling interrupts and thus is suitable for real-time and control systems and also for multitasking. The perceived market for Intel 8086 systems is largely to upgrade earlier Intel products and to serve as a steppingstone to 16-bit applications. The National products, according to current specifications, are attractive across the range because of their direct upward compatibility with the Intel 8080, as well as their string-processing and interrupt-handling capabilities.

Another major evaluation dimension is the availability and type of support chips. Such chips greatly facilitate particular functions—e.g., memory management, bus arbitration, floating-point operations, array processing, and a whole spectrum of I/O operations. Although all chip vendors are involved in the development of "coprocessor," "slave," or support chips, only a few such chips are commercially available. Since the 8086 has been in existence much longer than the other processors, it possesses a distinct advantage in this realm. Table 4 presents a listing of the various support chips. In most cases, the new 16-bit microprocessors will interface with support chips designed earlier for eight-bit microprocessors. This may result, however, in a substantial performance loss, as the earlier chips use relatively obsolete technology, operate at lower speeds, and use fewer data lines. The new chips cost more than the earlier ones—thus the price-performance trade-offs of the two options must be considered in the design of any new system.

The software conversion costs of upgrading to a 16-bit microprocessor are not insignificant. A system presently using an Intel 8080 must convert either to an Intel 8086 or a National Semiconductor 16008/16016. These alternatives will yield a speed increase of a factor of 4-6. It is possible to obtain higher speeds with an NS16032 or a Motorola 68000, but the costs of rewriting software plus the associated costs of debugging can more than offset the gain. Likewise, the only appropriate upward path from an MC6800 is to an MC68000. The Z8000 has a basic structure different from the previous Z80; hence, one must fully analyze present programs before making a final choice.

The major features discussed in this section are listed and evaluated in Table 5 (A is excellent; B is good; C is fair; D is poor).

Commercial issues. The availability of vendor support and second sourcing is critical, especially for high-volume systems. (Second sources for the 16-bit microprocessor-based systems were listed in the second paragraph of this article.) It is unwise to depend on a single source for the supply of all chips. So far, no second source has been identified for the National microprocessors, and this constraint must be kept in mind.

We come finally to the pertinent issue of new product versus old product. The Intel 8086 has been available since 1978, the Zilog 8000 since 1979, and the Motorola

**Table 4.
Support chips for 16-bit microprocessors.**

TYPE OF CHIP	INTEL 8086	Z8000	MC68000	NS16000
MEMORY MANAGEMENT		Z8010	68451	NS16082 (NOT USEABLE W/NS16008)
BUS ARBITER	8289	Z8001/8002 MAY BE USED		NS16024
FLOATING-POINT	8087		68000X	NS16081
DMA CONTROLLER	8089/8237	Z8016	68450	NS16023
INTERRUPT CONTROL UNIT	8259A			NS16202
I/O PROCESSOR/INTERFACE	8089	Z8038		
PERIPHERAL CONTROLLER	8041A/8741A	Z8034	68120	
FLOPPY DISK CONTROLLER	8271/8271-6/8271-8			
CRT CONTROLLER	8275	Z8052		
ARRAY PROCESSOR				
BUBBLE MEMORY CONTROLLER			68453	

68000 since January 1980. The number of Intel users is the largest. Hence, the company's spectrum of support chips is also the largest, and there is a much lower probability of a bug in the software. The MC68000 can use the large number of support chips designed earlier for the MC6800 family. However, very few support chips designed exclusively for the MC68000 are presently available. National Semiconductor support products will be available this year. But by that time, Intel will also have new iAPX series products, which will offer higher speeds, wider data paths, and superior addressing facilities. Microprocessing is a dynamic world, and we can always expect newer and more powerful chips. ∎

**Table 5.
Ranking of 16-bit microprocessors.**

	INTEL 8086	Z8000	MC68000	NS16000
SPEED	C	B	A	A
NUMBER OF REGISTERS	B	A	A	C
ADDRESS RANGE	D	A	A	B
COMPATIBILITY W/EARLIER MICROPROCESSORS	A	B	B	B
SUPPORT CHIPS	A	B	C	D
MULTIPROCESSING CAPABILITY	B	B	B	C
SECOND SOURCE	A	A	A	D

Acknowledgment

The authors sincerely thank John-Francis Mergen and Svein Ove Strommen for their valuable assistance in the preparation of this article.

Bibliography

Brooks, F. P., "An Overview of Microcomputer Architecture and Software," *Micro Architecture,* EUROMICRO 1976 Proceedings, pp. 1-3a.

Childs, R. E., "Multiple Microprocessor Systems: Goals, Limitations and Alternatives," *Digest of Papers COMPCON Spring 79,* pp. 94-97.

Enslow, P. H., Jr., ed., *Multiprocessors and Parallel Processing,* John Wiley, New York, 1974.

Franklin, M. A., S. A. Kahn, and M. J. Stucki, "Design Issues in the Development of a Modular Multiprocessor Communications Network," *Sixth Ann. Symp. Computer Architecture,* Apr. 23-25, 1979, pp. 182-187.

Fung, K. T., and H. C. Torng, "On the Analysis of Memory Conflicts and Bus Contentions in a Multiple-Microprocessor System," *IEEE Trans. Computers,* Vol. C-27, No. 1, Jan. 1979, pp. 28-37.

Harris, J. A., and D. R. Smith, "Hierarchical Multiprocessor Organizations," *Fourth Ann. Symp. Computer Architecture,* Mar. 23-25, 1977, pp. 41-48.

Intel Corp., "8086 User's Guide," and other 8086 technical publications, 3065 Bowers Ave., Santa Clara, CA 95051.

Lipovski, G. J., "On Virtual Memories and Micronetworks," *Proc. Fourth Ann. Symp. Computer Architecture,* Mar. 23-25, 1977, pp. 125-134.

Motorola Semiconductor, "MC68000 Microprocessor User's Manual," and other MC68000 technical publications, Motorola IC Division, 3501 Ed Bluestein Blvd., Austin, TX 78721.

Myers, G., *Advances in Computer Architecture,* John Wiley, New York, 1978.

National Semiconductor Corp., "The NS16000 Family of 16-Bit Microprocessors," and other NS16000 technical publications, 2900 Semiconductor Dr., Santa Clara, CA 95051.

Patel, J. H., "Processor-Memory Interconnections for Multiprocessors," *Proc. Sixth Ann. Symp. Computer Architecture,* Apr. 23-25, 1979, pp. 168-177.

Thurber, K. J., and G. M. Masson, *Distributed Processor Communication Architecture,* Lexington Books, Lexington, MA, 1979.

Toong, H. D., J. F. Mergen, and C. J. Smith, "Issues of Advanced Microprocessor Architecture," Technical Report #4, M.I.T. internal monograph, July 1979.

Toong, H. D., S. O. Strommen, and E. R. Goodrich II, "A General Multimicroprocessor Interconnection Mechanism for Non-Numeric Processing," *Proc. Fifth Workshop on Computer Architecture for Non-Numeric Processing,* 1980, pp. 115-123.

Zilog Corp., "Z8000 User's Guide," and other Z8000 technical publications, 10460 Bubb Rd., Cupertino, CA 95014.

Hoo-min D. Toong is an assistant professor of management in the Sloan School of Management at MIT, which he joined in 1978. He is in charge of the Digital Systems Laboratory of the Center for Information Systems Research of MIT. Before joining the Sloan School, he was a faculty member of the Electrical Engineering and Computer Science Department of MIT. His research interests are VLDB architectures, multiprocessors, distributed operating systems, and the organizational impact of such systems.

Toong received the BS in 1967, the MS and EE in 1969, and the PhD in electrical engineering and computer science in 1974 from MIT. He is a member of Tau Beta Pi, Eta Kappa Nu, Sigma Xi, IEEE, and ACM.

Amar Gupta is a visiting research fellow in the Sloan School of Management of MIT. His research interests include multiprocessor architectures, performance measurement, and office automation. He has participated in research dealing with tightly coupled SIMD and MIMD machines.

Gupta received his B.Tech in 1974 from the Indian Institute of Technology, Kanpur, his MS in 1980 from MIT's Sloan School, and his PhD in 1980 from the Indian Institute of Technology, Delhi.

The authors' address is Massachusetts Institute of Technology, Sloan School of Management, 50 Memorial Dr., Cambridge, MA 02139.

The performance of two addressing mechanisms

on three different microprocessors is examined. One of the

mechanisms—and one of the micros—provided superior performance.

A Performance Comparison of Three Contemporary 16-bit Microprocessors

Martin De Prycker*

University of Ghent

The choice of a new computer system is influenced by considerations of various importance: compatibility with the former system, software availability, cost, maintenance, and system performance.[1] To a great extent, the system's performance depends on the central processor's architecture. To study the performance of a particular architecture, two methods are frequently used. One is that which was used in the CFA project,[2-4] in which three architectural parameters were defined and compared for a set of machine language routines. The other method consists of measuring the execution times of assembly language benchmarks on different processors, as was done at Carnegie-Mellon[5] and by Nelson and Nagle.[6] Other contributions to architecture evaluation have been made by Shustek,[7] who compared instruction execution times, and by Lunde,[8] who evaluated an ISP description of the processors. However, in order to obtain performance figures with any of these methods, the actual processor, or a simulator, has to be available.

The above-mentioned methods involve comparisons of performance made at a low level; here, I compared the performances of processors executing high-level-language programs. In block-structured high-level languages, a major part of execution time is spent on procedure and block entry/exit. (This has been noted by Batson, Brundage, and Kearns,[9] Tanenbaum,[10] and Blake.[11]) When we also include the execution time of variable addressing, it is clear that a large amount of the execution time of block-structured high-level-language programs is spent on procedure and block entry/exit and variable addressing. The overall system performance is thus strongly influenced by the implementation of the addressing mechanism. Therefore, several variable addressing mechanisms have been proposed, e.g., the display mechanism introduced by Dijkstra[12] and the addressing mechanism presented by Tanenbaum.[10]

In a recent paper,[13] I analyzed a method for describing variable addressing implementation performance, one that employs three independent parameter sets: a set of program statistics determined by high-level-language benchmarks, a set of architectural parameters based on the processor architecture and the variable addressing mechanism, and a set of technology-dependent parameters. The usefulness of this model lies in the independence of the three sets, and in the fact that the processor is available in neither physical nor virtual (i.e., simulated) form. Hence, a complete performance analysis can be done analytically. In addition, in order to evaluate the program statistics, the high-level-language benchmarks can be run on any computer system.

Using this analytical model, I compared the addressing mechanisms implemented on a number of processors. I chose three comparable 16-bit micros—the Intel i8086,[14] the Zilog Z8000,[15] and the Motorola MC68000.[16]

In the next section I will explain the performance model, as adapted to processors with an instruction prefetch pipeline.[17] I describe a set of Algol and Pascal benchmarks in the third section of this article and

*Now with Bell Telephone Manufacturing Company, Antwerp, Belgium.

Addressing mechanisms that implement the block structure in high-level languages

In block-structured high-level languages, program statements can be recursively grouped into composite statements by means of two block delimiters (begin-end and procedure-return). The recursive program structure so generated can be represented by a *program tree* (Figure 1). Each composite statement or block can thus be given a number, its *static lexical level*, which is the depth at which the block definition is located in the program tree.

Hence, the lexical level of a block is always determined by the level of the (static) surrounding block: A *begin* generates a lexical level which is one level higher than the surrounding block; a corresponding *end* returns the level of the block to the surrounding level. A *procedure call* generates a lexical level which is one higher than the level at which the procedure is declared; a *return* puts the level back to the calling level.

Variables may be accessed only when they are declared within the same block or in *static* surrounding blocks, that is, when they reside at a lexical parent level. With respect to the program tree, this means that we can access all variables declared in path nodes from the root to the actual active node. This also means that *scope rules* are fully determined by the static program structure known at compile time. Within a block, each variable gets a *sequence number*, and a *lexical address* is formed by the pair (lexical level, sequence number). When a block ends (by an end or return), all variables within that block are no longer visible.

For the implementation of the scope rules of a block-structured language, one needs two stacks: a stack with static information (known at compile time), and a stack with dynamic information (known only at run time). Generally, one combines these stacks with the evaluation/allocation stack on which the defined variables and the temporary results are stored. The three stacks are merged into one stack via a linked-list technique. The stack of static and dynamic environments is implemented through *marker words* that are linked. Among other information, each marker contains two pointers: a static link, pointing to its parent static environment, and a dynamic link, pointing to the previous dynamic environment. The top-most stack marker serves as the base address of the allocation/evaluation stack of the current environment. For the sake of efficiency, the latter stack is implemented contiguously.

It is clear that, with the above simple structure, accessing variables in parent static environments necessitates tracing down the static pointer chain, possibly to a depth of several levels. In order to lessen or avoid this run-time overhead, two mechanisms have been proposed, namely the display mechanism and Tanenbaum's proposal.

The display mechanism. In order to provide fast access to any lexical level, this scheme uses an extra stack (display). Each display location contains a pointer to the base of a visible environment. When a variable at lexical level i is accessed, DISPLAY[i] is used as base for level i. Thus, only one level of indirection is needed to access a variable at any static level. The main benefit of the display mechanism is that the address of any variable can be determined very easily: address = DISPLAY[i] + sequence number. Thus, the variable access time is independent of the lexical level.

During the execution of statement Q in our example, the display and data stack appear as shown in Figure 2. Variables are accessible through the display: All variables in the three levels can be reached.

Tanenbaum's mechanism. In order to reduce the overhead associated with display rebuilding—which must be done after every procedure return—Tanenbaum reduced the display to two pointers: a local pointer LP and a global pointer GP. Local and global variables can be reached through these pointers, and intermediate variables must be accessed by tracing the static pointer chain through indirections. The rationale behind this approach is that the addressing of variables at levels between the current level and the global level (i.e., intermediate variables) is a relatively rare event.

In our example the data stack during the execution of statement Q will appear as shown in Figure 3. Local (e,f) and global (a,b) variables can be addressed directly; intermediate variables (c,d) can be reached only by tracing the static pointer chain.

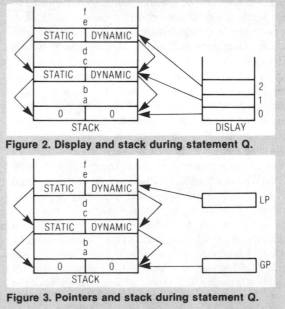

Figure 2. Display and stack during statement Q.

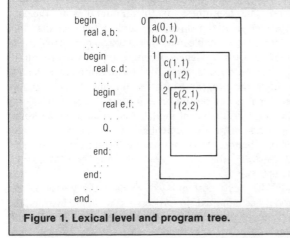

Figure 1. Lexical level and program tree.

Figure 3. Pointers and stack during statement Q.

discuss their statistical parameters. In the fourth section Dijkstra's and Tanenbaum's addressing mechanisms, as implemented on the three microprocessors, are compared. It is shown that Tanenbaum's mechanism always performs better than Dijkstra's display mechanism. In the last section, I compare the relative performance of the three microprocessors, as a function of memory speed. I conclude by ranking the processors according to their performance. The correspondence with low-level performance analyses performed elsewhere is striking, not only qualitatively but also quantitatively. I also discuss a cost/performance model.

Variable addressing implementation model

In an earlier work,[13] I expressed overall system performance as a function of three independent factors: the high-level-language programs (benchmarks); the processor architecture, i.e., the instruction set and register organization; and the technology. Here, I will examine this model as it has been adapted to processors with instruction prefetch buffers of different lengths.[17]

The overall system execution cost K, induced by procedure and block entry/exit and variable addressing, can be written as a product of three independent arrays: one composed of high-level-language program statistics S, one determined by the processor's architecture M, and one influenced by the technology K_T. That is,

$$K = K_T \cdot M \cdot S^T, \qquad (1)$$

where the superscript T denotes array transposition.

This model was obtained in a very straightforward way: The execution cost of any high-level-language program can be determined as a weighted sum of the execution costs of the individual high-level-language instructions, with the frequency of these instructions in the test program as the weight factor. Thus, we can write

$$K - T \cdot S^T. \qquad (2)$$

The array S contains high-level-language program statistics concerning variable addressing, and thus is independent of either architecture or technology. The statistics which make up the S array comprise the following:

- The number of block entry/exits (n_b).
- The number of procedure call/returns (n_p).
- The number of variables accessed in the program (n_t).
- The number of local variables accessed (n_l). Local variables are variables which are accessed at the same level at which they are declared.
- The number of global variables accessed (n_g). Global variables are variables which are declared at the outermost level.
- The number of intermediate variables accessed (n_i). Intermediate variables are nonglobal variables

which are accessed at an higher lexical level than that at which they are declared.
- The total lexical-level difference of intermediate variables (di_t), that is, the sum of the lexical-level differences between declaration and access.
- The total lexical-level difference between declaration and access of procedures (dp_t).

The operations described here can be viewed as "generic instructions," and each high-level-language program can thus be written as a sequence of these generic instructions.

In Equation 2, T denotes an array of execution costs T_i of the generic instructions i, or

$$T = (T_1 \ldots T_i \ldots T_n). \qquad (3)$$

One possible description of the execution cost K is the execution time of the test program. Since my study involves only microprocessors, this execution time can be expressed in terms of the number of clock cycles, because of the indivisibility of the clock cycle time t_c (in nanoseconds).

The number of clock cycles T_i needed to execute each generic instruction i depends on various parameters:

- The number of clock cycles TC_i needed to execute each generic instruction i. It is assumed that the memory is fast enough (no wait states) and the instruction pipeline is always full.
- The number of extra clock cycles needed to perform a memory read (TMR_i) and a memory write (TMW_i) and used by slower memory.
- The number of extra clock cycles in the delay TPC_i. This delay is caused by an empty pipeline resulting from the execution of a sequence of instructions when not enough memory is free.
- The number of clock cycles in the delay TPS_i. This delay is caused by a memory that is slower than specified in the user's manual; hence, extra wait states are introduced in order to have a full pipeline.

The total number of cycles T_i can thus be written as a sum of clock cycles:

$$T_i = TC_i + TMR_i + TMW_i + TPC_i + TPS_i. \qquad (4)$$

The value of each of these parameters is determined by the processor's architecture and technology. If we express each parameter as a product of a technology-dependent part and an architecture-dependent part, then Equation 1 will be satisfied, since the technological parameters are independent of i:

$$TC_i = C_i \cdot K_C \qquad (5a)$$
$$TMR_i = MR_i \cdot K_{MR} \qquad (5b)$$
$$TMW_i = MW_i \cdot K_{MW} \qquad (5c)$$
$$TPC_i = PC_i \cdot K_{PC} \qquad (5d)$$
$$TPS_i = PS_i \cdot K_{PS} \qquad (5e)$$

If we define a technological array K_T and an architectural array M_i as

$$K_T = (K_C \ K_{MR} \ K_{MW} \ K_{PC} \ K_{PS}) \qquad (6)$$

and

$$M_i = (C_i \ MR_i \ MW_i \ PC_i \ PS_i)^T, \qquad (7)$$

then we can rewrite Equation 4:

$$T_i = K_T \cdot M_i \qquad (8a)$$

or

$$T = K_T \cdot M \qquad (8b)$$

if

$$M = (M_1 \ . \ . \ . \ M_i \ . \ . \ . \ M_n). \qquad (9)$$

Applying Equation 8b to Equation 2 finally leads to the basic model of Equation 1.

For each of the five parameters of Equation 5, the question of whether to separate them into technology-dependent and architecture-dependent parts must be individually determined.

Execution time in the optimal case. When the memory is fast enough (no wait states) and the instruction pipeline is full, the total number of clock cycles needed for each generic instruction i is the sum of the number of clock cycles C_{ij} needed for the machine instructions j which compose the generic instruction i. These numbers C_{ij} can be easily found in the microprocessor user's manual.

Influence of slower memory on data memory operations. The read/write timing diagrams of the typical user's manual give the minimum number of clock cycles needed by the processor to execute a memory read or write. We call these values m_r and m_w. Let us denote the memory access time as x (in nanoseconds). The memory is fast enough if $x/t_c \leq m_r$ for a data read—no wait states have to be introduced. The number of clock cycles to be inserted depends on the memory speed, e.g., when $m_r < x/t_c \leq m_r + 1$, only one cycle has to be introduced. The number of clock cycles to be inserted can thus be written as

$$D_r = \max\{0, \lceil x/t_c - m_r \rceil\}, \qquad (10)$$

where $\lceil z \rceil$ denotes the smallest integer greater than or equal to z. A similar expression D_w exists for data write operations.

This delay occurs for each data memory operation. The total number of memory operations required for each generic instruction i is the sum of the number of memory operations required for the individual machine instructions j (R_{ij} read operations, W_{ij} write operations).

Pipeline influence. The number of clock cycles required for each machine instruction, as described in the user's manual of a microprocessor with an instruction pipeline, is only the number of clock cycles needed to "really" execute the instruction. It is assumed that the instruction word is already prefetched and available in the pipeline buffer. However, since the memory bus is not always free to fill the pipeline, sometimes the pipeline buffer is empty. This causes a delay so that the buffer can be filled before the instruction is executed. Microprocessor manufacturers give a typical value of 5 to 10 percent for this delay, but note that the value can be much higher, depending on the instruction sequence.

To determine this delay TPC_i *exactly*, the internal microcode of each processor would have to be available. However, since no information on this microcode was available, I used a best/worst-case analysis to determine an upper and lower bound for TPC_i.

In the *best case* I assumed that all free clock cycles in one machine instruction were grouped consecutively. For instance, when an instruction needed eight clock cycles and two memory operations of three cycles each, I supposed that the two free clock cycles were contiguous, as shown in Figure 1. Only one cycle needed to be inserted to do the prefetch.

The number of cycles to be inserted for each machine instruction can be determined by using the values of R_{ij}, W_{ij}, and I_{ij} (the number of clock cycles for that instruction), and a table. One such relation for the Z8000, which has a pipeline length of one word, is shown in Table 1.

In the *worst case* I assumed that the free bus cycles were *not* grouped, as shown in Figure 2. In this example, two clock cycles have to be inserted. The number of cycles to be inserted can again be determined using a table, as shown for the Z8000 in Table 2.

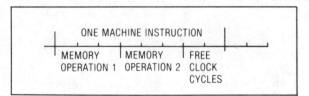

Figure 1. Memory operation in the best-case model.

**Table 1.
Number of clock cycles to be inserted in the Z8000
for the best-case model.**

$R_{ij} + W_{ij}$	I_{ij}										
	1	2	3	4	5	6	7	8	9	10	11
0	2	1	0	0	0	0	0	0	0	0	0
1	-	-	3	2	1	0	0	0	0	0	0
2	-	-	-	-	-	3	2	1	0	0	0
3	-	-	-	-	-	-	-	-	3	2	1

Influence of slower memory on the use of a pipeline. When the memory is slower than specified, problems can arise in filling the pipeline buffer during instruction execution. These problems cause a delay TPS_i that is dependent on the memory speed x. Again, information on the microcode would be needed to determine this delay exactly, and again I used a best/worst-case analysis to find bounds for this delay.

In the *best case* I took into account only the instructions Q which have just enough free clock cycles to do the prefetch without delay when fast memory is used. This is a lower bound, since I eliminated the instructions which operate without delay even when the memory is slower, i.e., instructions which have at least one free

Figure 2. Memory operation in the worst-case model.

**Table 2.
Number of clock cycles to be inserted in the Z8000
for the worst-case model.**

	I_{ij}										
	1	2	3	4	5	6	7	8	9	10	11
$R_{ij} + W_{ij}$											
0	2	1	0	0	0	0	0	0	0	0	0
1	-	-	3	2	2	2	2	2	2	2	2
2	-	-	-	-	-	3	2	2	2	2	2
3	-	-	-	-	-	-	-	-	3	2	2

**Table 3a.
M for the display mechanism, implemented on the Z8000
for the best and worst cases.**

$$M_{BEST} = \begin{bmatrix} 85 & 194 & 24 & 48 \\ 3 & 11 & 2 & 2 \\ 4 & 7 & 1 & 1 \\ 0 & 0 & 0 & 0 \\ 3 & 6 & 0 & 0 \end{bmatrix} \qquad M_{WORST} = \begin{bmatrix} 85 & 194 & 24 & 48 \\ 3 & 11 & 2 & 2 \\ 4 & 7 & 1 & 1 \\ 12 & 30 & 3 & 8 \\ 13 & 31 & 4 & 6 \end{bmatrix}$$

**Table 3b.
M for Tanenbaum's proposal, implemented on the Z8000 for the best and worst cases.**

$$M_{BEST} = \begin{bmatrix} 64 & 139 & 14 & 14 & 22 & 18 \\ 3 & 8 & 1 & 1 & 1 & 1 \\ 3 & 6 & 1 & 1 & 1 & 0 \\ 0 & 0 & 0 & 0 & 0 & 0 \\ 3 & 5 & 0 & 0 & 1 & 0 \end{bmatrix} \qquad M_{WORST} = \begin{bmatrix} 64 & 139 & 14 & 14 & 22 & 18 \\ 3 & 8 & 1 & 1 & 1 & 1 \\ 3 & 6 & 1 & 1 & 1 & 0 \\ 12 & 24 & 2 & 2 & 4 & 2 \\ 11 & 23 & 2 & 2 & 4 & 2 \end{bmatrix}$$

clock cycle available. The number of cycles to be inserted for these instructions Q depends on the memory speed and is equal to D_r (Equation 10).

In the *worst case* I assumed that every instruction causes a delay of D_r clock cycles, except the instructions which use the memory data bus very little and thus have enough free cycles. However, since in principle infinitely slow memory can be used, no instruction will have enough free cycles. Therefore I reduced the minimum memory speed to a practical value. This minimum is obtained for a maximum access time x_M. Thus an instruction which causes no delay in doing a prefetch must have at least Z free cycles, with

$$Z = \max\{m_r, [x_M/t_c]\} - m_r. \qquad (11)$$

This value is maximum (an upper bound) for a minimum value of t_c. This minimum value t_{cm} means a maximum processor clock frequency.

Given these descriptions, it is easy to determine the M array for both addressing mechanisms in both the best and worst cases; Tables 3a and 3b show M for the Z8000. It is obvious that only the fourth rows of the M arrays differ in the best and worst cases.

The K_T, M, and S values can be applied to Equation 1 to obtain a lower bound K_L for the total number of clock cycles in the best case, and an upper bound K_U for the total number of clock cycles in the worst case. The total execution time of a test program's block-structured and variable addressing instructions, running on a processor with clock cycle time t_c, will always lie in the range $[K_L \cdot t_c, K_U \cdot t_c]$. This range can be used to compare addressing mechanisms and processors, as described in the following sections.

Benchmarks and program statistics

Processors and addressing mechanisms are usually more suited to some languages and applications than to others. In a statistical analysis, one hopes to eliminate this bias by considering different languages and applications. In this study, I was limited to two languages, and I considered only a few applications. However, even with applications belonging to totally different domains, the results were almost language- and application-independent, as is shown in the next two sections. In my system, I used HP Algol,[18] a slightly changed version of Algol 60, and Swedish Pascal,[19] a version of Jensen and Wirth's Pascal.[20]

The programs tested concern nonhomogeneous applications such as numerical problems, compiler construction, and data manipulation. They were written by graduate and postgraduate students. Let us call the graduate students programmers A and B, and the postgraduate students programmers C and D. DIGFD, DIGFP, and DIGFK are numerical programs used for digital filtering and speech recognition, and BUBBLE is a bubblesort; all were written in Algol. The Pascal programs are TREE, a program that generates the syntax tree of a program, and SPLIT, which generates the LR(0)-items and adds the look-aheads in a syntax-analyzer generator.[21] The numerical programs were written by programmer C, TREE and BUBBLE by D, and SPLIT by A and B. Dynamic program statistics obviously depend on their input data. Therefore each program was run several times with different input data.

In order to measure the program statistics as described in the preceding section, I developed a measurement system that can analyze any block-structured high-level-language program and measure any high-level-language program statistic.[22] In the same work, I identified a set of useful statistics. For a comparative study of variable addressing mechanisms on microprocessors, I needed only a few of these statistics, namely those defined in the section above. These statistics, measured for the programs described above, are shown in Table 4.

A comparison of two variable addressing mechanisms

In order to compare the display mechanism with Tanenbaum's proposal, I applied the M array of each to Equation 1. By doing so, I obtained a measurement proportional to the execution time of programs which implement Tanenbaum's mechanism, and one proportional to the execution time of programs which implement the display mechanism. As stated in the second section of this article, I was also able to analyze the influence of memory speed on these measurements, for the three microprocessors under both the best- and worst-case models.

To compare the two addressing mechanisms, I calculated R, which is the ratio of the execution time of Tanenbaum's proposal to that of the display mechanism:

$$R = K_{TA} \cdot t_c / K_{DI} \cdot t_c. \qquad (12)$$

Figures 3a and 3b show this ratio, under both the best- and worst-case models, for an i8086 with a memory fast enough to eliminate wait states. This ratio lies in the range [0.73, 0.86] for Algol programs and in the range [0.57, 0.59] for Pascal programs and is almost independent of program and input data. Both figures show that Tanenbaum's mechanism really performs better than the display mechanism. The better behavior of Tanenbaum's mechanism in the Pascal programs is due to the low use of intermediate variables in Pascal, which is a consequence of the ability to compile Pascal programs separately. Figures and results for the Z8000 and MC-68000 are very similar.

A measurement system for high-level-language program statistics

The measurement system we developed has two important features: It is independent of language and it can be adapted to any program statistic. Such a system needs three types of input:

(1) a description of the language to be analyzed;
(2) some indications of the statistics that must be measured; and
(3) a program in the language to be analyzed.

In contrast, language-dependent measurement systems lack Input 1—i.e., the language description is built-in.

Since both the description of the language and the description of the statistics are intimately connected with the syntactic structure of the language, a formal means of describing this structure can be used to describe both the language and the statistics. In our system we used the BNF notation developed by Backus and Naur.[1]

Our measurement system uses the above-mentioned connections between the program syntax and the statistics. The way in which this is done can best be explained by considering the compilation process. A compiler first creates the syntax tree of the program (i.e., by means of a syntax analyzer). Then, this tree is converted to machine code via *semantic* routines, which generate specific pieces of code for each BNF rule. In a high-level-language interpreter system, the semantic routines *directly* execute the semantic functions associated with the syntactic construct.

In our measurement system, things are similar: We first construct the syntax tree of the program, using an automatic-construction parser. Rather than defining a semantic routine for each syntax rule, we append one or more *software probes* to some or all syntax rules. These software probes perform one of the following functions:

(1) measurement of static statistics,
(2) insertion of *write* statements in particular places in the test program, or
(3) insertion of block delimiters (*begin-end*) to keep the test program syntactically correct and semantically unchanged.

When the converted test program is compiled and executed, the inserted *write* statements generate trace files, which will later be analyzed to collect dynamic high-level statistics.

1. P. Naur, "Revised Report on the Algorithmic Language Algol 60," *Comm. ACM*, Vol. 6, No. 1, Jan. 1963, pp. 1-17.

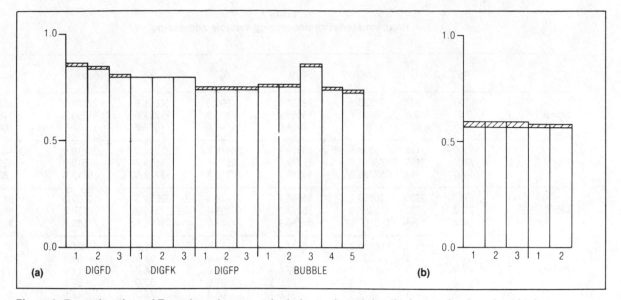

Figure 3. Execution time of Tanenbaum's proposal relative to that of the display mechanism: for Algol programs on the i8086 (a) and for Pascal programs on the i8086 (b).

Analyzing the influence of processor and memory speed on R, I again drew similar conclusions: R is almost independent of processor and memory speed. Figures 4a and 4b show R for the three microprocessors (each with memory that is fast enough) and for an "average" program, i.e., a program exhibiting the average of the statistics shown in Table 4. We see that the ratio is indeed very similar for the three microprocessors. The influence of the memory speed x (in nanoseconds) on a 12-MHz MC68000 is very small (Figure 5). Similar figures can be drawn for the i8086 and the Z8000. Notice also that the influence of memory on slower processors' R is still smaller.

Given these results, I concluded that under both the best- and worst-case models, and for all three microprocessors, both languages, all programs and input data, and any memory speed, Tanenbaum's mechanism

results in considerably better performance than that provided by the classical display mechanism. The gain in performance reaches a value of at least 14 percent for Algol programs and 39 percent for Pascal programs.

Comparison of the three microprocessors

To compare the execution ties of procedure and block entry/exit and variable addressing in high-level-language programs running on the three microprocessor systems, I used the model described in the second section of this article. Applying the M arrays for the three processors to Equation 1, I obtained sets of performance figures, one for each processor and one for each addressing mechanism in the best and worst cases, and one for the individual programs. With such figures, one can compare two processors for the different cases mentioned above by examining the ratio of their respective performance values.

In the course of my analysis, I arrived at an important conclusion: *The relationships among the performances of the microprocessors are almost independent of program and input data.* This conclusion can be deduced from Figures 6a and 6b, which describe the performance of each processor relative to the 8086 worst case (assuming that the memory is fast enough), for Algol programs implementing the display mechanism on the Z8000, and for Pascal programs implementing Tanenbaum's proposal on the MC68000. The figures for different programs and input data differ by only a few percent. Notice also that best- and worst-case results lie within a reasonable range. Because of this program and data independence, only the results of "average" Algol or Pascal programs need to be discussed below. Average Algol or Pascal programs are as defined in the preceding section.

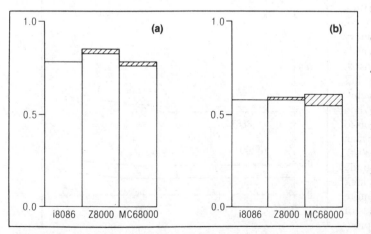

Figure 4. K_{TA}/K_{DI} for Algol programs on the three processors (a); K_{TA}/K_{DI} for Pascal programs on the three processors (b).

IEEE MICRO

Table 4.
Program statistics concerning variable addressing.

		n_b	n_p	n_t	n_l	n_g	n_i	di_t	dp_t
DIGFD	1	951	963	71583.6	19331.4	24690.6	27561.6	27561.6	1637.1
	2	851	863	56390.6	15083.2	20225.2	21253.6	21253.6	1467.1
	3	651	663	32061.6	7884.0	13140.0	11037.6	11037.6	1060.8
DIGFK	1	2102	2115	78014.5	19819.9	28675.6	29519.0	29519.0	4230.0
	2	2102	2115	78014.5	19819.9	28675.6	29519.0	29519.0	4230.0
	3	1402	1414	53785.6	13235.2	20556.8	19712.0	19712.0	2828.0
DIGFP	1	2752	2765	115857.0	38067.3	45239.4	32550.3	32550.3	5530.0
	2	2752	2765	115857.0	38067.3	45239.4	32550.3	32550.3	5530.0
	3	1852	1864	79150.0	85640.4	31957.6	21552.8	21552.8	3728.0
BUBBLE	1	2	1	4620.0	2127.0	1572.0	921.0	921.0	0.0
	2	2	1	267.0	117.0	96.0	54.0	54.0	0.0
	3	2	1	420.0	189.0	144.0	114.0	114.0	0.0
	4	2	1	291.0	129.0	105.0	57.0	57.0	0.0
	5	2	1	228.0	96.0	90.0	42.0	42.0	0.0
SPLIT	1	1	10	220000.0	21120.0	198880.0	0.0	0.0	2.0
	2	1	10	110000.0	13310.0	96690.0	0.0	0.0	2.0
	3	1	10	110000.0	13310.0	96690.0	0.0	0.0	2.0
TREE	1	1	380	20802.6	10782.3	10020.3	0.0	0.0	266.0
	2	1	7501	408859.0	210806.2	198052.8	0.0	0.0	5250.7

n_b = NUMBER OF BLOCK ENTRY/EXITS
n_p = NUMBER OF PROCEDURE CALL/RETURNS
n_t = NUMBER OF VARIABLES ACCESSED
n_l = NUMBER OF LOCAL VARIABLES ACCESSED
n_g = NUMBER OF GLOBAL VARIABLES ACCESSED
n_i = NUMBER OF INTERMEDIATE VARIABLES ACCESSED
di_t = TOTAL LEXICAL-LEVEL DIFFERENCE OF INTERMEDIATE VARIABLES
dp_t = TOTAL LEXICAL-LEVEL DIFFERENCE BETWEEN DECLARATION AND ACCESS OF PROCEDURES

Figure 7a shows the influence of memory speed on the execution-time ratio $K_{Z8000}/K_{MC68000}$ for an average Algol program, with the display mechanism, implemented on 4, 8, 10, and 12-MHz processors. The same ratio is shown in Figure 7b for Tanenbaum's proposal. Both addressing mechanisms have a better performance when implemented on the Z8000 than when implemented on the MC68000, provided that the memory is fast enough for the processor's clock frequency. With slow memories and high processor clock frequencies, however, the MC68000 performance degrades more slowly than that of the Z8000. Indeed, an MC68000 with a slow memory actually performs better than a Z8000 with a slow memory. This behavior can be easily explained. The Z8000 needs only three clock cycles for a memory operation ($m_r=m_w=3$), whereas the MC68000 needs four cycles ($m_r=m_w=4$). When fast memories are used, the Z8000 can operate at maximum speed and thus execute a memory operation in only three clock cycles. A better Z8000 performance is thus obtained. When slower memories are used, Z8000 performance begins to degrade as soon as a memory operation requires more than three clock cycles. This is in contrast to the MC68000, the performance of which does not begin to degrade until a memory operation requires more than *four* clock cycles. Thus, MC68000 performance degrades more slowly than Z8000 performance for memory speeds of at least $3 \cdot t_c$, e.g., 250 nanoseconds for a 12-MHz processor and 300 nanoseconds for a 10-MHz processor (see again Figures 7a and 7b).

Comparing Figures 7a and 7b, we see that the Z8000 is better suited to the display mechanism than to Tanenbaum's proposal, compared to the MC68000. The main reason for this lies in the method of computation of the base address of the lexical level, which is slower in the MC68000. In the display mechanism, this operation is performed at each variable access and thus requires more operations in the MC68000. Again note that the

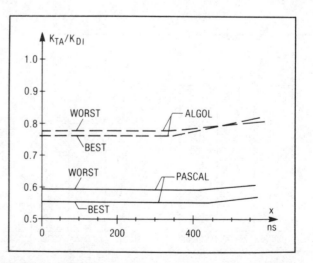

Figure 5. Influence of memory speed *x* on K_{TA}/K_{DI} for a 12-MHz MC68000.

best- and worst-case ratios do not differ much: The exact performance ratio lies between tight limits. Similar figures can be derived for an average Pascal program.

Similar conclusions can be reached in comparing the Z8000 to the i8086 (Figures 8a and 8b). One major difference is striking: The performance of the i8086 is much poorer than that of the MC68000.

Since the i8086 and the MC68000 both need an equal number of clock cycles for a data read and write ($m_r = m_w = 4$), the influence of memory speed on the execution-time ratio $K_{MC68000}/K_{i8086}$ is very small, as is shown in Figures 9a and 9b. Note also that both processors are equally suited to both addressing mechanisms.

Using the results shown in Figures 7, 8, and 9, I made a global performance analysis and compared my results with those from other studies. To obtain one performance value for each processor, I averaged the performances of all the programs in both languages with both variable addressing mechanisms. I also used average performance values from the studies by other researchers; these values were obtained by averaging the performances of all programs, normalized to equal processor clock frequencies. Figures 10a and 10b show the mean performance ratio of programs analyzed by Nelson and Nagle,[6] by Grappel and Hemenway[5] and adjusted by Patstone,[23] by Hunter and Ready, Inc.,[24] and by Hansen et al.[25] They also show an upper and lower bound for my results. The upper bound is obtained by dividing

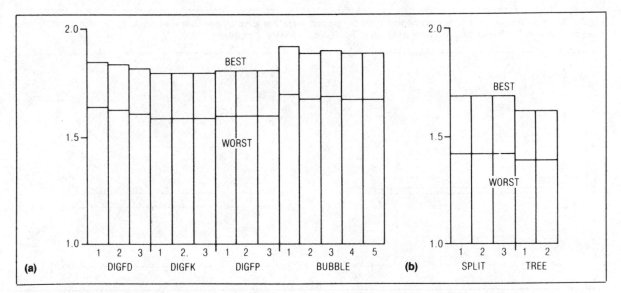

Figure 6. Relative performance of the Z8000 compared to the i8086 worst case, with the display mechanism implemented for Algol programs (a); relative performance of the MC68000 compared to the i8086 worst case, with Tanenbaum's mechanism implemented for Pascal programs (b).

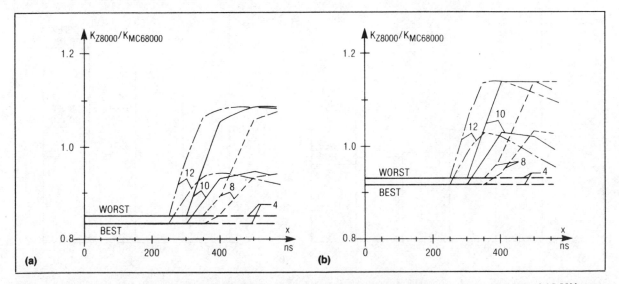

Figure 7. $K_{Z8000}/K_{MC68000}$ as a function of the memory speed x for the display mechanism on 4, 8, 10, and 12-MHz processors (a) and for Tanenbaum's proposal on 4, 8, 10, and 12-MHz processors (b).

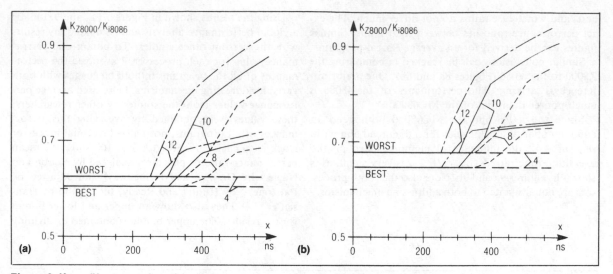

Figure 8. K_{Z8000}/K_{i8086} as a function of the memory speed x for the display mechanism on 4, 8, 10, and 12-MHz processors (a) and for Tanenbaum's proposal on 4, 8, 10, and 12-MHz processors (b).

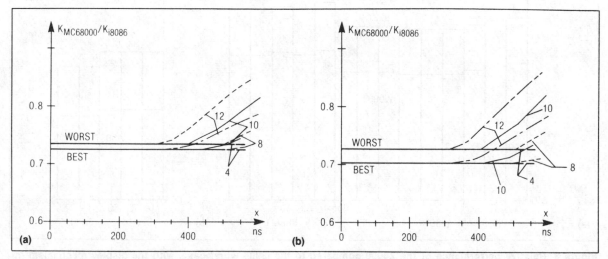

Figure 9. $K_{MC68000}/K_{i8086}$ as a function of the memory speed x for the display mechanism on 4, 8, 10, and 12-MHz processors (a) and for Tanenbaum's proposal on 4, 8, 10, and 12-MHz processors (b).

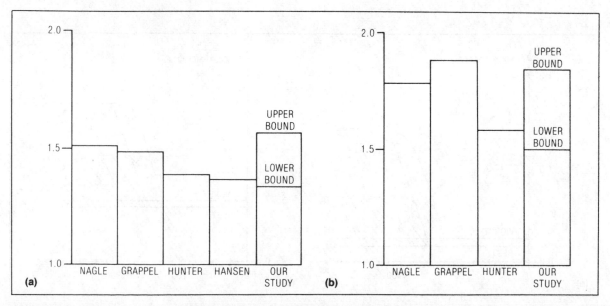

Figure 10. Relative performance of the MC68000 to the i8086 as determined in five studies (a); relative performance of the Z8000 to the i8086 as determined in four studies (b).

the best-case results for one processor by the worst-case results for the other. The lower bound is similarly obtained by dividing the worst-case results for the first processor by the best-case results for the second processor. The real performance ratio will always lie in the range defined by these bounds. Note that there is a great resemblance among the studies, even when my performance figures include only the times to execute procedure and block entry/exit and perform variable addressing in high-level-language programs. This proves that the results from an *analytical* model provide great accuracy.

The results can also be combined to provide a cost/performance analysis. Figure 11 shows a global comparison of the three processors with a set of possible clock frequencies. (We assume that each processor is or will be available with a 4, 8, 10, or 12-MHz clock.) The results depicted are for an average Pascal program having the display mechanism, but similar results will be obtained for an average Algol program and/or Tanenbaum's proposal. Even when programs producing different statistics are used, the results will be similar. Thus, various microprocessor system configurations will yield a relative performance of, say, 3.5: a 12-MHz Z8000 with 395-nanosecond memory, a 12-MHz MC68000 with 445-nanosecond memory, a 10-MHz Z8000 with 380-nanosecond memory, or a 10-MHz MC68000 with 415-nanosecond memory. These solutions are for the worst-case model.

By taking a set of processors T_k with a memory speed xw_k, we can find the lowest-cost configuration, depending on the cost of the processor P_k, the cost of the memory M_k, and the size of the memory S. The processor cost P_k is a function of the processor type T_k, which is characterized by the manufacturer m_k and the clock frequency f_k—thus, $P_k = P(m_k, f_k)$. The memory cost M_k is a function of the memory speed xw_k, i.e., $M_k = M(xw_k)$. Thus, for each possible configuration k we obtain a cost figure C_k:

$$C_k = P(m_k, f_k) + S \cdot M(xw_k). \qquad (13)$$

The lowest-cost processor/memory configuration will have the smallest C_k.

Since we used the worst-case model to obtain the memory speed xw_k, we can be sure that the relative performance will be at least minimally acceptable, since the real performance value will always lie in the range [worst case, best case]. Systems using memories with a speed xb_k obtained under the best-case model *can* also have the same performance figure, even with a slower memory, since $xb_k > xw_k$. For instance, a relative performance of 3.5 can be provided by a 10-MHz MC68000 and a memory with access time of 540 nanoseconds (>415 nanoseconds), if the best-case results are taken. Since the memory is slower, the cost will be lower. However, given a memory speed xb_k, it cannot be *guaranteed* that the performance will actually have the value in mind, since the figures are obtained under best-case models and the real performance value can thus be smaller. The choice of memory speed depends on whether the application is time-sensitive. If it is, the worst-case speed xw_k must be used to ensure that the desired performance will be obtained. If the application is cost-sensitive rather than time-sensitive, the best-case speed xb_k must be used, since it always results in a cheaper configuration than if the worst-case speed is used. Of course, this approach cannot ensure that the desired performance will be obtained.

We have analyzed the performance of addressing mechanism implementations for block-structured high-level languages. The performance measure defined here can be written as a (scalar) product of three arrays, each array depending on one parameter set. These three sets are completely independent—that is, they comprise technological, architectural, and program-statistical sets.

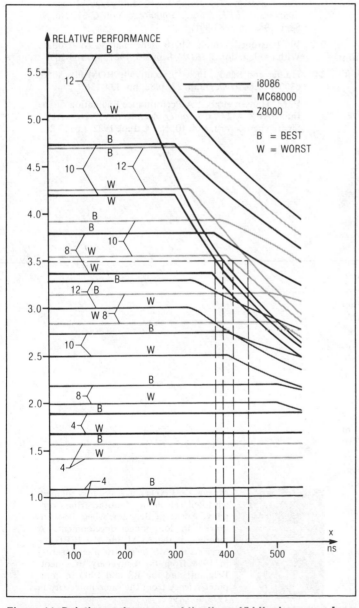

Figure 11. Relative performance of the three 16-bit micros as a function of the memory speed x.

127

This model provided a basis for comparing, in three contemporary 16-bit microprocessors, the implementation of the traditional display mechanism to the implementation of the mechanism proposed by Tanenbaum. A best/worst-case analysis overcame the lack of information about the microcode and its relationship to instruction prefetch behavior.

The performance figures presented here were consistent with one another and with those derived in other studies. They showed that Tanenbaum's proposal provided a uniformly better performance than the display mechanism. The figures also indicated the relative performance of the three microprocessors—the Z8000 did the best, the MC68000 the second-best, and the i8086 the worst. These results agreed well with earlier data. The methods presented here also showed how to determine the influence of memory speed on performance, and how the results could be used to obtain a cost/performance figure.∎

Acknowledgment

The author wishes to thank Dr. J. Van Campenhout for his many helpful comments and for his thorough proofreading.

References

1. D. Ferrari, *Computer Systems Performance Evaluation*, Prentice-Hall, Englewood Cliffs, NJ, 1978.

2. W. E. Burr and R. Gordon, "Selecting a Military Computer Architecture," *Computer*, Vol. 10, No. 10, Oct. 1977, pp. 16-23.

3. S. H. Fuller and W. E. Burr, "Measurement and Evaluation of Alternative Computer Architectures," *Computer*, Vol. 10, No. 10, Oct. 1977, pp. 24-35.

4. W. B. Dietz and L. Szewerenko, "Architectural Efficiency Measures: An Overview of Three Studies," *Computer*, Vol. 12, No. 4, Apr. 1979, pp. 26-32.

5. R. D. Grappel and J. E. Hemenway, "A Tale of Four Micros: Benchmarks Quantify Performance," *EDN*, Apr. 1, 1981, pp. 179-265.

6. V. P. Nelson and H. T. Nagle, "Digital Filtering Performance Comparison of 16-bit Microcomputers," *IEEE Micro*, Vol. 1, No. 1, Feb. 1981, pp. 32-41.

7. L. J. Shustek, "Analysis and Performance of Computer Instruction Sets," PhD thesis, Stanford University, Stanford, CA, 1978.

8. A. Lunde, "Empirical Evaluation of Some Features of Instruction Set Processor Architectures," *Comm. ACM*, Vol. 20, No. 3, Mar. 1977, pp. 143-153.

9. A. P. Batson, R. E. Brundage, and J. P. Kearns, "Design Data for Algol 60 Machines," *Proc. 3rd Ann. Symp. Computer Architecture*, 1976, pp. 151-154.

10. A. S. Tanenbaum, "Implications of Structured Programming for Machine Architecture," *Comm. ACM*, Vol. 21, No. 3, Mar. 1978, pp. 237-245.

11. R. P. Blake, "Exploring a Stack Architecture," *Computer*, Vol. 10, No. 5, May 1977, pp. 30-38.

12. E. W. Dijkstra, "Recursive Programming," *Numerische Math*, Vol. 2, 1960, pp. 312-318.

13. M. L. De Prycker, "A Performance Analysis of the Implementation of Addressing Methods in Block-structured Languages," *IEEE Trans. Computers*, Vol. C-31, No. 2, Feb. 1982, pp. 155-163.

14. *The 8086 Family User's Manual*, Intel Corp., Santa Clara, CA, 1979.

15. *Z8000 CPU Technical Manual*, Zilog Corp., Cupertino, CA, 1980.

16. *MC68000 Microprocessor User's Manual*, Motorola Semiconductor Products, Inc., Phoenix, AZ, 1979.

17. M. L. De Prycker, "Representing the Effects of Instruction Prefetch in a Microprocessor Performance Model," to appear in *IEEE Trans. Computers*.

18. *HP Algol*, Hewlett-Packard Co., Cupertino, CA, 1971.

19. *Pascal for PDP-11 Under RSX/IAS*, Tech. Report S-126 25, L.M. Ericsson Co., Stockholm, Sweden, 1979.

20. K. Jensen and N. Wirth, *Pascal User Manual and Report*, Springer Verlag, Berlin, 1976.

21. A. V. Aho and J. D. Ullman, *Principles of Compiler Design*, Addison-Wesley, Reading, MA, 1977.

22. M. L. De Prycker, "On the Development of a Measurement System for High-Level Language Program Statistics," *IEEE Trans. Computers*, Vol. C-31, No. 9, Sept. 1982, pp. 883-891.

23. W. Patstone, "16-bit Micro Benchmarks: An Update With Explanations," *EDN*, Sept. 16, 1981, pp. 169-203.

24. Hunter and Ready, Inc., "Executive in ROM Fits 8086, 68000," *Electronics*, Jan. 27, 1982, pp. 134-136.

25. P. M. Hansen et al., "A Performance Evaluation of the Intel iAPX 432," *Computer Architecture News* (ACM Sigarch newsletter), Vol. 10, No. 4, June 1982, pp. 17-26.

Martin De Prycker is a systems engineer with Bell Telephone Manufacturing Company, Antwerp, Belgium, where he is involved in long-range development. A member of the ACM and the IEEE, he received the MS in electrical engineering in 1978 from the University of Ghent, Belgium, and the BS and PhD in computer science from the same university in 1979 and 1982.

De Prycker's address is Bell Telephone Manufacturing Company, EA5, Fr. Wellesplein 1, B2000 Antwerpen, Belgium.

The supermicros have arrived. Their 32-bit structure—and their performance—quite justifiably earn them the name "micromainframes."

An Architectural Comparison of 32-bit Microprocessors

Amar Gupta and Hoo-min D. Toong

Massachusetts Institute of Technology

The pace of the current microelectronic revolution is unparalleled; it even outstrips the pace of development of the mainframe computer itself. In just a little over a decade, microprocessors have evolved from the Intel 4004, a four-bit machine, to 32-bit chips. In the case of mainframe computers, the "maturity" of a 32-bit word length came with the IBM 360 series, *two* decades after the first computers. The pace of microprocessor development is made even more impressive by the newest generation of microprocessors, which offers sophistications such as object-oriented architecture and easy network interfacing. Such features are considered innovative even in mainframe computers.

The semiconductor industry continues to invest heavily in the development of more complex and more powerful microprocessors. The characteristics and performance of single-chip 16-bit microprocessors have been summarized in earlier articles we have written.[1,2] Announcements of 32-bit chips have been made by several manufacturers in the US and abroad. Chips like the NS 16032 offer 32-bit internal data paths but only 16-bit external paths. One microprocessor, the Intel iAPX 432, uses three chips instead of one to implement a very sophisticated architecture. Other chips, designed by companies like IBM, Hewlett-Packard, Bell Labs, and Rockwell, are intended for internal use but are harbingers of similar public-domain products. A major contender from Japan is the 20,000-gate CMOS microprocessor fabricated by Nippon Telegraph and Telephone.

The MC68000, with 32-bit internal and 16-bit external data paths, was considered by us in an earlier article in *IEEE Micro*.[1] Its performance relative to other 32-bit microprocessors is considered later in this article. The MC68020, with 32-bit external data paths, and other unreleased 32-bit microprocessors of major commercial impact are not included here due to the preliminary nature of their specifications. A useful insight into the current direction of microprocessor innovation can be

129

EHO214-7/84/0000/0129$01.00©1983 IEEE

achieved by studying and comparing the following better-documented 32-bit products:

- the NS 16032 chip designed by National,[3,4]
- the Bellmac-32A chip designed by Bell Labs,[5,6]
- the "no name" 32-bit CPU chip designed by Hewlett-Packard,[7,8] and
- the iAPX 432 chip set designed by Intel.[9-14]

In the following sections, we examine and compare the architectures of these four processors.

General characteristics

The general characteristics of the four microprocessors are summarized in Table 1.

The NS 16032. This microprocessor represents the high end of the NS 16000 family. Internally, it uses 32-bit data paths and 32-bit address arithmetic to access memory without the overhead of segmentation registers. Externally, it uses a multiplexed address and data bus with 24 bits of external address and 16 bits of external data; this multiplexing has enabled the device to be packaged in a 48-pin package, at the cost of reduced external data rates.

The NS 16032 chip implements 82 basic instructions and has an address range of 16M bytes with 24-bit address pointers; this address range can be enhanced to 32M bytes with a memory management unit. The chip has a three-stage pipeline. Implementation of an eight-byte instruction fetch-ahead queue provides an overlapped instruction fetch and execute facility. Other highlights include modular software capabilities, a fully orthogonal instruction set, a virtual memory facility, and string processing capabilities. These features can be expanded through the use of auxiliary chips. The NS 16081, for example, provides 32-bit and 64-bit floating-point capabilities, while the NS 16082 memory management unit sup-

ports demand-paged virtual memory. Together, these three chips implement a software architecture comparable in sophistication to a VAX-11/780, with about half that machine's performance and a much lower price.[4] Communication between the NS 16032 CPU and an NS 16202 interrupt control unit may involve transfer of information on the local bus as well as on the system bus, and incur the overheads and delays inherent in such transfers.

The Bellmac-32A. Besides being a true 32-bit microprocessor, the Bellmac-32A is much more sophisticated technologically than the NS 16032. In general, CMOS circuits provide faster speed and lower power consumption than circuits implemented with traditional PMOS and NMOS technology. The Bellmac-32A single-chip CPU is fabricated in twin-tub CMOS and uses "domino circuits" that operate at twice the speed of previous CMOS circuits and enable a single clock pulse to activate many circuits simultaneously. The chip uses two non-overlapping clocks, each of 10 MHz and both generated from a 40-MHz external clock.[24]

The Bellmac-32A chip has been designed to provide support for the C programming language. Single instructions can move blocks of data from memory to memory, or push and pop a group of registers with respect to the stack. Sophisticated hardware facilities include a barrel-shift circuit that shifts 0 to 31 bits in a single cycle. The operating system, which can be included in the address space of every process, includes a hardware interface to assist process-oriented operating system control software. It also includes a set of exception handling mechanisms. The exception structure provides four levels of execution privilege and is intended for real-time control applications. Neither floating-point nor decimal arithmetic is supported, although an auxiliary processor to perform such operations is being investigated.[6] At present, "extension" instructions are provided for these functions. There is little compatibility with any existing microprocessor.

Table 1.
General characteristics of the four 32-bit microprocessors.

	NS 16032[15]	BELLMAC-32A[16,24]	HP 32-BIT CPU[17]	INTEL iAPX 432[18]
YEAR OF COMMERCIAL INTRODUCTION	1982	1982*	1982*	1981
TECHNOLOGY	3.5-μm NMOS	2.5-μm DOMINO CMOS	1.5/1.0-μm NMOS	HMOS
NO. OF TRANSISTORS	60,000	146,000	450,000	219,000 ON 3 CHIPS
SIZE OF CHIP	84,000 MIL^2	160,000 MIL^2	48,400 MIL^2	100,000 MIL^2 EACH
POWER DISSIPATION	1.25 WATTS	0.7 WATT AT 8 MHz	4 WATTS	2.5 WATTS/CHIP
PIN COUNT	48	63 ACTIVE 84 TOTAL	83	64 PER CHIP
BASIC CLOCK FREQUENCY	10 MHz	10 MHz	18 MHz	8 MHz
DIRECT ADDRESS RANGE (BYTES)	2^{24}; 2^{25} WITH MMU	2^{32}	2^{29} REAL; 2^{41} VIRTUAL	2^{24} REAL; 2^{40} VIRTUAL
NO. OF GENERAL-PURPOSE REGISTERS	8	16 USER-VISIBLE	28 (NOT ALL GENERAL-PURPOSE)	NO REGISTERS VISIBLE TO USER
NO. OF BASIC INSTRUCTIONS	82	169	230	221
NO. OF ADDRESSING MODES	9	18	10	5

*CURRENTLY FOR INTERNAL USE ONLY.

The Bellmac-32A chip was developed in a relatively short time through the extensive use of computer-aided design techniques. These techniques make the Bellmac-32A "technology updatable." They include a mask generation program that enables old mask sets to be easily updated to new rules, and a facility that provides automatic generation of new simulation files. With these techniques, an existing design can benefit from the advances in fabrication technology that permit thinner line widths. On the chip itself, special internal features provide access to most registers for test and debug purposes. Unlike the Hewlett-Packard chip, which will be discussed in the next section, the Bellmac has no facility for automatic self-test during power-up.

The HP 32-bit chip. This no-name, no-number device has the highest circuit density of any microprocessor—450,000 transistors on a single, 48,400 mil^2 chip. Implemented in double-layer-metal NMOS with a one-micrometer pitch, this microprocessor uses two nonoverlapping clocks, each of 18 MHz frequency and both generated from an external 36-MHz clock. The chip is microcoded with 9K (38-bit) words of ROM control store addressed via a set of 14-bit registers in the sequence stack. The microinstructions are decoded by a PLA. Most of the microinstructions execute in one clock cycle of 55 nanoseconds. Pipelining of memory operations permits initiation of a 32-bit memory read every two states (every 110 nanoseconds), even though the memory access time is longer. Like the other chips considered so far, the HP device has a three-level pipeline—this is implemented through a CIR (current instruction register), an NIR (next instruction register), and a PIR (prefetch instruction register). A self-test routine, executed by the CPU during power-up, automatically tests operations internal to the chip.

The HP chip offers several sophisticated hardware and software features. A hardware-implemented n-bit barrel shifter can shift a 32-bit quantity right or left 0 to 31 places in a single clock cycle. The load instruction includes automatic bounds checking and takes only 550 nanoseconds. The arithmetic and logical instructions can manipulate the 32- and 64-bit floating-point operands specified in the proposed IEEE floating-point standard. Text editing capabilities are inherent in the move and string instructions that manipulate byte arrays and string-type data. All communication to and from the chip uses the memory-processor bus. This 32-bit-wide multiplexed address/data bus permits pipelined data transfers at 36M bytes per second. Facilities to communicate with the memory and with peripheral devices are provided by a memory controller chip and an I/O processor chip, respectively.

The iAPX 432. In many respects, the Intel iAPX 432 is very different from the chips described above. The others are single-chip CPUs, but the iAPX 432 is a three-chip set. These three chips are tied together through a processor-memory interconnection bus that is different from the traditional Intel Multibus. In addition, the iAPX 432 was designed to support the Ada programming language. Just as the Burroughs 5000 initiated a trend, two decades ago, toward architectures specifically designed to support high-level languages, so the iAPX 432 may start a trend toward architectures specifically designed to be programmed in a particular high-level language.

The General Data Processor System, or GDP, is a subset of the iAPX 432. It consists of two chips—the iAPX 43201, with 110,000 transistors, which is responsible for instruction decoding; and the iAPX 43202, with 49,000 transistors, which performs actual instruction execution. The iAPX 43203 I/O interface processor, containing 60,000 transistors, performs I/O interface functions and possesses limited capabilities for execution of microcode. There is an additional chip—a multiprocessor memory interface—that provides the signals required for packet bus interconnection. The Intel iAPX 432 is architecturally very different from its predecessors, namely the 8080, 8085, and 8086. This difference, although providing hardware enhancements, newer functions, and higher overall throughput, greatly limits programming compatibility between the iAPX 432 and earlier Intel products.

The total physical address size is limited to 2^{24} bytes. The upper limit on the logical address space is 2^{40} bytes. However, at any instant the logical addressing environment of a program is restricted to 2^{32} bytes. The instructions are of variable length, ranging from six bits to 344 bits. Each instruction's operator can have zero, one, two, or three operands. The GDP chip set has built-in security mechanisms that restrict access to programs and data on a "need-to-know" basis. Other noteworthy features include hardware-implemented concurrent programming and self-dispatching processors with hardware-implemented process scheduling. In addition, the processor can perform specialized functions such as floating-point and string operations without needing to attach specialized auxiliary chips.

Architectural details

Technology. All the chips reflect a conscious attempt toward the integration of an enormously large number of transistors. Even with a significantly smaller chip size, Hewlett-Packard has packaged the largest number—450,000—on a single chip, almost twice what Intel has packaged on its three chips put together. In order to achieve this density, HP used an electron beam to generate masks that provide 1.5-micrometer wide lines and 1.0-micrometer-wide spaces, with ±0.25-micrometer tolerances. The large number of devices and the narrowness of the lines contribute to the chip's relatively high power dissipation of four watts. To package the device, Hewlett-Packard uses a copper core, on which the CPU and auxiliary chips are directly mounted, and four layers of interconnect, which are separated by low-capacitance Teflon dielectrics. The HP chip, the NS 16032, and the iAPX 432 are all implemented in NMOS, although Intel prefers to call it N-channel, silicon-gate HMOS.

The NS 16032 and iAPX 432 have larger structures, and hence lower transistor densities, than the HP chip. National and Intel took this approach because their chips are intended to be openly sold in the world market. Needing large numbers of chips, the companies chose a structure size that would give them high yields.

131

Because of its CMOS implementation, the Bellmac-32A consumes the least power of the four microprocessors. The twin-tub CMOS process (Figure 1) provides high switching speeds in both N- and P-channel devices because each tub is separately implanted for optimum doping. Classical CMOS logic designs have an equal number of N- and P-channel devices. Newer CMOS designs use 80 percent N-channel devices and only 20 percent P-channel devices. This ratio of N-channel to P-channel devices makes it possible to have high circuit densities while retaining the CMOS advantages of fast speed and low power consumption.

Principles of operation. The basic structure of the NS 16032 is shown in Figure 2. The instructions are fetched via the 24-bit-wide multiplexed address/data bus. An instruction fetch-ahead queue provides overlap of instruction fetch and execution and aligns incoming instructions to 16-bit boundaries. The queue consists of a double-ended eight-byte FIFO with 16-bit input and output

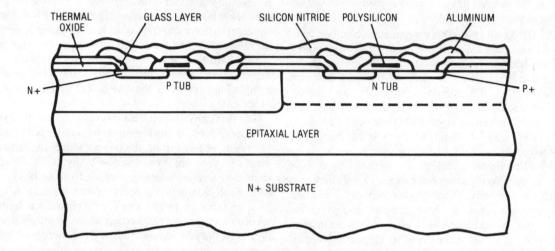

Figure 1. The Bellmac-32A is implemented in twin-tub domino CMOS. This process gives the microprocessor high switching speed in both N- and P-channel devices, because each tub is separately implanted for optimum doping. The process easily scales down for denser designs. The N+ substrate layer prevents the thyristor-like latch-up usually found in CMOS circuits. (Figure adapted from A. F. Shackil, "Microprocessors," *IEEE Spectrum*, Jan. 1982, page 33.)

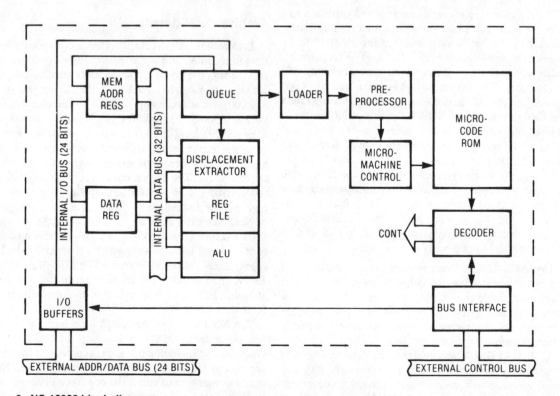

Figure 2. NS 16032 block diagram.

buses. The loader extracts the instruction from the queue and decodes it into a basic opcode, an operand length, address modes, and ALU control fields. The loader can decode two bytes every 100 nanoseconds. So that complex instructions can be efficiently executed without consuming excessive microcode ROM space, a two-level microcode (similar to that used in the Motorola 68000[1]) enables sharing of common effective address-calculation routines by all instructions and avoids both time-consuming subroutine calls and space-consuming repeated microcode flows. A preprocessor controls the sequence of instruction execution, while the micromachine controls the individual execution steps. As microinstruction n is executed, microinstruction $n + 1$ is decoded, and microinstruction $n + 2$ is selected by the microcode ROM address decoder. This procedure results in an effective 100-nanosecond microinstruction execution rate. A hardware backup mechanism saves contents of the processor status register, the stack pointer, and the program counter, and automatically restores them to their original values in the case of an instruction retry.

The structure of the Bellmac-32A is shown in Figure 3. Like the NS 16032, it consists of two distinct functional units—a fetch unit which controls interactions with the external memory and an execution unit which controls the manipulation and processing of data. Both units, as well as the bus, have full 32-bit capability. The instruction stream is byte-oriented. The first byte specifies the addressing mode and the register, and the subsequent bytes specify additional data. All byte and half-word operands are sign- or zero-extended to 32-bits when they are fetched. Instructions are monadic if there is one operator, dyadic if there are two operators, or triadic if there are three operators. Instructions fetched from the memory are stored in the instruction queue and translated into a series of microinstructions via a PLA. An arithmetic address unit performs all address calculations. An ALU in the execute block performs the actual execution of microinstructions. The emphasis on support of process-oriented operating systems generates a need to store instructions, data, and register values associated with a process whenever there is a switch from one process to another. The Bellmac-32A provides these storage functions in hardware.

The HP 32-bit chip, shown in Figure 4, is similar in operation to the previous two chips. It too uses a three-stage overlapping sequence for instruction prefetch and execution; it too uses a microcoded structure. The microcode control-store ROM is organized as 9216 words, each of 38 bits. Microinstructions accessed from the ROM are decoded by a PLA; they drive control lines which determine the operations of the 32-bit register stack and the ALU. The flow of instructions to the PLA is controlled by a sequencing machine, which contains a microprogram counter, a set of incrementers, three registers for microcode subroutine return addresses, and a machine instruction opcode decoder. The opcode decoder generates the starting address in the control store for the microcode routine that implements each machine instruction. The test condition multiplexer facilitates conditional jumps and skips in the microcode. The ALU contains an n-bit shifter, a 32-bit logical selector, and a 32-bit full look-ahead adder which also performs integer multiplication and division via special hardware.

The operation of the iAPX 432 involves communication among the iAPX 43201 instruction fetch and decode unit, the iAPX 43202 instruction execution unit, and the iAPX 43203 I/O interface unit. This communication is

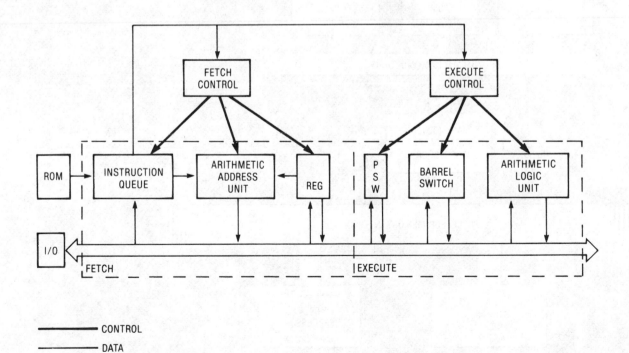

Figure 3. Bellmac-32A CPU architecture.

Figure 4. The HP 32-bit microprocessor.

ulated in the form of eight-bit characters, 16/32-bit ordinals, 16/32-bit integers, 32/64/80-bit floating-point variables, bit strings, arrays, records, or "objects," which are data structures containing information organized in some manner. Such objects can be referenced as a single entity; their internal organization is hidden and protected from all other procedures by hardware mechanisms. Each object has defined for it a set of operations (procedures or instructions) that are permitted to directly manipulate it. Examples of hardware-defined objects are

- processor objects, which represent the physical processors;
- process objects, which represent the individual computing tasks;
- context objects, which represent the activation of a program unit;
- dispatching-port objects, which provide a stream of work for a set of processors; and
- communications-port objects, which support interprocess communication and synchronization.

The iAPX 432 instruction set supports objects through messages (SEND, WAIT), context (CALL, RETURN), storage pools (ALLOCATE, TYPE), and processes (SCHEDULE, DISPATCH). At the macro level, the notion of objects permits each user to visualize a "virtual machine" that is exclusively his own. The concept of objects also makes multiprogramming and multiprocessing easier.

handled over the processor-memory interconnect bus, as shown in Figure 5. The characteristics of the three iAPX 432 chips are summarized in Table 2. Data can be manip-

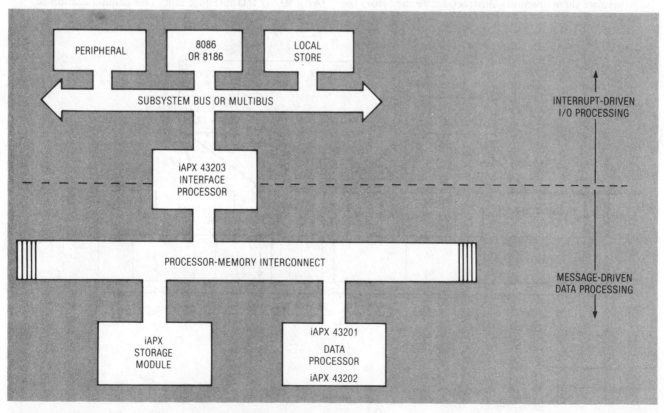

Figure 5. The Intel iAPX 432 three-chip 32-bit microprocessor.

Register organization. The NS 16032 contains sixteen registers—eight general-purpose ones (all 32 bits wide) and eight dedicated ones. The dedicated registers are as follows:

- The program counter register (24 bits) points to the current instruction being executed.
- The frame pointer register (24 bits) is used to access parameters and local variables on the stack.
- The static base register (24 bits) is used by software modules as a pointer to their respective global variables.
- The interrupt register (24 bits) points to the dispatch table for interrupts and traps.
- The two stack pointer registers (2 pointers each, 24 bits wide) point to the top of the stack used for interrupt routines and to the top of the stack used for other programs, respectively.
- The processor status register contains status codes.
- The module register points to the module description of the currently executing software module. The module register and the processor status register together use 32 bits.

To reduce register allocation problems, the instruction set has been designed to be symmetric with respect to memory and general register references.

The Bellmac-32A microprocessor contains a special program counter register and fifteen other registers, each 32 bits wide, that can be referenced in any addressing mode. Of these fifteen registers, three are used to support operating system functions (interrupt stack pointer, process control block pointer, processor status word) and can be written when the processor is in kernel execution level. Another three registers are used by certain instructions as a stack pointer, a frame pointer, and an argument pointer.

At the heart of the HP chip is a register stack, with 28 identical general-purpose registers, and an ALU, with four operand/result registers. Each of the general-purpose registers is 32 bits wide; not all are accessible by software. The register stack uses two databases and contains auxiliary logic such as top-of-stack and instruction registers. In any register, each of the 32 bit-cells can receive data from, or dump data to, either of the two data buses, as determined by the PLA outputs.

On account of the iAPX 432's multichip organization, its register structure cannot be equitably compared with that of the other chips. A microinstruction execution unit performs several functions traditionally associated with registers. Its functional subunit, the reference generation unit, or RGU, contains a 43-bit by 20-entry register array to support logical-to-physical address translation and access right verification. The other functional unit, the data manipulation unit, or DMU, contains its own set of operand registers, implemented as double-ended queues, to optimize arithmetic calculations on variable-length operands over a fixed-length (16-bit) bus. Intel claims that compiler complexity is reduced by keeping registers "behind the scenes" rather than as visible features of the architecture.[19]

Instruction set. Thirty-two-bit processors offer powerful instruction sets and support a wide spectrum of distinct data structures. These capabilities are summarized in Table 3.

The original specifications of the NS 16032 were too ambitious to be accommodated on a single chip with current technology. Several functions were offloaded from the main chip to auxiliary chips or slave processors. The total number of instructions was reduced from 100 to 82.

Floating-point instructions are trapped by the main processor and executed by the NS 16081 floating-point unit. The NS 16032 processor accepts data in bits, bytes,

Table 2.
Characteristics of the components of the iAPX 432.

CHARACTERISTIC	iAPX 43201		iAPX 43202		iAPX 43203	
DIE SIZE (IN μm)	318×323		366×313		358×326	
TOTAL DEVICE PLACEMENTS	110,000		49,000		60,000	
FUNCTION OF UNIT	INSTRUCTION FETCH AND DECODE		INSTRUCTION EXECUTION		I/O INTERFACE	
FUNCTIONAL SUB-UNITS	INSTRUCTION DECODER	MICROINSTRUCTION SEQUENCER (MIS)	DATA MANIPULATION UNIT (DMU)	REFERENCE GENERATION UNIT (RGU)	DATA ACQUISITION UNIT (DAU)	MICRO-EXECUTION UNIT (MEU)
FUNCTION OF SUBUNIT	DECODES VARIABLE-LENGTH, BIT-ALIGNED INSTRUCTIONS	SEQUENCES VERTICALLY ENCODED MICRO-INSTRUCTIONS AND INPUTS THEM TO THE MEU	CONTAINS OPERAND AND UNITS TO IMPLEMENT THE MACRO-INSTRUCTION SET EFFICIENTLY	CONTAINS REGISTERS AND FUNCTIONAL UNITS FOR LOGICAL-TO-PHYSICAL ADDRESS TRANSLATION AND ACCESS RIGHT VERIFICATION	PERFORMS PREFETCH AND POST-WRITE BUFFERING OF DATA AND GENERATES MAIN SYSTEM MEMORY ACCESSES	PERFORMS SYSTEM ACCESS, ENVIRONMENT MANIPULATION, INTER-PROCESSOR COMMUNICATION, AND ADDRESS MAP SET-UP

half-words, and words. Its ability to operate on variable-length character strings suits it to text processing applications. The NS 16032 offers instructions to operate on packed decimal quantities, on arrays, and on blocks. Instructions are of variable length. Common zero-operand instructions, such as the branch instruction, have a one-byte opcode. One-operand and two-operand instructions use a two-byte basic instruction. All instructions can use all applicable addressing modes. For code compactness, instructions are aligned on byte boundaries rather than on half-word or word boundaries.

The Bellmac-32A offers 169 instructions, 24 more than twice the number of the NS 16032. It too supports bytes, half-words, words, and bit fields. Strings are supported by special block instructions, and the string format conforms to the C language. C compatibility is manifest in the implementation of the instruction repertoire. The result of the unary operations NEGATE and COMPLEMENT (implemented as move instructions) can either replace the existing datum or be placed in a new location. The dyadic form stores the result in the second operand, and the triadic form places the result in the third operand, with the first two unaltered: these dyadic and triadic instructions are available for all operators. High-level procedure linkage operations assist in manipulating the stack frame, saving registers, and transferring control between procedures. Also, explicit instructions that permit the operating system to switch processes (CALL PROCESS and RETURN TO PROCESS) are provided. On the negative side, the Bellmac-32A does not support floating-point or decimal arithmetic.

The HP 32-bit chip offers a still larger repertoire of 230 instructions as well as 32- and 64-bit floating-point arithmetic. The load and store instructions can transfer double-words in addition to bits, bytes, half-words, and words. MOVE and STRING manipulate both unstructured byte arrays and structured string data. Hardware support includes four top-of-stack registers to handle push and pop operations and to provide "data valid" indications. The large number of transistors enables hardware implementation of features that have traditionally been done by software. For example, run-time bounds checking of addresses, performed on all memory accesses, is supported in hardware.

The iAPX 432 supports integer data in hardware; this has traditionally been done by software. Like the HP processor, the iAPX 432 performs run-time bounds checking of addresses. The iAPX 432 supports integer data in the form of half-words and words, and floating-point data in the form of words, double-words, and as 80-bit quantities. The usual 80-bit-wide quantities, called temporary reals, are used to store intermediate results to improve the accuracy of final results. Instructions are bit-variable in length and are not constrained to coincide with byte or word boundaries. The total number of instructions is 230, and the longest is 344 bits long. By allowing both stack and memory-to-memory arithmetic, the iAPX 432 can provide denser code and faster speeds for evaluating expressions. An instruction contains four fields. The first two fields, the class field and the format field, specify how many operands are in the instruction and how they are to be accessed. The third field, the reference field, contains the logical addresses of up to three operands. The last field specifies the operator itself. The processor reads an instruction segment in units of 32 bits. The instructions are decoded by the 43201 decoding chip, and the resulting stream of microinstructions are executed by the 43202 execution chip.

Memory organization. The NS 16032 provides a 16M-byte uniform address space and nine types of address mode (register, memory, immediate, absolute, register relative, memory relative, top-of-stack, external, and scaled index). An autoindexing address mode is not supported, as National feels that compilers seldom produce such code.[15] Moreover, properly supporting both autoindexing and demand-paged virtual memory is difficult.

Table 3.
Capabilities of the four microprocessors, not including functions provided by coprocessors or auxiliary chips.

	NS 16032	BELLMAC-32A	HP 32	iAPX 432
SYSTEM STRUCTURES				
UNIFORM ADDRESSABILITY	✔	✔	✔	✔
MODULE MAP AND MODULES	✔	X	X	✔
VIRTUAL	✔	✔	✔	✔
PRIMITIVE DATA TYPES				
BITS	✔	✔	✔	✔
INTEGER BYTE OR HALF-WORD	✔	✔	✔	✔
INTEGER WORD	✔	✔	✔	✔
LOGICAL BYTE OR HALF-WORD	✔	✔	✔	✔
LOGICAL WORD	✔	✔	✔	✔
CHARACTER STRINGS (VARIABLE)	✔	✔	✔	✔
BCD BYTE OR HALF-WORD	✔	X	X	X
BCD WORD	✔	X	✔	X
32-BIT FLOATING-POINT	X	X	✔	✔
64-BIT FLOATING-POINT	X	X	✔	✔
80-BIT FLOATING-POINT	X	X	X	✔
DATA STRUCTURES				
STACKS	✔	✔	✔	✔
ARRAYS	✔	✔	✔	✔
PACKED ARRAYS	✔	X	X	X
RECORDS	✔	X	X	✔
PACKED RECORDS	✔	X	X	X
STRINGS	✔	✔	✔	✔
PRIMITIVE CONTROL OPERATIONS				
CONDITION CODE PRIMITIVES	✔	✔	✔	✔
JUMP	✔	✔	✔	✔
CONDITIONAL BRANCH	✔	✔	✔	✔
ITERATIVE LOOP CONTROL	✔	X	✔	✔
SUBROUTINE CALL	✔	✔	✔	✔
MULTIWAY BRANCH	✔	✔	✔	✔
ORTHOGONAL INSTRUCTION SET		✔	✔	✔
CONTROL STRUCTURE				
EXTERNAL PROCEDURE CALL	✔	✔	✔	✔
SEMAPHORES	✔	✔	✔	✔
TRAPS	✔	✔	✔	✔
INTERRUPTS	✔	✔	✔	✔
SUPERVISOR CALL	✔	✔	✔	✔
OBJECTS	X	X	X	✔
HIERARCHICAL OPERATING SYSTEM	X	✔	X	✔
OTHER				
USER MICROCODE	X	X	X	X
DEBUG MODE	X	✔	✔	X
COMPATIBILITY WITH OTHER MICROPROCESSORS	X	X	X	X
SELF-TEST DURING POWER-UP	X	X	✔	X

✔ = FEATURE AVAILABLE
X = FEATURE NOT AVAILABLE

The lengths of address-mode offset constants are encoded in the upper two bits of the offset so that small offsets (-64 to 63) will require only one byte in the instruction stream and larger offsets will take two or four bytes. The integration of the memory management unit (see Figure 6) provides operating system and virtual memory support and enables addressing of up to 32M bytes. Virtual-address-to-real-address translation is accomplished through two levels of page tables and offset specifications. Each page, 512 bytes in size, is assigned a protection code, and this provides an access control mechanism. The memory management unit has eight registers and provides a flow tracing facility for both sequential and nonsequential instructions.

The Bellmac-32A chip offers several addressing modes: literal, byte/half-word/word immediate, register, register deferred, short offset (for frame and argument pointers), absolute, absolute deferred, byte/half-word/word displacement deferred, and expanded operand. The Bellmac-32A chip includes a set of exception handling mechanisms and a hardware interface for a process-oriented operating system; this operating system can be included in the address space of each process, enabling each to execute independently.

The HP 32-bit processor views the memory space for each program as an active code segment (one of 4096 code segments), a stack segment, a global data segment, and a set of 4096 external data segments. Segment pointers, maintained in 32-bit, on-chip registers, include ones to a base and limit register for the code, to stack and global data segments, to the current instruction address in the code segment, to the address of the most recent stack marker in the stack segment, and to the address of the top-of-stack in memory. External data segments are accessed via a set of memory-resident tables. A memory controller chip can control up to 20 RAM chips, each of 128K bits, or up to eight ROM chips, each of 640K bits, providing an effective memory space of up to 256K bytes of RAM or 512K bytes of ROM (Figure 7). The processor-memory bus has a transfer rate of 36M bytes per second, and the overlapped access method permits high throughput. The memory controller maps logical-to-physical addresses in 16K-byte blocks, and permits byte, half-word, word, and semaphore operations.

The iAPX 432 uses a segmented memory scheme having up to 2^{24} segments; each segment is 2^{16} bytes long, yielding a total virtual space of 2^{40} bytes. A two-step mapping process separates the relocation mechanism from the access control mechanism. Segments are of two types—access and data. The hardware recognizes them differently and rigorously enforces the distinction. The iAPX 432 provides four addressing modes: the base and index direct, used to access scalars; the base indirect, index direct, used to access records; the base direct, index

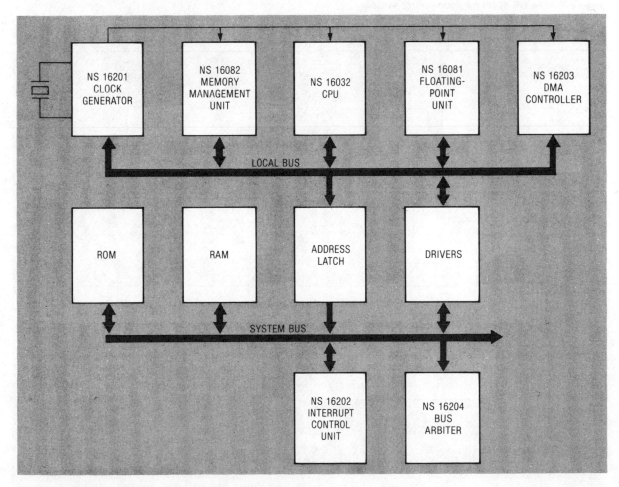

Figure 6. The National Semiconductor NS 16000 system.

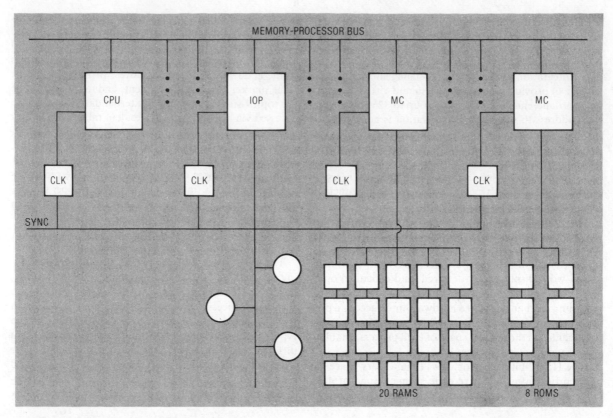

Figure 7. The HP 32-bit microcomputer system.

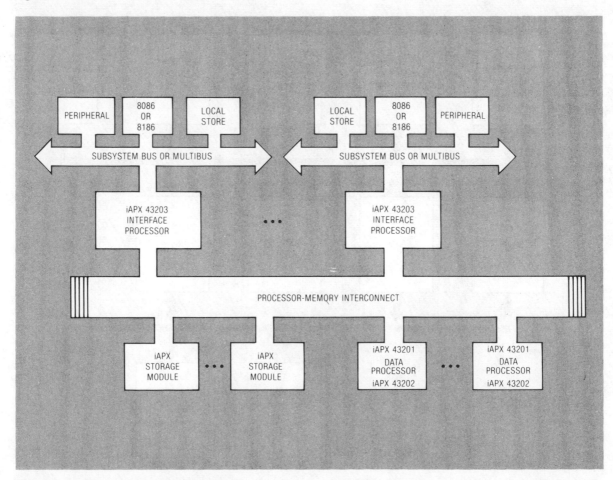

Figure 8. A typical multiple-iAPX-432 system.

indirect, used to access static arrays; and the base and index indirect, used to access dynamic arrays. The emphasis is on addressing objects through the use of access descriptors in the form of directory index and segment index. This object-oriented architecture facilitates implementation of high-level languages like Ada, Pascal, and PL/I.

Multiprocessing capabilities. To increase computational bandwidth and/or system resilience, the integration of several microprocessors frequently becomes necessary. The throughput and efficiency of integrated systems depend directly on the hardware and software interconnection mechanisms supported by the microprocessors. Many interconnection schemes have evolved over the years, but the single timeshared bus offers distinct advantages as an interconnection mechanism for multimicroprocessor systems. Under such a scheme, different modules can equally share the bus resource on a time-multiplexed or demand-multiplexed basis. National and HP indicate that their respective system-buses/processor-memory buses can provide the communications required for multiprocessing; the Bellmac also provides some multiprocessing support. Here, we will concentrate on the Intel product.

A typical iAPX-432-based multiprocessor configuration is shown in Figure 8. Different iAPX 432 processor pairs (each pair comprising the 43201 and the 43202) are connected to a single processor-memory interconnect bus. An existing 8086 processor cannot be connected directly to this bus; it must be connected through the Multibus and an interface processor, the iAPX 43203. Thus, if one 8086-based system is required to read information from a second 8086-based system in a configuration such as that shown in Figure 8, the request will involve the Multibus, an interface processor, the processor-memory interconnect bus, the second interface processor, and finally the second Multibus. The reply will involve the same interface/communication units, in the reverse order. In all, six distinct buses and four distinct interface processors will be used to complete a simple READ between the two 8086 systems. Such slave-to-slave operations are not efficiently supported by the suggested system organization.

Intel refers to the processor-memory interconnect bus as a Packetbus. This bus operates on a split-transaction basis. For example, a processor needing to access some data from memory will send a message to the appropriate storage module. The actual transfer of the message on the bus occurs when the arbitration mechanism grants the bus to the particular CPU. When the request for the data is received by the storage module, it accesses the data, but during this period of data access the bus is freed up for use by others. Finally, when the storage module is ready with the data, it requests the bus, gets it, and sends the "reply" to the CPU. The freeing up of the bus during the period of memory access—which is significantly longer than the bus service time—enables more processors to communicate on the same bus in a given span. In the iAPX 432, variable-length (1 to 10 bytes) data messages are used for request/reply; a 32-bit word can be transferred in 250 nanoseconds.

Hewlett-Packard also uses a demand-multiplexed bus,[17] with a single CPU using 30 percent of the total bus bandwidth for typical instruction mixes. In any multiprocessor environment, the number of bus users increases as the number of processors increases, resulting in greater bus contention. Also, additional overhead is incurred in controlling and coordinating multiple resources. The latter overhead is difficult to estimate, and most studies simply neglect to take it into account. Figure 9 reflects Intel's estimates of the effective number of processors versus the actual number of processors. Since a dual-processor configuration is shown as having twice the processing power of a single-processor one, the exclusion of software overhead is evident. Notice that the curve flattens off quickly. No matter the number of physical processors used, it is impossible to get an aggregate performance exceeding four times the power of a single processor on a single processor-memory bus. Hewlett-Packard[17] claims that with four processors overall multitasking performance ranges from 2.9 to 3.7 times the uniprocessor performance, depending on the instruction mix. Studies of other single-timeshared-bus systems[20] show that with proper interface circuitry and bus protocols, one can integrate up to 25 processors on a single bus, with positive incremental increases in overall system throughput.

Performance estimates

The timing estimates for several elementary operations, summarized in Table 4, must be interpreted with caution. Actual throughput is a function of the exact instruction sequence, displacements, data lengths, clock frequency, and other factors. Also, since the figures have been provided by the manufacturers, it is appropriate to assume that they reflect optimal estimates. Notice that the comparison is being made at dissimilar clock frequencies. In the case of Intel, several chips are involved and the timings include some operating overhead.

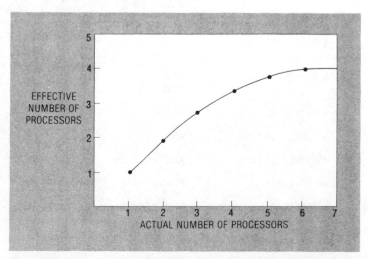

Figure 9. Intel's estimate of iAPX 432 bus efficiency for a single memory bus.

Table 4. Timing estimates for the four microprocessors (in microseconds unless otherwise specified).

OPERATION	NS 16032[15]	BELLMAC-32A[16,24]	HP 32[17]	iAPX 432
GENERAL: CLOCK SPEED	10 MHz	10 MHz	18 MHz	8 MHz
MOVE: MEMORY TO REGISTER	1.5	0.95	0.56	0.75
ADD: 32-BIT INTEGER	1.6	0.4	0.055 (HARDWARE TIME) 0.275 (INSTRUC-TION TIME)	0.5
ADD: FLOATING-POINT	9.3 WITH NS 16081	NOT SUPPORTED IN HARDWARE	6.0 (FOR 64-BIT) 4.7 (FOR 32-BIT)	19.125 (FOR 80-BIT)
MULTIPLY: 32-BIT INTEGER	8.3	1.8-9.5, DEPENDING ON OPERANDS	1.8 (HARDWARE TIME) 2.9 (INSTRUC-TION TIME)	6.375
MULTIPLY: FLOATING-POINT	7.1 (FOR 64-BIT) WITH NS 16081	NOT SUPPORTED IN HARDWARE	10.4 (FOR 64-BIT) 5.1 (FOR 32-BIT)	27.875 (FOR 80-BIT)
DIVIDE: 32-BIT INTEGER	9.2	DEPENDENT ON OPERANDS	9.4 (64-BIT/32-BIT) 5.2 (32-BIT/32-BIT)	10.625
DIVIDE: FLOATING-POINT	10.8 WITH NS 16081	NOT SUPPORTED IN HARDWARE	16.0 (FOR 64-BIT) 6.5 (FOR 32-BIT)	48.25 (FOR 80-BIT)

Table 5. Relative code sizes (from Hansen et al.[21]).

MACHINE	LANGUAGE	WORD SIZE	RATIO TO VMS PASCAL (<1 = > SMALLER)				
			SEARCH	SIEVE	PUZZLE	ACKER	AVG ± SD
VAX-11/780	C	32	0.60	0.38	0.77	0.45	0.5 ± 0.2
	PASCAL (UNIX)	32	0.95	1.24	1.49	0.72	1.1 ± 0.3
68000	C	32	0.79	0.55	1.01	0.50	0.7 ± 0.2
	PASCAL	16	0.72	0.29	0.60	0.36	0.5 ± 0.2
	PASCAL	32	0.74	0.31	0.64	0.38	0.5 ± 0.2
8086	PASCAL	16	0.94	0.85	0.79	0.91	0.9 ± 0.1
432 (REL. 3)	ADA	16	0.76	0.44	0.84	0.42	0.6 ± 0.2

(NUMBERS SMALLER THAN ONE INDICATE MORE COMPACT CODE THAN ON THE VAX.)

Table 6. Execution times (from Patterson[22]).

MACHINE	LANGUAGE	WORD SIZE	TIME (MILLISECONDS)			
			SEARCH	SIEVE	PUZZLE	ACKER
VAX-11/780	C	32	1.4	250	9400	4600
	PASCAL (UNIX)	32	1.6	220	11,900	7800
	PASCAL (VMS)	32	1.4	259	11,530	9850
68000 (8 MHz)	C	32	4.7	740	37,100	7800
	PASCAL	16	5.3	810	32,470	11,480
	PASCAL	32	5.8	960	32,520	12,320
68000 (16 MHz)	PASCAL	16	1.3	196	9180	2750
	PASCAL	32	1.5	246	9200	3080
8086 (5 MHz)	PASCAL	16	7.3	764	44,000	11,100
432/REL. 2 (4 MHz)	ADA	16	35.0	3200	350,000	260,000
432/REL. 3 (8 MHz)	ADA	16	4.4	978	45,700	47,800
80286 (8 MHz)	PASCAL	16	1.4	168	9138	2218
80286 (10 MHz)	PASCAL	16	1.1	135	7311	1774
HP 32-BIT CPU* (18 MHz)	PASCAL	32	NA	NA	7450	2590
NS 16032* (7 MHz)	PASCAL	32	NA	NA	24,000	9900

*VENDOR-PROVIDED INFORMATION

Hansen and his colleagues[21] used four programs (string search, sieve, puzzle, and Ackermann's function) to evaluate iAPX 432 performance in comparison to that of two 16-bit microprocessors and the VAX-11/780. Using a VAX-11/780 operating in a VMS Pascal environment as the base, they determined relative code sizes (Table 5). These figures indicate that in spite of bit-variable-length instructions, the code size was larger on the iAPX 432 as compared to the 68000, probably because of the inability of the former to refer to a local variable or constant with fewer than 16 bits of address. The execution timings are summarized in Tables 6 and 7.[22] In all these performance evaluation exercises, the iAPX 432 was tested as a high-level-language uniprocessor for integer and character programs; thus, any potential benefits arising from transparent multiprocessing, data security, or increased programmer productivity are not reflected.[21] Also, the timings for the Hewlett-Packard and National chips must be viewed with caution, as they have not been verified by any independent organization.

Overall, the performance of the newer microprocessors approaches that of mainframes. The Intel 432 takes 5.0 microseconds for a 32-bit integer multiply and 27.0 microseconds for an 80-bit floating-point multiply. The equivalent figures for an IBM 370/148 are 16.0 microseconds and 38.5 microseconds. In terms of basic computational power, the iAPX 432 is superior to an IBM 370/148. The Bellmac-32A chip and the HP 32-bit chip are expected to be superior to an IBM 370/158. However, the IBM 370 family is supported by many compilers and application programs; it will take some time for similar facilities to be available for 32-bit microprocessors. A typical end user will have to decide among several options: waiting for the desired application software to become commercially available, developing the desired software in house, or using an earlier generation microprocessor that is already supported by necessary software.

Selection strategy

The 32-bit word size of the newer microprocessors permits higher throughput, greater precision, and larger addressing space than those supported by earlier chips. The power that traditionally characterized mainframes is now exhibited by the four 32-bit microprocessors we have considered here. Overall performance is determined by the hardware and by the efficiency of the several layers of software that determine how a user sees the chip. The trend in microprocessors is toward microcoding and performing traditionally software-based functions in hardware. For example, the operating system function of job dispatching is performed entirely by hardware in the iAPX 432. The hardware shift circuit is another example. No longer is it possible to base evaluations on register-to-register-level instructions alone. Today one must analyze the match between the user's application and the functions being implemented in hardware. The situation is analogous to the mainframe world, where evaluations once were based on clock frequencies and elementary instruction timings, but today are based on benchmarks and simulation studies. The trend in the "micromainframe" world is the same.

The Intel iAPX 432 is not the only multichip, 32-bit processor. The HP 32-bit machine requires a memory controller and I/O processor to do meaningful work. Similarly, the NS 16032, to demonstrate its virtual memory and floating-point capabilities, requires two auxiliary chips. The final decision of Bell Labs regarding the floating-point processor for the Bellmac is not known. However, to tap their full potentials, the NS 16032 and the HP 32-bit CPU both need at least two auxiliary chips.

The HP and Bell Lab micros are reserved for use with company products. The much simpler National chip is compatible with the firm's 16008. However, not one of these chips has established a market niche to date, nor does any offer compatibility with earlier chips. The iAPX 432 is the most complex of the four, and it will take some time before it will be fully accepted. Also, it offers no direct compatibility with Intel's 8080, 8086, or other chip. This noncompatibility tends to negate Intel's advantage of a large established user base and software library. The 432's increased hardware capabilities, however, favor its use in areas such as database and transaction processing.

We have evaluated the four chips (Table 8) on the basis of available technical information. A is excellent, B is good, C is fair, and D is poor. As vendors announce newer chips, designers will face even greater difficulty in the selection exercise. Motorola has announced the MC68020, its first true 32-bit microprocessor; it is upward-compatible with, and similar in architecture to, the MC68000. National plans to offer the NS32032, with 32-bit external data paths, in 1983.[15] NCR has announced the microprogrammable NCR/32 four-chip set.[23]

Table 7.
Performance at eight MHz (from Patterson[22]).

WAIT STATES	MACHINE	LANGUAGE	TIME (MILLISECONDS)			
			SEARCH	SIEVE	PUZZLE	ACKER
	68000	PASCAL	5.3	810	32,470	11,480
4	432 (REL. 2)	ADA	17.5	1600	175,000	130,000
	432 (REL. 3)	ADA	4.4	978	45,700	47,800
	8086	PASCAL	4.6	448	27,500	6938
0	68000	PASCAL	2.6	392	18,360	5500
	80286	PASCAL	1.4	168	9138	2218

Table 8.
Ranking of the four 32-bit microprocessors.

	NS 16032	BELLMAC-32A	HP 32-BIT CPU	iAPX 432
SPEED	B	B	B	C
ADDRESS RANGE	B	A	A	B
COMPATIBILITY WITH OTHER MICROPROCESSORS	C	C	C	C
SOFTWARE SUPPORT	B	B	B	A
LARGE-SCALE MULTIPROCESSING CAPABILITY	B	B	B	A

The microprocessor industry has been characterized by an incredibly fast pace of technical development. We have gone from four-bit chips to 32-bit chips in just over eleven years. However, we see one development that will parallel the mainframe world—just as most mainframes eventually settled on a 32-bit structure, so should microprocessors eventually settle on 32 bits as a lasting standard. ∎

Acknowledgments

After this paper was accepted for publication, we asked the four vendors to correct any inaccuracies and to update facts and figures. We are grateful to the representatives of these vendors for their time and effort and their helpful comments and suggestions.

References

1. H. D. Toong and A. Gupta, "An Architectural Comparison of Contemporary 16-bit Microprocessors," *IEEE Micro,* Vol. 1, No. 2, May 1981, pp. 26-37.

2. H. D. Toong and A. Gupta, "Evaluation Kernels for Microprocessor Performance Analyses," *Performance Evaluation,* Vol. 2, No. 1, May 1982, pp. 1-8.

3. L. Kohn, "A 32b Microprocessor with Virtual Memory Support," *Proc. IEEE Int'l Solid-State Circuits Conf.,* Feb. 1981, pp. 232-233.

4. A. Kaminker et al., "A 32-bit Microprocessor with Virtual Memory Support," *IEEE J. Solid-State Circuits,* Oct. 1981, pp. 548-557.

5. B. T. Murphy et al., "A CMOS 32b Single Chip Microprocessor," *Proc. IEEE Int'l Solid-State Circuits Conf.,* Feb. 1981, pp. 230-231.

6. A. D. Berenbaum et al., "The Operating System and Language Support Features of the Bellmac-32 Microprocessor," *Proc. Symp. Architectural Support for Programming Languages and Operating Systems,* Mar. 1982, pp. 30-38.

7. J. W. Beyers et al., "A 32-bit VLSI CPU Chip," *IEEE J. Solid-State Circuits,* Oct. 1981, pp. 537-542.

8. J. M. Mikkelson et al., "An NMOS VLSI Process for Fabrication of a 32-bit CPU Chip," *IEEE J. Solid State Circuits,* Oct. 1981, pp. 542-547.

9. D.L. Budde et al., "The 32b Computer Execution Unit," *Proc. IEEE Int'l Solid-State Circuits Conf.,* Feb. 1981, pp. 112-113.

10. W. S. Richardson et al., "The 32b Computer Instruction Decoding Unit," *Proc. IEEE Int'l Solid-State Circuits Conf.,* Feb. 1981, pp. 114-115.

11. J. A. Bayliss et al., "The Interface Processor for the 32b Computer," *Proc. IEEE Int'l Solid-State Circuits Conf.,* Feb. 1981, pp. 116-117.

12. D. L. Budde et al., "The Execution Unit for the VLSI 432 General Data Processor," *IEEE J. Solid-State Circuits,* Oct. 1981, pp. 514-521.

13. J. A. Bayliss et al., "The Interface Processor for the Intel 432 32-bit Computer," *IEEE J. Solid-State Circuits,* Oct. 1981, pp. 522-530.

14. F. J. Pollack et al., "Supporting Ada Memory Management in the iAPX-432," *Proc. Symp. Architectural Support for Programming Languages and Operating Systems,* Mar. 1982, pp. 117-131.

15. S. Bal (National Semiconductor Corp.), personal communication, Nov. 19, 1982.

16. B. T. Murphy (Bell Laboratories), personal communication, Nov. 17, 1982.

17. D. Seccombe (Hewlett-Packard), personal communication, Nov. 8, 1982.

18. R. Martin (Intel Corp.), personal communication, Nov. 10, 1982.

19. *Intel 432 System Summary: Manager's Perspective,* Manual No. 171867-001, Intel Corp., Santa Clara, CA, 1981, p. 29.

20. H. D. Toong, S. O. Strommen, and E. R. Goodrich II, "A General Multi-Microprocessor Interconnection Mechanism for Non-Numeric Processing," *Proc. Fifth Workshop Computer Architecture for Non-Numeric Processing,* 1980, pp. 115-123.

21. P. M. Hansen et al., "A Performance Evaluation of the Intel iAPX 432," *Computer Architecture News* (ACM Sigarch newsletter), Vol. 10, No. 4, June 1982, pp. 17-26.

22. D. A. Patterson, "A Performance Evaluation of the Intel 80286," *Computer Architecture News* (ACM Sigarch newsletter), Vol. 10, No. 5, Sept. 1982, pp. 16-18.

23. W. R. Iversen, "32-bit Chip Set Will Offer Huge Microprogram Store," *Electronics,* Sept. 8, 1982, pp. 47-48.

24. J. Mao (Bell Laboratories), personal communication, Jan. 11, 1983.

Amar Gupta is a postdoctoral associate in the Sloan School of Management of the Massachusetts Institute of Technology. His interests include multiprocessor architectures, performance measurement, decision support systems, analytic modeling, office automation, and international technology transfer. He has been involved in research on tightly-coupled SIMD and MIMD machines.

Gupta received his BTech in electrical engineering in 1974 from the Indian Institute of Technology, Kanpur, his MS in management in 1980 from MIT's Sloan School, and his PhD in computer technology in 1980 from the Indian Institute of Technology, Delhi. In 1979, he was awarded the Rotary Fellowship for International Understanding, and in the 1980-1981 academic year, he received the Brooks' Prize, honorable mention, for his master's thesis at MIT. He is the editor, with Hoo-min Toong, of *Advanced Microprocessors,* which will be published by the IEEE Press in the spring of 1983.

Hoo-min D. Toong is on the faculty of the Sloan School of Management at the Massachusetts Institute of Technology, which he joined in 1978. He is in charge of the Digital Systems Laboratory of the Center for Information Systems Research of MIT. His research interests include very large database architectures, multiprocessors, distributed operating systems, and the organizational impact of such systems.

Toong received the BS in 1967, the MS and EE in 1969, and the PhD in electrical engineering and computer science in 1974, all from MIT. Before joining the Sloan School, he was a member of the Electrical Engineering and Computer Science Department of MIT. Toong is a member of Tau Beta Pi, Eta Kappa Nu, Sigma Xi, the IEEE, and the ACM.

The authors' address is the Center for Information Systems Research, Sloan School of Management, Massachusetts Institute of Technology, Mail Station E53-301, 77 Massachusetts Ave., Cambridge, MA 02139.

MICROPROCESSORS
& MICROCOMPUTERS
MICROPROCESSORS
& MICROCOMPUTERS

SELECTED REPRINTS ON
MICROPROCESSORS
& MICROCOMPUTERS

SECTION 3
ARCHITECTURE NOVEL/PROPOSED

Reprinted from *Computer*, June 1982, pages 33-45. Copyright © 1982 by The Institute of Electrical and Electronics Engineers, Inc.

Novel VLSI processor architectures, some implemented by only a few different types of simple cells, are leading the way towards a new generation of computers.

VLSI Processor Architectures

Philip C. Treleaven, University of Newcastle upon Tyne

As an illustration of the rapidly increasing complexity of integrated circuits, Charles Seitz of the California Institute of Technology developed the following analogy:

> In the mid-1960's the complexity of a chip was comparable to the street network of a small town. Most people can navigate such a network by memory without difficulty. Today's microprocessor, using a five-micron technology, is comparable to the entire San Francisco Bay Area. By the time a one-micron technology is solidly in place, designing a chip will be conparable to planning a street network covering all of California and Nevada at urban densities. The ultimate one-quarter micron technology will likely be capable of producing chips with the intricacy of an urban grid covering the entire North American continent.[1]

VLSI microprocessors containing 100,000 transistors, such as the recently announced 32-bit microprocessors from Intel (the iAPX 432) and Bell Laboratories (the Mac-32), are becoming more and more commonplace.[2,3] In fact, the term "VLSI processor architecture" is normally viewed as being synonymous with such designs.[4]

But as Gordon Moore, President of Intel Corporation, said at a relatively recent conference, "Beyond memory, I haven't the slightest idea of how to take advantage of VLSI . . . . How to best make use of the processing technology is what the problem is."[5] The reason for this pessimism is the escalating cost of designing and testing such complex VLSI processors.

However, Mead and Conway's *Introduction to VLSI Systems*,[6] and the companion Multiproject Chip (MPC)[7] courses and silicon foundries[8] they helped to establish, have together stimulated the rapid development of a new VLSI proccessor architecture "culture." A brief survey of these novel VLSI processor architectures will illustrate the exciting work going on in the area, most of which is still at the research stage.

A "good" VLSI architecture in the context of this article should have one or more following properties[9]:

(1) It should be implementable by only a few different types of simple cells.

(2) It should have simple and regular data and control paths so that the cells can be connected by a network with local and regular interconnections. (Long-distance or irregular communication is thus minimized.)

(3) It should use extensive pipelining and multiprocessing. In this way, a large number of cells are active at one time so that the overall computational rate of the simple cells is high.

As we shall see, a whole spectrum of processor architectures is under development based on this philosophy of simplicity and replication.

Special-purpose processors

A special-purpose VLSI processor is usually designed as a peripherial device attached to a conventional host computer. It may be a single chip built from a replication of simple cells, or a system built from identical simple chips, or it may be a chip that uses both of these techniques. Special-purpose processors have a number of advantages[9] that help reduce their cost:

- Only a few different, simple cells need to be designed and tested since most of the cells and chips are copies of a few basic models.
- Regular interconnection implies that the design is modular and extensible, so one can create a large

EHO214-7/84/0000/0145$01.00©1982 IEEE

processor by combining the designs of small cells and chips.

- Many identical cells and chips that use pipelining and multiprocessing can meet the performance requirements of a special-purpose processor.

Examples of these special-purpose processor designs can be found in the literature.[5,10-12]

Systolic arrays. H. T. Kung and his co-workers at Carnegie-Mellon University are investigating the relationship of algorithm design to special-purpose chip architecture.[9,13] They state that in designing such chips the most crucial decision is the choice of the underlying algorithm, since it is the suitability of the algorithm that largely determines chip design cost and performance. In other words, they feel the algorithm should receive the largest part of the design effort. They also argue that low-level optimizations at the circuit or layout design levels are probably not worthwhile, as these will lead to only minor improvements in the overall performance and an increase in design time. Borrowing from physiology, Kung's group coined the term "systolic" array for algorithms and architectures with good VLSI properties. Figure 1 shows a number of simple and regular structures for interconnecting processors for VLSI algorithms. Each tends to be good for a particular function—e.g., linear arrays for real-time filters, trees for searching, and shuffle exchanges for Fourier transforms.

A specific VLSI chip[9]—one that performs on-line pattern matching of strings with "wild card" characters—illustrates the design philosophy and methodology of Kung's group. The chip is based on a linear array, the simplest possible geometry, which is good for pipelined

operations. It accepts two streams of characters from the host machine and produces a stream of bits, as shown in Figure 2. One of the input streams, the text string, is an endless string of characters over some alphabet. The other, the pattern input stream, contains a fixed-length vector of characters over the alphabet, with X being a "wild card" character. The output is a stream of bits, each of which corresponds to one of the characters in the text string.

The chip is divided into character cells, each of which compares two characters and accumulates a temporary result. The pattern and string follow a preset path of cells from the time they enter the chip until the time they leave it. On each beat, every character moves to a new cell.

It took only about two months to design the pattern-matcher chip and its fabrication was completed in the spring of 1979. Preliminary analysis showed that the chip achieved a data rate of one character every 250 ns, which is higher than the memory bandwidth of most conventional computers. This seems to justify Kung et al.'s claim that careful design of the underlying algorithm leads to high performance.

RSA cipher chip.[14] This chip, designed by Ronald Rivest and his colleagues at the Massachusetts Institute of Technology, implements a public-key encryption algorithm. This operation is computationally demanding, requiring up to several hundred multiplications of several hundred bit numbers. The chip was designed as a general-purpose, big-number processor, using a bit-slice architecture for the ALU. It is a good example of a chip design based on the duplication of simple cells.

Externally, the chip is configured as a memory chip that can be read or written at one of four eight-bit word positions. For instance, one of these positions is the "window" for data I/O, while another is for receiving commands such as "encrypt." To support encryption, the RSA chip has a 512-bit ALU organized in a bit-slice manner. It has eight general-purpose 512-bit registers, as well as up-down shifter logic and a multiplier. Other subsystems include control logic (containing a PLA of 224 72-bit microcode words), a stack/counter array for subroutines and loops, and an array of powerful super-buffers to drive the signals that control the ALU.

Internally, the ALU is only capable of performing the operations $(A * B) \pm C$, shift-left, shift-right, and test least-significant bit. The remaining required operations are implemented by microcode control subroutines. These operations include RSA encryption/decryption (modular exponentiation); generating a large prime

COMMUNICATION GEOMETRY	EXAMPLES
1—DIM LINEAR ARRAYS	MATRIX—VECTOR MULTIPLICATION RECURRENCE EVALUATION
2—DIM SQUARE ARRAYS	DYNAMIC PROGRAMMING PATTERN MATCHING
2—DIM HEXAGONAL ARRAYS	MATRIX MULTIPLICATION GAUSSIAN ELIMINATION
TREES	SEARCHING ALGORITHMS PARALLEL FUNCTION EVALUATION
SHUFFLE-EXCHANGE NETWORKS	FAST FOURIER TRANSFORMS BITONIC SORT

Figure 1. Examples of VLSI algorithms.

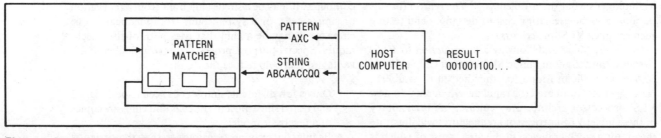

Figure 2. Data to and from the pattern matcher.

COMPUTER

number; generating a complete RSA key-set; greatest common divisor; and input or output of a large number through the eight-bit window.

The "floor plan" of the RSA cipher chip is shown in Figure 3. The left side contains a block of 320 slices of the ALU and the upper-right block contains the remaining 192 slices. The central spine carries control signals to the ALU from the superbuffer driver array at its lower right. The microcode PLA occupies the right-center area of the chip, and the remaining logic (stack, pads, etc.) occupies the lower-right portion. In Figure 3, S denotes a stack, X an eight-bit "window," C a small bus-control PLA, and D some debugging logic.

The entire chip contains about 40,000 MOS transistors, has 18 pins, runs at four MHz, and uses a little more than one watt of power. Rivest estimates that the project required about five man-months of effort, with the chip finally being fabricated in the fall of 1979. It was primarily a programming project because he and his colleagues almost exclusively wrote programs in Lisp, which when executed, created the desired Caltech Intermediate Form output file. Altogether, they wrote about 75 pages of Lisp code. The largest pieces specified the final placement and interconnection of the modules (14 pages), the description of the ALU (11 pages), and the microcode assembler and simulator (10 pages). Estimates are that the chip can perform RSA encryption faster than 1200 bps (even faster if shorter keys are used), and the designers predict speeds of 20,000 bps within a few years.

Optical mouse chip. Dick Lyon is investigating new VLSI architecture methodologies for applications such as signal processing[15] and smart digital sensors.[16] A novel example of the latter is the optical mouse chip,[16] designed in the VLSI system design area at Xerox Corporation's Palo Alto Research Center.

The optical mouse (Figure 4a) is a pointing device for controlling the cursor on a personal workstation display, such as the one found on the Xerox Star 8010 information system. The design was motivated by the desire for a highly reliable mouse with no moving parts except button switches, and it was realized through the innovative use of electro-optics, circuit design, geometric combinatorics, and algorithms—all in a single special-purpose sensor chip.

This chip reports the motion of visible spots relative to its coordinate system by combining two techniques. One

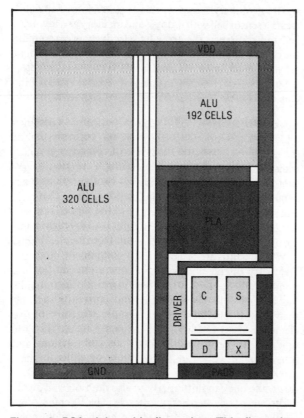

Figure 3. RSA cipher chip floor plan. (This floor plan originally appeared in the fourth quarter 1980 issue of *Lambda* [now *VLSI Design*].)

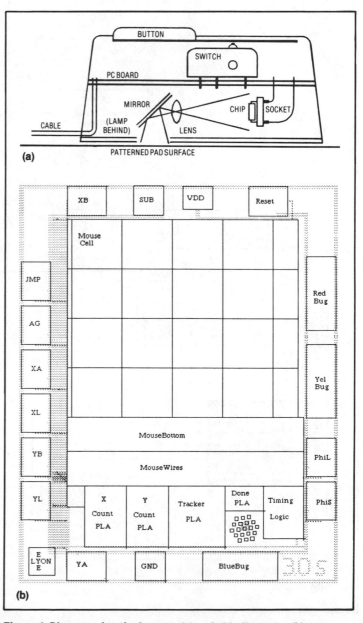

Figure 4. Diagram of optical mouse (a) and chip floor plan (b).

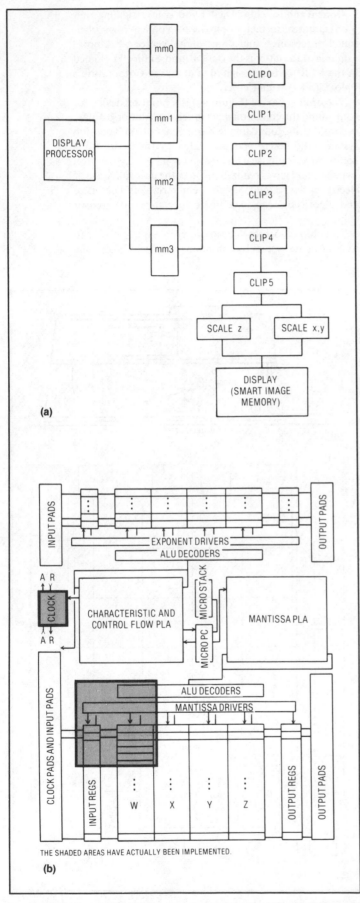

(a)

(b)

THE SHADED AREAS HAVE ACTUALLY BEEN IMPLEMENTED.

Figure 5. The Geometry Engine: (a) system data flow; (b) chip floor plan.

is a simple, "mostly digital" circuit that produces digital image (bitmap) snapshots of bright features on a dark field using self-timed circuit concepts and mutually inhibiting light sensors. The other technique uses a tracking algorithm with an easy-to-track contrasting pattern, a detector array and inhibition network matched to the pattern, and a digital machine that inputs images of that pattern and tracks relative image motion. (An especially interesting aspect of the design is the integration of sensors, memory, and logic in a single array using standard MOS technology.)

The basis of the sensors is that in NMOS, light striking the circuit side of the chip converts photons to hole-electron pairs; the holes are attracted to negative-biased p-type silicon substrates, while the electrons are attracted to n-type regions. A so-called dynamic node that has been positively charged will detect light by collecting a negative charge (electrons) and "leaking" to a lower voltage. An imager is simply an array of subcircuits, each consisting of a dynamic node, a transistor to reset the node to "high" and isolate it, and an inverter circuit to sense the voltage of the node and communicate it to other circuits.

Figure 4b shows the floor plan of the optical mouse chip. "Mouse cells" represent the four-by-four, two-dimensional sensor array, and "Tracker PLA" tracks spots by comparing images and outputting X and Y movements, as well as outputting "Any-Good" and "Jump" counter control and test signals. The "X counter PLA" and the "Y counter PLA" control up/down counting and transmit "$XA\ XB\ XL$" and "$YA\ YB\ YL$" coordinates to the host computer.

The layout style used in this first version of the chip treats a sensor cell with its logic and memory as a low-level cell and constructs the array by selectively programming the cells in different positions. The resulting chip is about 3.5 mm × 5.4 mm in a typical NMOS process (Lambda = 2.5 microns, or five-micron lines). A second version of the chip has also been designed to improve light sensitivity.[16]

Geometry Engine.[17] This vector function unit, designed by James Clark of Stanford University, performs three of the common geometric functions of computer graphics: transformation, clipping, and scaling. A single-chip version is used in 12 slightly different configurations to accomplish 4 × 4 matrix multiplications; line, character, and polygon clipping; and scaling of the clipped results to display device coordinates. This unit is an excellent example of a special-purpose device built from identical chips.

When configured as a four-component unit, the Geometry Engine allows simple operations on floating-point numbers. Each of its four identical function units has an eight-bit characteristic and (currently) a 20-bit mantissa. It operates with a simple structure of five elements: an ALU, three registers, and a stack. This basic unit can perform parallel additions, subtractions, and other similar two-variable operations on either the characteristic or the mantissa. Since one register can shift down and one can shift up, it can also multiply and divide at the rate of one step per microcycle. The 12-chip system consists of 1344 copies of a single bit-slice layout composed of the five elements. Four pins on the chip are wired to indicate to the microcode which of the 12 functions to carry out, according to the chip's position in the subsystem organization.

Figure 5a shows the geometry subsystem described above. The terms "mm," "clip," and "scale" denote matrix multiply, clipping, and scaling. Each of the four "mm" blocks, for instance, is a separate Geometry Engine chip that does a four-component vector dot product. Although each multiplication is done at the rate of one partial product per microcycle, the matrix multiplier has 16 of these products simultaneously active. Thus, the total transformation time, which is the bandwidth limiting system operation, is about 12 microseconds.

Figure 5b is a plan view of the Geometry Engine. The shaded parts have been implemented as two separate MPC projects. (The very small rectangles are copies of the principal bit-slice.) These projects are five-bit versions of the main function unit and the "pipelined" clock. Almost all the Geometry Engine's complexity is in the microcode that drives it. This microcode represents the logic equations for its finite-state machine, which will be implemented in a PLA. Writing this microcode and making minor additions to the principal bit-slice to accommodate it took up approximately 50 percent of the total design time. Estimations are that the Geometry Engine is capable of performing about four million floating-point operations per second; 48 identical units, four per chip, will each do a floating-point operation in about 12 microseconds.[17] Also note that the Geometry Engine is designed to work in conjunction with an image memory processor whose design is described by Clark and Hannah.[18]

Simple microprocessors

Traditionally, the trend in designing microprocessors, and even mainframe computers, has been towards the use of increasingly complex instruction sets and associated architectures. However, the judicious choice of a simple set of instructions and a corresponding simple machine organization can achieve such a high instruction rate that the overall processing power can exceed that of processors implementing more complex instructions.[19] An additional advantage is that the microprocessor has a short

design time. (Patterson and Ditzel[20] give the arguments for such an approach to computer design, with a rebuttal by the designers of the Digital Equipment Corporation VAX computers.) In the following, we examine two contrasting designs for "simple microprocessors."

RISC I.[19,21] The reduced instruction set computer is being developed by Dave Patterson and his co-workers at the University of California, Berkeley. This type of microprocessor combines a small set of often-used instructions, with an architecture tailored to the efficient execution of these instructions. In addition, a single-chip implementation of a simpler machine makes more effective use of the limited resources of present-day VLSI chips—such as the number of transistors, area, and power consumption. The RISC I project has also shown that simplicity of the instruction set leads to a small control section and shorter machine cycle, as well as to a reduction in design time.

RISC I is a register-oriented, 32-bit microprocessor that has 31 operation codes, uses 32-bit addresses, and supports eight-, 16-, and 32-bit data. It has 138 general-purpose 32-bit registers and executes most instructions in a single cycle. The LOAD and STORE instructions—the only operations that access memory—violate this single cycle constraint; they add an index register and the immediate offset during the first cycle, performing the memory access during the next cycle to allow enough time for main-memory access.

Figure 6 shows the machine organization of RISC I. The machine naturally subdivides into the following function blocks: the register-file, the ALU, the shifter, a set of program counter (PC) registers, the data I/O latches, the program status word (PSW) register, and the control section (which contains the instruction register, instruction decoder, and internal clock circuits). In addition, the register file needs at least two independent buses because two operands are required simultaneously. In Figure 6, buses A and B are read-only and bus C is write-only.

An unusual feature of RISC I is the so-called overlapped window registers, a fast and simple procedure calling mechanism using the general-purpose registers. A procedure has access to 32 registers: global (registers 0-9

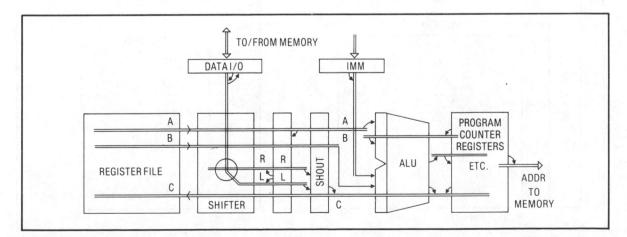

Figure 6. RISC I data path organization.

are shared by every procedure); low (registers 10-15 contain result parameters); local (registers 16-25 are used for local working); and high (registers 26-31 are input parameters). Each time a procedure is called, new registers are allocated in which the low registers of the calling procedure overlap the high registers of the called procedure.

Two different NMOS versions of RISC I are currently being pursued.[21] The "gold" version, whose data path is shown in Figure 6, has actually been fabricated. But the "blue" version is still under development. It's organization is similar to gold's but a more sophisticated timing scheme shortens the machine cycle and reduces chip area. Details of the gold design[21] include a chip size of 406 × 350 mm, 44K devices, a design time of 15 man-months, and a layout time of 12 man-months. Power consumption for the chip is estimated at between 1.2 and 1.9 watts. One very notable impact of the reduced instruction set approach is that the chip area dedicated to control dropped from the typical 50 percent in commercial microprocessors to only 6 percent in RISC I.

Scheme-79. This single-chip microprocessor[22,23] developed by Gerry Sussman and his colleagues at MIT directly interprets a dialect of the Lisp language. As noted by the designers,[23] Lisp is a natural choice among high-level languages for implementation in hardware. It is simple but powerful and, as in traditional machine languages, represents programs as data uniformly. All compound data in the system are built from list nodes, consisting of a CAR pointer and a CDR pointer. Each pointer is 32-bits, comprising a 24-bit data field, a seven-bit type field, and a one-bit field used by the storage allocator.

The Scheme-79 chip, whose architecture is shown in Figure 7, implements a standard von Neumann architecture in which a processor is attached to a memory system. The processor is divided into two parts: the data paths and the controller. The data paths are a set of special-purpose registers, with built-in operators interconnected with a single 32-bit bus. The controller is a finite-state machine that sequences through microcode, implementing both the interpreter for the Lisp subset and the garbage collector that supports an automatic storage allocation system. At each step it performs an operation on some of the registers (for example, transferring the address of an allocated cell in NEWCELL into the STACK register) and selects a next state based on both its current state and the conditions developed within the data paths.

Ten registers in the chip have specialized characteristics. On each cycle, these registers can be controlled so that one of them is gated onto the bus and selected fields of the bus are gated to another register. (The bus is extended off the chip through a set of pads.)

The finite-state controller for the Scheme-79 chip is a synchronous system composed of a state register and a large piece of combinational logic—the control map. From the current state stored in the state register, the control map develops control signals for the register array

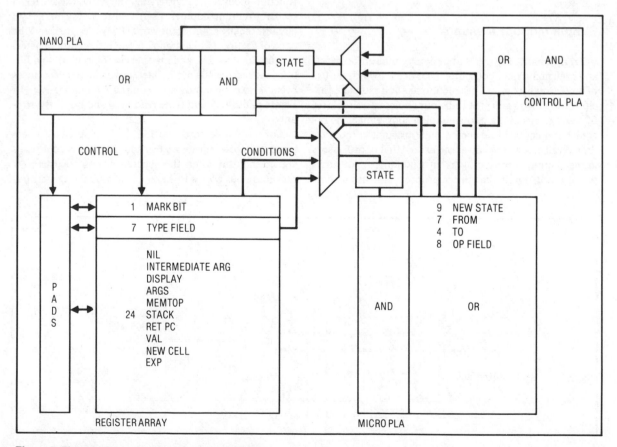

Figure 7. The major blocks of the Scheme-79 chip.

and pads, the new state, and controls for selecting the sources for the next sequential state. The Scheme-79 chip interfaces to the external world through a 32-bit bidirectional data bus that specifies addresses, reads and writes (heap) memory, references I/O devices, reads interrupt vectors, and accesses the internal microcode state during debugging.

To estimate the Lisp chip's performance, Sussman's group computed the values of Fibonacci numbers. For example, they calculated (fib 20) = 6765 with two different memory loadings, a clock period of 1595 nanoseconds (not the chip's top speed), and a memory of 32K-Lisp cells. If the memory was substantially empty (when garbage collection is most efficient) the Scheme-79 chip took about one minute to execute the program. With memory half-full of live structure (a typical load for a Lisp system), the Scheme-79 chip took about three minutes. (A MacLisp interpreter running on a DEC KA10 took about 3.6 minutes for the same calculation.)

The Scheme-79 chip, using a process with a minimum line width of five microns (Lambda = 2.5 microns), was 5926 microns wide and 7548 microns long, a total area of 44.73 mm^2. The entire project,[22] including prototype tool building and chip synthesis, was completed in five weeks and is frequently cited to justify the power of the Mead and Conway VLSI design philosophy. Areas for future work include improving the electrical characteristics of the Scheme-79 chip and implementing a multiprocessor system composed of Lisp chips.

Tree machines

As Seitz[24] has observed, the existence of communication problems makes scaling large single processors to submicron dimensions self-defeating. Communication assumes a progressively more dominant and limiting role in VLSI as chip area, signal energy, and propagation time become increasingly expensive. As these costs rise, improving performance with an ensemble of concurrently operating small processors becomes more attractive than using a larger single processor. The principle of locality has a number of effects on VLSI. First, it encourages the repeated use of identical computing elements, each with capabilities for processing, communication, and memory. Second, it becomes desirable for a group of elements to be functionally equivalent to a single element (to overcome problems of increasing miniaturization). Third, it motivates the use of concurrency to counteract the simplicity of the individual computing elements. And lastly, it encourages designers to utilize locality of reference to reduce system-wide communications.

A tree machine architecture combines the above VLSI properties with a general-purpose computing environment. A tree machine is a collection of simple computing elements connected as a binary tree. There is no global communication, only communication between a parent and its child in the tree, and between the root of the tree and the external world. This architecture gives rise to integrated circuits with regular interconnections, local communication, and many repetitions of a single cell. These integrated circuits, in turn, can be assembled into regular patterns at the printed-circuit board and backplane levels to construct machines with thousands of processors. Examples of such tree machines are being investigated at Berkeley,[25,26] Caltech,[24,27] and Carnegie-Mellon.[28]

The X-tree. This University of California, Berkeley, project[25,26] is developing a tree machine built of modular components known as X-nodes. As shown in Figure 8, this is a binary tree enhanced with additional links to form a half- or full-ring tree. These links further shorten the average path length by distributing message traffic more evenly throughout the tree, and they provide the potential for fault-tolerant communication if a few nodes or links are removed. Notice in Figure 8 that the children of node n have node addresses $2n$ and $2n + 1$, respectively.

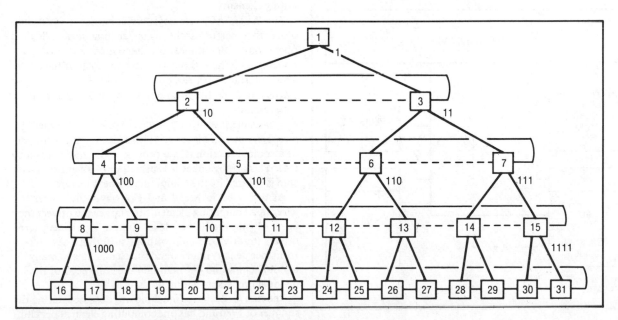

Figure 8. The X-tree—a binary tree with full-ring connections.

All communication throughout the tree is in the form of messages. For effective routing, the complete address is divided into a node address and a second part identifying a particular memory location, if that node has any memory belonging to the global address space. (In the X-tree, secondary memory as well as input/output is restricted to the frontier (i.e., the leaves) of the tree.)

Message routing is based on the binary address. As seen in Figure 8, the root node is assigned address 1; the address of a left child is formed by appending a 0 to the root node address and a right child's address is formed by appending a 1 to it. To address one node from another, the message has to move up the tree to their common ancestor—that is, to the node where the address matches all leading bits in the target address. From there the message moves down to the destination.

On first glance, each X-node (see Figure 9) is simply a computing element that communicates with four or five

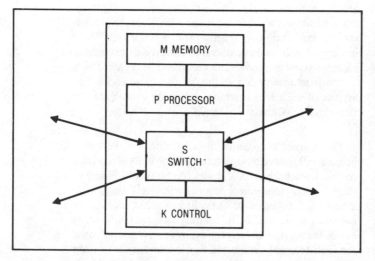

Figure 9. The X-node—a computing element shown in PMS notation.

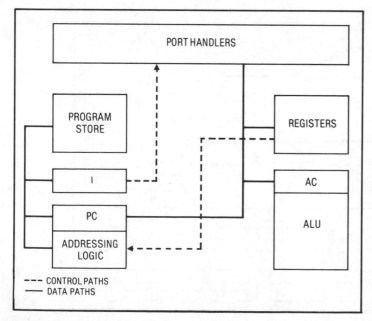

Figure 10. Block diagram of the Caltech processor.

neighbors. However, normal microprocessor input/output techniques are inadequate because of bandwidth requirements. Computation must occur in parallel with communication. Thus, each X-node contains a self-controlled switching network with its own I/O buffers and controllers. The heart of this switching network is a time-multiplexed bus. Since this bus is completely contained within one chip, its parasitic capacity is low. The resulting bandwidth for a given amount of drive power is thus an order of magnitude higher than that running through the package pins associated with the input/output ports. Each of these ports consists of a set of input and output buffers and the necessary finite-state machines to control them.

By the mid 1980's, it appears likely that approximately 64K bytes will be able to be implemented on the same chip with the X-node processor if dynamic RAM or charge-coupled devices are used. Prototype TTL circuitry for the communication system, consisting of I/O ports and a routing controller, has already been implemented. The RISC I processor is definitely a key stage in the development of a complete X-node.

Caltech tree machine. The California Institute of Technolgy tree machine is based on Sally Browning's doctoral dissertation,[27] and the description of the machine presented here is largely taken from this source.

The Caltech tree machine is programmed in tree machine programming language (TMPL), a high-level language resembling Hoare's communicating sequential processes notation.[29] Computing elements of the machine have four main parts: a program store, a bank of registers for storing data, an ALU, and some communications handlers. The control and data paths run between these components, aided by three special-purpose registers. The I register holds an instruction, the PC register is the program counter, and the AC is an accumulator providing the source and destination for the ALU. Figure 10 is a block diagram of one of these computing elements.

The ALU, AC, and registers comprise a functional block that performs the usual arithmetic and logical operations. Communications handlers are related components, and there is one of them for each of the ports. They interface with the outside world, handle message traffic, load the program store, and pass code to their subordinates.

A possible layout of a binary tree of computing elements is shown in Figure 11. There, each element consists of a communication (C), a processor (P), and a memory (M). This arrangement is repeated until an entire silicon chip is covered by the computing element hierarchy.

As discussed in Mead and Conway,[6] the longer the wires in a computing element, the larger the drivers they need. Giving the highest-level computing element large drivers (to drive off-chip without suffering a severe performance penalty) can extend such a machine to many individual chips and yet maintain the full speed of the individual processors within it.

The first Caltech tree machine was designed during the summer of 1980 and has one computing element per chip. As finer design geometries become available, several pro-

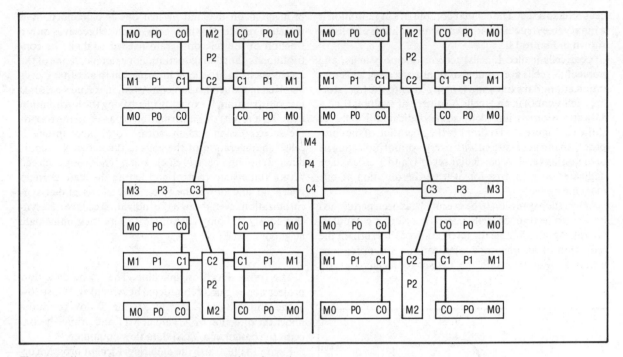

Figure 11. Layout for a binary tree of computing elements.

cessors and their memories will be placed on a single chip. Caltech's goal was to build and test a tree machine by the fall of 1981 and have a machine of at least 1023 processors working in 1982.[24]

Non-von Neumann computers

The final area of VLSI processor architecture covered in this article also concerns the design of decentralized computers built from identical computing elements. Some of these architectures are even tree machines. However, what distinguishes the two areas is the design approach. In the tree machines discussed previously, the design centered on the hardware—i.e., the configuration of computing elements to exploit increasing levels of integration and also to handle problems such as communication. In non-von Neumann computers, though, the design centers on the software. In other words, the design concentrates on the way the computing elements are programmed to exploit parallelism.

The VLSI architectures discussed below are not based on traditional, sequential control-flow program organization, but on alternative naturally parallel organizations such as reduction[30] or data flow.[31-33] All three are specifically designed to exploit VLSI. These program organizations are distinguished by the form of instructions, by the way instructions manipulate their arguments, and by the patterns of control. At present, over 30 non-von Neumann computers are being developed worldwide, and a number of machines are currently operational.[34]

The cellular reduction machine. This machine[30,35] is being developed by Gyula Mago and his colleagues at the University of North Carolina, Chapel Hill. It uses the class of FP functional programming languages designed by Backus[36]; its program organization is string reduction; and its machine organization is a binary tree structure.

Figure 12 illustrates the string reduction form of program organization for a statement $a = (b+1)*(b-c)$. In this example, each instruction is a "name:(expression)" pair, where the expression is either constant (4) or defines an operator and its input operands. Notice that an instruction has no explicit output operands, but always returns the result to the invoking instructions. Thus, in reduction, instruction execution is often viewed as "demand driven." An instruction is executed when the result it generates is required as input by the invoking instruction. In string reduction, each instruction invoking another will take a copy of the instruction and store the copy in place of the operand address. These copies can then be manipulated independently and in parallel.

A program for the cellular reduction machine is a linear string of symbols mapped onto a vector of memory cells in the computer, one symbol per cell, possibly with empty

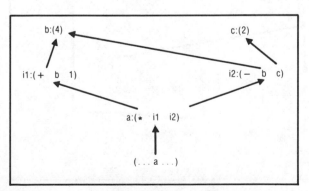

Figure 12. Reduction program for a = (b + 1)*(b − c).

cells interspersed. The cellular computer's organization is a binary tree structure with two different kinds of cells, as shown in Figure 13.

Leaf cells (called L cells) serve as memory units, and nonleaf (T) cells are capable of dual processing and communication. An expression is mapped onto the tree, storing each symbol in an L cell. A subtree of symbols (i.e., a subexpression) is linked by some dedicated T cells, as shown in Figure 13. To simplify the operation of the computer, an integer is stored with every symbol indicating its own nesting level. A particular set of L and T cells will be dedicated to a subtree for at least the duration of one machine cycle.

When the expression to be executed has been partitioned into a collection of cells, itself a cellular computer, microprograms handle the interaction of these cells in the reduction of an innermost application. Microprograms normally reside outside the network of cells and are brought in on demand. When one is demanded, it is placed in registers in the L cells. Each cell receives only a fraction of the microprogram needed to make its contribution to the total reduction. For example, if one of the L cells wants to broadcast information to all other L cells involved in reducing a subexpression, it executes a SEND microinstruction,[35] explicitly identifying the information item. As a result, this information is passed to the root of the subexpression and broadcast to all appropriate L cells. The operation of the cells in the network is coordinated, not by a central clock, but by endowing each cell with a finite-state control and letting the state changes sweep up and down the tree. This allows global synchronization, even though the individual cells work asynchronously and only communicate with their immediate neighbors.

The Irvine data flow machine. The Irvine data flow project was originally conducted by Arvind and Gostelow at the University of California, Irvine. It now continues under the direction of Arvind at MIT and primarily concerns the design of a VLSI data flow computer.[31]

Figure 14 illustrates the data flow form of program organization for the statement $a = (b + 1)*(b - c)$. In this example, each instruction consists of an operator, two inputs that are either constants or "unknown" operands defined by empty bracket symbols, and an address such as i3/1 defining a consumer instruction and operand position for the result. In data flow programs, copies of a result are logically stored by the producer instruction directly into each consumer instruction. These so-called data tokens also provide a control signal to the consumer instruction, which is executed when it has received all of its input operands. Data flow program execution is *data driven* and as such is highly parallel.

The Irvine data flow machine, like other data flow computers, is based on a packet communication machine organization.[33] For a parallel computer, packet communication is a very simple strategy for allocating "packets of work" to resources. Each packet to be processed, such as an executable instruction, is placed with similar packets in a "pool of work." When a resource becomes idle, it takes a packet from its input pool, processes the packet, and places a modified packet in an output pool.

Figure 15 illustrates a computing element of the proposed Irvine data flow machine. The machine consists of N computing elements and an $N \times N$ packet communication network. Each computing element is essentially a complete computer with an instruction set. These computing elements have up to 16K words each of program storage and data structure storage, and also contain certain "special" elements, which are divided into sections. These specialized elements include an input section, which accepts input from other computing elements; a waiting-matching section, which forms data tokens into sets for a consumer instruction; an instruction fetch section, which fetches executable instructions from the local program memory; a service section containing a floating-point ALU such as an Intel 8087 that executes instructions; and an output section, which routes data tokens containing results to the destination computing element.

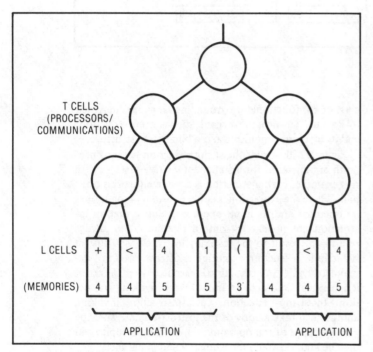

Figure 13. The cellular tree machine.

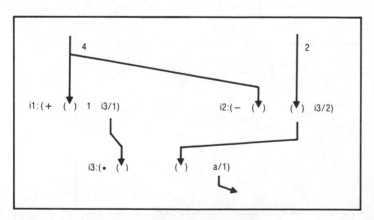

Figure 14. Data flow program for a = (b + 1)*(b − c).

Arvind is currently designing a data flow machine with 64 computing elements at MIT, and he hopes to complete the design for MOS fabrication by the end of 1982.

The recursive machine project.[37] This project, conducted by Wayne Wilner at Xerox Corporation's Palo Alto Research Center in California, builds on earlier work by Bob Barton and Wilner at Burroughs Corporation. This is one of the most sophisticated non-von Neumann computers currently under investigation. The organization of both its program and machine are based on the principle of recursion.

Information is represented in terms of fields, which are recursively defined to be either bracketed strings of characters or bracketed strings of fields

field :: = "(" char 1   char 2   . . .   char n ")"
field :: = "(" field 1   field 2   . . .   field n ")"

where the character alphabet is disjoint from the bracket alphabet. For example, the number "six" can be represented as (6), a 2×2 matrix as (((a11)(a12))((a21)(a22))), and an empty stack as ( ). Likewise, a machine instruction is recursively defined to be either a string of characters or an n-tuple of machine instructions. The statement $a = (b+1)*(b-c)$ could be represented as $((b + 1) (*)(b - c) . . .)$.

Program execution is based on an "actor," or message passing model, such as logically underlies the Xerox PARC Smalltalk[38] programming language. In this model, execution of the instruction $(4 + 1)$ is viewed as the message " + 1" being sent to the integer value 4, which executes and is replaced by the result 5. Messages can be either data driven or demand driven and are sent from one field to another. The addresses used to route messages are the logical addresses of the fields, not their physical designations.

A recursive machine (RM) can be either a single element or a system of recursive machines, as shown in Figure 16.

Several RM elements can be configured into a network by joining their point-to-point connections serially, by busing their hierarchical connections, and by using another recursive machine element to couple the buses to the next higher level of storage and communication. The resulting configuration has exactly the same outward appearance as a single RM element.

A recursive machine element is a small general-purpose computer, forming the bottom level of the storage, control, and communication hierarchy. It consists of a microprogrammable processor with various functional units, or FUs, and writable control store. It has variable-length registers, which are accessed through field-

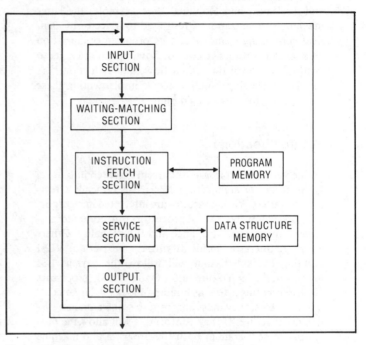

Figure 15. An Irvine data flow computing element.

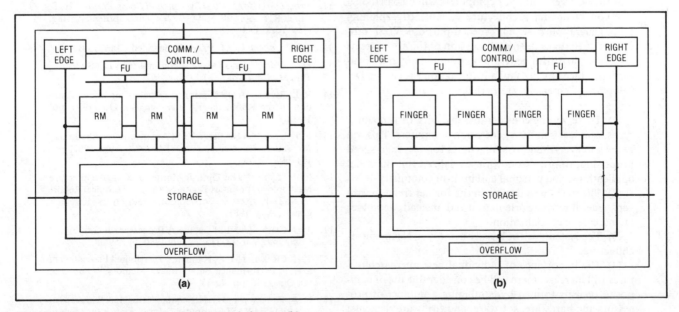

Figure 16. Recursive machine system (a) and element (b).

155

oriented machines called "fingers." It has input and output ports through which it transmits messages on behalf of fields located within its storage. And it also has point-to-point connections to neighboring elements through which fields migrate when algorithms create more data than can fit inside a single element. Lastly, each recursive machine has two "boundary registers" to hold the logical addresses of the characters at the left and right edges of the RM. These locate the approximate position of an addressed field.

In closing, Treleaven and Hopkins[39] are currently investigating another recursive machine that is based on the work of Wilner[37] and Barton.[40] There are some distinct differences between Wilner's recursive, or actor, machine and Treleaven and Hopkins'. For example, the latter machine's organization is restricted to a vector of identical computing elements and its program organization uses so-called recursive control flow, which attempts to synthesize control flow, data flow, and reduction.[34] A simple, single-chip building block implementing these concepts is presently being designed.

Future directions

The veritable explosion of current research into novel VLSI processor architectures[5,10-12,41] is radically affecting computers. Various groups are interested in incorporating special-purpose VLSI processors into computer systems to increase performance and functionality. Others are more interested in identifying the next era of VLSI building blocks[42,43] that will follow the current LSI microprocessor. To use all of the VLSI processors discussed in this article as building blocks in larger computer systems, they must conform to some common system architecture. If they conform, it will allow the processors to cooperate at both the program and machine organization levels.

Thus, there is a belief among some computer architects that the next generation of computers will be based on a non-von Neumann architecture capable of exploiting both general-purpose and special-purpose VLSI processors.[44] Perhaps the best discussion of the attributes of these so-called fifth generation computers is in a document produced by the Japan Information Processing Development Center.[45] It states that

(1) There will be considerable diversity of functions, types, and levels in fifth generation computers. This will be seen in everything from machines for very high-speed processing, to processors with specialized functions and applications, and personal and built-in computers.

(2) There will be a decline in the former trend toward very general-purpose orientation and, instead, we will see an increase in specialization.

(3) The systems will be based on non-von Neumann architecture.

(4) The importance of individual new microarchitectures will increase; there will be considerable use of composite systems formed by combining a number of processors and hardware, software, and firmware elements; and the importance of system architecture will grow.

Just as Mead and Conway's VLSI design philosophy[6] provides a whole new way to "do electronics," fifth generation architectures are likely to provide a whole new way to "build computing systems." Although we are starting to understand the strengths and weaknesses of various decentralized computer architectures,[34] it is not yet clear just which sets of concepts will contribute to fifth generation computers. It seems likely that they will be significantly influenced by both tree and recursive machines, which are essentially equivalent. Lastly, however, the programming of these decentralized architectures remains a largely unsolved problem. ■

References

1. "About the Cover," *Lambda*, 1st Qtr. 1980.

2. R. Bernhart, "More Hardware Means Less Software," *IEEE Spectrum,* Vol. 18, No. 12, Dec. 1981, pp. 30-37.

3. R. C. Johnson, "32-bit Microprocessors Inherit Mainframe Features," *Electronics*, Vol. 54, No. 4, Feb. 1981, pp. 138-141.

4. *Very Large Scale Integration (VLSI) Fundamentals and Applications*, D. F. Barbe, ed., Springer-Verlag, New York, 1980.

5. *Proc. Caltech Conf. VLSI*, C. Seitz, ed., Jan. 1979.

6. C. A. Mead and L. Conway, *Introduction to VLSI Systems,* Addison-Wesley, Reading, Mass., 1980.

7. L. Conway, et al., "MPC79: A Large-Scale Demonstration of a New Way to Create Systems in Silicon," *Lambda,* 2nd Qtr. 1980, pp. 10-19.

8. W. D. Jansen and D. G. Fairbairn, "The Silicon Foundry: Concepts and Reality," *Lambda,* 1st Qtr 1981, pp. 16-26.

9. M.J. Foster and H. T. Kung, "The Design of Special-Purpose VLSI Chips," *Computer,* Vol. 13, No. 1, Jan. 1980, pp. 26-40.

10. *Proc. VLSI 81,* J. P. Gray, ed., Academic Press, New York, 1981.

11. *Proc. CMU Conf. VLSI Systems and Computations,* H. T. Kung, R. F. Sproull, and G. Steele, eds., Springer-Verlag, New York, Oct. 1981.

12. *Proc. Caltech Conf. VLSI*, C. Seitz, ed., Jan. 1981.

13. H. T. Kung, "Let's Design Algorithms for VLSI Systems," *Proc. Caltech Conf. VLSI,* Jan. 1979.

14. R. L. Rivest, "A Description of a Single-Chip Implementation of the RSA Cipher," *Lambda,* 4th Qtr. 1980, pp. 14-18.

15. R. F. Lyon, "A Bit-Serial VLSI Architecture Methodology for Signal Processing, *Proc. VLSI 81,* Aug. 1981, pp. 131-140.

16. R. F. Lyon, "The Optical Mouse, and an Architecture Methdology for Smart Digital Sensors," Technical Report VLSI-81-1, Xerox Corporation Palo Alto Research Center, Aug. 1981.

17. J. H. Clark, "A VLSI Geometry Processor for Graphics," *Computer,* Vol. 13, No. 7, July 1980, pp. 59-68.

18. J. H. Clark and M. R. Hannah, "Distributed Processing in a High-Performance Smart Image Memory," *Lambda,* 4th Qtr. 1980, pp. 40-45.

19. D. A. Patterson and C. H. Sequin, "RISC I: A Reduced Instruction Set VLSI Computer," *Proc. Eighth Int'l Symp. Computer Architecture,* May 1981, pp. 443-457.

20. D. A. Patterson and D. R. Ditzel, "The Case for the Reduced Instruction Set Computer," *Computer Architecture News*, Vol. 8, No. 6, Oct. 1980, pp. 25-32.

21. D. T. Fitzpatrick et al., "A RISCy Approach to VLSI," *VLSI Design*, 4th Qtr. 1981, pp. 14-20.

22. J. Holloway et al., "The Scheme-79 Chip," MIT AI Memo 559, Cambridge, Mass., Jan. 1980.

23. G. J. Sussman et al., "Scheme-79—Lisp on a Chip," *Computer*, Vol. 14, No. 7, July 1981, pp. 10-21.

24. S. A. Browning and C. L. Seitz, "Communication in a Tree Machine," *Proc. Caltech Conf. VLSI*, Jan. 1981.

25. A. M. Despain and D. A. Patterson, "X-TREE: A Tree Structured Multiprocessor Computer Architecture," *Proc. Fifth Int'l Symp. Computer Architecture*, Apr. 1978, pp. 144-151.

26. D. A. Patterson et al., "Design Considerations for the VLSI Processor of X-TREE," *Proc. Sixth Int'l Symp. Computer Architecture*, Apr. 1979, pp. 90-100.

27. S. A. Browning, "The Tree Machine: A Highly Concurrent Computing Environment," PhD dissertation, Department of Computer Science, California Institute of Technology, 1980.

28. J. L. Bentley and H. T. Kung, "Two Papers on a Tree Structured Parallel Computer," Technical Report CMU-CS-79-142, Department of Computer Science, Carnegie-Mellon University, Aug. 1979.

29. C. A. R. Hoare, "Communicating Sequential Processes," *Comm. ACM*, Vol. 21, No. 8, Aug. 1978, pp. 666-677.

30. G. A. Mago, "A Cellular Computer Architecture for Functional Programming," *Proc. Compcon Spring 80*, pp. 179-185.

31. Arvind et al., "A Processing Element for a Large Multiple Processor Dataflow Machine," *Proc. Int'l Conf. Circuits and Computers*, Oct. 1980.

32. A. L. Davis, "A Data-Driven Machine Architecture Suitable for VLSI Implementation," *Proc. Caltech Conf. VLSI*, Jan. 1979, pp. 479-494.

33. J. B. Dennis, "Data Flow Supercomputers," *Computer*, Vol. 13, No. 11, Nov. 1980, pp. 48-56.

34. P. C. Treleaven et al., "Data Driven and Demand Driven Computer Architecture," *ACM Computing Surveys*, Vol. 14, No. 1, Mar. 1982.

35. G. A. Mago, "A Network of Microprocessors to Execute Reduction Languages," *Int'l J. Computer and Information Sciences*, Vol. 8, No. 5, pp. 349-385, and Vol. 8, No. 6, pp. 435-471, 1980.

36. J. Backus, "Can Programming be Liberated from the von Neumann Style? A Functional Style and its Algebra of Programs," *Comm. ACM*, Vol. 21, No. 8, Aug. 1978, pp. 613-641.

37. W. Wilner, "Recursive Machines," internal report, Xerox Corporation Palo Alto Research Center, 1980.

38. "The Smalltalk-80 Programming Language," *Byte*, Vol. 6, No. 8, Aug. 1981.

39. P. C. Treleaven and R. P. Hopkins, "A Recursive Computer Architecture for VLSI," *Proc. Ninth Int'l Symp. Computer Architecture*, Apr. 1982.

40. B. Barton, "On Modular Machines," *Proc. Arhus Workshop Software Eng.*, May 1978.

41. P. C. Treleaven, "VLSI: Machine Architecture and Very High Level Languages," *Proc. Joint UK SRC/University of Newcastle upon Tyne Workshop*, Technical Report 156, Computing Lab., University of Newcastle upon Tyne, summarized also in *Sigarch*, Vol. 8, No. 7, Dec. 1980.

42. D. A. Patterson and C. H. Sequin, "Design Considerations for Single-Chip Computers of the Future," *IEEE Trans. Computers*, Vol. C-29, No. 2, Feb. 1980, pp. 108-116.

43. J. R. Tobias, "LSI/VLSI Building Blocks," *Computer*, Vol. 14, No. 8, Aug. 1981, pp. 83-101.

44. *Proc. Int'l Conf. Fifth Generation Computer Systems*, Japan Information Processing Center, Oct. 1981.

45. "Interim Report on the Study and Research on Fifth-Generation Computers," Japan Information Processing Development Center, 1980.

Philip C. Treleaven is a research associate in the Computing Laboratory at the University of Newcastle upon Tyne, England, where he leads the Computer Architecture Group. His research interests include decentralized computer architectures, new forms of programming languages, fault-tolerant computing, and very large scale integration. From 1970 to 1973 he was employed by International Computers Limited. From 1973 to 1976 he was a graduate student in the computer science department of Manchester University, where he started the department's data flow research, which led to the construction of a prototype data flow computer.

Treleaven holds a BT from Brunel University, England, and an MS and PhD from Manchester University. He is a member of the ACM, the IEEE, and the British Computer Society, for which he has served as a council member.

*The reduced instruction set computer is an alternative to the
general trend toward increasingly complex instruction sets.
It executes most instructions in a single, short cycle.*

A VLSI RISC

David A. Patterson and Carlo H. Séquin

University of California, Berkeley

A general trend in computers today is to increase the
complexity of architectures commensurate with the increasing potential of implementation technologies, as
exemplified by the complex successors of simpler machines. Compare, for example, the DEC VAX-11[1] to the
PDP-11, the IBM System/38[2] to the System/3, and the
Intel iAPX-432[3,4] to the 8086. The complexity of this
class of computers, which we call CISCs for complex instruction set computers, has some negative consequences: increased design time, increased design errors,
and inconsistent implementations.[5]

Investigations of VLSI architectures indicate that the
delay-power penalty of data transfers across chip boundaries and the still-limited resources (devices) available on
a single chip are major design limitations. Even a million-
transistor chip is insufficient if a whole computer has to be
built from it.[6] This raises the question of whether the extra hardware needed to implement a CISC is the best use
of "scarce" resources.

The above findings led to the Reduced Instruction Set
Computer Project. The purpose of the RISC Project is to
explore alternatives to the general trend toward architectural complexity. The hypothesis is that by reducing the
instruction set one can design a suitable VLSI architecture
that uses scarce resources more effectively than a CISC.
We also expect this approach to reduce design time, design
errors, and the execution time of individual instructions.

Our initial version of such a computer is called RISC I.
To meet our goals of simplicity and effective single-chip
implementation, we somewhat artificially placed the
following design constraints on the architecture:

(1) *Execute one instruction per cycle*. RISC I instructions should be about as fast and no more complicated
than microinstructions in current machines such as the
PDP-11 or VAX.

(2) *Make all instructions the same size*. This again
simplifies implementation. We intentionally postponed
attempts to reduce program size.

(3) *Access memory only with load and store instructions; the rest operate between registers*. This restriction
simplifies the design. The lack of complex addressing
modes also makes it easier to restart instructions.

(4) *Support high-level languages*. The degree of support is explained below. Our intent is to optimize the performance of RISC I for use with high-level languages.

RISC I supports 32-bit addresses, 8-, 16-, and 32-bit data,
and several 32-bit registers. We intend to examine support
for operating systems and floating-point calculations in
the future.

It would appear that these constraints, based on our
desire for simplicity and regularity, would result in a
machine with substantially poorer code density, poorer
performance, or both; but in spite of these constraints,
the resulting architecture competes favorably with other

An earlier version of this article, entitled "RISC I: A Reduced
Instruction Set VLSI Computer," appeared in the *Proc. Eighth
Int'l Symp. Computer Architecture*, May 1981, pp. 443-457.

158

Recent developments

Since this article was submitted, we have received our first good silicon, and it looks like beginner's luck applies to VLSI. These chips correctly ran all diagnostic programs used to verify our original design. We (foolishly) created new diagnostics and uncovered a design error associated with the optional setting of condition codes on the load and shift instructions. Defying historical precedent for solving the problem by announcing a new architectural "feature," we decided to cover this minor error by modifying the RISC I assembler. (This was possible because ALU operations properly set all condition codes, whereas load and shift instructions do not set the negative condition bit. The patch consists of inserting an arithmetic test instruction when a conditional jump needs the N condition from a load or shift operation.)

The fastest of these chips runs all diagnostics at 1.5 MHz, or 2 μsec per RISC I instruction. Several factors explain the difference between expected and measured performance. The chief one is inexperience; this was the first chip that any of us had built. A second is raw speed of transistors from this fabrication. Test structures ran about half the speed of other runs. The last stage of design involved connecting cells, and we concentrated our resources on logical correctness rather than circuit speed. We recently reexamined the design and found four long clocked control lines that an analog circuit simulator predicts will limit the maximum clock speed to 4 MHz. Furthermore, many of our diagnostics can be run with a 3-MHz clock, suggesting that only a few RISC instructions are limiting performance. Finally, as we have still tested only 20 percent of the chips, we may well find faster RISC I's.

Even at 1.5 MHz and the assembler correction of the error, RISC I still runs programs faster than commercial microprocessors. RISC I was put onto a board with memory, I/O, and memory management on June 11, 1982, and ran its first program.

The bottom line of the RISC I effort is that students, as part of the graduate curriculum, designed and evaluated an architecture, learned Mead-Conway design, built new CAD tools, and tested their design. The end product, a 44,500-transistor integrated circuit, has one minor design error; it worked on the first good silicon and runs programs faster than commercial microprocessors.

More details can be found in an article in the September/October 1982 issue of *VLSI Design* entitled "Running RISCs."

---

microprocessors and minicomputers. This is due largely to a scheme of register organization we call overlapped register windows.

Support for high-level languages

Clearly, new architectures should be designed with the needs of high-level language programming in mind. It should not matter, however, whether a high-level language system is implemented mostly by hardware or mostly by software, provided the system hides any lower levels from the programmer.[7] Given this framework, the role of the architect is to build a cost-effective system by deciding what pieces of the system should be in hardware and what pieces in software.

The selection of languages for consideration in RISC I was influenced by our environment; we chose "C" because of its large user community and, hence, considerable local expertise. Given the limited number of transistors that can be integrated into a single-chip computer, most of the pieces of a RISC high-level language system are in software, with hardware support for only the most time-consuming events.

To determine what constructs are used most frequently and, if possible, what constructs use the most time in average programs, we first looked at the frequency of classes of variables in high-level language programs. Data collected for Pascal and C are shown in Table 1.

The most important observation was that integer constants appeared almost as frequently as arrays or structures. What is not shown is that more than 80 percent of the scalars were local variables and more than 90 percent of the arrays or structures were global variables.

We also looked at the relative dynamic frequencies of high-level language statements for the same eight programs; average occurrences over one percent are shown in Table 2. This information does not tell what statements use the most time in the execution of typical programs. To answer that question, we have to look at the code produced by typical versions of each of these statements. A "typical" version of each statement was supplied by Wulf as part of his study into judging the quality of compilers.[8] We used C compilers for the VAX, PDP-11, and 68000 to determine the average number of instructions and mem-

Table 1.
Dynamic percentage of operands in Pascal and C.

	P1	P2	P3	P4	C1	C2	C3	C4	AVERAGE
INTEGER CONSTANT	14	18	11	20	25	11	29	28	20 ± 7
SCALAR	63	68	46	54	37	45	66	62	55 ± 11
ARRAY/STRUCTURE	23	14	43	25	36	43	5	10	25 ± 14

PROGRAM	EXPLANATION
P1	COMP - a Pascal P-code style compiler
P2	MACRO - the macro expansion phase of the SCALD I design system
P3	PRINT - a prettyprinter for Pascal
P4	DIFF - a program that finds the differences between two files
C1	PCC - the portable C compiler for the VAX
C2	CIFPLOT - a program that plots VLSI mask layouts on a dot plotter
C3	NROFF - a text formatting program
C4	SORT - the Unix sorting program

Table 2.
Relative frequency of Pascal and C statements.

STATEMENTS*	P1	P2	P3	P4	AVERAGE	C1	C2	C3	C4	AVERAGE
ASSIGN	39	52	35	53	45 ± 8	22	50	25	56	38 ± 15
IF	35	30	36	16	29 ± 8	59	31	61	22	43 ± 17
CALL	15	14	16	15	15 ± 1	6	17	9	16	12 ± 5
WITH	2	0	5	13	5 ± 5	2	2	3	5	3 ± 1
LOOP	5	5	5	4	5 ± 0	9	0	1	1	3 ± 4
CASE	4	0	1	0	1 ± 1	2	-	-	0	$< 1 \pm 1$

*Because statements can be nested, we count each occurrence of a statement. Loop statements are counted once per execution rather than once per loop iteration. For example, if two IF statements and three assignment statements appear in a loop that iterates 5 times, we would count 26 statements with 15 assignments, 10 IF statements, and one loop. The WITH statement qualifies a record name.

ory references per statement. By multiplying the frequency of occurrence of each statement with the corresponding number of machine instructions and memory references, we obtain Table 3, which is ordered by memory references.

The data in Table 3 suggest that the procedure call/ return is the most time-consuming operation in typical high-level language programs. These results corroborate studies by Lunde[9] and Wichmann.[10] The statistics on operands found in Table 1 emphasize the importance of local variables and constants. RISC I supports HLLs by enhancing performance of the most time-consuming features of typical HLL programs, as opposed to making the architecture "close" to a particular HLL; thus, RISC I attempts to handle local variables, constants, and procedure calls efficiently while leaving less frequent operations to instruction sequences or subroutines.

Basic architecture of RISC I

The RISC I architecture has 31 instructions, most of which do simple ALU and shift operations on registers. As shown in Table 4, they have been grouped into four

Table 3.
Weighted relative frequency of HLL statements
(ordered by memory references).

STATEMENTS*	HLL (OCCURRENCE)		WEIGHTED (MACHINE INSTR.)		WEIGHTED (MEM. REF.)	
HLL	P	C	P	C	P	C
CALL/RETURN	15 ± 1	12 ± 5	31 ± 3	33 ± 14	44 ± 4	45 ± 19
LOOPS	5 ± 0	3 ± 1	42 ± 3	32 ± 6	33 ± 2	26 ± 5
ASSIGN	45 ± 5	38 ± 15	13 ± 2	13 ± 5	14 ± 2	15 ± 6
IF	29 ± 8	43 ± 17	11 ± 3	21 ± 8	7 ± 2	13 ± 5
WITH	5 ± 5	—	1 ± 0	—	1 ± 0	—
CASE	1 ± 1	$< 1 \pm 1$	1 ± 1	1 ± 1	1 ± 1	1 ± 1
GOTO	—	3 ± 1	—	0 ± 0	—	0 ± 0

*For the CALL statement we counted passing parameters, saving/restoring general registers, and saving/restoring the program counter. The IF and CASE statements include instructions to evaluate expressions and to jump. For LOOP statements we count all the machine instructions executed during each iteration.

categories: arithmetic-logical, memory access, branch, and miscellaneous. Instructions, data, addresses, and registers are 32 bits. The execution time of a RISC I cycle is given by the time it takes to read and add two registers, and then store the result back into a register. Register 0, which always contains zero, allows us to synthesize a variety of operations and addressing modes.

Load and store instructions move data between registers and memory. Rather than lengthen the general cycle to permit a complete memory access, these instructions use two CPU cycles. There are eight variations of memory access instructions to accommodate sign-extended or zero-extended 8-bit, 16-bit, and 32-bit data. Although there appears to be only the index-plus-displacement addressing mode in data transfer instructions, absolute and register-indirect addressing can be synthesized using register 0 (see Table 5).

Branch instructions include call, return, conditional, and unconditional jump. The conditional instructions are the standard set used originally in the PDP-11 and found in most 16-bit microprocessors today. Most of the innovative features of RISC I are found in call, return, and jump; they will be discussed later.

Figure 1 shows the 32-bit format used by register-to-register instructions and memory access instructions. For register-to-register instructions, DEST selects one of the 32 registers as the destination of the result of the operation performed on the registers specified by SOURCE1 and SOURCE2. If IMM = 0, the low-order five bits of SOURCE2 specify another register; if IMM = 1, SOURCE2 expresses a sign-extended 13-bit constant. As mentioned above, the frequency of integer constants in HLL programs suggests architectural support, so immediate operands are available in every instruction. SCC determines whether or not the condition codes are set. Memory access instructions use SOURCE1 to specify the index register and SOURCE2 to specify the offset. One other format combines the last three fields to form a 19-bit PC-relative address and is used primarily by the branch instructions.

The examples in Table 6 show that many of the important VAX instructions can be synthesized from simple RISC I addressing modes and opcodes. Comparative measurements of benchmarks will demonstrate the effectiveness of the chosen instruction set.

Table 4.
Assembly language definition for RISC I.

INSTRUCTION	OPERANDS	COMMENTS	
ADD	Rs,S2,Rd	Rd ← Rs + S2	integer add
ADDC	Rs,S2,Rd	Rd ← Rs + S2 + carry	add with carry
SUB	Rs,S2,Rd	Rd ← Rs − S2	integer subtract
SUBC	Rs,S2,Rd	Rd ← Rs − S2 − carry	subtract with carry
SUBR	Rs,S2,Rd	Rd ← S2 − Rs	integer subtract
SUBCR	Rs,S2,Rd	Rd ← S2 − Rs − carry	subtract with carry
AND	Rs,S2,Rd	Rd ← Rs & S2	logical AND
OR	Rs,S2,Rd	Rd ← Rs | S2	logical OR
XOR	Rs,S2,Rd	Rd ← Rs xor S2	logical EXCLUSIVE OR
SLL	Rs,S2,Rd	Rd ← Rs shifted by S2	shift left
SRL	Rs,S2,Rd	Rd ← Rs shifted by S2	shift right logical
SRA	Rs,S2,Rd	Rd ← Rs shifted by S2	shift right arithmetic
LDL	(Rx)S2,Rd	Rd ← M[Rx + S2]	load long
LDSU	(Rx)S2,Rd	Rd ← M[Rx + S2]	load short unsigned
LDSS	(Rx)S2,Rd	Rd ← M[Rx + S2]	load short signed
LDBU	(Rx)S2,Rd	Rd ← M[Rx + S2]	load byte unsigned
LDBS	(Rx)S2,Rd	Rd ← M[Rx + S2]	load byte signed
STL	Rm,(Rx)S2	M[Rx + S2] ← Rm	store long
STS	Rm,(Rx)S2	M[Rx + S2] ← Rm	store short
STB	Rm,(Rx)S2	M[Rx + S2] ← Rm	store byte
JMP	COND,S2(Rx)	pc ← Rx + S2	conditional jump
JMPR	COND,Y	pc ← pc + Y	conditional relative
CALL	Rd,S2(Rx)	Rd ← pc, next pc ← Rx + S2, CWP ← CWP − 1	call and change window
CALLR	Rd,Y	Rd ← pc, next pc ← pc + Y, CWP ← CWP − 1	call relative and change window
RET	Rm,S2	pc ← Rm + S2, CWP ← CWP + 1	return and change window
CALLINT	Rd	Rd ← last pc; next CWP ← CWP − 1	disable interrupts
RETINT	Rm,S2	pc ← Rm + S2; next CWP ← CWP + 1	enable interrupts
LDHI	Rd,Y	Rd<31:13> ← Y; Rd<12:0> ← 0	load immediate high
GTLPC	Rd	Rd ← last pc	to restart delayed jump
GETPSW	Rd	Rd ← PSW	load status word
PUTPSW	Rm	PSW ← Rm	set status word

Register windows. Investigations into the use of high-level languages suggest that the procedure call is the most time-consuming operation in high-level language programs. Potentially, RISC programs may have even more

Table 5.
Synthesizing VAX addressing modes.

ADDRESSING	VAX	RISC EQUIVALENT
REGISTER	Rx	Rx
IMMEDIATE	#LITERAL	S2 (13-BIT LITERAL)
INDEXED	Rx + DISPL	Rx + S2 (13-BIT DISPLACEMENT)
ABSOLUTE	@#ADDRESS	r0 + S2 (r0 ≡ 0)
REG INDIRECT	(Rx)	Rx + 0

calls, because the complex instructions found in CISCs are subroutines in RISCs. Thus, the procedure call must be as fast as possible, perhaps no longer than a few jumps. Because of its register window scheme, RISC I approaches this goal and reduces data memory traffic.

Using procedures involves two groups of time-consuming operations: saving or restoring registers on each call or return, and passing parameters and results to and from the procedure. The frequency of local scalar variables justifies the architectural support of placing locals in registers, and Baskett[11] and Sites[12] have proposed that

OP CODE<7>	SCC<1>	DEST<5>	SOURCE1<5>	IMM<1>	SOURCE2<13>

Figure 1. RISC I basic instruction format.

Table 6.
Synthesizing VAX instructions.

OPERATION	VAX		RISC I EQUIVALENT	
REG-REG MOVE	MOVL	Rm,Rn	ADD	R0,Rm,Rn (r0 ≡ 0)
COMPARE	CMPL	Rm,Rn	SUB	Rm,Rn,r0,{c}
COMPARE TO 0	TSTL	Rn	SUB	Rn,r0,r0,{c}
	TSTL	A	LDL	(r0)A,r0,{c}
CLEAR	CLRL	Rn	ADD	r0,r0,Rn
	CLRL	A	STL	r0,(r0)A
TWOS COMPLEMENT	MNEGL	Rm,Rn	SUB	r0,Rm,Rn
ONES COMPLEMENT	MCOML	Rm,Rn	XOR	Rm,#−1,Rn
LOAD CONST	MOVL	$N,Rm(|N| < 2^{12})	ADD	r0,#N,Rm
	MOVL	$N,Rm(|N| ≥ 2^{12})	LDHI	#N<31:13>,Rm
			ADD	r0,#N<12:0>,Rm
INCREMENT	INCL	Rn	ADD	Rn,#1,Rn
DECREMENT	DECL	Rn	SUB	Rn,#1,Rn
CHECK INDEX BOUNDS,	INDEX	Rm,#0,#U,	SUB	Rm,#U,r0{c};
(A[0:U])		#1,A,Rn;	JMP	lequ,OK;*
TRAP IF ERROR,	MOVB	(Rn),Rp	CALL	error;
AND READ A[Rm]			OK: LDBU	(Rm)A,Rp

*This approach is better than the normal algorithm. We can think of an index as an unsigned integer since 0 ≤ index ≤ U. A two's complement negative number (1X...X) is then a large unsigned number, so we only need make one unsigned test instead of two signed tests. Nonzero lower bounds are handled by subtracting the lower bound from the index, and multiple indices are handled by repeating the sequence and including a multiply and an add. This idea resulted from a discussion between Bill Joy, Peter Kessler, and George Taylor. Taylor coded the examples and found that on the VAX-11/780, the sequence of simple instructions was always faster than the index instruction. This optimization is found in the Unix C optimizer.

microprocessors keep multiple banks of registers on the chip to avoid register saving and restoring. A similar scheme was adopted by RISC I. Each procedure call allocates a new "window" of registers from the large register file for use by that procedure, and the return resets a pointer, restoring the old set. But some of the registers are not saved or restored on each procedure call; these registers (r0 through r9) are called global registers.

Furthermore, the sets of registers used by different procedures overlap, allowing parameters to be passed in registers. In other machines, parameters are usually passed on the stack, and the calling procedure uses a register (frame pointer) that points to the beginning of the parameters (and also the end of the locals). Thus, all references to parameters are indexed references to mem-

ory. Our approach partitions the set of window registers (10-31) into the three parts defined by their respective overlap. Every procedure sees the set of registers shown in Figure 2.

High registers 26 through 31 contain parameters passed from "above" the current procedure—that is, from the calling procedure. Local registers 16 through 25 are used for local scalar storage. Low registers 10 through 15 are used for temporaries and parameters passed to the procedure "below" the current procedure (the called procedure). On each procedure call a new set of registers, numbered 10-31, is allocated. The low registers of the "caller" become the high registers of the "callee" because of the hardware overlap between subsequent register windows. Thus, without moving information, parameters in registers 10-15 appear in registers 25-31 of the called window. Figure 3 illustrates this approach for the case where procedure A calls procedure B, which calls procedure C.

If the nesting depth is sufficiently large, all register windows will be used. RISC I handles a call overflow with a separate stack in memory. Overflow and underflow are handled with a trap to a software routine that adjusts that stack. Because this routine can save or restore several sets of registers, the overflow/underflow frequency is based on local variations in the depth of the stack rather than absolute depth. The effectiveness of this scheme depends on the relative frequency of overflows and underflows. Studies by Halbert and Kessler[13] show that with eight register banks overflow will occur in less than one percent of the calls. This suggests that programs exhibit locality in the dynamic nesting of procedures, just as they exhibit locality in memory references.

Another problem with variables in registers occurs in referencing them with pointers, since this requires variable addresses. Because registers normally do not have memory addresses, we could let the compiler determine which variables have pointers and put these variables in

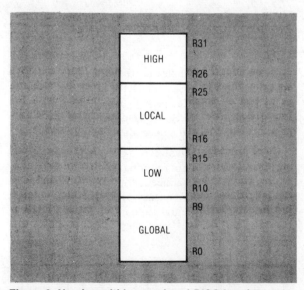

Figure 2. Naming within one virtual RISC I register window.

COMPUTER

memory, but this precludes separate compilation and slows access to these variables. RISC I solves that problem by giving addresses to the window registers. By reserving a portion of the address space, we can determine, with one comparison, whether a register address points to a CPU register or to one that has overflowed into memory. Because the only instructions accessing memory—load and store—already take an extra cycle, we can add this feature without reducing their performance. This permits the use of straightforward compiler technology and still leaves most of the variables in registers.

This addressing technique also solves the "up-level addressing" problem. Pascal and other languages allow nested procedure declarations, thereby creating a class of variables that are neither global variables nor local to a single procedure. Compilers keep track of each procedure environment using static and dynamic links or displays. Such a compiler for RISC I would also associate the memory address for the window of local variables. These variables would then be accessed by using the display or dynamic chains to find the corresponding memory addresses.

Delayed jump. The normal RISC I instruction cycle is just long enough to execute the following sequence of operations: read a register, do an ALU operation, and store the result back into a register. We increase performance by prefetching the next instruction during the execution of the current instruction. This introduces difficulties with branch instructions. Several high-end machines have elaborate techniques to prefetch the appropriate instruction after the branch,[14] but these techniques are too complicated for a single-chip RISC. Our solution was to redefine jumps so that they do not take effect until after the *following* instructions; we refer to this as the delayed jump.

The delayed jump allows RISC I to always prefetch the next instruction during the execution of the current instruction. The machine language code is suitably arranged so that the desired results are obtained. Because RISC I is always intended to be programmed in high-level languages, we will not burden the programmer with this complexity; the "burden" will be carried by the programmers of the compiler, the optimizer, and the debugger.

Table 7 illustrates the delayed branch. Machines with normal jumps would execute the sequence in Table 7a in the order 100, 101, 102, 105, ... To get that same effect in RISC I, we would have to insert a no operation instruction (Table 7b). The sequence of instructions for RISC I is now 100, 101, 102, **103**, 106, ... In the worst case, every jump could take two instructions. The RISC I compiler, however, includes an optimizer that tries to rearrange the sequence of instructions to do the equivalent operations while making use of the instruction slot where the NOP appears. As shown in Table 7c, the optimized RISC I sequence is 100, 101, **102**, 105, ... Because the instruction following a jump is always executed and the jump at 101 is not dependent on the add at 102, this sequence is equivalent to the original program segment in Table 7a.

Architectural heritage. Since architects of new machines build on the work of others, we believe it is important to trace the genealogy of RISC I. Its earliest ancestor is the 1951 Ferranti-Manchester MADM—the first machine with index registers—which also used a register to supply zero.[15] Seymour Cray revived the idea in 1964 with the CDC-6400 and continued to use it in the CDC-7600 and the Cray 1. The delayed jump was first used in the Maniac I, which was completed just a year after the MADM, but we adopted the idea from microprogrammed control units, where delayed jumps are the norm.

The leading proponent of reduced instruction set computers for floating-point data is Cray. For the last 15 years, he has combined simple instruction sets with so-

Table 7.
Normal and delayed jumps.

ADDRESS	(a) NORMAL JUMP		(b) DELAYED JUMP		(c) OPTIMIZED DELAYED JUMP	
100	LOAD	X,A	LOAD	X,A	LOAD	X,A
101	ADD	1,A	ADD	1,A	**JUMP**	**105**
102	**JUMP**	**105**	**JUMP**	**106**	**ADD**	**1,A**
103	ADD	A,B	**NOP**		ADD	A,B
104	SUB	C,B	ADD	A,B	SUB	C,B
105	**STORE**	**A,Z**	SUB	C,B	**STORE**	**A,Z**
106			**STORE**	**A,Z**		

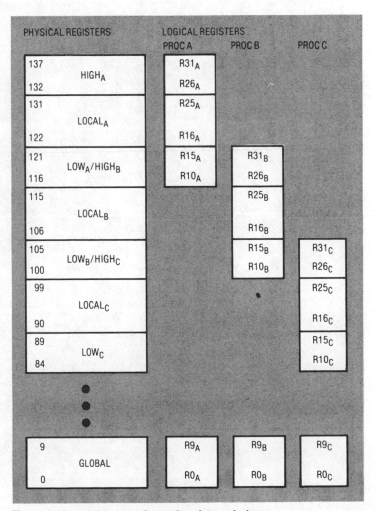

Figure 3. Use of three overlapped register windows.

163

phisticated pipelined implementations to create the most powerful floating-point engines in the world. While Cray concentrates on impressive floating-point rates at impressive costs, RISC I concentrates on improved performance at lower cost for integer programs written in HLLs.

A machine with similar goals that predates RISC I is the IBM 801. This project, led by John Cocke and George Radin, began in 1975 by reexamining the relationship between instruction sets, compilers, and operating systems. They pushed the state of the art of compiler technology and created an extremely fast, reduced-instruction-set ECL minicomputer. Alas, the architecture community was left to speculate on the truth of widely varying rumors about the technical details[16] as well as the success or failure of the project.[17] Fortunately, accurate information is beginning to emerge.[18] It will be interesting to see the similarities between RISC I and the 801; one difference is that RISC I uses traditional compiler technology and the 801 uses a traditional register set.

In searching the annals of computer architecture we cannot find a clear reference to overlapped register windows. To our best knowledge, no machine uses the scheme for fast, multiport registers in the CPU. Most modern machines support procedure call by having instructions that manage a portion of main memory as a stack to pass parameters and allocate locals. Theoretically, a cache should then make such a scheme as fast as the overlapped register windows. Registers are faster than caches because of the difference in speed between a small memory and a large memory, the difference in speed between a deterministic access and a probabilistic access, and the difference in speed between a nontranslated register access and a translated virtual memory access. Theoretically, hardware can overcome almost any obstacle, but it occasionally stumbles in implementation. The advantages of registers become apparent when we look at concrete realizations; as we shall see, procedure call/return on the VAX-11/780, using a software stack enhanced by a hardware cache, is about an order of magnitude slower than the overlapped register windows of RISC I.

There are a few machines that share features of RISC I's overlapped register window scheme. The BBN C/70, a recent machine, allocates a new set of registers on every procedure call, but it does not overlap register sets.

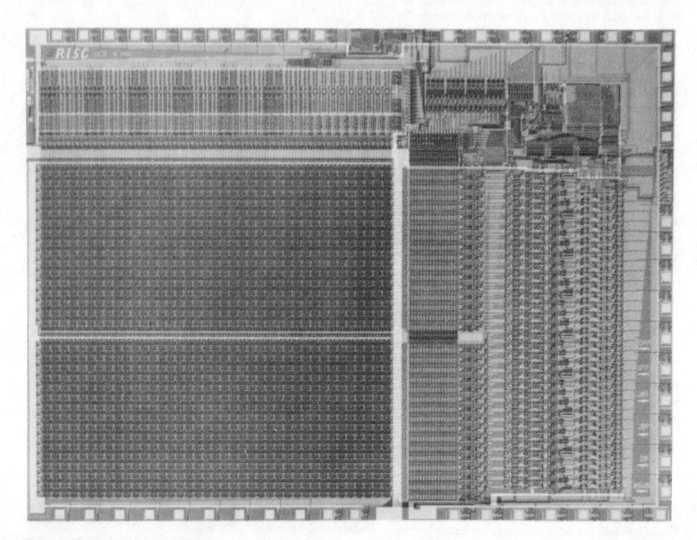

Figure 4. Photomicrograph of RISC I.

| | ZILOG Z8000 | MOTOROLA 68000 | INTEL iAPX-432 | | | RISC I |
			43201	43202	43203	
TOTAL DEVICES	17.5K	68K	110K	49K	60K	44K
TOTAL MINUS ROM	17.5K	37K	44K	49K	44K	44K
DRAWN DEVICES	3.5K	3.0K	5.6K	9.5K	5.7K	1.8K
REGULARIZATION FACTOR	5.0	12.1	7.9	5.2	7.7	25
SIZE OF CHIP (MILS)	238×251	246×281	318×323	366×313	358×326	406×305
(AREA IN MIL^2)	60K	69K	103K	115K	117K	124K
SIZE OF CONTROL (MIL^2)	37K	35K	67K	45K	47K	7K
PERCENT CONTROL	53%	50%	65%	39%	40%	6%
TIME TO FIRST SILICON (MONTHS)	30	30	33	33	21	19
DESIGN EFFORT (MAN MONTHS)	60	100	170	170	130	15
LAYOUT EFFORT (MAN MONTHS)	70	70	90	100	50	12

A popular architecture that comes close to RISC I is the Texas Instruments 990-9900 family. These machines allocate their general "registers" in memory, so adding the contents of one register to another results in three memory accesses. A single register points to the register work space; most of the machines allow the pointer to overlap work spaces. The latest generation of this family, the TI 99000, includes on-chip main memory, but the first models appear to still have slow register access.[19] The machine that comes closest to the overlapped register windows is the Bell Labs MAC-8. The state of NMOS technology in 1975 precluded having a rich instruction set *and* a register file on the chip; the architects chose the rich instruction set. The main difference between the MAC-8 and TI 990 is that the Bell architects realized that overlapping the registers could improve the performance of the procedure call and provided instructions to specifically overlap the register windows in memory. It is our understanding that some C compilers used this feature. This machine was never implemented with on-chip registers, and the logical successor to this machine, the BellMAC-32, has abandoned this approach.

VLSI implementation

The transition from theoretical architecture to concrete circuits began on January 6, 1981. Mask descriptions were completed June 22, and we received first silicon on October 23. Figure 4 is a photomicrograph of RISC I. We followed the Mead-Conway design philosophy for NMOS with lambda at two microns and no buried contacts. This first version, RISC I "Gold" as it is known internally, implements the complete instruction set and six windows with a total of 78 registers. The only piece of the architecture not implemented is the mapping of registers into the memory address space.

We collected statistics on the design and layout of RISC I.[20] Table 8 compares these results to VLSI implementations of more complex architectures. The most visible impact of the reduced instruction set is the reduced control

area: control is only six percent of RISC I compared to 50 percent in others. RISC I is also more regular. Lattin defines the regularity factor as the total number of transistors (less those in ROM) divided by the number of individually drawn transistors.[21] By this measure RISC I is two to five times more regular than the Z8000, 68000, or 432. The time from the first discussion of the RISC I architecture to the masks was 14 months—less than the development periods of other machines. This was due in part to the reduced instruction set and in part to the Berkeley CAD software, a good match for this style of VLSI design. The primary interface was Caesar, an excellent color graphics layout editor developed by Ousterhout.[22]

Evaluation

Register windows. Two benchmarks—"puzzle" and "quicksort"—showed the effectiveness of window registers in reducing procedure cost. The two recursive programs behave quite differently. Quicksort has a large percentage of procedure calls. Puzzle has such a low density of calls that it is almost atypical for modern structured programs, but it does have a large nesting depth. In both cases, the window scheme proved to be beneficial. Table 9 shows the maximum depth of recursion, the number of register window overflows and underflows, and the total

Table 9.
Memory traffic due to call/return.

	CALLS PLUS RETURNS, % INSTRS	MAXIMUM NESTED DEPTH	RISC I OVERFLOWS + UNDERFLOWS	DATA MEMORY TRAFFIC RISC I, WORDS	VAX, WORDS
PUZZLE	43K 0.7%	20	124	8K 0.8%	444K 28.0%
QUICKSORT	111K 8.0%	10	64	4K 1.0%	696K 50.0%

165

number of words transferred between memory and the RISC CPU as a result of the overflows and underflows. It also shows the memory traffic due to saving and restoring registers in the VAX. For this simulation we assumed that half of the registers were saved on an overflow and half were restored on an underflow. We found that for RISC I, an average of 0.37 words are transferred to memory per procedure invocation for the puzzle program and 0.07 for quicksort. Note that half of the data memory references in quicksort are the result of the call/return overhead of the VAX.

Table 10 compares the average "cost" of the RISC procedure mechanism—measured in execution time, number of instructions executed, and data memory accesses—to that of three traditional machines. The data was collected by looking at the code generated by C compilers for these machines for procedure call and return statements, assuming that two parameters are passed and requiring that three registers be saved.

The window scheme also reduces off-chip memory accesses. In traditional machines, 30 to 50 percent of the instructions generally access data memory, but no more than 20 percent of the instructions are register-to-register.[23,24] Because RISC I arithmetic and logical instructions cannot access memory, one might expect a higher percent of data transfer instructions. This is not the case. The static frequencies of RISC I instructions for nine typical C programs show that less than 20 percent of the instructions are loads and stores, but more than 50 percent are register-to-register. RISC I has successfully changed the allocation of variables from memory into registers, thus minimizing the slower off-chip memory accesses. This demonstrates that complex addressing modes are not necessary to obtain an effective machine.

Delayed jump. The effectiveness of rearranging the code around jump instructions can be evaluated by counting the NOP instructions in a program. Static figures before optimization show that in typical C programs about 18 percent of the instructions are NOPs inserted after jump instructions. A simple peephole optimizer reduces this to about eight percent. The optimizer does well on unconditional branches (removing about 90 percent of the NOPs) but not so well with conditional branches (removing only about 20 percent of the NOPs). Note that these are the static numbers; the dynamic numbers can be worse.

This optimizer was improved to replace the NOP by the instruction at the target of a jump. This technique can be applied to conditional branches if the optimizer determines that the target instruction modifies temporary resources—for example, an instruction that only modifies the condition codes. In quicksort, this removes all NOPs except those that follow return instructions, dropping NOPs from 12 percent statically to three percent. The dynamic effectiveness of the delayed branch must now include the NOPs plus the instructions after conditional branches that need not be executed for a particular jump condition. The total percentages of either type of instruction are again program dependent, ranging from 4 to 22 percent.

Overall performance. Prototype versions of a RISC I compiler for C, optimizer, linker, assembler, and simulator were developed early in the project to predict the code size and performance of RISC I. The minicomputers and microprocessors chosen for this comparison are described in Table 11. We didn't have working hardware for either the 68000 or RISC I, so we used simulators to predict performance. The cycle time for the first RISC I prototype is expected to be 400 nsec to read and add two 32-bit registers, store the result in a register, and prefetch the next instruction. This estimate is both optimistic and pessimistic: optimistic in that it is unlikely that students can successfully build something that fast on their first

Table 10.
Procedure call/return overhead (including parameter passing).

	EXECUTION TIME (μSECS)	INSTRUCTIONS EXECUTED	DATA MEMORY ACCESSES
VAX-11	26	5	19
PDP-11	22	19	15
68000	19	9	12
RISC I	2	6	0.2

Table 11.
Characteristics of six machines.

	MICROPROCESSORS—NMOS VLSI				MINICOMPUTERS—SHOTTKY TTL MSI		
	RISC I	68000	Z8002		VAX-11/780	PDP-11/70	C/70
YEAR OF INTRODUCTION	1981	1980	1979		1978	1975	1980
BASIC INSTRUCTIONS	31	61	110		248	65	40
GENERAL REGISTERS	32	15	14		13	6	8
ADDRESSING MODES	2	14	12		18	12	17
ADDRESS SIZE (BITS)	32	24	16		32	16	20
BASIC CLOCK FREQUENCY	7.5MHz	10MHz	6MHz		5MHz	7.5MHz	6.7MHz
REG. TO REG. ADD (μsec)	0.4	0.4	0.7		0.4	0.5	?
MODIFY INDEX, BRANCH IF ZERO (BRANCH TAKEN)	1.2	1.0	2.2		1.4	0.8	?

try, and pessimistic because an experienced IC design team could build a much faster machine.

We chose 11 C programs for the performance comparison. The first five programs are HLL versions of the *EDN* benchmarks.[25] The other C programs range from toy programs (e.g., towers of Hanoi) to programs from the Unix environment that are used every day (e.g., SED, a batch-oriented text editor).

The compilers used are quite similar: the VAX, C/70, Z8002, 68000, and RISC I C compilers are based on a Unix portable C compiler,[26] and the one for the PDP-11 is based on the Ritchie C compiler.[27] Experiments comparing the Ritchie and portable C compilers for the PDP-11 have shown that the average difference in the size of generated code is within one percent.[28]

Tables 12 and 13 compare the relative performance and code size of these minicomputers and microprocessors on the 11 C programs. A surprising result is that, even though size optimization was virtually ignored, RISC I programs are—at worst—a factor of two larger than programs for the other machines. To us, the most important figure of merit for a new architecture is execution time. Table 13 shows that RISC I executes C programs faster than currently available microprocessors—faster even than most minicomputers.

Discussion

The presentation of the RISC concept has led to many stimulating discussions. Listed below are frequently heard comments followed by a short discussion of that comment.

CISCs provide better support of HLLs since they include HLL primitives (CASE, CALL).

CISC architectures support HLLs by narrowing the gap between the semantics of the assembly language and

Table 12.
C benchmarks: RISC I program size (in bytes) and RISC I size ratio.

| BENCHMARK | RISC I | PROGRAM SIZE RELATIVE TO RISC I | | | | |
		68000	Z8002	VAX-11/780	11/70	C/70
E—STRING SEARCH	144	.8	.9	.7	.8	.7
F—BIT TEST	120	1.2	1.5	1.2	1.4	1.0
H—LINKED LIST	176	.7	.8	1.2	1.7	.8
K—BIT MATRIX	288	1.1	1.3	1.0	1.3	1.1
I— QUICKSORT	992	.7	1.1	.9	1.1	.9
ACKERMAN(3,6)	144	—	2.1	.5	.6	.5
PUZZLE(SUBSCRIPT)	2736	—	.5	.5	.6	.6
PUZZLE(POINTER)	2796	.9	.5	.5	.5	.6
RECURSIVE QSORT	752	—	.8	.6	.8	.6
SED(BATCH EDITOR)	17720	—	1.0	.6	.5	.5
TOWERS HANOI(18)	96	—	2.5	.8	1.0	.7
AVERAGE		.9 ± .2	1.2 ± .6	.8 ± .3	.9 ± .4	.7 ± .2

Table 13.
C benchmarks: RISC I execution time (in milliseconds) and RISC I performance ratio.

| BENCHMARK | RISC I | NUMBER OF TIMES SLOWER THAN RISC I | | | | |
		68000	Z8002	VAX-11/780	11/70	C/70
E—STRING SEARCH	.46	2.8	1.6	1.3	0.9	2.2
F—BIT TEST	.06	4.8	7.2	4.8	6.2	9.2
H—LINKED LIST	.10	1.6	2.4	1.2	1.9	2.5
K—BIT MATRIX	.43	4.0	5.2	3.0	4.0	9.3
I— QUICKSORT	50.4	4.1	5.2	3.0	3.6	5.8
ACKERMAN(3,6)	3200	—	2.8	1.6	1.6	—
RECURSIVE QSORT	800	—	5.9	2.3	3.2	1.3
PUZZLE(SUBSCRIPT)	4700	—	4.2	2.0	1.6	3.4
PUZZLE(POINTER)	3200	4.2	2.3	1.3	2.0	2.1
SED(BATCH EDITOR)	5100	—	4.4	1.1	1.1	2.6
TOWERS HANOI(18)	6800	—	4.2	1.8	2.3	1.6
AVERAGE		3.5 ± 1.8	4.1 ± 1.6	2.1 ± 1.1	2.6 ± 1.5	4.0 ± 2.8

September 1982

the semantics of an HLL. Support can also, however, be measured as the inverse of the "costs" of using typical HLL constructs on a particular machine. If the architect provides a feature that "looks" like the HLL construct but runs slowly, the compiler writer will omit the feature or, worse, the HLL programmer concerned with performance will avoid the construct. A recent study shows that CISCs penalize the use of HLLs far more than RISCs.[29]

It is more difficult to write a compiler for a RISC than a CISC.

A recent paper by Wulf[30] helps explain why this is not true. He says that compiling is essentially a large "case analysis." The more ways there are to do something (more instructions and addressing modes), the more cases must be considered. The compiler writer must balance the speed of the compiler with his desire to get good code. In CISCs there may not be enough time to analyze the potential usage of all available instructions. Thus, Wulf recommends, "There should be precisely one way to do something, or all ways should be possible." In RISC we have taken the former approach. There are few choices; for example, if an operand is in memory, it must first be loaded into a register. Simple case analysis implies a simple compiler, even if more instructions must be generated in each case.

RISC I is tailored to C and will not work well with other HLLs.

Studies of other HLLs[23,31] indicate that the most frequently executed operations are the same simple HLL constructs found in C, for which RISC I has been optimized. Unless an HLL significantly changes the way people program, we expect to see similar results. For languages that have unusual data types, such as Cobol, we need to find the simple operations that are used repeatedly in that environment and incorporate them into a RISC. Even if the RISC I architecture does not map Cobol efficiently, we believe this philosophy can lead to a RISC that does.

Comparisons of RISC I with the VAX are unfair in that the VAX provides a virtual address space; RISC I would be much slower if it had virtual memory.

To answer the question "How much slower?" we looked at solutions used by other microprocessors. National Semiconductor has announced the 16082, a memory management chip with an address cache that normally translates virtual address into physical addresses in 100 nsec.[32] If we were to put this chip in a system with a RISC CPU, it would add another 100 nsec to every memory access. Memory is referenced every 400 nsec in RISC I, so such a combination would reduce RISC performance by 20 percent. Because 80 to 90 percent of memory references in RISC I are to instructions,[1] more sophisticated approaches, such as translating addresses only when crossing a page boundary, might limit performance reduction to only five percent. A final observation is that even if the addition of virtual memory doubled the cycle

time of NMOS RISC I, it would still be faster than most present-day microprocessors.

The good performance is due to the overlapped register windows; the reduced instruction set has nothing to do with it.

Certainly, a significant portion of the speed is due to the overlapped register windows of RISC I. A key point is that there would have been no room for register windows if control had not dropped from 50 to 6 percent. Furthermore, control is so simple in RISC that microprogramming is unnecessary; this eliminates the control loop as the limiting factor of the machine cycle, as is frequently the case in microprogrammed machines.

There is no difference between overlapped register windows and a data cache.

A cache is ineffective if it is too small. An effective data cache would require a much larger area than our register file, especially if it must provide the same number of ports as the register file. The more complicated virtual address translation and decoding would likely stretch the basic CPU cycle time. Finally, the more complicated cache control would have extended the design phase of RISC I.

RISC I represents a new style of computers that take less time to build yet provide higher performance. While traditional machines "support" HLLs with instructions that look like HLL constructs, this machine supports the use of HLLs with instructions that HLL compilers can use efficiently. The loss of complexity has not reduced RISC's functionality; the chosen subset, especially when combined with the register window scheme, emulates more complex machines. It also appears we can build such a single-chip computer much sooner and with less effort than traditional architectures.

As we go to press, we are just testing the RISC I chips. Unfortunately, the polysilicon layer was processed improperly, and we believe this accounts for the fact that the chips are only partially operational. We have not yet found any circuit design errors.

This research area is by no means closed. For example, an investigation of a RISC with two ALU operations per cycle and dual-port main memory has begun at Stanford,[33] and we are working on a new implementation with a denser register file and a more sophisticated timing scheme.[34] Some of the other topics to be investigated include the applicability of RISCs to other HLLs (e.g., Lisp, Cobol, Ada), the effectiveness of an operating system on RISC (e.g., Unix), the architecture of coprocessors for RISC (e.g., graphics, floating point), migration of software to RISC (e.g., a 370 emulator written in RISC machine language), and the implementation of RISC in other technologies (CMOS, TTL, ECL). This list is too big for one project; we hope to cooperate with industry and academia in exploring RISCy architectures. ■

Acknowledgments

The RISC Project has been sustained by a large group of volunteers. We would like to thank all those in the Berkeley community who have helped push RISC from a concept to a chip. We would also like to give special thanks to a few.

John Ousterhout created, maintained, and revised Caesar, our principal design aid, and consistently provided useful technical and editorial advice. Lloyd Dickman was actively involved with the design of RISC during his sabbatical at Berkeley, supplying technical and managerial expertise. We also want to thank Richard Newton for dedicating his VLSI class to the RISC project.

The RISC research was investigated over a four-quarter sequence of graduate courses at Berkeley. Many have participated but a few contributed significantly. Manolis Katevenis did the initial block structure and the initial timing description and provided many important simplifications and ideas about the implementation and the architecture. Ralph Campbell wrote the initial C compiler, the optimizer, assembler, and linker. Yuval Tamir wrote a simulator, ran the benchmarks,[35] and provided many suggestions in the initial design of RISC I. Gary Corcoran wrote the initial ISPS description of RISC I. Jim Peek, Korbin Van Dyke, John Foderaro, Dan Fitzpatrick, and Zvi Peshkess were the principal VLSI designers of the first RISC I chip. Michael Arnold, Dan Fitzpatrick, John Foderaro, and Howard Landman all wrote CAD tools that were crucial to the VLSI implementation of RISC I. Peter Kessler helped derive the overlapped register windows and helped with the CAD software. Jim Beck and Bob Cmelik created the VLSI testing hardware and software. Bob Sherburne is currently working with Katevenis on a more efficient VLSI implementation of RISC. Earl Cohen and Neil Soiffer collected statistics on C programs, and Shafi Goldwasser collected similar statistics for Pascal.

We would also like to thank Korbin Van Dyke for his useful suggestions on improving this paper.

This research was funded in part by the Defense Advance Research Projects Agency, ARPA Order No. 3803, and monitored by the Naval Electronic System Command under Contract No. N00039-78-G-0013-0004. We would like to thank Duane Adams, Paul Losleben, and DARPA for providing the resources that allow universities to attempt projects involving high risk.

References

1. W. D. Strecker, "VAX-11/780: A Virtual Address Extension to the DEC PDP-11 Family," *AFIPS Conf. Proc.,* Vol. 47, 1978 NCC, pp. 967-980.

2. B. G. Utley et al., *IBM System/38 Technical Developments,* IBM GS80-0237, 1978.

3. P. Tyner, *iAPX-432 General Data Processor Architecture Reference Manual,* Order No. 171860-001, Intel, Santa Clara, Calif., 1981.

4. E. Organick, *A Programmer's View of the Intel 432 System*, McGraw-Hill, Hightstown, N.J., 1982.

5. D. A. Patterson and D. R. Ditzel, "The Case for the Reduced Instruction Set Computer," *Computer Architecture News,* Vol. 8, No. 6, Oct. 15, 1980, pp. 25-33.

6. D. A. Patterson and C. H. Séquin, "Design Considerations for Single-Chip Computers of the Future," *IEEE Trans. Computers,* Joint Special Issue on Microprocessors and Microcomputers, Vol. C-29, No. 2, pp. 108-116.

7. D. R. Ditzel and D. A. Patterson, "Retrospective on High-Level Language Computer Architecture," *Proc. Seventh Annual Int'l Symp. Computer Architecture,* May 6-8, 1980, pp. 97-104.

8. W. Wulf, private communication, Nov. 1980.

9. A. Lunde, "Empirical Evaluation of Some Features of Instruction Set Processor Architecture," *Comm. ACM,* Mar. 1977, Vol. 20, No. 3, pp. 143-153.

10. B. A. Wichmann, "Ackermann's Function: A Study in the Efficiency of Calling Procedures," *BIT,* Vol. 16, No. 1, Jan. 1976, pp. 103-110.

11. F. Baskett, "A VLSI Pascal Machine," public lecture, University of California, Berkeley, Fall 1978.

12. R. L. Sites, "How to Use 1000 Registers," *Caltech Conf. VLSI,* Jan. 1979.

13. D. Halbert and P. Kessler, *Windows of Overlapping Registers,* CS292R Final Reports, June 9, 1980.

14. D. Morris and R. N. Ibbett, *The MU-5 Computer System,* Springer-Verlag, New York, 1979.

15. F. C. Williams and T. Kilburn, "The University of Machester Computing Machine," *Inaugural Conf. Machester University Computer,* July 1951, pp. 5-11.

16. "Altering Computer Architecture is Way to Raise Throughput, Suggests IBM Researchers," *Electronics,* Vol. 49, No. 25, Dec. 23, 1976, pp. 30-31.

17. "IBM Mini a Radical Departure," *Datamation,* Vol. 25, No. 11, Oct. 79, pp. 53-55.

18. G. Radin, "The 801 Minicomputer," *Proc. Symp. Architectural Support for Programming Languages and Operating Systems,* Mar. 1-3, 1982.

19. R. V. Orlando and T. L. Anderson, "An Overview of the 9900 Microprocessor Family," *IEEE Micro,* Vol. 1, No. 3, Aug. 1981, pp. 38-42.

20. D. T. Fitzpatrick et al., "A RISCy Approach to VLSI," *VLSI Design,* Vol. 2, No. 4, Oct. 81, pp. 14-20.

21. W. W. Lattin et al., "A Methodology for VLSI Chip Design," *Lambda—The Magazine of VLSI Design,* Second Quarter 1981, pp. 34-44.

22. J. Ousterhout, "Caesar: An Interactive Editor for VLSI Circuits," *VLSI Design,* Vol. 2, No. 4, Nov. 1981, pp. 34-38.

23. W. C. Alexander and D. B. Wortman, "Static and Dynamic Characteristics of XPL Programs," *Computer,* Vol. 8, No. 11, Nov. 1975, pp. 41-46.

24. L. Shustek, "Analysis and Performance of Computer Instruction Sets," PhD Thesis, Stanford University, Jan. 1978.

25. R. G. Grappel and J. E. Hemmengway, "A Tale of Four Microprocessors: Benchmarks Quantify Performance," *Electronic Design News,* Vol. 26, No. 7, Apr. 1, 1981, pp. 179-265.

26. S. C. Johnson, "A Portable Compiler: Theory and Practice," *Proc. Fifth Annual ACM Symp. Programming Languages,* Jan. 1978, pp. 97-104.

27. B. W. Kernighan and D. M. Ritchie, *The C Programming Language,* Prentice-Hall, Englewood Cliffs, N.J., 1978.

28. S. C. Johnson, private communication, Jan. 1981.

29. D. A. Patterson and R. S. Piepho, "RISC Assessment: A High-Level Language Experiment," *Proc. Ninth Int'l Symp. Computer Architecture,* Apr. 26-29, 1982, pp. 3-8. (Scheduled to appear in an upcoming issue of IEEE Micro.)

30. W. A. Wulf, "Compilers and Computer Architecture," *Computer,* Vol. 14, No. 7, July 1981, pp. 41-48.

31. D. R. Ditzel, "Program Measurements on a High-Level Language Computer," *Computer*, Vol. 13, No. 8, Aug. 1980, pp. 62-72.

32. Y. Lavi et al., "16-bit Microprocessor Enters Virtual Memory Domain," *Electronics,* Vol. 53, No. 9, Apr. 24, 1980, pp. 123-129.

33. J. Hennessy et al., "The MIPS Machine," *Digest of Papers Compcon Spring 82*, Feb. 1982, pp. 2-7.

34. R. W. Sherburne et al., "Datapath Design for RISC," *Proc. Conf. Advanced Research in VLSI,* Jan. 25-27, 1982, pp. 53-62.

35. Y. Tamir, "Simulation and Performance Evaluation of the RISC Architecture," Electronics Research Laboratory Memorandom No. UCB/ERL M81/17, University of California, Berkeley, Mar. 1981.

David A. Patterson has been a member of the faculty in the Computer Science Division, Department of Electrical Engineering and Computer Sciences, University of California, Berkeley, since 1977. He was named associate professor in 1981 and currently teaches computer architecture at the graduate and undergraduate levels. His research combines popular software, experimental architecture, and VLSI to create more effective computer systems.

Patterson spent the fall of 1979 on leave of absence at Digital Equipment Corporation developing microprogram design tools and reviewing computer designs. In the next academic year he developed courses that led to the design and implementation of RISC I, a 45,000-transistor microprocessor. In 1982 he received the Distinguished Teaching Award from the Berkeley division of the Academic Senate of the University of California. Patterson received a BA in mathematics and an MS and PhD in computer science from UCLA.

Carlo H. Séquin is a professor of computer science at the University of California, Berkeley. Since 1980, he has headed the Computer Science Division as associate chairman for computer sciences in the Department of Electrical Engineering and Computer Science. He joined the faculty in 1977. His research interests lie in the field of computer architecture and design tools for very large scale integrated systems. In particular, his research concerns multi-microprocessor computer networks, the mutual influence of advanced computer architecture and modern VLSI technology, and the implementation of special functions in silicon.

From 1970 to 1976, Séquin worked on the design and investigation of charge-coupled devices for imaging and signal processing applications at Bell Telephone Laboratories, Murray Hill, New Jersey. He has written many papers in that field and is an author of the first book on charge-transfer devices. Séquin received his PhD in experimental physics from the University of Basel, Switzerland, in 1969. He is a member of the ACM and the Swiss Physical Society, and a fellow of the IEEE.

Reprinted from *IEEE Micro*, November 1982, pages 9-18. Copyright © 1982 by The Institute of Electrical and Electronics Engineers, Inc.

A reduced instruction set computer, RISC I, was compared to five traditional machines.

It provided the highest performance with the smallest penalty for using high-level language.

Assessing RISCs in High-Level Language Support

David A. Patterson and Richard S. Piepho*

University of California, Berkeley

Computer designers today generally increase the complexity of architectures commensurate with the increasing capabilities of implementation technologies. Negative consequences of such complexity are increased design time, more design errors, inconsistent implementations, and the delay in implementation typical of single-chip designs.[1] The class of computers characterized by this architectural complexity we call CISCs—complex instruction set computers. In this article, we will contrast CISCs to another class of computers we call RISCs—reduced instruction set computers. Examples of RISCs are the 801[2] at IBM, RISC I[3] at the University of California, Berkeley, and the MIPS machine[4] at Stanford; examples of CISCs are the DEC VAX-11[5] and the Intel iAPX-432.[6] Discussions arguing the merits of each style of design are found elsewhere.[1,7,8] Fairclough, apparently unaware of other work in the area, recently published evidence to support RISCs.[9]

Preliminary results from the RISC project at Berkeley are very encouraging. The design of RISC I began in spring 1980 and was completed in spring 1981. After we specified the architecture, we developed a C compiler, an optimizer, an assembler, a linker, and a simulator, and we designed a NMOS single-chip VLSI microprocessor.

The reduced instruction set had its most visible impact on the amount of control logic: It dropped by a factor of

*Richard S. Piepho is now with Bell Laboratories, Naperville, Illinois.

An earlier version of this article, entitled "RISC Assessment: A High-Level Language Experiment," was presented at the *Ninth Annual Symposium on Computer Architecture*, April 1982, in Austin, Texas.

10.[10,11] The chip area saved by the simplicity of the control circuitry was devoted to a large set of 32-bit registers. The register file was partitioned in a way that allows a new set of registers to be allocated for each procedure call, thus avoiding the overhead of saving registers in memory. By giving memory addresses to these registers, and by overlapping sequential sets of registers, compilers can easily allocate local variables and parameters in registers.

Support for HLL

Computer architects agree on the need to support HLLs—high-level languages. Indeed, nearly every new architecture in the last five years has claimed that it was designed with HLLs in mind.[5,6,12,13,14] There is widespread disagreement, however, on the best way to provide HLL support.

Traditional architecture support for HLLs ranges from a simple stack pointer to direct execution of the source HLL program. Rather than define a HLL computer in terms of implementation, we define it in terms of its characteristics. An *HLL computer system*[15] (1) discovers and reports errors in terms of the HLL source program, and (2) does not have any outward appearance of transformations from the user programming language into internal languages. Its only important property is that the programmer is always interacting with the computer in terms of a high-level language. Thus it makes no difference to the user of a high-level language computer system whether that system is implemented with a CISC that maps one-to-one with the tokens of the language, or if HLL support is provided largely by software on a very fast but simple machine.

A measure of the "quality" of an HLL computer system is the ratio of the execution time of programs written in the lowest-level language (usually assembly language) to the execution time of the same programs written in the HLL. This ratio is called the HLLESF—the HLL execution support factor.[15] A computer system with an HLLESF close to zero penalizes the use of an HLL, whereas a computer system with an HLLESF close to one does not reward the use of assembly language.

This article presents an informal experiment we conducted to determine whether RISCs or CISCs are better architectures for an HLL. Our hypothesis was that RISCs could provide as good an HLL environment as CISCs. We used two metrics to compare benchmark programs on a RISC with those on various CISCs. The first metric was simply performance—the speed at which the machines ran a set of HLL benchmarks. The second metric examined the penalty for using an HLL on a given machine—it is the HLLESF discussed above. We chose 11 benchmark programs and six computers for the experiment.

The HLL benchmark programs were compiled using the same compiler technology. Table 1 shows the absolute performance of the eleven HLL benchmarks on three minicomputers and three microprocessors. For the MC68000 and RISC I, we derived *predicted* performances through simulation, since at the time of the experiment we did not have working hardware for these two microprocessors. The 7.5-MHz RISC I microprocessor not only ran an average of two to four times faster than the other microprocessors and minicomputers, but of the 55 combinations of 11 programs with five machines, only one combination was faster than or equal to a 7.5-MHz RISC I.

We obtained the HLLESF by recoding the HLL benchmarks into assembly language and then comparing the performance of the HLL programs to that of the assembly programs. Machines penalizing an HLL the most will execute assembly language programs in much less time

than the HLL versions of those same programs; hence, the machines in Table 2 with HLLESFs closest to zero have the highest HLL penalties. This table suggests that there is significantly more reason to discard HLLs in the five traditional computers than in RISC I.

The results shown in Tables 1 and 2 indicate that a 7.5-MHz RISC I has the best absolute HLL performance and does the most to encourage the use of HLLs. These results, especially when combined with reduced design time, are a powerful argument that new architectures intended to be programmed in HLLs should follow the path of RISCs.

Conditions of the experiment

Since compiler technology affects the HLLESF, and since both compiler technology and hardware implementation technology affect absolute performance, the ideal experiment would vary only the architecture. As a result, we wanted to run a common set of benchmarks using a single compiler and programming language, to produce code for a variety of computer architectures in a given implementation technology. There were five variables in our experiment:

(1) benchmark programs,
(2) programming language,
(3) compiler technology,
(4) computer architecture, and
(5) implementation technology.

The sections below give our rationale for the decisions made in the experiment.

Benchmarks. We needed benchmarks coded in both an HLL and an assembly language for a variety of architectures. One common set of benchmarks is the Computer Family Architecture (CFA) Benchmarks.[16] In 1975, the

Table 1.
C benchmarks—7.5-MHz RISC I execution times and performance ratios.

BENCHMARK	RISC I 7.5 MHz msecs	68000 10 MHz	Z8002 6 MHz	VAX-11/780 5 MHz	11/70 7.5 MHz	C/70 7.4 MHz
		NUMBER OF TIMES SLOWER THAN 7.5-MHz RISC I				
E—STRING SEARCH	0.46	2.8	1.6	1.3	0.9	2.2
F—BIT TEST	0.06	4.8	7.2	4.8	6.2	9.2
H—LINKED LIST	0.10	1.6	2.4	1.2	1.9	2.5
K—BIT MATRIX	0.43	4.0	5.2	3.0	4.0	9.3
I—QUICKSORT	50.4	4.1	5.2	3.0	3.6	5.8
ACKERMANN (3,6)	3200	—	2.8	1.6	1.6	—
RECURSIVE QSORT	800	—	5.9	2.3	3.2	1.3
PUZZLE (SUBSCRIPT)	4700	—	4.2	2.0	1.6	3.4
PUZZLE (POINTER)	3200	4.2	2.3	1.3	2.0	2.1
SED (BATCH EDITOR)	5100	—	4.4	1.1	1.1	2.6
TOWERS HANOI (18)	6800	—	4.2	1.8	2.3	1.6
AVG. ±STD. DEV.		3.5±1.8	4.1±1.8	2.1±1.1	2.6±1.5	4.0±2.8

Army/Navy Computer Family Architecture Committee established a set of criteria to measure computer architectures.[17] They hoped to determine the criteria under which a commercial computer architecture could be evaluated for possible selection as a standard military computer.

The committee selected 12 programs as representative of frequent, "real-world" routines. These programs manipulate character, integer, and floating-point data, and also test interrupt handling and addressing modes.

A recent performance study, reported in the April 1, 1981 issue of *Electronic Design News* (*EDN*),[18] utilized the CFA benchmarks. The authors' goal was to have a fair set of criteria for selecting the best of the 16-bit microprocessors on the market. They presented the results of running a subset of the original benchmarks on the leading 16-bit machines.

Seven benchmarks (labeled A, B, E, F, H, K, and I in the CFA committee report) were coded by the individual manufacturers and run. An independent arbitrator, Hemmenway and Associates, confirmed the correctness of the routines and timing information. Five of the 12 original CFA benchmarks were omitted from the *EDN* study due to the lack of virtual memory (C and L) and floating-point arithmetic (D, G, and J). We further reduced the number of the benchmarks in our experiment by leaving out benchmarks A (I/O interrupt kernel) and B (I/O interrupt with FIFO processing), because of the difficulty of writing them in an HLL. Therefore, benchmark E (string search), benchmark F (bit test, set, and reset), benchmark H (linked-list insertion), benchmark I (quicksort), and benchmark K (bit matrix transposition) define our benchmark set. The sections below briefly describe each benchmark.[16,18]

String Search (E) examines a long character string for the first occurrence of a substring. If the search is successful, the procedure returns the substring's starting position. Otherwise the procedure returns a "not found" indicator. The starting addresses and the lengths of the string and substring are passed as parameters to the benchmark. This benchmark exercises an architecture's ability to move through character strings sequentially.

Bit test, set, and reset (F) tests, sets, or resets a bit within a tightly packed bit string beginning at a word boundary. A function code passed to the routine selects the operation performed. The base address of the bit string and the bit number are also passed as parameters to the benchmark. This benchmark tests, sets, and then resets three bits. It checks an architecture's bit-manipulation capabilities.

Linked-list insertion (H) inserts five new entries into a doubly linked list. The field length of each entry is 32 bits; the size of the forward and backward pointers depends on the architecture's addressing range. The address of a block of control information, and the address of the entry to be inserted, are passed as parameters. This benchmark tests pointer manipulation.

Quicksort (I) performs a nonrecursive quicksort algorithm on a large vector of fixed-length records. Unlike the original algorithm developed by C. A. R. Hoare, this one contains no procedure calls. The point at which the quicksort algorithm degrades into a simple insertion sort is

passed as a parameter to the benchmark. The number of records and the starting address of the array are also passed to the benchmark. It thoroughly tests an architecture's addressing modes and character and stack manipulation capabilities.

Bit matrix transposition (K) takes a tightly packed, square bit matrix and transposes it. The matrix is of variable size and starts on a word boundary. However, the starting bit of the matrix within the first byte of the word is variable and is passed as a parameter to the benchmark. The size and starting byte address of the matrix are also passed as parameters to the benchmark. This benchmark exercises an architecture's bit manipulation and looping capabilities.

EDN published the assembly language version of each benchmark for each manufacturer. Since the results of this study could have influenced the sales of products, we were confident that each manufacturer had provided a highly tuned assembly language routine. To calculate the HLLESF,[19] we coded these benchmarks in an HLL—the C language—and recorded the execution speeds of the two versions.

The CFA benchmarks, however, lack tests for procedure call mechanisms. Recent studies on several architectures show that one out of every 20 executed instructions is a procedure call or return,[20,21,22] accounting for as much as 40 percent of execution time.[23,24,25] Hence, we also selected a set of programs more typical of the way HLLs are used in standard programming practice. This set of benchmarks includes Puzzle, Ackermann's Function, SED (a stream editor), Qsort (a sorting program), and Towers of Hanoi. All but the first program were written originally on the PDP-11/70. Ackermann's Function and Towers of Hanoi are well-known simple programs, but the others deserve further discussion.

Forest Baskett developed Puzzle, a recursive bin-packing program that solves a three-dimensional puzzle. He believes that the execution profile of this program typifies most HLL programs.[26] It has been written in several languages and has been run on several computers. Qsort is a *recursive* quicksort program frequently used in Unix. This version sorts 2600 fixed-length character strings. SED is a stream-oriented text editor that is one of the Unix software tools. It copies input files to the standard output after they have been edited according to a script of commands.

**Table 2.
HLLESF—ratio of assembly execution time
to HLL execution time.**

BENCHMARK	RISC I	68000	Z8002	VAX-11/780	11/70
E—STRING SEARCH	0.62	0.17	0.32	0.23	0.53
F—BIT TEST	1.00	0.23	0.27	0.34	0.50
H—LINKED LIST	1.00	0.92	0.96	0.88	0.83
K—BIT MATRIX	0.94	0.21	0.29	0.34	0.24
I—QUICKSORT	0.92	0.16	0.44	0.47	—
AVERAGE ± STD. DEV.	0.9±0.1	0.3±0.3	0.5±0.3	0.4±0.2	0.5±0.2

A reduced instruction set

David A. Patterson

The philosophy of the reduced instruction set is to provide a very small set of very fast instructions and to rely on the compiler to produce optimized instruction sequences. Such instruction sets bring to mind early computers and vertical microprogrammed machines.

The RISC I architecture has 31 instructions, most of which do simple ALU and shift operations on registers. Instructions, data, addresses, and registers are 32 bits wide. The execution time of a RISC I cycle is given by the time it takes to read and add two registers and then store the result back into a register. The global register 0, which always contains zero, allows us to synthesize a variety of operations and addressing modes.

Load and store instructions move data between registers and memory. Rather than lengthen the general cycle to permit a complete memory access, these instructions use two CPU cycles. There are eight variations of memory access instructions to accommodate sign-extended or zero-extended eight-bit, 16-bit, and 32-bit data. Although only the *index plus displacement* addressing mode appears to be included in data transfer instructions, *absolute* and *register indirect* addressing can be synthesized using register 0. (The last two entries in Table 1 show how this is done; the rest of the table shows how other addressing modes are synthesized.) Branch instructions include call, return, and conditional and unconditional jump. Most of the innovative features of RISC I are found in call and return; they will be discussed later. Figure 1 shows the 32-bit format used by register-to-register and memory access instructions.

For register-to-register instructions, DEST selects one of the 32 registers as the destination of the result of the operation performed on the registers specified by SOURCE1 and SOURCE2. If IMM (immediate) = 0, the low-order five bits of SOURCE2 specify another register; if IMM = 1, SOURCE2 expresses a sign-extended 13-bit constant. The frequency of integer constants in HLL programs suggests architectural support, so immediate operands are available in every instruction. SCC determines whether the condition codes are set. Memory access instructions use SOURCE1 to specify the index register and SOURCE2 to specify the offset. One other format combines the last three fields to form a 19-bit PC-relative address, and is used primarily by the branch instructions.

The examples in Table 2 show that many important VAX instructions can be synthesized from simple RISC I addressing modes and opcodes.

Procedure calls are time-consuming in typical high-level language programs. Potentially, RISC programs

Table 1.
Synthesizing addressing modes.

ADDRESSING	RISC I	VAX EQUIVALENT
REGISTER	Rs	Rs
IMMEDIATE	S2 (13-bit literal)	#literal
INDEXED	Rx + S2 (13-bit displacement)	Rx + displ
ABSOLUTE	r0 + S2 (r0 ≡ 0)	@#address
REG INDIRECT	Rx + 0	(Rx)

Table 2.
Synthesizing VAX instructions.

OPERATION	VAX		RISC I EQUIVALENT	
REG-REG MOVE	movl	Rm,Rn	add	r0,Rm,Rn(r0 ≡ 0)
COMPARE	cmpl	Rm,Rn	sub	Rm,Rn,r0{c}
CLEAR	clrl	Rn	add	r0,r0,Rn
INCREMENT	incl	Rn	add	Rn,#1,Rn

Table 3.
Assembly programs for the VAX and the RISC I.

LINE NO.	VAX-11 (VARIABLES IN VAX MEMORY)			VAX-11 (VARIABLES IN VAX REGISTERS)			RISC I (r0 ≡ 0)		
1		moval	_String,−4(fp)		moval	_String,r9		add	r0,#String,r28
2		clrl	−8(fp)		clrl	r8		add	r0,r0,r27
3	L49:	movl	−4(fp),r0				L49:	ldbs	0(r28),r6
4*		incl	−4(fp)					add*	r28,#1,r28
5		cmpb	8(ap),(r0)	L49:	cmpb	r10,(r9)+		sub	r29,r6,r0, {c}
6		jneq	L50		jneq	L50		jmpr*	ne,L50
7		incl	−8(fp)		incl	r8		add	r27,#1,r27
8	L50:	sobgeq	4(ap),L49	L50:	sobgeq	r11,L49	L50:	sub	r30,#1,r30,{c}
9								jmpr	ge,L49

*The *delayed jump* of RISC I actually requires moving the add on line 4 below the jump on line 6. For more information, see Patterson and Séquin,[3] p. 13.

may have even more calls, because the complex instructions found in CISCs are subroutines in RISCs. Thus, the procedure call must be as fast as possible, perhaps no longer than a few jumps. Because of its *register window* scheme, RISC I comes close to this goal.

Using procedures involves two groups of time-consuming operations: saving or restoring registers on each call or return, and passing parameters and results to and from the procedure. In RISC I each procedure call results in the allocation of a new "window" of registers from the large register file, for use by the new procedure. The return just resets a pointer, restoring the old set. In addition, some of the registers are not saved or restored on each procedure call. These registers (r0 through r9) are called *global* registers.

Furthermore, the sets of registers used by different procedures are overlapped to allow parameters to be passed in registers. In other machines, parameters are usually passed on the stack, with the calling procedure using a register (frame pointer) to point to the beginning of the parameters (and also to the end of the locals). Thus, all references to parameters are indexed references to memory. The RISC approach is to partition the set of window registers (10-31) into the three parts defined by their respective overlap. Figure 2 shows this overlapped register window scheme.

Registers 26 through 31 (HIGH) contain parameters passed from "above" the current procedure, that is, from the calling procedure. Registers 16 through 25 (LOCAL) are used for local scalar storage. Registers 10 through 15 (LOW) are used for temporaries and parameters passed to the procedure "below" the current procedure (the called procedure). On each procedure call a new set of registers, numbered 10-31, is allocated. The LOW registers of the "caller" become the HIGH registers of the "callee" because of the hardware overlap between subsequent register windows. Thus, without the moving of any information, parameters in registers 10-15 appear in registers 25-31 of the called window. Figure 2 illustrates this approach for the case in which procedure A calls procedure B, which in turn calls procedure C.

If the nesting depth is sufficiently large, all register windows will be used. RISC I handles such overflow (as well as underflow) with a separate stack in memory, by trapping to a software routine that adjusts that stack. Because this routine can save or restore several sets of registers, the overflow/underflow frequency is based on the local variations in the depth of the stack rather than on the absolute depth. The effectiveness of this scheme depends on the relative frequency of overflows and underflows. Studies show that with eight register banks, overflow will occur in less than one percent of the calls. This suggests that programs exhibit locality in the dynamic nesting of procedures just as they exhibit locality in memory references.

Table 3 compares a VAX-11 assembly language program to its RISC I equivalent. The program counts the number of occurrences of a character in a string. There are two versions of the VAX-11 program; one is used with local variables allocated in memory, the other with them allocated in registers. The window register architecture of RISC I makes registers the natural depository of variables. The VAX depends on the programmer and compiler writer to be ingenious enough to use registers.

For more information on RISC I, see "A VLSI RISC" in the September 1982 issue of *Computer,* pages 8-21.

| OP CODE < 7 > | SCC < 1 > | DEST < 5 > | SOURCE1 < 5 > | IMM < 1 > | SOURCE2 < 13 > |

Figure 1. RISC I basic instruction format.

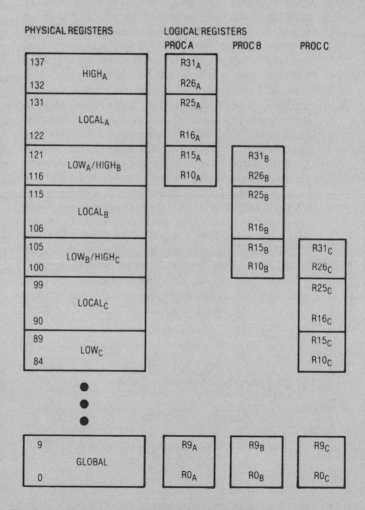

Figure 2. Use of three overlapped register windows.

The frequency of procedure calls plus returns in these programs varies from one in five instructions in Qsort to one in 235 in Puzzle. We used these five programs plus the subset of the CFA benchmarks discussed previously to estimate the performance of HLL programs executing on the machines in our experiment.

Programming language/compiler technology. To our knowledge, no compiler has been targeted to as many computer architectures as PCC—Johnson's Portable C Compiler.[27] A two-pass compiler with table-driven syntax analysis and code generation, it has been targeted to mainframes (IBM 370, Honeywell 6000, Univac 1110), minicomputers (VAX-11, PDP-11, BBN C/70), and microcomputers (Ii8085, Z8000, MC68000, Bellmac-32, RISC I). The first pass, identical in each version of this compiler, parses the C code and builds the symbol table. The second pass generates code according to table-driven algorithms, so only the tables are changed in each version. In each case, a simple peephole optimizer improves the code sequences and removes jump-to-jumps. Thus, saying that our experiment used the same compiler technology means that every version of the compiler used the same algorithms and that most of the code in each version was identical. One intangible was that different people built the compiler tables for each machine. We believed that their skills were roughly equal and that in any case the results were not biased in favor of RISC I.

An interesting question is how much performance is penalized to achieve portability. If the penalty is large, then perhaps PCC does not provide a fair evaluation of an architecture. DEC has recently announced a highly optimizing VMS C compiler written especially for the VAX family.[28] Robert Henry took the optimized assembly language output of the VMS C compiler, converted it to Unix assembler format, and timed the routines on the VAX-11/780 under Unix.[29] Table 3 presents the results for several programs that were compiled and executed using both the Unix PCC and the VMS C compilers. The VMS C compiler does an excellent job for loops with fixed bounds and allocates registers on the basis of common subexpression analysis. For large procedures, this combination produces excellent code, such as the subscripted version of the Puzzle program. PCC relies on register

declaration to allocate registers, which can lead to slightly better performance, as in the pointer version of the Puzzle program. The exception is Towers of Hanoi, where the VMS C compiler uses more registers than PCC. Unfortunately, saving and restoring registers on the VAX-11/780 is fairly slow. Thus, the savings gained from more efficient execution between procedure calls is swamped by the extra overhead of saving registers. From Table 3 we conclude that PCC is a satisfactory C compiler for the VAX.

Although the popularity of C is on the rise, some critics maintain that it is a low-level programming language. If you don't share our opinion that C is a reasonable HLL, then you must believe that the HLLESF of C serves as an upper bound, since the HLLESF of a "real" HLL would be lower.

Architecture/implementation technology. We wanted to compare RISC I with a set of popular minicomputers and microprocessors. Unfortunately, implementations of these computers in the same technology do not exist. Thus, we do not distinguish architecture from implementation; one must consider the advantages arising from implementation technology when comparing performance.

The minicomputers we tested were the VAX-11/780, a 32-bit Schottky-TTL machine with a 200-nanosecond microcycle time; the PDP-11/70, a 16-bit Schottky-TTL machine with a 135-nanosecond cycle time; and the Bolt Beranek and Newman C/70, a 20-bit Schottky-TTL machine with a 150-nanosecond microcycle time. Both the VAX and PDP-11 have a cache. The VAX-11/780 and PDP-11/70 dominate today's minicomputer market. Digital Equipment Corporation specifies the VAX as being one or two times more powerful than the 11/70. The C/70 is a newly announced microcoded machine optimized for the execution of C. BBN claims the same performance for the C/70 as that of the PDP-11/70.

We also tested three microprocessors: the Zilog Z8002 and, via simulators, the Motorola MC68000 and RISC I. RISC I, a 32-bit machine with 32-bit addresses, uses NMOS technology almost at the same state of the art as that used by the Z8002 and MC68000. The transistor count is 17,500 for the Z8002, 45,000 for RISC I, and 68,000 for the MC68000. The Z8002 uses the smallest silicon area and RISC I the largest. The Z8002 is a 16-bit computer with 16-bit addresses, whereas the MC68000 works effectively as either a 16-bit or 32-bit machine with 24-bit addresses. Both the MC68000 and Z8002 come with a variety of clock rates. A 10-MHz MC68000 and a six-MHz Z8002 were used in the *EDN* study. We designed RISC I to run at 400 nanoseconds per instruction, implying a memory of the same speed at the 10-MHz MC68000, which can access memory in four clock ticks.

As mentioned above, C is a language of demonstrated portability. When moving it to a new architecture, the compiler writer must decide how many characters to fit into an integer variable. There are four characters per integer in the VAX, RISC I, and MC68000 versions of C, and two characters per integer in the C/70 and Z8002 versions. C also uses the default integer size to hold addresses. The small size of the C benchmark programs does not tax the limits of a 16-bit address space, and thus

**Table 3.
C benchmarks on the VAX-11/780—
VMS C compiler vs. Unix PCC.**

BENCHMARK	VMS C	UNIX PCC	VMS/UNIX (NUMBER OF TIMES SLOWER THAN UNIX)
ACKERMANN (3,6)	5750	5750	1.00
RECURSIVE QSORT	1750	2000	0.86
PUZZLE (SUBSCRIPT)	5650	10900	0.52
PUZZLE (POINTER)	4700	4750	1.01
SED (BATCH EDITOR)	6300	5850	1.08
TOWERS HANOI (18)	16050	12250	1.31
AVG. ±STD. DEV.	—	—	1.0±0.2

smaller-word machines should enjoy a slight performance advantage, since with narrower data paths signals need not propagate as far. This advantage is strongest in VLSI implementations.

Running the experiment

To derive the two metrics, we ran the experiment several times, making adjustments as we went to give the various machines the "benefit of the doubt." Hence, each performance figure in Tables 1 and 2 are the best of several we obtained. Some of the results of the earlier runs, and the adjustments we made in response to them, are discussed below.

VAX. The C version of benchmark F on the VAX at first took 40 percent longer than the time indicated in Table 1. On examining the code, we found a patch to the compiler that was not allocating characters in registers. This patch was made because the allocation of characters in registers frequently leads to poorer performance on the VAX-11/780. We "corrected" the code for F and K, but the correction made no difference in the execution time of K.

MC68000. The architecture of the MC68000 spans the 32-bit *and* the 16-bit worlds. Our C compiler treats it as a 32-bit computer, while the assembly language programmer uses 32-bit data only when it improves performance. Thus, the HLLESF for the MC68000 may have been higher if our C compiler had used it strictly as a 16-bit computer. The simulated runs of the benchmarks on the MC68000 yielded execution times that were at first 15 percent slower than the times shown in the tables. The compiler for the MC68000 was the only one lacking an optimizer, so we estimated the performance improvement an optimizer would have provided by measuring the performance of the other five machines with and without optimization. The average improvement was 11 percent, but we picked 15 percent to give the "MC68000 optimizer" the benefit of the doubt.

Z8002. We measured the benchmarks on a four-MHz version of the Z8002 and got execution times 50 percent higher than what now shows in Table 1. Because we wanted a performance figure for a six-MHz Z8002 (as was used in the *EDN* study) instead of a four-MHz one, we reduced the measured execution time by 33 percent.

C/70. Although the C/70 does have a C compiler with a traditional assembly-language level, we excluded it from the HLLESF calculations simply because the manufacturer did not supply documentation of this level. The 10-bit bytes of the C/70 introduced problems with the C coding of benchmarks F (bit test, set, and reset) and K (bit matrix transposition). The shifts used to divide by eight in these benchmarks had to be replaced with actual divides by 10. Dividing is obviously much slower than shifting. If we assume that the C/70 can execute these two programs as fast as the 11/70, the average ratio of its performance to that of a 7.5-MHz RISC I drops from the 4.0 indicated in Table 1 to 3.2.

Questions raised by the RISC concept

The presentation of the RISC concept has led to many stimulating discussions with our coworkers and colleagues. Here, we present a brief review of the most popular topics.

Compilers. A comparison of the assembly language manual for the MC6800 to that for the MC68000, and of the manual for the PDP-11 to that for the VAX-11, shows an obvious increase in the "level" of the architecture. Concepts in HLLs become instructions in the new machines, e.g., CASE and CALL.

One would expect a CISC to have better HLL performance than a RISC, and thus it should be easier to write compilers for a CISC than for a RISC. A recent paper by Wulf[30] helps explain why neither statement is true. He considers compiling essentially a large "case analysis." The more *ways* to do something (the more instructions and addressing modes), the more cases we must consider. Since the compiler writer must balance the speed of the compiler with his desire to get good code, he may not have the time to perform the case analysis needed to generate all of the CISC instructions. Wulf further says that this trend towards "higher-level" assembly language, while commendable, may not be useful because a clash between the semantics of a HLL and the semantics of an instruction may render the instruction unusable. He argues that architectures should provide primitives rather than "solutions."

During the development of the RISC I compiler, we often observed that the task was not difficult, even though the instruction set was at a "lower level." This illustrates Wulf's recommendation that architectures provide either one way or every way to perform an operation. In RISC I we took the former approach. There are few choices in RISC I; for example, if an operand is in memory it must be loaded into a register. Simple case analysis implies a simple compiler, even if more instructions must be generated in each case.

Applicability to other HLLs. Studies of other algorithmic HLLs[31,32] disclose the most frequently executed operations as the same simple HLL constructs found in C, for which RISC I has been optimized. Unless an HLL significantly changes the way people program, we expect to see similar results with any HLL. In the case of languages with unusual data types, such as Cobol, we need to find the simple operations used repeatedly in that environment and incorporate them into a RISC. Even if Cobol does not map efficiently onto the RISC I architecture, we believe the reduced instruction set philosophy can lead to an effective Cobol RISC.

Registers vs. a reduced instruction set. One reason for the good performance of RISC I is its overlapped register sets. Perhaps the instruction set is not even a first-order consideration!

We certainly agree that a significant portion of RISC I's speed is due to its overlapped register windows. RISC I's small amount of control logic (only six percent of the total circuitry on the chip, compared to the 50 percent typical of CISCs) created room for register windows—a key point in this discussion. Furthermore, the simplicity of control in RISC I rendered microprogramming unnecessary; this in turn eliminated the control loop—frequently the most critical timing path in microprogrammed machines—as the determining factor of the machine cycle. Moreover, any argument suggesting that instruction sets are not a primary performance factor is an argument for designing architectures that allow easy and efficient implementation—i.e., RISCs.

Virtual memory/protection. Our comparison of the six computers was somewhat unfair in that only the VAX provides a virtual address space that is larger than the physical address space. Given that RISC I doesn't provide the same function, perhaps RISC I should be considered in another class. Furthermore, RISC I provides no protection.

What about adding virtual memory capability to RISC I? In a virtual memory system, we first must have restartable instructions. Restarting a machine with simple instructions and addressing modes is quite easy, and RISC I is restartable. By how much would a virtual memory capability slow RISC I down? To find an accurate answer to this question, we looked at solutions used by other microprocessors. National Semiconductor has announced the 16082, a memory management chip that has an address cache and that normally translates virtual addresses into physical addresses in 100 nanoseconds.[33] If we put this chip in a system with a RISC I, it would add another 100 nanoseconds to every memory access. Memory is referenced every 400 nanoseconds in a 7.5-MHz RISC I, so such a combination would reduce RISC performance by 25 percent. Because 80 percent to 90 percent of memory references in RISC I are to instructions,[23] more sophisticated approaches, such as translating addresses only when crossing a page boundary (as is done in the VAX-11/780) or providing a virtual address cache (as is done in the Dorado[14]), would be needed to keep performance close to our goals.

Memory management subsumes protection. The most widely used computers rely on the separation of system and user states and associate protection with pages. If you believe this provides adequate security, then RISC I will suffice.

First silicon

The first RISC I was fabricated over the summer of 1981. The 44,500-transistor chip was designed in less time, with less manpower and fewer errors, than comparable CISC machines. Its original masks, for example, had only one design error. Programs first ran on a RISC I chip in the spring of 1982. Our first chips ran instructions at a clock rate of 1.5 MHz, considerably less than our projected 7.5 MHz. Even at that slow rate, however, RISC I ran programs faster than commercial microprocessors.[34] Discussions with IC professionals confirmed that a 7.5-MHz rate could be achieved with the NMOS fabrication technology we used. Hence, we have begun designing a new chip, with the goal of reaching 7.5 MHz.

Since our first implementation of RISC I was slower than planned, we feel we should wait for full-speed chips before altogether dismissing traditional architectures. Attaining expected performance on full-speed chips would certainly have been a more convincing argument for RISCs than falling short of expected performance on less than full-speed chips. However, we believe that the results from our experiment nonetheless make a strong case for the premise that the RISC I architecture can provide higher performance to HLL programs.

We attribute the lack of design errors and increased layout regularity to the simple RISC I architecture. As this was the first chip that any of us had designed, we think that inexperience (in addition to nonoptimal processing and missing CAD tools) were probably to blame for the poorer-than-expected performance.[34] As one of us stated in an earlier paper,[23]

> This (7.5-MHz) estimate is both optimistic and pessimistic: optimistic in that it is unlikely that students can successfully build something that fast on their first try, and pessimistic because an experienced IC design team could build a much faster machine.

We believe the next chip will be much closer to our goals.

RISCs represent a new architectural style, one that enables designers not only to build working silicon faster than they can for CISCs, but also to obtain higher performance than CISCs. Whereas traditional machines "support" HLLs with instructions resembling HLL constructs, RISCs support HLLs with instructions that HLL compilers can use efficiently. We have performed a simple experiment to determine whether reduced or complex instruction set computers provide a better architectural base for high-level languages. We examined the support for HLLs by measuring both the absolute performance of eleven HLL programs and the performance benefits of recoding these programs by hand into assembly language. We compared the performance of six different architectures, using the same benchmarks, programming language, and compiler technology, and concluded that RISC I was the best.

Work on RISCs is by no means limited to one group of researchers. For example, John Hennessy of Stanford is investigating a pipelined RISC with software control of pipeline interlocks.[4] Many other topics remain to be investigated, such as the applicability of RISCs to HLLs like Lisp, Cobol, and Ada, the effectiveness of an operating system on RISCs (e.g., Unix), the architecture of coprocessors for RISCs (e.g., graphics, floating point), migration of software to RISCs (e.g., a 370 emulator written in a RISC machine language), and the implementation of RISCs in technologies such as CMOS, TTL, and ECL. This list surpasses the scope of one project; we hope to help industry and academia in exploring RISCy architectures. ■

Acknowledgments

The RISC project was aided by several people at Berkeley and other places. We would like to thank them all, and give special thanks to a few. Yuval Tamir created the RISC I simulator and helped with the assembly language benchmarks for RISC I and the VAX.[35] Michael Carey provided the support on the C compiler and suggestions on the measurements. More detailed information on this experiment can be found elsewhere.[19]

We would like to thank D. Clark, P. Hansen, R. Mayo, J. Ousterhout, M. Katevenis, R. Probst, C. Séquin, R. Sherburne, K. Van Dyke, and R. Wayman for their suggestions in improving this article.

The research reported in this article was supported in part by Bell Laboratories, and in part by the Department of Defense Advanced Research Projects Agency under ARPA Order No. 3803. The work was monitored by the Naval Electronic System Command under Contract No. N00039-81-K-0251.

We would also like to thank Duane Adams, Paul Losleben, and DARPA for providing the resources that allow universities to attempt projects involving high risk.

References

1. D. A. Patterson and D. R. Ditzel, "The Case for the Reduced Instruction Set Computer," *Computer Architecture News* (ACM Sigarch), Vol. 8, No. 6, Oct. 15, 1980, pp. 25-33.

2. G. Radin, "The 801 Minicomputer," *Proc. Symp. Architectural Support for Programming Languages and Operating Systems,* Mar. 1982, pp. 39-47.

3. D. A. Patterson and C. H. Séquin, "A VLSI RISC," *Computer,* Vol. 15, No. 9, Sept. 1982, pp. 8-21.

4. J. Hennessy et al., "The MIPS Machine," *Digest of Papers—Compcon Spring 82,* Feb. 1982, pp. 2-7.

5. W. D. Strecker, "VAX-11/780: A Virtual Address Extension to the DEC PDP-11 Family," *AFIPS Conf. Proc.,* Vol. 47, 1978 NCC, pp. 967-980.

6. W. W. Lattin et al., "A 32-bit VLSI Micromainframe Computer System," *Proc. IEEE Int'l Solid-State Circuits Conf.,* Feb. 1981, pp. 110-111.

7. D. W. Clark and W. D. Strecker, "Comments on 'The Case for the Reduced Instruction Set Computer'," *Computer Architecture News* (ACM Sigarch), Vol. 8, No. 6, Oct. 15, 1980, pp. 34-38.

8. R. Bernhard, "More Hardware Means Less Software," *IEEE Spectrum,* Vol. 18, No. 12, Dec. 1981, pp. 30-37.

9. D. A. Fairclough, "A Unique Microprocessor Instruction Set," *IEEE Micro,* Vol. 2, No. 2, May 1982, pp. 8-18.

10. D. T. Fitzpatrick et al., "VLSI Implementations of a Reduced Instruction Set Computer," *Proc. CMU Conf. VLSI Systems and Computations,* Oct. 1981, pp. 327-336.

11. D. T. Fitzpatrick et al., "A RISCy Approach to VLSI," *VLSI Design,* Vol. 2, No. 4, Fourth Qtr. 1981, pp. 14-20.

12. E. Stritter and T. Gunter, "A Microprocessor for a Changing World: The Motorola 68000," *Computer,* Vol. 12, No. 2, Feb. 1979, pp. 43-52.

13. B. L. Peuto, "Architecture of a New Microprocessor," *Computer,* Vol. 12, No. 2, Feb. 1979, pp. 10-21.

14. D. W. Clark, B. W. Lampson, and K. A. Pier, "The Memory System of a High-Performance Personal Computer," *IEEE Trans. Computers,* Vol. C-30, No. 10, Oct. 1981, pp. 715-733.

15. D. R. Ditzel and D. A. Patterson, "Retrospective on High-Level Language Computer Architecture," *Proc. 7th Ann. Symp. Computer Architecture,* May 1980, pp. 97-104.

16. S. H. Fuller and W. E. Burr, "Measurement and Evaluation of Alternative Computer Architectures," *Computer,* Vol. 10, No. 10, Oct. 1977, pp. 24-35.

17. W. E. Burr, A. H. Coleman, and W. R. Smith, "Overview of the Military Computer Family Architecture Selection," *AFIPS Conf. Proc.,* Vol. 46, 1977 NCC, pp. 131-137.

18. R. G. Grappel and J. E. Hemmenway, "A Tale of Four Microprocessors: Benchmarks Quantify Performance," *Electronic Design News,* Apr. 1, 1981, pp. 179-265.

19. R. S. Piepho, "Comparative Evaluation of the RISC I Architecture via the Computer Family Architecture Benchmarks," MS degree project report, University of California, Berkeley, Aug. 1981.

20. D. Clark and H. Levy, "Measurement and Analysis of Instruction Use in the VAX-11/780," *Proc. 9th Ann. Symp. Computer Architecture,* Apr. 1982, pp. 9-17.

21. D. Ditzel and R. McLellan, "Register Allocation for Free: The C Machine Stack Cache," *Proc. Symp. Architectural Support for Programming Languages and Operating Systems,* Mar. 1982, pp. 48-56.

22. G. McDaniel, "An Analysis of a Mesa Instruction Set Using Dynamic Instruction Frequencies," *Proc. Symp. Architectural Support for Programming Languages and Operating Systems,* Mar. 1982, pp. 167-176.

23. D. A. Patterson and C. H. Séquin, "RISC I: A Reduced Instruction Set VLSI Computer," *Proc. 8th Ann. Symp. Computer Architecture,* May 1981, pp. 443-457.

24. A. Lunde, "Empirical Evaluation of Some Features of Instruction Set Processor Architecture," *Comm. ACM,* Vol. 20, No. 3, Mar. 1977, pp. 143-153.

25. B. A. Wichmann, "Ackermann's Function: A Study in the Efficiency of Calling Procedures," *BIT,* Vol. 16, No. 1, 1976, pp. 103-110.

26. F. Baskett, private communication, Nov. 1981.

27. S. C. Johnson, "A Portable Compiler: Theory and Practice," *Proc. Fifth Ann. ACM Symp. Programming Languages,* Jan. 1978, pp. 97-104.

28. P. Anklam et al., *Engineering a Compiler: VAX-11 Code Generation and Optimization,* Digital Press, Billerica, MA, 1982.

29. R. R. Henry, "Yet Another Benchmark: The VMS and UNIX C Compilers for Eight Favorite Programs on Two Different VAXes," internal working paper, University of California, Berkeley, Aug. 1982.

30. W. A. Wulf, "Compilers and Computer Architecture," *Computer,* Vol. 14, No. 7, July 1981, pp. 41-48.

31. W. C. Alexander and D. B. Wortman, "Static and Dynamic Characteristics of XPL Programs," *Computer,* Vol. 8, No. 11, Nov. 1975, pp. 41-46.

32. D. R. Ditzel, "Program Measurements on a High-Level Language Computer," *Computer,* Vol. 13, No. 8, Aug. 1980, pp. 62-72.

33. Y. Lavi et al., "16-bit Microprocessor Enters Virtual Memory Domain," *Electronics,* Apr. 24, 1980, pp. 123-129.

34. J. K. Foderaro, K. S. Van Dyke, and D. A. Patterson, "Running RISCs," *VLSI Design,* Vol. 3, No. 5, Sept./Oct. 1982, pp. 27-32.

35. Y. Tamir, "Simulation and Performance Evaluation of the RISC Architecture," Electronics Research Laboratory memorandum UCB/ERL M81/17, University of California, Berkeley, Mar. 1981.

David A. Patterson has been a member of the faculty in the Computer Science Division, Department of Electrical Engineering and Computer Sciences, University of California, Berkeley, since 1977. He was named associate professor in 1981 and currently teaches computer architecture at the graduate and undergraduate levels. His research combines popular software, experimental architecture, and VLSI to create more effective computer systems.

Patterson spent the fall of 1979 on leave of absence at Digital Equipment Corporation developing microprogram design tools and reviewing computer designs. In the next academic year he developed courses that led to the design and implementation of RISC I, a 45,000-transistor microprocessor. In 1982 he received the Distinguished Teaching Award from the Berkeley division of the Academic Senate of the University of California. Patterson received a BA in mathematics and an MS and PhD in computer science from UCLA.

Patterson's address is the Computer Science Division, Department of Electrical Engineering and Computer Sciences, University of California, Berkeley, CA 94720.

Richard S. Piepho is a member of the technical staff at Bell Telephone Laboratories in Naperville, Illinois. A member of the IEEE, Tau Beta Pi, and Eta Kappa Nu, he received a BSEE from Purdue University in 1980 and an MS in computer science and electrical engineering from the University of California, Berkeley, in 1981.

An Advanced Computer Architecture CMOS/SOS Microprocessor

David W. Best,
Charles E. Kress,
Nick M. Mykris,
Jeffrey D. Russell, and
William J. Smith

Rockwell International

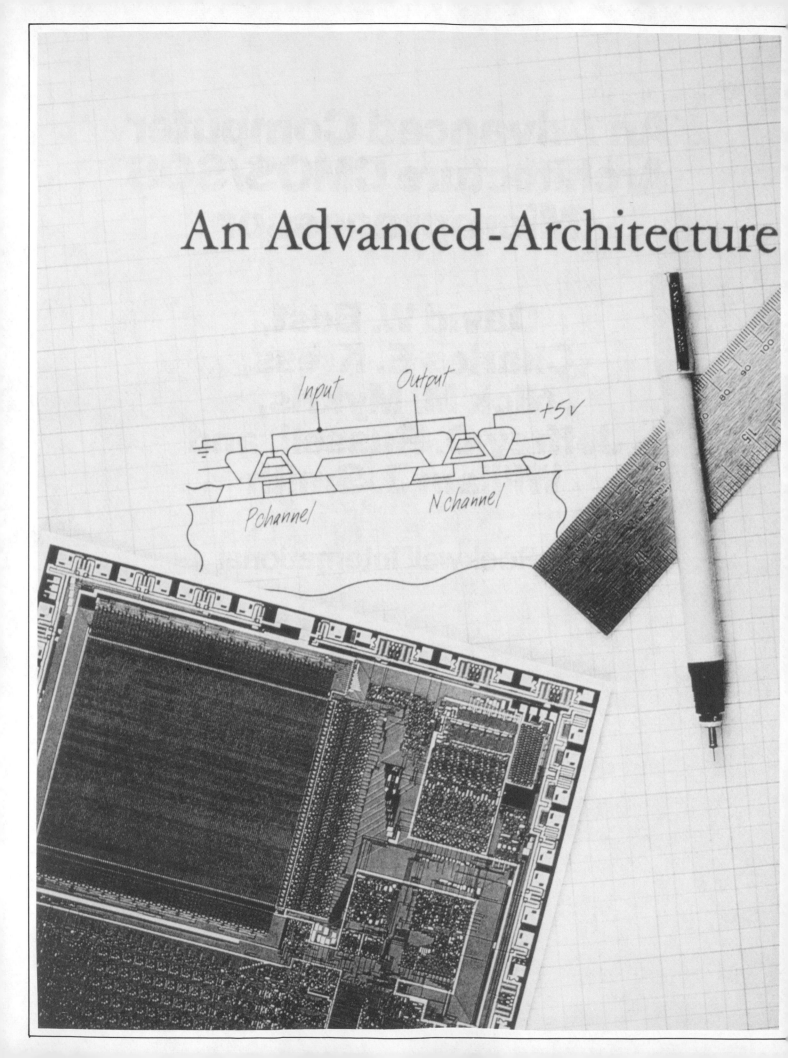

An Advanced-Architecture

A language-directed stack architecture, implemented in two-micrometer CMOS/SOS,

yields a 16-bit microprocessor having high throughput and high compiled code density.

CMOS/SOS Microprocessor

David W. Best, Charles E. Kress, Nick M. Mykris,
Jeffrey D. Russell, and William J. Smith

Rockwell International

Since the introduction of the microprocessor in 1971, integrated circuit technology has advanced at an astonishing rate. Unfortunately, the technology of computer architecture, as exemplified by commercial microprocessors, has improved very little during that time. Most architectures are classical von Neumann, register-oriented architectures whose support of high-level languages is suspect, and certainly far less than what can be achieved.[1,2,3,4,5]

At about the same time the microprocessor first emerged, Collins Radio Corporation (now the Collins Avionics Group of Rockwell International) began CAPS—the Collins Adaptive Processing System—to change the way digital systems were developed. The growing importance of high-level language, which has since become pervasive, was recognized. Among the goals of the CAPS concept were the exclusive use of high-level language for all software development, and the development of a computer architecture that could efficiently support such languages. The latter has, since 1972, been implemented and refined in several processor designs and applied to many systems. It has resulted in substantial reductions in memory space requirements for compiled programs, acceptance of high-level language for software design, development of stuctured software, reductions in software design costs, and improvements in software reliability.

The regularity, symmetry, and high-level nature of the CAPS instruction set provide it with hardware independence, yet make it amenable to simple implementation. Ten different realizations have been successfully used in sophisticated avionics applications such as the Boeing 757/767 flight control system, the USAF GPS—Global Positioning System—Generalized Development Model, the GPS Phase 2 User Equipment, the US Coast Guard Medium-Range Surveillance and Short-Range Recovery systems, the Lockheed L-1011 flight control system, and the NASA Fault Tolerant Multiprocessor.

Feasibility for a VLSI version of the CAPS architecture was established in 1978. Rockwell's Processor Technology Department in Cedar Rapids, Iowa, and its Microelectronics Research and Development Center in Anaheim, California, began cooperative development in 1979. Initial lots of the resulting device—the AAMP, for Advanced-Architecture Microprocessor—were fabricated in February 1981.

The AAMP is a high-performance, general-purpose, 16-bit processor implemented on a single, silicon-on-sapphire die. We believe it to be a unique achievement in the microprocessor field, in that it merges the elegance and efficiency of a high-level-language-directed stack architecture with the performance and density of two-micrometer CMOS/SOS VLSI technology.

Several of the important characteristics of the AAMP are summarized in Table 1. Subnanosecond gate delays and a highly-parallel microprogrammed internal structure are the foundation for the AAMP's performance, while the complementary-MOS circuitry accounts for its low power consumption. Combined with a language-directed, instruction-set architecture, high execution speed and code density result for compiled high-level-language programs. Throughput, based on a realistic instruction mix including 12 percent floating-point operations, is in excess of 355,000 operations per second when

183

August 1982
EHO214-7/84/0000/0182$01.00©1982 IEEE

used with medium-speed memory. Furthermore, the AAMP's CMOS/SOS technology maintains this performance over the full military temperature range, provides inherent radiation resistance, and has high noise immunity. Thus, we feel that the AAMP is as suited to severe environments as it is to commercial applications.

Presented below are discussions of the AAMP's instruction-set architecture, microarchitecture, implementation, interface, and performance. An appendix—a portion of the programmer's reference card—provides an overview of the instruction set.

Architecture

Support of high-level-language software design is a fundamental requirement in sophisticated microprocessor applications. The AAMP is intended to be programmed exclusively in a high-level language. Its stack architecture was specifically developed to provide efficient compilation of block-structured high-level languages such as PL/I and Jovial, and it inherently supports a majority of the features of Ada as well. The AAMP architecture is similar in concept to the architectures of the Burroughs mainframes, the Hewlett-Packard 3000, the Microdata 32/S, the Xerox Mesa,[6] and Tanenbaum's hypothetical EM-1.[3] It is designed for multitasking and provides, automatically, parameter passage, procedure linkage, interrupt linkage and state saving, exception handling, reentrancy, recursiveness, and dynamic memory allocation.

Our studies of languages led us to give special emphasis to the instrucion set's support of high-level constructs. Instructions are included that would take several steps in other architectures. Stack orientation is in concert with the usual compilation methodologies.* Indeed, our experience with the design indicates that the instruction set can match the intermediate-level output of typical compilers. Furthermore, most instructions are one byte long. These features contribute to the AAMP's code density—a critical factor on which microprocessor speed is highly dependent.

Process stack. During compilation of block-structured languages, most compilers produce intermediate code which specifies operand manipulations based on last-in, first-out stacking algorithms. A key element in the CAPS architecture is the use of a process stack, not only for subroutine linkage and operand passage, but also for operand and pointer manipulation and for dynamic allocation of local-environment operand storage. As a result, the CAPS instruction set closely matches intermediate compiler languages, eliminating many of the inefficiencies of machine-language-code generation realized with register-oriented architectures.

As shown in Figure 1, the process stack is composed of nested local environments providing a procedure work space, with stack marks for procedure state-saving and return-linkage and an accumulator stack area for operand and pointer manipulation. Machine instructions operate on values located on top of the accumulator stack area. Local variables and parameters passed to a procedure are contained in the current procedure's local environment area. Only the area needed by a procedure is allocated to the local environment. Pointers (TOS and LENV) maintained by the CPU are used to locate accumulator stack and local environment areas.

The local environment and the accumulator stack provide a dynamically allocated work area (a stack frame) for

---

*Expression evaluation in postfix (or in parse-trees that trivially map to postfix) is typically employed. An accumulator stack is ideal for such compilers, and problems of resource allocation are minimized, although optimization difficulties may arise.[5] There is disagreement about the speed and encoding efficiency of expression evaluation in a stack architecture as compared to that in a multiple-register or memory-to-memory architecture.[2] However, the stacking of procedure environments has gained wide acceptance.

Table 1.
AAMP characteristics.

Technology	CMOS/SOS; two-micrometer gate length
Processor architecture	Stack-oriented with nested, recursive procedures
Word length	8-, 16-, 32-, and 48-bit data; 8-, 16-, 24-, and 56-bit instructions
Number of instructions	153
Addressing modes	Local, nonlocal, global, universal, component, and indexed
Addressability	16,777,216 16-bit words (24-bit addresses)
Data area types	Local variables (dynamically allocated); global and universal variables
Interrupts	1 maskable; 1 unmaskable (expandable)
Typical speeds (100 ns ROM, 250 ns RAM)	ADD (16/32): 0.65/0.85 μs
	MPY (16/32): 4.85/15.05 μs
	DIV (16/32): 5.65/15.85 μs
	FADD (32/48): 7.85/11.45 μs
	FMUL (32/48): 19.25/29.85 μs
	FDIV (32/48): 19.85/34.25 μs
	SKIP: 1.35 μs
Throughput	355 KOPS (Gibson mix, 12% floating-point)
Clock	Crystal or external up to 20 MHz
Size	214 x 261 mils
Supply voltage	5.0 ± 0.5 V dc
Power	200 mW, maximum
Package	68-pin square array
Interface	LSTTL and CMOS-compatible
Temperature range	-55 to +125°C

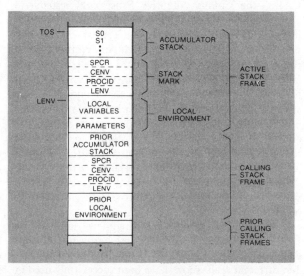

Figure 1. The AAMP process stack.

a procedure. Below the currently active stack frame are frames for prior procedures. Procedure linkage and stack-frame allocation are performed by CALL instructions. Values are returned to calling procedures and to stack-frames deallocated by RETURN instructions.

CALL and RETURN operation. Figure 2 illustrates, by means of "snapshots" of the process stack, the operation of the CALL and RETURN instructions. Before calling another procedure, the current procedure first pushes the arguments (parameters) to be passed and then the ad-

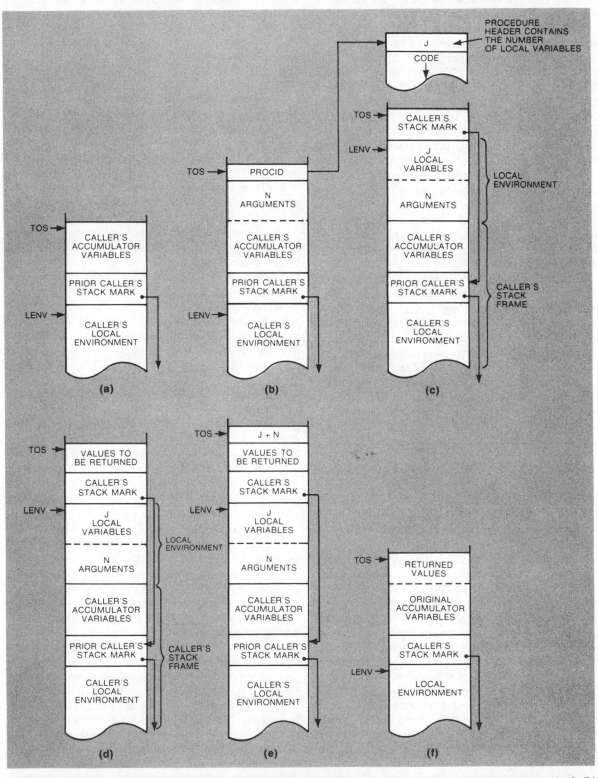

Figure 2. Illustration of CALL and RETURN: (a) before calling procedure pushes arguments on the process stack; (b) just prior to execution of CALL instruction; (c) just after CALL instruction; (d) after completion of called procedure; (e) with deallocation value pushed on the stack; and (f) just after RETURN instruction.

185

dress of the target procedure (PROCID). This results in the change of state shown in Figure 2b. The CALL instruction is then executed.

The PROCID is popped from the stack and employed to locate the called procedure code, the first word of which is a 16-bit header. The header contains the number of words (J) to be allocated in the stack for use as temporary variables. Allocation is accomplished by decrementing TOS by J. A stack mark for return linkage is then created by pushing the current value of LENV, the address of the target procedure PROCID, the current value of the code environment CENV, and the current value of the program counter SPCR. LENV is then set to TOS + 4 to establish the new local environment area for the called procedure, resulting in the state shown in Figure 2c. Execution ensues with SPCR = PROCID + 2. Note that arguments to the called procedure are automatically passed as part of its local environment.

Near the completion of the called procedure, values to be returned (if any) are computed and pushed onto the top of the stack, as shown in Figure 2d. The procedure then pushes the number of words to be deallocated (N arguments and J temporaries). Thus, the state of the process state just prior to the execution of the RETURN instruction is that shown in Figure 2e.

Execution of the RETURN results in the state illustrated in Figure 2f. The return values are copied on top of the caller's original accumulator variables, and TOS is set accordingly. LENV, CENV, and SPCR are restored from the stack mark, and execution of the calling procedure continues with the first instruction following the CALL.

Typical execution times for CALL and RETURN are 6.0 microseconds and 7.6 microseconds, respectively. The latter assumes that one 16-bit value is to be returned. No additional time is needed for state saving and restoration by software, as would be required in a register-oriented machine.

Tasking. The AAMP architecture supports the concept of task concurrency, wherein two or more tasks can be executing simultaneously. Each task consists of a set of procedures and an assigned dynamic work space—i.e., a process stack. There are as many stacks as there are concurrently executing tasks.

Multitasking operations, including context switching, are performed automatically by the processor. A special task, called the executive, performs scheduling by selecting one of several user tasks to be activated or resumed.

Execution of a user task is suspended at the occurrence of an interrupt, of a hardware-generated trap due to a detected error (e.g., a stack overflow), or of a software trap. The state of the user task is saved and the executive task is reactivated. The typical execution time for such a context switch is 18.5 microseconds. The executive then provides servicing for the interrupt or trap and schedules the same or another task for resumption. A context switch back to a user task occurs automatically after the executive executes a RETURN from its outermost procedure.

Exceptions. Interrupts and traps are primarily relevant to other processes, or to the system as a whole, and are therefore serviced in a system-wide context by the executive task. In contrast, exceptions are erroneous events, such as arithmetic overflow, relevant primarily to the currently executing process. Therefore, exceptions normally invoke software that handles them in the context of that process.

When an exception is detected, the state of the executing procedure is saved via the call mechanism, and the processor is automatically vectored to a handling procedure on the active stack. Each task establishes its own exception-handling algorithms as appropriate to its functions.

Addressing. Code and data can be treated as conceptually separate memory areas and may be implemented as such. Similarly, memory areas for the executive are separate from those for user tasks. Each task is allocated a unique environment within which its code and data areas reside.

The foregoing scheme is implemented with a code-environment register, CENV, and a data-environment register, DENV, both of which are managed by the processor. For a given task, the code environment contains up to 65,536 bytes of code and the data environment up to 65,536 words of data. Addresses are formed by concatenating CENV with the program counter, or DENV with an offset.

Access to data or procedures in another task's environment is supported through universal addressing. This mode allows specification of a complete 24-bit address for locating a procedure or data object.

Data types. The AAMP directly supports 16- and 32-bit integer, 16- and 32-bit fractional, 32- and 48-bit floating-point, and 16-bit logical variables. The floating-point formats have an eight-bit, excess-128 exponent and, respectively, 24 and 40 bits of fractional mantissa. Addition, subtraction, multiplication, division, and type conversions are provided for all of the arithmetic types.

Instruction set. The high performance of the AAMP architecture is based in part on the efficiency of the machine-level instruction set. The instruction set is the result of extensive analysis performed on a wide range of compiled benchmark programs and applications software. It is high level in nature, closely matching the intermediate code of compilers. Processor performance is further enhanced by frequency encoding of the instruction opcodes. The use of local, nonlocal, global, universal, component, and indexed addressing modes allows data-structure definition and access to be optimized for high-level languages targeted to the AAMP.

The AAMP has 153 instructions, which can be divided into several classes as shown in Table 2. The instructions vary in length from eight to 56 bits. More than 70 percent of them, including all the arithmetic, logic, and relational instructions, are only eight bits long. Up to 16 local-variable locations can be accessed with an eight-bit instruction. Up to 256 local variables can be accessed with a 16-bit instruction.

Code density

Many benchmark programs have been used to compare AAMP code density to that of other architectures. Table 3 summarizes the amount of program memory required by the AAMP and other processors for a group of benchmarks representative of avionics problems. The compilers for each language (J73/I and PL/I) differed only in their code-generator designs. Other architectures required from 35 to 160 percent more code space than the AAMP.

Compactness of compiled AAMP code can be attributed to the basic architectural features of the processor. Short instruction lengths and efficient use of the process stack, together with high-level instructions for procedure call, return, and loop iteration functions, contribute to the code densities achieved by all CAPS processors. Additionally, automatic allocation of procedure work space and run-time exception checking eliminate the excess instructions that would otherwise be required to implement these functions.

Microarchitecture

The virtual nature of the AAMP's instruction-set architecture allows nearly unconstrained microarchitectural freedom. This factor, conjoined with customized logic, provided the opportunity for the development of an efficient internal structure that would yield high processor throughput. Keeping the chip size reasonable, however, demanded that the microarchitecture be amenable to a very regular layout having dense, repetitive circuitry.

The experience gained from previous discrete TTL versions of the CAPS architecture provided a foundation for the AAMP. The microarchitecture evolved iteratively as the instruction set was refined, as microprogramming efforts progressed, as testability was considered, and as the potential of CMOS/SOS design was recognized. The resulting design confirmed our belief that the CAPS architecture is amenable to simpler and more elegant implementation than register-oriented machines of comparable performance.

The AAMP's microarchitecture is shown in the block diagram of Figure 3. Its major components are discussed below.

Data path. The data-path section provides the data manipulation and processing functions required to execute the AAMP instruction set. It includes the data and address interface, the instruction latch and parsing logic, the arithmetic-logic unit, the incrementer, the shift/rotate logic, and a 16-word multiport register file.

The register file is a key element of the microarchitecture. Its multiport design is important in achieving the parallelism needed for high execution speed and compact microcode. During each microcycle, six file locations are output, and, at the end of the microcycle, three are written back. Locations include four stack registers, STK3-STK0; a counter, CNTR; two shift registers, QH and QL; three general-purpose registers, R2-R0; and architectural pointers, SPCR, CENV, DENV, LENV, TOS, and SKLM. The latter are, respectively, the syllable-program-counter, the code-environment, the data-environment, the local-environment, the top-of-stack, and the stack-limit registers. The four-bit A and B address inputs provide arbitrary selection of two source operands, with the B addressed location also being a destination. Special ports are used for shifting, counting, and external address generation. The incrementer has SPCR or CNTR as its source and destination operands. Similarly, either QH or

Table 2.
Classes of AAMP instructions.

CLASS	NO. OF INSTRUCTIONS
STACK MANAGEMENT	8
TYPE CONVERSION	9
SHIFT, ROTATE, AND FIELD OPERATIONS	6
LOGIC, ARITHMETIC, AND RELATIONAL OPERATIONS	46
LITERAL DATA (CONSTANTS)	9
MEMORY ACCESS	51
OPERAND LOCATION	3
PROGRAM CONTROL	19
MISCELLANEOUS	2
TOTAL	153

Table 3.
Memory requirements, in 16-bit words, of various benchmark programs.

	AAMP (J73/I)	AAMP (PL/I)	1750A (J73/I)	362F (J73/I)	8086 (PL/I)	Z8000 (PL/I)	PDP-11/70 (PL/I)
MATRIX MULTIPLY	69	64	136	164	167	142	183
HASH ROUTINE	343	336	286	342	378	718	1115
COORDINATE TRANSFORMATION 1	115	100	168	148	264	275	340
COORDINATE TRANSFORMATION 2	131	171	250	234	451	419	421
COORDINATE TRANSFORMATION 3	128	120	214	182	334	329	392
FILTER PROGRAM	312	403	430	458	483	547	961
NAVIGATION 1	679	639	972	938	1645	1536	1992
NAVIGATION 2	168	188	212	140	529	400	237
KALMAN FILTER	164	146	252	258	306	372	290
CDU DRIVER 1	334	408	482	574	636	701	846
CDU DRIVER 2	79	102	104	102	134	123	186
AREA-NAVIGATION SUBROUTINE	82	68	168	154	214	236	340
FLIGHT-CONTROL ROUTINE	339	313	368	324	902	842	793
TOTALS	2943	3058	4042	4018	6443	6640	8096

QL can be passed through the Q shifter and written back. The address port, which is an output only, provides 24 bits formed by concatenating two file locations for data and code accesses.

Single-position shifts to the left or the right are implemented. Eight shift linkages allow efficient implementation of fixed-point and floating-point multiplication, division, normalization and alignment, and field extraction and insertion. A single-link flip-flop is included for multiple-precision shifts of operands exceeding 32 bits.

Register-file entries STK0, STK1, STK2, and STK3 can contain up to four operands from the top of the accumulator stack, with the remainder of the accumulator stack operands residing in memory. The existence of the stack registers is of no concern to the programmer or compiler, since these registers are automatically managed so that they function as if the entire accumulator stack were in memory. Operands are moved from these registers to the memory stack only after the registers become full. Similarly, only when the stack registers become empty is movement required from the memory stack.

This encachement technique allows most stack operations to be high-speed, register-to-register operations, thereby increasing execution speed and minimizing the number of memory accesses. The number of operands occupying the internal stack registers is maintained by a four-bit register called the stack vector. Register-file addressing via the stack vector is provided to support operations on the four stack registers. The microcontroller automatically ensures that the internal stack contains a suitable number of operands for the instruction to be executed.

The 16-bit ALU provides addition, three logical operations, and indications of sign, all-zero, carry, and overflow status. The R and S inputs to the ALU are fed from multiplexing logic in order to provide several source alternatives. Several formats are specifically included to support efficient multiplication and division algorithms.

A 16-bit instruction latch receives two bytes from program memory for each fetch initiated. The incoming bytes are either opcodes, immediate data, or one of each. Opcode bytes are passed to the microcontroller to initiate instruction execution. Immediate data bytes are fed to the ALU as S source operands. Parsing logic formats the immediate data to avoid shifting or masking through the ALU. This feature enhances execution speed.

Because most instructions are one byte in length, the 16-bit instruction latch provides partial look-ahead. When the microcontroller is ready to start executing another instruction, the opcode is either in memory or already fetched and resident in the latch. In general, if SPCR is even, the addressed byte is still in memory; if SPCR is odd, the addressed byte is in the upper half of the latch. Conditional-fetch logic uses this information to decide when it is necessary to perform a read.

Microcontroller. Macroinstruction bytes are fetched from the code environment, two at a time, and stored in an instruction latch. Execution begins with the translation of the opcode byte into a starting microprogram location. The microcontroller then steps through control-store locations to cause proper execution of the instruction. If an interrupt condition is pending, the microcon-

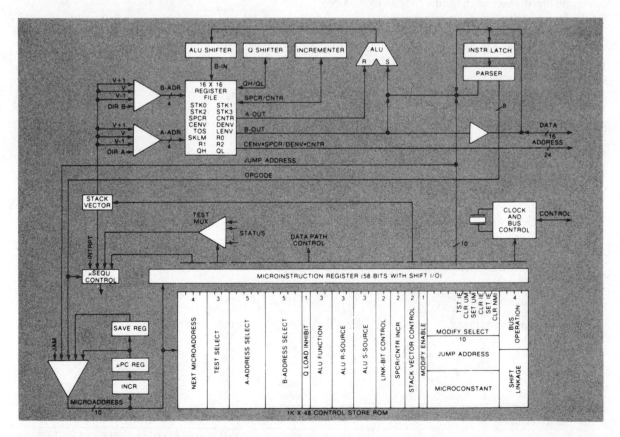

Figure 3. Block diagram of the AAMP microarchitecture.

troller automatically enters an appropriate service microroutine before executing the next instruction.

The control store is implemented with a 1K × 48 ROM. It contains microsequences for each of the machine-language instructions and for stack adjustment, initialization, interrupt servicing, and exception handling. The output of the ROM is loaded into a microinstruction register at the end of each microcycle. The register outputs determine which operations are to occur during the current microcycle. Microinstruction fetch and execution are overlapped.

The function of the microsequencer is to generate the 10-bit microaddress fed to the control-store ROM. At each microprogram step, the next microaddress is selected from one of the following sources:

- the microprogram counter containing the address of the current microinstruction incremented by one,
- 10-bit jump address emanating from a field of the current microinstruction and allowing nonsequential access to the control store,
- a save register previously loaded from the microprogram counter to establish the return linkage from a called microsubroutine,
- the current opcode byte from the instruction latch, conjoined with two fixed bits, for dispatching to an initial microprogram address, or
- jam logic generating the starting microaddress for initialization, interrupt servicing, and stack adjustment.

The selection of the next microinstruction to be executed is, in some cases, conditional on the state of a particular status line. To determine this state, eight status lines are fed to the test multiplexer. Conditional and unconditional jump, map, call, and return operations can be selected by the microprogrammer.

Clock logic includes oscillator circuitry and divide-by-four logic to produce the necessary internal timing signals. The 200-nanosecond microcycle implies a crystal frequency of 20 MHz. The clock logic allows pauses to be inserted as required during memory accesses. Intertwined with the clock logic is bus-acquisition and read/write-control logic.

Microprogramming. The microcode-control-store ROM is configured as 1024 words, each 48 bits in length. The 48-bit microinstruction word is divided into 17 subfields, as shown in Figure 3. The format is "horizontal," having minimum overlap in field definitions to allow maximum parallel operation in the data paths. A two-pass microassembler is used to translate symbolic microprogram source into object code.

The eight-bit opcode for each machine-level instruction is used as its microcode ROM entry-point address. The stack vector, in combination with the instruction opcode, determines if the stack-register condition is correct for each instruction. If it is, the microsequencer enters the ROM at the appropriate opcode entry-point microaddress. If not, microsequence jam logic automatically vectors to stack algorithm microsequences; this is done to empty or fill (from the process stack) stack registers in

order to provide proper stack-register contents for the instruction to be executed. This cache operation is intrinsic to the high performance found in the AAMP. Statistics indicate that the stack registers, for single-precision operations, contain appropriate accumulator conditions approximately 97 percent of the time.

Twenty-five percent of the ROM is used for instruction entry points. These entry points can perform some of the operations necessary for instruction execution. They usually contain a jump command to additional control-store locations for execution completion. Forty percent of the ROM is used for logical, arithmetic, and relational instructions. Twelve percent is used for executive firmware routines; seven percent for program control routines; only three percent for memory access instructions; six percent for miscellaneous instructions; and seven percent for special operations.

Design for testability. Testability of the AAMP was given high priority throughout the microarchitecture development. Key features were incorporated which, although easily implemented, have a profound diagnostic impact. Foremost among these are the shift capability of the microinstruction register and the external pins for serial I/O and control, which allow test equipment to shift out and verify the entire ROM contents. Moreover, special microinstructions can be serially loaded into the register and executed. As a result, microdiagnostics can be performed for initial chip debug and production testing. Also inherent in the design is the ability to repeatedly execute a single microinstruction at high speed. This capability is useful when it is necessary to observe signals with an oscilloscope during initial verification.

Testability was also enhanced by extending the microinstruction register by 10 bits so that the current address output of the microsequencer can be loaded (see again Figure 3). This allows efficient testing of the microsequencer. Furthermore, the three-state data-output drivers are automatically enabled whenever the microinstruction register is placed in the shift mode for testing. By so doing, there is a direct, observable port out of the register file. Thus, register contents can be observed without the need for bus write cycles.

The power of the AAMP's testability features allows thorough verification of its major elements. Separation of the address and data buses is also advantageous in this regard. High visibility and testability are achieved even for packaged parts.

Implementation. Two-micrometer CMOS/SOS was chosen as the AAMP device technology, since it could provide high-speed, low-power operation over the full military temperature range. Modules ("super cells") were established during microarchitecture development and used as the basis for layout partitioning. These modules were logically simulated, individually laid out, checked for proper layout with computer-aided design tools, and integrated via an interconnect cell. The overall design was described and emulated in AHPL — A Hardware Programming Language.[7] A microprocessor-based tester was developed to verify the chip design.

The CMOS/SOS-II process. The AAMP is implemented with Rockwell's CMOS/SOS–II technology. Transistors are formed on isolated silicon islands (Figure 4). This feature and the use of self-aligning silicon gates result in very low parasitic capacitances. Aluminum is used for one interconnect layer and a molybdenum-silicide polysilicon "sandwich" for the gate and second interconnect layer. These features produce high circuit densities and subnanosecond logic-gate delays.

Design methodology. Computer-aided design methods were used throughout design and layout. TRACAP, Rockwell's Transient Circuit Analysis Program, was used for sizing individual circuits. Logical simulation of each AAMP module was done with SIMSTRAN, the System Simulation with Signal Tracing Analysis Program. The same nodal equations used in SIMSTRAN were used in MTRACE, the Matrix Trace Program for symbolic layout verification. To verify the overall operation of the AAMP and its microprograms, the chip was emulated through AHPL descriptions of its modules and their interconnections and microcode.

Computer simulations were used to evaluate the effects of temperature- and supply-voltage variations on device operation. Simulations revealed the circuit areas most sensitive to mobility and threshold variations, and the designs of those areas were adjusted to accommodate those variations.

Power consumption is another important parameter. The worst case occurs at -55°C and +5.5 volts, at which point current conduction increases during logic-state changes. However, circuit simulations indicated that the AAMP's maximum power consumption would be well within the design goal of 0.2 watts. This was verified in testing.

Circuit layout. Circuit layout was done with symbolic layout design aids. The geometrical features were represented symbolically on a grid matrix, the digital translation of which was used for layout verification, design-rule violation checking, and mask generation.

Three grid spacings were used in the AAMP layout. The 4.5-micrometer grid used for the microprogram ROM enabled the 49,152 ROM bits and their accompanying decode logic to fit into an area of 112 by 106 mils. Each ROM cell has a channel width of six micrometers, a channel length of two micrometers and a contact size of

two by three micrometers. Access time is less than 50 nanoseconds.

A six-micrometer grid was used for the remaining chip logic and a nine-micrometer grid for interconnect line spacing. The nine-micrometer grid allowed the AAMP's designers to combine optimal logic and ROM interconnections with spacing conservative enough to maintain high yields.

Logic equations were written for each of the 6000 signal nodes. The resulting computer file was then used for logic simulation and for verification of the symbolic layout, to ensure a correct translation of the logic into laid-out circuits.

A photomicrograph of the fabricated chip is shown in Figure 5. 67,925 transistor sites are implemented on the 214-by-261-mil die.

External interface

The AAMP is housed in a 68-pin, square, grid-array ceramic package measuring 1.1 by 1.1 inches. In addition to small size, the package has sufficient pins to allow the use of separate (nonmultiplexed) address and data buses. Greater flexibility and higher throughput are thereby achieved. Each signal is dedicated to a single function. This enables users of the device to have a thorough understanding of the interface, and makes device interface design straightforward and efficient.

Pin functions. The AAMP employs 16 data and 24 address lines (Figure 6). The address lines provide a basic addressability of 16 megawords. Use of the C/D and E/U status lines can increase the address space to a maximum of 64 megawords.

The address presented on A23-A00 always selects a 16-bit word. The processor assumes the responsibility for properly managing instruction-byte fetches and byte-data accesses. Although not required by the memory system, high-byte (HB) and low-byte (LB) status lines are output to identify the byte(s) being accessed and to facilitate software debugging.

The data-transfer signals and protocol have been carefully selected to enhance operational reliability and to ease interfacing. Data transfers are 16-bit parallel and asynchronous. Interlocked handshaking control via XRQ and XAK is employed to support devices of widely differing speeds. Furthermore, the burden of transfer timing is placed on the AAMP itself to minimize device interface complexity. For example, two select lines, S1 and S0, are provided to control address and data set-up time with respect to the transfer request. This allows the system designer to choose, out of four delays, the one appropriate to the bus length and expected skew.

Memory protection is directly supported by the signals provided. Protection can be accomplished with an external memory-management unit or can be distributed throughout the memory system. A signal that allows code accesses to be distinguished from data accesses (C/D) is issued, as is one that differentiates between executive and

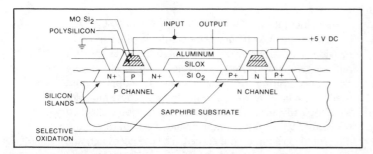

Figure 4. Transistors are formed on isolated silicon islands in CMOS/SOS devices. The AAMP was implemented with this technology.

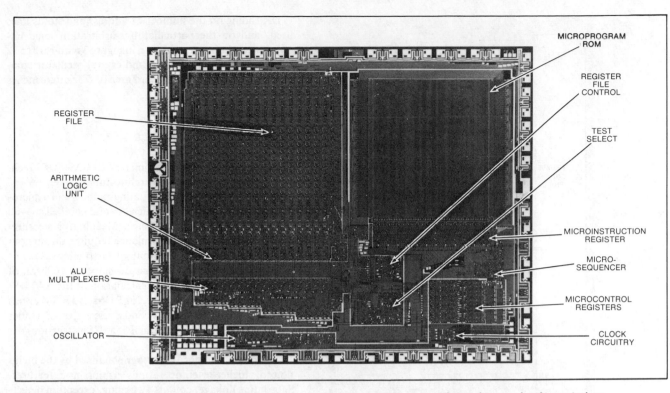

Figure 5. A photomicrograph of the AAMP shows its physical structure. 67,925 transistor sites are implemented on the 214-by-261-mil die.

user tasks (E/U). A protection violation or nonexistent memory is signalled to the AAMP through its transfer-error input XER.

Both maskable and nonmaskable interrupts are included. In a typical system, the NMI—the edge-triggered nonmaskable interrupt—is likely to be devoted to power-failure warning. The IRQ—the maskable interrupt request—is level-sensitive and can be externally expanded to support an arbitrary number of asynchronous events, however. IRQ is compatible with interrupt controllers, such as the Am9519, that permit software to determine the highest-priority pending interrupt and to manipulate the mask and interrupt registers.

In a shared-bus environment, the AAMP must be able to relinquish bus control to some other master device. The bus-request signal, BR, and the bus-grant signal, BG, are included for this purpose, and they directly support most arbitration schemes. Since BR is an output, the AAMP is given no special role in bus arbitration; rather, it is treated in a manner consistent with other master devices.

Bus interface design. The AAMP was intended to be applied in systems of medium-to-high complexity. Hence, external three-state buffering was required on address, data, and control signals. Timing and drive levels were specifically designed to be directly compatible with commercially available CMOS and TTL interface components.

A typical interface to a shared bus is illustrated in Figure 7. Data are buffered through three-state transceivers, and direction is controlled with the AAMP's read/write output. The unidirectional address and status lines are fed to the bus through three-state drivers. Input

signals such as interrupts and transfer-acknowledge signals employ bus receivers.

Bus-arbitration logic is required in a shared-bus system. The logic's active-low grant output becomes the AAMP's BG input and also directly controls the three-stating of the drivers and transceivers.

The AAMP's signal timing protocol provides hold time on address and status after an assertion of XAK, the transfer acknowledge, has been received. Some bus protocols require hold time after a negation of XRQ, the transfer request, has been received. The latter scheme is readily accommodated by means of HLD, the AAMP's hold output, which controls transparent latches. A package penalty need not result, since a designer can employ three-state drivers which include such latches.

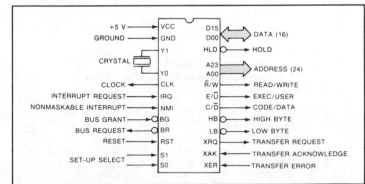

Figure 6. Summary of AAMP pin functions. The device employs 16 data and 24 address lines (shading), giving it sufficient pins to allow the use of nonmultiplexed address and data buses.

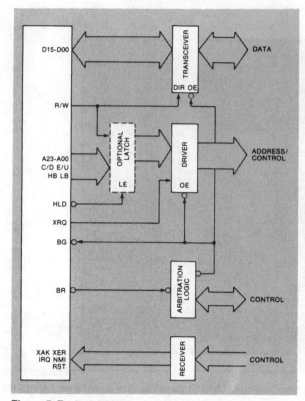

Figure 7. Typical AAMP interface to a shared system bus.

Depending on the number of address and status lines used, and on the particular bus-arbitration logic implemented, the interface shown in Figure 7 requires 8 to 12 packages. Including AAMP and crystal-oscillator components, an approximate board area of 6.5 square inches is required.

Throughput performance

The AAMP's two-micrometer CMOS/SOS technology, language-directed architecture, frequency-encoded instructions, on-chip floating-point—and a microarchitecture optimized for efficiency and parallelism—all contribute to high performance. Meaningful measurement of the AAMP's performance requires throughput calculations based on some mix of instructions. One of the more popular mixes is that developed by Gibson of IBM.[8] Table 4 summarizes a calculation of the AAMP's throughput based on this mix, for ROM and RAM access times of 100 and 250 nanoseconds, respectively.* Under these assumptions, throughput is 355,025 instructions per second.

AAMP performance is further enhanced by the inclusion of higher-level operations as intrinsic features. Subroutine linkage, context switching, exception detecting/vectoring, register maintenance, and high-level loop control would have each required a considerable number of assembly-level instructions had they not been included in the hardware. Context switching provides a good example of the AAMP's high-level control and performance. Less than 20 microseconds are required (after completion of the current instruction) to recognize a hardware or software interrupt, save the state of the existing task, activate the executive stack, and vector to the TRAP or to one of four interrupt-handling routines.

Table 5 compares AAMP throughput to that of other commercially available microprocessors, and to that of the CAPS-7, a high-speed CPU using 2900-family bipolar LSI devices. The CAPS-7 has the same instruction set as the AAMP. Single- and double-precision fractional arithmetic is substituted for floating-point arithmetic in the first two columns. Throughputs are shown for the 8086 without and with the 8087 math chip. (Math chips are also available for the Z8000 and M68000.)

The AAMP is a language-directed, high-performance, single-chip microprocessor implemented on a single CMOS/SOS die. Modular implementation techniques were combined with microprogrammed control to produce an advanced design on a moderately sized chip. Full use of computer-aided design tools minimized design risks. Use of a high-level-language-oriented architecture yielded a microprocessor with high run-time efficiency and high code density for compiled programs. Furthermore, the AAMP's operating characteristics remain

Table 4.
AAMP throughput with a Gibson mix. The calculation assumed a ROM access time of 100 ns and a RAM access time of 250 ns.

INSTRUCTION	EXECUTION TIME, μs	MIX PERCENTAGE	WEIGHTED TIME, μs
REFSL	1.225	31.1	0.3810
ADD	0.65	6.1	0.0397
MPY	4.85	0.6	0.0291
DIV	5.65	0.2	0.0113
ADDF	7.85	6.9	0.5417
MPYF	19.25	3.8	0.7315
DIVF	19.85	1.5	0.2978
GR	0.85	3.8	0.0323
SKIP	1.15	16.7	0.1921
SHIFT	2.85	4.4	0.1254
AND	0.45	1.6	0.0072
EXCH	0.85	5.3	0.0451
REFSXI	2.125	18.0	0.3825

Average execution time	2.8167	μs
Throughput	355,025	IPS

Table 5.
Throughput comparisons, Gibson mix.

PROCESSOR	16-BIT OPERANDS	32-BIT OPERANDS	12% FLOATING-POINT OPERANDS
INTEL 8086 (8-MHz CLOCK)*	416 KOPS	176 KOPS	NOT APPLICABLE
INTEL 8086/8087 (5-MHz CLOCK)*	270 KOPS	235 KOPS	210 KOPS
ZILOG Z8000 (6-MHz CLOCK)*	510 KOPS	325 KOPS	NOT APPLICABLE
MOTOROLA 68000 (8-MHz CLOCK)*	610 KOPS	380 KOPS	NOT APPLICABLE
AAMP (20-MHz CLOCK)**	740 KOPS	470 KOPS	355 KOPS
CAPS-7 (20-MHz CLOCK)**	900 KOPS	590 KOPS	450 KOPS

*ASSUMES NO WAIT STATES AND NO INSTRUCTION FETCH OVERHEAD.
**AAMP AND CAPS-7 CALCULATIONS ASSUME 100-ns ROM AND 250-ns RAM ACCESS TIMES AND INCLUDE BUS ACQUISITION AND DELAY TIMES.

*These times are measured at the memory system interface from the receipt of XRQ to the assertion of XAK. Overhead for bus acquisition, address set-up, and so on, is included in the instruction execution times.

stable in harsh environments, making the device suitable for avionics, space, and military applications.

Device testing has verified the computer analysis and confirmed the attainment of the design goals. Chips tested at a 20-MHz clock rate have dissipated less than 125 milliwatts, with some as low as 50 milliwatts. Moreover, testing has indicated that the AAMP can be operated at clock rates higher than 20 MHz. The device has successfully passed its instruction diagnostic program, and actual performance statistics have been accumulated through the execution of several benchmark programs. ∎

Acknowledgments

We wish to thank Frank Micheletti, Daryl Butcher, Jai Hakhu, John Kremarik, Ralph Seymour, Mat Tam, Pen Chow, Sadau Kuwahara, Mike Splinter, and Ross Orndorf, from the Rockwell Microelectronics Research and Development Center, Anaheim, California, for their help in the development and fabriction of the AAMP. Thanks are also due to George Benning, Ron Coffin, Don Stover, Bob Jakoubek, and Scott Holland, from the Advanced Technology and Engineering Division, Collins Avionics Group, Rockwell International, Cedar Rapids, Iowa, for their support and assistance during the AAMP project.

Publication of this article is for information only; its appearance does not constitute endorsement of CAPS or of the AAMP by *IEEE Micro* or by the IEEE.

References

1. D. R. Allison, "A Design Philosophy for Microcomputer Architectures," *Computer,* Vol. 10, No. 2, Feb. 1977, pp. 35-41.

2. H. G. Cragon, "An Evaluation of Code Space Requirements and Performance of Various Architectures," *Computer Architecture News* (ACM Sigarch newsletter), Vol. 7, No. 5, Feb. 1979, pp. 5-21.

3. A. S. Tanenbaum, "Implications of Structured Programming for Machine Architecture," *Comm. ACM,* Vol. 21, No. 3, Mar. 1978, pp. 237-246.

4. *Computer* (special issue on stack machines), Vol. 10, No. 5, May 1977, pp. 14-52.

5. W. A. Wulf, "Compilers and Computer Architecture," *Computer,* Vol. 14, No. 7, July 1981, pp. 41-47.

6. R. K. Johnson and J. D. Wick, "An Overview of the Mesa Processor Architecture," *Computer Architecture News* (ACM Sigarch newsletter), Vol. 10, No. 2, Mar. 1982, pp. 20-29.

7. F.J. Hill and G. R. Peterson, *Digital Systems: Hardware Organization and Design,* 2nd ed., John Wiley & Sons, New York, 1978.

8. J. C. Gibson, "The Gibson Mix," IBM Tech. Report 00.2043, June 18, 1970.

Appendix: CAPS programmer's reference*

Programmers Reference Card for CAPS-7, CAPS-9 (AAMP) and CAPS-10

PROCESS STACK

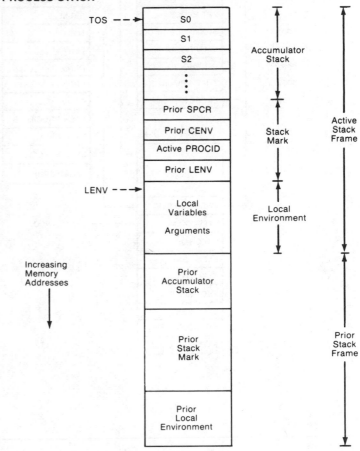

MEMORY NUMBERING NOTATION

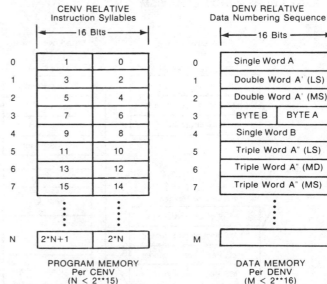

EXECUTIVE ENTRY TABLE

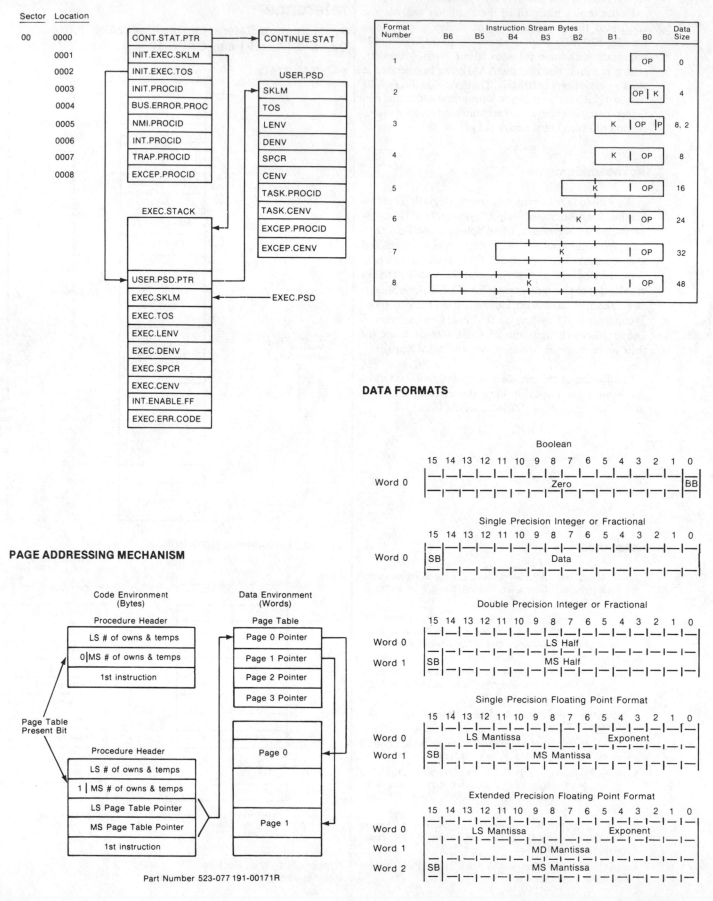

Sector	Location
00	0000
	0001
	0002
	0003
	0004
	0005
	0006
	0007
	0008

CONT.STAT.PTR → CONTINUE.STAT
INIT.EXEC.SKLM
INIT.EXEC.TOS
INIT.PROCID
BUS.ERROR.PROC
NMI.PROCID
INT.PROCID
TRAP.PROCID
EXCEP.PROCID

USER.PSD
SKLM
TOS
LENV
DENV
SPCR
CENV
TASK.PROCID
TASK.CENV
EXCEP.PROCID
EXCEP.CENV

EXEC.STACK

USER.PSD.PTR
EXEC.SKLM ← EXEC.PSD
EXEC.TOS
EXEC.LENV
EXEC.DENV
EXEC.SPCR
EXEC.CENV
INT.ENABLE.FF
EXEC.ERR.CODE

INSTRUCTION FORMAT TYPES

Format Number			Instruction Stream Bytes					Data Size
	B6	B5	B4	B3	B2	B1	B0	
1							OP	0
2							OP | K	4
3						K	OP | P	8, 2
4						K	OP	8
5					K	|	OP	16
6				K	|		OP	24
7			K	|			OP	32
8		K	|				OP	48

PAGE ADDRESSING MECHANISM

Code Environment (Bytes)

Procedure Header
LS # of owns & temps
0|MS # of owns & temps
1st instruction

Page Table Present Bit

Procedure Header
LS # of owns & temps
1 | MS # of owns & temps
LS Page Table Pointer
MS Page Table Pointer
1st instruction

Data Environment (Words)

Page Table
Page 0 Pointer
Page 1 Pointer
Page 2 Pointer
Page 3 Pointer

Page 0

Page 1

Part Number 523-077 191-00171R

DATA FORMATS

Boolean

	15	14	13	12	11	10	9	8	7	6	5	4	3	2	1	0
Word 0								Zero								BB

Single Precision Integer or Fractional

	15	14	13	12	11	10	9	8	7	6	5	4	3	2	1	0
Word 0	SB							Data								

Double Precision Integer or Fractional

	15	14	13	12	11	10	9	8	7	6	5	4	3	2	1	0
Word 0								LS Half								
Word 1	SB							MS Half								

Single Precision Floating Point Format

	15	14	13	12	11	10	9	8	7	6	5	4	3	2	1	0
Word 0			LS Mantissa							Exponent						
Word 1	SB					MS Mantissa										

Extended Precision Floating Point Format

	15	14	13	12	11	10	9	8	7	6	5	4	3	2	1	0
Word 0			LS Mantissa							Exponent						
Word 1						MD Mantissa										
Word 2	SB					MS Mantissa										

EXCEPTIONS

NO	EXCEPTIONS	RESULT
0	EXCEPT 0	NOT APPLICABLE
1	EXCEPT 1	NOT APPLICABLE
2	EXCEPT 2	NOT APPLICABLE
3	CVTDS	SATURATE
4	CVTFD/CVTFED	SATURATE
5	ABS/NEG (8000)	MODULO 2**16
6	ABSD/NEGD (8000 0000)	MODULO 2**32
7	ADD/SUB/INCS/INCSI/INCSLE DECS/DECSI DECSLE	MODULO 2**16
8	ADDD/SUBD	MODULO 2**32
9	MPYI (NEGATIVE OVERFLOW)	MODULO 2**16
10	MPYI (POSITIVE OVERFLOW)	MODULO 2**16
11	MPYID (NEGATIVE OVERFLOW)	MODULO 2**32
12	MPYID (POSITIVE OVERFLOW)	MODULO 2**32
13	DIVI (8000/FFFF)	SATURATE
14	DIVI BY 0	SATURATE
15	DIVID (8000 0000/FFFF FFFF)	SATURATE
16	DIVID BY 0	SATURATE
17	MPY (8000 * 8000)	SATURATE
18	MPYD (80000000 * 80000000)	SATURATE
19	DIV	SATURATE
20	DIV BY 0	SATURATE
21	DIVD	SATURATE
22	DIVD BY 0	SATURATE
23	EXPONENT OVERFLOW	MODULO 2**8
24	DIVF BY 0	SATURATE
25	EXTENDED EXPONENT OVERFLOW	MODULO 2**8
26	DIVFE BY 0	SATURATE

EXECUTIVE EXECUTION ERROR CODES

CODE	EXPLANATION
0	HALT instruction has been executed.
1	An illegal instruction has been detected.
2	A Non-Local search error has occurred.
3	Executive stack overflowed.
4	Executive stack underflowed.
5	Illegal header called. (AAMP and CAPS-10 only)
6-7	Reserved for future expansion.
8	A bus error has occured. (AAMP only)
9	Executive initial PROCID is zero.
10	Bus Error PROCID is zero. (AAMP only)
11	Nonmaskable interrupt PROCID is zero.
12	Interrupt PROCID is zero.
13	Trap PROCID is zero.

TRAPS

NO	TRAPS
0	OUTER PROCEDURE RETURN
1	ILLEGAL INSTRUCTION
2	NON-LOCAL SEARCH ERROR
3	STACK OVERFLOW
4	STACK UNDERFLOW
5	ILLEGAL HEADER CALLED (AAMP and CAPS-10 only)
6	RESERVED
7	RESERVED
8	USER TRAP0
9	USER TRAP 1
:	: : :

24	16	15		0
Instruction Byte Address:	CENV		SPCR	

23	16	15		0
Data Word Address:	DENV		OFFSET	

EFFECTIVE ADDRESS COMPUTATION, E_A

Suffix Symbol	Operand Size	Mode	Instruction Format	Effective Address
SU	16	Universal	1	EA = S1, S0
DU	32	Universal	1	EA = S1, S0
TU	48	Universal	1	EA = S1, S0
S	16	Global	1	EA = DENV, S0
D	32	Global	1	EA = DENV, S0
T	48	Global	1	EA = DENV, S0
SI	16	Immediate	5	EA = DENV, K
DI	32	Immediate	5	EA = DENV, K
TI	48	Immediate	5	EA = DENV, K
BX	8	Indexed	1	**EA = DENV, S0 + S1/2
SX	16	Indexed	1	EA = DENV, S0 + S1
DX	32	Indexed	1	EA = DENV, S0 + 2*S1
TX	48	Indexed	1	EA = DENV, S0 + 3*S1
SXI	16	Indexed Immediate	5	EA = DENV, K + S0
DXI	32	Indexed Immediate	5	EA = DENV, K + 2*S0
TXI	48	Indexed Immediate	5	EA = DENV, K + 3*S0
SC	16	Constant Offset	4	EA = DENV, S0 + K
DC	32	Constant Offset	4	EA = DENV, S0 + K
TC	48	Constant Offset	4	EA = DENV, S0 + K
SL	16	Local	2	EA = DENV, LENV+K
DL	32	Local	2	EA = DENV, LENV+K
TL	48	Local	2	EA = DENV, LENV+K
SLE	16	Local Extended	4	EA = DENV, LENV+K
DLE	32	Local Extended	4	EA = DENV, LENV+K
TLE	48	Local Extended	4	EA = DENV, LENV+K
SP	16	Paged	3	*EA = DENV, PAGE+K
DP	32	Paged	3	*EA = DENV, PAGE+K
TP	48	Paged	3	*EA = DENV, PAGE+K

*PAGE is selected by the 2 bit offset from the Page Table Pointer.
**The least significant bit of S1 determines the byte location, where 0 is the even byte or low byte and 1 is the odd byte or high byte.

ASCII CHARACTER SET (7-BIT CODE)

LSD \ MSD		0 000	1 001	2 010	3 011	4 100	5 101	6 110	7 111
0	0000	NUL	DLE	SP	0	@	P		p
1	0001	SOH	DC1	!	1	A	Q	a	q
2	0010	STX	DC2	"	2	B	R	b	r
3	0011	ETX	DC3	#	3	C	S	c	s
4	0100	EOT	DC4	$	4	D	T	d	t
5	0101	ENQ	NAK	%	5	E	U	e	u
6	0110	ACK	SYN	&	6	F	V	f	v
7	0111	BEL	ETB	'	7	G	W	g	w
8	1000	BS	CAN	(	8	H	X	h	x
9	1001	HT	EM	)	9	I	Y	i	y
A	1010	LF	SUB	*	:	J	Z	j	z
B	1011	VT	ESC	+	;	K	[	k	{
C	1100	FF	FS	,	<	L	\	l		
D	1101	CR	GS	-	=	M	]	m	}
E	1110	SO	RS	•	>	N	↑	n	~
F	1111	SI	VS	/	?	O	←	o	DEL

NUL — Null
SOH — Start of Heading
STX — Start of Text
ETX — End of Text
EOT — End of Transmission
ENQ — Enquiry
ACK — Acknowledge
BEL — Bell
BS — Backspace
HT — Horizontal Tabulation
LF — Line Feed
VT — Vertical Tabulation
FF — Form Feed
CR — Carriage Return
SO — Shift Out
SI — Shift In

DLE — Data Link Escape
DC — Device Control
NAK — Negative Acknowledge
SYN — Synchronous Idle
ETB — End of Transmission Block
CAN — Cancel
EM — End of Medium
SUB — Substitute
ESC — Escape
FS — File Separator
GS — Group Separator
RS — Record Separator
US — Unit Separator
SP — Space (Blank)
DEL — Delete

OPCODE	MNEMONIC	FORMAT	USAGE	DESCRIPTION
1 — REFERENCES AND ASSIGNS:				
LITERALS:				
1x	LIT4A	2	LIT4A N1	S0 <- N1
2x	LIT4B	2	LIT4B N1	S0 <- N1
18	LIT8	4	LIT8 B2	S0 <- B2
19	LIT8N	4	LIT8N B2	S0 <- one s comp B2
1A	LIT16	5	LIT16 B2-B3	S0 <- B3, B2
24	LIT24	6	LIT24 B2-B4	S0 <- B3, B2 / S1 <- zero byte, B4
25	LIT32	7	LIT32 B2-B5	S0 <- B3, B2 / S1 <- B5, B4
27	LITD0	1	LITD0	S0 <- zero / S1 <- zero
26	LIT48	8	LIT 48 B2-B7	S0 <- B3, B2 / S1 <- B5, B4 / S2 <- B7, B6

LOCAL DATA:				
4x	ASNSL	2	ASNSL N1	(DENV, LENV + N1) <- S0
Cx	ASNDL	2	ASNDL N1	(DENV, LENV + N1) <- S0 / (DENV, LENV + N1 + 1) <- S1
5C	ASNSLE	4	ASNSLE B2	(DENV, LENV + B2) <- S0 .
F7	ASNDLE	4	ASNDLE B2	(DENV, LENV + B2) <- S0 / (DENV, LENV + B2 + 1) <- S1
B5	ASNTLE	4	ASNTLE B2	(DENV, LENV + B2) <- S0 / (DENV, LENV + B2 + 1) <- S1 / (DENV, LENV + B2 + 2) <- S2
0x	REFSL	2	REFSL N1	S0 <- (DENV, LENV + N1)
3x	REFDL	2	REFDL N1	S0 <- (DENV, LENV + N1) / S1 <- (DENV, LENV + N1 + 1)
1E	REFSLE	4	REFSLE B2	S0 <- (DENV, LENV + B2)
22	REFDLE	4	REFDLE B2	S0 <- (DENV, LENV + B2) / S1 <- (DENV, LENV + B2 + 1)
77	REFTLE	4	REFTLE B2	S0 <- (DENV, LENV + B2) / S1 <- (DENV, LENV + B2 + 1) / S2 <- (DENV, LENV + B2 + 2)
53	LOCL	1	LOCL	Locate local data / S0 <- LENV + S0

GLOBAL DATA:				
A4	ASNBX	1	ASNBX	(DENV, S0 + S1/2) <- LS Byte (S2) / High byte if MOD (S1, 2) = 1, / Otherwise low byte
A5	**ASNBX2	1	ASNBX2	(DENV, S0 + S1/2) <- LS Byte (S2) / Zero byte, LS byte (S2)
D3	ASNS	1	ASNS	(DENV, S0) <- S1
D4	ASNSC	4	ASNSC B2	(DENV, S0 + B2) <- S1
54	ASNSI	5	ASNSI B2-B3	(DENV, B3, B2) <- S0
Bx	*ASNSP	3	ASNSP P1-B2	(DENV, (PDTR + P1) + B2) <- S0
A7	ASNSU	1	ASNSU	(S1, S0) <- S2
A6	ASNSX	1	ASNSX	(DENV, S0 + S1) <- S2
D5	ASNSXI	5	ASNSXI B2-B3	(DENV, S0 + B3, B2) <- S1
A8	ASND	1	ASND	(DENV, S0) <- S1 / (DENV, S0 + 1) <- S2
A9	ASNDC	4	ASNDC B2	(DENV, S0 + B2) <- S1 / (DENV, S0 + B2 + 1) <- S2
F6	ASNDI	5	ASNDI B2-B3	(DENV, B3, B2) <- S0 / (DENV, B3, B2 + 1) <- S1
Ex	*ASNDP	3	ASNDP P1-B2	(DENV, (PDTR + P1) + B2) <- S0 / (DENV, (PDTR + P1) + B2 + 1) <- S1
8B	ASNDU	1	ASNDU	(S1, S0) <- S2 / (S1, S0 + 1) <- S3
8C	ASNDX	1	ASNDX	(DENV, S0 + 2*S1) <- S2 / (DENV, S0 + 2*S1 + 1) <- S3
AA	ASNDXI	5	ASNDXI B2-B3	(DENV, 2*S0 + B3, B2) <- S1 / (DENV, 2*S0 + B3, B2 + 1) <- S2
98	ASNT	1	ASNT	(DENV, S0) <- S1 / (DENV, S0 + 1) <- S2 / (DENV, S0 + 2) <- S3
99	ASNTC	4	ASNTC B2	(DENV, S0 + B2) <- S1 / (DENV, S0 + B2 + 1) <- S2 / (DENV, S0 + B2 + 2) <- S3
B6	ASNTI	5	ASNTI B2-B3	(DENV, B3, B2) <- S0 / (DENV, B3, B2 + 1) <- S1 / (DENV, B3, B2 + 2) <- S2
Fx	*ASNTP	3	ASNTP P1-B2	(DENV, (PDTR + P1) + B2) <- S0 / (DENV, (PDTR + P1) + B2 + 1) <- S1 / (DENV, (PDTR + P1) + B2 + 2) <- S2
9A	ASNTU	1	ASNTU	(S1, S0) <- S2 / (S1, S0 + 1) <- S3 / (S1, S0 + 2) <- S4
9B	ASNTX	1	ASNTX	(DENV, S0 + 3*S1) <- S2 / (DENV, S0 + 3*S1 + 1) <- S3 / (DENV, S0 + 3*S1 + 2) <- S4
9C	ASNTXI	5	ASNTXI B2-B3	(DENV, 3*S0 + B3, B2) <- S1 / (DENV, 3*S0 + B3, B2 + 1) <- S2 / (DENV, 3*S0 + B3, B2 + 2) <- S3
9E	ASNF	1	ASNF	(DENV, S0) <- field from S3 / S0 = 16 - field length / S1 = start bit position

*CAPS-7 Instruction Only
**AAMP Instruction Only
***CAPS-7 and AAMP Instruction Only

OPCODE	MNEMONIC	FORMAT	USAGE	DESCRIPTION
D1	REFBX	1	REFBX	S0 <- (DENV, S0 + S1/2) / High byte if MOD (S1, 2) = 1, / Otherwise low byte; zero fill
55	REFS	1	REFS	S0 <- (DENV, S0)
56	REFSC	4	REFSC B2	S0 <- (DENV, S0 + B2)
1C	REFSI	5	REFSI B2-B3	S0 <- (DENV, B3, B2)
6x	*REFSP	3	REFSP P1-B2	S0 <- (DENV, (PDTR + P1) + B2)
D0	REFSX	1	REFSX	S0 <- (DENV, S0 + S1)
D8	REFSU	1	REFSU	S0 <- (S1, S0)
57	REFSXI	5	REFSXI B2-B3	S0 <- (DENV, S0 + B3, B2)
67	REFD	1	REFD	S0 <- (DENV, S0) / S1 <- (DENV, S0 + 1)
68	REFDC	4	REFDC B2	S0 <- (DENV, S0 + B2) / S1 <- (DENV, S0 + B2 + 1)
21	REFDI	5	REFDI B2-B3	S0 <- (DENV, B3, B2) / S1 <- (DENV, B3, B2 + 1)
7x	*REFDP	3	REFDP P1-B2	S0 <- (DENV, (PDTR + P1) + B2) / S1 <- (DENV, (PDTR + P1) + B2 + 1)
D6	REFDU	1	REFDU	S0 <- (S1, S0) / S1 <- (S1, S0 + 1)
D7	REFDX	1	REFDX	S0 <- (DENV, S0 + 2*S1) / S1 <- (DENV, S0 + 2*S1 + 1)
69	REFDXI	5	REFDXI B2-B3	S0 <- (DENV, 2*S0 + B3, B2) / S1 <- (DENV, 2*S0 + B3. B2 + 1)
75	REFT	1	REFT	S0 <- (DENV, S0) / S1 <- (DENV, S0 + 1) / S2 <- (DENV, S0 + 2)
76	REFTC	4	REFTC B2	S0 <- (DENV, S0 + B2) / S1 <- (DENV, S0 + B2 + 1) / S2 <- (DENV, S0 + B2 + 2)
74	REFTI	5	REFTI B2-B3	S0 <- (DENV, B3, B2) / S1 <- (DENV, B3, B2 + 1) / S2 <- (DENV, B3, B2 + 2)
Ax	*REFTP	3	REFTP P1-B2	S0 <- (DENV, (PDTR + P1) + B2) / S1 <- (DENV, (PDTR + P1) + B2 + 1) / S2 <- (DENV, (PDTR + P1) + B2 + 2)
78	REFTU	1	REFTU	S0 <- (S1, S0) / S1 <- (S1, S0 + 1) / S2 <- (S1, S0 + 2)
6F	REFTX	1	REFTX	S0 <- (DENV, S0 + 3*S1) / S1 <- (DENV, S0 + 3*S1 + 1) / S2 <- (DENV, S0 + 3*S1 + 2)
6E	REFTXI	5	REFTXI B2-B3	S0 <- (DENV, 3*S0 + B3, B2) / S1 <- (DENV, 3*S0 + B3, B2 + 1) / S2 <- (DENV, 3*S0 + B3, B2 + 2)
AB	SWAPSU	1	SWAPSU	S0 = Address of semaphore / S1 = DENV of semaphore / S0 <- (S1, S0) / (S1, S0) <- S2
66	LOCU	1	LOCU	Form universal address / S1 <- DENV / S0 = Address
FF	LOCX	1	LOCX	S0 + S1
D2	LOCNL	1	LOCNL	Locate nonlocal data / S0 <- Address of nonlocal data / S0 = displacement from nonlocal LENV / S1 = PROCID of nonlocal LENV
BA	*BLKXFR	1	BLKXFR	S2 = Source address / S1 = Destination Address / S0 = Number of words
BC	*INDEX	4	INDEX B2	S0 <- S0 + B2*S1

2 — ARITHMETIC INSTRUCTIONS:				
INTEGER:				
E4	ADD	1	ADD	S0 <- S1 + S0
E5	SUB	1	SUB	S0 <- S1 - S0
E6	MPYI	1	MPYI	S0 <- S1 * S0
E7	DIVI	1	DIVI	S0 <- S1 / S0
50	ABS	1	ABS	S0 <-	S0	
51	NEG	1	NEG	S0 <- Two s complement of S0
7C	INCS	1	INCS	(DENV,S0) <- (DENV,S0) + 1
7B	INCSI	5	INSI B2-B3	(DENV,B3,B2) <- (DENV,B3,B2) + 1
7A	INCSLE	4	INCSLE B2	(DENV,LENV+B2) <- (DENV,LENV+B2)+1
7F	DECS	1	DECS	(DENV,S0) <- (DENV,S0) -1
7E	DECSI	5	DECSI B2-B3	(DENV,B3,B2) <- (DENV,B3,B2) -1
7D	DECSLE	4	DECSLE B2	(DENV,LENV+B2) <- (DENV,LENV+B2) -1
DOUBLE PRECISION INTEGER:				
80	ADDD	1	ADDD	S1, S0 <- S3, S2 + S1, S0
81	SUBD	1	SUBD	S1, S0 <- S3, S2 - S1, S0
82	MPYID	1	MPYID	S1, S0 <- S3, S2 * S1, S0
83	DIVID	1	DIVID	S1, S0 <- S3, S2 / S1, S0
DC	ABSD	1	ABSD	S1, S0 <-	S1, S0	
DD	NEGD	1	NEGD	S1, S0 <- Two's complement S1, S0
FRACTIONAL:				
F9	***MPY	1	MPY	S0 <- S1 * S0
FA	***DIV	1	DIV	S 0 <- S1 / S0

OPCODE	MNEMONIC	FORMAT	USAGE	DESCRIPTION
DOUBLE PRECISION FRACTIONAL:				
96	***MPYD	1	MPYD	S1, S0 <- S3, S2 * S1, S0
97	***DIVD	1	DIVD	S1, S0 <- S3, S2 / S1, S0
BIT/FIELD MANIPULATION:				
8E	INSERT	1	INSERT	S0 <- field from S3 inserted into S2 / S0 = 16 - field length / S1 = start bit position
AC	XTRACT	1	XTRACT	S0 <- field from S2 / S0 = 16 - field length / S1 = start bit position
B9	*AXTRACT	1	AXTRACT	S0 <- field from S2 with sign extension / S0 = 16 - field length / S1 = first bit position
B8	ARS	1	ARS	S0 <- - S1 shifted S0 bits to the right, sign filled
FB	SHIFT	1	SHIFT	if S0 > 0, logic left shift S1 by S0 places, else logical right shift S1 by |S0| places
FC	SHIFTR	1	SHIFTR	S0 <- S1 shifted S0 bits to the right, zero filled
FD	SHIFTL	1	SHIFTL	S0 <- S1 shifted S0 bits to the left, zero filled

*CAPS-7 Instruction Only
**AAMP Instruction Only
***CAPS-7 and AAMP Instruction Only

FLOATING POINT:

84	ADDF	1	ADDF	S1, S0 <- S1, S0 + S3, S2
85	SUBF	1	SUBF	S1, S0 <- S3, S2 - S1, S0
86	MPYF	1	MPYF	S1, S0 <- S1, S0 * S3, S2
87	DIVF	1	DIVF	S1, S0 <- S3, S2 / S1, S0
DE	ABSF	1	ABSF	S1, S0 <- |S1, S0|
DF	NEGF	1	NEGF	Floating point negate S1, S0

EXTENDED PRECISION FLOATING POINT:

92	ADDFE	1	ADDFE	S2, S1, S0 <- S2, S1, S0 + S5, S4, S3
93	SUBFE	1	SUBFE	S2, S1, S0 <- S5, S4, S3 - S2, S1, S0
94	MPYFE	1	MPYFE	S2, S1, S0 <- S2, S1, S0 * S5, S4, S3
95	DIVFE	1	DIVFE	S2, S1, S0 <- S5, S4, S3 / S2, S1, S0
AD	NEGFE	1	NEGFE	Floating point negate S2, S1, S0
AE	ABSFE	1	ABSFE	S2, S1, S0 <- |S2, S1, S0|

DATA TYPE CONVERSION:

65	CVTSD	1	CVTSD	Convert 16 bit integer to 32 bit integer
DA	CVTDS	1	CVTDS	Convert 32 bit integer to 16 bit integer
D9	CVTDF	1	CVTDF	Convert 32 bit integer to 32 bit floating point real
DB	CVTFD	1	CVTFD	Convert 32 bit floating real to 32 bit integer
6C	CVTDFE	1	CVTDFE	Convert 32 bit integer to 48 bit floating real
AF	CVTFED	1	CVTFED	Convert 48 bit floating real to 32 bit integer
6D	CVTFFE	1	CVTFFE	Convert 32 bit floating real to 48 bit floating real
B4	CVTFEF	1	CVTFEF	Convert 48 bit floating real to 32 bit floating real
F8	CVTBIT	1	CVTBIT	Convert non-zero word to sign mask '8000'

3 — LOGICAL INSTRUCTIONS:

BOOLEAN:

E8	AND	1	AND	S0 <- S0 and S1
E9	OR	1	OR	S0 <- S0 or S1
EA	XOR	1	XOR	S0 <- S0 xor S1
F4	NOT	1	NOT	S0 <- One s complement of S0

RELATIONAL: TRUE = '0001', FALSE = '0000'

EC	GR	1	GR	If S1 > S0 then S0 <- TRUE else S0 <- FALSE
89	GRD	1	GRD	If S3, S2 > S1, S0 then S0 <- TRUE else S0 <- FALSE
8A	GRF	1	GRF	If S3, S2 > S1, S0 then S0 <- TRUE else S0 <- FALSE
91	GRFE	1	GRFE	If S5, S4, S3 > S2, S1, S0 then S0 <- TRUE else S0 <- FALSE
EB	EQ	1	EQ	If S1 = S0 then S0 <- TRUE else S0 <- FALSE
88	EQD	1	EQD	If S3, S2 = S1, S0 then S0 <- TRUE else S0 <- FALSE
90	EQT	1	EQT	If S5, S4, S3 = S2, S1, S0 then S0 <- TRUE else S0 <- FALSE

OPCODE	MNEMONIC	FORMAT	USAGE	DESCRIPTION
F5	HIGHER	1	HIGHER	Unsigned compare of S0 and S1 If S1 > S0 then S0 <- TRUE else S0 <- FALSE

4 — CONTROL TRANSFER INSTRUCTIONS:

CONDITIONAL:

EF	SKIPNZ	1	SKIPNZ	If S1 <> 0 then SKIP S0 bytes else SPCR <- SPCR + 1
EE	SKIPZ	1	SKIPZ	If S1 = 0 then SKIP S0 bytes else SPCR <- SPCR + 1
5B	SKIPNZI	4	SKIPNZI B2	If S0 <> 0 then SKIP B2 bytes else SPCR <- SPCR + 1
5A	SKIPZI	4	SKIPZI B2	If S0 = 0 then SKIP B2 bytes else SPCR <- SPCR + 1

UNCONDITIONAL:

59	SKIP	1	SKIP	SPCR <- SPCR + S0
1D	SKIPI	4	SKIPI B2	SPCR <- SPCR + B2
BB	*GOTO	1	GOTO	Jump to a program point outside the currently active procedure S0 = Pointer to SPCR and PROCID of prior active procedure

EXECUTIVE INTERFACE:

FE	HALT	1	HALT	Stop the processor
BD	EXCEPT0	1	EXCEPT0	Call exception handler "0"
BE	EXCEPT1	1	EXCEPT1	Call exception handler "1"
BF	EXCEPT2	1	EXCEPT2	Call exception handler "2"
58	TRAP	1	TRAP	Call executive trap handler S0 = Trap number

5 — HIGH LEVEL LANGUAGE ORIENTED INSTRUCTIONS:

SUBROUTINE LINKAGE:

5D	CALL	1	CALL	Call a subroutine in the current CENV; S0 = PROCID
23	CALLI	5	CALLI B2-B3	Call subroutine in the current CENV; B3, B2 = PROCID
5E	CALLP	1	CALLP	Call subroutine outside the current CENV; S0 = Pointer to PROCID and CENV
1F	CALLPI	5	CALLPI B2-B3	Call subroutine outside the current CENV; B3, B2 = Pointer to PROCID and CENV
64	CALLU	1	CALLU	Call subroutine outside the current CENV; S0 = PROCID S1 = CENV
5F	RETURN	1	RETURN	Return from subroutine. If LENV = 0, then return to executive

LOOP CONTROL:

8F	DO	5	DO B2-B3	Do loop initialization and range check
9F	ENDO	1	ENDO	Add increment and loop if within range

6 — MISCELLANEOUS INSTRUCTIONS:

20	NOP	1	NOP	No operation
1B	INTE	1	INTE	Enable processor interupt

STACK MANAGEMENT:

6A	DUP	1	DUP	S1 <- S0
6B	DUPD	1	DUPD	S3, S2 <- S1, S0
79	DUPT	1	DUPT	S5, S4, S2 <- S2, S1, S0
ED	EXCH	1	EXCH	S0 <- S1 S1 <- S0
8D	EXCHD	1	EXCHD	S1, S0 <- S3, S2 S3, S2 <- S1, S0
9D	EXCHT	1	EXCHT	S2, S1, S0 <- S5, S4, S3 S5, S4, S3 <- S2, S1, S0
52	POP	1	POP	TOS < - TOS + 1
B7	POPD	1	POPD	TOS <- TOS + 2

OPCODES IN NUMERICAL ORDER

OP	Inst	OP	Inst	OP	Inst	OP	Inst
00	REFSL.0	40	ASNSL.0	80	ADDD	C0	ASNDL.0
01	REFSL.1	41	ASNSL.1	81	SUBD	C1	ASNDL.1
02	REFSL.2	42	ASNSL.2	82	MPYID	C2	ASNDL.2
03	REFSL.3	43	ASNSL.3	83	DIVID	C3	ASNDL.3
04	REFSL.4	44	ASNSL.4	84	ADDF	C4	ASNDL.4
05	REFSL.5	45	ASNSL.5	85	SUBF	C5	ASNDL.5
06	REFSL.6	46	ASNSL.6	86	MPYF	C6	ASNDL.6
07	REFSL.7	47	ASNSL.7	87	DIVF	C7	ASNDL.7
08	REFSL.8	48	ASNSL.8	88	EQD	C8	ASNDL.8
09	REFSL.9	49	ASNSL.9	89	GRD	C9	ASNDL.9
0A	REFSL.A	4A	ASNSL.A	8A	GRF	CA	ASNDL.A
0B	REFSL.B	4B	ASNSL.B	8B	ASNDU	CB	ASNDL.B
0C	REFSL.C	4C	ASNSL.C	8C	ASNDX	CC	ASNDL.C
0D	REFSL.D	4D	ASNSL.D	8D	EXCHD	CD	ASNDL.D
0E	REFSL.E	4E	ASNSL.E	8E	INSERT	CE	ASNDL.E
0F	REFSL.F	4F	ASNSL.F	8F	DO	CF	ASNDL.F
10	LIT4A.0	50	ABS	90	EQT	D0	REFSX
11	LIT4A.1	51	NEG	91	GRFE	D1	REFBX
12	LIT4A.2	52	POP	92	ADDFE	D2	LOCNL
13	LIT4A.3	53	LOCL	93	SUBFE	D3	ASNS
14	LIT4A.4	54	ASNSI	94	MPYFE	D4	ASNSC
15	LIT4A.5	55	REFS	95	DIVFE	D5	ASNSXI
16	LIT4A.6	56	REFSC	***96	MPYD	D6	REFDU
17	LIT4A.7	57	REFSXI	***97	DIVD	D7	REFDX
18	LIT8	58	TRAP	98	ASNT	D8	REFSU
19	LIT8N	59	SKIP	99	ASNTC	D9	CVTDF
1A	LIT16	5A	SKIPZI	9A	ASNTU	DA	CVTDS
1B	INTE	5B	SKIPNZI	9B	ASNTX	DB	CVTFD
1C	REFSI	5C	ASNSLE	9C	ASNTXI	DC	ABSD
1D	SKIPI	5D	CALL	9D	EXCHT	DD	NEGD
1E	REFSLE	5E	CALLP	9E	ASNF	DE	ABSF
1F	CALLPI	5F	RETURN	9F	ENDO	DF	NEGF
20	NOP	*60	REFSP.0	*A0	REFTP.0	*E0	ASNDP.0
21	REFDI	*61	REFSP.1	*A1	REFTP.1	*E1	ASNDP.1
22	REFDLE	*62	REFSP.2	*A2	REFTP.2	*E2	ASNDP.2
23	CALLI	*63	REFSP.3	*A3	REFTP.3	*E3	ASNDP.3
24	LIT24	64	CALLU	A4	ASNBX	E4	ADD
25	LIT32	65	CVTSD	**A5	ASNBX2	E5	SUB
26	LIT48	66	LOCU	A6	ASNSX	E6	MPYI
27	LITD0	67	REFD	A7	ASNSU	E7	DIVI
28	LIT4B.8	68	REFDC	A8	ASND	E8	AND
29	LIT4B.9	69	REFDXI	A9	ASNDC	E9	OR
2A	LIT4B.A	6A	DUP	AA	ASNDXI	EA	XOR
2B	LIT4B.B	6B	DUPD	AB	SWAPSU	EB	EQ
2C	LIT4B.C	6C	CVTDFE	AC	XTRACT	EC	GR
2D	LIT4B.D	6D	CVTFFE	AD	NEGFE	ED	EXCH
2E	LIT4B.E	6E	REFTXI	AE	ABSFE	EE	SKIPZ
2F	LIT4B.F	6F	REFTX	AF	CVTFED	EF	SKIPNZ
30	REFDL.0	*70	REFDP.0	*B0	ASNSP.0	*F0	ASNTP.0
31	REFDL.1	*71	REFDP.1	*B1	ASNSP.1	*F1	ASNTP.1
32	REFDL.2	*72	REFDP.2	*B2	ASNSP.2	*F2	ASNTP.2
33	REFDL.3	*73	REFDP.3	*B3	ASNSP.3	*F3	ASNTP.3
34	REFDL.4	74	REFTI	B4	CVTFEF	F4	NOT
35	REFDL.5	75	REFT	B5	ASNTLE	F5	HIGHER
36	REFDL.6	76	REFTC	B6	ASNTI	F6	ASNDI
37	REFDL.7	77	REFTLE	B7	POPD	F7	ASNDLE
38	REFDL.8	78	REFTU	B8	ARS	F8	CVTBIT
39	REFDL.9	79	DUPT	*B9	AXTRACT	***F9	MPY
3A	REFDL.A	7A	INCSLE	*BA	BLKXFR	***FA	DIV
3B	REFDL.B	7B	INCSI	*BB	BGOTO	FB	SHIFT
3C	REFDL.C	7C	INCS	*BC	INDEX	FC	SHIFTR
3D	REFDL.D	7D	DECSLE	BD	EXCEPT0	FD	SHIFTL
3E	REFDL.E	7E	DECSI	BE	EXCEPT1	FE	HALT
3F	REFDL.F	7F	DECS	BF	EXCEPT2	FF	LOCX

POWERS OF 2

2^n	n
256	8
512	9
1 024	10
2 048	11
4 090	12
8 192	13
16 384	14
32 768	15
65 536	16
131 072	17
262 144	18
524 288	19
1 048 576	20
2 097 152	21
4 194 304	22
8 388 608	23
16 777 216	24

$2^0 = 16^0$
$2^4 = 16^1$
$2^8 = 16^2$
$2^{12} = 16^3$
$2^{16} = 16^4$
$2^{20} = 16^5$
$2^{24} = 16^6$
$2^{28} = 16^7$
$2^{32} = 16^8$
$2^{36} = 16^9$
$2^{40} = 16^{10}$
$2^{44} = 16^{11}$
$2^{48} = 16^{12}$
$2^{52} = 16^{13}$
$2^{56} = 16^{14}$
$2^{60} = 16^{15}$

*CAPS-7 Instruction Only
**AAMP Instruction Only
***CAPS-7 and AAMP Instruction Only

HEXADECIMAL AND DECIMAL CONVERSION

HEXADECIMAL COLUMNS											
6		5		4		3		2		1	
HEX	DEC	HEX	DEC	HEX	DEC	HEX	DEC	HEX	DEC	HEX	DEC
0	0	0	0	0	0	0	0	0	0	0	0
1	1,048,576	1	65,536	1	4,096	1	256	1	16	1	1
2	2,097,152	2	131,072	2	8,192	2	512	2	32	2	2
3	3,145,728	3	196,608	3	12,288	3	768	3	48	3	3
4	4,194,304	4	262,144	4	16,384	4	1,024	4	64	4	4
5	5,242,880	5	327,680	5	20,480	5	1,280	5	80	5	5
6	6,291,456	6	393,216	6	24,576	6	1,536	6	96	6	6
7	7,340,032	7	458,752	7	28,672	7	1,792	7	112	7	7
8	8,388,608	8	524,288	8	32,768	8	2,048	8	128	8	8
9	9,437,184	9	589,824	9	36,864	9	2,304	9	144	9	9
A	10,485,760	A	655,360	A	40,960	A	2,560	A	160	A	10
B	11,534,336	B	720,896	B	45,056	B	2,816	B	176	B	11
C	12,582,912	C	786,432	C	49,152	C	3,072	C	192	C	12
D	13,631,488	D	851,968	D	53,248	D	3,328	D	208	D	13
E	14,680,064	E	917,504	E	57,344	E	3,584	E	224	E	14
F	15,728,640	F	983,040	F	61,440	F	3,840	F	240	F	15
7654		3210		7654		3210		7654		3210	
Byte				Byte				Byte			

Nick M. Mykris is the project leader for microprogram tools and development in the Processor Technology Department of the Rockwell-Collins Advanced Technology and Engineering Division. His primary interests include computer architecture, microprogramming, and microprogram development tools. He was responsible for the microprogram development and verification of the AAMP.

A member of Pi Mu Epsilon, Tau Beta, and the IEEE, Mykris received the BS degree in electrical engineering and mathematics from the South Dakota School of Mines and Technology in 1978.

Jeffrey D. Russell is project leader for advanced architectures in the Processor Technology Department of the Rockwell-Collins Advanced Technology and Engineering Division. His major interests include computer architecture, CPU implementation, and fault-tolerant computing. The author of several technical publications, he was responsible for the microarchitecture of the AAMP.

Russell is a member of Eta Kappa Nu, Tau Beta Pi, and Sigma Xi. He received the BS, MS, and PhD degrees in electrical engineering from the University of Wisconsin in 1970, 1971, and 1973, respectively.

David W. Best is project leader for advanced VLSI processor development in the Processor Technology Department, Advanced Technology and Engineering Division, Collins Avionics Group, Rockwell International. His primary interests include VLSI design, computer architecture, and fault-tolerant computing. He has authored several technical publications, was responsible for the logic design, implementation, and testing of the AAMP, and was project engineer for coordinating AAMP development efforts with the Rockwell Microelectronics Research and Development Center in Anaheim, California.

Best received his BS in computer science from Colorado State University in 1978 and is completing an MSEE from Iowa State University.

William J. Smith is project engineer for systems software and architecture in the Processor Technology Department of the Rockwell-Collins Advanced Technology and Engineering Division. His interests include high-order languages, computer architecture, and support software. He was responsible for the tasking and interrupt architecture of the AAMP.

A member of Tau Beta Pi and Eta Kappa Nu, Smith received the BSEE from Iowa State University in 1966. He has done postgraduate work in computer science and electrical engineering at the University of Wisconsin and at Iowa State University.

Charles E. Kress is manager of the Digital Computer Technology Section in the Processor Technology Department of the Rockwell-Collins Advanced Technology and Engineering Division. His responsibilities include computer architecture, processor implementation, processor development systems, and microprocessor applications.

Kress is a member of Sigma Tau, Eta Kappa Nu, Pi Mu Epsilon, and the ACM. He received his BSEE from the University of Nebraska in 1959 and his MSEE from Ohio State University in 1961.

The authors' address is Processor Technology Department, Advanced Technology and Engineering Division, Collins Avionics Group, Rockwell International, 400 Collins Road NE, Cedar Rapids, IA 52406.

A Unique Microprocessor Instruction Set

Dennis A. Fairclough

Brigham Young University

New instruction sets have been based on tradition.

Here, the latter has yielded a simple, optimal,

A Unique Micro

Dennis A. Fairclough, Brigham Young University

The fundamental building block of any computer is its instruction set. In the architecture of a new computer, the selection of the instruction set is the most critical decision. The decision is even more critical in microprocessor architecture, due to the restrictions on power dissipation, number of input/output pins, die size, speed, and chip complexity.

The instruction set format is composed of the instruction, the word size to be accessed, the address mode, the address modifiers, and the condition codes, in a binary format. The *instruction set* is the group of instructions that the system may execute, while the *instruction set format* is the arrangement of the instruction field, address field, and other fields in memory.

Instruction sets appear to vary widely from computer to computer, but a closer analysis shows that they have many similarities. The instruction set of one microprocessor can be remarkably similar to that of a different microprocessor. Different microprocessors can even share identical instructions which are supersets of some earlier microprocessor.

Computer instruction sets are evolutionary rather than revolutionary in design; most are simply extensions of earlier sets. One reason for this is the need to be program-compatible with older computers. Another is the complexity of the design task itself. This complexity also forces a heuristic approach —designers must make heuristic decisions because they lack data on how instructions will be used.

An example of how heuristic architectural decisions are made is detailed in a paper by Foster.[1] Foster relates,

Today's instruction set— How much is excess baggage?

Reprinted from *IEEE Micro*, May 1982, pages 8-18. Copyright © 1982 by The Institute of Electrical and Electronics Engineers, Inc.

IEEE MICRO

processor Instruction Set

"Someone once asked why Stretch was designed with eight index registers. The answer that is reported to have been given was 'clearly four are not enough and 16 would be too expensive.' In the same spirit we choose 32 bits as the word length of our microcomputer." Design decisions made in this manner are typical of those made in the design of computer instruction sets.

A very good programmer once told me, "the instruction set on the Nova is the best that will ever be." Heaven help us if this is true of any instruction set. Instruction sets are like high-level languages—no one is the best; there are only languages that are less restrictive than others.

In providing for program portability, programmers have created their own software instruction sets. The p-code used in the UCSD Pascal system[2] is a good example of a software metainstruction set. By forcing a standard software interface, software portability is more easily achieved. This is not all bad, as evidenced by the large number of microprocessors using UCSD Pascal. The UCSD approach forces transportability at the expense of efficiency in the execution of the target-machine program.

The above are just a few examples of architectural complexity and how this complexity forces heuristic design decisions. The complexity that exists in computer architecture in general, and instruction set design in particular, encourage heuristic designs and evolutionary microprocessor architectures. Because computer architects generally do not know how their instructions will be used, they find it safer to follow an existing design than to create a new set from scratch.

The first goal of this article is to present data on how instruction sets have been used. The second is to define a scientific approach to instruction set design and then to use that approach to construct a new microprocessor instruction set. If we do not understand the past, we are condemned to relive it.

Previous work

A study of the Maniac computer by Herbst, Metropolis, and Wells[3] analyzed by Foster[4] showed that in the Maniac 16 of the 36 possible instructions accounted for 90 percent of all instructions written, and 24 instructions accounted for 99 percent of all instructions written. Foster[4] observed that the CDC-3600 instruction set could be reduced to one-half or one-quarter the size of the present instructions without loss of flexibility. He demonstrated that if the CDC-3600 instruction set was reduced from 142 instructions to 64 instructions, only two percent of the instructions executed would not be in the smaller instruction set. Alexander and Woitman[5] reported similar results in a study of the IBM System/360.

In research by the author, studies were made of programs used on four microprocessors: the Texas Instruments TMS9900, the MOS Technology MOS6502, the Motorola MC6800, and the Motorola MC68000. A significant number and variety of programs were analyzed.

May 1982

Table 1.
The use of microprocessor instructions.

INSTRUCTIONS EXECUTED	TMS9900 INSTR.	CUM.	MOS6502 INSTR.	CUM.	MC6800 INSTR.	CUM.	MC68000 INSTR.	CUM.
≤ 0%	8.7%	8.7%	7.1%	7.1%	27.1%	27.1%	30.3%	30.3%
≤0.1	14.5	23.2	12.5	19.6	27.1	54.2	3.9	34.2
≤0.5	29.0	52.2	10.7	30.3	27.1	81.3	21.1	55.3
≤1.0	20.3	72.5	14.3	44.6	6.5	87.8	11.8	67.1
≤2.0	7.2	79.7	26.8	71.4	0.9	88.7	10.5	77.6
≤3.0	5.8	85.5	16.1	87.5	1.9	90.6	13.2	90.8
≤4.0	7.2	92.7	3.6	91.1	4.6	95.2	0.0	90.8
≤5.0	2.9	95.6	3.6	94.7	0.9	96.1	6.6	97.4
>5.0	4.3	99.9	5.4	100.1	3.7	99.8	2.6	100.0
TOTAL	99.9%		100.1%		99.8%		100.0%	

A summary of the data is given in Table 1. The table shows that 8.7 percent to 30.3 percent of all the microprocessor instructions were never used; also 44.6 percent to 87.8 percent of the instructions were used 1 percent or less.

The data could be misleading if you simply look at the percentage of use. Ideally the frequency of use would have a uniform distribution. For the microprocessors analyzed, the uniform instruction-usage distribution should be:

- TMS9900   1.45 percent
- MOS6502   1.79 percent
- MC6800   0.93 percent
- MC68000   1.32 percent

These percentages place a figure-of-merit value on the instruction usage. If the instruction usage U is

$$U/10 \leq UD \qquad (Equation\ 1.)$$

Where U = instruction usage and UD = uniform instruction distribution usage, then the inclusion of the instruction in the instruction set should be eliminated. Using this criteria, we find that for the

- TMS9900,   18 of 69 total instructions   (26%),

Table 2.
The Gibson Mix.

(1)	LOADS AND STORES	31.2%
(2)	FIXED-POINT ADD AND SUBTRACT	6.1
(3)	COMPARES	3.8
(4)	BRANCHES	16.6
(5)	FLOATING-POINT ADD AND SUBTRACT	6.9
(6)	FLOATING MULTIPLY	3.8
(7)	FLOATING DIVIDE	1.5
(8)	FIXED-POINT MULTIPLY	0.6
(9)	FIXED-POINT DIVIDE	0.2
(10)	SHIFTING	4.4
(11)	LOGICAL AND, OR, ETC.	1.6
(12)	INSTRUCTIONS NOT USING REGISTERS	5.3
(13)	INDEXING	18.0
	TOTAL	100.0%

- MOS6502,   13 of 56 total instructions   (23%),
- MC6800,   29 of 107 total instructions   (27%),
- MC68000,   31 of 76 total instructions   (41%),

satisfy equation 1 and should be eliminated from the instruction set.

The instruction set usage presented above prompts one to ask, Is this a science or an art? Based on the data presented, we must answer that instruction set architecture is an art masquerading as a science. Knuth,[6] in an article entitled "Computer Programming as an Art," said, ". . . a transition of programming from an art to a disciplined science must be effected. . . . we have actually succeeded in making our discipline a science, and in a remarkably simple way: merely by deciding to call it 'computer science.' " Computer architecture and instruction set design are a combination of parody, art, and science.

The studies by Herbst, Metropolis, Wells, Alexander, Wortman, and Foster, and the research reported here, clearly indicate that a scientific approach to the design of instruction sets is required.

The procedure is first to determine how existing instruction sets are used and what particular groups of instructions predominate (and are significant). The methodology is based on instruction group usage. Only when the findings are in hand can a new instruction set be designed.

Before we begin this procedure, however, we must first investigate the history of instruction mixes, instruction frequencies, and instruction groups.

Instruction mixes. The most widely quoted study on the usage of instructions is that of Gibson.[7] Gibson attempted to quantify a tool—the "Gibson Mix"—in order to ". . . plan and design new computers, to estimate the worth of a computer to a user, and to plan data processing systems." Unfortunately, the Gibson Mix combined both instruction usage, instructions not using registers, and indexing. The Gibson Mix also combined instructions and addressing modes, two entirely different processes; mixing them only obscured the relationships between instructions and addressing modes.

The Gibson Mix grouped instructions by common characteristics, according to the function they performed. The Gibson Mix is shown in Table 2.

We must make a point in defense of Gibson's approach—most computer architects mix instructions and addressing modes. A good example of this mixing is the LDA (LOAD ACCUMULATOR IMMEDIATE) instruction format. The LDA instruction LOADs the IMMEDIATE data (the source address) into the A register (the implied destination address).

The mixing of address modes with instructions is a common occurrence. In early computers, instructions and address fields were mixed due to the small memory space available. Memory space is not a major problem today and there is no reason to mix address modes, instructions, and other information; in fact, there are many reasons not to mix them. One might argue that the mixing of instructions and address types saves bits in the instruction format and thus reduces the fetch time of the address. The discussion on address types will demonstrate that this is not the case.

After Gibson, and following his lead, other researchers developed other mixes—Arbuckle[8] one for the IBM 650, Agarwal[9] and Lunde[10] one for the PDP-10, Schreiber[11] one for the IBM 360, Foster[12] one for the CDC-3600, and others[13-15] ones for other machines. Such instruction mixes provided the basis on which the author generated instruction groups.

Instruction frequencies. Instruction frequencies have been investigated by Alexander[16] for the IBM 360, Shustek[17] for the Amdahl 470 and Intel 8080, Shima[18] for the Z8000, and Stritter[19] for the MC68000. Instruction frequencies record the frequency of use for individual instructions. They suffer from many problems—one is that in most computers instructions and addressing modes are mixed; another is that individual instructions do not always appear in differing computer architectures. The lack of uniformity from one computer to another makes individual instruction frequencies measurements of limited usefulness.

Instruction groups. Instruction groups were originally created by the author in May, 1976, but have not been published until now. The groups are variations on the Gibson Mix but with one very important difference: instructions in these groups are not mixed with address modes. All instructions are pure instructions.

Instructions are divided into eight categories:

- *Data movement instruction group.* Instructions in this group are LOAD, STORE, and MOVE.
- *Program modification instruction group.* Instructions in this group are BRANCH, JUMP, CALL (subroutine), and RETURN (subroutine).
- *Arithmetic instruction group.* Instructions in this group include ADD, SUBTRACT, MULTIPLY, and DIVIDE.
- *Compare instruction group.* This group includes both arithmetic and logical compare instructions.
- *Logical instruction group.* Instructions such as AND, OR, XOR, and NOT are included in this group.

- *Shift instruction group.* Instructions in this group are SHIFT and ROTATE.
- *Bit instruction group.* Bit set, clear, and test are in this group.
- *Input/output and miscellaneous instruction group.* In this group are input and output instructions and those instructions that do not logically fit into any of the other seven groups.

The collecting of instructions into groups masks out the idiosyncrasies of individual instruction sets. Using these groups allows the instruction sets of many different computers to be easily and accurately analyzed.

Definitions

To provide an unambiguous working vocabulary, the following definitions are provided:

- *Instruction set.* A computer's instruction set is the set of all instructions that can be executed.
- *Instruction format (instruction set format).* The instruction format is the binary configuration that the instruction-bit field, the address-mode-bit field, the address-modifier-bit field, and all other instruction-bit fields are formatted into. The instruction format is in a form that the control unit may easily decode for instruction execution and address resolution.
- *Address field.* The address field is that portion of the instruction format that defines the unique bit configurations for the specific address types.
- *Instruction field.* The instruction field is that portion of the instruction format that defines the unique bit configurations for the instruction (operation code).
- *Instruction (operation code).* The instruction (opcode) is an object that instructs the control unit which operation to perform.
- *Address type.* The address type refers to a general addressing method used to obtain the final effective address for a memory unit. The address type is made up of the address mode and the address modifier.
- *Address mode.* The address mode is the algorithm by which the address of a memory unit is calculated. These addressed units include flip-flops (bits), registers, and main memory.
- *Address modifier.* The address modifier provides the modification to a memory address (effective address) just prior to actually addressing memory. Indexing is an example of an address modifier.
- *Source address.* The source address is the modified effective address from which address data is read.
- *Destination address.* The destination address is the modified effective address to which data is written.
- *Pure instruction.* A pure instruction is an object (field) that contains only operation-code information.
- *Pure address mode and modifier.* A pure address mode is an object (field) that contains only addressing information.

Instruction groups

The instruction group method allows the classification of instructions by function. It provides a convenient way to compare, on a common basis, the instruction sets of many different computers. However, it can only be used to compare instruction sets on machines having similar architectures. This work concentrated on von Neumann-style register-to-register and memory-to-memory architectures.

The data on instruction groups were obtained by analyzing programs written for the TMS9900, the MOS6502, the MC6800, and the MC68000. Programs were randomly selected and were of many differing types. The programs analyzed included applications programs, assemblers, interpreters, compilers, monitors, kernels, op-

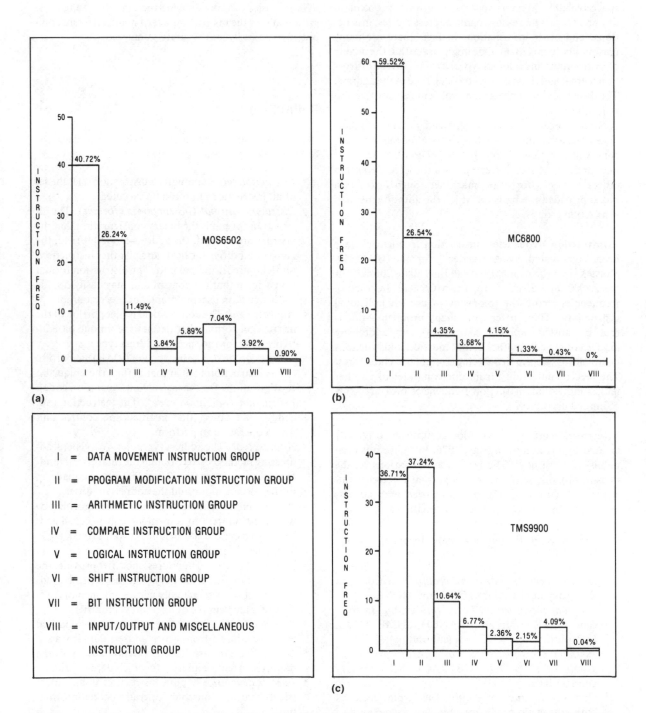

Figure 1. Instruction frequency by instruction group for (a) the MOS6502 microprocessor, a single-operand, 8-bit machine; (b) the MC6800, another single-operand, 8-bit machine; (c) the TMS9900, a double-operand, 16-bit microprocessor; (d) the MC68000, also a double-operand, 16-bit micro; (e) the Nova 1210 minicomputer, a single-operand,

erating system libraries, process control and process monitoring routines, and system utilities.

There are two distinct ways to obtain instruction usage data: one is a static instruction-frequency count; the other is a dynamic instruction-frequency count. The static count is obtained by counting instructions as they appear in a program listing. The dynamic count is obtained by counting instructions as they are executed by the com-puter. There is an excellent correlation between static and dynamic instruction frequency counts, as shown by Myers[20] and Alexander and Wortman.[5]

The data displayed in Figure 1 are based on static frequency counts. The figure shows the distribution of instruction usage by instruction group for seven machines. In each part of Figure 1, the instruction groups are given roman numeral designations—these appear along the

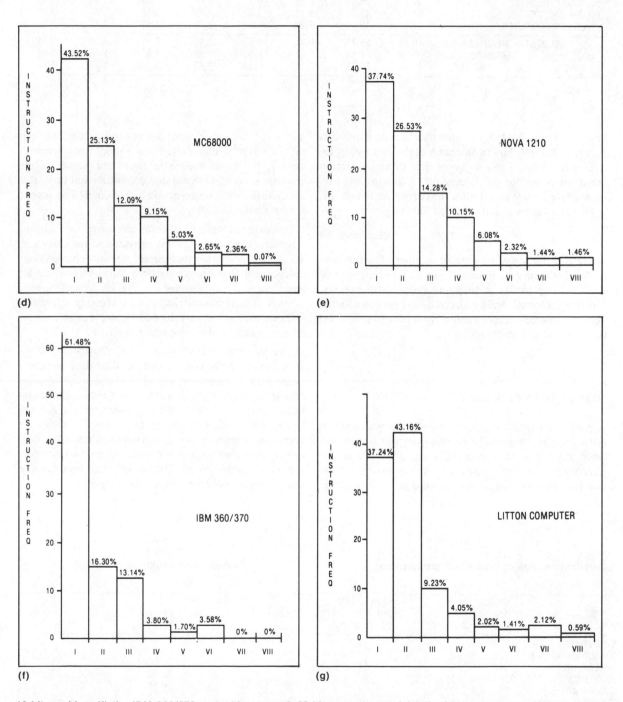

16-bit machine; (f) the IBM 360/370, a double-operand, 32-bit computer; and (g) the Litton computer. All data were derived by the author,[21] except those for the IBM 360/370[5] and the Litton computer.[22].

Table 3.
Summary of instruction group means.

ASSEMBLY LANGUAGE PROGRAMS BY COMPUTER TYPE	I DATA MOVE	II PROG. MODIF.	III ARITH.	IV COMP.	V LOGIC.	VI SHIFT	VII BIT	VIII I/O & MISC.
1. MOS6502 (8-BIT)	40.72	26.24	11.49	3.84	5.85	7.04	3.92	0.90
2. MC6800 (8-BIT)	59.52	26.54	4.35	3.68	4.15	1.33	0.43	0.00
3. TMS 9900 (16-BIT)	36.71	37.24	10.64	6.77	2.36	2.15	4.09	0.04
4. MC68000 (16-BIT)	43.52	25.13	12.09	9.15	5.03	2.65	2.36	0.07
5. NOVA1210 (MINI)	37.74	26.53	14.28	10.15	6.08	2.32	1.44	1.46
6. IBM 360/370	61.48	16.30	13.14	3.80	1.70	3.58	0.00	0.00
7. LITTON COMPUTER	37.24	43.16	9.23	4.05	2.20	1.41	2.12	0.59
SUBTOTAL MEAN=100%	45.28	28.73	10.75	5.92	3.91	2.93	2.05	0.44
STANDARD DEV.	9.89	8.14	3.02	2.57	1.69	1.82	1.46	0.53
VARIANCE	97.72	66.27	9.11	6.63	2.86	3.32	2.14	0.28

horizontal axis. Table 3 is a summary of the data shown in Figure 1. Table 4 shows a summary of the average, by instruction group. Table 4 shows that three instruction groups account for 84 percent of all instructions executed. Five groups account for the remaining 16 percent.

Fitting a function to the data of Table 4 yields

$$f(n) = 2^{-n} \qquad \text{(Equation 2.)}$$

where n is the instruction group number. The function $f(n)$ of Equation 2 is shown in Figure 2. This function will serve as the guideline in designing a new instruction set. The most emphasis will be placed on the groups with the highest projected usage. Table 5 shows the function $f(n)$ for each instruction group.

Instruction set design

What is an optimal instruction set? How is an optimal instruction set designed? One might answer that an optimal instruction set is one that contains the fewest instructions. Minsky[23] showed, using automata theory, that two instructions, *decrement* (and jump if zero) and

add one, ". . . can do anything an existing computer can do." Turing[24] demonstrated that a simple machine with an infinite serial magnetic tape and some simple algorithms could perform any computational task. But are these theoretical instruction sets optimal? The answer is most obviously no!

Due to the complexity of computer instruction sets, no satisfactory answer has been provided to the question, What is an optimal instruction set? A number of machine-independent algorithms have been shown to be optimal; however, such algorithms can be implemented in a number of different instruction sets. Memory utilization and execution speed vary depending on the programmer, instruction set, and computer system used.

The position of this paper is that a near-optimal instruction set can be constructed based on the instruction group data previously presented. A near-optimal instruction set is one that provides the user the powerful functions he requires. The thesis is that a near-optimal instruction set (or NOIS, as we will call it) is one that allows the user (programmer) to do what is required in an easy, efficient manner, with minimal memory usage, and with reasonable execution speed. The NOIS is a general-purpose instruction set rather than a special-purpose one.

Table 4.
Statistical average of instruction group usage.

		FREQUENCY OF INSTRUCTION GROUP USAGE, %	INSTRUCTION GROUP FREQ. OF USE, CUM. %
I	DATA MOVEMENT GROUP	45	45
II	PROGRAM MOD. GROUP	29	74
III	ARITHMETIC GROUP	10	84
IV	COMPARE GROUP	6	90
V	LOGICAL GROUP	4	94
VI	SHIFT GROUP	3	97
VII	BIT GROUP	2	99
VIII	I/O AND MISC. GROUP	1	100
	TOTAL	100%	

Table 5.
Probability instruction function.

GROUP	$f(n)$	CUM. %
I	50.00%	50.00%
II	25.00	75.00
III	12.50	87.50
IV	6.25	93.75
V	3.13	96.88
VI	1.56	98.44
VII	0.78	99.22
VIII	0.39	99.61

The NOIS provides

- pure instructions,
- pure address modes,
- pure address modifiers,
- an efficient and uniformly coded instruction format,
- orthogonality between instructions and addressing usage, and
- a uniform and consistent appearance to the user.

A pure instruction is one that contains only instruction information and is not contaminated with address-mode or other noninstruction information. A pure address mode or pure address modifier contains only addressing information. The power of this instruction set design is achieved by maintaining purity in all the instruction format fields.

The fewest number of bits should be used to huffman-encode every field in the instruction format; however, in no case should these fields be mixed to obtain additional efficiency. The efficiency obtained by mixing format fields is sacrificed to provide control-unit design efficiency. In the long term this provides improvements in both memory space and execution speed.

Pure instruction formats are effective in providing characteristics such as orthogonality. Orthogonality allows each instruction to use every address mode or modifier in exactly the same manner. This uniformity applies to addressing, word sizes, access methods, and condition-code testing and setting. Orthogonality must be maintained above format-field encoding efficiency. Uniformity, consistency, and purity must be maintained over *all* other considerations. These design restrictions do not have a significant effect on execution speed.

Contrary to advertisements in popular trade journals, a large instruction set is a liability, not an asset. An instruction should be added to an instruction set only when a new function cannot possibly be supported by existing instructions, or when the function can be supported, but only with significant deterioration of programmer or computer system efficiency.

Instructions. The designer, when unencumbered by parody, previous architectures, and program-compatibility restrictions, has a rich opportunity to create a near-optimal instruction set. He begins by selecting a single function for each of the eight instruction groups, one that, with the required operands, can encompass the functions of the whole group.

Data movement group. A single instruction will be used to provide the functions required by the data movement group:

MOVE, source, destination

MOVE moves data from the source address to the destination address. The effective address (EA) of both the source- and destination-address fields is determined by the address mode and address modifier.

The MOVE instruction accounts for 50 percent of all instructions executed (see Table 5).

Program modification group. The functions required by the program modification group can also be provided by the MOVE instruction. To provide JUMP or BRANCH operations, the source address is the address of

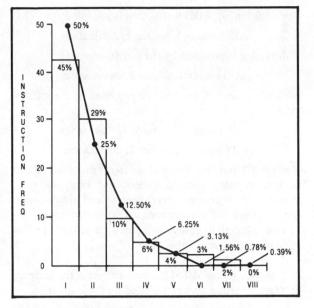

Figure 2. Generalized instruction usage function $f(n) = 2^{-n}$.

where to BRANCH to, and the destination address is the program counter (PC):

MOVE address, PC

To provide a JUMP or BRANCH operation on condition, the instruction is written

MOVE source, destination, CC

where CC is the condition code. The movement of data from source address to destination occurs only when the condition code is satisfied.

The MOVE instruction may also provide a JUMP or BRANCH to a subroutine on condition:

MOVE source 1, dest 1, source 2, dest 2, CC

where source 1 = program counter, destination 1 = stack or first word of the subroutine, source 2 = subroutine address, destination 2 = program counter, and CC = condition code. The MOVE instruction is executed only if the condition code is satisfied. A RTN (return subroutine on condition) is provided by a two-operand MOVE instruction and with a condition code:

MOVE source, destination, CC

where source = stack or first word of the subroutine, destination = program counter, and CC = condition code.

Note that the first two instruction groups, or 75 percent of all instructions executed, are satisfied by the MOVE instruction and various address types. Decoding of the instruction field (opcode) is simplified significantly by the large reduction in the number of instructions required.

Arithmetic group. Arithmetic instructions require three address fields:

- source 1 = address of value 1 (arith),
- source 2 = address of value 2 (arith), and
- destination = addr of result (arith) = value 1 op value 2.

For addition, an ADD instruction is provided:

ADD source 1, source 2, destination

Subtraction is provided by the instruction:

SUB source 1, source 2, destination

Multiplication and division are provided by the instructions:

MULT source 1, source 2, destination

DIV source 1, source 2, destination

The MULT and DIV instructions create problems related to results, value sizes, precision, and sign extension, however. Such problems have been solved before—their solutions are well-documented in the literature.

Five instructions now account for 87.5 percent of all instructions executed (Table 5).

Compare group. All of the instructions in the compare instruction group may be satisfied by the instruction:

SUB source 1, source 2, destination

where source 1 = value 1, source 2 = value 2, and destination = status register = value 1 − value 2. An arithmetic COMPARE is really just a subtraction that has the status register as its destination address.

Five instructions now account for 93.75 percent of all instructions executed.

Logical group. The logical instruction group cannot be supported by any of the previously defined instructions. The address fields required are

- source 1 = address of value 1 (boolean),
- source 2 = address of value 2 (boolean), and
- destination = result (boolean) = value 1 operator value 2.

The three essential boolean operators are AND, OR, and XOR (the exclusive OR):

- AND = source 1, source 2, destination,
- OR = source 1, source 2, destination, and
- XOR = source 1, source 2, destination.

The eight instructions defined thus far now represent 96.88 percent of all instructions executed.

Shift group. The shift instruction group also cannot be supported by any previously defined instruction. A SHIFT instruction, then, must be added to the instruction set:

SHIFT source, destination, type, count

The address modes to be provided are

- source = address value to be shifted,
- destination = destination address of the shifted value,
- direction = shift direction (right/left),
- type = shift type (arith/logical), and
- count = shift count 1 through maximum − 1.

Nine instructions now represent 98.44 percent of all instructions executed.

Bit group. Of all the instruction groups, this one is the most widely acclaimed and least used. Only one instruction, MOVE bit (MOVEB), is provided for this group:

MOVEB source, destination

where source = source bit address, and destination = destination bit address.

Ten instructions now account for 99.22 percent of all instructions executed.

Input/output and miscellaneous group. No additional instructions are provided for this group. All the microprocessors analyzed used memory-mapped I/O, which opens pins on the integrated circuit package for other important functions without placing a significant restraint on the I/O capability of the microprocessor. Interrupts are handled by hardware; the return from an interrupt uses a four-operand MOVE instruction to place the return address in the program counter and the status in the status register.

Since no additional instructions are needed for I/O, just ten instructions account for 100 percent of all instructions executed.

Summary of basic instructions. By group, the ten instructions are

I	Data movement	**MOVE**
II	Program modification	(MOVE)
III	Arithmetic	**ADD, SUB, MULT, and DIV**
IV	Compare	(SUB)
V	Logical	**AND, OR, XOR**
VI	Shift	**SHIFT**
VII	Bit	**MOVEB**
VIII	I/O and misc.	none

Extended instructions. There are a few other instructions that are not essential to the instruction set, but which add significantly to its programming flexibility. By examining the data on arithmetic instruction frequency, we can see that 2.5 percent of the instructions are increment instructions and 2.5 percent are decrement instructions. These high percentages justify the extension of the set to include such instructions. The instructions to increment by one to four and decrement by one to four are

INC value, destination

DEC value, destination

Combined instructions. Shustek[17] and Stritter[19] performed research to determine if any two or more instructions could be effectively combined into a single instruction. The author researched this possibility on the previously discussed microprocessors and concluded that very few useful combined instructions could be identified. Only two were determined to be significant enough to be included in the instruction set:

I/DBRC source 1, destination, CC

MOVEM source 1, source 2, destination, count

I/DBRC (increment/decrement and BRANCH on condition code) tests the source to be equal to the condition code. If the equality is satisfied, the BRANCH to the destination address is not taken. If the equality is not satisfied, the branch is taken and the source address is incremented or decremented by one, prior to the BRANCH to the destination address. The I/DBRC instruction is very useful in loop control.

The MOVEM (MOVE multiple) instruction moves the number of bytes in the count field from the source address(es) to the destination address(es). MOVEM is useful in string manipulation.

Restrictiveness and efficiency

One might argue that the instruction set is unnecessarily restrictive; however, it is adequate to efficiently perform every necessary function. The question that then arises is, How well? This was determined by comparing the number of NOIS instructions required to implement various compiler functions to the number of MC68000 instructions required to implement those functions. Programs were first written in MC68000 Pascal and compiled. The compiled code was then disassembled into MC68000 assembler mnemonics and also coded in NOIS assembler mnemonics. The results of this comparison are shown in Table 6.

No attempt was made to optimize the code as generated by the MC68000 Pascal compiler. The MC68000 instructions were replaced by the NOIS instructions on a line-by-line basis. With some optimization, the efficiency of the NOIS instructions over the MC68000 instructions could have been increased by another 15 to 20 percent over that indicated by Table 6. This optimization would have made the NOIS 25 percent to 42 percent more efficient than the MC68000 instructions.

When instructions are separated from instruction formats and analyzed as pure instructions, an interesting number of things become clear. One is that the power in a computer system resides in surprisingly few instructions. In the case of the NOIS, there are only ten basic and four extended instructions. If the instruction groups for the NOIS follow the $f(n) = 2^{-n}$ function, one instruction, MOVE, will represent 75 percent of all instructions executed, and four instructions, MOVE, ADD/SUB, MULT, and DIV, will represent 87.5 percent of all instructions executed.

A single bit may be used for the MOVE operation code, and a maximum of four to eight bits for all other operation codes. This minimal encoding frees all the remaining bits for use in encoding the address mode, address modifier, word size, and condition code fields.

The power of the NOIS is provided by a few pure instructions and a very rich addressing capability—further research has revealed that most of the power comes from the richness of the latter. Moreover, the importance and capability of pure addressing modes are almost as significant as the pure instructions. Address usage data is the basis on which to develop addressing modes and modifiers.

Table 6.
Number of instructions used in assembly language routines—NOIS vs. MC68000.

PASCAL CONSTRUCT	NOIS INSTRUCTIONS VS. MC68000 INSTRUCTIONS
FOR	−22%
WHILE	− 9%
IF THEN/ELSE	−15%
REPEAT-UNTIL	−10%

Floating-point instructions were not included in the NOIS. Such instructions can be provided on a separate chip. Other capabilities, such as transcendental and BCD functions, can also be placed on a separate chip.

The near-optimal instruction set is based on an analysis of instruction usage by groups rather than by individual instructions. The grouping of instructions by function allowed addressing modes and individual machine idiosyncrasies to be stripped out. The function $f(n) = 2^{-n}$, where n is the instruction group number, allowed the author to predict how the NOIS will be used.

The greatest effort was placed on creating and optimizing the instructions in the first four groups, which represent 93.75 percent of all instructions that will be executed. Less effort was allocated to the remaining instructions in the other groups.

The NOIS is a powerful yet simple tool. Its instructions are few and easy to use and remember. They are also orthogonal to the addressing modes.

A simulator for the NOIS was written in Pascal and was used to explore various algorithms. This exercise produced concise and efficient code. The next task will be to build the hardware needed to execute the near-optimal instruction set. ■

Acknowledgments

The author would like to acknowledge a number of people at Brigham Young University, Wicat, Inc., and Novell Data Systems, Inc., for their assistance. The number of individuals is so large that their names cannot be listed here, unfortunately. There are two individuals who must be recognized above all others—Dr. Dustin Hueston of Wicat and Dr. Jens J. Jonsson of Brigham Young University.

References

1. C. C. Foster, "A View of Computer Architecture," *Comm. ACM,* Vol. 15, No. 5, July 1972, pp. 557-565.

2. K. L. Bowles, *Problem Solving Using PASCAL,* Springer-Verlag, New York, 1977.

3. E. H. Herbst, N. Metropolis, and M. B. Wells, "Analysis of Problem Codes on the MANIAC," *Math. Tables Other Aids Computer,* Vol. 9. No. 49, Jan. 1945, pp. 14-20.

4. C. C. Foster, R. H. Gonter, and E. M. Riseman, "Measures of Op-Code Utilization," *IEEE Trans. Computers,* Vol. C-20, No. 5, May 1971, pp. 582-584.

5. A. G. Alexander and D. B. Wortman, "Static and Dynamic Characteristics of XPL Programs," *Computer,* Vol. 8, No. 11, Nov. 1975, pp. 41-46.

6. D. E. Knuth, "Computer Programming as an Art," *Comm. ACM,* Vol. 17, No. 12, Dec. 1974, pp. 667-673.

7. J. C. Gibson, "The Gibson Mix," IBM Tech. Report TR-00.2043, June 18, 1970.

8. R. A. Arbuckle, "Computer Analysis and Throughput Evaluation," *Computers and Automation*, Jan. 1966, pp. 12-19.

9. D. P. Agarwal, "Design of an Efficient Instruction Set," tech. report, Dept. of Computer Science, Carnegie-Mellon University, 1973.

10. A. Lunde, "Evaluation of Instruction Set Processor Architecture by Program Tracings," tech. report, Dept. of Computer Science, Carnegie-Mellon University, July 1974.

11. H. Schreiber, "Hardware Measurement of CPU Activities," *Modelling and Performance Evaluation of Computer Systems,* North-Holland Pub. Co., Amsterdam, 1977.

12. C. C. Foster and R. Gonter, "Conditional Interpretation of Operation Codes," *IEEE Trans. Computers,* Vol. C-20, No. 1, Jan. 1971, pp. 108-111.

13. D. W. Ashley, "A Methodology for Large Systems Performance Prediction," IBM Tech. Report TR-00.1773, Sept. 10, 1968.

14. *MC68000 Microprocessor User's Manual,* 2d ed., Motorola Semiconductor Products, Inc., Jan. 1980.

15. D. P. Siewiorek, C. G. Bell, and A. Newell, *Computer Structures: Principles and Examples,* McGraw-Hill, New York, 1982, pp. 54-55.

16. A. G. Alexander, "How a Programming Language Is Used," Tech. Report CSRG-10, Computer Research Group, University of Toronto, Feb. 1972.

17. L. J. Shustek, "Analysis and Performance of Computer Instruction Sets," PhD dissertation, Stanford University, Aug. 1978.

18. M. Shima, "Demystifying Microprocessor Design," *IEEE Spectrum,* Vol. 16, No. 7, July 1979, pp. 22-30.

19. E. Stritter and T. Gunter, "A Microprocessor Architecture for a Changing World: The Motorola 68000," *Computer,* Vol. 12, No. 2, Feb. 1979, pp. 43-52.

20. G. J. Myers, *Advances in Computer Architecture*, John Wiley and Sons, New York, 1978, pp. 273-291.

21. D. A. Fairclough, "Microprocessor Instruction Groups," unpublished paper, Dept. of Electrical Eng., Brigham Young University, Apr. 1980.

22. C. C. Church, "Computer Instruction Repertoire—Time for a Change," *AFIPS Conf. Proc.*, Vol. 36, 1970 SJCC, pp. 343-349.

23. M. L. Minsky, *Computation of Finite and Infinite Machines*, Prentice-Hall, Englewood Cliffs, N.J., 1967, p. 207.

24. A. M. Turing, "On Computable Numbers," *Proc. London Math. Soc.*, Ser. 2, Vol. 42, 1936, pp. 230-265.

Dennis A. Fairclough is an assistant professor in the Department of Electrical Engineering at Brigham Young University. He does research, teaches, consults, and publishes in the areas of computer architecture, high-performance microprocessor systems, and intelligent disk subsystems. He received the BSEE in 1962 from the University of Utah, the MSEE in 1968 from the University of Santa Clara, and is completing work for a PhD in electrical engineering from Brigham Young University. He is a member of the IEEE, the ACM, Phi Kappa Phi, Tau Beta Pi, and Eta Kappa Nu.

Fairclough's address is Dept. of Electrical Engineering, 468 Clyde Bldg., Brigham Young University, Provo, UT 84602.

MICROPROCESSORS & MICROCOMPUTERS

MICROPROCESSORS & MICROCOMPUTERS

SELECTED REPRINTS ON MICROPROCESSORS & MICROCOMPUTERS

SECTION 4
PERIPHERAL PROCESSORS

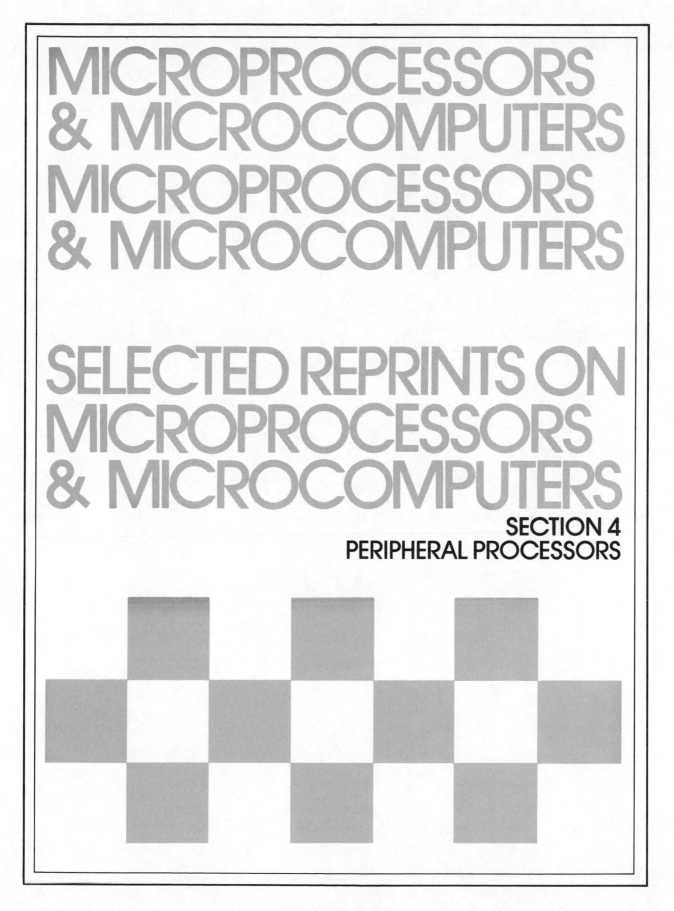

This device, a hardware implementation of the proposed

IEEE floating-point standard, can operate as a coprocessor

on a 32-bit bus or as a peripheral on an 8- or 16-bit bus.

The MC68881
Floating-point Coprocessor

Clayton Huntsman and Duane Cawthron

Motorola, Inc.

Two things have happened that will have a strong influence on the design of modern numerical engines. First, a standard for floating-point arithmetic, now being proposed, is likely to become widely accepted. Second, currently available technology has made it economical to build VLSI floating-point processors. Here, we will present the highlights of the proposed IEEE standard for floating-point arithmetic[1,2] and discuss what its features do for real-number computations. We will briefly examine several ways to implement IEEE arithmetic, and we will then describe the MC68881, Motorola's floating-point processor for the M68000 family of microprocessors.

IEEE arithmetic

Motivations for standardizing floating-point arithmetic include the need for increased portability of numerical software and the need for graceful handling of anomalies and exceptions. Meeting these needs enables users with diverse numerical expertise to develop consistent and predictable software.

Data formats. Greater portability means that there must be a standard format to which programs using floating-point arithmetic must adhere. IEEE Task P754 proposes binary floating-point data formats, each consisting of a biased exponent, an unsigned mantissa, and a one-bit indicator for the sign of the mantissa. A mantissa consists of an explicit or implied leading bit to the left of the binary point and a fractional part to the right.

The proposed standard fully defines a 32-bit, single-precision format—which must be provided in all implementations—and a 64-bit, double-precision format. It also minimally specifies single-extended-precision and double-extended-precision formats, leaving it to the implementer to fully define them. If both of the nonextended formats are to be supported, and if one of the extended formats is to be provided as well, the standard requires that it be the wider of the two. The characteristics of the various formats are shown in Table 1.

The proposed standard also specifies the numerical characteristics for conversions between the specified binary formats and implementer-defined, decimal string formats. Because of the decimal conversion ranges, for which support is required by the standard, a minimal binary-coded decimal format is implied even though it is not explicitly specified.

Data types. The defined formats include five data types which permit representation of regular and particular numbers and of special situations.

213

Normalized numbers are the most common data type with which the user must deal. This type has the most significant bit of the mantissa positioned such that the one lies to the left of the radix point. In the nonextended formats, only the fractional part of the mantissa is stored in memory, which means that the most significant bit is implied and is equal to one. Thus, one more bit of significance can be extracted from the stored information than could be extracted otherwise. In the extended formats, which are required to meet the minimum fraction width specified by the standard, the integer bit may be either explicit or implied, but in either case it is equal to one.

Unlike a normalized number, a denormalized number, or denorm for short, has a nonzero mantissa with the most significant bit positioned somewhere to the right of the radix point. (Hence, the implied bit in nonextended formats is a zero.) A denorm's exponent is the format's minimum. Therefore, a denorm allows a graceful underflow to zero while maintaining some precision. (It is, in fact, sometimes possible to denormalize a number and not lose any precision.)

Zeroes are another data type. A number with a zero mantissa and the format's minimum exponent is a zero. Zeroes also have signs, which become important in mathematical packages such as those that provide complex arithmetic.

At the extremes of a format are the infinities. These numbers have zero fractions and the format's maximum exponent. Like zeroes, infinities are signed.

The last data type is called a NAN, for not-a-number. A NAN is simply what the name implies. It is a symbolic representation of a special number or situation in floating-point format. NANs include all numbers with nonzero fractions and the format's maximum exponent. There are two types of NANs—signaling and quiet. Quiet NANs provide a way to indicate uninitialized variables or illegal variable accesses as well as a means for floating-point routines to communicate error reports through successive calculations. Signaling NANs cause an exceptional condition to be reported. They were added so that extensions outside the scope of the proposed standard could be added. The standard does not define how a signaling NAN is distinguished from a quite NAN. The distinction is left to the implementer. For all operations required by the standard, the presence of one or more signaling NAN arguments causes an exceptional condition to be reported. A quiet NAN does not cause an exception. Instead, since the result of an operation with one or more NAN operands is a NAN, the information is propagated through any number of operations that may follow.

The various data types are summarized in Table 2.

Although these formats and associated data types allow numerical data to be transported from one machine to another, a floating-point system must be more than portable and more than just a format. It must ensure that the behavior of systems during format conversions is consistent. It must provide the user with a minimal set of exceptional conditions so that he can diagnose anomalies. The proposed IEEE floating-point standard defines such

a system. It provides predictability and utility for the numerically naive user as well as for the expert. NANs and exceptional condition reporting provide debug and run-time diagnosis of packages developed under any implementation of the standard. Since Draft 10.0 of the standard requires that certain exceptions be announced by conforming sytems, users of such systems can easily trace algorithmic design flaws.

Exceptional conditions. There are five classes of exceptional conditions reported by conforming implementations. These are division by zero, underflow, overflow, inexact result, and invalid operation. Whenever an attempt is made to divide a finitely representable number by zero, the division-by-zero exception is reported. If an operation returns a result so small that it can be represented in the particular format only as a denorm and it loses significance during denormalization, the underflow exception is signaled. If an operation returns a rounded result that has an exponent greater than that of the largest finite number in the format, the overflow exception is reported. If an operation returns a rounded result that is imprecise, the inexact result is signaled. For instance, a number converted from BCD to single precision may not be exactly representable in the new format. If this is so, it is reported as an inexact result. Whenever arguments that will yield undefined results are presented to an operation, an invalid operation is signaled. Examples include operations such as attempting to multiply a zero times an infinity and attempting to divide two zeroes or two infinities. As stated above, the proposed standard requires all operations incorporating a signaling NAN to report exceptions. In these cases, the reporting vehicle is the invalid operation.

Basic operations. The proposed standard requires certain basic operations, including add, subtract, multiply, divide, find square root, find remainder, round to integer,

**Table 1.
IEEE floating-point formats.**

FORMAT	FIELD WIDTHS IN BITS		
	SIGN	EXPONENT	MANTISSA*
SINGLE	1	8	23
DOUBLE	1	11	52
SINGLE-EXTENDED	1	≥ 11	≥ 31
DOUBLE-EXTENDED	1	≥ 15	≥ 63

*THE MINIMUM NUMBER OF BITS SPECIFIED IN THIS FIELD REFLECTS AN IMPLIED INTEGER BIT IN THE MANTISSA.

**Table 2.
IEEE floating-point data types.**

TYPE	DESCRIPTION
NORMALIZED	MSB TO LEFT OF RADIX POINT, FORMAT'S EXPONENT RANGE
DENORMALIZED	MSB TO RIGHT OF RADIX POINT, MINIMUM EXPONENT
ZERO	ZERO MANTISSA, MINIMUM EXPONENT
INFINITY	ZERO FRACTION, MAXIMUM EXPONENT
NOT-A-NUMBER	NONZERO FRACTION, MAXIMUM EXPONENT

and compare. It specifies conversion between different floating-point formats, conversion between floating-point and integer formats, and conversion between binary and decimal formats. It also stipulates rules for the various rounding methods for these operations.

The proposed IEEE floating-point standard addresses the need for a functionally superior, floating-point methodology by providing various formats, regular error-handling mechanisms, fundamental operations, and simplicity. Compliance by major corporations will mean that scientific and business users will enjoy numerical software that is more producible, portable, and maintainable.

Implementing the proposed IEEE standard

The following discourse examines three general implementation schemes that are within the framework of the specification. The standard allows for software, hardware, or hybrid solutions to the implementation problem. It also stipulates that no hardware portion of a hybrid shall be said to conform apart from its supporting software.

So far we have discussed only the more salient features of the standard. Even so, it should already be obvious that a significant amount of overhead is required before and after the execution of each operation. We would expect, therefore, that a conforming software implementation would run slower than other, nonconforming software floating-point implementations currently in place. This is in fact the case. In an exhaustive evaluation of a conforming software package developed at Motorola for internal use, it was found that a significant portion of an operation's total execution time involved exception checking, preservation of rounding direction, and the like. Such performance degradation may make it difficult to convince some users of non-IEEE software implementations to convert to the philosophy of the proposed standard.

For VLSI implementations, at least, the hybrid approach could use a processor to perform certain kernel functions such as add, subtract, multiply, and divide, and rely on a software envelope to handle most of the special

cases. If the hardware was able to multiply two normalized numbers, for example, the software would check the operands of each multiply instruction for zeroes, infinities, denorms, and NANs. Only normalized numbers might actually be passed to the hardware. This method definitely would be faster than a software-only approach and would be relatively inexpensive. Users could achieve the benefits provided by IEEE arithmetic while increasing system performance. However, they would still have to develop commonly used functions such as trigonometric and transcendental routines. These routines would represent a burden in addition to that imposed by the standard functions, and they would further degrade the overall performance of the hybrid implementation.

It seems, therefore, that if hardware could be used to solve part of the implementation problem, it should be allowed to provide a total solution. This means that special cases could be handled in an efficient manner. It means that the problems associated with the integration of commonly used functions such as trigonometrics and transcendentals could be handled with built-in expertise. And it means that maximum performance could be attained for about what a complete hybrid system would cost.

The MC68881 floating-point machine

The MC68881, a single-chip HCMOS VLSI processor, is a hardware implementation of the proposed IEEE standard for floating-point arithmetic. It is available in either a 64-pin DIP or a 68-pin grid array. It not only provides those features required by the standard but includes most of the optional features suggested by it as well. It needs no software envelope. Its instruction set is a logical extension of the M68000 family architecture. This allows it to be used as a coprocessor with the next generation of Motorola microprocessors or as a peripheral for other central processing units.

The MC68881 is most effectively utilized when it is configured as a coprocessor for the MC68020, a 32-bit, general-purpose microprocessor (see Figure 1). The MC68020 and MC68881 contain bus interface units that utilize a protocol that allows them to exchange machine instructions, operands, and results along a 32-bit data bus. By executing asynchronously, the bus interfaces permit the MC68020 and the MC68881 to run at different clock speeds and to execute many operations concurrently. Because of the generality of its bus interface, the MC68881 can also be configured as a peripheral for the MC68008[3] (Figure 2) or as a peripheral for the MC68000[4] and MC68010[5] (Figure 3).

The following paragraphs discuss the protocol required to interface the floating-point coprocessor to an M68000 system. It should be understood that the operation word and extension word or words are peculiar to the M68000 family of processors. Nonfamily members as well as non-Motorola processors need only observe the actions required to pass the command word(s) to the coprocessor and to perform the necessary responses.

When the MC68000 was designed, certain operation code combinations were reserved for future expansion.

Partial list of M68000 family signals

SIGNAL	DESCRIPTION
A0-A31	Address bus
FC0-FC2	Processor status (function code)
D0-D31	Data bus
R/W	Read/write
AS	Address strobe
DS	Data strobe
UDS	Upper data strobe
LDS	Lower data strobe
CS	Chip select
SIZE	Bus size
DSACK0	Data and size acknowledge
DSACK1	Data and size acknowledge
DTACK	Data transfer acknowledge
RESET	Reset

Of course, at that time the intent of the reserved instructions was not known, so these operation codes simply initiated traps. Later, the F-line codes (those with the uppermost four bits set to ones, or hexidecimal F) were relegated to the class of instructions that supports coprocessors.

Members of the microprocessor family supporting coprocessors (e.g., the MC68020) recognize coprocessor instructions and perform the protocol required for coprocessor instruction sequencing. The other members of the family (i.e., the MC68000, MC68008, and MC68010) simply perform an F-line trap and rely on the software to complete the interface between the machines. The coprocessor in the trapping instance is characterized as a peripheral.

An M68000 coprocessor instruction (see Figure 4) consists of an F-line operation word, a possible coprocessor command word, and zero or more extension words. The coprocessor command word (or words) provides the operation code specifically for the coprocessor. The operation word consists of four fields. The first field is the F-line indicator. The coprocessor identification, or

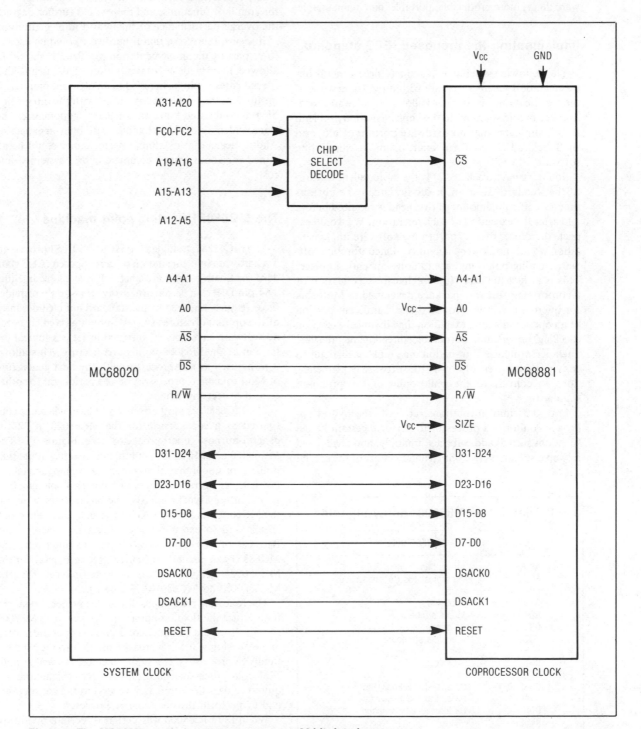

Figure 1. The MC68881 used as a coprocessor on a 32-bit data bus.

216

December 1983

CP-ID, field determines the particular coprocessor for which the instruction is intended. Up to eight coprocessors may exist in a system. The MC68881 can be one of eight different coprocessors, or all eight coprocessors can be MC68881s. The type field declares the class of coprocessor instruction and includes the general type (for the most common coprocessor operations), the conditional type, the save type, and the restore type. The modifier field provides additional information about a particular operation word type—the modifier for the general instruction type, for example, is an effective address field. (This modifier can also specify that additional extension words are needed to determine the effective address.)

Coprocessor instruction processing begins with the fetching of the F-line instruction. If the main processor does not directly support the coprocessor interface, the F-line trap handler is entered. In any case, the main processor must then interpret the operation word and write the command word to the coprocessor command register. The MC68881 must then decode the command word and provide a response for the host machine in the coprocessor response register. The main processor then reads the response register. The register indicates either that no further action is required or that some additional service must

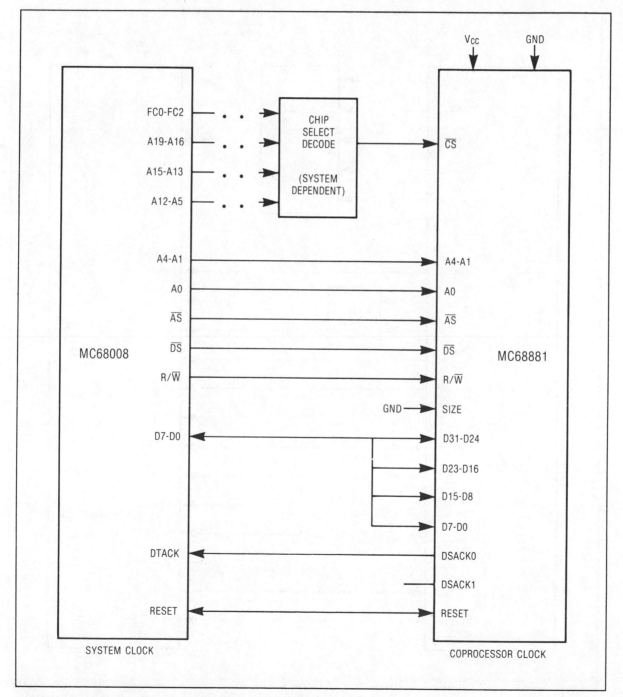

Figure 2. The MC68881 used as a peripheral on an 8-bit data bus.

217

be performed. Such a service may be the evaluation of an effective address or the commencement of exception processing.

In the M68000 family, coprocessor interface registers are, by definition, memory-mapped. Therefore, the protocol for coprocessor operation is the same whether the MC68881 is used as an M68000 family coprocessor or peripheral. Because the burden of operation word decoding and effective address evaluation is on the main processor, instruction sequencing external to the coprocessor is necessarily slower when the part is used as a peripheral. However, once the host-to-coprocessor protocol software has been installed, the architecture of the host processor has been effectively extended with additional instructions and register resources.

Programmer's model. The MC68881 programmer's model appears as an extension of the host processor and provides eight floating-point data registers, a status register, a control register, and an instruction address register (Figure 5).

Floating-point registers. The floating-point data registers are 80-bit, extended-procision registers. All floating-point operations are performed via these

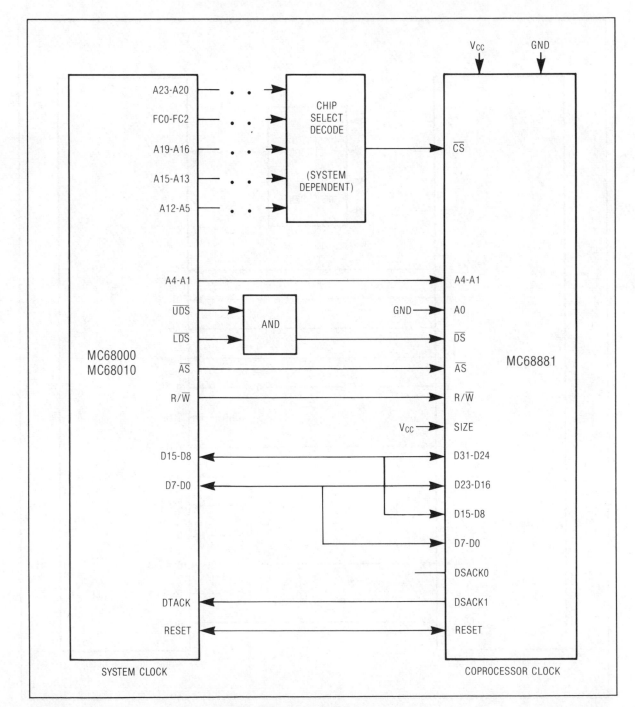

Figure 3. The MC68881 used as a peripheral on a 16-bit data bus.

December 1983

registers. During execution of a floating-point instruction, the MC68881 execution unit obtains its operands from the floating-point register block, an MC68020 data register, or a memory area. It performs the calculation specified by the floating-point coprocessor command word and then deposits the result into a floating-point register. (Exceptions to this are the move-out instruc-

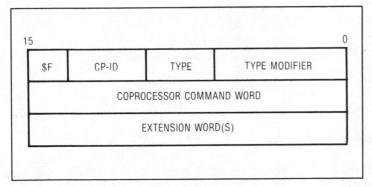

15   0

| $F | CP-ID | TYPE | TYPE MODIFIER |

| COPROCESSOR COMMAND WORD |

| EXTENSION WORD(S) |

Figure 4. MC68881 instruction format.

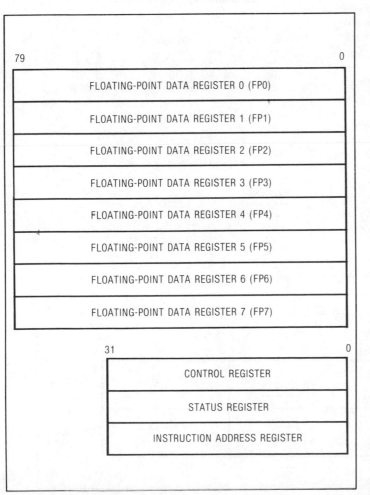

79   0

| FLOATING-POINT DATA REGISTER 0 (FP0) |

| FLOATING-POINT DATA REGISTER 1 (FP1) |

| FLOATING-POINT DATA REGISTER 2 (FP2) |

| FLOATING-POINT DATA REGISTER 3 (FP3) |

| FLOATING-POINT DATA REGISTER 4 (FP4) |

| FLOATING-POINT DATA REGISTER 5 (FP5) |

| FLOATING-POINT DATA REGISTER 6 (FP6) |

| FLOATING-POINT DATA REGISTER 7 (FP7) |

31   0

| CONTROL REGISTER |

| STATUS REGISTER |

| INSTRUCTION ADDRESS REGISTER |

Figure 5. MC68881 programmer's model.

tions.) The result may be left in the register for another calculation, or it may be moved off the chip.

Status register. In the MC68881, the status register

- reports exceptions which have occurred during the execution of an instruction,
- indicates exceptions which have accrued since the last time the exception history was cleared,
- reports floating-point condition codes, and
- provides a portion of the quotient generated by the modulo and IEEE remainder instructions.

An exception is reported in the exception byte. Each bit position in this byte represents a particular exception type. Any exception that occurs during the execution of an instruction sets the appropriate bit. The exception byte is cleared before the start of any instruction capable of causing an exception.

The floating-point standard requires conforming implementations to maintain a history of exception occurrences. The control of this history must be under the user's auspices. The MC68881 incorporates the accrued exception (AEXC) byte to accomplish this. Whenever an exception occurs, the corresponding bit in the AEXC byte is set to one and remains set until the user explicitly clears it.

The value of the AEXC bytes lies in the way it simplifies exception handling. During expression evaluation, it is not always desirable to trap just because an exception has occurred, nor is it desirable to poll for the occurrence of an exception at the completion of each instruction. The accrued exception byte allows the user to check only once, at the end of a set of calculations, for the occurrence of an exception. Table 3 shows the exceptions that can be recorded in the accrued exception byte.

A quotient byte is also provided in the status register. The information written into the quotient byte is provided by the modulo and IEEE remainder operations. The quotient byte provides a sign-magnitude quantity that may be used by user-defined periodic functions to classify the portion of the period in which the remainder lies. The least significant seven bits of the quotient are placed in the least significant bits of the quotient byte, while the sign information (a one indicates that the quantity is negative) is placed in the most significant bit of the quotient byte.

The condition code byte is also contained in the status register. It indicates the data type of the result of a move to a floating-point data register and the data type of the result of a floating-point arithmetic instruction. The IEEE floating-point standard requires only the determination of the data type resulting from a compare operation. However, data type determination at the completion of an instruction allows conditional branching, conditional setting of a byte, decrementing and branching on condition, and trapping on condition to occur without an explicitly performed compare operation. The MC68881 implements all conditional predicates specified by the proposed standard.

Control register. The control register is written to enable or disable traps on exceptions, to select the rounding mode, or to select the rounding precision. It and the status register are shown in Figure 6.

When an exceptional condition has occurred, as indicated in the exception byte of the status register, either program execution continues unabated or exception processing begins. The choice of program flow is determined by the value of the exception enable byte. For each exception indicated in the status register exception byte, there is a corresponding exception enable bit in the control register exception byte. When an exception occurs and the associated enable for the exception is set, exception processing begins in the host processor.

The control register also contains a byte of information that specifies the precision (single, double, or extended) to which a floating-point result will be rounded (Table 4). Rounding to single or double precision facilitates the emulation of machines that support only single-precision or double-precision calculations. This byte also specifies which of four rounding modes is used. The rounding modes allow the floating-point mantissa to be adjusted by one unit in the last place, according to the rounding rules for the mode selected.

The four rounding modes are shown in Table 5. Round-to-nearest rounds to the nearest representable value, unless the result is exactly halfway between two consecutive points. In that instance the result becomes the value having a zero in the least significant bit position (the even value). Round-toward-zero simply truncates the result. This is the rounding mode inherent in Fortran programs. Round-toward-plus-infinity and round-toward-minus-infinity force the result to be rounded in the direction of the associated infinity. This rounding mode is used in interval arithmetic, which can be employed to determine the largest interval on which an infinitely precise answer lies.

Instruction address register. The last element in the programmer's model is the instruction address register, a pointer to the last floating-point instruction executed. The host processor uses this pointer to locate an instruction that has caused an exception. (Were it not for this pointer, the host—because it operates concurrently with the coprocessor—might not be able to locate such an instruction.)

Data formats and types. Internal number representation in the MC68881 is in an extended format conform-

ing to the IEEE specification. However, representation of data that are moved and converted outside the device can be in the IEEE format or in any of a number of other supported formats. Each datum, regardless of initial memory-resident format, is coerced into the extended floating-point format as it is brought on board the processor. Once the internal set of operations has been performed and the final datum is ready to be moved into any of the other supported formats. (This scheme inherently supports coercion in high-level languages.)

Table 3.
MC68881 accrued exception byte.

EXCEPTION	DESCRIPTION
IOP	INVALID OPERATION
OVFL	OVERFLOW
UNFL	UNDERFLOW
DZ	DIVISION BY ZERO
INEX	INEXACT RESULT

Table 4.
MC68881 rounding precision.

ROUNDING PRECISION	DESCRIPTION
SGL	ROUND TO SINGLE PRECISION
DBL	ROUND TO DOUBLE PRECISION
EXT	ROUND TO EXTENDED PRECISION

Table 5.
MC68881 rounding modes.

ROUNDING MODE	DESCRIPTION
RN	ROUND TO NEAREST EVEN
RZ	ROUND TOWARD ZERO
RP	ROUND TOWARD PLUS INFINITY
RM	ROUND TOWARD MINUS INFINITY

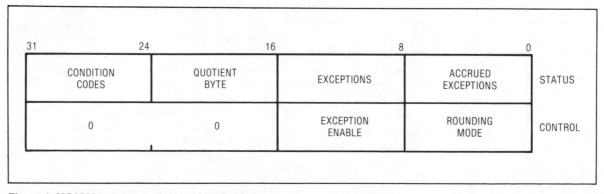

Figure 6. MC68881 status and control registers.

Table 6.
Move instructions.

INSTRUCTION	DESCRIPTION
FMOVE	FLOATING-POINT MOVE TO/FROM FP DATA REGISTER
FMOVE	MOVE TO/FROM MC68881 CONTROL/STATUS REGISTER
FMOVE	MOVE TO/FROM MC68881 IADDR REGISTER
FMOVECR	FLOATING-POINT MOVE FROM ON-CHIP CONSTANT ROM
FMOVEM	FLOATING-POINT MOVE MULTIPLE TO/FROM CONTROL/STATUS/IADDR REGISTERS
FMOVEM	FLOATING-POINT MOVE MULTIPLE TO/FROM FP DATA REGISTERS

Table 7.
Conditional instructions.

INSTRUCTION	DESCRIPTION
FBcc	FLOATING-POINT CONDITIONAL BRANCH
FDBcc	FLOATING-POINT CONDITIONAL TEST, DECREMENT, AND BRANCH
FScc	FLOATING-POINT CONDITIONAL SET
FTcc	FLOATING-POINT CONDITIONAL TRAP
FTPcc	FLOATING-POINT CONDITIONAL TRAP WITH PARAMETER

Seven data formats are supported. Byte, word, and long integers are 8, 16, and 32 bits long, respectively. These are the same integer formats supported by the M68000 family of central processing units.

Single-, double-, and extended-precision binary floating-point numbers are 32, 64, and 80 bits long, respectively. Extended-precision numbers external to the MC68881 (those residing in the memory space) are actually padded with zeroes so that they will occupy 96 bits.

The MC68881 provides a packed binary-coded decimal format which fully supports the conversion operations described by the proposed standard. Each number in this format occupies a 96-bit region in memory space (see Figure 7). The specifications for conversion between this format and any other format are stringent and involve complicated algorithms. Therefore, hardware support of BCD conversions relieves the programmer of a large burden. In addition, hardware support of decimal strings assists financial calculations in business programming languages.

The MC68881 supports all of the IEEE-specified data types. Ordinary numbers are represented by the normalized data type, and gradual underflow is provided by the denormalized data type. Special data types are plus and minus zero, plus and minus infinity, and not-a-number (NAN).

Instruction set. Besides the floating-point arithmetic operations required by the proposed standard, the MC68881 instruction set includes operations for moving data into and out of the machine, for branching, and for supporting virtual memory. It also includes a full set of trigonometric and transcendental functions.

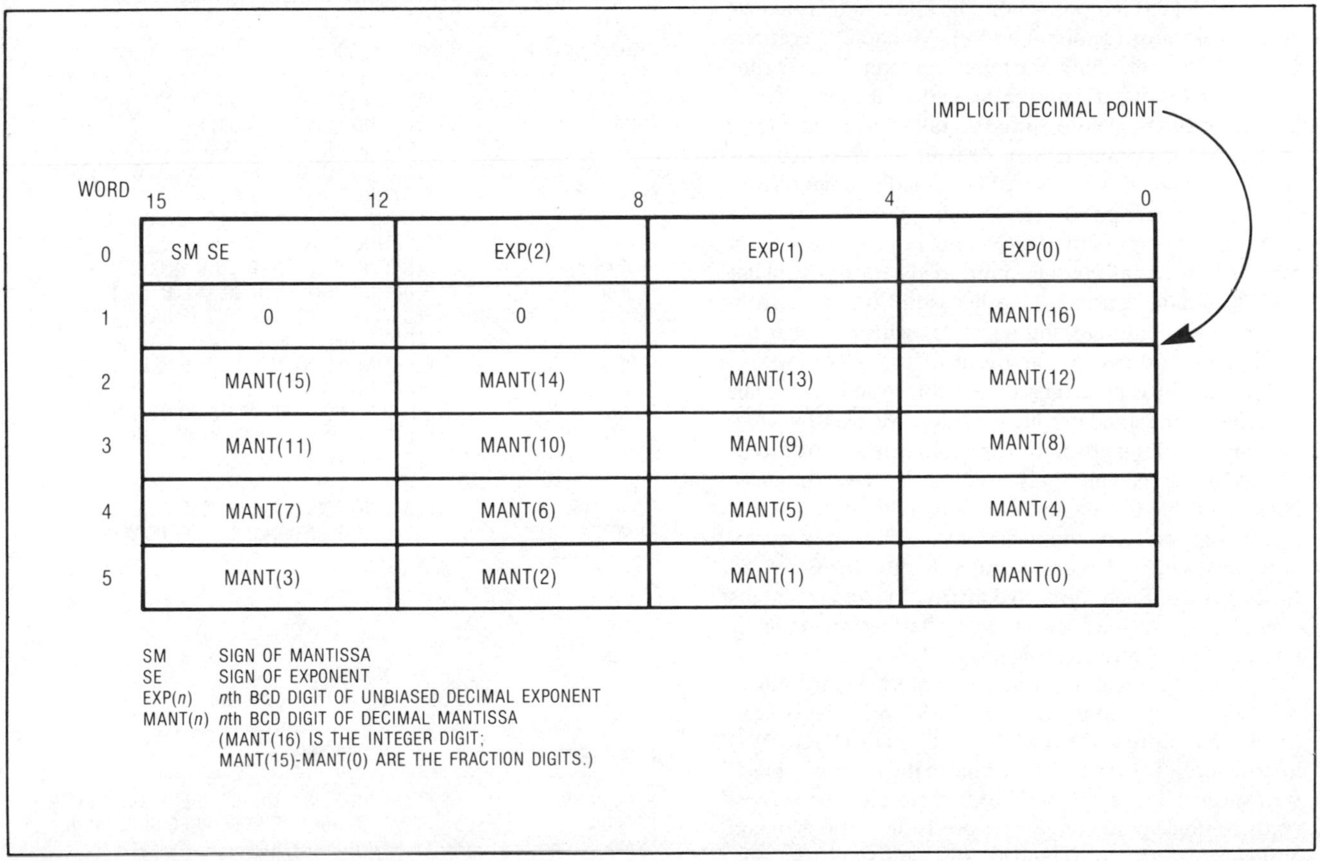

Figure 7. MC68881 decimal floating-point data format.

Floating-point move instructions (Table 6) allow data to be transferred into and out of the floating-point data, control, status, and instruction address registers. Each operand is converted to extended precision when it is moved into a floating-point data register. When the operand is moved out of the floating-point data register and into memory, it is converted to the format of the destination. This permits calculations between arguments having differing formats.

Move multiple register (FMOVEM) instructions speed the movement of data to or from multiple registers. One instruction can move data into or out of any or all of the floating-point data registers. Another instruction can move data into or out of any or all of the control, status, and instruction address registers.

Frequently used constants such as pi and one are stored in the MC68881 execution unit and are made available to the user by the move constant ROM (FMOVECR) instruction. This instruction always moves information from an internal read-only store to one of the floating-point data registers.

The branch according to condition instruction (FBcc) and the trap according to condition instructions (FTcc and FTPcc) alter the flow of a program according to the floating-point condition code byte in the status register. The set according to condition instruction (FScc) allows a byte to be either set or cleared according to the floating-point condition codes. If the condition is true, the byte specified by the effective address is set to all ones; if the condition is false, the byte is set to all zeroes. The conditional instructions are listed in Table 7.

The MC68881 supports monadic and dyadic floating-point operations (Tables 8 and 9). Monadic operations are those that take only one input operand. Square root and the trigonometric and transcendental functions are in this category. The operand is taken from memory, from a floating-point register, or from an MC68020 data register, and the result is placed in a floating-point register called the destination register. Dyadic operations are those that require two operands. One operand is taken from memory, from a floating-point register, or from an MC68020 data register; the other is always taken from one of the floating-point registers, which is also the destination address for the result of the operation.

Trigonometric and transcendental instructions are not specified by the standard. However, the MC68881 instruction set includes a group of trigonometric and transcendental functions commonly used in high-level-language libraries (Table 10). Each instruction in this group is completely supported by input bounds checking and exception processing in the same manner that the IEEE-defined functions are. Each supported instruction accepts inputs over its domain. Each is completely defined and requires no additional software envelope.

For speed-critical applications requiring only single-precision calculations, the MC68881 provides single-precision multiply (FSGLMUL) and divide (FSGLDIV) instructions (Table 11). These ignore the rounding precision selected by the user and produce results rounded correctly to single precision. Single-precision versions of add and subtract are not included, since no significant improvement in throughput would be observed.

Table 8.
Floating-point monadic instructions.

INSTRUCTION	DESCRIPTION
FABS	FLOATING-POINT ABSOLUTE VALUE
FGETEXP	GET FLOATING-POINT EXPONENT
FGETMAN	GET FLOATING-POINT MANTISSA
FINT	FLOATING-POINT INTEGER PART
FNEG	FLOATING-POINT NEGATE
FNOP	FLOATING-POINT NO OPERATION
NSCALE	FLOATING-POINT SCALE EXPONENT BY INTEGER
FSQRT	FLOATING-POINT SQUARE ROOT
FTST	FLOATING-POINT TEST

Table 9.
Floating-point dyadic instructions.

INSTRUCTION	DESCRIPTION
FADD	FLOATING-POINT ADD
FCMP	FLOATING-POINT COMPARE
FDIV	FLOATING-POINT DIVIDE
FMOD	FLOATING-POINT MODULO REMAINDER
FMUL	FLOATING-POINT MULTIPLY
FREM	FLOATING-POINT IEEE REMAINDER
FSUB	FLOATING-POINT SUBTRACT

Table 10.
Trigonometric and transcendental instructions.

INSTRUCTION	DESCRIPTION
FACOS	FLOATING-POINT ARC COSINE
FASIN	FLOATING-POINT ARC SINE
FATAN	FLOATING-POINT ARC TANGENT
FATANH	FLOATING-POINT HYPERBOLIC ARC TANGENT
FCOS	FLOATING-POINT COSINE
FCOSH	FLOATING-POINT HYPERBOLIC COSINE
FETOX	FLOATING-POINT e TO THE x
FETOXM1	FLOATING-POINT (e TO THE x) MINUS 1
FLOG10	FLOATING-POINT LOG TO THE BASE 10
FLOG2	FLOATING-POINT LOG TO THE BASE 2
FLOGN	FLOATING-POINT LOG TO THE BASE e
FLOGNP1	FLOATING-POINT LOG TO THE BASE e OF $(x + 1)$
FSIN	FLOATING-POINT SINE
FSINCOS	SIMULTANEOUS FLOATING-POINT SINE AND COSINE
FSINH	FLOATING-POINT HYPERBOLIC SINE
FTAN	FLOATING-POINT TANGENT
FTANH	FLOATING-POINT HYPERBOLIC TANGENT
FTENTOX	FLOATING-POINT TEN TO THE POWER x
FTWOTOX	FLOATING-POINT TWO TO THE POWER x

Table 11.
Miscellaneous instructions.

INSTRUCTION	DESCRIPTION
FSGLMUL	FLOATING-POINT SINGLE-PRECISION MULTIPLY
FSGLDIV	FLOATING-POINT SINGLE-PRECISION DIVIDE
FSAVE	FLOATING-POINT SAVE
FRESTORE	FLOATING-POINT RESTORE

Virtual memory support requires a processor to be able to stop in the middle of an instruction that is trying to access a logical address not currently mapped into a physical memory location. Since a memory fault can occur during a floating-point operand fetch, the floating-point coprocessor, as well as the main processor, must provide this capability.

The MC68881 can be halted during the execution of an instruction. Its current internal state can be saved and later restored so that instruction execution can be restarted from its stopping point. FSAVE and FRESTORE provide this support to virtual memory systems (see again Table 11). Three sizes of internal state can be managed. If the coprocessor has not executed an instruction since it was last reset, FSAVE causes a minimal amount of the internal state to be preserved in the memory space. More information must be saved if the machine has executed an instruction since it was last reset and is currently idle. A maximum amount of the internal state must be saved whenever the coprocessor is interrupted while executing an instruction. FRESTORE allows for saved-state movement back to the MC68881.

Exception processing. The MC68881 supports the handling of all IEEE-defined exceptions. There are also other exceptions that can occur during system operation. These include exceptions arising from bus interface protocol violations and from illegal coprocessor commands. The protocol violation is the highest-priority exception and is considered a fatal error. Because of this, it preempts all other exceptions. Illegal commands are reported by the coprocessor, since it decodes the command portion of a floating-point instruction.

The IEEE proposal for standardizing arithmetic will bring stability to the floating-point world. Programmers will be able to create software which will be safe and reliable and which will provide consistent answers when moved across system boundaries. Systems designers requiring high-performance mathematical computation at low cost will be able to take advantage of hardware implementations of the standard such as the MC68881. The rich instruction sets and advanced system features the standard will make possible will provide architectural extensions for generations of central processing units to come. ■

References

1. "A Proposed Standard for Binary Floating-point Arithmetic" (Draft 8.0 of IEEE Task P754), *Computer,* Vol. 14, No. 3, Mar. 1981, pp. 51-62.

2. "A Proposed Standard for Binary Floating-point Arithmetic" (Draft 10.0 of IEEE Task P754), Dec. 2, 1982, 17 pp. (Available from David Stevenson, Chairman, IEEE Task P754, c/o Zilog, 1315 Dell Ave., Campbell, CA 95008.)

3. W. Browne, Jr., and B. Moyer, "μP Fits 16-bit Performance into 8-bit Systems," *Electronic Design,* Vol. 30, No. 8, April 15, 1982, pp. 183-187.

4. E. Stritter and T. Gunter, "A Microprocessor Architecture for a Changing World—The Motorola 68000," *Computer,* Vol. 12, No. 2, Feb. 1979, pp. 20-29.

5. D. MacGregor and D. S. Mothersole, "Virtual Memory and the MC68010," *IEEE Micro,* Vol. 3, No. 3, June 1983, pp. 24-39.

For further reading

J. Boney, V. Shahan, and P. Harvey, "Floating-point Power for the M68000 Family," *Proc. Maecon,* Sept. 1983, Vol. 9/2, pp. 1-9.

J. T. Coonen, "An Implementation Guide to a Proposed Standard for Floating-point Arithmetic," *Computer,* Vol. 13, No. 1, Jan. 1980, pp. 68-79.

MC68881 Design Specifications, Motorola, Inc., Austin, TX, July 1983.

Clayton Huntsman, a former submariner and nuclear reactor operator, has been working since 1977 in Motorola's Microprocessor Design Group in Austin, Texas. His primary responsibility is transcendental algorithm implementation in the MC68881 project. He is interested in alternative computer architectures and artificial intelligence, and he enjoys delivering soapbox orations concerning the shortage of user-friendly software and operating systems. His hobbies include running, swimming, and bicycling.

Duane Cawthron has been working since 1979 in Motorola's Microprocessor Design Group in Austin, Texas. He is currently involved with the system-level design of the MC68881. His interests include microcoded instruction sequencers, efficient VLSI design methodology, and the Unix operating system. He received his BSEE from the University of Texas at Austin in 1979.

The authors' address is MOS Microprocessor Design Group, Mail Drop M2, Motorola MOS Integrated Circuits Division, 3501 Ed Bluestein Blvd., Austin, TX 78721.

The Intel 8089: An Integrated I/O Processor

K. A. El-Ayat

Intel Corporation

Reprinted from *Computer*, June 1979, pages 67-78. Copyright © 1979 by The Institute of Electrical and Electronics Engineers, Inc.

As most mainframe manufacturers have demonstrated, the logical solution to I/O control problems is to deploy intelligent I/O subsystems. Intel's 8089 brings this capability to microcomputer systems.

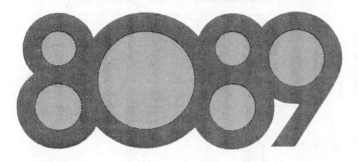

Special Feature

The Intel 8089: An Integrated I/O Processor

K. A. El-Ayat
Intel Corporation

The design of I/O subsystems is an integral and important step in computer system design. CPUs and I/O peripherals have generally non-compatible bus and timing requirements—a fact that can result in significant degradation in system performance. The logical solution to this problem has been the deployment of an intelligent I/O subsystem which isolates the CPU from the I/O peripherals.[1-3] The CPU is therefore free to proceed at full speed with its primary task of internal program processing and data manipulation. Control of all I/O operations is then performed by an I/O processor, an integral part of the I/O subsystem. The CPU maintains supervisory control over the system and issues commands and messages to the I/O processor, which then proceeds with all necessary peripheral control operations to complete the desired I/O transaction. The I/O processor is responsible for device initialization, record selection, I/O transfer, simple data transformation, error checking and retries, and it signals the CPU upon successful completion of the I/O transfer.

Microprocessors of today (such as the Intel 8086[4]) have attained respectable performance levels by innovative architectural and technological advances. However, such advances in microprocessor perform-

Intel 8089 device characteristics

ALU Width	20 bits
Memory addressing capability	1M byte
Addressable I/O ports	64K
Process	HMOS
Clock period	200 nsec standard, 125 nsec selected
Number of channels	2
Pins	40
Supply	+ 5V

Conventional and dual-bus microcomputer systems

In a conventional microcomputer system the CPU executes application and I/O programs. Availability of a single bus in the system means that CPU, I/O peripherals, and DMA controller share the use of that bus. Bus is therefore heavily utilized, and high-speed I/O may impede application program execution.

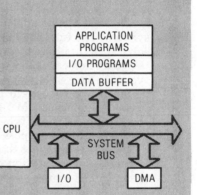

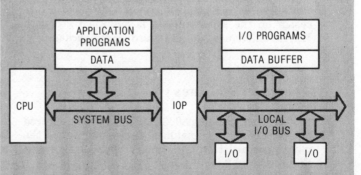

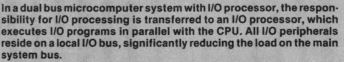

In a dual bus microcomputer system with I/O processor, the responsibility for I/O processing is transferred to an I/O processor, which executes I/O programs in parallel with the CPU. All I/O peripherals reside on a local I/O bus, significantly reducing the load on the main system bus.

EHO214-7/84/0000/0225$01.00©1979 IEEE

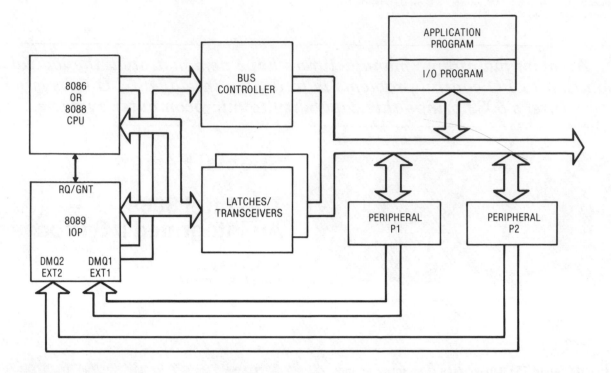

Figure 1. System configuration in the LOCOL mode offers the capability of an I/O processor while sharing the system bus interface logic with the host CPU.

ance may be seriously overshadowed by the constraints of traditional non-intelligent I/O subsystems. The Intel 8089 I/O processor is designed to solve such problems by providing the necessary intelligence and capability to microcomputer I/O subsystems. The architecture of the I/O processor is designed to meet typical I/O system requirements, such as high speed DMA transfers, peripheral synchronization, etc., and is better suited to I/O processing than a general-purpose microprocessor.

This article describes the Intel 8089 I/O processor. It contains a description of the various IOP-based system architectures and an overview of their operation. The internal architecture of the IOP and a typical application example are then given to illustrate its various features and capabilities that facilitate I/O subsystem design. The I/O processor contains two independent I/O channels and a processor on the same chip. It is manufactured with HMOS and housed in a standard 40-pin package.

System architectures

Systems containing 8089 IOP's may be configured in two ways—a minimal local configuration and the more general REMOTE configuration as shown in Figures 1 and 2.

In the LOCAL configuration, all the system components such as CPU, IOP, main meory, and peripheral controllers reside on the main system bus. The CPU operates as the master processor while the

IOP operates as the slave processor. The two processors share the control and use of the bus by means of special bus arbitration circuitry on each processor. The LOCAL configuration offers the advantages of an independent IOP while requiring only a minimal component count, which can be effectively used in cost-sensitive applications. Its main disadvantage is that it contains a single bus which is used by all the system components, thereby limiting overall system throughput.

The REMOTE configuration, on the other hand, contains two separate buses—a main system bus and a local I/O bus (REMOTE bus). This affords a great reduction in system bus utilization while minimizing processor idle time, thereby significantly improving overall system efficiency and throughput. Reduction in system bus utilization results from (a) placement of I/O programs in local memory residing on the local I/O bus and (b) placement of all I/O peripherals on the local I/O bus. The main system bus is utilized only by the CPU and the IOP whenever system memory reference operations are desired. Bus arbitration in this configuration is performed by a bus arbiter chip set which arbitrates the use of the system bus between the two processors as well as any other processors residing on the bus. The local I/O bus (REMOTE bus) is used for all I/O transfers to peripherals and is controlled by the IOP as shown. The REMOTE configuration shown can be easily expanded to a larger system employing multiple IOPs. Every two IOPs may share the same local I/O bus with bus arbitration between them performed by special on-chip arbitration circuitry as shown in Figure 3.

COMPUTER

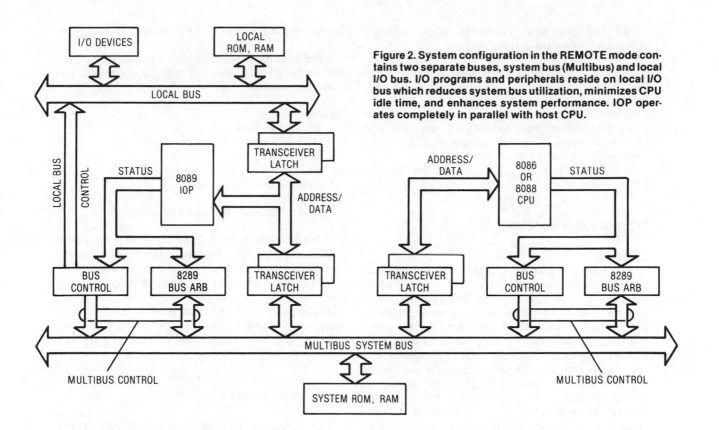

Figure 2. System configuration in the REMOTE mode contains two separate buses, system bus (Multibus) and local I/O bus. I/O programs and peripherals reside on local I/O bus which reduces system bus utilization, minimizes CPU idle time, and enhances system performance. IOP operates completely in parallel with host CPU.

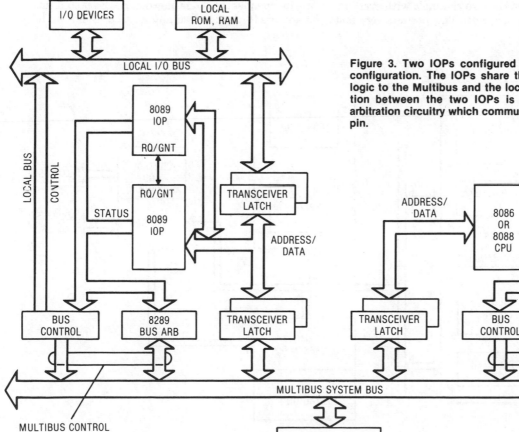

Figure 3. Two IOPs configured in a REMOTE system configuration. The IOPs share the same bus interface logic to the Multibus and the local I/O bus. Bus arbitration between the two IOPs is performed by on-chip arbitration circuitry which communicates via the RQ/GNT pin.

The I/O processor enhances microcomputer system performance in three ways:

(a) by dedicating an I/O processor whose architecture is better suited for I/O processing and high-speed data transfers;

(b) by relieving the CPU from the burdensome task of I/O processing, thus liberating it to perform its intended internal program processing and data manipulation; and

(c) by operating completely in parallel with the CPU.

I/O processor architecture

The 8089 I/O processor (Figure 4) contains two separate I/O channels, a CPU, bus interface unit, an assembly/disassembly register file, and an instruction fetch unit. To enable autonomous operation of the I/O channels, each channel maintains its own register set, control and status words, and a flexible channel controller. Both channels may operate concurrently, executing channel programs or performing high-speed DMA transfers by time multiplexing the access and use of the external bus. Since only one channel can access the external bus during any bus cycle, the control and bus interface logic are shared between the two channels. The IOP is thus capable of alternating between the two channels with every internal cycle (4-8 clock cycles). This permits very fast service response times to the channel requesting service.

When both channels are running concurrently, the IOP employs the following priority algorithm for channel selection:

highest priority
- DMA transfers
- chained channel program
- DMA termination

second priority
- channel attention service

lowest priority
- normal channel program execution

If both channels are requesting service for tasks with equal priorities, channel selection is done according to two programmable priority bits. The priority bits may specify a rotating priority or assign one channel to have higher priority than the other. The above priority selection scheme ensures fast responses for time-critical I/O operations while providing overall user programmability to perform channel selection.

Register structure

The I/O processor maintains separate register sets for each of its two I/O channels, enabling them to execute independently of one another. Each set contains 8 registers (Figure 5), and almost all of them can be

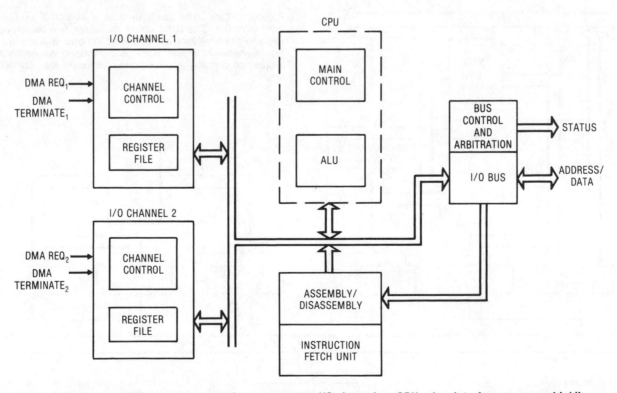

Figure 4. The Intel 8089 I/O processor contains two separate I/O channels, a CPU, a bus interface, an assembly/disassembly register file, and an instruction fetch unit.

used for general computation during channel program execution. Eight of the 16 registers are 21 bits wide and can be used to address one megabyte of system memory or 64K bytes of I/O space. The 21st bit is used to select the address space as system or local I/O space. The other 8 registers are 16 bits wide.

The GA and GB registers are used to reference the source and destination locations during any data transfer operation. The GC register can also be used as a general register/pointer by the channel program. The task pointer serves as the channel program counter which is initialized whenever the channel is started; it can also be manipulated by the channel program. The BC register contains the number of bytes to be transferred during DMA operation and can terminate the DMA transfer if byte count termination is selected. The IX register is used as an index in the indexed addressing mode. The mask/compare register is used to perform masked byte comparisons during channel program execution and DMA operations. During program execution, the comparisons are used for conditional jumping, and in DMA, they may terminate the current DMA transfer. The control register is a special 16-bit register which defines the channel's operation during DMA transfer operations.

Assembly and disassembly

The IOP maintains an assembly register file for the assembly/disassembly of data bytes in the DMA

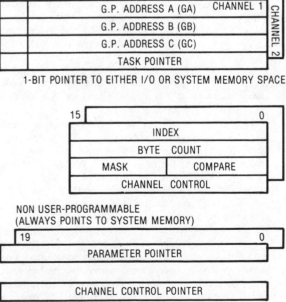

Figure 5. I/O processor register model—separate register sets for each I/O channel enable their autonomous operation.

transfer mode. For example, when data is transferred, during a DMA operation, from an 8-bit bus to a 16-bit bus, the IOP assembles 2 bytes in its assembly register file before transferring a word to the destination. The opposite occurs when transferring data from a 16-bit bus to an 8-bit bus, in that one word is fetched and 2 separate bytes are transferred to the destination.

This capability of assembly/disassembly of data bytes has the following advantages:

- allows great flexibility in interfacing the IOP to 8- or 16-bit components;
- enhances transfer speeds by utilizing the busses to the best advantage;
- reduces bus utilization by effectively using 16-bit buses.

I/O processor model

A simplified computational model of the I/O processor is given in Figure 6. After reset, a channel at-

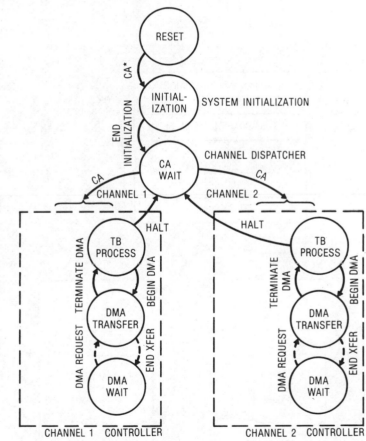

*CA = Channel Attention

Figure 6. Simplified computational model of I/O processor. After system initialization the processor can dispatch its two I/O channels to execute channel programs (TB processing) and perform high-speed DMA transfers. Channel can be multiplexed between peripherals and can perform complex I/O tasks.

tention input pulse forces an internal initialization sequence, after which the processor is ready to dispatch either of the two I/O channels to perform the desired I/O task. The I/O channel normally begins its operation in the task block state with the execution of the I/O program and enters the DMA state under IOP program control. In this state, the channel proceeds with high-speed data transfers in either burst or request-synchronized modes until the occurrence of a valid termination condition which returns the channel to the TB state. HALT commands force the channel into the idle state until further dispatching occurs.

Instruction set

The IOP instruction set combines a set of general-purpose data processing instructions with a set of flexible and specialized I/O instructions. The I/O intensive instruction set, which includes bit manipulation and testing and generalized MOV data, permits simple and efficient I/O data transfers between any two components residing anywhere in the system. The bit manipulation instructions allow the manipulation of any bit in memory or in a peripheral interface residing on either of the two buses in the system (main system bus or local I/O bus).

The general-purpose data processing instructions enable the IOP to serve as an independent processor which requires little attention from the main CPU. The set includes general data transfer instructions, arithmetic and logical operations, and subroutine capability, as well as powerful conditional and unconditional branch operations. The set also includes special instructions for interrupt control, DMA initialization, bus width selection, and a simple semaphore test mechanism.

The Intel 8089 I/O processor is capable of interfacing to both 8- and 16-bit systems without any restrictions. Typical systems may be configured with any combination of 8/16-bit CPUs, 8/16-bit peripherals, and 8/16-bit memories, allowing the system designer to choose advanced 8/16-bit CPUs while using the

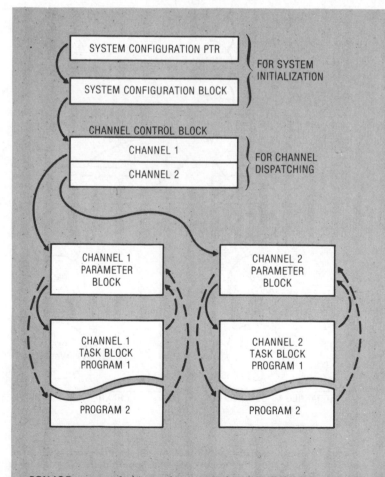

CPU-IOP communication scheme consists of a linked data structure containing control, parameter, and status information. The parameter and task blocks perform the required I/O functions.

CPU-IOP communication

The CPU and IOP communicate with one another by writing communication messages for one another in system memory. The CPU prepares the message area and signals the IOP by pulsing its channel attention input pin. The IOP reads the message, performs the requested I/O functions, and executes the appropriate I/O channel program. This general memory-based communication mechanism permits the flexibility of tailoring the message areas to suit the desired I/O configuration.

The communication scheme, shown in Figure 8, consists of control blocks connected to form a linked data structure. Each block contains control and parameter information as well as a pointer to its successor block to allow the location of the blocks anywhere in memory. The communication blocks consist of the system configuration pointer, system configuration block, channel control block, parameter block, and task block. The first two blocks are used for system initialization; the third is used for channel dispatching; and the final two blocks perform all operations required to control the requested I/O function.

The first two blocks contain system configuration parameters, such as system data bus width (8/16) and I/O data bus width (8/16), and define bus protocol between master and slave processors sharing the same bus. The IOP references these blocks only during system initialization; this occurs after an IOP reset and upon receipt of a pulse at its CA (channel attention, similar to a CPU interrupt) input pin from the CPU. In a multi-IOP system all IOPs share the use of the first two control blocks, whereas the remaining blocks must be separately configured to suit the particular IOP's con-

great variety of 8-bit peripherals available today. This feature is accomplished within the IOP by permitting any internal register to be used as 8/16 bits wide, designing the instruction set to operate on 8/16-bit data, and providing an assembly register file for the assembly/disassembly of data. A third data type employed by the IOP is the 20-bit-wide address used to address one megabyte of address space. The addressing scheme is compatible with the Intel 8086. A 20-bit address is formed by adding an address word to a relocation word after the latter is left-shifted four places. The IOP has load pointer instructions for loading 20-bit registers with 20-bit addresses computed as mentioned above. Pointers are stored externally in three consecutive bytes of memory.

The IOP has versatile branch capabilities. Conditional branching can be made under any one of the following conditions:

(1) Contents of a memory location are zero.
(2) Contents of a memory location are nonzero.
(3) Contents of a register are zero.

figuration requirements. To initialize any IOP in the system, the CPU alters the system configuration block to reference the appropriate communication area and sends a CA pulse to the appropriate IOP.

The channel control block is used for channel dispatching and is referenced by the IOP whenever a CA pulse is received other than the first pulse after reset (the first CA pulse after reset is used for IOP initialization). The block contains pointers, channel command words, and BUSY/ DONE flags that govern the operation of the two IOP channels. The status of another input pin (SEL pin) determines which channel the CA pulse is intended for. Channel commands include START channel, HALT, HALT and SAVE status, and CONTINUE. The command word also includes an interrupt control field and a priority field which defines the relative priority between the two IOP channels.

The final two blocks in the hierarchy, the parameter block and the task block, perform the specific I/O functions requested. The task block contains the user I/O control program whereas the parameter block contains all necessary parameter, data, and status information needed to maintain the I/O functions. The I/O channel can be programmed to perform complex I/O operations with multiple tasks and without assistance from the CPU by appropriately coding the above two blocks. A typical example may be a hard disk track seek operation, followed by high-speed record transfer, error check, retry, and simple data transformation. Further, individual I/O tasks can be chained to permit fast execution of I/O control programs along with high-speed data transfers. The communication hierarchy maintains separate parameter blocks and task blocks for each I/O channel. Each channel contains two registers (parameter pointer and task pointer) for referencing the parameter and task blocks. ∎

The 8089 instruction set

MNEMONIC		DESCRIPTION
ADD	M,R	ADD register to memory
ADD	R,M	ADD memory to register
ADDI	M,I	ADD immediate to memory
ADDI	R,I	ADD immediate to register
AND	M,R	AND memory with register
AND	R,M	AND register with memory
ANDI	M,I	AND memory with immediate
ANDI	R,I	AND register with immediate
CALL		CALL unconditional
CLR		Clear the selected bit
DEC	M	Decrement addressed location
DEC	R	Decrement register
HLT		HALT channel execution
INC	M	Increment addressed location
INC	R	Increment register
JBT		Test bit and jump if true
JMCE		Mask/compare and jump on equal
JMCNE		Mask/com and jump on nonequal
JMP		Unconditional jump
JNBT		Test bit and jump if not true
JNZ	M	Jump on nonzero memory
JNZ	R	Jump on nonzero register
JZ	M	Jump on zero memory
JZ	R	Jump on zero register
LPD	P,M	Load pointer from address location
LPDI	P,I	Load pointer immediate 4 bytes
MOV	M,M	Move from source to destination
MOV	M,R	Store contents of R in addressed location
MOV	R,M	Load R from addressed location
MOVI	M,I	Move immediate to addressed location
MOVI	R,I	Move immediate to register
MOVP	M,P	Store contents of pointer R
MOVP	P,M	Restore pointer
NOP		No operation
NOT	M	Complement memory
NOT	R	Complement register
NOT	R,M	Complement memory, put in R
OR	M,R	OR memory with register
OR	R,M	OR register with memory
ORI	M,I	OR memory with immediate
ORI	R,I	OR register with immediate
SET		SET the selected bit
SINTR		SET interrupt service flip flop
TSL		Test and set LOCK
WID		SET source, destination logical widths
XFER		Enter DMA transfer

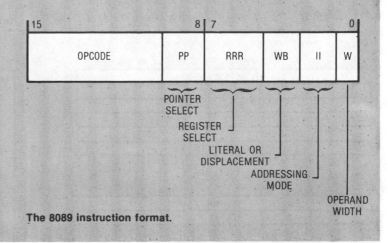

The 8089 instruction format.

Task block program

The following program is an example of task block program for a floppy disk read opera;tion. The hardware configuration utilized the Intel 8271 floppy disk controller. The organization of the peripheral bus interface and the parameter block is given also. Some of the test instructions are illustrated here along with a subset of the data transfer and conditional branch instructions.

BEGIN	LPD	GB,PB + 4	GB is the memory pointer Load it from the PB.
	MOVIB	PB + 11, OA	Intialize the retry count to 10.
	MOVI	MC, 0818	Load mask compare register.
	MOV	GA, PB + 12	Load GA with peripheral address.
RETRY	JNBT	GA + 4,7	Wait until controller is not busy (bit 7).
	MOVIB	GA + 4, 12	Send read sector command to controller.
	MOVB	GA + 5,PB + 9	Send track address to controller.
	JNBT	GA + 4,5	Wait until parameter register is empty (bit 5).
	MOVI	CC, 8820	Load CC register to perform port to block; GA is source, source sync. Terminate on external terminate condition. CC = channel control.
	MOVB	GA + 5,PB + 8	Send sector address to controller
	XFER		Enter transfer mode after next instruction.
	WID	00A0	The logical width of the source is 8 bits; the destination is 16 bits.
	JMCE	GA + 5,EXIT	Return from DMA mode. Is status ok? If yes, go to exit.
	DEC	PB + 11	Status error.
	JNZ	PB + 11,RETRY	Try up to 10 times.
EXIT	JNBT	GA + 4,7	Wait for controller not busy.
	MOVI	GA + 4, 2C	Send read status to controller.
	JBT	GA + 4,4	Wait until status is read.
	MOVB	PB + 10,GA + 5	Send status to PB for CPU.
	HLT		

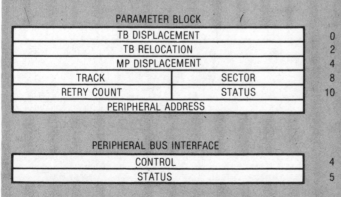

PARAMETER BLOCK

TB DISPLACEMENT		0
TB RELOCATION		2
MP DISPLACEMENT		4
TRACK	SECTOR	8
RETRY COUNT	STATUS	10
PERIPHERAL ADDRESS		

PERIPHERAL BUS INTERFACE

CONTROL	4
STATUS	5

(4) Contents of a register are nonzero.

(5) Contents of a memory location match the contents of the mask/compare register after masking.

(6) Contents of memory location do not match the contents of the mask/compare register after masking.

(7) Status of 1 bit located anywhere in the address space is true.

(8) Status of 1 bit located anywhere in the address space is false.

In all the branch instructions mentioned above, an 8/16-bit sign displacement is included to permit a branch range of +/− 32K bytes. Single byte displacements are used whenever the branch range is small to permit code compaction. In conditions 1 and 2 above, the memory location (operand) tested can be either 1 or 2 bytes.

The IOP also provides subroutine capability for commonly executed routines. The CALL instruction saves the contents of the TP in the first four locations of the parameter block and branches to the desired subroutine. Exit from the subroutine is performed by the instruction which restores the TP from the parameter block to its original value. The general MOV data instruction is provided to permit single byte/word transfers between any source and destination and is useful for I/O device initialization and general I/O transfers. Data transfers are permitted between any two components in the system, allowing such transfers as memory to/from I/O, memory to memory, and I/O to I/O. The IOP also has the capability of manipulating a single bit in a byte that is located anywhere in either the system or I/O space. The byte is fetched from the address indicated by a designated pointer, and the desired bit is set, cleared, or tested before storing it back at the same location. This feature is useful for manipulating peripheral control interfaces.

The IOP employs four simple but effective addressing modes for addressing operands: (a) immediate, (b) offset, (c) indexed, and (d) indexed autoincrement. In the immediate addressing mode, the operand (which may be 1, 2, or 4 bytes long) immediately follows the instruction. In the offset addressing mode, a 1-byte unsigned offset is added to the contents of a base pointer to form the operand address. The third ad-

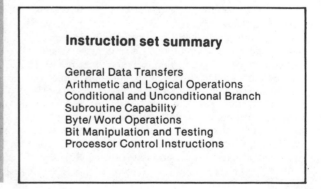

Instruction set summary

General Data Transfers
Arithmetic and Logical Operations
Conditional and Unconditional Branch
Subroutine Capability
Byte/ Word Operations
Bit Manipulation and Testing
Processor Control Instructions

dressing mode is the indexed mode, where the contents of the index register (IX) are added to the contents of the selected base pointer to form the operand address. The IX register may be optionally incremented after each operand reference, as in the fourth addressing mode, to facilitate table indexing operations. In all the addressing modes of the IOP, the contents of base pointers are not altered during the data reference operation.

Because of the multiprocessing nature of systems containing a CPU and one or more IOPs, a semaphore mechanism is implemented to resolve problems arising from critical code sections. The mechanism allows the IOP to LOCK the system bus after seizing it and prevent access to it by any other processor while it examines and conditionally manipulates the status of a critical flag in memory. This is accomplished by a special TEST and SET LOCK instruction and the LOCK output pin.

DMA mode operation

The Intel 8089 I/O processor is capable of maintaining high-speed DMA data transfers (up to 1.25 megabytes/sec using a standard 5-MHz clock) while providing the system designer with flexible features and options for controlling the DMA transfer. The DMA mode is entered by executing the instruction XFER. Each DMA data transfer consists of at least one fetch cycle and one store cycle (e.g., peripheral to IOP, IOP to memory). The IOP permits a data assembly mode (or disassembly) in which two data bytes are assembled in two consecutive fetch cycles before a 16-bit word is transferred to the destination. This is especially useful when transferring data from an 8-bit bus to a 16-bit bus. The user may select one or more of five different conditions for terminating DMA transfers, such as single transfers, number of bytes transferred, external terminate input, and match/no-match masked byte comparisons. The user also specifies DMA control parameters that govern the DMA operation, such as pointer selection for source and destination addresses, pointer autoincrementing, DMA request-synchronization, chained operation, locked-bus transfers, and translate mode data transfers. All of the above DMA parameters are specified by the channel's control register and are under direct channel program control.

The selected termination parameters specify under which conditions DMA transfers are terminated (DMA transfers are complete), and most of the conditions, such as number of bytes transferred, external terminate input, and single transfers are self-explanatory. In the match/no-match termination conditions, incoming data bytes are compared with a "compare" byte, masked with a "mask" byte, and the result used to terminate DMA transfers. Termination may occur on either a match or a no-match which allows programming data constructs such as SCAN WHILE and SCAN UNTIL by loading the mask/compare register with the appropriate data. Terminate parameters also specify a branch offset of

0, 4, or 8 to be added to the TP after completion of the DMA transfer. This allows the user to uniquely identify the terminate source, in case of multi-terminate conditions, by appropriate selection of branch offsets.

The remaining DMA control parameters provide the user with great flexibility in specifying the DMA transfer operation. The DMA request-synchronization option allows the DMA transfers to be synchronized with the source device (e.g., input from disk) or the destination device (e.g., memory to CRT). The chaining feature allows the user to chain individual I/O tasks so that the completion of one task is promptly followed by the execution of another. For example, a record transfer from a disk may be followed by error check or data search which initiates another record transfer, etc. I/O tasks can be assigned a high execution priority to ensure their prompt execution whenever conflicts arise between the two I/O channels.

The LOCKed bus DMA option ensures high-speed uninterrupted service to the I/O channel during the entire DMA transfer. In this mode, the locking channel seizes the system bus for the duration of all its DMA transfers and relinquishes it only after terminating the final DMA transfer. The translate mode allows fast byte translation or code conversion during DMA transfers. The incoming data byte is used as an offset into a user-defined translate table from which the translated data is fetched and transferred to the destination (Figure 7).

Application example

A typical application example utilizing the 8089 I/O processor is given in Figure 8. The system is configured in the dual-bus REMOTE configuration with

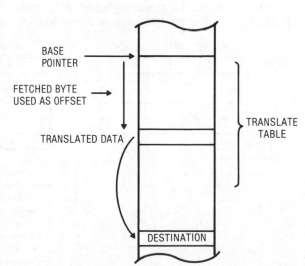

Figure 7. Translate option allows fast code conversions during DMA. Fetched byte is used as an offset into a translate table to fetch the translated data.

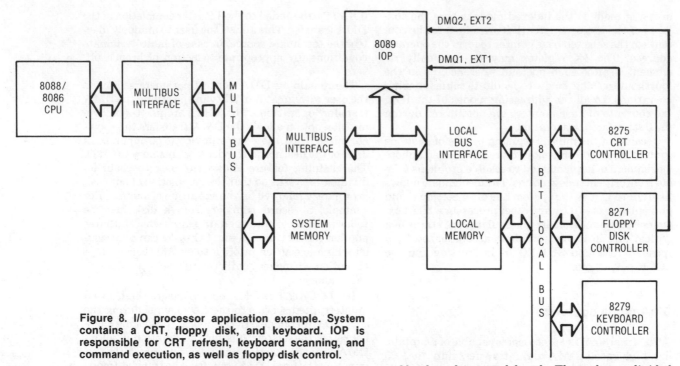

Figure 8. I/O processor application example. System contains a CRT, floppy disk, and keyboard. IOP is responsible for CRT refresh, keyboard scanning, and command execution, as well as floppy disk control.

the MULTIBUS used as the main system bus and an 8-bit local I/O bus used for I/O operations. The system consists of a CPU (8086/8088), an IOP (8089), system memory, CRT controller (8275), floppy disk controller (8271), a keyboard controller (8279), and local I/O memory. The main system bus is utilized by the CPU and the IOP (e.g., disk to system memory) whenever system memory references are made. All I/O programs and buffers are stored in the local I/O memory to reduce the load on the main bus. The local I/O bus is thus dedicated to I/O processing and I/O data transfers.

The I/O tasks to be performed are CRT screen refresh, CRT buffer update, floppy disk transfers, and keyboard scan and decode. The tasks are divided between the two channels as follows:

(a) Channel 1 is responsible for CRT refresh and keyboard control functions.

(b) Channel 2 is responsible for floppy disk transfers and CRT buffer update.

The memory organization of the control blocks, channel control, parameter, and task blocks for the two channels is shown in Figure 9. Channel 1 parameter block contains its I/O program's starting address (task block address), CRT parameters (number of lines, characters per line, buffer pointer, etc.), keyboard parameters, and a data storage buffer. Similarly, Channel 2's parameter block contains its I/O program address and floppy disk parameters (pointers, track, sector, etc.). The floppy disk I/O

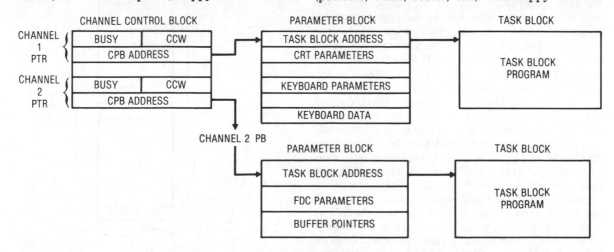

Figure 9. Memory organization of the control blocks for channels 1 and 2 in the application example. Channel 1 is responsible for CRT refresh and keyboard control while Channel 2 maintains FDC transfers and CRT buffer update.

234

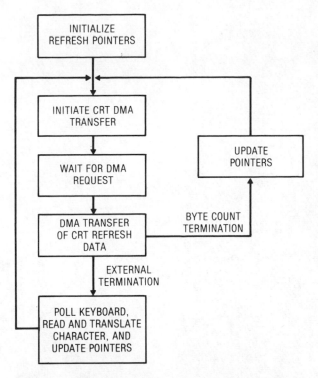

Figure 10. Flowchart for channel 1 I/O program. After pointer initialization, the channel enters the DMA transfer mode to refresh a character row (80 characters) on the CRT screen and continues to the next row. After each screen page transfer (20 lines) the program polls the keyboard and executes the requested command.

The boxes in the flowchart read:

- INITIALIZE REFRESH POINTERS
- INITIATE CRT DMA TRANSFER
- WAIT FOR DMA REQUEST
- DMA TRANSFER OF CRT REFRESH DATA
- UPDATE POINTERS
- BYTE COUNT TERMINATION
- EXTERNAL TERMINATION
- POLL KEYBOARD, READ AND TRANSLATE CHARACTER, AND UPDATE POINTERS

routine is similar to the sample program mentioned above. The Channel 1 I/O program is described in the flowchart in Figure 10. After pointer and parameter initialization, the channel enters the DMA mode to transfer one complete line (80 characters) of data from the CRT buffer to the CRT controller. Byte count termination is used to terminate the DMA transfer after each line is transferred. The I/O program then updates its buffer pointers, byte counter, etc., and initiates another DMA transfer for the next line. After the entire screen is refreshed (20 lines), the CRT controller generates an end-of-screen (retrace) signal which triggers the external termination condition on the channel. The program then branches to a keyboard service routine for reading and translating keyboard data and returns after completion to the beginning of the program.

Using a standard 5-MHz clock cycle, the IOP needs 1.6 μs for each DMA transfer (8 clocks/transfer). The IOP thus requires 2.5 ms to refresh a 20-line, 80-character/line screen; and assuming that a complete screen refresh must be initiated every 1/60 second, then only 20 percent of the IOP's bandwidth is used for CRT refreshing. A similar analysis reveals that 5 percent of the IOP bandwidth is used to transfer data to a single-density floppy disk. The remaining I/O program execution steps are found to require 5 percent of the bandwidth, and the user is thus free to incorporate additional features to perform complex I/O operations or add more peripheral devices. Almost all of the I/O activity in this system occurs on the local I/O bus. Only a small fraction of this activity occurs on the main bus when main

memory accesses are required, such as parameter fetch from the parameter block or data transfer to/from main memory.

Conclusion

The logical solution to I/O control problems is the deployment of intelligent I/O subsystems as offered by most mainframe manufacturers. The Intel 8089 I/O processor brings such capability to microcomputer systems such as the Intel 8086. It isolates the CPU from I/O peripherals, executes all I/O programs, performs high-speed DMA transfers, and intervenes into the CPU's operation only when necessary, thereby significantly improving system throughput. The discussion includes an explanation of the various IOP-based system configurations, the internal architecture of the I/O processor, and a detailed application example. The I/O processor achieves transfer rates of 1.25 megabytes/sec at a maximum latency of 2.4 μs, with a standard clock cycle of 5 MHz. ∎

Acknowledgments

The design of the Intel 8089 would not have been possible without the skilled and dedicated efforts of David Stamm, Stanley Kopec, John Atwood, and Aryeh Finegold. Jeffrey Katz and William Pohlman played key roles in the architecture definition of the 8089.

References

1. J. P. Buzen, "I/O Subsystem Architecture," *Proc. IEEE*, Vol. 63, No. 6, June 1975, pp. 871-878.

2. H. S. Stone, *Introduction to Computer Architecture*, Science Research Associates, Inc., 1975.

3. D. E. Freeman and O. R. Perry, *I/O design: Data Management in Operating systems*, Hayden Book Co. Inc., 1977.

4. S. P. Morse, W. B. Pohlman, and B. W. Ravenel, "The Intel 8086 Microprocessor: a 16-bit Evolution of the 8080," *Computer*, Vol. 11, No. 6, 1978, pp. 18-27.

Khaled A. El-Ayat, a senior design engineer responsible for the definition and design of LSI microprocessors at Intel Corporation, has played a major role in the design of the 8089. His areas of interest are VLSI chip architecture and implementation, computer architecture, and distributed processing systems. He is also a lecturer at the University of Santa Clara. Before joining Intel in 1977, he worked for the University of California, Santa Barbara, where he developed a mini-computer-controlled system for an on-campus TV network, and for the University of Toronto, where he developed system hardware and software for three minicomputer installations.

El-Ayat received his BSc degree from Cairo University, his MSc from the University of Toronto, and his PhD from the University of California, Santa Barbara—all in electrical engineering. A member of IEEE, he has authored several technical papers.

235

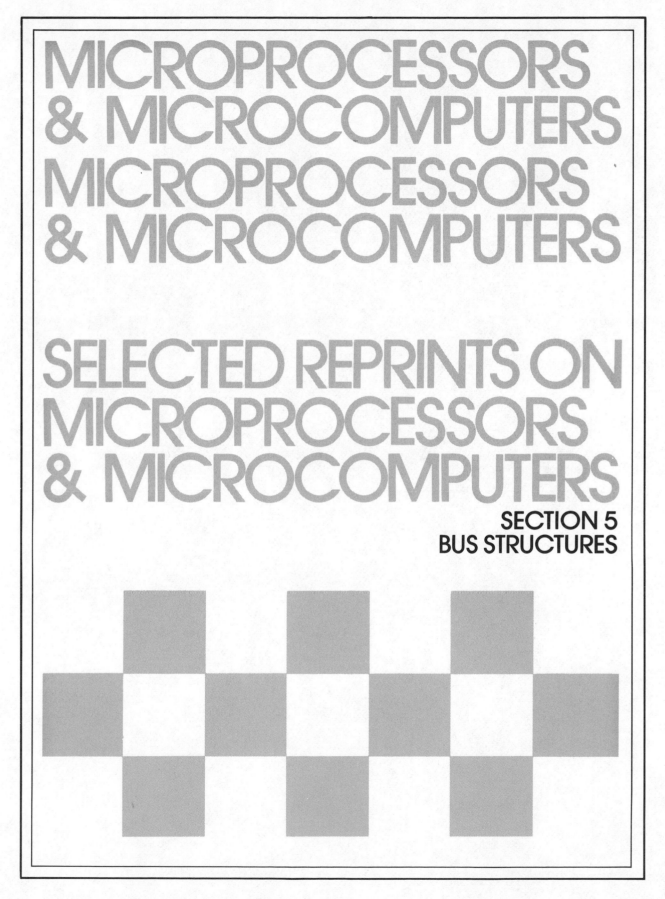

MICROPROCESSORS
& MICROCOMPUTERS
MICROPROCESSORS
& MICROCOMPUTERS

SELECTED REPRINTS ON
MICROPROCESSORS
& MICROCOMPUTERS

**SECTION 5
BUS STRUCTURES**

Bus structures must be transparent to the programmer of

multiprocessor systems. Such transparency can be attained with the

adoption of a standard data representation for future bus designs.

Microprocessor Bus Structures and Standards

Paul L. Borrill

University College London

Buses are most commonly defined as data highways connecting two or more digital system elements. They come in all shapes and sizes to connect devices to each other (component buses), printed circuit cards to each other (backplane buses), racks of equipment to each other (system buses), peripheral units to processing systems (parallel interface buses), and processing systems to other processing systems in networks (serial interface buses).

Much as the programming levels of a computer can be described by a number of virtual machines, and computer memory as a number of levels in a hierarchy of speed and capacity, so bus systems can be described in levels, by the attributes of length, speed, width, and protocol. All computer systems contain many levels of buses. Generally speaking, the larger the system the more levels it will support. Figure 1 shows a medium-sized system with many interface connections implemented as buses; it illustrates the concept of a hierarchy of buses.

The greatest attribute of computers is their generality—by tailoring them with the appropriate program they can be used for almost any application. The bus is the backbone and plays a vital part in the architecture. If the bus is well-designed, flexible, and fast, it extracts the maximum power from the processor architecture it serves and enhances the generality of the system. If the bus is ill-considered, rigid, or slow, it will hinder its applications and become obsolete soon after the arrival of the next generation of processors.

Definitions and models

A relationship between bus structure level and maximum bus length can be established (Figure 2). This provides a basis for the definition of bus levels—we might even consider the straight line to define a "rule of thumb" giving the optimal length at each level.

This paper was presented at the Euromicro 80 Symposium and published
in its proceedings, *Microprocessors: Software, Firmware and Hardware*
(Sami, Thompson, Hanna, Mezzalira, eds.), Amsterdam, 1980. Reprinted
by permission of Euromicro.

When we consider real buses we can see clearly how this "bus level" line predicts the lack or excess of length. Although the DEC Unibus is specified to a maximum of 50 feet, for example, it is rare for an installation to require more than 20 feet, which correlates with the rule-of-thumb line showing an excess of 30 feet. This might be usefully traded off as an increase in bus throughput. The IEEE-488 instrumentation bus falls short of its optimal length by almost a factor of five. It is a common criticism of the IEEE-488 bus that its length and the number of loads it supports are inadequate.

Of course, the bus level line should not be unquestioningly accepted as a criterion for bus length. It is only a guideline and does not take fully into account the continuous size reduction of real equipment due to advances in integration and packaging.

Level 0—component-level buses

Strictly speaking, component-level buses are not the lowest in the system, because inside the devices themselves exist yet lower levels of buses. However, component-level buses are the lowest which the systems designer can manipulate directly. They can be distinguished from other levels by the following attributes:

- They are entirely confined to one printed circuit board. This sets a limit on the length of the signal lines and makes proper line termination impractical, thus presenting the devices with essentially capacitive loads.
- LSI devices may have sufficient output drive capability to make buffering unnecessary, except on the interface to the backplane level.
- All signals are specific to the processor or other LSI device in use, making the component-level bus the most dedicated and inflexible of all.
- A number of basic housekeeping signals appear at this level, such as dynamic memory refresh at typically 2 or 4 ms.

239

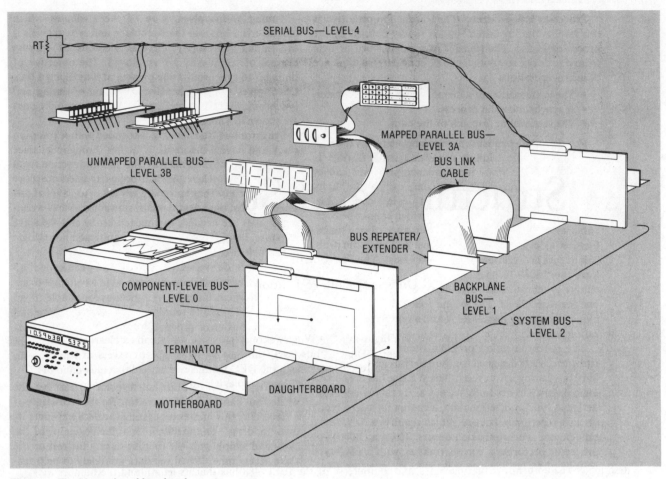

SERIAL BUS—LEVEL 4

RT

MAPPED PARALLEL BUS—
LEVEL 3A

BUS LINK
CABLE

UNMAPPED PARALLEL BUS—
LEVEL 3B

BUS REPEATER/
EXTENDER

COMPONENT-LEVEL BUS—
LEVEL 0

BACKPLANE
BUS—
LEVEL 1

SYSTEM BUS—
LEVEL 2

TERMINATOR

DAUGHTERBOARD

MOTHERBOARD

Figure 1. The hierarchy of bus levels.

Examples of component-level buses are the National Semiconductor Microbus[1] and the Zilog Z-bus.[2]

Multiplexing. Because of the high cost of packaging a device in a 64-pin configuration, multiplexing of the data and addresses is used to reduce the number of intercomponent connections. Additional devices may be needed to demultiplex the signals; this offsets the initial advantage. Therefore, a multiplexed microprocessor shows its greatest cost advantage when it interfaces to devices which have their buses multiplexed in the same way, as when an 8085 interfaces to an 8155. Multiplexing means fewer lines, fewer lines mean fewer connections, and fewer connections mean more reliability; hence, it might be argued that multiplexed designs are more reliable.

In addition to the 8085, microprocessors which use multiplexing include the 8048, 6801, 8086, and Z8000. Whatever may be claimed to the contrary by the manufacturer, multiplexing slows a device down, though not by as much as one might expect. Multiplexing data and addresses on the same lines requires two distinctly separate transactions, each with a synchronization process. However, on a read cycle a nonmultiplexed device simply waits for the cycle to complete before continuing. A multiplexed device usually uses this time to turn the bus around to ready it for data.

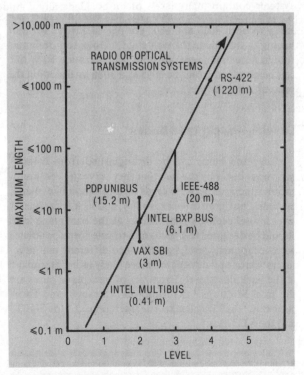

Figure 2. The relationship between bus structure level and maximum length.

Processor independence. The transaction primitive at this level is the "transfer" and is rigidly defined by the processor in use. The transfer of a single word or byte from one device to another can be considered a sequence of micro-operations:

- The presentation of a memory address by a master.
- A synchronization process.
- The retrieval or dispatch of the data.

Processor independence at the component level is practically impossible without penalizing some devices in favor of others. Many independence problems can be overcome by increasing the logic complexity of the bus interface in order to make different devices compatible. There is one main issue, however, which cannot be overcome without degrading the performance of one manufacturer's device in favor of another's. This is the problem of synchronization. Two schools exist. The first follows the "8080 technique" of using two mutually exclusive synchronization signals, one for read ($\overline{RD}$) and one for write ($\overline{WR}$). The second follows the "6800 technique" of using a logical R/$\overline{W}$ and a separate synchronization strobe E.

The synchronization problem occurs only when peripheral devices designed for the 6800 bus are used on the 8080 bus during write cycles. The $\overline{WR}$ line has the correct logic polarity to act as R/$\overline{W}$, but as its falling edge also defines a synchronization time, it cannot be used directly on a 6800 peripheral device, which requires a R/$\overline{W}$ setup time before synchronization occurs. Thus, an 8080-type processor performs a correct transfer with a 6800-type peripheral device by using $\overline{WR}$ for R/$\overline{W}$, inserting an artificial wait state, and generating a synchronization strobe E from the logical NAND of $\overline{RD}$ and $\overline{WR}$.

The necessity of introducing a wait state is the issue. One can only conclude that the 6800 component-level bus is more flexible, since a 6800-type processor can interface easily to both 8080 and 6800 peripheral devices without having to introduce the wait state.* However, designers should note that a separate presynchronization R/$\overline{W}$ line can be obtained from the 8085 and 8086 by decoding the processor status lines.

Level 1—backplane buses

Backplane buses can be distinguished from component-level buses by the fact that they serve the communication functions between cards on a common backplane, provide a buffered drive capability, and lack component-level housekeeping signals. Buses at the backplane level should be designed to avoid a one-to-one correspondence with component-level signals, since different manufacturers' cards and devices are more likely to be intermixed at the backplane level. Examples of backplane buses are the Intel Multibus,[3] the Motorola Versabus[4] and Exorciser-bus,[5] the Zilog Backplane Interconnect,[6] the S-100,[7] and the STD-Bus.[8]

---

*It is interesting to note that while Intel sticks dogmatically to the separate $\overline{RD}$ and $\overline{WR}$ philosophy with the 8086 in order to retain complete compatibility with their existing peripheral devices, Zilog has done an about turn and followed the 6800 technique on the Z8000, which sports a R/$\overline{W}$ line and a separate strobe $\overline{DS}$.

Timing philosophies. One of the attributes which characterizes buses at the backplane and system levels is the timing philosophy. Several methods of varying degrees of complexity are employed. The objective of timing is to synchronize the passing of data along a bus. Chen[9] gives a comprehensive discussion of timing and synchronization philosophies. The most common ones are shown in Table 1.

Synchronous transfers are associated with a common clock and have a theoretically higher throughput, since there is one control signal traveling in one direction from the master to the slave. Asynchronous transfers are more flexible, because they automatically adapt to slaves of different speeds, but are potentially slower because two control signals are needed, the master strobe and the slave response, requiring two bus traverses plus additional logic delays before completion of the transfer.

Asynchronous buses have a snag—they can hang if no response is received from the slave, as in an attempt to access nonexistent memory. A timeout monostable (dead man timer) is used to terminate such an occurrence and activate a bus error process. Synchronous buses do not hang when no response is received from nonexistent memory, however, nor is there any immediate indication an error has occurred.

Split-cycle transfers are an attempt to retrieve the wasted bus bandwidth when waiting for the access time of a slave. The bus master requesting the data transmits its own "address" on the data lines at the beginning of the cycle and simply gets off the bus during the rest of the slave access time. When the data are ready to be transferred, the slave then becomes a pseudomaster and addresses the real master as if it were a slave. In this way a split-cycle protocol can accommodate slaves of various speeds, such as memories with different cycle times, and gain both the speed of synchronous buses and the versatility of asynchronous buses.

Buses using the split-cycle technique include the Honeywell Megabus[10] and the DEC synchronous backplane interconnect.[11] To date there are no microprocessor buses using this technique.

Backplane/system-level multiplexing. At the backplane or system level, the multiplexing technique must be processor-independent. In an extreme case, achieving independence may mean demultiplexing the buses at the component level and remultiplexing them at the interface to the backplane level, considerably degrading the performance of the processor. Multiplexing at the backplane level also penalizes a high-peformance nonmultiplexed processor.

For the same reasons discussed in the section on component-level buses, multiplexing may utilize the access time of a slave to effectively mask the double operation process, thereby reducing the speed penalty. However, if the access time is short (perhaps as the result of masking it by means of memory interleaving[12] or using a processor cache or memory microcache), then the true speed disadvantage of multiplexing becomes more obvious. Moreover, trying to mask the multiplex delay with the access time will be ineffective on a split-cycle bus, or on a write cycle with an asynchronous bus, when both the data and address can be latched on the memory card together, making it unnecessary for the processor to be available for the rest of the cycle.

The multiplexing argument is more reasonable at the component level, where deskewing* and data setup times are less stringent and where fancy techniques are unlikely to be used to improve the bus throughput.

Implementation. Intel has attempted to divorce their Multibus from the component-level bus by defining a distinctly higher-level, asynchronous transaction protocol. Although the component-level bus is a synchronous one for the 8080, 8085, and 8086, the bus interface makes this transparent by introducing wait states at the component level whenever necessary. However, the problem of separate $\overline{RD}$ and $\overline{WR}$ synchronization signals spoils the Multibus' prospects of becoming a true processor-or-independent standard.

The backplane bus is the most easily recognizable bus in the system. The backplane itself is often a printed circuit motherboard with visibly parallel tracks connected in a regular array across the back of the connectors. The connectors themselves fall into two main classes:

- Direct-edge connectors, which use gold-plated fingers on a short tongue extending from the main body of the PCB.
- Indirect or two-part connectors, which use male and female connectors attached to the daughter board and backplane, respectively (although the reverse "male on the backplane" is used in some circumstances).

The indirect connector has one overwhelming advantage over the direct-edge connector—it can have more than two rows of connections to the motherboard, providing a greater density of connections along a card edge. The indirect connector is therefore more suited to the packaging techniques needed for VLSI, since the physical card size is less dominated by connections. Also, indirect connectors are claimed to be more reliable,[6] because their enclosed connection surfaces are shielded from dirt and dust.

When working with complex systems with many levels of detail, it becomes necessary in hardware, as it does in software, to confine oneself to the level of detail relevant to the current problem. In software, the buzzwords "modular" and "stepwise refinement" refer to this practice. In hardware, we can use an analogous technique, as shown in Figure 3. When we are designing a part of the system at the circuit level, we are concerned with the logic levels and delays provided by the "data transfer protocol." At the card level we think in terms of the "transfers" among different subsections on the card, as when a microprocessor reads a memory location. At the backplane level, we are likely to think in terms of "sequences" of transfers, with a complete microprocessor instruction being the basic transaction primitive, for ex-

ample. In larger systems which support system-level buses, we think more in terms of a "group" of sequences, like a DMA block transfer.

The basic transaction primitive at the backplane level is the "sequence." The sequence is the minimum series of operations that represent a complete function—a processor instruction, for example. The sequence may require several bus cycles, each with a synchronization process, especially if the bus is multiplexed and thus requires two or more operations for each memory transfer.

The details of the sequence depend on the master module and the system architecture. For instance, the master module may execute its main program from its local memory, or from global memory through the bus, in which case both instructions and data comprise a sequence. The sequence is the smallest unit which may be

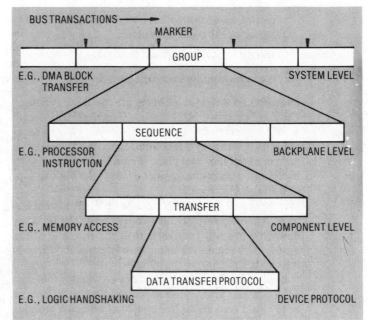

Figure 3. Hierarchy of levels for bus design work, analogous to "modularity" in software design work.

Table 1.
The four most common timing and synchronization philosophies.

	READ	WRITE
SYNCHRONOUS	HERE'S THE ADDRESS. GIVE ME THE DATA BEFORE TIME T.	HERE'S THE ADDRESS AND DATA. I HOPE YOU CATCH IT.
ASYNCHRONOUS	HERE'S THE ADDRESS. I'LL HANG AROUND UNTIL YOU CONFIRM THE DATA IS ON THE BUS.	HERE'S THE ADDRESS AND DATA. I'LL HANG AROUND UNTIL YOU CONFIRM YOU'VE GOT IT.
SPLIT-CYCLE SYNCHRONOUS	HERE'S THE ADDRESS. CALL ME BACK WHEN YOU'VE FOUND THE DATA.	HERE'S THE ADDRESS AND DATA. I HOPE YOU CATCH IT.
SPLIT-CYCLE ASYNCHRONOUS	HERE'S THE ADDRESS. CONFIRM THIS ADDRESS EXISTS, THEN CALL ME BACK WHEN YOU'VE FOUND THE DATA.	HERE'S THE ADDRESS AND DATA. I'LL HANG AROUND UNTIL YOU CONFIRM YOU'VE GOT IT.

---

*Skew is the difference between the minimum delay and the maximum delay of two logic signals traveling through their respective conductor and logic paths. This difference may be sufficient to make the earlier signal arrive after the later signal. Skew is mostly caused by device delay spread and by using different gate types in two otherwise similar logic paths.[13,14]

executed entirely without interruption on the bus; it is an indivisible operation suitable for interprocessor communication via semaphores.

Level 2—system buses

Level 2 buses represent the most global manifestations of the processor's parallel bus system. A system bus may be a single backplane in a small, simple system, but more generally it comprises all the separate sections which make up the entire bus, such as backplanes, bus repeaters, bus linking cables, and termination networks. The attributes which distinguish this level are:

- Absolutely no appearance of device-level housekeeping, such as dynamic RAM refresh addresses.
- A signal protocol to take into account the propagation delay from the bus transmitter to the bus receiver and to accommodate the transmission line behavior of the signal conductors.
- A maximum opportunity for processor independence, while still allowing processors direct access to the same memory and peripheral devices.

Examples of system-level buses are the DEC Unibus,[15] Ferranti Eurobus,[16] NBS Fastbus,[17] and Intel BXP-Bus.[18] Each of these buses provides for extension from the backplane level, either by direct connection via a ribbon cable jumper to another backplane (i.e., a bus extender) or by buffering to boost the number of loads the bus can support (i.e., a bus repeater).

Transmission line behavior dominates the system bus level. Almost invariably the two-way transmission delay down the bus will be greater than the rise time of the signals. This requires termination of the bus at both ends if it can be driven from the middle.

Longer buses also present more crosstalk problems. Solutions here are to make the conductor spacing greater or to shield each signal line by having alternate grounds among them. This method of shielding, though helping to reduce capacitive crosstalk (proportional to frequency), does little for inductive crosstalk (proportional to signal current). Terrell[20] has presented a simple method of measuring the crosstalk on microprocessor backplanes; Catt[21] provides a more complete description of crosstalk in general.

The most often encountered problem when crosstalk occurs is the induced change in the state of the address lines when all the data lines change together.[22] This can cause an address decode change fast enough to remove the previously correct data from the data bus before the processor latches it in. Use of an address "latch" instead of a simple read-through buffer at the slave card can help to overcome this problem by capturing the address bus on the slave card for the remainder of the bus cycle. This also opens up the possibility of "pipelining" the bus transfers—after the address has been latched, another master can get ready for the next cycle by setting up its addresses on the bus.

Many bus designers prefer "inverted" data and address drivers instead of the more logical noninverted ones, because they are faster and consume less power and because the bus assumes the correct negated level when the drivers are inactive.

Open-collector drivers have been displaced by tri-state devices in many modern buses, but the advantage is not clear for backplane and system-level buses. Open collector devices show poor rise times only when driving capacitive loads such as unterminated component-level buses. When the bus transmission delay is greater than half the rise time of the signal, as on backplane or system-level buses that should be correctly terminated anyway, open-collector devices show no disadvantage in speed over tri-state devices because Zo appears as a pure resistance. When we consider system reliability and maintainability, open collectors can have a distinct advantage over tri-state. Consider the case when a card is placed in the system and accidentally set to the incorrect address—a harmless "soft" error occurs when open-collector devices OR themselves on the bus, but a more serious bus fight with high currents may occur in the tri-state system. There are also implications in allowing more flexible control protocols with open-collector systems—an interrupting controller may "steer" the processor to a correct memory location on an interrupt autovector cycle by manipulating the low-order addresses put out by the master.

A method for overcoming the bus fight problem with tri-state buses is to have all boards which drive the bus also drive a valid line via a series resistor (approximately 170 ohms for TTL). If the valid line falls below a threshold, then two cards must be attempting to drive the bus at the same time. A threshold detector (TTL Schmitt) can be used to set a bus error (interrupt or reset), removing both the offending cards from the bus and avoiding damage to the drivers.[23]

Level 3—parallel interface buses

Whenever designers consider the connection of peripherals such as a bank of displays, thumbwheel switches, keyboards, or disk storage units, they can consider using a minibus structure that daisy chains around the peripherals. There are two distinct classes of parallel interface bus which can suit this purpose:

The mapped parallel interface bus. This is a partial extension of the system bus, in that some or all of the data signals may be carried through latches to the outside world along with a number of address lines. In a system with an eight-bit processor, the eight data bits will typically pass through a bidirectional latch to the peripheral units. Four address lines will be buffered and fed out also, to be decoded at the other end of the cable selecting one of 16 devices. A minimum number of control signals will provide a synchronization process to strobe the data at the selected peripheral unit and to specify the direction of the data transfer.

The unmapped parallel interface bus. This is a data highway system divorced from the normal signals which provide transfer between the processor and its memory. It is often implemented with a great deal more interface circuitry than the mapped interface bus, although this circuitry may reside entirely within an LSI device. Only the control registers of the interface circuitry will manifest themselves as memory or I/O space locations.

There are no commercial standards available for mapped parallel buses. Typically, an engineer would implement his own design, based on the requirements and the number of peripheral units.

An unmapped parallel interface bus will often be implemented with an LSI peripheral interface device such as the Zilog PIO or Intel 8292/8291. The most widely known example of an unmapped parallel interface bus is the IEEE-488.[24]

Level 4—serial interface buses

Buses at this level are the longest and the slowest that still use DC logic levels for communication. Distances over 1000 meters can be accommodated with the RS-422 standard.[25] Buses working over longer distances are likely to use transmission methods—such as modulated carrier, optical, or radio systems—which do not cause large degradations in signal quality over the transmission medium.

Serial buses are widely used in computer networks with packet-switching protocols. In addition, there is a trend toward adoption of serial buses for connecting data acquisition and digital I/O modules to LSI devices designed for those purposes. The Motorola MC14469 addressable asynchronous transmitter/receiver can recognize its own address and respond to the command which follows, although its speed is limited to 4800 baud and its protocol is fixed. The Mostek SCU-1 is a programmable serial bus controller in the form of a microprocessor. It also has a limited speed—1200 bits/s—but can be programmed to operate with a variety of protocols and error detection/correction schemes.

Serial bus techniques for household AC wiring have recently received some attention. This may provide a much needed stimulus for standardization before household appliances begin to use such techniques and manufacturing companies rush in to sell their mutually incompatible systems. We may hope eventually to see a common protocol, using either an interface through the AC wiring or the RS-422 standard, for both household and industrial systems.

Whenever the transmission speed is not critical, such as in radio networks or serial buses, an interesting technique—contention arbitration[26]—can be used for the arbitration procedure. Here, a master first "listens" to the bus to ascertain if it is busy. If not, the master begins to transmit its message while still listening to the bus. Should its message be interfered with, it removes itself from the line for an "arbitration period" and tries again later.

Bus error control mechanisms

Whenever a faulty transaction takes place on the bus, the system is in danger of suffering a crash. By offering error recovery schemes such as retry and backtracking, the bus can help the system detect and recover from such otherwise catastrophic failures.

Typical faults include

- attempted transaction with nonexistent memory,
- attempted overwrite of operating system code,
- attempted execution of critical instructions, such as halt or reset,
- system deadlock (or "deadly embrace"),
- bus error due to crosstalk, externally induced noise, or power supply fluctuations, and
- soft errors due to alpha particles in memory device packaging materials.

The first problem manifests itself as false data to a program and is difficult to detect without a memory management unit on a synchronous bus. On an asynchronous bus the absence of a slave response is a real indication that a faulty transaction has been attempted; the dead man timer terminates the bus cycle normally and activates a nonmaskable interrupt or bus error signal. Bus error facilities are more useful because automatic retry of the bus cycle can be made by the hardware, like the facilities provided on the Versabus.

The problem of overwriting forbidden memory areas really requires a memory management unit. But there are other "tricks" such as decoding the normal/system and program/data states from the processor status lines and using them to generate additional memory address bits.

Preventing the execution of forbidden instructions requires a processor which can distinguish normal states from system states. To date, the only microprocessors capable of this are the LSI-11, the MC68000 and the Z8000. Alternatively, external hardware may be used at the component level to detect illegal or forbidden code during an opcode fetch.

System deadlock is a difficult problem and becomes even more difficult in multiprocessor implementations. It is not easy to see how bus interface hardware could recognize system deadlock; perhaps some procedure or recourse timeout could be arranged. Chen[9] discusses the system deadlock problem in depth.

Bus noise is handled using parity, or other error detection schemes, across the bus. Externally induced noise will probably be asynchronous and is unlikely to occur for two cycles running, so a simple bus cycle retry will work. Synchronous noise such as crosstalk will not be eliminated. However, with error correction schemes across the bus, only really drastic errors will need hardware (or software) error processing, since faulty data will be automatically righted before completion of the bus cycle.

The soft memory problem troubles designers whenever they consider high-density memory devices, particularly dynamic RAMs. Error correction using a modified hamming code has been used in mainframe mini- and microcomputers,[27,28] but the concept of carrying the error detection circuitry on the master card instead of integrating it with the slave card has not. There are two obvious advantages to placing the error correction circuitry on the processor card:

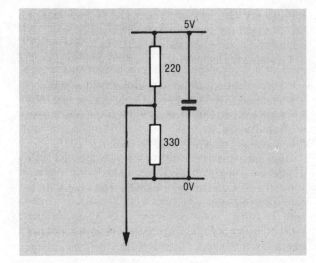

Figure 4. Termination network used on the Unibus, Multibus, Versabus, and ZBI.

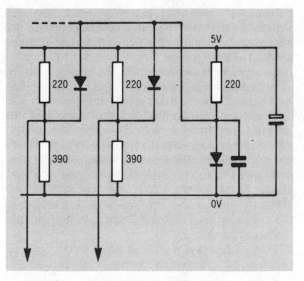

Figure 5. A termination network used on the Eurobus.

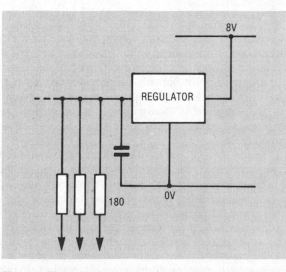

Figure 6. The technique of "active" termination, common on the S-100 bus.

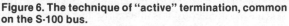

- In a system in which memory cards outnumber processor cards (as is usual), there is a reduction in cost since the error circuitry is included only once on the processor card instead of many times on each memory card.
- Faults occurring on the bus are taken care of as well (but at the expense of additional lines on the bus).

Termination techniques

Whenever lines driven by TTL buffers are longer than about 30 cm, they do not represent a lumped capacitive load. Rather, they act as transmission lines driven by nonlinear sources,[29] with distributed inductance and capacitance. Such lines present themselves with a characteristic impedance of 100 to 150 ohms for printed circuit boards, depending on line cross-section geometry.

A transition of the driver output propagates down a line at approximately 5-15 ns per meter depending on the nature of the insulating medium. When the transition reaches the far end of an unterminated line, it doubles its amplitude and travels back to the source, whereupon it is reflected again, with a negative sign due to the low output impedance of the TTL driver. This continuous reflection causes the familiar "ringing." Preventing ringing requires termination of the line at one end, preferably where the first reflection occurs.[30] Figures 4, 5, and 6 show typical termination networks used in mini- and microcomputer buses at the backplane or system level. Figure 4 is the standard Thevenin equivalent used on the Unibus, Multibus, Versabus, and ZBI. Figure 5 shows a modification on the Eurobus, using a 0.7V source so that the diode clamps at 0V instead of at some negative voltage. Figure 6 shows the technique of "active" termination common on the S-100 bus, whereby some of the supply current wasted in the schemes shown in Figures 4 and 5 is saved by using a constant voltage source at ~2.6-3.6V in series with individual resistors to the bus lines.

Software visibility

One cannot consider only hardware aspects when discussing buses. At some point, the design of the bus and its control by the processor cease to be transparent to the programmer. The appearance of the memory map, the interrupt, and reset processing are all affected by the design of the bus.

Memory map. Depending on the philosophy of input/output on the processor in use, the address map will appear as a single contiguous map of addresses from zero to 2^{n-1}, where n is the number of address lines directly controlled by the processor instruction set, or as two or more independent address maps which may segregate program space, data space, I/O space, etc.

In the case of a single contiguous map of addresses, I/O is said to be "memory mapped." In the case where I/O operations are carried out in a separate I/O space, a special set of I/O instructions are provided in the processor. The following points sum up the arguments for and against each philosophy of I/O:

- Memory mapped processors can use the full power of the memory manipulation instructions for I/O.
- A processor with a separate I/O space is not restricted to doing its I/O with its special instructions; by having memory mapped I/O, it can also take advantage of its memory manipulation instructions.
- Separate I/O space processors can access their I/O devices at high speed because only two memory cycles are needed for the instruction—one to specify the opcode and one to specify the I/O port address.
- Most eight-bit memory-mapped-only processors have an addressing mode which enables them to do fast I/O in the same way—for example, the direct addressing mode of the 6800, in which the upper-address byte is assumed to be zero, or the 6809, in which the upper-address byte is defined by the direct-page register.
- Separate I/O space processors leave the memory address map entirely free for memory.
- A 256-byte area of the address map reserved for I/O in memory mapped systems represents about 0.4 percent of the total address space—hardly relevant, even if the address space for programs is tight.
- Separate I/O space processors need more control lines on the bus. A single memory-space/I/O-space signal (8085) may be required or two more $\overline{RD}$ and $\overline{WR}$ lines for I/O space operations (8080/Z80).
- Memory-mapped-only processors require more address decoding circuitry for a fully decoded system, because both upper and lower bytes of the address bus must be decoded (unless one set of upper-byte decode circuitry in the system provides an IOPAGE signal for the bus).

The conclusion is simple—it does not matter which method of I/O is used. The methods can be made compatible by defining a contiguous memory map with a portion dedicated to I/O, accessed through I/O instructions or memory reference instructions. Moreover, the I/O-MEM signal appears like an additional memory address bit and need not be treated differently, either conceptually or in the design of the bus.

Memory type, reset, and interrupt processing. Most processors make some assumptions about the locations of startup or boot vectors and hence require nonvolatile memory to be in a particular area of the memory map. It is desirable to have read/write memory starting at address zero going up; unfortunately, many processors mess up this low address area with vectors for reset or restart. This can be circumvented by adding more control lines to the bus to enable ROM and disable RAM during restart operations. The Multibus provides $\overline{INH1}$ and $\overline{INH2}$; the Versabus provides $\overline{ROMDIS}$ and $\overline{RAMDIS}$. However, there is no reason that a simple ROM/$\overline{RAM}$ signal cannot be treated as yet another address bit, improving the generality of the bus.

Multiprocessor systems present several unique problems to the bus designer. He must consider multiply

targeted interrupts and resets; i.e., if one of several processors on the bus requests an I/O controller to carry out an operation and to interrupt the same requesting processor upon completion, then he must implement some mechanism to enable only that processor to intercept the interrupt. Also, in a system required to have high availability, a method should be available for processors to be reset independently of each other, so that graceful degradation can be maintained throughout processor failure, diagnosis, and rehabilitation.

If the bus designer decides to use the split-cycle timing philosophy, then he simply targets the interrupt and reset functions to a particular processor. The I/O controller simply acts as a pseudomaster and makes a transfer directly to the address of the target processor. (Note that these types of interrupt require no dedicated lines to achieve the operation.)

Multiprocessor, DMA, and interrupt arbitration

If multiple demands on bus resources can exist randomly in the same system, conflicts will occur, and some arbitration scheme must be implemented to resolve them. A priority scheme such as first-come-first-served cannot resolve two simultaneous requests, so a priority must be assigned on the basis of selection criteria which may be fixed or dynamically alterable.

There are many selection algorithms, each of which has particular advantages in particular applications. If a bus system is to be truly general-purpose, its arbitration control scheme must be flexible enough to give the system implementer the widest range of priority selection algorithms. Factors influencing the choice of an arbitration scheme include

- its adaptability to various priority selection algorithms,
- the number of bus lines it needs to have to achieve the control,
- the maximum number of requests it can handle,
- the extent to which it requires the motherboard to be dedicated, and
- whether it is to be centralized or distributed.

These points are interrelated. For example, a parallel arbitration scheme can be either encoded or decoded in form. An encoded scheme requires fewer lines and allows the arbiter to be distributed, but provides globally only the result of the arbitration process and no information on the contenders. This makes it more difficult to implement dynamically alterable priority schemes such as round-robin.

Figure 7 shows a typical "daisy chain" scheme used on many of the manufacturer-dependent buses such as the Multibus, Z-bus, and Unibus. When a request is made by a card pulling the bus request line low through an open-collector gate, the master issues a bus grant signal which propagates through the logic of each card until it reaches the requestor and is prevented from propagating further. In this way the priority algorithm is predefined by the position of the cards on the backplane. Drawbacks to this scheme are numerous: it is inherently slow because of the

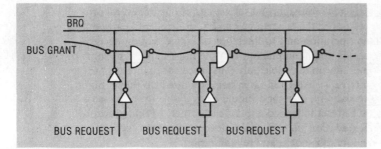

Figure 7. Daisy chain arbitration scheme used on many manufacturer-dependent buses.

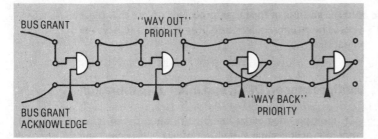

Figure 8. An arbitration scheme that provides flexibility in card positioning.

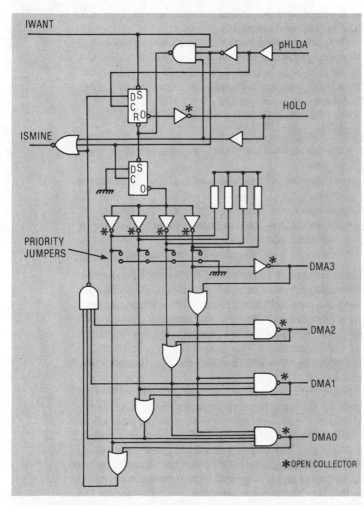

Figure 9. A parallel-encoded arbitration method used on the S-100 and Fastbus.

number of logic levels the bus grant signal must pass through; the cards are position-sensitive, making maintenance difficult for nontechnical personnel (on a card replacement basis); it requires a dedicated backplane and is suitable for only one class of multiprocessor architectures, i.e., those requiring the use of a centralized master.

In some circumstances, priority assignment by card position is incompatible with requirements for mechanical proximity to external controls and connectors or with thermal spreading considerations. In these cases, the modified scheme shown in Figure 8 provides more flexibility in card positioning by allowing the request logic to sit on the "way out" or "way back" paths of the bus grant signal. The bus grant acknowledge line also provides a method of verifying that a bus grant has been accepted by a requestor.

A new parallel-encoded method for determining the winner of an arbitration is shown in Figure 9. This astonishingly simple technique has already been used in the S-100[7] and in the Fastbus[17] and is likely to be used in the IEEE-896 bus under development at this moment.[31] The technique involves having all cards which request the bus place their encoded priority on the bus through open-collector drivers. Each card examines these lines to determine if another card is simultaneously making a higher-priority request. If so, it removes its request and allows the higher-priority card to take control of the bus. In order to prevent oscillation of the system, each requestor examines each bit individually and disables it and all lower priority bits should it find a disagreement. This scheme overcomes all the problems of the daisy chain, requires a simple, undedicated backplane, and is suited to any kind of multiprocessor architecture, at the expense of more logic complexity on each card.

The "starred" technique (Figure 10) is used on the Eurobus and provides more information about the contenders, thus allowing the use of a more sophisticated algorithm. Unfortunately, a dedicated backplane is again required, and the number of lines on the bus is directly proportional to the number of masters supported.

Arbitrations for DMA requests, multiprocessor bus requests, and interrupts are all very similar and can be either combined into a single scheme or divided into three separate ones. The Multibus has eight parallel lines for interrupts and a daisy-chain scheme for multiprocessor and DMA requests. The Z-bus, however, uses daisy chains for both.

Data representation

Some of the most frustrating problems encountered when using various processors are the subtle incompatibilities among the various data types and data storage schemes supported. An example is the way various processors and buses treat the storage of 16-bit words in byte address space. There are only two ways an eight-bit processor can store a 16-bit number:

- least significant byte in address A and most significant byte in address A + 1, (Type 1 storage), or
- most significant byte in address A and least significant byte in address A + 1, (Type 2 storage).

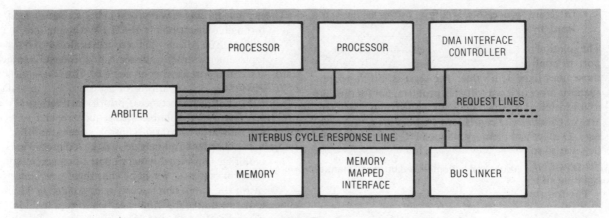

Figure 10. The "starred" arbitration technique used on the Eurobus.

The first method is used in the 8080/8085 and Z80, the second in the 6800 and 6502. The reverse is the problem of how a 16-bit processor sees the two constituent bytes of its word when it addresses them as bytes. The PDP-11 and 8086 see them as in the first method and the Z8000 and 68000 as in the second.

Given an array of ASCII characters (which are essentially byte-oriented data types), the most logical way to store text strings is to have characters stored in successive byte addresses. This means the text string "Sugar and spice." would look like the forms in Table 2. The problem thus presents itself in two ways:

- Memory dumps are easier and more logical to read with Type 2 storage. This applies especially for number storage, since if the memory dump is printed with increasing memory addresses from left to right across and down the page (as is usual), Type 1 storage will have the most significant byte on the right, which is very confusing.
- Interprocessor communication among different processors via global memory may result in bytes getting turned the wrong way around. Given a bus structure which can support eight-bit, 16-bit, 32-bit, and 64-bit transactions, Type 1 storage of the message in 64-bit space will produce this:

    2000 'na raguS
    2008 '.ecips d

and Type 2 this:

    2000 'Sugar an
    2008 'd spice.

On this basis I suggest that Type 2 storage be considered a candidate for byte/word/longword/quadword organization in future bus standards.

Compatibility is a concern when eight-bit peripheral devices which have 16-bit internal registers—such as timer/counters—are considered. In these devices, the processor can take "snapshots" of a counter's state. If the MS byte were in address A and the LS byte in address A + 1, for example, the processor would take a snapshot (with, say, an index register of the 6809) by reading the MSB, which would cause the device to transfer the whole 16-bit word from the counter register, the MS byte to the data bus, and the LS byte to a buffer register. The next bus cycle would attempt to read the LS byte of the counter but in fact would get the contents of the buffer register.

The snapshot operation therefore relies on the processor reading the MS byte first, from address A. If the LS byte were read first, the old buffer register contents would be read, which would be incorrect. This problem is minor but can cause much frustration to a designer using combinations such as a 6840 timer/counter and a Z80.

Word/byte control lines. In a general-purpose computer system allowing intermixing of various processor types, it is desirable to have compatible addressing of those types. Let us imagine a processor system in which eight-bit and 16-bit processors can be intermixed freely.[32] A number of problems may occur in such a situation:

- Some processors may have a larger total address space than others.
- Some processors may divide their address space into sections for system/application data, system/application code, I/O, stacks, etc.
- Some processors may dedicate areas of the memory map to vectors.

**Table 2.
Comparison of two types of storage
for byte-oriented data.**

ALL PROCESSORS BYTE SPACE	TYPE 1 PDP-11, 8086 WORD SPACE	TYPE 2 68000, Z8000 WORD SPACE
2000 'S	2000 'uS	2000 'Su
2001 'u		
2002 'g	2002 'ag	2002 'ga
2003 'a		
2004 'r	2004 'r	2004 'r
2005 '		
2006 'a	2006 'na	2006 'an
2007 'n		
2008 'd	2008 'd	2008 'd
2009 '		
200A 's	200A 'ps	200A 'sp
200B 'p		
200C 'i	200C 'ci	200C 'ic
200D 'c		
200E 'e	200E '.e	200E 'e.
200F '.		

- Different processors will use different lines for word/byte control.

The solution to the first problem is either to use an output port to control the additional lines or to simply leave those lines fixed at a value. The segregation of address spaces is more or less a software problem, but for the sake of uniformity I/O space may be mapped onto a different area of an otherwise contiguous memory map, thus making I/O space and memory mapped I/O compatible. The best way to solve the third problem is to prevent access to the processor's local memory from the global bus, thus isolating all processor-dependent functions.

The fourth problem requires more detailed attention. Consider the four methods of controlling byte/word access shown in Table 3. From this table it can be seen that the Multibus and Versabus methods are similar, with $\overline{BHE}$ equivalent to $\overline{UDS}$ and A0 equivalent to LDS. However, there are two problems to overcome before these methods can be intermixed:

- The Versabus signals define a synchronization time as well as select the required byte. This looks like a retrograde step on the part of the Versabus, because it leads to a problem similar to the $\overline{RD}$, $\overline{WR}$ versus R/$\overline{W}$-plus-strobe syndrome.
- The Multibus defines its least significant byte in the lower address and the Versabus in the higher address, creating the software problem demonstrated in the previous section.

The buses designed for the older generation of microprocessors reflect the architectural deficiencies and inflexibility of those devices. New standards should be designed with flexibility and processor independence as major requirements. Mixing synchronization signals with other bus functions such as the 8080-style $\overline{RD}$ and $\overline{WR}$ is not compatible with such requirements.

No other single factor causes as sharp a trade-off between cost and performance as multiplexing. Multiplexing at the backplane or system level should be avoided if high-performance nonmultiplexed microprocessors like the 68000 are to be employed.

The most promising development in bus standards has been the establishment of the IEEE P896 committee,[31] chaired by Andrew Allison. This group has already made progress toward a truly processor-independent standard—a status report appears on pages 67-82 of this issue of *IEEE Micro*.

The subject of buses is complex and covers a variety of problems, from pure electronics to pure computer science. New standards comparable in excellence to the NBS Fastbus, but cheaper to implement, will be required if we are to cope with the varied requirements of commercial multiprocessor systems. We hope that these new standards will go beyond simple card size, connector pin allocation, and timing diagram specifications to include protocols for multiprocessor communication, data types and storage, multiple bus organizations, and advanced error control. ■

Acknowledgments

I thank Professor R.L.F. Boyd, CBE, FRS, for his encouragement in this work.

The following terms used in this article are registered trademarks: Unibus, SBI – of Digital Equipment Corp.; Eurobus – of Ferranti Computer Systems Ltd.; Megabus – of Honeywell Inc.; BXP, Multibus – of Intel Corp.; Exorciser, Versabus – of Motorola Inc.; Microbus – of National Semiconductor Corp.; Fastbus – of the National Bureau of Standards; ZBI, Z-bus – of Zilog Inc.

References

1. G. Force, "Microprocessor Bus Standard Could Cure Designers' Woes," *Electronics*, Vol. 51, No. 15, July 20, 1978, pp. 113-118; also see "National Semiconductor Microbus," *New Electronics*, Sept. 4, 1979, pp. 50-59.

2. "An Introduction to the Z-bus," preliminary draft, Zilog, Inc., Cupertino, CA, Oct. 13, 1978.

3. "Intel Multibus Interfacing," application note AP-22A, Intel Corp., Santa Clara, CA.

Table 3.
Methods for controlling byte/word access.

Z-BUS			VERSABUS		
	B/$\overline{W}$	A0		$\overline{UDS}$	$\overline{LDS}$
WORD	0	0	WORD	0	0
NO OPERATION	0	1	MS BYTE	0	1
MS BYTE	1	0	LS BYTE	1	0
LS BYTE	1	1	NO OPERATION	1	1

MULTIBUS			EUROBUS		
	$\overline{BHE}$	A0		BYTE WK	BYTE AD
WORD	0	0	MS BYTE	0	0
MS BYTE	0	1	LS BYTE	0	1
LS BYTE	1	0	NO OPERATION	1	0
NO OPERATION	1	1	WORD NORMAL	1	1

4. "Versabus Preliminary Specification," Motorola Microsystems, Phoenix, AZ, Nov. 1979.

5. "M6800 Exorciser User's Guide," Motorola Microsystems, Phoenix, AZ.

6. "Zilog Backplane Interconnect," preliminary data sheet, Zilog, Inc., Cupertino, CA, Apr. 18, 1980.

7. K. A. Elmquist, et al., "Standard Specification for S-100 Bus Interface Devices" (draft of proposal by IEEE Task 696.1), *Computer*, Vol. 12, No. 7, July 1979, pp. 28-52.

8. "Series 7000 STD BUS Technical Manual," Pro-Log Corp., Monterey, CA.

9. R. Chia-Hua Chen, "Bus Communication Systems," PhD thesis, Carnegie-Mellon Univ., 1974.

10. J. W. Conway, "Approach to Unified Bus Architecture Sidesteps Inherent Drawbacks," *Computer Design,* Vol. 16, No. 1, Jan. 1977, pp. 71-76.

11. "Synchronous Backplane Interconnect," chapter 7 in *VAX 11/780 Hardware Handbook,* Digital Equipment Corp., Maynard, MA, 1978.

12. B. R. Rau, "Program Behavior and the Performance of Interleaved Memories," *IEEE Trans. Computers,* Vol. C-28, No. 3, Mar. 1979, pp. 191-199.

13. T. R. Blakeslee, "Clock Skew," *Digital Design with Standard MSI and LSI,* John Wiley and Sons, Somerset, NJ, 1979, pp. 140-143.

14. E. Metzler and J. Oliphant, "Single Supply 16K Dynamic RAM is Ready for Denser Systems," *Electronic Design,* Sept. 1978, pp. 64-69.

15. C. G. Bell, J. C. Mudge, and J. E. McNamara, "Buses, the Skeleton of Computer Structures," chapter 11 in *Computer Engineering—A DEC View of Hardware Systems Design,* Digital Equipment Corp., Maynard, MA, 1978.

16. "Specification for the Eurobus," Ferranti Computer Systems Ltd., Bracknell Division, Bracknell, Berkshire, England, May 1978.

17. D. B. Gustavson, "Introduction to the Fastbus," SLAC-PUB-2378, Stanford Linear Accelerator Center, Stanford, CA, Aug. 1979.

18. R. L. Papenberg and M. Rydhan, "Versatile Memory Bus Handles Mixed Memories Compatibly," *Electronic Design,* Sept. 18, 1979, pp. 86-89.

19. L. W. Berkbigler, "Simplify Mini or μC Bus Extensions," *EDN,* Vol. 24, No. 2, Jan. 20, 1979, pp. 106-108.

20. P. M. Terrell, "Low Inductance Wiring, GND Plane Packaging Set Crosstalk Limits in Microprocessor Based Systems," *Electronic Design,* Jan. 4, 1980.

21. I. Catt, "Crosstalk (Noise) in Digital Systems," *IEEE Trans. Electronic Computers,* Vol. EC-16, No. 6, Dec. 1967, pp. 743-763.

22. P. Bramley, "Crosstalk on Microprocessor Buses," internal report, Spectra-Tek Ltd., Swinton Grange, Swinton, Malton, North Yorkshire, England.

23. D. R. Wilson and N. M. Rothan, "A Standard Micro System Bus," branch report No. 00081, British Post Office Telecommunications, Computer Systems Engineering, Jan. 1979.

24. "Standard Digital Interface for Programmable Instrumentation and Related System Components" (ANSI/IEEE Std. 488-1978), Institute of Electrical and Electronics Engineers, Inc., New York.

25. D. A. Laws and R. J. Levy, "EIA RS-422 and 423 Applications," application note, Advanced Micro Devices, Sunnyvale, CA, June 1978.

26. D. MacLaren, "Contention Arbitration of Serial Buses," technical report DEC TR71, Digital Equipment Corp., Maynard, MA, Aug. 14, 1977.

27. E. L. Wall, "Applying the Hamming Code to Microprocessor-Based Systems," *Electronics,* Vol. 52, No. 24, Nov. 22, 1979, pp. 103-110.

28. R. Korody and D. Raaum, "Purge Your Memory Array of Pesky Error Bits," *EDN,* Vol. 25, No. 10, May 20, 1980, pp. 153-158.

29. O. A. Horna, "Nonlinear Termination of Transmission Lines," *IEEE Trans. Computers,* Vol. C-21, No. 9, Sept. 1972, pp. 1011-1015.

30. J. DeFalco, "Reflection and Crosstalk in Logic Circuit Interconnections," *IEEE Spectrum,* July 1970, pp. 44-50.

31. A. Allison, "Status Report on the P896 Backplane Bus," *IEEE Micro,* Vol. 1, No. 1, Feb. 1981, pp. 67-82.

32. I. R. Whitworth, "Designing Flexibility into Memory Systems," *Microprocessors and Microsystems,* Vol. 3, No. 10, Dec. 1979, pp. 435-441.

Paul Borrill is a postgraduate student at the University College London, Mullard Space Science Laboratory. Prior to university, he spent several years as a radio and electronics officer in the British Merchant Navy. His PhD interests include space research applications of microprocessors, computer bus structures, and fault-tolerant multiprocessor systems. He has special responsibility for the microprocessor control of a UV spectrometer to be flown on Spacelab 2 and for the ground-based minicomputer systems which support this space shuttle mission.

Paul graduated with an honors degree in physics from the University of Manchester in 1977.

Reprinted from *IEEE Micro*, February 1982, pages 41-51. Copyright © 1982
by The Institute of Electrical and Electronics Engineers, Inc.

Inadequate documentation by instrument manufacturers is the source of most GPIB

difficulties. A wise purchasing strategy may be the best solution to these problems.

The General-Purpose
Interface Bus

Richard Gilbert

University of South Florida

The IEEE-488 interface standard, known as the General-Purpose Interface Bus, or GPIB, offers a uniform method of sending parallel code from one device to another. The standard has been revised twice, and communications based on it are now quite reliable. Most current problems with GPIB stem from inadequate documentation by individual manufacturers. This causes unnecessary implementation difficulties, especially when instruments from different sources are involved. This article addresses these problems by reviewing the IEEE-488 standard itself, discussing the methods of its implementation, and presenting specific applications to illustrate how the standard is applied to data-collection situations.

Review of the IEEE-488 standard

The fundamental requirements for a GPIB system are presented in Figure 1. The GPIB is here strictly defined as the wire connections between device 1 and device 2. (Although the term GPIB is often used to refer to a complete system, we limit its meaning to the cable that connects the devices in a GPIB system.) Figure 1 implies that an interface circuit is needed in each device attached to the GPIB; this interface is also defined by the IEEE-488 standard. Finally, the diagram suggests that a GPIB system requires a minimum of two devices, two interfaces, and one cable connection for each successful operation. In fact, there can be 15 devices on the GPIB. The maximum length of cable connecting a group of devices within a normal bus system is either two meters times the number of devices on the bus or 20 meters, whichever is less. Repeaters and optical bus extenders are available.

Figure 2 shows a simple GPIB system. This representation accents the fact that the usual minimal system requires a controller with its interface. The controller decides which device on the GPIB is to communicate with any other device(s).

The GPIB cable has IEEE-488-defined wire and connector requirements. The geometry of the connectors is such that it is best to purchase a GPIB cable when the GPIB instrument is obtained. There are 24 wires in the GPIB; 16 are used to transmit information and eight serve as ground wires. The wires are grouped as data lines, control lines, and management lines. The control lines are

- NRFD, not ready for data;
- DAV, data valid; and
- NDAC, not data accepted.

Figure 1. Minimum requirements for a GPIB system.

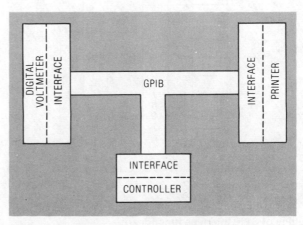

Figure 2. Usual minimal system configuration.

EHO214-7/84/0000/0251$01.00©1982 IEEE

The management lines are

- ATN, attention;
- SRQ, service request;
- IFC, interface clear;
- EOI, end or identify; and
- REN, remote enable.

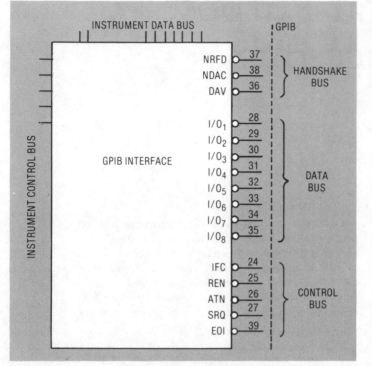

Figure 3. General view of GPIB interface.

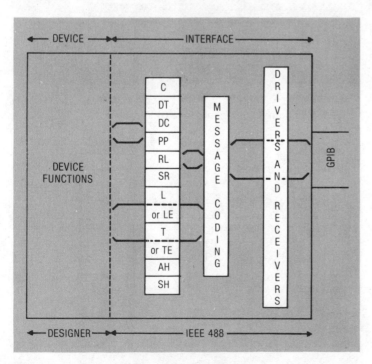

Figure 4. Outline of GPIB interface functions.

Each of the 24 wires on the GPIB is connected via the standard connector to the GPIB interface on the IEEE-488-compatible device. The bus protocol is labeled *active low*, which indicates that the function defined by the wire in question is active when the wire is at zero volts. For example, if the GPIB interface is to recognize the *attention* function and then perform some predefined activity, the wire labeled ATN must be brought to zero volts.

Figure 3 presents a general view of an interface used in an IEEE-488 system. Several firms manufacture these interface chips. There are three groups of GPIB control connections:

(1) The *data bus* is the group of wires that provides the paths for the actual codes to be sent from one instrument interface to another.

(2) The *handshake bus* is used to establish communication across the interface before the actual code is transmitted on the data bus.

(3) The *control bus* contains the special-function wires that control and enhance the GPIB operations. Although there are five control functions in the control bus, a minimal system requires only ATN. If two controllers are to coexist on the bus, the IFC must be operational. The EOI and SRQ are control lines that allow the various instruments on the GPIB to communicate their status to the bus controller. The REN gives the controller a method of removing an instrument from local operator control.

Figure 4 accents the various duties of the GPIB interface, which has three general responsibilities. First, it prepares the digital code to be sent on the GPIB, an activity performed in the driver and receiver sections. Second, it encodes and decodes information that travels on the GPIB. Third, the interface performs the set of IEEE-488-defined functions.

The driver and receiver sections of the interface operate under IEEE-488 guidelines. If a GPIB system uses GPIB instruments, there will be no problems with the drivers and receivers. By contrast, if the user intends to communicate with equipment developed in-house, he must pay more attention to the bus line receiver and drivers.

The message-coding section of the GPIB interface is of interest for what it does, but not for how it does it. The coding section has the responsibility of providing the bus lines with a specific pattern of high and low voltage signals—logic zeros and ones—when a message character is to be sent over the GPIB.

Table 1 summarizes one character code used on the GPIB. This code, the American Standard Code for Information Interchange, or ASCII, contains control characters, letters of the alphabet, digits, and miscellaneous characters commonly found on typewriter keyboards. The table shows control characters in the first two columns and typewriter characters and digits in the next two columns. Capitals, small letters, and miscellaneous characters are in columns four, five, six, and seven. Although ASCII control characters are used in several communication schemes, they are not employed in a GPIB system.

Table 2 is an enlarged section of the ASCII code table, with two additional pieces of information. The first is the seven-bit pattern for each code element and the second is the decimal equivalent for each code element. A brief review of Table 2 indicates its function. For example, the percent character is located in column two, row five of both Tables 1 and 2 (note that there is a column zero and a row zero). This character can be represented as 37_{10}, as 25 in the hexadecimal code, or as the seven-bit pattern 0100101. This seven-bit pattern has a decimal value of 37. The bit patterns and decimal values for the other ASCII characters are column-oriented. Thus, the question-mark character has a 0111111 bit pattern and a decimal value of 63. The space bar, —, has a decimal value of 95 and a 10111111 bit pattern. The last ASCII character, DEL, has a 1111111 pattern and a decimal value of 127.

Interface functions. Figure 4 also summarizes the 10 interface functions supported by the IEEE-488 parallel communications standard. These include

- SH, the source handshake;
- AH, the acceptor handshake;
- T, the talk, and TE, the extended talk;
- L, the listen, and LE, the extended listen;
- SR, the service request;
- RL, the remote/local;
- PP, the parallel poll;
- DC, the device clear;
- DT, the device trigger; and
- C, the control functions.

The first four functions—SH, AH, T, and L—are the minimum requirements for successful GPIB system operation. The SH and AH functions are operated automatically by the interface.

Figure 5 presents the general task for the GPIB interface. It shows an eight-bit byte of code that is to be transferred via the GPIB from the device assigned as the talker to the device assigned as the listener. The bit pattern represents the ASCII code for the question-mark character. The eighth, and most significant, bit is assigned a default value when the seven-bit ASCII code is employed. The actual transfer of the question mark from the talker to the talker interface is talker-dependent and not defined by the IEEE-488 standard. However, the character transfer procedure from the talker interface to the listener interface via the GPIB data lines is defined by the GPIB standard. As the figure implies, the NRFD, NDAC, and DAV lines are needed to produce a successful character transfer down the data lines. The NRFD and NDAC lines are controlled by the listener; the DAV line is manipulated by the talker. The actual procedure for this code transfer is known as a GPIB handshake.

GPIB handshake. The GPIB handshake involves the systematic cycling of the voltage states on the NRFD and NDAC lines with those on the DAV line. The NRFD and NDAC lines are controlled by the listener's interface; the DAV line is the responsibility of the talker's interface. Row (1) of Figure 6 presents the conditions of these lines before the three-wire GPIB handshake begins. When the handshake is complete, the question mark will have been successfully sent from the talker to the listener.

Figure 6 shows that when the listener holds NRFD and NDAC at zero volts, it is not ready for any code transfer

from the talker and it is not processing any previous code character. Thus, the listener is not ready to participate in a handshake cycle.

The DAV line is controlled by the talker. In Figure 6, the line is initially at five volts and the talker has not placed valid data on the GPIB data lines.

Table 1.
American Standard Code for Information Interchange.

	0	1	2	3	4	5	6	7
0	NUL	DLE	SP	0	@	P	`	p
1	SOH	DC1	!	1	A	Q	a	q
2	STX	DC2	"	2	B	R	b	r
3	ETX	DC3	#	3	C	S	c	s
4	EOT	DC4	$	4	D	T	d	t
5	ENQ	NAK	%	5	E	U	e	u
6	ACK	SYN	&	6	F	V	f	v
7	BEL	ETB	'	7	G	W	g	w
8	BS	CAN	(	8	H	X	h	x
9	HT	EM	)	9	I	Y	i	y
A	LF	SUB	*	:	J	Z	j	z
B	VT	ESC	+	;	K	[	k	{
C	FF	FS	,	<	L	\	l	|
D	CR	GS	—	=	M	]	m	}
E	SO	RS	.	>	N	↑	n	~
F	SI	US	/	?	O	_	o	DEL

Table 2.
Enlarged section of ASCII code.

				B_7	0	0	0	0	1
				B_6	0	0	1	1	0
				B_5	0	1	0	1	0
					MOST SIGNIFICANT DIGITS				
B_4	B_3	B_2	B_1		0	1	2	3	4
0	0	0	0	0	NUL_0	DLE_{16}	SP_{32}	0_{48}	$@_{64}$
1	0	0	0	1	SOH_1	$DC1_{17}$	$!_{33}$	1_{49}	A_{65}
2	0	0	1	0	STX_2	$DC2_{18}$	$"_{34}$	2_{50}	B_{66}
3	0	0	1	1	ETX_3	$DC3_{19}$	$\#_{35}$	3_{51}	C_{67}
4	0	1	0	0	EOT_4	$DC4_{20}$	$\$_{36}$	4_{52}	D_{68}
5	0	1	0	1	ENQ_5	NAK_{21}	$\%_{37}$	5_{53}	E_{69}

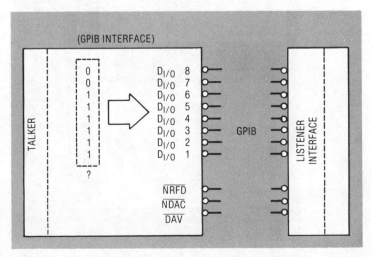

Figure 5. General task of GPIB interface.

253

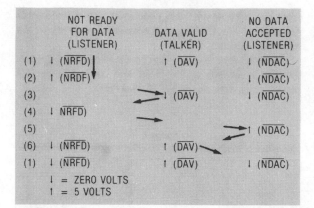

Figure 6. Summary of handshake cycles. Each line cycles states once per handshake.

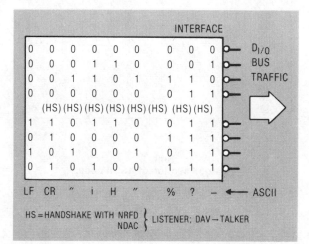

Figure 7. Procedure for code transfer down the bus.

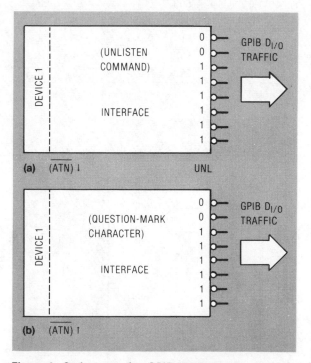

Figure 8. Code types for GPIB transmission; (a) commands and addresses; (b) messages and data.

Row (1) shows the initial state for the listener. Rows (2) through (6) illustrate one complete three-wire GPIB handshake cycle; row (2) indicates a change in the NRFD voltage from zero to five volts. This is interpreted by the talker as a signal to place the code character onto the GPIB data bus. Once this is accomplished, the talker brings DAV to zero volts, an operation shown in row (3). After DAV goes low, the listener interface proceeds to accept the code character that the talker interface has placed on the bus. Simultaneously, the listener returns NRFD to low to prevent the acceptance of an additional character, and begins to process the current code character, in this case the question mark. When the listener interface has successfully passed the received code character to its device, it brings NDAC to five volts, as shown in row (5). Once NDAC is sensed high by the talker interface, the talker DAV line is returned to five volts [row (6)]. This is the last step in the handshake cycle, which is then repeated for the next character.

The three-wire handshake only appears to be complex—it is, in fact, a straightforward procedure. Each wire goes through one voltage cycle for every handshake cycle. The NRFD line starts at zero volts and goes high when the listener desires a code character. It returns low after the listener interface collects the code from the bus. The talker's DAV line starts high and drops to zero volts when the talker interface has placed valid code on the bus. The line returns high when the code is invalid and a new code character is to be placed on the bus. Finally, the listener NDAC line starts low and goes high when the listener's interface has processed the transmitted code character and passed it to the listener. The NDAC line then returns low to begin the entire process again.

Figure 7 presents the general procedure for sending a series of ASCII characters onto the GPIB. The figure shows the bit patterns for a string of characters (– , ?, %, ", H, i, ", CR, and LF) that are to be sent down the bus one at a time, with a handshake on each. The CR and LF are the ASCII carriage return and line feed control characters, respectively. They can be sent as code characters on the GPIB, but exercise no GPIB control activity.

As mentioned earlier, the handshake procedure, although required on each code transfer, is transparent to the user. It is, however, an asynchronous process that can cause problems for the user. Consider again steps (5) and (6) in Figure 6. The time involved in the transfer of code from the GPIB through the listener interface to the listener is listener-dependent. If the listener takes an inordinately long time to process the code character, the bus handshake process halts and waits for the NDAC to indicate that the code character has been accepted by the listener. A user could interpret such a delay as a fault in the GPIB system.

GPIB code. The discussion so far has centered on the transmission of ASCII characters from a talker to a listener via the GPIB. In practice, the situation is more complicated because some characters sent down the bus are not ASCII code.

Figure 8 shows the different types of eight-bit characters that can be sent on the GPIB. The type of character sent depends on the voltage condition on the ATN line. A

Table 3.
GPIB command and address code.

| | | | | ATN MOST SIGNIFICANT DIGIT | | | | |
| | ADDRESS COMMAND GROUP | UNIVERSAL COMMAND GROUP | | LISTEN ADDRESS GROUP | TALK ADDRESS GROUP | | SECOND COMMAND GROUP | |
HEX	0	1	2	3	4	5	6	7
0	—	—	32	48	64	80	96	112
1	GTL	LLO	33	49	65	81	97	113
2	—	—	34	50	66	82	98	114
3	—	—	35	51	67	83	99	115
4	SDC	DCL	36	52	68	84	100	116
5	PPC	PPU	37	53	69	85	101	117
6	—	—	38	54	70	86	102	118
7	—	—	39	55	71	87	103	119
8	GET	SPE	40	56	72	88	104	120
9	TCT	SPD	41	57	73	89	105	121
A	—	—	42	58	74	90	106	122
B	—	—	43	59	75	91	107	123
C	—	—	44	60	76	92	108	124
D	—	—	45	61	77	93	109	125
E	—	—	46	62	78	94	110	126
F	—	—	47	UNL	79	UNT	111	127

LEAST SIGNIFICANT DIGIT (vertical label on left)

low voltage on this line indicates that command or address code characters are being sent down the bus. Thus, the two cases in Figure 8 show the same bit pattern, 00111111, to be sent down the bus. In the first case, it is the GPIB unlisten command, or UNL; in the second, it is the ASCII question-mark character.

Table 3 summarizes all GPIB command and address code characters. Its arrangement parallels that of Table 1. Thus, the character located in row one, column two of Table 3 represents GPIB listen address 33, with a hexadecimal code value of 21. The actual bit pattern—00100001—that represents listen address 33 also represents the exclamation point in ASCII code. The GPIB listener interface distinguishes listen address 33 from the ASCII exclamation point by the voltage state of the ATN line.

Figure 9 returns to the example of a series of eight-bit code bytes to be sent down the bus. Unlike Figure 7, it emphasizes the condition of the ATN line during the code transfer. The same sequence of bytes is to be sent down the bus, but the first three bytes—01011111, 00111111, and 00100101—have different meanings. In Figure 9, ATN is low while the first three bytes are sent. As a result, the three-bit patterns are not interpreted by the listener as the ASCII space, question mark, and percent, respectively. Instead, they are accepted by the listener interface as two GPIB commands, untalk and unlisten, and a single GPIB address, listen address 37.

Extended talk/listen function. The necessity for a GPIB talker and a GPIB listener is apparent; the IEEE-488 standard extends the talk/listen concept still further. At the discretion of the manufacturer, GPIB-compatible devices can have a primary and secondary address structure. The primary addresses are byte patterns assigned to the instrument and indicate whether the instrument is to talk or listen. For example, if an instrument is assigned

GPIB listen address 37, the device becomes a GPIB listener when its data bus receives 00100101 while ATN is low. Similarly, the same instrument becomes the GPIB talker if 01000101, or talk address 69, is received while ATN is low. The secondary address provides a second byte of address code, to be sent after the primary address has been transmitted over the bus. This secondary address provides the device with additional information it might need to perform its function. If the instrument is multi-functional, its operational mode might be defined by the secondary address.

The series of bytes shown in Figure 10 includes a secondary address character. This example suggests that the message portion of the code to be sent to a GPIB instrument must be preceded by a series of GPIB command and

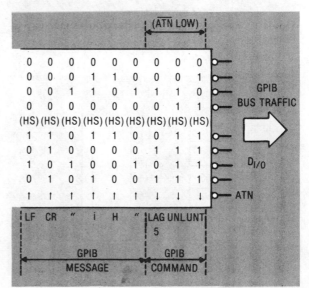

Figure 9. Example of GPIB command and address code.

address code characters. The first command characters to be sent are the universal UNT and UNL commands. These two commands, as well as those located in column one of Table 3, are recognized by all GPIB-compatible instruments when ATN is low. The UNT and UNL commands are sent down the bus to assure that all bus instruments stop their bus traffic so that the controller can reconfigure the bus. Once the previous talker and all of its listeners have stopped their activity, the new listen address and the new secondary address are placed on the bus. For the specific example shown in Figure 10, the listen address bit pattern is 00100101 and the secondary address pattern is 01100001. These two addresses can be expressed as decimal values (37_{10} and 97_{10}), as hexadecimal code (25_{hex} and 61_{hex}), or as their corresponding listen address group and secondary command group values (LAG 5 and SCG 1). In any case, the actual bit patterns placed on the bus are 00100101 and 01100001, respectively. Once this is accomplished, listen address 37 and secondary address character 97 are recognized by the assigned GPIB instrument, which is placed in its proper operational mode.

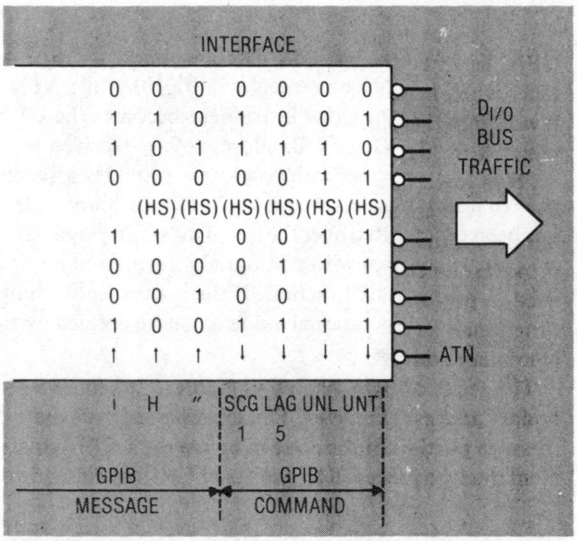

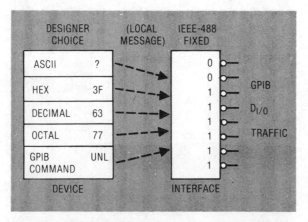

Figure 10. Example of code transfer with a secondary address.

Figure 11. Methods for communicating with the GPIB interface.

Control function. The GPIB provides a method for two or more instruments to listen to another instrument as it sends code down the bus. The usual GPIB system has an instrument that not only acts as a talker or a listener, but can also control bus activities. Such control activities are defined by the controller function in the controller interface to the GPIB.

IEEE-488 implementation

The first decision in instrumentation implementation concerns the acquisition of equipment. The GPIB user can choose a single system, a mixed system, or a prototype system.

The single system is from one vendor—all equipment, including talk and listen devices and cables—comes from the same manufacturer. The single systems save time and intellectual effort, but this speed and ease have a price. The restriction to one vendor limits the user to instruments provided by that vendor, and the user must be content with the characteristics of the available instruments.

The mixed system, with instruments from a variety of manufacturers, is more common. Its advantages are equipment cost and choice of instruments. The user has the freedom to shop for the best instruments at a cost his laboratory can afford, but this freedom has its price. Although the manufacturer of GPIB instruments must build them to be compatible with IEEE-488, there are many ways to meet that standard. All GPIB functions supported by an instrument are not necessarily recognized by another instrument. In fact, similar instruments from various manufacturers are not likely to support all of the same GPIB functions. An instrument is considered IEEE-488-compatible if it can be addressed and can perform the talk/listen handshake operations. Other GPIB functions can be absent or partially supported, according to the guidelines in the IEEE standard. Ultimately, a user dealing with a mixed system must expend more time and effort in establishing initial communication among the instruments.

Another factor in choosing a mixed or single system is the available documentation and manufacturer's support. Although most equipment is reliable and has a satisfactory operational warranty, the single-system vendor generally provides more help in bringing the system on line. In contrast, a GPIB vendor is not likely to offer much help in getting his meter to communicate with another manufacturer's printer. As a result, a physically easy instrument interface might be intellectually difficult. The user should be prepared to spend the time and energy to sort it out.

The prototype system is one in which at least one instrument on the bus is not commercially available. The user might have a commercial controller but be developing his own instrument, which must ultimately be GPIB-compatible. The successful operation of a prototype system requires a great deal of user time, but little initial investment in GPIB parts.

The bit-pattern representation problem. Figure 11, which shows an IEEE-488 interface receiving a byte of code, illustrates a major GPIB implementation problem: the GPIB standard does not control the way in which the manufacturer communicates with the interface. Thus, the instrument designer knows that the 00111111 bit pattern has a specific IEEE-488 meaning under defined circumstances, but he has several options as to how his instrument receives this byte in the first place. It is clear from the illustration that the ASCII question mark, the hexadecimal code value 3F, the decimal number 63, the octal code value 77, and the GPIB unlisten command can all represent the desired bit pattern. Any of these representations can be typed into the talker to send 00111111 to the IEEE-488 interface. The manufacturer's literature might not make clear exactly which is to be used.

Example Implementations. Consider the implementation (with the Tektronix 4051 controller) of the following GPIB code structure:

$$\text{WBYTE @ 95,63,37,97:34,72,105, - 34.}$$

The WBYTE command effects direct access to the GPIB interface from the keyboard of the 4051. The command includes the decimal equivalent of the GPIB code character to be sent down the bus. The ATN line on the GPIB is brought to zero volts by the @ symbol and returned to five volts by the colon.

Figure 12 illustrates the code structure presented above. The drawing presents the bit patterns for the UNT, UNL, LAG 5, and SCG 1 GPIB command and address characters. The "Hi" message bit pattern is also shown. Note the changes in voltage on the ATN line. The last character, the final quote, is sent down the bus when the EOI line is brought low.

Still another communication complication is the GPIB address group concept. Table 4 presents the four address groups used to classify the various GPIB addressing situations. The four are:

- DAG, the device address group;
- LAG, the listen address group;
- TAG, the talk address group; and
- SCG, the secondary command group.

The DAG, TAG, and LAG assignments are interlocked, while use of the SCG value is an option of the designer. For example, if a GPIB instrument is assigned the 10th device address, that instrument also is given LAG 10 and TAG 10. No SCG need be assigned to the instrument unless the designer desires the extra byte of addressing capability.

Some confusion centers on the decision as to when to employ the assigned DAG, LAG, or TAG. The device address is not used when direct communication via the GPIB interface is desired. In such cases, if the instrument is to function as a listener, the listen address must be used. Likewise, if the instrument is to be configured as the talker, the specific talk address must be used. When direct code access to the bus is not necessary, the controller provides software that can be used to configure the bus. These manufacturer-defined commands use the DAG and, when necessary, the SCG to communicate with the instruments in the system. Figure 13 offers a clarifying ex-

ample for three different controllers. In all three cases, the ubiquitous but innocuous "Hi" message is sent to GPIB device number five. Employment of the device address considerably reduces the user's GPIB communication responsibilities. Comparison of the 4051 example in Figure 13a with the WBYTE statement for the same message in Figure 12 confirms this observation. In the situation of Figure 13, the user need not be concerned with the

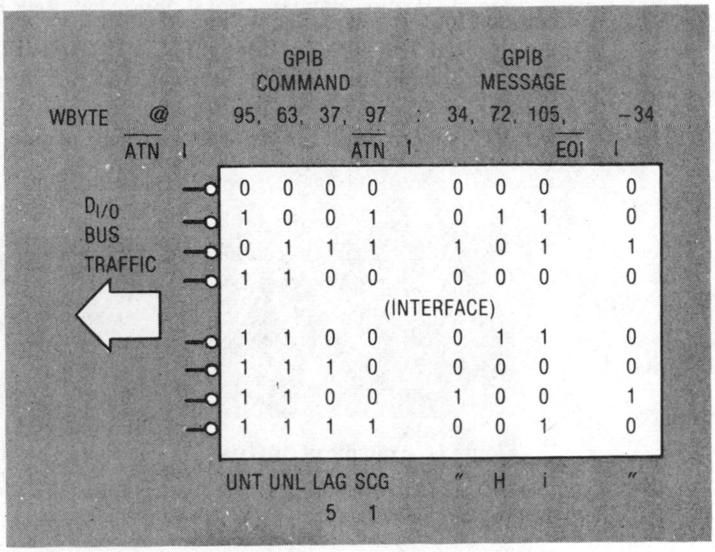

Figure 12. Expanded illustration of WBYTE command.

Table 4.
Summary of GPIB address groups.

DAG		LAG		TAG		SCG	
0	1	2	3	4	5	6	7
0	16	0	16	0	16	0	16
1	17	1	17	1	17	1	17
2	18	2	18	2	18	2	18
3	19	3	19	3	19	3	19
4	20	4	20	4	20	4	20
5	21	5	21	5	21	5	21
6	22	6	22	6	22	6	22
7	23	7	23	7	23	7	23
8	24	8	24	8	24	8	24
9	25	9	25	9	25	9	25
10	26	10	26	10	26	10	26
11	27	11	27	11	27	11	27
12	28	12	28	12	28	12	28
13	29	13	29	13	29	13	29
14	30	14	30	14	30	14	30
15	31	15	31	15	31	15	31

(a) 10) PRINT @ 5: "Hi"
(b) 10) OUTPUT 705: "Hi"
(c) 10) OPEN 1,5
    20) PRINT #1, "Hi"

DEVICE ADDRESS 5 AS LISTENER

Figure 13. Example of DAG used to configure a bus listener: (a) Tektronix 4051; (b) HP-85; (c) PET.

GPIB commands or specific address structure. The controller still performs these required transactions and directs them to DAG 5 in operations that are transparent to the user. The actual ASCII message to be sent is simplified in Figure 13.

Figure 13b is an example of the use of the HP-85 controller. In this instance, the format is similar to that employed by the 4051. Instead of PRINT, the OUTPUT command is employed; the 7 is added to inform the HP-85 to send the ASCII message to output port number 7. (Port 7 has been designated by HP as their IEEE port. Other communication standards are supported at other HP-85 output ports.) The HP-85 returns ATN to five volts in response to a semicolon; the 4051 uses a colon for this purpose. The HP-85 does not designate a unique character to lower ATN to zero, while the 4051 requires the @ character for that task. The HP-85 and 4051 use the same format to send the ASCII message.

Figure 13c presents a PET example. The use of the DAG is a bit more involved, but still uncomplicated. Line 10 of this example is used to establish a dummy file for the device 5 instrument. Once this is accomplished, the print statement in line 20 is used to access file 1 and send the "Hi" message to device 5. The # and common characters control the status of the ATN line.

In each of the examples in Figure 13, the chosen command selects instrument 5 as a GPIB listener. This is done with no further assistance from the user.

The assignment of a GPIB talker by means of the DAG is equally straightforward. Figure 14 represents the analogous examples for this case. In cases (a), (b), and (c), the incoming bus code is to be placed in the A$ string variable. The 4051 example differs from its counterpart in Figure 13a only in the replacement of the PRINT command with the INPUT command. This change reflects the different direction in which the code is traveling. In Figure 13a, the message leaves the 4051 and arrives at device 5; thus, device 5 was assigned the role of GPIB listener. In Figure 14a, the 4051 is assigning device 5 as the talker and itself as the listener. Once device 5 has been assigned as the GPIB talker, the message code from GPIB instrument 5 is collected by the 4051 and stored in the A$ variable. ATN is still controlled by the @ and colon characters. Figures 14b and 14c follow a similar line of reasoning. The ENTER command for the HP-85 program and the INPUT statement in the PET program are used to collect the input code string into A$.

Figure 15 illustrates the implementation of the secondary address in conjunction with the device address. In each example, DAG 5 and SCG 1 are used. A quick glance at Figure 15a shows that for the 4051's controller, the implementation of the secondary address merely requires placing the SCG address of interest behind the DAG value. The comma is a delimiter.

The HP-85 utilization of SCG values is more involved. The SEND 7 portion of line 10 in Figure 15b is necessary for the HP-85 to address its GPIB output port. The characters after the semicolon send GPIB commands to the interfaces of interest. The UNT and UNL commands are sent first. My talk address, or MTA, is sent next. The HP-85 recognizes this command as a signal to put its own interface talk address on the bus. Because the HP-85 controller can also function as a system controller, it requires the MTA. Unlike the 4051, the HP-85 need not always be the active controller. As a consequence of this flexibility, the HP-85's GPIB interface must be addressed each time the HP-85 is to communicate with bus instruments. The MTA is sent automatically when the HP-85 OUTPUT command is used. The last two commands, LISTEN 5 and SCG 1, configure instrument 5 as a listener to perform the function defined by SCG 1. The result of all this command code traffic is a GPIB system configured with the HP-85 interface as the talker and the instrument at listen address 37 as the listener. In addition, device 37 has been instructed to perform its SCG 1 function. This particular function is defined by the manufacturer of the addressed listener device.

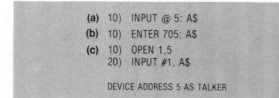

(a) 10) INPUT @ 5: A$
(b) 10) ENTER 705; A$
(c) 10) OPEN 1,5
    20) INPUT #1, A$

DEVICE ADDRESS 5 AS TALKER

Figure 14. Example of DAG used to configure a bus talker: (a) Tektronix 4051; (b) HP-85; (c) PET. In each case, the tag is entered by the interface.

(a) 10) PRINT @ 5, 1; "Hi"
(b) 10) SEND 7; UNT UNL MTA LISTEN 5 SCG 1
    20) OUTPUT 7; "Hi"
(c) 10) OPEN 1,5,1
    20) PRINT #1, "Hi"

Figure 15. Example of DAG and SCG with (a) Tektronix 4051, (b) HP-85, and (c) PET controllers.

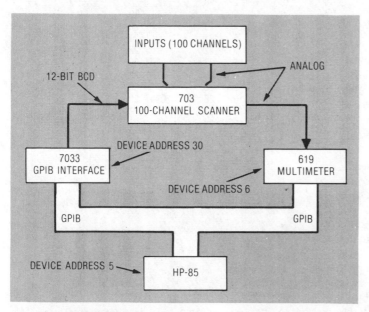

Figure 16. A Keithley data system.

The PET example (Figure 15c) is a logical extension of that in Figure 13c. The introduction of the secondary address is accomplished in line 10 of the PET program in Figure 19c. This extra address code is added to the dummy file structure after the DAG value. Finally, a careful review of Figure 12 will reveal the use of the 4051 WBYTE command structure in the issuance of an SCG value. In Figure 12, SCG 1 is sent. This task is accomplished by placing its decimal value (97) into the command string after the decimal value (37) of the listen address.

IEEE-488 applications

GPIB applications are restricted by instrument-supported data rates, by the number of instruments on the bus, by cable length limitations, and by the imagination of the user. Three examples of general-purpose application are presented below, along with appropriate software. The program sections supplied, however, require user embellishment.

The Keithley data system. The first example, the Keithley data system, is presented in Figure 16; the associated software is in Figure 17. The system uses an HP-85 controller, a Keithley 614 multimeter, a Keithley 703, a 100-channel scanner, and a Keithley 7033 GPIB interface. Figure 16 shows a schematic arrangement of the instruments. The 703 scanner provides a 100-channel analog input port to the data system. The channel is selected by a 12-bit BCD code, and the selected channel response is directed to the 619 multimeter. The multimeter functions and the 7033 interface are controlled by the HP-85. In this example, any of the three GPIB devices—the 7033, the 619, or the HP-85—can perform talk or listen operations. The usual function of the 7033 interface is to accept GPIB instructions from the HP-85 and translate these commands to the 703-channel scanner into BCD code. The 619 meter must accept GPIB commands from the HP-85, comply with these commands by performing the selected operations, accept the analog signal from the data port, and send the appropriate digital reading back to the HP-85.

Figure 17 shows the program components needed to accomplish these tasks. Line 100 provides the formatting information used on incoming code from the 619 multimeter. Lines 220 and 230 provide a way of supplying the desired meter conditions to the HP-85 interface. The actual characters put into the C$ variable depend on the instrument manufacturer; this information must be obtained from the appropriate instrument manual. This task can be formidable, since many GPIB instrument manufacturers do not clearly specify which characters to use for which instrument functions. Line 210 defines two string variables that provide the program with the X character (E$) and the quotation mark (D$). These two ASCII characters are required by both the 7033 and 619 as part of their command structures. For example, if the two-character instruction F1 is to be sent to the 619 meter, then the 619 requires that the X character precede F1 and that all three characters be enclosed in quotation marks. Line 240 is used to assemble the command character string, C$, in-

cluding the required X character and surrounding quotation marks. The 703 scanner has similar command format requirements. Line 330 accepts the command characters as defined by the 703 instruction manual, and line 340 arranges them with the X character and quotes into the V$ character string.

The remaining program lines in Figure 17 present the requirements for actual bus communications. Line 500 activates output port 7 on the HP-85 and sequentially sends the UNT, UNL, MTA, LISTEN 6, and SCG 1 GPIB command and address codes to the bus. When line 500 is successfully executed, the GPIB is configured with device 6, the 619 multimeter, as the listener and the HP-85 as the talker. After execution of line 500, the 619 multimeter waits for code to be placed on the GPIB. After line 550, the contents of C$ have been accepted by the 619. The inclusion of the X character in C$ causes the 619 to execute the command at once. Line 600 sends the UNT and UNL commands to the GPIB and reconfigures the system with the MTA and listen 30 address commands. This time a new listener, the 7033 interface, is on the GPIB, but the HP-85 remains the bus talker. As with line 550, line 650 sends the correctly structured commands to a GPIB device. The output address in line 650 has a different form from that of line 550. Line 650 uses address 730; line 550 merely uses 7 to access the GPIB output port. (Note the use of a secondary address command in line 500.) The need for SCG 1 to be sent to the 619 meter forced line 550 to be directed to the GPIB output instead of DAG 6 because—unlike the 4051—the HP-85 recognizes only the SEND command as the method to transmit SCG bytes down the bus. Line 600 does not have an SCG because device 30 does not require one. The final program elements, lines 800 and 850 in Figure 17, configure the bus so that the HP-85 is the listener and the multimeter is the talker. Line 850 allows the data code to be brought from device 6 into the HP-85 and stored in the two variables Z$ and Z in a format defined in line 100.

Figure 18 summarizes the program elements needed if the 4051 is the controller. Line 150 is used to change the significance of certain ASCII characters recognized by the 4051. (Note that 37 is the listen address for the 4051 microprocessor and that SCG 0 is the secondary address

```
100   IMAGE YA, MD.5DE

210   E$ = "X", D$ = CHR $(34)
220   PRINT "INPUT METER CONDITIONS"
230   INPUT C$
240   C$ = D$ & C$ & E$ & D$

320   PRINT "INPUT SCANNER CONDITIONS"
330   INPUT V$
340   V$ = D$ & V$ & E$ & D$

500   SEND 7; UNT UNL MTA LISTEN 6 SCG 1
550   OUTPUT 7; C$
600   SEND 7; UNT UNL MTA LISTEN 30
650   OUTPUT 730; V$

800   SEND 7, UNT MLA TALK 6 SCG 1
850   ENTER 706 USING 100; Z$, Z
```

Figure 17. Key HP-85 commands for Keithley system.

```
150   PRINT @ 37,0: 10, 255, 13

500   PRINT @ 6, 1: C$
600   PRINT @ 30, 32: V$

800   INPUT % 6, 1: B$
850   PRINT @ 32: USING 100: B$
```

Figure 18. Tektronix 4051 program parts for Keithley system.

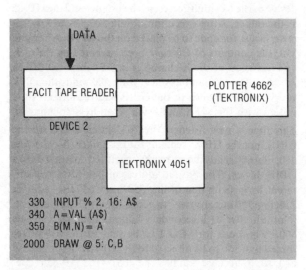

```
330   INPUT % 2, 16: A$
340   A =VAL (A$)
350   B(M,N) = A

2000   DRAW @ 5: C,B
```

Figure 19. 4051 tape-reader-to-plotter program elements.

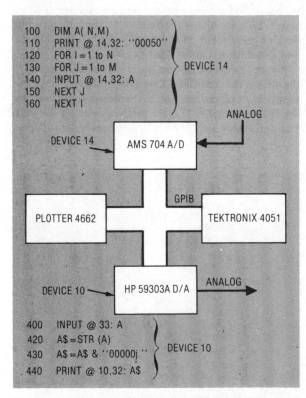

```
100   DIM A( N,M)
110   PRINT @ 14,32: ''00050''
120   FOR I =1 to N
130   FOR J =1 to M          DEVICE 14
140   INPUT @ 14,32: A
150   NEXT J
160   NEXT I
```

```
400   INPUT @ 33: A
420   A$ =STR (A)
430   A$ =A$ & ''00000j''      DEVICE 10
440   PRINT @ 10,32: A$
```

Figure 20. 4051 program elements for an A/D-D/A system.

for a status byte register in that microprocessor.) Lines 500 and 600 are used to send information to devices 6 and 30, respectively. The SCG 32 in line 600 is used to prevent the 4051 from sending a default SCG with the PRINT statement. Lines 800 and 850 address the multimeter and direct the 4051 to accept its data. The percent character in line 800 is used by the 4051 to recognize that some characters—those defined by line 150 in the coming data train—have an alternate meaning.

Transferring code from paper tape to printer. The second GPIB example, an uncluttered GPIB application, is presented in Figure 19, which also lists the 4051 program elements. The task is to transfer code from the paper tape to a printer. In this case, the characters are assigned to the A$ string variable. Then, the numerical value for each string is assigned to the A variable. The values for each string are finally assigned to a matrix for further manipulation or display. In this example, the tape is only involved in the transmission of ASCII codes that represent digits.

An A/D and D/A system. Figure 20 shows the elements of an A/D and D/A system. Lines 100 through 160 in the 4051 program provide a method of acquiring the data from the AMS 704 and placing it in the variable A. The character string in line 110 is used to select a desired AMS channel. The AMS 704 in this example has been assigned DAG 14, but requires no SCG. A problem might develop, since the 4051 automatically sends SCG 12 with every PRINT command. To assure that no SCG is sent, SCG 32 is inserted to the immediate right of DAG 14 in the PRINT statement in line 110.

The D/A operation is presented in lines 400 to 440. In this case, data is taken from the 4051's internal magnetic tape file, device 33 on the GPIB, and sent to the HP 59303A. Lines 400 and 420 provide a way to take the data from the tape and convert it to an ASCII character string. The data string is added to an HP 59303A command string in line 430. Line 440 is used to send this concatenated string to device 10, the HP 59303A. It also provides the method of sending this data and command string to the outside world as an analog signal. Again, note that SCG 32 has been added to the PRINT statement in line 440. This was done to prevent the 4051 from sending any SCG to the HP 59303A. The result of line 440's execution is a steady DC output voltage from the HP 59303A. This voltage represents the digital data stored in the variable A.

User concerns

The addition of GPIB equipment to the experimenter's arsenal provides an enormous expansion of his ability to inexpensively collect and process data. Automated evaluation of development products, computer control of complex experiments, and development of routine quality control schemes are easily accomplished. However, there are subtle problems with the GPIB system. Before obtaining GPIB equipment, the user must consider the instrument's

- compatibility,
- command of the bus,

- secondary address requirements,
- implementation of the other GPIB functions,
- support literature, and
- data collection rate.

These considerations are briefly discussed below for a simple talk/listen GPIB system.

Function compatibility in the GPIB interface is a primary concern. The instruments to be placed on the GPIB may or may not require a secondary address; this decision is made by the instrument manufacturer. If the instrument of choice has a secondary address, the user must learn what it is and how to put that code into the bus. He must also confirm that his controller can send secondary addresses and must understand exactly how that is accomplished. The user should investigate the extended talk and extended listen capabilities of any GPIB instrument or controller he intends to procure. He should also compile a list of the desired GPIB functions and compare it with the list of functions provided by each instrument under consideration. No manufacturer is required to supply all of the possible GPIB-supported functions, so the user must know which are actually supported by each instrument.

A final compatibility consideration is the possibility of several controllers existing on the same bus. A system controller can transfer bus control to other controllers and then reestablish itself as the bus controller at a later time. The minimal GPIB controller function does not require one controller to allow another to function on the bus. As a result, some controllers (the HP-85, for example) can be configured as system controllers, while others (such as the Tektronix 4051) cannot.

Most manufacturers provide detailed manuals on the operation and maintenance of their equipment, but this practice does not always include the GPIB instructions for the GPIB instruments. The user should examine the GPIB information provided with an instrument *before* the instrument is purchased. If this material is unclear or unavailable, an alternate vendor should be considered. It is very difficult to implement a GPIB instrument if the manufacturer does not supply strong support documents.

The data collection rates accepted by the IEEE-488 standard are so wide that considerable attention must be paid to particular instrument values. The user must be familiar with each instrument's data rate in order to understand the code transfer characteristics of his GPIB system. ∎

Bibliography

AMS 704 Manual, AMS, Lake Elmo, Minn.

HP-85 I/O Programming Guide, Hewlett-Packard, Corvallis, Ore., 1981.

IEEE Standard Digital Interface for Programmable Instruments, IEEE, New York, 1978.

Keithley 619 Multimeter Manual, Keithley Instruments, Cleveland, Ohio, 1980.

Tektronix 4051 Reference Manual, Tektronix, Inc., Beaverton, Ore., 1975.

Richard Gilbert is an assistant professor in the chemical/mechanical engineering department of the College of Engineering at the University of South Florida, Tampa, Florida. His research areas include sensor development, computer interface technology, and instrumentation for process control and environmental monitoring. He is also actively interested in application developments for data analysis techniques such as factor and Fourier analysis.

Gilbert's address is Chemical/Mechanical Engineering Dept., University of South Florida, Tampa, FL 33620.

Reprinted from *IEEE Micro*, August 1983, pages 32-47. Copyright © 1983 by
The Institute of Electrical and Electronics Engineers, Inc.

Which end of the data egg gets broken first—big or little?

Do you start with the MSB or the LSB? For the proposed

IEEE 896 bus, the most practical approach may be the little-endian one.

Data Format and Bus Compatibility in Multiprocessors

Hubert Kirrmann

Brown Boveri Research Center

Several bus standards are being developed by the IEEE, such as the proposed IEEE 802 standard for local-area networks. Other standardization efforts by organizations such as the ISO and the IEC apply to industrial buses and long-haul networks. Yet other standards aim at closely coupled systems. The P896 backplane bus,[1] a proposal being developed by the IEEE Computer Society, the European Workshop on Industrial Computing Systems, and the Institution of Electrical Engineers, has been designed to be the

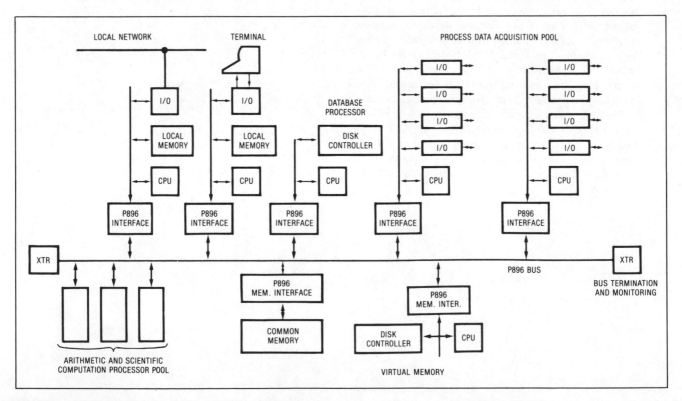

Figure 1. A nonhomogeneous tightly coupled multiprocessor.

262

EHO214-7/84/0000/0262$01.00©1983 IEEE

backbone of a tightly coupled multiprocessor system in which different boards communicate through a common memory (Figure 1).

Standards should guarantee compatibility between products from different manufacturers and of different technical conception. Computing systems interconnected by standard buses are often nonhomogeneous, and the standard has the difficult task of guaranteeing communication between building blocks having different speeds, signal protocols, and data formats.

The lower protocol layers, which ensure mechanical, electrical, and timing compatibility, rule *how* information is transmitted, not *what* information is transmitted. Beyond this physical compatibility, the modules must agree on a common format for data transmission and storage. Such a convention requires a much broader standardization than the physical layers, since it directly concerns the instruction set and the architecture of the processors.

Until now, the manufacturers of processors have not agreed on any common data representation, with the result that it is not possible for a processor to interpret data in memory without knowing its source. An automatic translation within the bus interface is usually not feasible, since the interface would need an impractical amount of knowledge about what the processor is intending to do.

The problem gets worse when software layers are involved. It is reasonable to assume that programs that run on different processor types are compiled independently. These programs must, however, communicate with each other by means of common data structures such as mailboxes and ports. Unfortunately, compilers have little respect or knowledge of other compilers' conventions, so most of the time compatibility has to be achieved by rather primitive and inefficient mechanisms. The data compatibility problem is present each time data are exchanged between machines of different type or even of different serial number. It appears in multiprocessor computers, in networks, and each time a tape or a floppy disk written on one type of machine must be read on another.

In this article, I analyze the problem of data representation and show to what extent it can be solved at the bus interface level. I then consider how future 32-bit processors should be interfaced, and I give the rationale for the choice of the bus data format in the EDISG* proposal for the IEEE P896 Future Bus standard.

Data format compatibility

Each time data are transferred between computers of different types, a common data format must be employed. This is not easy to achieve, since the user normally has no control over data formats, especially if she or he programs in a high-level language. Suppose that a

*EDISG, the European Distributed Intelligence Study Group, is committee TC 10 of EWICS, the European Workshop on Industrial Computing Systems. EWICS is supported by the European Community.

Little-endians vs. big-endians

In Jonathan Swift's *Gulliver's Travels,* Gulliver, the author's hero, is shipwrecked and washed ashore on Lilliput, whose six-inch-tall inhabitants are required by law to break their eggs only at the little ends. Of course, all those citizens who habitually break their eggs at the big ends are angered by the proclamation. Civil war breaks out between the little-endians and the big-endians, resulting in the big-endians taking refuge on a nearby island, the kingdom of Blefuscu. The controversy is ethically and politically important for the Lilliputians—Swift has 11,000 Lilliputian rebels die over the egg question.

Swift was satirizing the causes of the devastating religious wars of his day. His point was that warring over matters of religious conviction is just as absurd as warring over egg-breaking—that everyone should follow his own preferred way.

In his October 1981 article in *Computer,* "On Holy Wars and a Plea for Peace," Danny Cohen applied Swift's terms to the debate over data format in the microcomputer world. Cohen asserted that the difference between sending information with the little or big end first is indeed trivial, but that *agreement* on a single way of sending is not trivial at all. To avoid anarchy in the microcomputer kingdom, everyone must break the data egg on the same end. Which end is unimportant, agreement on it is. Cohen suggested a coin toss.

Here, Hubert Kirrmann investigates the problems encountered in interfacing both little-endian and big-endian devices to a standard microcomputer system bus. The bus is the proposed IEEE 896 backplane, and Kirrmann recommends that it be little-endian. He favors that approach not as a matter of technical conscience but as one of technical practicality. Ease of interfacing, low cost, and coming developments in the microcomputer kingdom favor the little end. Hence, the coin toss may *not* be the solution of choice for the citizens of the 896 province.

processor is sampling data and that it sends them for processing to another processor. The sending program has been written in Pascal and defines the data to be sent as being of type "exchange":

```
TYPE exchange = RECORD OF
                date: (daytime = ARRAY[1:12]
                OF CHAR);
                IO__channel: (channel = 0..255);
                sample: (measure = REAL)
                END;
```

Even if the receiver program has also been programmed in Pascal and also defines the data as being of type "exchange," it is unlikely that the data will be correctly interpreted if the computers are different or even if the computers are the same but are running two different compiler versions. So an underlying common data format must be established to allow programs to exchange data in a consistent way. At the end of this article, a proposal for a standardized data format is given. Ideally, the agreement on the data format should be enforced by the compilers, not by the processor or by the user. As this is not the case today, the user must have a knowledge of the underlying data structure at least for all routines that communicate with the outside world. So we will first review the data formats used by most of today's processors.

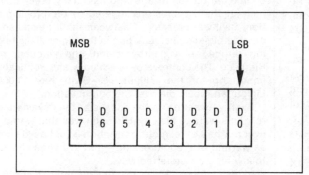

Figure 2. One byte represented in little-endian notation.

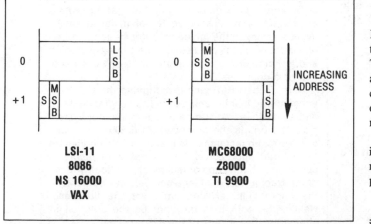

Figure 3. 16-bit integer formats.

Processor fixed-data types

In the following, we shall compare the data formats used by different processors. We will consider only the data structures recognized at the instruction set level by the hardware. We will distinguish between those data types that are *public* and that can be exchanged with other processors, like integers, reals, and pointers, and those that are *private* and are unique to a processor, like the instruction format and descriptors and call frames.

Software-dictated data structures, like sets, files or records, and system configuration tables, are not considered, although these data structures are already being cast in silicon today. We will come back later to the case of the software data structure.

We shall use "byte" to mean an 8-bit unit of information, "word" a 16-bit unit, "triplet" a 24-bit unit, and "quad" a 32-bit unit.

Byte. The only data format every microprocessor today agrees upon is that memory consists of a linear array of bytes. This doesn't apply to big mainframes, which consider memory to be an array of words, quads, or even rare entities like 24-bit or 36-bit chunks, or to some minicomputers like the PDP-8, which consider the memory to be an array of 12-bit units.

Within a byte, we should give each bit a number. Here is where the trouble begins: Should we name D0 the most significant bit (MSB) or the least significant bit (LSB)? Both conventions are meaningful. Most microprocessors today name D0 the LSB, but the TI 9900 and the PDP-8, as well as most big mainframes, have the reverse convention and name D0 the MSB or sign bit. The reasons (or rather unreasons) for this difference are well explained in an article by Cohen.[2] We will follow Cohen's notation and refer to the first convention as "little-endian" (LE) and the second convention as "big-endian" (BE).

We will observe the following definitions:

- In a little-endian format, the least significant digit or bit has the lowest number and is stored at the lowest address.
- In a big-endian format, the most significant digit or bit has the lowest number and is stored at the lowest address.

Interestingly enough, the big-endian/little-endian controversy takes place within the same company (DEC and TI have products that employ opposing conventions) and even within the same processor, as we will see. The concept of little-endian or big-endian is thus not a property of a processor. A processor is LE or BE only with respect to certain data types.

Since we cannot remain neutral, we adopt for counting bits the LE notation, which is the most common for microprocessors (Figure 2). In order to have a reference point, we shall try to remain little-endian in this article.

16-bit integer (word). The LSI-11,[3] 8086,[4] NS 16000,[5] iAPX 432[6] store the most significant part of a word (MSP) with the sign bit at the higher address and are, according to our definition, little-endians for words. The MC68000,[7] the Z8000,[8] and the TI 9900[9] store the MSP at the lowest address and are therefore big-endians for words. We see already that the MC68000 and Z8000 are inconsistent, since they are little-endians for counting bits but big-endians for counting bytes (Figure 3).

32-bit integers. Here again, the data representations are quite different. The 432, 8086/8087, NS 16000, and VAX[10] follow the little-endian philosophy, while the 68000 goes the big-endian way, and DEC's LSI-11 takes a middle way—little-endian for words but big-endian for quads (Figure 4).

Address. Processors normally consider an address to be a 16-bit or 32-bit integer and use the same representation for it as for an integer of the same size. Memory addresses are public data only within a tightly coupled multiprocessor. It makes no sense to transmit a pointer to data in a network; however, in a network, a device name can be considered an address. The address format must therefore also be standardized in a tightly coupled multiprocessor. It is relatively easy to enforce a common address by mapping, as long as all modules agree that the address space is divided into bytes. Here, the little-endian notation has the nice effect that it does not require that all lines be renamed as address size is increased.

Floating-point formats and BCD. Although a proposal for a floating-point format has been submitted to the IEEE,[11] there is no agreement upon how the 32- or 64-bit string representing the number should be stored, so everybody does it his own way (Figure 5). The only consistent way is the Intel way, which stores the numbers in the little-endian format. DEC[2,10] uses a mix between LE and BE.

For BCD, as above, every manufacturer has his own format (Figure 6).

Compound structures. Compound structures are arrays, records, files, or some combination thereof. There are only a few hardware-defined compound structures, the most common being the array of characters, or string.[10] A BCD representation of a number is not an array, as long as the structure is treated as a whole by the machine. Fortunately, all processors agree that in an array structure, the first element of the array is stored at the lowest address.

Some processors require character strings to have a length field, others require them to have a trailing delimiter. For these cases, the structure can be viewed as a record consisting of two elements, an array of characters, and a delimiter or length field.

Urgency of standardization. There is no common data representation among processors. As processor complexity increases, more data types are put in silicon and the compatibility problem increases. The 8080 has only two hardware-defined data types (bytes and words), whereas the VAX has about 10. And the coprocessors now being put on the market are further increasing the number of hardware-defined data formats, and are doing so rapidly. Hence, adoption of a standard data representation is an urgent matter.

Data formats on a parallel bus between a processor and memory

The data format in memory does not depend solely on the processor. Every bus standard today imposes—unnecessarily as we will see—a data format for transmis-

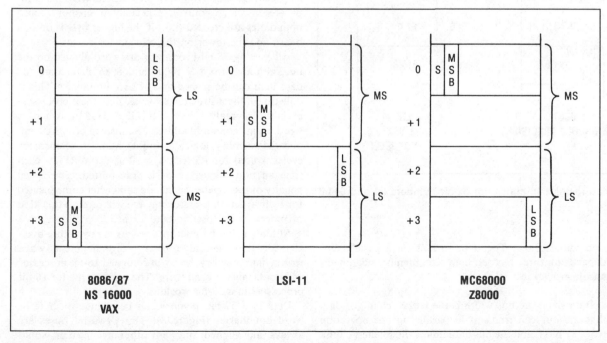

Figure 4. 32-bit integer formats.

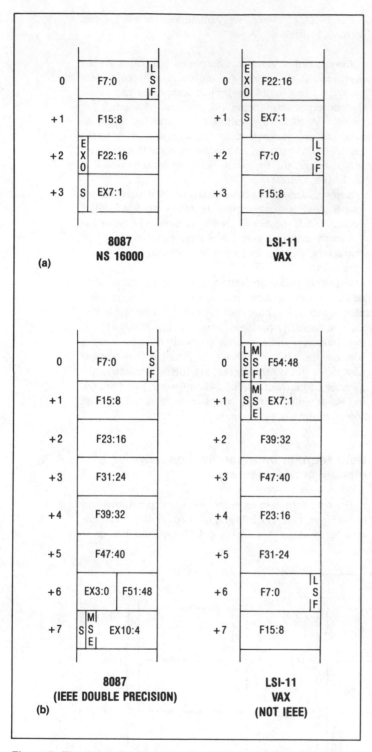

Figure 5. Floating-point formats—for 32-bit numbers (a) and 64-bit numbers (b).

sion and storage. The data format on a parallel bus depends on three factors: data size, memory alignment, and justification.

Data size. The bus width is the largest chunk of data that the bus can transmit in parallel in one operation (e.g., 32 bits), and the bus data unit is the smallest chunk of data that the bus can transmit at a time as a unit (usually one 8-bit byte). In a 16-bit-wide bus, for example, a transfer can consist of a 16-bit word or of an 8-bit byte. In a 32-bit-wide bus, information can be transferred by bytes, words, triplets, or quads. In both cases, the bus data unit is the byte.

The bus width and data unit size dictate the memory structure. A memory has exactly one independent bank for each bus data unit, e.g., one bank per byte. Any other arrangement would require a READ/MODIFY/ WRITE operation for each WRITE that is smaller than the bank size. Just think how a nibble (4 bits) should be written into a half-byte without disturbing the other half.

A memory should always have the same width as the bus itself, since the speed gain of a wide bus would otherwise be offset by having to store data in consecutive locations in the same chip (which requires two memory cycles).

Alignment. Alignment is an additional restriction imposed by a processor on the data representation in memory in order to simplify the interface between the processor, the bus, and the memory.

In a byte-aligned memory, any data item (byte, word, or quad) can begin at any byte boundary, i.e., at any address. In a word-aligned memory, a byte can begin at any address but a word or a quad is constrained to begin at an even address (word address). In a fully-aligned memory, a data item can only be stored at a memory address which is an integer multiple of the item's length.

Alignment is related to the width of the bus. If the bus is 8 bits wide, there is no reason to align data. All 8-bit processors are byte-aligned. Their words can begin at any byte address. All 16-bit processors are word-aligned on the bus in order to simplify memory addressing (Figure 7).

If a word is aligned on an odd address, the memory chip address is not the same in both banks. This complicates memory control, especially if memory-board boundaries are crossed (i.e., if the higher byte is on one board and the lower on the other).

All existing 16-bit processors are word-aligned on the bus, although the NS 16000 and 8086 claim that any data item can be placed at any byte boundary. This is only true at the instruction set level, since these processors execute in reality two FETCH/STOREs when a word begins at an odd address. So instead of more complicated memory logic, a double number of memory cycles is used for READs as well as for WRITEs each time an odd-aligned word is transmitted. The speed penalty of this operation can be somewhat compensated for by instruction prefetching. We will refer to this kind of processor as "pseudo-byte-aligned."

Although all 8-bit microprocessors are by nature byte-aligned, they should respect word-alignment when writing into memory, or a word-aligned 16-bit processor will not be able to read them. The same is true for 16-bit processors in a 32-bit world.

Data in a 32-bit memory can be aligned on byte or word boundaries (Figure 8). Thirty-two-bit buses are always fully aligned, since any other arrangement would require a complicated byte routing system such as a 4

266

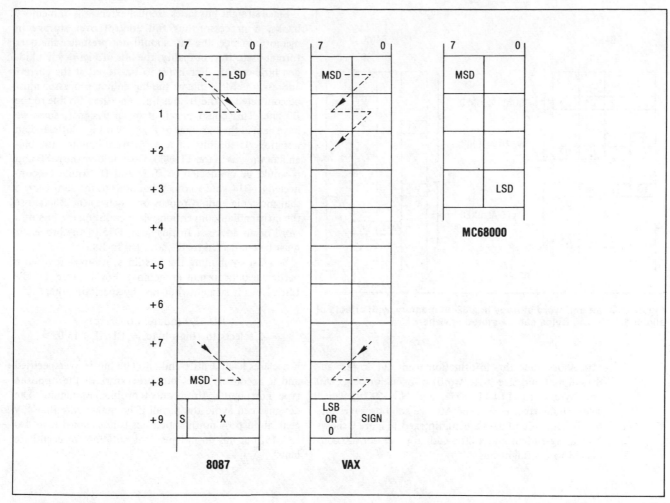

Figure 6. BCD string formats.

× 4 crossbar matrix or a 16-byte switch. Some 32-bit processors like the VAX are byte-aligned, and so they require two bus cycles for every data item that crosses a quad boundary. Interestingly, this occurs three-fourths of the time if the quads are stored randomly.

Full alignment complicates assemblers and compilers and results in some loss of storage, but reduces logic complexity in both the processor and the memory and speeds up execution. Furthermore, the programmer need not be aware of memory-board boundary crossings.

Straight (nonjustified) bus. In a straight, or nonjustified bus, the bus lanes are direct extensions of the memory banks. In a 16-bit bus, the lanes are termed "odd" and "even." In a 32-bit bus they are named 0, 1, 2, and 3, with bank 0 being accessed when the two lower bits of the address are 0. The data path that comes out of all processor chips today is straight. Straight buses include the LSI-11 bus, which has a little-endian data format, and the 16-bit Versabus, which is big-endian. The P896 bus is also straight and it has an uncommitted little-endian format.

Some processors such as the MC68000 make the lane assignment explicit by issuing one control signal per byte lane, e.g., upper data strobe, lower data strobe. Other

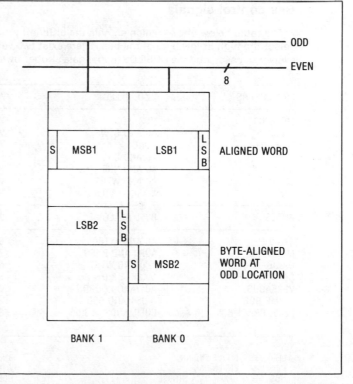

Figure 7. Storage of a 16-bit word in a byte-aligned memory (little-endian representation).

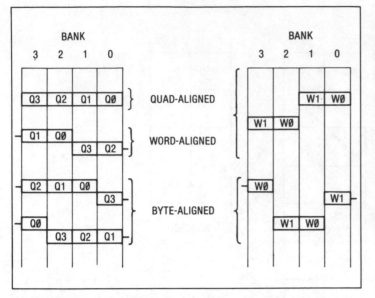

Figure 8. Quad and word storage in a 32-bit memory, with effects of alignment shown. Bytes can be stored anywhere.

Since straight bus lanes are just extensions of memory banks, a processor has full control over storage in memory. Hence, the bus should not prejudice the data format used. But, in reality, the bus of Figure 9 is a hidden little-endian. For bytes to be stored at the correct address, the MSB line of the big-endian processor must be connected to the B7 bus line, and the LSB line to the B8 line. This could puzzle many a designer, since we have named the bus lines of Figure 9 using a little-endian notation. If the bits of a word were counted the big-endian way, as in the TI 9900, D0 would be the MSB and it would be connected to B15, and D1 would be connected to B14, and so on. What adds to the confusion is that most big-endian processors such as the Z8000 use the little-endian convention when counting the bits of a word or an address. In this case, D15 of the processor must be connected to B7, and D0 to B8.

So, just by naming the bus lines, we have favored a particular data format in memory. For instance, DEC's LSI-11 bus is straight, but just by specifying that

$$\text{BDAL0 (address bit zero)}$$
$$= 1 \text{ selects the high byte} = \text{BDAL}<15:08>,$$

processors code this information using the lowest address bit(s) and size (byte/word) information, e.g., A0 and byte/word (LSI-11, 8086, and NS 16000), which select the correct lane. (The A0/size solution saves one line if address and data are multiplexed.) Figure 9 shows how a big-endian and a little-endian processor are connected to a straight bus.

it declares itself a little-endian. The bus is overspecified and it needlessly rules out processors of the opposite type. Fortunately, this is only a problem of naming. The designer can avoid the pitfall if he makes sure that any general-purpose nonjustified bus is not named from D0 to D15, but has an independent notation for each byte lane.

Bus control signals

The table below shows which signals the different processor types use to control the bus. These signals select the high or low byte of the bus. There exist two variants, the A0/byte signal, which is used by almost every processor, and the UDS/LDS (upper data strobe, lower data strobe) signal, which is used by the MC68000.

PROCESSORS	BYTE SELECT	ALIGNMENT	WORD FORMAT
MC68000	UDS, LDS	WORD-ALIGNED	BE
Z8000	A0 AND B/W	WORD-ALIGNED	BE
TI 9900	NONE	WORD-ALIGNED	BE
8086	A0 AND BHE	PSEUDO-BYTE-ALIGNED	LE
NS 16032	A0 AND HBE	PSEUDO-BYTE-ALIGNED	LE
LSI-11	A0 AND WTBT	WORD-ALIGNED	LE
VAX	MASK <3:0>	PSEUDO-BYTE-ALIGNED	LE

BUSES	BYTE SELECT	JUSTIFICATION	WORD FORMAT
S-100	A0 AND sXTRQ	BYTE-JUSTIFIED	BE
MULTIBUS	ADR0 AND BHEN	BYTE-JUSTIFIED	LE
Q-BUS	AD0 AND WTBT	NOT JUSTIFIED	—
SBI	MASK <3:0>	NOT JUSTIFIED	—
VERSABUS, VME BUS	A01 AND LWORD, DS1 AND DS0	WORD-JUSTIFIED	BE
P896, DRAFT 5.2	COMMANDS <3:0>	SUBSET: WORD-JUSTIFIED; FULL WIDTH: NOT JUSTIFIED	LE —

KEY:
LE	=	LITTLE-ENDIAN		BHE	=	BYTE HIGH ENABLE
BE	=	BIG-ENDIAN		WTBT	=	WRITE BYTE
UDS	=	UPPER DATA STROBE		HBE	=	HIGH BYTE ENABLE
LDS	=	LOWER DATA STROBE		A0	=	ADDRESS BIT ZERO

What happens if one tries to store the words correctly by inverting the byte lane connections of one of the processors (Figure 10)? (Forget about the byte switch BS for the moment.) Alas, this method only works with fully aligned words; an odd-aligned word will be stored differently by both processors—in the correct lane, but at the wrong address. At best, this method can be used to integrate aligned processors such as the MC68000 into a little-endian system. If the processor is fully aligned, however, one can even store bytes at the correct address. This can be done by routing a single byte to the correct lane with the help of the byte switch shown in Figure 10. To do so, one must rely on the byte/word signal that most processors give to know when to swap the byte.

Unfortunately, this can lead to trouble. First of all, not all processors issue byte/word information. The TI 9900, for instance, has no such line; it systematically accesses its memory as an array of words. To write a byte, it always does a READ/MODIFY/WRITE. The TI 9900 will store its words the big-endian way no matter what the bus format. Other processors like the LSI-11/2 do have a byte/word line, but the information on it is simply ignored. Like the TI 9900, this processor always accesses the memory by words and does a READ/MODIFY/WRITE operation on the interesting half. Even worse, some processors like the LSI-11/23 issue the byte/word indication, but only for WRITEs. They always read a word and internally select the accessed byte.

Pseudo-byte-aligned processors like the 8086 issue a byte/word indication, but it cannot be relied on. "Byte" does not mean that a single byte has been transmitted—the interface cannot distinguish the writing of two halves of a word from the writing of two separate bytes. These processors will still store the odd-aligned words in a little-endian format and will do so independently of the bus format.

So the circuit of Figure 10 can only be used in some restricted cases; it is not recommended for general use. The designer should stick to the rule that the bytes should be at the correct place, and he should take into account that the words can be inconsistent.

Justified bus. Justification, as in typography, means that data which are not as wide as the bus are bound to the left or the right of the path. A bus is byte-justified if a single byte always travels on the same B7-B0 lane, a single word on B15-B0, and a quad on B31-B0. In a straight bus, however, a single byte can travel on either the B7-B0 lane or the B15-B8 lane, depending on whether it must be placed at an odd or at an even address. A bus is word-justified when only words are justified, but a byte within a word is not justified.

Justified buses include the Multibus,[12] which is byte-justified and little-endian; the S-100 bus,[13] which is byte-justified and big-endian; and the 32-bit Versabus/VME bus,[14,15] which is word-justified and big-endian. Note that all these standards specify a storage format in memory. Justification does not imply it—a justified bus is in principle no different from a straight bus with a multiplexed data path. The same observations as for the straight bus hold.

Justification requires that a single byte be recognized as such and be routed to the correct lane by a byte switch. This requirement is recognized in the Multibus, S-100 bus, and Versabus (Figure 11). Justification assumes that the processor indicates the width of its data; as we have seen above, this is not always the case. Processors such as the TI 9900 and the LSI-11 cannot be integrated into a justified bus.

The control lines of a justified bus indicate two things: the start address and the size of the data. The availability of such information looks appealing in terms

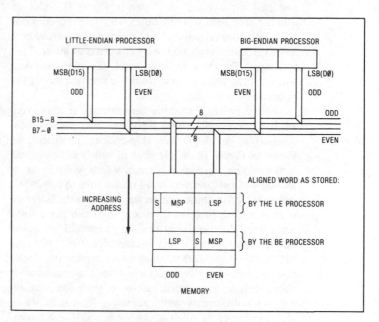

Figure 9. Straight (nonjustified) bus with a little-endian and a big-endian processor connected to it.

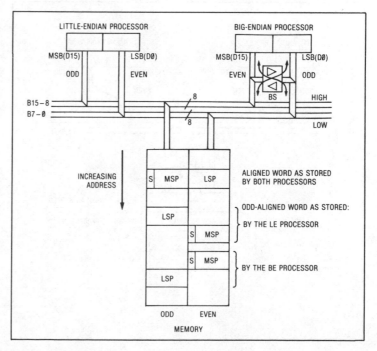

Figure 10. Trying to store words consistently over a straight bus.

269

of ensuring data format compatibility. One gives the start address of a data item and its size, and the bus interface is responsible for accessing the memory in the correct way. However, the data format will be defined only if one also indicates which half of the word is the MSP and which is the LSP. As shown in Figure 11, the justified bus respects the storage of bytes in memory, but handles words inconsistently.

The above-mentioned buses impose a data format in memory by coupling the odd/even with the high/low-byte indications. Strictly following these standards, one should be able to achieve a common data format by connecting the processors as shown in Figure 12. Alas, as was the case with straight buses, this method does not allow consistent storage of odd-aligned words. And here again one cannot rely on the byte/word indication of the processor. For these reasons, great care must be taken when interfacing a processor with a justified bus of the opposite data format.

There is potential trouble, for example, in connecting an 8086 or an NS 16000 (little-endians, pseudo-byte-aligned) to an S-100 bus (big-endian, jusitified), as shown in Figure 12. While aligned words will be stored in the correct big-endian format, words which begin at an odd address (and which are transmitted in two bytes) will be stored the little-endian way, because the interface is unable to distinguish the transfer of two halves of a word from the transfer of two single bytes. This should not greatly affect a big-endian processor like the MC68000 or the Z8000, since these processors cannot read odd-aligned words anyway. But the programmer should not access a word byte-wise, since the program will work differently when accessing local memory or global memory or when accessing an odd- or an even-aligned word.

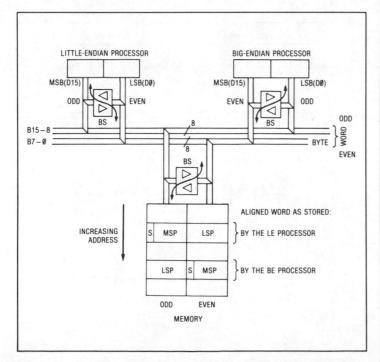

Figure 11. Interfacing a little-endian and a big-endian to a justified bus.

Why justify a bus?

Justification does not guarantee data format consistency—on the contrary, some processor types are ruled out when a bus is justified. So why are buses justified?

Justification allows communication between buses of different physical width. For instance, the Multibus is justified to let 16-bit processors communicate with 8-bit peripherals. Justification requires a certain overhead in order to route data to the correct place, since the processor bus is always straight. This overhead consists of a single byte switch in a 16-bit system, but four are required in a 32-bit system. Figure 1 shows the logic required to route data for processors of different data width in a little-endian system. Let us compare this configuration with the same configuration on a straight bus (Figure 2). Here, each module must have access to all byte lanes. This puts the overhead of interfacing on the smaller systems. In a justified bus, transfers are always optimized for the participant with the smallest data path, e.g., for 8-bit devices in a byte-justified bus. The burden of compatibility is put on modules with wider data paths, e.g., on 16-bit modules in the Multibus.

In a mixed system comprising modules of different data widths, there are two reasons why one should introduce justification:

- To minimize cost. Since the majority of modules are of small width, overall cost can be reduced by burdening compatibility on the widest modules. This was the case at the time the Multibus was introduced.
- To accommodate smaller modules that do not have access to the whole width of the data path. The Versabus/VME bus is word-justified, since 16-bit systems do not have access to the full width of the 32-bit data path. (The higher data lines D16-D31 are on the second, facultative connector.)

Justification introduces some additional constraints. For instance, it obliges large-width modules to always speak in the language of small-width modules when dealing with them. A 16-bit module in a Multibus system must always access an 8-bit module by bytes. A smarter interface could, of course, automatically split a 16-bit word into two bytes when accessing an 8-bit device, but to do so it would have to receive a reply status from the accessed module telling it whether it was talking with an 8-bit or a 16-bit device.

Another constraint is that in a justified bus all transfers must be fully aligned. Doing otherwise would require that the interface be capable of swapping data. For instance, both halves of a word would have to be swapped if the word were accessed at an odd location (see Figure 7 in the main text of this article). This would cost four byte switches in a 16-bit system, and 16 byte switches in a 32-bit system. Fortunately, among processors today none send odd-aligned words; they use pseudo-byte alignment instead.

Justification has been introduced to accommodate small-width systems. We can categorize justified systems as follows:

- byte-justified = 8-bit optimized,
- word-justified = 16-bit optimized, and
- quad-justified = 32-bit optimized.

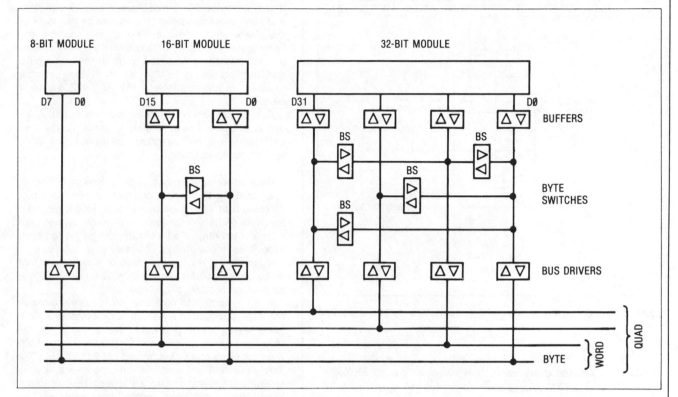

Figure 1. Interfacing 8-, 16-, and 32-bit modules to a justified little-endian bus.

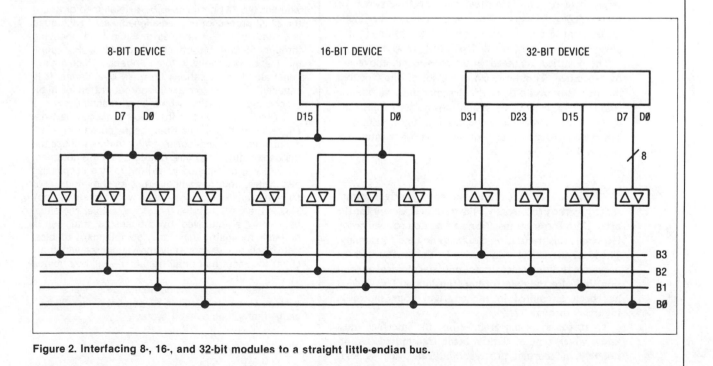

Figure 2. Interfacing 8-, 16-, and 32-bit modules to a straight little-endian bus.

271

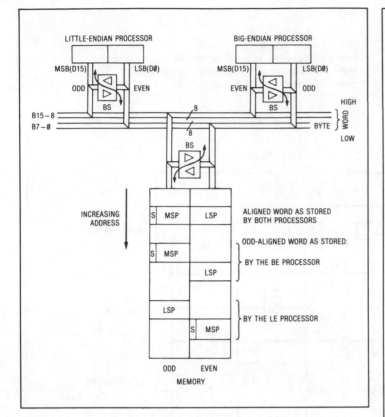

Figure 12. Trying to store words and bytes consistently over a justified bus.

On the other hand, it is easier to put an MC68000 or a Z8000 (big-endian) on a Multibus (justified little-endian), since these processors are fully aligned. The byte/word indication can then be used to indicate a single byte or word transfer, and the byte switch of Figure 12 will work. The Multibus can be made transparent to the processor, but the programmer must always access a word word-wise, not byte-wise.

The justified standard buses mentioned above are overspecified. To interface a processor of one type to a bus of the opposite type, the designer must violate the standard. In general, he should always try to have the bytes at the correct place (Figure 11), and he can only achieve consistent storage for words in a few rare cases (Figure 12).

We have seen that there is no common data format shared by the processors we have studied, except for the byte. Data format translation can be done by *software*. However, this translation can be quite time-consuming. The ideal alternative would be to let the *hardware* of the processor/bus interface do not only the physical adaptation, but also the data format translation. This is what has been attempted in the configurations shown in Figures 9 through 12.

To do data format translation, the interface must know which type of data is being transmitted. Unfortunately, no current processor indicates this. A logic analyzer connected to the processor bus is unable to

Should a bus be optimized for 16-bit or 32-bit transfers?

There is still no integrated 32-bit processor with a 32-bit-wide data path. The data path of the processors that claim to be 32-bit machines is still 16 bits wide, and such processors can just as well be called 64-bit machines, since their arithmetic unit can manage floating-point numbers of that size. So we will classify processors according to the width of their data path, and not according to the width of their internal registers. In our terminology the iAPX 432 is a 16-bit device.

But processors with 32-bit-wide data paths are bound to come. The interesting question is how their data paths will be organized and how future 32-bit system buses will look.

How advantageous is a 32-bit processor? It would seem that the throughput of a 32-bit processor would be twice that of a 16-bit processor, since it executes transfers on data twice the size of 16-bit data. In reality, this is only true if all transfers can be made 32 bits wide. This is not always possible. In a 32-bit system like the VAX, a small percentage of transfers is done on bytes (characters) and not on 32-bit entities. This percentage is application-dependent.

It is interesting to note that this problem most affects one application for which 32-bit systems are currently being developed—graphics processors. The screen is normally accessed as a RAM which is 16 bits wide (for color and symbols) and not 32 bits wide. The only operation in which 32-bit operations are interesting is copying one portion of a screen to another. Most other operations involve only one pixel or character at a time. This bus subutilization is, however, secondary. What most affects throughput is whether the 32-bit processor is byte-aligned or not. If the 32-bit processor is quad-aligned, i.e., if each quad is bound to a byte address divisible by 4, then the throughput will be effectively doubled. But communication is difficult in 16-bit systems, which are not constrained to operations on quad boundaries. It is especially difficult to make programs written for 16-bit processors compatible with a 32-bit machine.

On the other hand, if the 32-bit processor is byte-aligned, i.e., if any quad can begin on any byte address, then only one-fourth of all transfers will use the full bandwidth of the bus. Quads which are not quad-aligned will be fetched or written in two successive bus cycles, and they will account for three-fourths of all quad transfers (one-half of all word transfers, also). This is the case with the VAX, for example. The situation can be improved by processors that use a prefetch for instructions and (sometimes) variables. With such processors, only the variables—which account for about half of all transfers—will be affected by alignment.

Because of these considerations, we expect a 32-bit system to be only about 50 percent—not 100 percent—faster than a 16-bit system.

How should a mixed 16/32-bit system be optimized? There are two basic options:

- optimize buses for 16-bit-wide transfers, and
- optimize buses for 32-bit-wide transfers.

Both options are found in system buses. The Versabus, for instance, has 16-bit optimization, while the Fastbus[1] has 32-bit optimization.

16-bit optimization. The first option means that buses are optimized for 16-bit processors. A processor with a 16-bit-wide data path interfaces only to a 16-bit bus (Figure 1). The 32-bit bus is then word-justified, which has the nice side effect that a bus subset with less pins can be made for 16-bit processors.

The burden of interfacing is put on the 32-bit modules. Every 32-bit module must have a word switch in the form of two additional 8-bit buffers. These buffers can be efficiently implemented within the pro-

cessor itself with no cost or delay penalty. Thirty-two-bit-wide memories must also have a word switch, although integrating that switch will be difficult. The total delay introduced by these additional buffers is normally negligible (about 30 nanoseconds).

An obvious disadvantage of this scheme is that a 32-bit processor can only communicate with a 16-bit memory by accessing it word-wise; i.e., it must know in advance whether it communicates with a 16- or a 32-bit memory. The communication protocol must ensure that the two participants in a data transfer always communicate on the level of the smallest data width.

32-bit optimization. In a 32-bit optimized system, the data path on the system bus is always 32 bits wide. Sixteen-bit systems that interface to this bus must have access to all 32 lines (Figure 2). Sixteen-bit devices are penalized by 16 additional bus drivers.

All memories ought to be 32 bits wide in a 32-bit optimized system. A 16-bit memory makes little sense,

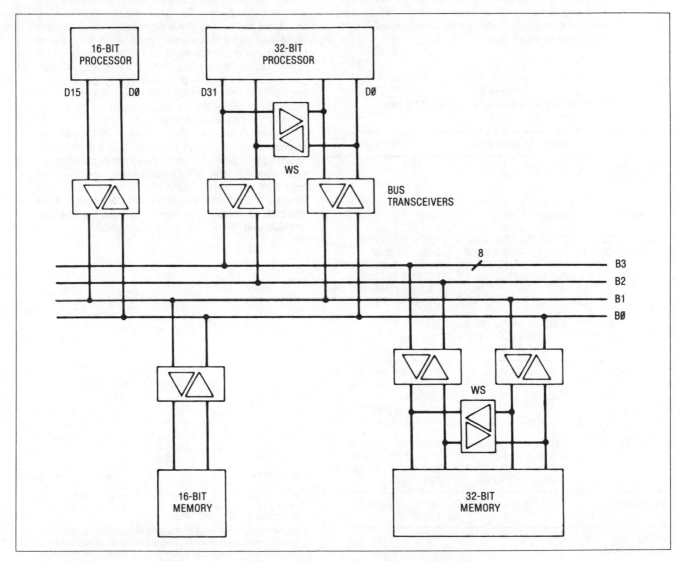

Figure 1. 32-bit bus optimized for 16-bit processors, with 16- and 32-bit devices attached.

but it may be required for operations such as accessing internal registers. However, a processor needs no knowledge of the memory's width, since a 16-bit memory will appear to the bus to be a (slow) 32-bit memory.

There is no time delay involved in a 32-bit optimized system. This solution requires additional power drivers, however. The 32-bit optimization also prevents the building of a 16-bit bus subset, which may be either an annoyance or a blessing, according to one's system philosophy.

Comparison. The 16- and 32-bit optimizations have about the same number of advantages and disadvantages (Table 1). We assume that future 32-bit processors will be tailored for high throughput but will nevertheless retain 16-bit compatibility to ease their introduction and lower system costs. For high throughput, a processor should be able to communicate without overhead with a 32-bit memory. To do this, a 32-bit processor must be able to independently steer each byte lane, either with a strobe (or a mask bit) per lane, or with a data length indication (byte/word/triplet/quad) plus the address at which the data should begin. (Each representation can be partially mapped onto the other, the second being somewhat more elegant.)

In the interest of 16-bit compatibility, a 32-bit processor should probably have a 16-bit mode which uses word justification. Its internal shifter should allow the processor to perform justification at no cost. Although high throughput requires full alignment, 16-bit compatibility asks for byte alignment. Again, byte alignment is cheap to achieve internally, but programmers should be encouraged to use full alignment whenever possible.

To be integrated into a justified bus system, a 32-bit processor must issue data size information, even for READs. In the interest of compatibility and ease of program debugging, the processor should indicate on which type of data it is operating. This requirement goes further than just bus format compatibility and paves the way for a consistent system-wide object architecture.

Rationale for a 32-bit bus data format. There were several reasons why the EDISG chose a little-endian representation for its proposal[2] for the IEEE P896 backplane bus. One was that all 16-bit BE microprocessors (the MC68000, Z8000, and TI 9900) are word-aligned. Except for the TI 9900, which has no byte/word indication, these processors can be easily integrated into a little-endian world with a byte switch like that shown in Figures 10 and 12 in the main text (if some precautions in programming are taken), while LE processors are mostly pseudo-byte-aligned and cannot be easily fitted into a BE system. So in order to maximize manufacturer independence, a little-endian representation was recommended.

Another motive for the choice of a little-endian representation was that the Versabus and the VME bus are big-endian and therefore do not conform to the representation used in little-endian processors like the Intel 8086 or the NS 16000. Furthermore, the EDISG thought that 16-bit processors will dominate system design for some years to come, and therefore it recommended that the bus be 16-bit optimized.

Table 1.
16-bit vs. 32-bit optimization for a 32-bit bus.

	16-BIT OPTIMIZED	32-BIT OPTIMIZED
TIME PENALTY WHEN TRANS-MITTING		
A WORD	NONE	NONE
A QUAD TO A 16-BIT MODULE	TWICE THE TRANSFER TIME BECAUSE A QUAD MUST BE SPLIT INTO TWO WORDS*	TWICE THE ACCESS TIME FOR 16-BIT MEMORIES BECAUSE OF STORAGE IN CONTIGUOUS ADDRESSES ON THE SAME CHIP
A QUAD TO A 32-BIT MODULE	SAME AS ABOVE FOR A 16-BIT MODULE; NONE FOR A 32-BIT MODULE	NONE
LOGIC AMOUNT	TWO LOW-POWER 8-BIT BUFFERS FOR EACH 32-BIT MODULE	TWO 8-BIT BUS DRIVERS FOR EACH 16-BIT PROCESSOR (ONE IF ADDRESS/DATA MULTIPLEXED)
	ADDITIONAL LOGIC MAY BE REQUIRED FOR AUTOMATIC SPLITTING IN 32-BIT DEVICES	ADDITIONAL LOGIC REQUIRED FOR 16-BIT MODULES TO ASSEMBLE 32-BIT DATA
BUS SUBSET	16-BIT SUBSET POSSIBLE	NO 16-BIT SUBSET POSSIBLE
IMPACT ON DATA FORMAT	NONE	NONE

*Splitting is required anyway in 75 percent of the cases if the quads are not fully aligned.

References

1. US NIM Committee, "Fastbus Tentative Specification," US Dept. of Commerce, National Bureau of Standards, Washington, DC, Aug. 1981.

2. "P896 Draft 5.2," proposal of the P896 subgroup of the European Distributed Intelligence Study Group. (Available from the author at the address given in the biographical sketch at the end of this article.)

distinguish among the transfer of a 16-bit integer, a 16-bit address, four BCD digits, or the higher 16 bits of the mantissa of a floating-point number. The logic analyzer cannot even distinguish an instruction fetch from a data read in some processors like the LSI-11, unless it uses some tricky "manufacturer-reserved" lines.

The one indication a processor gives about the data it processes, the byte/word signal, can be used to convert the data format of words and bytes only when

- the processor issues and itself respects the byte/word indication (this is not the case for the TI 9900 and the LSI-11);
- the byte/word information indicates that the data transmitted are a single byte, and not the high or low part of a word (this rules out all pseudo-byte-aligned processors); and
- data are always read in the same format as they are written (this is left to the programmer's care).

Of all the processors we have discussed here, only the MC68000 and the Z8000 are suited for automatic format adaptation of bytes and words at the interface. With a little care in programming, the designer can quite easily integrate these processors into a little-endian world, and the processors can consistently store at least bytes and words, which are the most common data types.

All existing bus standards indirectly impose a data format for memory because they are overspecified. Hence, following the data type convention of one standard rules out processors of the opposite type. To overcome this limitation and standardize all data types, the interface would need to track the instruction flow of the processor and decide which type of data it is transmitting. The complexity of such an interface would approach that of the processor. Furthermore, such an interface would suppose that the processor itself has some knowledge of the data type. However, the processor has such knowledge only for hardware-defined types.

So until processors with standardized data types are available, the best thing is to leave the bus uncommitted and stick to the rule that bytes must be stored in the correct place. This can always be done, unless one uses a justified bus.

Automatic type conversion between processors having different data representations is restricted to very simple cases. It is possible to achieve partial compatibility of data items that are not wider than the bus width if one relies on the byte/word indication of some processors—as long as the data items are retrieved in the same format as they have been stored. This method is therefore not applicable to pseudo-byte-aligned processors and is currently restricted to the MC68000 and

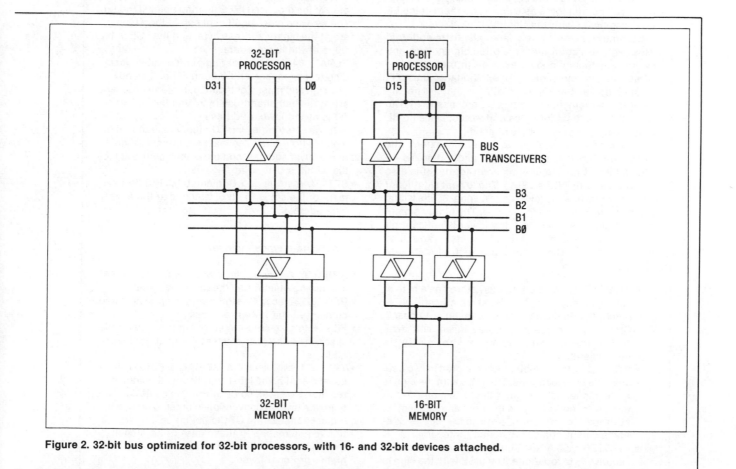

Figure 2. 32-bit bus optimized for 32-bit processors, with 16- and 32-bit devices attached.

the Z8000. The interface does not have sufficient knowledge to perform any other conversion, since the processor issues no information about the type of data it is manipulating and often has no such information.

Since an automatic format conversion at the interface between processor and bus is in most cases impractical, standard buses like the Multibus and S-100 bus should not impose a storage format for memory (e.g., by coupling the "low" byte with an "even" address). The only practical effect of imposing a data format is to favor the processor for which the bus was originally designed.

Although it is easier to only use homogeneous multiprocessors, the simple fact that data interchange media are standardized encourages people to build heterogeneous ones. Before it is too late, a common data interchange format should be standardized. I recommend that this standard be the little-endian format, since it is the natural way binary numbers are represented and since most existing processors can conform to it with little expense.

It is highly desirable that a processor in a multiprocessor system respect full alignment; i.e., an item of data must always be placed at an address that is a multiple of its size. Besides ensuring compatibility, full alignment speeds up execution on pseudo-byte-aligned processors. This is mostly a problem for compiler writers.

It is also desirable that data be read in the same format as it has been written. Buses should be justified only to connect buses of different physical widths. Justification does not guarantee any kind of data format com-

---

A proposal for a common data representation for multiprocessors

This proposal for a common data format for multiprocessors uses a little-endian rather than a big-endian representation. There is no compelling reason to choose one over the other, as long as whatever representation is chosen is consistent within itself (i.e., a processor should be LE or BE for all data and not LE for some and BE for other). One reason for choosing a little-endian format is its natural way of representing numbers. D7 is more significant than D0. Although we speak our numbers as BE, we add them in the LE way, beginning with the rightmost digit.

Communication chips are all little-endians. (However, disk controllers are often big-endians, and cyclic redundancy codes, as used in protocols like HDLC, are also big-endian.) An additional argument in favor of little-endian representation is that it is not difficult to integrate most existing BE processors into an LE system (at least for bytes and words, since no BE processors are pseudo-byte-aligned).

This proposal matches, to a certain extent, the representation used in Intel's 8087 and National's NS 16000. Except for the floating-point format, it is also compatible with DEC's LSI-11. The lowest significant bit of a datum has the lowest numbering, 0. Bits within a datum are numbered in decimal. The higher significant bit appears to the left, the lower significant bit to the right (e.g., AD $<31...0>$ and not AD$<0...31>$). The following types of data are defined:

- INTEGER_8: An 8 bit integer, stored as a byte at any byte address. The least significant bit is number 0 and the most significant bit is number 7.
- CHAR_8: A character, stored in an 8-bit byte. ASCII format with even or no parity is recommended.
- INTEGER_16: A 16-bit integer, stored in two consecutive byte locations. The MSB with the sign is at the higher address, and the LSB in bit D0 is at the lowest address. This integer can represent an address <unsigned_integer> or a 2's-complement number <signed_integer>.
- INTEGER_32: A 32-bit integer, stored in four consecutive byte locations. The MSB with the sign is at the higher address, and the LSB in bit D0 is at the lowest address. This integer can represent an address <unsigned_integer> or a 2's-complement number <signed_integer>.
- INTEGER_64: A 64-bit integer, stored in four consecutive byte locations. The MSB with the sign is at the higher address, and the LSB in bit D0 is at the lowest address.
- FLOAT_32: A 32-bit floating-point number according to the proposed IEEE floating-point standard. The sign and most significant part of the exponent are at the higher address byte, and the LSB in bit D0 is at the lower address.
- FLOAT_64: A 64-bit floating-point number according to the proposed IEEE floating-point standard. The sign and most significant part of the exponent are at the higher address byte, and the LSB in bit D0 is at the lowest address.
- BCD_X: A string of x BCD numbers, each filling a nibble (four bits). The least significant nibble is at the lower address, and the least significant nibble within a byte is at D<3:0>.
- SET_X: A string of x Boolean bits. The first element of the set is in bit 0, which is at the lowest byte address.

Compound data types include

- ARRAYS: An array is stored with its lowest numbering element at the lowest address.
- RECORD: A record is stored with the first declared element at the lowest address.
- FILE: File elements are stored in the order a file is scanned, the first element being at the lowest address.
- TRANSMISSION ON A SERIAL MEDIUM: In a serial medium, the least significant bit is transmitted first. However, some arithmetic operations require the reverse convention in order to reduce the logic. Examples are CRC calculation and arbitration (comparison). In these cases, the breach in the convention should not appear at the next higher protocol layer.

patibility. On the contrary, it makes it difficult for a processor using one format to work on a bus which has the opposite format.

In future communication protocols, information about the type of the data should be transmitted along with the data itself in a standardized coded form.[16] This would greatly ease debugging and monitoring of distributed systems. In the meantime, it is good practice only to transmit 8-bit entities, like characters and 8-bit integers. The increased bandwidth of today's communication systems should lead designers to transmit data more and more in cleartext (ASCII) instead of compressed code. ■

References

1. A. A. Allison, "Status Report on the P896 Backplane Bus," *IEEE Micro,* Vol. 1, No. 1, Feb. 1981, pp. 67-82.

2. D. Cohen, "On Holy Wars and a Plea for Peace," *Computer,* Vol. 14, No. 10, Oct. 1981, pp. 48-54.

3. "Floating Point," chap. 10 in *Microcomputer Processor Handbook 1979/80,* Digital Equipment Corp., Maynard, MA, 1979.

4. *The 8086 Family User's Manual—Numeric Supplement,* Pub. No. S-21, Intel Corp., Santa Clara, CA, July 1979.

5. *16032 High-Performance Microprocessor,* National Semiconductor Corp., Santa Clara, CA, Apr. 1982.

6. *iAPX 43201/02 VLSI General Data Processor,* Intel Corp., Santa Clara, CA, 1981.

7. *MC68000 User's Guide,* chap. 2, Motorola, Inc., Austin, TX, 1979.

8. *AmZ8000 Microprocessor Specifications,* Advanced Micro Devices, Inc., Sunnyvale, CA, 1979, p. 17.

9. *9900 Family Systems Design and Data Book,* chap. 5, Texas Instruments, Inc., Dallas, TX, 1978.

10. *VAX-11/780 Architecture Handbook,* chap. 4, Digital Equipment Corp., Maynard, MA, 1977.

11. IEEE Task P754, "A Proposed Standard for Binary Floating-Point Arithmetic," *Computer,* Vol. 14, No. 3, Mar. 1981, pp. 51-62.

12. *Microcomputer System Bus (IEEE Standard 796-1983),* Institute of Electrical and Electronics Engineers, Inc., New York, 1983. (This is the IEEE standard for the Multibus.)

13. *Interface Devices (IEEE Standard 696-1983),* Institute of Electrical and Electronics Engineers, Inc., New York, 1983. (This is the IEEE standard for the S-100 bus.)

14. *Versabus Specification Manual,* Pub. No. M68KVBS(D4), Motorola, Inc., Phoenix, AZ, May 1981.

15. *VME Bus Specification Manual,* Pub. No. M68KVMEB(D1), Motorola, Inc., Phoenix, AZ, Oct. 1981.

16. M. Herlihy and B. Liskov, "Communicating Abstract Values in Messages," Tech. Memo. 200, Computation Structures Group, MIT, Cambridge, MA, Oct. 1980.

Hubert D. Kirrmann is a research engineer at the Brown, Boveri & Company Research Center in Baden, Switzerland. He taught for several years at the District University of Bogota, Colombia, and he has worked as an R&D engineer in the field of transducers. He is currently involved in a multiprocessor project for process control and in computer bus standardization activities. His research interests include computer architecture and fault-tolerant systems.

A member of the IEEE, the ACM, and EWICS, Kirrmann received the MS degree in electrical engineering from the Swiss Federal Institute of Technology, Zürich, in 1970.

Kirrmann's address is Brown, Boveri & Company, Research Center, CH-5405 Baden-Dättwil, Switzerland.

MICROPROCESSORS & MICROCOMPUTERS
MICROPROCESSORS & MICROCOMPUTERS

SELECTED REPRINTS ON MICROPROCESSORS & MICROCOMPUTERS

**SECTION 6
SOFTWARE**

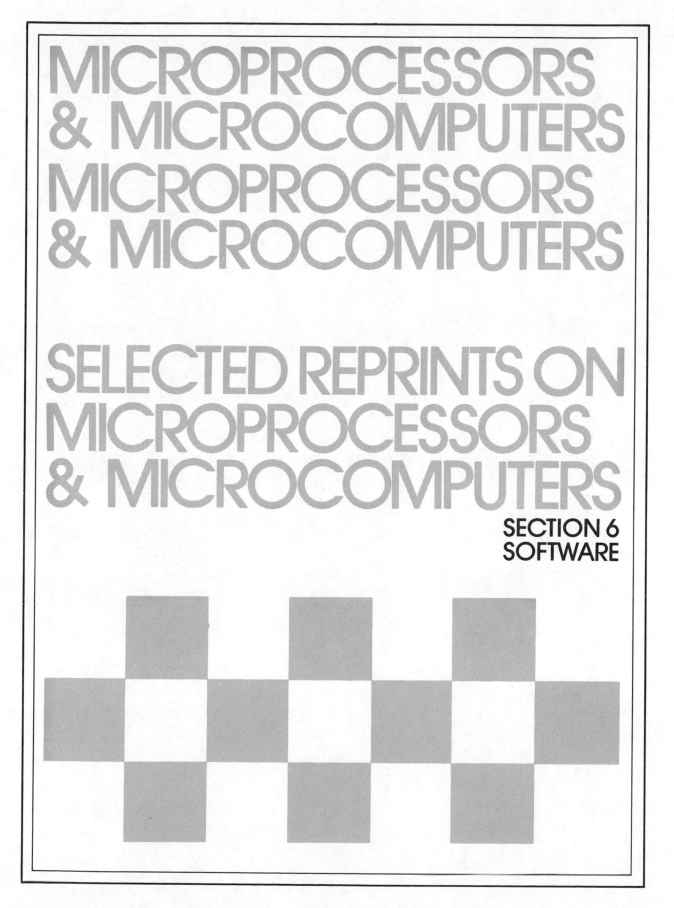

*Language selection for a specific microprocessor application is often
based on an individual's hesitancy to learn a new language or
on imposed requirements. It shouldn't be.*

Selecting a Programming Language, Compiler, and Support Environment: Method and Example

Gordon E. Anderson, TRW-Fujitsu, and Kenneth C. Shumate, Hughes Aircraft

Quite often, high-level programming languages are chosen for applications in a hasty and unscientific manner. With ever-increasing software costs, decisions of this nature should be based upon sound consideration of the technical advantages and disadvantages of available candidate languages. Although there are times when the situation limits the choice of programming languages to one or two possibilities, there are many other cases where the number of language options is quite broad.

This article presents a methodology that was developed and used to select a high-level programming language, compiler, and support environment for a real-time, military communication processing application. In this particular situation, requirements for the application were well-defined prior to the actual language selection process. Specifically, the target CPU was to be a National Semiconductor NSC800, a CMOS microprocessor that contains the Zilog Z80 instruction set.

Given these requirements, steps were taken toward developing a methodology to select a high-level programming language for the NSC800 application. The process needed to select not only a generic language but also a specific implementation of a language processor and programming support environment. The results of the analysis presented in this article are naturally somewhat specific to the choice of processor and the programming application, but the methodology itself is generally applicable. The predominant consideration in the selection of the language for the microprocessor was the minimizing of life-cycle software maintenance costs. This was especially significant, since the NSC800 was to be configured with 128K bytes of RAM. As a result, it was important to select a language that would facilitate changes

and enhancements to the developed software over a number of years. Note that the choice of programming language exerts a major influence on life-cycle software costs and therefore should be chosen with the same care as a major hardware acquisition. Yet, we have observed a number of instances where a programming language was chosen with very little consideration given to any long-range consequences.

Language selection is often based upon or limited by an individual's restricted frame of reference, language availability, imposed requirements, a hesitancy to learn a new language, or an exaggerated concern for efficiency. However, there is no guarantee that technical selection methods fare much better. Experience has shown that, in reality, many important factors in the language selection are never considered at all. With the obvious exception of the thorough analysis leading to the final selection of Ada by the Department of Defense, language selection is usually based on cursory analysis. Certainly, there have been few methodologies that encompass both broad issues related to the selection of an existing programming language as well as concrete benchmark results.

To make the situation even more difficult, there is also a lack of literature discussing and comparing languages available for microcomputers. This is not to say that there are no articles of interest that cover this subject, however. Reghizzi,[1] for example, provides excellent insights into the characteristics of some languages. And for a more broad-ranging article, one that includes a list of specific, available compilers in addition to languages in general, we recommend the article by Cherlin.[2] Other survey articles include those by Ogdin[3] and Schindler.[4] Additionally *Electronic Design's* article[5] relates languages to their

281

EHO214-7/84/0000/0281$01.00©1982 IEEE

operating environments, and Stiefel's[6] relates languages to their development environment. However, there is a definite lack of published examples of methods for selecting an existing programming language for a specific application.

In many ways the language selection process presented in this article has the flavor of the selection of a preferred computer architecture as reported by Fuller and Burr.[7] In order to avoid the pitfall of individual bias and in order to consider all the technical features of various languages, a study group of eight people was formed. This group collectively represented a broad range of experience in issues important to language selection. These included systems programming, programming language issues, software maintenance, microprocessors, software project management, operations research methods, and the requirements of the application. This study group actually applied the quantitative methodology for language selection that is described in this article to the specific application in question.

Towards a methodology

Languages considered. Our study methodology involved a broadly based survey of available languages, the use of benchmark testing, and calculation of a figure of merit to determine a quantitative measure of goodness for each language evaluated. The benchmark was based upon the specific application, as were judgments of the relative importance of various factors used to compute the figure of merit. In addition to being used to evaluate the final candidate languages, the benchmark was also employed during preliminary testing. At this stage, benchmark results were used to help eliminate a number of languages from later detailed consideration.

At the beginning of the study, literally hundreds of programming languages and language/compiler combinations were considered. This large initial list of languages was reduced through close examination of three major criteria: compiler availability, minor language variations, and clear lack of suitability.

The first criterion was that if no compiler existed that had the Z80 (and hence the NSC800) as a target processor, then the language was removed from consideration. This automatically eliminated a number of languages such as Ada, CMS – 2, SPL/I, Jovial, and Tacpol, which would otherwise have been primary candidates. Note that the Z80 was mandatory as a *target* processor; however, any host processor was permissible. Minor variations, the second criterion for removal from the candidate list, means small compiler variations and modifications of well-known languages. Examples of this are the minor compiler/interpreter variations of UCSD Pascal. Languages falling into this category were therefore eliminated. Finally, lack of suitability caused a number of languages to be removed because they were inappropriate for the application or because they served only a very small community of users. APL, Basic, Cobol, Lisp, GPSS, and others are cases in point. Cobol, for example, was eliminated because, although excellent for business applications, it is unsuitable for communication line drivers.

After the elimination process described above, there were 22 languages in six groups left to consider. They are listed below, along with the vendor providing them.

C

BDS C	Lifeboat Associates
C	Interactive Systems
C	Whitesmith

Fortran

Fortran IV	Cromemco
Fortran 66	Zilog
Fortran 77	SofTech Microsystems
Fortran 80	Microsoft
Fortran 80	Intel

Fortran preprocessors

Ratfor	Cromemco
Ratfor	Software Works

Forth and derivatives

Forth	Forth, Inc.
Stoic II	Avocet Systems

Pascal

ISO Pascal	Whitesmith
Pascal 64000	Hewlett-Packard
Pascal/M	Digital Marketing
Pascal/MT	MT Microsystems
Pascal/Z	Ithaca Intersystems
UCSD Pascal	SofTech

PL/I and derivatives

PL/I-80	Digital Research
PLM-80	Intel
PLMX	Systems Consultants
PLZ/SYS	Zilog

Initial testing. The remaining 22 candidate languages were subjected to a round of initial testing, and 13 of them were eliminated for one of four reasons. The first of these was for slow execution time. All of the interpretive or compiler/interpreter combinations were benchmarked for time of execution and were found to be excessively slow. Pascal/M, UCSD Pascal, SofTech Fortran 77 (part of the UCSD Pascal system), Forth, and Stoic all required 15-18 minutes to execute the benchmark. These times compared unfavorably to those for the compiler languages, all of which had execution times of less than 5 minutes. Fifteen to 18 minutes was judged—subjectively, but thoughtfully—to be so slow a time that there was likely to be an adverse operational effect if these languages were used. Consequently, languages with slow execution times were culled from the list of candidates.

A second reason for certain languages being dropped was that their program support environment was limited to a single vendor. For example, Hewlett-Packard Pascal is closely tied to the Hewlett-Packard microcomputer development system, and the Intel microcomputer development system is tied to Intel CPUs. We therefore thought it unlikely that an Intel MDS would ever support the NSC800. Hence, H-P Pascal, Intel Fortran, and PLM-80 were eliminated.

Third, we encountered a number of problems with ISO Pascal, Software Works Ratfor, and BDS C. In the case of ISO Pascal, the vendor was not ready to release it at the time of the study. With Software Works Ratfor, we found that it offered no advantages over Cromemco's Ratfor, and its generated Fortran was actually judged to be less readable. Finally, BDS C was evaluated as being targeted to the hobby market and lacking in the formal documentation necessary for the intended application. All three of these languages joined the growing list of discarded languages.

Finally, analysis showed that the Zilog and Cromemco Fortrans were in essence minor variations of Microsoft Fortran 80; consequently, they were eliminated from consideration because they were essentially the equivalent of Fortran 80. We decided that if Fortran were finally selected as the best language, further analysis could be performed to determine which of the similar Fortran versions was to be used.

At this point we should note that there would have been some way to make any of the languages described in this section usable. For example, use of assembly language for time-critical and heavily used portions of code might have allowed use of an interpretive language. However, in each case there were attractive alternatives that did not suffer the indicated disadvantages.

Figure of merit. A figure of merit for each of the candidate languages was calculated. First, the study participants identified the important technical features of programming languages, and then they assigned relative weights to these technical features by performing three iterations of the process known as the "Delphi" method.

The Delphi method is a procedure for obtaining quantitative (although often subjective) judgments from a group of experts. The procedure attempts to attain a degree of consensus by feeding back others' opinions and allowing group members to reassess their initial judgments. The method depends upon anonymous judgments, graphical feedback to indicate the degree of opinion diversity, and a willingness of people to compromise on opinions not strongly held. (The article by Quade[8] contains related information on the elicitation of subjective judgments.) The procedure was used to assign weights, representing relative importance, to each of the technical features described in a later section of this article. The weights were developed by distributing 1000 points among 18 language features in such a way that the points reflected the relative value of each feature. Obviously, there are potential problems associated with this process, ones that deal with the thoroughness of the features selected, their disjointedness (they shouldn't measure the same thing), and the assumption of additivity of the values. However, the eight study participants believed the method was appropriate for the language analysis. Furthermore, absolute accuracy is not necessary. If two or three languages are close in value, any one of them is probably a good choice.

After the assignment of these relative weights, three iterations of the Delphi process yielded scores. Each language was studied and assigned a score (from 0 to 1.0) for each technical feature. Finally, each language was assigned a final score by summing the products of every technical feature's relative weight and the language's score for that technical feature.

Stated algebraically, the figure of merit is

$$FOM = \sum_{i=1}^{N} W_i S_i$$

where W_i is the weighting factor for the ith technical feature and S_i is the language's score on the ith factor.

This procedure for deriving a figure of merit is widely known and used in the field of operations research and is described in detail in Churchman et al.[9]

Benchmarks. Of the 18 language features, three required objective measurement: time efficiency, space efficiency, and compile-time efficiency. In order to measure these features, we had to design and develop a benchmark program, code the benchmark in all candidate languages, and measure each benchmark for the three features. Keep in mind that it is possible to design a compact benchmark program so that the work associated with coding and measuring is not excessive.

The final candidates

After the preliminary analysis and weeding out described above, there were nine final candidate languages to be analyzed in further detail, which included having benchmark programs written and executed and having figures of merit calculated.

Seven of the final candidate language benchmarks were compiled under the CP/M operating system: Microsoft Fortran 80, MT Microsystems Pascal/MT, Ithaca Intersystems Pascal/Z, Digital Research PL/I-80, System Consultants PLMX, Cromemco Ratfor, and Whitesmith C. The eighth language was PLZ, whose compiler is hosted on a Zilog Z80-based operating system. Interactive Systems C was the ninth language, and its translator is a PDP-11-to-Z80 cross-compiler. Whitesmith C also had a PDP-11-to-Z80 cross-compiler, but the Z80-hosted version was used.

Selection criteria

The development of a benchmark to evaluate programming languages is important. Without one, important attributes such as execution time, generated program size, and compile time cannot be compared. These attributes, however, are only a few among *many* that should be evaluated in selecting a programming language. A general methodology should allow for inclusion of a large number of criteria—criteria that can be judged under two general headings: management and technical.

Management criteria. There are three management criteria by which a programming language should be judged: development time and cost, system effectiveness,

283

and life-cycle maintenance. All three of these relate to the success of software projects and operations systems over this life cycle.

Development time and cost should, obviously, be minimized whenever it is not at the expense of life-cycle maintainability. In addition, for any given budget, the less costly it is to develop or add any specific capability, the more capabilities can be included overall. This criterion thus favors technical features that facilitate software development, make projects easier to staff, minimize additional software tool development, or reduce efforts to force speed or space efficiency into the code.

Effectiveness is specifically concerned with how well end programs (coded in a particular language) work. Ultimately, of course, the determination is how effectively the complete system functions from an operational point of view. This criterion can be measured by factors such as ease of operation, so it favors technical features that lead to good algorithms, error-free code, and fast execution times.

Life-cycle maintenance is concerned with two actions: corrective action and enhancement action. Thus, a language that results in easily modifiable and extensible software will reduce life-cycle maintenance costs as well as enhance operational effectiveness by allowing a fast response to user-required modifications. This criterion favors technical features such as readability and a rich, versatile set of data structures.

What the management criteria did was to serve as a conceptual underpinning to the study, but they were not amenable to quantification and development of a figure of merit. Rather, the management criteria served as the top-level criteria from which the detailed, technical, and quantifiable criteria were derived.

Technical criteria. Technical criteria represent the viewpoint of the computer scientist, system designer, or system programmer. Technical features of a language should be judged from this viewpoint, but only if they reflect the top-level concepts of the management criteria. These features are inherent in a programming language, its compiler, and its software support system. In order to carefully evaluate a language against both management and technical criteria, it is necessary to develop a list of technical features against which each candidate language can be judged. In the study being described, a list of 18 technical features was developed, and each was judged against the management and technical criteria by the study group. These judgments were specifically oriented towards the needs of the application being considered—a real-time, military communication program. Application of this methodology to another programming problem might result in a different number of criteria and a different ordering of the criteria.

Recall that the purpose of the Delphi process (described earlier) was to obtain a rank ordering of the technical features and that after three iterations of the process, a set of weights was obtained. In order to initiate this process, the key members of the language evaluation team assigned an initial ordering based upon their general beliefs as to which were the most important factors. The initial

ordering was not a complete ranking, only an assignment of the technical criteria to one of three groups in relative order of importance. The features are listed and described below (ranking within groups is unimportant).

First order

Data representation. A programming language should be judged on the richness of its data representation, its ability to provide for integer and floating-point values, and complex data structures such as records, linked lists, files, and trees. Related factors include type checking, effective scope rules, passing of parameters among procedures, variant data structures, and packaging and compatibility of data between separate compilation units. Depending upon the programming problem, some of these capabilities are more important than others.

Control structures. Obviously languages that permit DO-WHILE, IF-THEN-ELSE, CASE, BEGIN-END, and REPEAT-UNTIL constructs are preferable to those that do not. Also worthy of consideration are the nesting of control structures and the ability to read the code from top to bottom instead of from bottom to top. This last attribute implies, of course, forward referencing.

Systems programming. Systems programming is the development and production of programs that have to do with the translation, loading, supervision, maintenance, control, and running of computers. As contrasted with applications programming, systems programming requires the ability to invert, shift, mask, and rotate word, byte, and bit quantities as well as the capability to handle interrupts and place values in absolute, specified memory addresses. The ideal systems programming language would provide the ability to write a complex operating system or a device handler without resorting to assembly language.

Program support environment. A programming language should be judged by its total programmer support environment. The availability, quality, and ease of use of editors, linkers, symbolic debuggers, emulators, utility programs, librarians, and PROM programmers are important factors in selecting a language. Of paramount desirability is a program support environment that provides a workbench of programming tools.

Second order

For many programming applications, some of these language features might well be considered with first order features.

Target CPU transportability. Transportability relates to the ability of a language to produce machine code for more than one CPU. Although the NSC800 had been previously selected for use, it is possible that future applications would use a different CPU.

Extent of Use. The most desirable language is not necessarily a good choice if the only available compiler is supported by a company without a long-term established record of performance and stability. Thus, widely used languages with compilers supported by large companies are more desirable than those from smaller, newer companies. Actually, there are two factors here. Widely used *languages* imply a large source of programmers familiar with the language. Widely used *compilers* supported by large companies or by government agencies imply good, long-term compiler support.

Learnability. Learnability relates to the ease of learning a language, given that one already knows how to program.

Documentation. In addition to basic user instructions, good documentation should include reserved word lists, concise error messages listed in alphabetical or numerical order, and concise syntax descriptions. Ease of use is most important.

Time efficiency. Time efficiency is measured by the execution time of the benchmark program.

Space efficiency. This is measured by the size of the object code generated by compiling the benchmark, exclusive of runtime input/output packages.

Assembly language linkage. Sometimes it is necessary to link assembly language modules to separately compiled, relocatable modules of high-level code.

Readability. The ability to easily read and understand code in a programming language is most desirable for maintenance and enhancement. In fact, readability is more important than writability. The ability for a compiler to generate cross-reference listings is relevant to this feature.

NSC800 instruction set use. In the intended application, the NSC800 was the target CPU. Since the NSC800 as well as the Z80 offers several architectural advantages over its predecessor, the 8080, compilers that exploit these advantages should receive due consideration.

Third order

Multitasking, when made easy to implement by a language, can be a distinct advantage.

Reentrancy and *recursion* could be advantageous in those situations where dynamic data structures are being manipulated.

Compile-time efficiency, of course was measured while compiling the benchmark. The time measured was the time to compile and link to an executable object file.

Transportability of program support environment software could provide the advantage of flexibility.

ROMable object code is a desirable attribute in microcomputer applications.

Results. The final rank order of the features after the weights were assigned by use of the Delphi procedure is as follows:

FEATURE	SCORE
Data representation	137.5
Systems Programming	124.0
Control structures	107.0
Program support environment	95.0
Documentation	74.0
Readability	67.4
Time efficiency	57.2
Space efficiency	55.5
Extent of use	49.0
Assembly language linkage	45.2
Target CPU transportability	31.5
Learnability	31.5
NSC 800 (Z80) instruction set	31.1
Multitasking	27.5
Reentrancy and recursion	25.0
ROMable object code	14.8
Compile-time efficiency	14.5
Transportability of program support environment software	12.3

Lessons learned. It is possible to argue interminably about the features to be included in the list above, and it should be noted that the 18 features finally selected were the result of compromise among many different viewpoints. Although it is unlikely that the results of the study are sensitive to minor modifications in the list of features, in retrospect, it would have been desirable to make some changes. We feel that it is impossible to ever obtain the ideal grouping of features, which are collectively exhaustive, mutually exclusive, and linearly unrelated, but the changes described below would improve the evaluation criteria. As a practical matter, some of these suggested changes were actually taken into account during the evaluation process on an informal basis.

Data representation. This encompasses so many factors that it should probably be separated into at least the three following elements:

- data structure—arrays, records, pointers, etc.;
- data types—the ability to define new types and the degree of type checking; and
- data scope—block structure, parameter passing, dynamic allocation, etc.

Machine access. System programming and assembly language linkage are so intimately related that perhaps they should have been combined. However, the combination would be so important that it would then need to be separated by other criteria. This issue is a difficult one that should be considered by anyone contemplating use of the methodology we describe.

Program support environment. The feature related to software transportability should have been subsumed under program support environment. More important, the topic should refer to the entire spectrum of software tools available for microprocessor development. This factor did have an effect on the study, and an important consideration in the final selection was the potential of using a programming support environment with large disks, a hierarchical file system with multiple protection levels, and automated configuration control tools.

Benchmark

The term "benchmark" quite often brings to mind a program designed to compare one computer system with another, this being the most common use of benchmarks. However, benchmarks can also be designed to compare other things; for example, comparing one operating system with another. In this particular case, it was desirable to compare two things: different languages and

285

different compilers. In comparing languages, the benchmark highlighted the advantages of one language over another; e.g., it compared Fortran with Pascal. In comparing compilers, however, the benchmark's purpose was to point out advantages of one vendor's compiler over another, say comparing Pascal/MT to Pascal/Z. To accomplish these tasks, we designed a synthetic benchmark program that contained a wide variety of control structures and data structures, which quickly illustrated one language's advantages over another. In addition, measured quantities such as execution time, program size, and compile time obtained from actual benchmark execution were also used to compare different compilers.

Three measurable quantities were obtained by coding, compiling, and executing the benchmark in all languages and compiler implementations. These were execution time, compile time, and object program size. The two time factors were measured directly, but object program size requires some additional consideration. Some compilers insert runtime code into object programs to provide for input/output and other functions. Additionally, some compilers insert large, extensive runtime packages into object code, while others insert small packages or none at all. In order to eliminate some of this variability, a special version of the benchmark was developed. In fact, we developed four variations of the benchmark to meet various requirements.

The first of these variations was the "regular" benchmark, which contained the benchmark program stated in a program design language closely resembling Pascal. Its purpose was to state the benchmark in algorithmic form. It was also called the code-only version. The second version of the benchmark contained in addition to the code many comments that provided detailed instructions for implementing the benchmark in the various languages. Third, a version of the benchmark free of all input/output was developed in order to eliminate most of the compiler-generated runtime differences described above. This was essential to comparing differences in generated object program sizes. And finally, an error-seeded version of the benchmark was developed. It contained the original benchmark "seeded" with five errors that were designed to test a compiler's ability to detect and report compile-time errors.

A synthetic benchmark has the following general algorithmic form:

```
Initialize Variables;
WRITE ('Begin Execution');
WHILE TimingControl < TimeLimit DO
    BEGIN
        FOR Index: = 1 TO WeightFactor1 DO
        BEGIN
            [Calculation set 1]
        END;
        FOR Index: = 1 TO WeightFactor2 DO
        BEGIN
            [Calculation set 2]
        END;
            •
            •
            •
```

```
        FOR Index: = 1 TO WeightFactor(i) DO
        BEGIN
            [Calculation set (i)]
        END;
    END;
WRITE ('End Execution');
```

The value of "time limit" should be chosen to facilitate measurement of benchmark execution time. If it is carefully selected, then execution time can be measured with a stop watch. The values of the different weight factors depend upon the relative importance assigned to the type of calculations performed inside the loop controlled by that weight factor. For example, a particular application might perform floating-point calculations 30 percent of the time. A synthetic benchmark could reflect this by looping 30 percent of the time while doing floating-point calculations. The calculation set would perform the actual calculations and might consist of three or four, or even one, line of code. Such a synthetic benchmark can be coded in a very compact manner. In fact, the benchmark used in this study was less than two pages in length. Thus, the time required to code the benchmark in nine different languages was not excessive. This is one of the major advantages of synthetic benchmarks.

The synthetic benchmark used in this study contained many loops that were controlled by weight factors. The sum of all these weight factors was 1000. For example, the weight factor that controlled array accessing was equal to 125. This means the array accessing loop was executed 125 times and that array accessing was given an importance of 12.5 percent of the total benchmark execution. By varying the loop controlling weight factors, the benchmark could be changed to give a different execution time emphasis, depending upon the proposed application. This method was first described by Curnow and Wichmann.[10]

In addition to the three timing and size measurements, the benchmark permitted subjective evaluation of important language features such as control structures, data structures, system programming capabilities, documentation, module linkage, programming support environment, and error-handling capabilities. The benchmark programs written in each language were also used in the Delphi study to assign scores to each language for each of the 18 technical features. Here, the error-seeded version was important in two ways. It provided an explicit indication of weakly typed languages that did not consider a type mismatch to be an error, and it provided a demonstration of a compiler's error diagnostics and of its capability for recovering from an error such as an unmatched BEGIN-END pair or unmatched parentheses.

Overall, the various versions of the benchmark permitted objective and subjective evaluation of the language and compiler attributes. Interestingly, one weakness of the benchmark program came to light during the evaluation. In coding and executing the different languages' versions of the benchmark, the question arose as to whether or not all of the benchmark program code was actually being executed. In order to ensure that this was actually being done, it was often necessary to use debuggers to trace the execution of the benchmark. If the benchmark had, in fact, calculated values that were dependent upon successful execution of all program paths, then this aspect of ensuring correct and complete execution would have been greatly simplified.

Analysis results

Our primary benchmark program was coded, compiled, linked, and executed in each of the nine finalist languages. When run, it yielded measured values for execution time, compile time, and object program size, and these values are presented in Table 1. Also, as a result of the figure of merit methodology, the other language features were evaluated. The weight-factor ranking (out of a possible score of 1000) is shown in Figure 1. Combining the results from Table 1 and Figure 1 yields a final figure of merit, which is shown in Figure 2. A word of caution: This figure of merit is highly dependent upon the specific application. A different application would yield different weights for the figure of merit analysis, a different synthetic benchmark program, and a different ranking of the languages/processors.

Table 1.
Benchmark results.

LANGUAGE	EXECUTION TIME (MIN: SEC)	NUMBER OF BYTES ABSOLUTE OBJECT CODE (NO I/O)	PROGRAM SUPPORT ENVIRONMENT	COMPILE TIME
INTERACTIVE C	:58.5	1286	UNIX	:45
WHITESMITH C	1:00	2538	CP/M	5:17
FORTRAN 80	4:03	3570	CP/M	1:47
RATFOR	3:43	3925	CP/M	3:01
PASCAL/MT	1:36	3298	CP/M	:52
PASCAL/Z	2:18	2304	CP/M	3:01
PLI-80	2:30	4514	CP/M	2:17
PLMX	:59	1759	CP/M	7:00
PLZ	2:48*	2165	ZILOG	4:00

*Corrected for 2.5-MHZ Z80

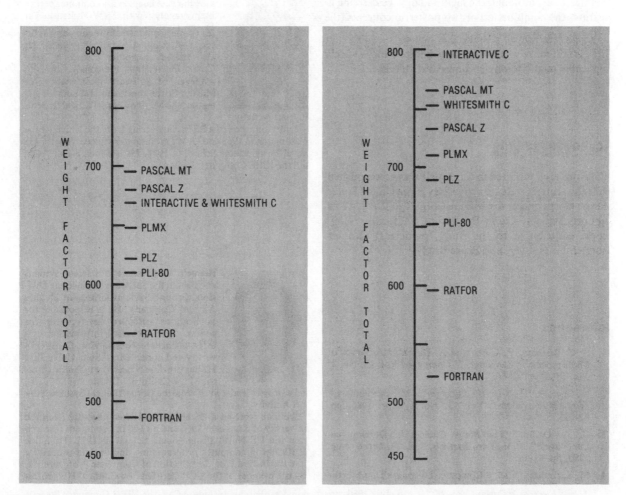

Figure 1. Figures of merit without benchmark results.   Figure 2. Figures of merit with benchmark results.

As can be seen from Figure 2, the results of the study show that for the particular, real-time communications application, Interactive Systems C was the best choice. Pascal/MT, Whitesmith C, Pascal/Z, and PLMX also did well and represent viable alternatives for the application. As might have been expected, Fortran, the oldest language evaluated, was last.

The selection of a specific language for a specific application was the major outcome of the study but is not important as a general result. What *is* important is the approach for language selection. It is not a trivial exercise to accomplish both benchmarking and a figure of merit analysis, but language selection is certainly as important a part of system development as hardware selection. For other than minor programming tasks or standardized environments, language selection should be based upon a rigorous analysis of alternatives, which are in turn based upon analytical and quantitative methods.

The methods described in this article represent an important step toward achieving a general methodology in language/processor selection. The method is still not completely general and objective. In this study, the grouping of language features into three categories of relative importance was in fact highly subjective. Somehow this step needs to be made more objective and quantifiable. Thus, although the methodology we describe illustrates the combination of two powerful concepts (the Delphi method and synthetic benchmarks) to quantify language selection, it remains incomplete, meaning that there is still more work to be done before a more widely applicable methodology becomes available. ∎

Acknowledgments

The research reported in this article was accomplished while the authors were on active duty in the United States Marine Corps and at the Marine Corps Tactical Systems Support Activity, Camp Pendleton, California. Many people contributed to the study, particularly Robert Sauer, John Hooper, and Bruce Brady.

References

1. S. C. Reghizzi, P. Corti, and A. Dapra', "A Survey of Microprocessor Languages," *Computer,* Vol. 13, No. 1, Jan. 1980, pp. 48-66.

2. M. Cherlin, "High-Level Languages for Microcomputers," *Mini-Micro Systems,* Vol. 13, No. 1, Apr. 1980, pp. 92-103.

3. C. A. Ogdin, "The Many Choices in Development Languages," *Mini-Micro Systems,* Vol. 13, No. 8, Aug. 1980, pp. 81-84.

4. M. Schindler, "Pick a Computer Language That Fits the Job," *Electronic Design,* Vol. 28, No. 16, July 1980, pp. 62-78.

5. "More and Better Operating Systems Turn More Chips Into Better MicroCs," *Electronic Design,* Vol. 28, No. 6, Mar. 1980, pp. 223-224.

6. M. L. Stiefel, "A Guide to Tool Selection," *Mini-Micro Systems,* Vol. 13, No. 8, Aug. 1980, pp. 68-76.

7. S. H. Fuller and W. E. Burr, "Measurement and Evaluation of Alternative Computer Architectures," *Computer,* Vol. 10, No. 10, Oct. 1977, pp. 24-35.

8. E. S. Quade, "When Quantitative Models Are Inadequate," *Systems Analysis and Policy Planning,* American Elsevier, 1968.

9. C. W. Churchman, R. L. Ackoff, and E. L. Arnoff, *Introduction to Operations Research,* John Wiley and Sons, New York, 1957.

10. H. J. Curnow, and B. A. Wichmann, "A Synthetic Benchmark," *Computer Journal,* Vol. 19, No. 1, Feb. 1976.

Gordon E. Anderson is a computer performance analyst with TRW-Fujitsu in San Diego, California, where he is responsible for the performance of the company's current and planned computer systems. He also teaches computer science at West Coast University. Previously, he was manager of software maintenance for Marine Corps command and control systems at the Marine Corps Tactical Systems Support Activity.

Anderson received a BS in engineering from the University of Washington in 1968 and an MS in computer science from the US Naval Postgraduate School in 1976. He is a member of ACM and the IEEE Computer Society.

Kenneth C. Shumate is a senior systems engineer in the Software Engineering Division, Ground Systems Group, of Hughes Aircraft Company. He is responsible for applications software development for command and control information systems. He also teaches at West Coast University and at San Diego State University. He has previously been the technical director of the California Division of SofTech, and a project leader at the Marine Corps Tactical Systems Support Activity.

Shumate received a BS in mechanical engineering from the University of Kansas in 1966 and an MS in operations research from the US Naval Postgraduate School in 1971. He holds certificates in computer programming and in data processing from the Institute for Certification of Computer Professionals, and is a member of the CCP Certification Council. His professional affiliations include ACM, the IEEE Computer Society, and Sigma Xi.

Reprinted from *Computer,* June 1978, pages 44-55. Copyright © 1978 by The Institute of Electrical and Electronics Engineers, Inc.

An ordered sequence of stages, well-supported development tools, good programming practices—management backing brings it all together in microprocessor-based system development.

A Unified Approach to Microcomputer Software Development

Tomlinson G. Rauscher
GTE Laboratories

The past several years have seen dramatic increases in the capabilities of microprocessors. Whereas five or six years ago there were only a few 4- and 8-bit processors with limited capabilities and slow speeds, today microprocessors range from 4 to 16 bits in word sizes, with bit-slice processors also available. These microprocessors have larger instruction sets, some with over 100 instructions, and fast instruction execution times, 1 to 2 microseconds for simple machine-language instructions.

Another characteristic of more recent microprocessors is the increased address space, which may be 64 kilobytes or more. With this increased capability the microprocessors are able to perform larger and more complex functions, and thus more and more software is being written for the microprocessors to perform these applications. This means that software development for microprocessor-based products is no longer primarily a one-person job of just writing a small program; rather it is frequently a coordinated effort of several people working together to produce a complete, usable software product. Nevertheless, the unified approach to microcomputer software development is applicable to—and should be used by—projects involving one or several people.

The magnitude of writing a significant piece of software for a microcomputer system can be roughly estimated from statistics given by Magers in this issue. At the typical rate of 10 instructions per person per day, one person can develop approximately 6 kilobytes of instructions in one year. A software product comprising 32 kilobytes of instructions would require more than 5 man-years to develop. If the software is structured so that it can be broken down into five reasonable parts, it would take five people at least one year to complete. In applications where microprocessors are being used, however, one year for the development of software is an incredibly long time; products introduced at that rate might be obsolete by the time they were delivered. To develop the same 32 kilobyte program in three months would ostensibly require 20 people. Due to problems of intercommunication, however, men and months are not interchangeable,[1] so that if 32 kilobytes of software are to be developed for a microcomputer in three months, it is likely to take many more than 20 people, if it is possible at all!

In many ways the development of microprocessor software is quite similar to the development of software on larger machines. Microprocessor software, however, is usually integrated into a system in such a way that the end user cannot determine whether it contains a microprocessor. Since microprocessor manufacturers seldom supply extensive support (system) software, it is frequently necessary to develop *all* the software for functions that range in level from handling interrupts to creating the user interface for a particular application. This affects the design stage of development. In addition, microprocessors frequently support real-time computing systems, which are driven by external events that happen asynchronously to the normal

EHO214-7/84/0000/0289$01.00©1978 IEEE

operation of the microprocessor. Producing software for this type of situation—a process that affects all the stages of software development—is much more difficult than producing software for the bulk of normal data processing.

Many people still appear to have the misconception that microprocessor software development is simple programming. This is akin to the notion that a programmer's role in software development is equivalent to a technician's role in traditional engineering development. Software development for microprocessors involves much more than just writing the machine language instructions to perform some functions. The software developer should be a competent designer, just as an electrical engineer should be a competent designer; indeed, software engineering *is* engineering.[2] In this sense, the hardware and software development aspects of microcomputer-based systems are synergistic, and this is one of the important aspects of a unified approach to software development. Another aspect mentioned previously is the range of functions which developers must implement. A third aspect is the ordered sequence of stages through which one progresses to develop a total product. The integration of these three aspects provides a unified approach to microcomputer software development.

General approach

Figure 1 illustrates the sequence of activities involved in the development of microcomputer software.[3]

System requirements. The first of these activities is devoted to analysis and the specification of requirements for the particular *system*. This first stage is not developing a specification for the hardware or for the software, but rather for the entire system. All too often I have seen companies developing microcomputer-based systems overlook the requirements specification and just design the hardware. Then they leave what the electrical engineers could not do or did not do to the programmers for completion of the product. This way of operating not only ignores the importance of the role of software in system development, but it is counterproductive and usually results in systems that are far from optimal in meeting the requirements of a particular application. In developing the requirements specification for the system, factors that should be addressed are (1) the functions that are to be performed, (2) the performance that is to be achieved, and (3) the cost constraints for development, production, and maintenance. Validation of system requirements includes consistency checking and appropriate management or customer approval.

Requirements specification is often overlooked.

System design. Following the specification of system requirements one should develop the system design. Traditionally the first step in this activity is selecting a microprocessor; however, this step is often overworked, as witnessed by the multitude of comparative microprocessor studies. Many people blindly assume that a microprocessor will solve all of their problems even though a minicomputer or hardwired logic may be more appropriate. Actually this system design activity comprises the specification of hardware requirements and software requirements. The functions specified in the system requirements are described in more detail and allocated to

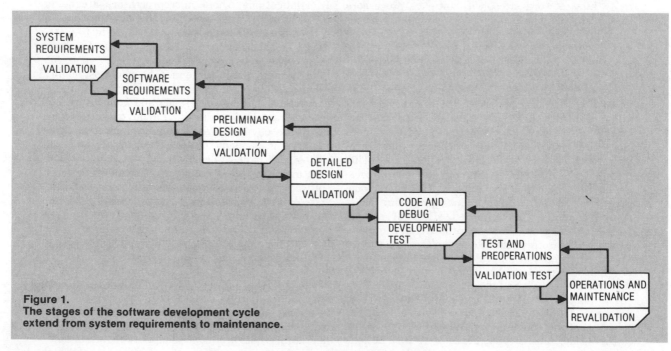

Figure 1.
The stages of the software development cycle extend from system requirements to maintenance.

the hardware or software subsystem, using the performance and cost guidelines.

Assuming that one has selected a microprocessor as a basis for the hardware of a system, one should examine the critical functions that are to be implemented in software. The performance of these critical functions on the microprocessor should be compared to the requirements specified in the previous step. This comparison, together with a cost comparison, should help determine if the system design is valid. If it is invalid, it must be changed. If none of several alternative designs fits the system requirements, then the system requirements should be changed accordingly. This iterative aspect of requirements definition, illustrated by the left-pointing arrows in Figure 1, helps identify errors early in the overall process when they are less expensive to correct.

Software requirements cannot be expressed clearly and concisely in a natural language.

Software design. After the requirements of the software subsystem are specified, the software features should be logically grouped into a small number of interdependent functions with well defined interfaces. This is the high-level (sometimes called preliminary) design stage. In the detailed design stage the functions are decomposed in a hierarchical manner; more detailed descriptions of the functions and their interfaces are added. This stepwise refinement should eventually lead to the point of specifying procedures which will later be implemented in code.

Implementation. In this stage the design is transformed into a language that can be efficiently translated into machine language. For microcomputer systems this has traditionally been some kind of assembler language, but in order to improve human efficiency, designers are making more frequent use of high-level languages. There are basically two approaches to this stage. One is that the person who does the implementation is a coder, a software technician, who transliterates the design on a one-to-one basis into a program. At the opposite end of the spectrum, the design has not been specified to the lowest level of detail and the programmer makes the transformation to a programming language based on his experience. Both approaches are feasible, and the selection of one depends on the type of personnel available and the size of the project.

Testing. Following implementation, microprocessor software is tested. Testing involves several subphases. The first of these—debugging the individual software modules—involves removing the programming language errors and then removing the logic errors that were introduced in the implementation stage. Logic errors may be detected by walking

through the code itself, or by simulating the code on another microcomputer system or a larger machine. Following the testing of individual modules, modules have to be integrated into larger and larger software subsystems. These also can be tested by walkthroughs or by simulation. The last step is debugging the entire software system on the host microcomputer system. This is really system debugging. Note that this type of bottom-up testing would be successful only if the design developed in the previous stage were correct. To ensure this, the design should also be tested (validated) by doing walkthroughs; alternatively, the code-testing stage can proceed top-down by using stubs where incomplete modules interface with completed ones.

Maintenance. The final stage in software development is maintenance. This really consists of two separate activities: (1) correcting errors that were not detected during the testing stage and (2) upgrading of software so it can perform new functions. This latter may be the more difficult, because adding new functions requires interfacing to existing functions, and if the interfaces do not allow introduction of new components, then redesign will be required.

Now let us examine these stages of software development in more detail and describe some tools and techniques to assist the development process.

Requirements definition

To define the requirements for a microcomputer-based system, one must describe why a system is needed, what features a system will have in order to fulfill these needs, and how the system is to be constructed. As Ross and Schoman[4] have put it, a requirements document must address these areas:

(1) *Context analysis.* The reason why the system is to be created and why certain technical, operational, and economic feasibilities are the criteria which form boundary conditions for the system.

(2) *Functional specifications.* A description of what the system is to be, in terms of the functions it must accomplish. Since this is part of the problem statement, it must only present boundary conditions for considerations to be taken up later in system design.

(3) *Design constraints.* A summary of conditions specifying how the required system is to be constructed and implemented. This does not necessarily specify which things will be in the system. Rather it identifies boundary conditions by which those things may later be selected or created.

The written descriptions that specify decisions on these subjects constitute a reference document that will be used throughout the remaining phases of the project.

There are several pitfalls in writing requirements specifications. Since these problems are magnified when found at later stages of development, it is particularly useful to avoid them at this stage. The most significant problem is an incomplete requirement document—generally a result of failure to consider all aspects of the three areas listed above. An incomplete requirement document forces designers to make assumptions and decisions which themselves are usually not documented and frequently differ from the intended requirements. Another problem, which sometimes results from trying to avoid the first, is overspecification. The symptom here is verbosity: Excessive detail can unnecessarily constrain the design and can produce deeply buried hard-to-detect inconsistencies that in turn lead to requirements that are inconsistent.

A requirements document should be complete, unambiguous, consistent, and testable. Because it is difficult for natural language descriptions to display these characteristics, new tools and techniques have been developed to support requirements specification. While approaches to requirements specification may vary, they should be applicable to projects not only from the technical viewpoint but also from the operational and economical viewpoints.

Although requirements cannot be expressed clearly and concisely in a natural language, suitably constrained subsets have served as useful vehicles. The simplest of these are the program description languages that utilize a structured English with perhaps some special types of objects—e.g., differentiation between data and procedures. Such languages are easy to use, and they are often designed for use on a computer. Processors for these languages perform document formatting, consistency checking, and cross referencing of data and procedures. PSL (Problem Statement Language),[5] a more sophisticated language, allows systems to be described in terms of eight aspects:

(1) system input/output flow,
(2) system structure,
(3) data structure,
(4) data derivation,
(5) system size and volume,
(6) system dynamics,
(7) system properties, and
(8) project management.

The associated PSA (Problem Statement Analyzer), shown in Figure 2, takes information expressed in the PSL, enters it into the analyzer data base, and produces reports of the following types:

(1) data base modification reports,
(2) reference reports,
(3) summary reports, and
(4) analysis reports.

SofTech's Structured Analysis and Design Technique[4] consists of techniques for performing system

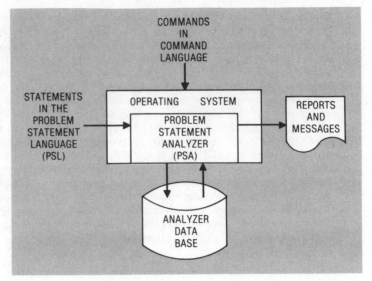

Figure 2. The Problem Statement Analyzer accepts statements in Problem Statement Language, enters them into the analyzer data base, and generates reports.

analysis and a process for applying them in requirements definition. The SADT* graphics language provides a limited set of primitive constructs for composing models, which are organized sequences of diagrams, each with concise supporting text. Other requirements languages and processing systems are discussed by Ross[6] and others in a theme issue of the *IEEE Transactions on Software Engineering*.

A useful model for describing the requirements of a real-time microprocessor software system is the finite state machine. An FSM in this context consists of:

(1) a set of states with a designated initial state and
(2) a set of transitions among states.

Control passes from one state to another when external events stimulate the system. Associated with each of these transitions is an action which the system must perform (the action may be null). An example of an FSM for part of an office telephone switching system is shown in Figure 3. The advantage of the FSM model is that it is easy to check for the following common errors in requirements specifications:

(1) *Ambiguity.* An FSM is ambiguous if for a given state and input (external event), more than one transition is possible.

(2) *Incompleteness.* An FSM is incomplete if for a given state and input, no transition is possible. (Often states may be "completed" by transitions to themselves with null actions.)

(3) *Disconnectedness.* An FSM is disconnected if there are states that cannot be reached from the initial state.

*SADT is trademarked by SofTech, Inc.

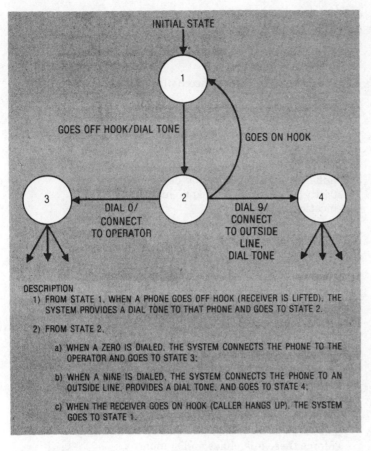

Figure 3. Finite state machine model for part of an office telephone switching system.

```
LOCAL TO DICTATION

REF
PAGE ************************************************
     *                                              *
136 *  1  GOES OFF HOOK                             *
     *  2  * STATION LIGHT AT ATTENDANT'S CONSOLE TURNS ON  *
     *  3  * DIAL TONE STARTS                        *
 59 *  4  DIALS ACCESS CODE DIGITS . "DICTATION"    *
     *  5  IF THERE IS A CLASS OR DICTATION EQUIPMENT RESTRICTION *
 65 *  6     * INTERCEPT SEQUENCE . IS PERFORMED     *
     *  7     (CALL ENDS).............................*
     *  8  ELSE IF DICTATION EQUIPMENT IS BUSY       *
     *  9     * BUSY TONE STARTS                      *
137 * 10  GOES ON HOOK                               *
     * 11     * STATION LIGHT AT ATTENDANT'S CONSOLE TURNS OFF *
     * 12     * DISCONNECTED AND INITIALIZED          *
     * 13     (CALL ENDS).............................*
     * 14  ELSE (EVERYTHING OK)                       *
     * 15     * CONNECTED TO DICTATION EQUIPMENT      *
     * 16  ENDIF                                      *
137 * 17  GOES ON HOOK                               *
     * 18     * STATION LIGHT AT ATTENDANT'S CONSOLE TURNS OFF *
     * 19     * DISCONNECTED AND INITIALIZED          *
     * 20     (CALL ENDS).............................*
     *                                               *
     ************************************************
```

Figure 4. Portion of an R2D2 document describes part of a microprocessor-based private automatic branch telephone exchange.[7]

The FSM models for microprocessor systems can easily be processed by computers and are small enough to be grasped easily when transcribed in a suitable requirements language, either printed or graphical. The FSM model has been used in the R2D2 approach, so called because it results in a "readable requirements definition document."[7] The R2D2 approach combines three elements—a notation, a processor, and a procedure for applying these to the analysis and documentation of real-time software. Figure 4 shows a page from an R2D2 document for a microprocessor-based private automatic branch telephone exchange.

Design specification

Specification of microprocessor software design involves analyzing requirements and describing software modules and their interfaces in detail. This phase of development is primarily concerned with the abstract structure and behavior of the target system, not with implementation details. It is assumed that one has an unambiguous, complete, consistent, machine-independent requirements document before initiating software design.

The first step in design specification is grouping the software functions identified in the requirements document into a small number (usually three to eight) of interdependent areas. The descriptions of these functional areas should be consolidated and the interfaces—i.e., the information passed among these functional areas should be described. This information constitutes the first level of functional decomposition and represents the high-level (or preliminary) design.

The second step in design specification involves

(1) the examination of the functions and information structures defined previously,

(2) the expansion of primitives expressed therein to provide more detail, and

(3) the grouping of this detailed information into subfunctions and their interfaces.

This process proceeds through several iterations to the point where functional decomposition becomes procedural decomposition—i.e., where functions are described in terms of algorithms which effect them, and information structures are described in terms of data structures used by the algorithms. This iterative design process incorporates several well known techniques:

(1) *Stepwise refinement.*[8] The sequence of steps which repeatedly breaks up tasks into subtasks and similarly refines data structures.

(2) *Top-down design.* Beginning with a firm, fixed requirements specification, top-down design organizes and develops the control structure of a program through stepwise refinement.

(3) *Hierarchical decomposition.* Provides guidelines on the amount of additional detail between successive refinement steps.

(4) *Modularity.* Provides guidelines on the passing of information among functions on a given level.

The result of the design process is a document, organized in a tree-structured manner as illustrated in Figure 5, whose lowest-level descriptions provide templates for the components of the software system. A useful goal is limiting specification of these templates (and other design components) to a single page of description.

A good design avoids errors in several ways:[1]

• the partitioning of modules avoids system bugs,

• the suppression of detail makes flaws in the structure more apparent,

• the small size of the components permits their comprehension by single individuals, and

• the design can be reviewed (through walk-throughs) and tested at each of its refinement steps, so testing can start earlier and focus on the proper level of detail at each step.

Since the cost of fixing errors increases exponentially with the time after project initiation, this last reason makes the design approach we have discussed especially important.

As observed recently by Boehm, "Most software design is still done bottom-up, by developing software components before addressing interface and integration issues."[3] This approach frequently leads to designs that are found to be invalid late in the development process; as already mentioned, such designs are costly to correct. Other pitfalls in developing a design are

• inconsistencies between levels in the amount of detail added,

• inconsistencies in interface definitions between design modules,

• introducing too much generality in a decomposition (which later results in an inefficient implementation).

These problems may be overcome by developing and adhering to standards for decomposition and by strictly considering the requirements and design specifications.

The cost of fixing errors increases exponentially with time.

Although "software design is still almost completely a manual process,"[3] some tools can facilitate the process. The most common tool is the program design language, which provides the following benefits:[9]

• The expression of a design in a design language permits extensive computer assisted checking.

• The design language can serve as a basis for the definition of design guidelines and standards and allow the preparation of systems that enforce these guidelines and standards.

• The syntactic structure of the language permits partitioning of a design description and manipulation in conjunction with a data management system.

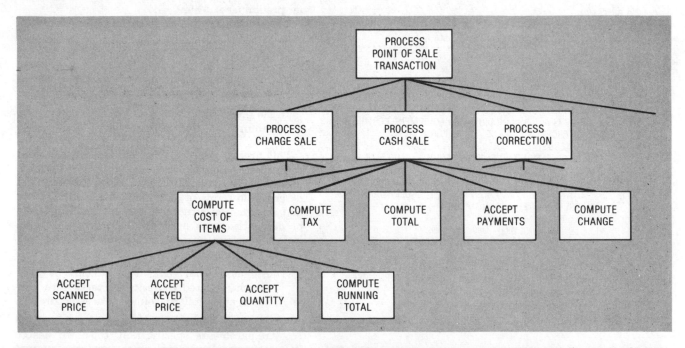

Figure 5. One end product of design techniques such as stepwise refinement, top-down design, hierarchical de- composition, and modularity is a tree-structured diagram in which the blocks correspond to the basic components of the software system.

In addition to PSL and SADT, which provide some design description capabilities, other facilities have been developed. Among the better known techniques is HIPO (hierarchy plus input-process-output), developed by IBM.[10] HIPO represents software design as a hierarchy of modules, represented graphically, each with a description of its inputs, outputs, and the associated transformation process. Figure 6 shows part of a HIPO diagram.

Another machine-processable design facility is the Program Design Language developed by Caine, Farber, and Gordon. According to the guide,[11] "A design in PDL is written in structured English which is then input to the PDL processor. Input to the processor consists of control information plus designs for procedures. The output is a working design document consisting of a table of contents, a listing of the segments (procedures) automatically formatted, a display of the procedure calling tree, and a cross-reference of the procedure calls." Other design techniques and tools are discussed by Boehm,[3] Peters and Tripp,[12] Riddle et al,[9] and Ulrickson.[13]

Returning to the FSM model, one can see that the design step of grouping functions involves looking for similar responses that appear throughout the FSM. This grouping into a high-level design (or architecture) is followed by the redefinition of the primitive responses in more specific terms so that they can be realized by software.

Implementation

My discussion of the implementation of microprocessor software is brief, since it is merely intended to complement the discussion in the preceding paper by Magers.

Implementing software involves transforming the design into program modules expressed in some computer programming language. This coding process is relatively straightforward if the design process has resulted in appropriate software templates, which should be incorporated into software components to provide most of the documentation. Some techniques and tools have been developed to facilitate implementation and to reduce its impact on testing and maintenance.

Consider again the assembler language versus higher-level language decision. In addition to

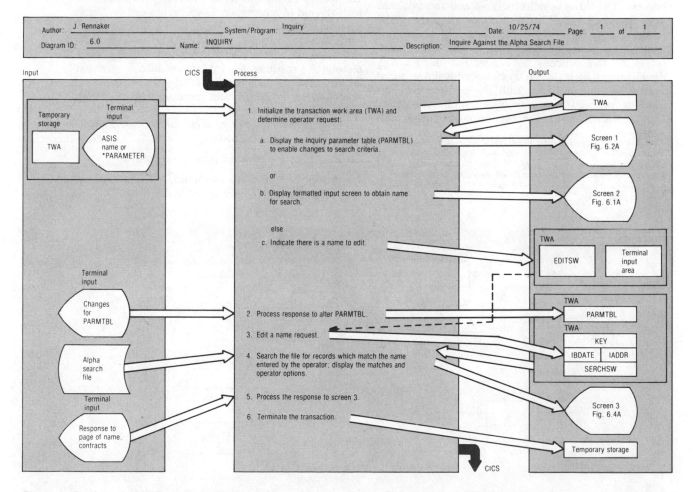

Figure 6. Portion of a HIPO chart depicts the process which transforms input to output as a series of processes.
(Figure courtesy IBM.)

295

improved programmer productivity* and reduced maintenance cost, the following factors should be considered:

- Software modules written in higher-level language can frequently be used in subsequent development projects, regardless of the microprocessor used as a system host. This "code capture" is particularly beneficial in product environments where updated versions of products are continually produced for a particular application.

- More and more higher level languages are being developed for use in microprocessor software development.[15][16]

- Compilers being developed by microprocessor manufacturers are becoming more reasonable in terms of memory size needed and the time to execute a program.

Two techniques which facilitate program implementation are structured coding and top-down development. Structured coding, which refers to standards governing the flow of control among statements in a program module, is a natural extension to the structuring one does in the design process. The three basic structures and two optional ones are shown in Figure 7. Note that the FSM model can be naturally implemented by these constructs. As Baker puts it, "Top-down development refers to the process of concurrent design and development of program systems containing more than a single compilable unit. It requires development to proceed in a way which minimizes interface problems normally encountered during the

*Studies have indicated that a programmer generates about the same number of *lines* of code per day regardless of the programming language being used. As one line of a higher-level language program may be translated into five or more lines of assembler language, higher-level languages can improve productivity significantly.[14]

integration process typical of 'bottom-up development' by integrating and testing modules as soon as they are developed."[17]

A useful tool for project management, communication, and control is the development support library and its associated support system, diagrammed in Figure 8.[18] A DSL should keep all machine-readable data associated with a project—source programs, object programs, test plans, etc. Associated with the DSL is a set of operations and clerical procedures for updating, maintaining, and using project information.

Testing

The goal of testing is to ensure that the microprocessor-based system works as described in the requirements specification; accordingly, the software subsystem must perform according to its specifications. The first stage of software testing (debugging) involves removing the programming language errors and logical errors introduced during implementation into individual program modules. The former of these activities is easily accomplished with the aid of a compiler. Logic errors can be found by program simulation using test cases. However, for individual modules, suitably managed code walkthroughs can identify errors more readily and completely. As modules are integrated into larger and larger software subsystems, testing becomes exponentially more difficult, and more sophisticated test methods are required.

The general sequence of steps performed in software testing is the following:[19]

- identification of what must be tested,

- design of test cases to include all test requirements that have been identified,

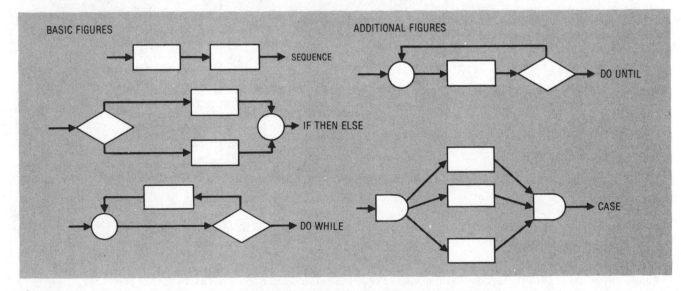

Figure 7. Structured coding employs three basic flow-of-control structures and two optional ones.

296

• execution of the program (or subprogram) using the designed test cases as input, and

• verification of results obtained.

The first two of these four steps are the more difficult. Examples of what to test (which provide increasing assurance about program correctness) are the following:

• every decision statement in the program,

• every statement in the program, and

• every program decision outcome.

Some tools have been developed to assist in software testing. Some compilers generate code that records statistics such as the number of times each program statement is executed and the number of program execution paths. Programs have been developed to examine other programs and generate data to test the program according to some criteria—e.g., to execute a specific path. Other programs can analyze the results of tests and report on failures. These programs are particularly useful in system tests. While these tools are not universal, they can relieve the programmer of much of the tedium associated with testing. Development of testing aids continues to be an area of intense research.[20,21]

The applicability of the FSM to testing is straightforward. The expected outputs for test cases are evident from the requirements specification. That makes the test-plan document easy to write; indeed, the test-plan document should be started following completion of the requirements specification, and more detail should be added as design and implementation progress.

Maintenance

Maintenance is the final stage in the software development process. Software maintenance presently accounts for about 40 percent of the total hardware/software cost, and the percentage is increasing, as illustrated in Figure 9.[3] And yet, as Laffan has so aptly put it, "Software maintenance has been an area of management neglect, little prestige, and only crisis appearance in budgeting cycles."[22] The first type of software maintenance is correction, which is pursued in response to system faults. If the previous steps of software development have followed a unified approach, this aspect of maintenance should be small. Change (updating) is the second type of software maintenance; because it results from changes in requirements, all stages

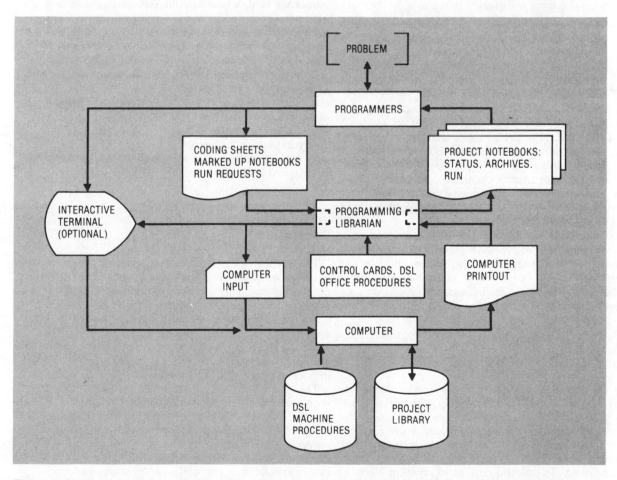

Figure 8. The development support library formally controls all machine-readable data related to a project.

297

of software development are affected. Change may be required for several reasons, including introduction of new functions, changes in the processing or data environment, and need for performance enhancements. The primary assistance needed for software maintenance is management support in terms of scheduling, resource allocation, enforcement of a unified approach to software development, and provision of testing facilities (machine time, interactive terminals).

Common problems

Many problems compound the already difficult process of microcomputer software development. The first is misinformed management. Not only are good programmers difficult to find, as Magers points out, but good managers are even scarcer. The reason is that engineering managers are sometimes ignorant of modern microprocessor technology as well as modern software technology.

The second problem is terminological confusion. Not only are basic terms such as microprogramming and firmware used with multiple meanings, but the software programs from a large variety of vendors frequently use different names to describe the same functions or processes. Moreover, the same name may have different meanings.

Second-sourcing system software could bring the benefits of competition to microprocessor system development.

Another problem is the lack of tools for supporting development. Few microcomputer system projects have appropriate tools, primarily because of management's misconceptions about their utility. This lack of tools results in excessive expenditure of personnel time, usually the most valuable resource in a project. Commercial timesharing services can provide a useful set of tools at reasonable cost for almost every project.

Yet another problem is the differences in the implementations of various computer languages among microprocessor vendors. When one begins work with a new language, it should be carefully evaluated against published standards or a language presently in use.

Some ideas for consideration

Although the tools and techniques discussed above are of some use individually, they should be integrated to form a complete microcomputer software development system that can track project plans, requirement specifications, design specifications, source code, object code, test plans, test results, etc. In addition, a total system should manage configuration control and software releases.

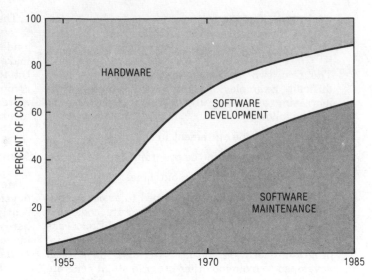

Figure 9. Hardware-software cost trends reveal the increasing proportion of costs going to software maintenance.

Such comprehensive systems have been developed for very large software development projects, but they are equally applicable to software development for microcomputers.

Another idea, which should seem natural in the microprocessor field, is to second-source system software, with several vendors developing software to meet a well-defined requirements specification. The purpose is to provide commonality of languages for use in developing microcomputer software and to encourage optimization of produced code. In general, the software developed would not be the same, but the function it performs would be. This idea would bring to software the same benefits that competition has already brought to the hardware side of the microcomputer industry—i.e., higher quality and lower cost.

Conclusion

The critical nature of microprocessor software development has been apparent in recent development projects. The unified approach to microprocessor software development described here should prove useful in most applications. Although this approach is based on software development for large machines, particular aspects, such as the finite-state-machine model, are of particular importance in microprocessor-based systems.

The availability of development tools, coupled with corresponding development techniques, can greatly simplify microprocessor software development. Even with these tools and techniques, however, software development will remain a problem until the support aspects can be unified into a single system and management provides appropriate backing. ■

References

1. Frederick P. Brooks, Jr., *The Mythical Man Month— Essays on Software Engineering*, Addison-Wesley, Reading, Massachusetts, 1974.

2. S. Jeffery and T. A. Linden, "Software Engineering Is Engineering," *Software Engineering Technical Committee Newsletter*, IEEE Computer Society, Vol. 3, No. 3, September 1977, pp. 6-7

3. Barry W. Boehm, "Software Engineering," *IEEE Trans. on Computers*, Vol. C-25, No. 12, December 1976, pp. 1226-1241.

4. Douglas T. Ross and Kenneth E. Schoman, Jr., "Structured Analysis for Requirements Definition," *IEEE Trans. on Software Engineering*, Vol. SE-3, No. 1, January 1977, pp. 6-15.

5. Daniel Teichrow and Ernest A. Hershey, III, "PSL/ PSA: A Computer-Aided Technique for Structured Documentation and Analysis of Information Processing Systems," *IEEE Trans. on Software Engineering*, Vol. SE-3, No. 1, January 1977, pp. 41-48.

6. Douglas T. Ross, editor, Special Collection on Requirement Analysis, *IEEE Trans. on Software Engineering*, Vol. SE-3, No. 1, January 1977, pp. 2-84.

7. Jonathan A. Bauer and Maurice I. Crystal, "An Approach to Analysis of Real-Time Software Requirements," submitted for publication.

8. Niklaus Wirth, "Program Development by Stepwise Refinement," *CACM*, Vol. 14, No. 4, April 1971, pp. 221-227.

9. William E. Riddle et al, "An Introduction to the Dream Software System," *Software Engineering Notes*, ACM, Vol. 2, No. 4, July 1977, pp. 11-24.

10. "HIPO—A Design Aid and Documentation Technique," IBM, Document GC20-1851-1, May 1975.

11. "PDL—Program Design Language Reference Guide," Caine, Farber, and Gordon, Pasadena, California, March 1976.

12. Lawrence J. Peters and Leonard L. Tripp, "Comparing Software Design Methodologies," *Datamation*, Vol. 23, No. 11, November 1977, pp. 89-94.

13. Robert W. Ulrickson, "Solve Software Problems Step by Step," *Electronic Design*, Vol. 25, No. 2, January 18, 1977, pp. 54-58.

14. Fernando J. Corbato, "PL/I as a Tool for System Programming," *Datamation*, Vol. 15, No. 5, May 1969, pp. 68-76.

15. Dave Bursky, "It's Getting Easier to Program Microprocessors with the New Software Design Aids," *Electronic Design*, Vol. 25, No. 2, January 1977, pp. 20-26.

16. Carol A. Ogdin, "Software Design Course," *EDN*, Vol. 22, No. 11, June 5, 1977, pp. 67-200.

17. F. Terry Baker, "Structured Programming in a Production Programming Environment," *IEEE Trans. on Software Engineering*, Vol. SE-1, No. 2, June 1975, pp. 241-252.

18. Douglas A. Cassell and John E. Cavanaugh, "The Microcomputer Development System," *Mini-Micro Systems*, Vol. 10, No. 8, August 1977, pp. 34-40.

19. Dorothy A. Walsh, "Structured Testing," *Datamation*, Vol. 23, No. 7, July 1977, pp. 111-118.

20. Edward F. Miller, Jr., "Program Testing: Art Meets Theory," *Computer*, Vol. 10, No. 7, July 1977, pp. 42-51.

21. Leon G. Stucki, ed., Special Section on Testing, *IEEE Trans. on Software Engineering*, Vol. SE-2, No. 3, September 1976, pp. 194-231.

22. Anne W. Laffan, "The Software Maintenance Problem," *Proc. of the Eleventh Hawaii International Conference on System Sciences*, pp. 37-39.

Tomlinson G. Rauscher is a manager of software systems at GTE Laboratories, Waltham, Massachusetts, where he directs projects in software engineering and computer-aided design. At Amdahl Corp. he worked on future systems architecture, and at NCR Corp. he led a software technology group. Earlier he helped develop a microprogrammable signal processing computer at the Naval Research Laboratory. An author of one book and several papers on microprogramming, architecture, operating systems, and programming languages, Rauscher received the BS from Yale, MS in computer science from the University of North Carolina, and the PhD in computer science from the University of Maryland. He is a member of the IEEE Computer Society, currently serving as chairman of the Technical Committee on Microprogramming. He is also a board member of ACM SIGMICRO. He received the CDP in 1977.

A Proposed Standard for Extending High-Level Language Implementations for Microprocessors

IEEE Task P755

Introductory remarks
by Richard E. James, III

Over the years language implementers have found it desirable to provide additional statements allowing users to get to some of the features of the hardware and operating system. Such new features partially eliminate the need for dropping into assembly language. With the wide use of microprocessors and microcomputers, and with the growing number of language implementations being made on them, it is time to ask, what is the minimal, common set of language extensions that will address the greatest number of needs of microprocessor users? The proposed standard published here tries to address this question with the following thoughts in mind:

- suitability for common languages (we chose Basic, Fortran, and Pascal for demonstration purposes);
- minimum number of syntax changes needed to implement the features.

Microprocessor applications interface to an arbitrary and inflexible environment characterized by such conditions as hardware-dictated memory layout, I/O via ports or memory mapping, interrupts, and prepackaged machine language subroutines with alien calling sequences. The extensions proposed here fall into several groups:

- Hardware requirements specify which addresses are read-only (ROM), which are read-write (RAM), which are inaccessible (so the compiler does not allocate code or data there), and which are hardware-specific (memory-mapped I/O). The proposed standard enables the user to tell the compiler where to put pieces of the object program, and also enables him to read and write specific locations. (We apologize for using PEEK and POKE, but they are the de facto standards.)

- Microcomputers are often used in low-level applications (e.g., as device drivers), where they need to get at the

hardware I/O and where perhaps there is no operating system to provide I/O subroutines. Therefore, the proposed standard calls for access to the hardware input and output instructions (if any). Access to file systems is beyond the "minimal" scope of this standard.

- The high-level language must provide for an interface to those things that the user decides to do in assembly language. The proposed standard provides a general mechanism. The new routines GETREG and PUTREG may not actually touch the registers ("state elements") indicated; instead, CALLER may move values between temporary areas used by GETREG and PUTREG and the hardware registers.

- A minimal interrupt servicing mechanism is provided, but, in deference to other standardization efforts, concurrency is not.

- Masking functions are provided to deal with hardware bits, even though such functions may be deemed redundant with respect to other features of the language (e.g., Pascal SETs and PACKED RECORDs).

There are two main advantages to standardized extensions — they minimize the retraining process for programmers who move between machines and/or languages and, more important, they encourage language implementers to include necessary features that might otherwise be left out. These advantages will enhance the usefulness of high-level languages and will be a blessing to programmers who prefer to stay away from assembly language.

The proposed standard provides some portability — concepts and syntax are portable between programs and between processors but individual programs are not necessarily portable, because of differences in environments. We should note that the proposed standard is not as strong as it may seem — there are a number of

300

"should's" which specify recommendations as well as ways around truly implementing some of the "shall" (obligatory) features. For example, a Fortran manual could say: "PEEK is not provided, but can be implemented by the arithmetic statement function PEEK (J) = K (1 − LOCF(K(1)) + J), given that K is dimensioned." It then is up to the user who wishes to adhere to the standard to use PEEK and its definition as needed, instead of the nonstandard LOCF. Note, however, that for the implementation to conform to the standard, the reference manual must include any such auxiliary code.

Richard Karpinski is to be thanked for early chairing the P755 working group. We also thank Robert Stewart, chairman of the IEEE Computer Society's Computer Standards Committee, for believing in standards enough to instigate this work, and Tom Pittman, for his expertise in grammar and word processing.

The IEEE Computer Society is publishing this proposed standard to allow comments prior to its submission to the IEEE Standards Board for adoption as an IEEE Standard. Your comments should be sent to

Richard E. James, III
3705 Eastwood Circle
Santa Clara, CA 95050
(408) 988-3048

Comments should be mailed to arrive no later than June 17, 1981.

If you would like to participate in this or other efforts of the Microprocessor Standards Committee, please contact either of its cochairmen, Steve Diamond or Michael Smolin at

Synertex Inc., MS 39
3001 Stender Way
Santa Clara, CA 95051

The Proposed Standard
IEEE Task P755

(Draft 3.0, December 5, 1980)

Abstract

This standard specifies extensions to high-level languages for the purpose of accommodating environmental restrictions common in microprocessor applications. The extensions include ways to access memory, I/O ports, and arbitrary subroutines; to service interrupts; and to bind entities to specific memory locations.

Foreword

(This Foreword is not a part of 755/D3.)

This standard represents the consensus of the High-Level Languages Working Group of the Microprocessor Standards Subcommittee of the IEEE Computer Society Computer Standards Committee.

While microprocessors are not qualitatively different from the more traditional computer systems (minicomputers and larger mainframes), their applications tend to be characterized by the need to interface to an arbitrary and inflexible environment. That environment may manifest itself in external hardware requirements or in pre-existing software. The failure of high-level languages (HLLs) to deal with this environment has historically precluded their use from such microprocessor applications.

Two reasons for the use of HLLs are

- to enable the application to be conceived and encoded in a language more oriented to the application than to the machine on which it is implemented, and

- to facilitate the transportation of encoded programs from one environment to another.

To the extent that microprocessor applications are entangled in the environment, this second purpose is defeated. This normally occurs, however, in only a small part of each well-coded application program; this part needs recoding for any transportation, regardless of the other constraints.

The purpose of this standard is to extend existing standard languages (which already afford a degree of portability and problem-orientation) in order to facilitate their interface to the inflexible environment of microprocessor applications. These extensions should not do violence to the language and should be implementable with minimal changes to the language processor. With most HLLs these extensions consist primarily of a set of predefined (library) subroutines and functions, which therefore require no language changes at all.

Suggestions for improvement of this standard are welcome. Readers are particularly encouraged to suggest implementations for items *a* through *e* of Section 1.3. All comments should be sent to the chairman of the High-Level Language Working Group, Richard E. James, III, at the address given in the introductory remarks.

The following working group members are responsible for this draft:

Richard E. James, III
Richard Karpinski
Dennis Paull
Tom Pittman
Harry Stewart
Robert G. Stewart

1 Scope

1.1 Languages

This standard specifies extensions to high-level languages for microprocessor applications. It covers computer languages for which there exist either ANSI or IEEE standards, or draft standards in preparation by existing ANSI or IEEE committees. Notwithstanding the extensions herein provided, the language extended by this standard shall conform to the existing standard for that language.

This standard explicitly extends three languages: Basic, Fortran, and Pascal. Other languages may be implicitly extended by the consistent application of the naming conventions and rules for extension specified in this standard.

1.2 Inclusions

This standard specifies

a) direct access to memory,
b) direct access to processor input and output instructions,
c) access to external subroutines not coded in the extended HLL,
d) facilities for servicing interrupts in the extended HLL, and
e) the ability to bind constant and variable parts of the program to specific regions of memory.

1.3 Exclusions

This standard does not, but some future revision of it may, specify

a) specific operating system capabilities,
b) facilities for concurrency,
c) access to internal processor functions not related to input/output or memory access (such as special instructions or functional modes),
d) access to file systems (other than by individual input/output operations), or
e) the effects of run-time errors (such as values too large for destination memory locations or registers, etc.).

This standard does not specify

f) machine architecture,
g) means of implementing specified extensions,
h) resource allocation in the extended HLLs (except in the case of memory), or
i) extensions to languages not compatible with microprocessors or not allowing for library subroutines (except Basic).

2 Definitions

HLL — High-level language to be extended by this standard. HLLs so extended are sometimes known as systems implementation languages.

Library routine — A function (which returns a value) or a procedure (which does not return a value) supplied with the implementation of the HLL. For the purposes of this standard, a short routine coded entirely in the language supported by the implemention, but which the user is obliged to include with the application program, is said to be a library routine if its complete specification (i.e., source listing) is included in the user documentation.

State — The condition of the target microprocessor, given in terms of the contents of its registers, internal flags, local memory, etc. A **state element** is a microprocessor component containing a distinguishable part of the state information, such as a single register.

Shall and **should** — In this standard, the use of the word "shall" signifies that which is obligatory in any conforming implementation; the use of the word "should" signifies that which is strongly recommended — i.e., that which is in keeping with the intent of the standard, despite architectural or other constraints beyond the scope of this standard that, on occasion, may render the recommendations impractical.

3 Form of extensions

With two exceptions, extensions specified in this standard consist of intrinsic or library subroutines and functions supplied by the implementer of the language. Whether a language processor directly generates the corresponding machine-language instructions or simply invokes a call to the library routine is implementation-dependent.

The two exceptions are as follows:

- Standard Minimal Basic (ANSI X3.60-1978) allows for library functions but has no facilities for calling named subroutines from a library. This standard follows the accepted practice of defining new statement types in the place of such subroutine calls. The new proposed Basic Standard (X3J2/82-06) allows named subroutines. For such implementations the form of the extensions should be the same as the proposed form for Fortran.
- Memory allocation (e.g., to read-only memories) is intrinsically done prior to execution; it is meaningless to refer to subroutines or functions for this extension. The standard specifies the means to effect this extension in Section 9.

Other than memory allocation, this standard identifies for each extension the subroutines or functions to effect the extension, and gives the names of the routines for each of the three languages, Basic, Fortran, and Pascal. To apply this standard to another language, the implementer should use the specified routine names in the normal calling sequence for the new language.

4 Memory access

All addressable memory shall be accessible to the program in the extended HLL for examination or modification, as appropriate. An addressable memory location is one which is uniquely identified by only one integer address value. For example, in a byte-addressable, 16-bit machine, the width of each memory location is eight bits. Memory access shall be provided by means of two routines, as specified in this section of the proposed standard. Memory may be examined by means of the integer function PEEK, with a single argument which evaluates to the integer address of the memory location to be examined. Memory may be modified (insofar as the hardware allows it) by means of a subroutine POKE, whose first argument is an integer address as in PEEK, and whose second argument evaluates to an integer appropriate to the width of a memory location. Both PEEK and POKE shall access the specified memory location, and not its neighbors, exactly once for each reference.* The bit mapping between integer value and the contents of the addressed memory is implementation-dependent.

In the following examples, the variable M is assigned the value of the memory datum at the location whose address is in variable L; that same memory location is then set to the value of the variable Q.

In Basic

        400   M = PEEK (L)
        410   POKE L,Q

In Fortran

        M = PEEK (L)
        CALL POKE (L,Q)

In Pascal

        M: = PEEK (L);
        POKE (L,Q)

If the microprocessor supports multiple-location memory access, or if the implementer desires such access be provided, additional routines (PEEK2, POKE2, PEEK3, POKE3, etc.) may be supplied to access consecutive memory locations.

5 Input and output

All of the input and output capabilities of the microprocessor shall be supported in the HLL.

5.1 Memory mapped I/O

Some microprocessors have no hardware or instructions for input or output of data except by memory access. Section 4.0 specifies all that is necessary to meet the I/O requirement of this standard for these processors.

5.2 Port and discrete I/O

Many microprocessors have special instructions to permit access to particular external logic that is distinct from memory. Most of this external logic is configured into "ports," each having some numerical address. A few microprocessors also have discrete input or output lines not associated with the normal ports. The language implementer shall assign "port numbers" to the discrete I/O signals also; these should be distinguished in some way, such as by being outside the range of normal port numbers. Special-purpose hardware registers with external side effects shall also be accessed in this way.

Input from the external world to the microprocessor shall be specified by a function having a single integer argument corresponding to the port number. An implementation may restrict this argument to a constant. The value of the function is a value appropriate to the actual input datum. The name of the function shall be INP.

Output to a port shall be specified by a subroutine with two arguments. The first argument is a port number as

above. The second argument evaluates to a value appropriate to the nature of the designated port; for discrete outputs, the value may be limited to 0 or 1. The name of this subroutine (or statement) shall be OUT.

In the following examples, the variable D is assigned the value of the input port number 3; that value is then sent to output port number 4.

In Basic

        500   D = INP (3)
        510   OUT 4,D

In Fortran

        D = INP (3)
        CALL OUT (4,D)

In Pascal

        D: = INP (3);
        OUT (4,D)

5.3 Simultaneous I/O

If a microprocessor has instructions which do simultaneous input and output, the function name IOP shall be used; its two arguments are the same as specified for OUT.*

6 Interrupts

The extended HLL should permit the application program to respond to some or all of the hardware interrupt capability of the processor. The number of interrupts thus supported and the amount of overhead processing imposed by the HLL (and possibly also by the operating system) are implementation-dependent.

An "interrupt number" shall be defined for each supported interrupt. The HLL application program may enable any such interrupt and attach an otherwise undistinguished routine to it by means of an interrupt enabling subroutine, as specified in this section. Thus, interrupt service routines may also be called in the ordinary way.

The name of the subroutine (or statement in Basic) shall be ARM. Its first argument is an integer interrupt number; its second argument is the name (or line number in Basic) of the routine that is to be attached to the interrupt.** An implementation may require the first argument to be a constant.

The interrupt service routine shall be detached by calling the subroutine DISARM with a single argument identifying the interrupt number, as above. This may also disable the interrupt. In block-structured languages like Pascal, the effect of exiting a scope in which the service routine is declared shall be implementation-defined.

An implementation may specify that service routines for certain interrupts have arguments and/or return a value. This is particularly useful for operating-system-generated interrupts or traps. The semantics of the argu-

---

*This is intended to accommodate memory-mapped I/O, where the act of access may be significant. Note that PEEK may thus have side effects which may interact with the order of evaluation of expressions.

*For example, the Z80 input instruction "IN A,n" sends out the previous contents of the accumulator during an input.

**Both Fortran and Pascal permit subroutine names to be passed to another subroutine as arguments.

ments and/or the value of the interrupt service routine is implementation-dependent.

In the following examples, the routine INTS (Basic line number 1000) is to be attached to interrupt number 3, and interrupt number 5 is to be disabled:

In Basic

```
600    ARM 3, 1000
610    DISARM 5
```

In Fortran

```
EXTERNAL INTS
CALL ARM (3, INTS)
CALL DISARM (5)
```

In Pascal

```
ARM (3, INTS);
DISARM (5)
```

7 Machine language subroutines

The extended HLL shall allow the application program to call externally supplied machine language routines.

7.1 Compatible linkage

If the subroutines can be identified by name, and if the implementation-dependent linkage provided by the HLL is compatible with that required by the external routine, then the calling sequence in the HLL program shall be the same as for normal named subroutine calls. Special directives (such as EXTERNAL) to identify such named subroutines may be required.

The subroutine linkage supported in this way shall be implementation-defined.

7.2 Incompatible linkage

In order to allow the application program to call an externally supplied subroutine that can only be identified by its address in memory, or that requires a machine state at entry or exit incompatible with the HLL calling conventions, the subroutine CALLER shall be provided as specified in this section.

CALLER takes a single argument that evaluates to the integer address of the machine language subroutine to be called. CALLER saves whatever state information the HLL needs to have preserved across the call; the specified machine language subroutine is entered in such a way that the normal machine language subroutine return mechanism will cause the saved state to be restored and the HLL program to resume execution. Furthermore, CALLER shall initialize all programmable state elements (i.e., registers, flags, etc., of the microprocessor) on entry to the specified routine and unload them on exit.

Three support routines shall be supplied to enable the user to adequately specify the initial state and to recover any results from the exit state. The implementer shall specify an integer or some other identification for each distinct state element (register, etc.); this may, at the implementer's option, be restricted to a constant. A subroutine with the name PUTREG shall be used to assign to the state element identified in its first argument the value of its second argument. When the machine language

routine requires an address rather than a value, the integer function MEMLOC shall be provided, which returns the memory address of its argument. The implementer shall specify the conditions under which the address value returned by MEMLOC may become invalid. The function GETREG shall return the value of the state element identified by its argument, as set by either PUTREG or CALLER. Unlike INP and OUT, GETREG and PUTREG need not immediately access the named physical registers.

In the following examples, the variable V is assigned the value of the memory address of the variable W, which is subsequently assigned to state element (register) number 4. Similarly, state element A is assigned the value in variable J. Then the machine language routine whose address is in variable M is called. Finally, variable X receives the value returned in state element number 2:

In Basic

```
700    V = MEMLOC (W)
710    PUTREG 4, V
720    PUTREG A, J
730    CALLER M
740    X = GETREG (2)
```

In Fortran

```
V = MEMLOC (W)
CALL PUTREG (4, V)
CALL PUTREG (A, J)
CALL CALLER (M)
X = GETREG (2)
```

In Pascal

```
V: = MEMLOC (W);
PUTREG (4, V);
PUTREG (A, J);
CALLER (M);
X: = GETREG (2)
```

8 Bit manipulation

In order to facilitate direct control of individual bits and subfields in peripheral registers, the following bit manipulation functions shall be provided:

```
IAND (A,B)
IOR (A,B)
IXOR (A,B)
INOT (A)
GETFLD (A,N,M)
PUTFLD (A,N,M,B)
```

8.1 Logical functions

The four logical functions, IAND, IOR, IXOR, and INOT, operate on the binary representations of integers of an implementation-defined length, are considered as bit vectors, and return an integer whose binary representation is the logical *and, inclusive or, exclusive or,* and *one's-complement,* respectively, of the arguments. The logical operations are performed bitwise-parallel on the binary integer representations of the arguments, irrespective of the actual internal representation of the numbers.

The implementer shall define the treatment of negative numbers. Thus,

$$IAND (5,6) = 4$$
$$IOR (5,6) = 7$$
$$IXOR (5,6) = 3$$
$$IAND (INOT (5), 15) = 10$$

8.2 Subfield functions

The other two functions provide field extraction/insertion and shifting. In each case, the second and third arguments are integers denoting the bit positions (counting the least significant bit as position 0) of the ends of a bit string considered as a substring of the binary integer representation of the first argument. GETFLD extracts, right-justifies, and returns the designated subfield as an integer. PUTFLD positions the rightmost part (least significant bit string of designated length) of the binary representation of its fourth argument to replace the designated subfield and returns the composite as an integer. The fourth argument is an integer expression. The bit position arguments shall be acceptable in either left-to-right or right-to-left order. Thus,

$$GETFLD (13, 2, 1) = GETFLD (13, 1, 2) = 2$$
$$PUTFLD (255, 4, 4, 0) = 239$$

9 Address binding

The implementation should accept a directive (called "ADDRESS") that specifies the memory location to be used for the immediately following declaration of one variable or procedure. Where the declaration of variables is not permitted, the variable name itself should be included in the directive. Note that such local bindings may constitute aliasing with other program parts which reside at the same memory location, however specified. Such aliasing should be reported to the user.

9.1 Global bindings

Directives shall be accepted to establish collections of memory. Each such collection shall be identified as either a constant part (called "ROM") or a variable part (called "RAM"). Both constant and variable parts of an application program that specifies only a variable-part directive shall be located in that collection of (RAM) memory. The implementation may designate further distinctions as appropriate.* These directives should be accepted at the beginning of programs or, if appropriate, in the input to linkers or loaders.

9.2 Local bindings

The implementation should accept a directive (called "ADDRESS") that specifies the memory location to be used for the immediately following declaration of one variable or procedure. Where the declaration of variables is not permitted, the variable name itself should be included in the directive. Note that such local bindings may constitute aliasing with another program part residing at the same memory location, whatever the manner in which that part has been placed in that location. Such aliasing should be reported to the user.

9.3 Syntax

Both the form of the directives and the form of the memory location specifications within the directives shall be implementation-defined. The implementation should accept memory location specifications in decimal, hexadecimal, and octal; the default should be decimal, but suitable notation should permit specification in any of these number systems.**

When there is no conflict with other HLL requirements, directives within the program text should be specified by a comment which begins with the currency symbol "$".

In the following examples, memory locations 4096 through 6143 are to be allocated to the constant part of the program (i.e., the instruction code), and locations 6144 through 8191 to the variable part, except for the variable X, which is to be assigned to location 92 (or as many locations as necessary, beginning with 92):

In Basic

```
900   REM$ROM 4096-6143
910   REM$RAM 6144-8191

950   REM$ADDRESS 92, X
```

In Fortran

```
C$ROM 4096 6143
C$RAM 6144-8191

C$ADDRESS 92
      REAL X
```

In Pascal

```
(*$ROM 4096-6143*)
(*$RAM 6144-8191*)

(*$ADDRESS 92*)
VAR   X: REAL;
```

(End of text of proposed standard)

---

*For example, if instructions reside in an address space separate from that for data, then instructions and data may each have constant and variable parts.

**For example, the *Microprocessor Assembly Language Draft Standard* (IEEE P694) uses Q ' 117 for octal, D ' 79 for decimal, and H ' 4F for hexadecimal.

Reprinted from *IEEE Micro*, August 1983, pages 48-65. Copyright © 1983 by
The Institute of Electrical and Electronics Engineers, Inc.

*A universal format for object modules, designed to apply to a
variety of microprocessors, permits linking and relocating to be
isolated from the specification of target architecture.*

The Microprocessor Universal
Format for Object Modules

Proposed Standard

IEEE P695 Working Group

This standard specifies a universal format for object
modules designed to apply to a variety of microprocessors, permitting the linking and relocating functions to
be isolated from the specification of target architecture.
For portability, object modules are represented as sequences of ASCII characters, although a binary representation is permitted. A uniform command structure is
specified to support linkage edition, relocation, expression evaluation, and loading.

Foreword

This forward is not part of P695, Draft 3.1,
Microprocessor Universal Format for Object Modules.

With the passage of time, microprocessor system
capabilities are increasing, just as did those of the
minicomputers of the previous generation and the mainframes before them. With larger memories come larger
programs, and with them, the necessity of partitioning
programs into smaller, more manageable units that are
linked together into the final program. Thus arises the
need for relocatable and linkable code modules.

Unlike their larger cousins, the minicomputers and
mainframes, microprocessors are often used in multiven-

dor situations where the same software must work with
a variety of operating systems and configurations and
usually where the original computer manufacturer does
not hold a dominant sway over the software formats. The
ability to relocate and link code from a variety of vendors is in the interest of the user, and to that end a standard object module format is desirable.

A second, perhaps even more compelling reason for
a standard object module format arises from the fact that
many users of microprocessors are not limited to one architecture or CPU. These users are compelled to support
all of their target processors with all stages of the software translation process, even though many operations
need not depend on the actual target CPU. With a standard format, only those functions that necessarily relate
to the target machine architecture need specialization;
linking and relocation of the object modules can be done
for all processors with a single program.

MUFOM, the Microprocessor Universal Format for
Object Modules, is designed to apply to a variety of target
machines. It permits the linking and relocating functions
to be isolated from the specification of target architecture, so that a user may employ a single program for these
functions across all CPUs.

306

Processes. MUFOM is specified with the realization that an object module may undergo five processes in its life cycle and that these processes may be separate programs or may be combined into a single program.

The first process in the life of an object module is its creation by a compiler or assembler. Such a process almost always must be concerned with the architecture of the target machine and is not specified in this standard.

The second process is normally that of linking separately translated modules into one module and resolving external references. A partial linking may take several modules and produce a new module with still unresolved external references, which may require yet another linking. Linking may not even be required for compilations that reference no external procedures.

The third process is relocation. This process assigns absolute memory addresses to module locations and adjusts address fields previously generated with address constants (or expressions) relative to the module entry points. Often relocation is done at the same time as linking. The object module that comes out of the relocator is normally an absolute module with all address fields completely specified.

The fourth process evaluates "loader" expressions. These may be generated in the process of linking and relocating, or they may be initially generated by the source

Proposed Standard
IEEE P695
Preliminary
Subject to Revision

language translator. Usually, it is only after relocation that all necessary operands for evaluation are available. The result of the evaluation is a memory image that only needs loading. Aside from considerations such as word size and back links, expression evaluation does not depend on the target machine.

The fifth process is the loading of the absolute module into memory in the target machine. This may be specific to the word size of the target machine. Other than that dependency, loading may be done independently of the CPU architecture. Often the loading function is included with relocation and expression evaluation. For pur-

---

Benefits of a universal format for object code

Users of a standardized, universal format for object modules reap the benefits of a wide variety of powerful software tools that are not restricted to a single target computer. The proposed standard object module format differs substantially from normal manufacturers' formats since it is independent of any particular computer or operating system. This is especially important in cross-software development, where a multitude of incompatible formats has restricted progress.

The proposed standard format affects the whole range of program development. The object module output stage of compilers and assemblers is standardized, the linkage editor is standardized, the relocator—which embodies different types of relocation—is standardized, and the loader is standardized. The developer of a new compiler or assembler can concentrate his efforts on producing the necessary bit patterns that form the object code of the target machine. He is relieved of having to learn a different incompatible format for a new machine. Furthermore, he can develop and use his software on any available host computer that supports the standard.

In the worst case, when no loader for the standard format is available, the loading stage may be preceded by a format conversion which produces an absolute load module in the target machine's own absolute format. Since the information contained in an absolute module is restricted to addresses and bit patterns that are to be loaded at those addresses, this format conversion is a simple one-to-one transformation. It should be recognized that separate compilation (including

type checking), relocation, and library facilities are available even when the target format does not support them. Also, the software developer is required to learn only the simplest subset of the target format.

Once the standard format's processors and library routines are established, the work required to produce a standard assembler for the standard format is roughly equivalent to that required to produce an absolute assembler for the target format.

Other advantages of this approach should also be taken into account. For example, there exist today microprocessors which are packaged by their manufacturers or by software houses, or which are targets for particular PROM programmers. Each of these microprocessors or programmers requires a different object module format. These differing requirements are due to the manufacturers' copyrights and to the generality of the PROM programmers, which accept different types of memory chips. In the best case, the microprocessors and programmers will convert to the proposed standard format, hence removing duplication of effort; in the worst case, they will be covered by a few format converters.

The proposed standard format will encourage the development of additional universal utilities such as program analyzers, symbolic debuggers, object module cross-referencers, and type checkers. The competition to produce high-quality cross-software products will only benefit the marketplace. The advent of powerful tools for library maintenance, separate compilation, and relocation will enhance the productivity of the microprocessor programmer.

Proposed Standard

IEEE P695

Preliminary
Subject to Revision

poses of consideration in this standard, a translator that converts the MUFOM format absolute code module into a target-machine-dependent format is considered to be doing the loading functions. The loading process marks the end of the life cycle of the object module.

MUFOM is defined consistently across all five processes so that a load module is in a format that is a proper subset of the format for an absolute module, which in turn is a proper subset of the format for a relocatable module, which similarly is a proper subset of the format for a linkable module. Thus, a single syntax defines all three formats, with the simple qualification that there are particular commands that are destined to be swallowed up by the linker and that there are other commands for the relocater and still others for the loader.

Portability. MUFOM is based on CUFOM, the CERN Universal Format for Object Modules. MUFOM is designed for maximum portability of object modules between conforming systems. For this reason, all commands are specified as ASCII text derived from a minimum character set. For internal use an equivalent binary format is encouraged, and Appendix B gives an example of a binary implementation.

Many existing object module formats were considered to ensure their ease of translation into MUFOM in a direct way. In general, a MUFOM command represents a single function. Portability of MUFOM modules to other formats was not considered to be of sufficient value or feasibility to warrant serious attention.

Committee list. The following persons are responsible for contributions to this document. Comments and suggestions are welcomed and should be addressed to the chairman of the committee:

Tom Pittman
Itty Bitty Computers
PO Box 6539
San Jose, CA 95150

Committee members:

Geoff Baldwin   Tom Pittman
Richard James III   Stephen Savitzky
Gregg Marshall   Ian Willers
Jean Montuelle

Proposed Standard

IEEE P695

Preliminary
Subject to Revision

1. Scope

This standard specifies the format of linkable, relocatable, and absolute object modules for binary computers of arbitrary word size and architecture. Two levels of compliance are specified, minimum and full.

The minimum compliance level affords sufficient flexibility to link separately compiled modules, to relocate addresses in simple ways, and to load the resulting absolute object modules with a minimal loader.

The full compliance level affords all of the functionality of the minimum level and adds to it arbitrary address expression handling, type checking capability, librarian control commands, and other useful functions for full generality.

A conforming implementation may extend the command or function set of MUFOM for greater efficiency in dealing with machine-specific requirements, but object modules containing such extensions shall not be said to be conforming to this standard. Such extensions are not specified in this standard.

This standard also does not specify

(1) the source language features to be supported via MUFOM modules,
(2) the structure of relocatable code libraries,
(3) the format of the optional binary equivalent,
(4) algorithms for linking, relocating, and loading,
(5) the architecture of the host machine, or
(6) the architecture of the target machine, including word size, size of memory, memory organization, or instruction format.

This standard is derived from documents in the public domain and contains no patented or proprietary material.

2. Definitions and reference documents

The following definitions give the meanings of the technical words as they are used in this standard and are intended to reflect the accepted use of the defined words.

2.1 Definitions

Absolute code. Data or executable machine code in memory or an image thereof. Distinguish from *relocatable code.*

Absolute loader. A *process* which can load one or more *sections* of *absolute code* only at the locations specified by the *sections.* See *relocator.*

Binary information. Bit patterns to be loaded into memory.

Character form. The (printable) character representation of *binary information* as opposed to the bit pattern representation.

Checksum. A deterministic function of a file's contents. If a file is copied and the *checksum* of the copy is different from the original, there has been an error in copying.

Code. Data or executable machine code. See *absolute code* and *relocatable code.*

Command. Control information for a *linker, relocator,* or *loader.* Distinguish from *code.*

Comments. Information that is readable by people. To be distinguished from *binary information* and *character form.*

External definition. The definition, within a *section,* of a symbol which is referenced by other *sections.* An exported global symbol.

External reference. The specification, within a *section,* of a symbol which is defined outside that *section.* An imported global symbol.

Format. The language is which *object modules* are specified.

Librarian. The *process* which performs operations, such as maintenance, upon a *library.*

Library. A set of *object modules.*

Linkage editor. A *process* which combines *object modules* into a single *object module* satisfying links between the *object modules.*

Linker. Same as *linkage editor.*

Load pointer. A pointer for a *section* which is dynamically maintained by the *loader.* It indicates where the next item of *code* is to be loaded. It is initialized to a *starting load address.*

Loader. Same as *absolute loader.*

MAU. Abbreviation for *minimum addressable unit.*

Minimum addressable unit. For a given *processor,* the amount of memory located between an address and the next address. It is not necessarily equivalent to a word or a byte. Abbreviated *MAU.*

Module. Same as *object module.*

MUFOM. Acronym for Microprocessor Universal Format for Object Modules.

August 1983

Proposed Standard

IEEE P695

Preliminary
Subject to Revision

Object module. A set of *sections* of *absolute code* or *relocatable code,* together with *commands.*

Process. A program which is executed by a *processor.* In this document the denotation is restricted to *linker, relocator,* expression evaluator, and *loader.*

Processor. A computing machine, albeit perhaps a virtual machine.

Program. A set of data and instructions which defines the operations to be performed by a *processor.*

Relocatable code. Position-independent code which can be loaded at an arbitrary memory location. It generally requires both *relocation* and expression evaluation to become *absolute code.*

Relocator. A *process* which assigns absolute addresses to a *section* of *relocatable code* to produce *absolute code.*

Relocation. The function of the *relocator.*

Replication. The loading of repetitive data by means of an abbreviated specification.

Section. A part of a *program* with ancillary information (*commands*) which becomes a *segment* when loaded.

Segment. A contiguous region in memory with arbitrary boundaries.

Shall. Is required to . . . , are required to . . . .

Should. Is advised to . . . , are advised to . . . .

Starting load address. The address at which the loading of a *section* begins.

Type. An attribute of a symbol, value, or *section.* The definition of a symbol type is left to the implementer.

Weak external. An *external reference* which need not be satisfied during linking.

2.2 Reference documents

(1) Christopher W. Fraser and David R. Hanson, "A Machine-Independent Linker," *Software—Practice & Experience,* Vol. 12, 1982, pp. 351-366.

(2) Leon Presser and John R. White, "Linkers and Loaders," *Computing Surveys,* Vol. 4, No. 3, Sept. 1972, pp. 149-157.

(3) Jean Montuelle, "CUFOM: The CERN Universal Format for Object Modules," Report No. DD/78/21, CERN Data Handling Division, Geneva, Switzerland, Oct. 1978.

(4) J. Montuelle and I. M. Willers, "Cross Software Using a Universal Object Module Format, CUFOM," *Proc. Euro IFIP 79—European Conf. on Applied Information Technology,* P. A. Samet, ed., North-Holland Pub. Co., Amsterdam, pp. 627-632.

3. Introduction

3.1 Commands

A MUFOM object module is a sequence of commands. These commands are introduced by a two-letter mnemonic and are terminated by a period. Thus,

```
MBI8080.
ASP,100.
LDC30001.
ME.
```

is a well-formed module. Detailed descriptions of the commands in this example are contained in following sections, but an informal paraphrase of this example might be

Module begin "Intel 8080".
Assign load pointer value to be 256 (decimal).
Load three bytes with the binary information
    represented by the hexadecimal specification
    "C3", "00", and "01".
Module end.

3.2 Free-form syntax

An object module is treated as one contiguous string of ASCII characters (reference ANSI X3.4—1968). All ASCII control characters (such as a line feed or a carriage return) are ignored in processing.

The length of a MUFOM command is variable and there is no limitation on that length. To represent a MUFOM object module as a text file on a host processor (with limited line size), a single command can occupy several successive lines (e.g., encompass several line feeds, carriage returns, or other control characters).

4. Basic constructions

4.1 Notation used for syntax definitions

The metalanguage for the syntax definitions is derived from the Backus-Naur form and from regular expression notation.

Terminal symbols (literal characters shown exactly as used) are enclosed in quotation marks; nonterminal symbols (names of syntactic forms) are (possibly hyphenated) words without quotation marks. Parentheses are used to show grouping. Spaces are not significant. Concatenation is indicated by the juxtaposition of symbols. Repetition is indicated by recursion or by the two metasymbols + or *

| item * | zero or more occurrences of item |
| item + | one or more occurrences of item |

Alternation is indicated by the metasymbol |

    item1 | item2   either item1 or item2 not both

Election is indicated by the metasymbol ?

    item?   either item or nothing

Example:

    variable → letter (letter | digit)*

4.2 Elementary syntactic objects

MUFOM uses a small number of data types to provide standard means of expressing constructs. They are as follows:

digit → "0" | "1" | "2" | "3" | "4" |
        "5" | "6" | "7" | "8" | "9"

hexletter → "A" | "B" | "C" | "D" | "E" | "F"

hexdigit → digit | hexletter

hexnumber → hexdigit +

nonhexletter → "G" | "H" | "I" | "J" | "K" | "L" |
            "M" | "N" | "O" | "P" | "Q" | "R" |
            "S" | "T" | "U" | "V" | "W" | "X" |
            "Y" | "Z"

letter → hexletter | nonhexletter

alphanum → letter | digit

identifier → letter alphanum*

character → any ASCII graphic character

char-string-length → hexdigit hexdigit

char-string → char-string-length character*

where the hexadecimal value of string-length shall be equal to the number of characters, which shall be less than 128, e.g., 14A STRING WITH SPACES,

MUFOM-variable → nonhexletter hexnumber?

a name which references an internal variable of a MUFOM process (see Section 6).

5. Expressions

Expressions are written in postfix Polish notation. The binary representation of each operand shall not exceed 64 bits. An implementation shall accept operands of at least 15 bits.

expression → hexnumber | MUFOM-variable |
            polish-expr | conditional-expr

polish-expr → (operand ",")* function

operand → expression

function → "@" identifier | operator

operator → "+" | "−" | "/" | "*" |
         "<" | ">" | "=" | "#"

When a function or an operator appears in an expression, it specifies the computation to be performed on the values given in any preceding expression or expressions according to the function definition. Some standard functions are provided with MUFOM. However, it is expected that the implementer will enhance this set in order to more easily accommodate his target machine.

5.1 Types of operands

The result of an operation performed on operands depends on the types and values of those operands. If the type or range of an operand is not allowed by the operation applied to it, the result is undefined. In MUFOM, only two types of operands are distinguished: logical and integer. Integer operands can be positive or negative. Logical operands can have only the two values TRUE and FALSE.

The type of an operand written as 'hexnumber' is integer, and its value is equal to that of the 'hexnumber' considered as a positive hexadecimal number. The type of an operand written as 'MUFOM-variable' depends on the last assignment to the corresponding variable. The type of an operand written as 'polish-expr' will be defined below. The type of an operand written as 'conditional-expr' is the type of the operand for which the condition is true.

For bit-wise logical operations (@AND, @OR, @XOR, @INS, @EXT), a MUFOM integer is represented by a binary number aligned on the right, zero-filled or truncated on the left, and considered as unsigned.

5.2. Functions with no operands

polish-cxpr → "@F"
polish-expr → "@T"

Proposed Standard

IEEE P695

Preliminary
Subject to Revision

@F, @T—These functions return the logical values FALSE and TRUE. They have no operands.

5.3 Monadic operators and functions

polish-expr → operand "," monad-f

monad-f → "@ABS" | "@NEG" | "@NOT" | "@ISDEF"

@ABS—The type of 'operand' must be integer. This function returns an integer which is the absolute value of 'operand.'

@NEG—The type of 'operand' must be integer. This function returns an integer which is 'operand' arithmetically negated.

@NOT—If the type of 'operand' is logical, the value returned is its logical complement. If the type of 'operand' is integer, the value returned is the one's complement of its value.

@ISDEF—This function returns the logical value TRUE if 'operand' contains no unassigned variables, and returns FALSE otherwise.

5.4 Dyadic operators and functions

polish-expr → operand1 "," operand 2 "," dyad-f

dyad-f → "+" | "−" | "/" | "*" |
      "@MAX" | "@MIN" | "@MOD" |
      "<" | ">" | "=" | "#" |
      "@AND" | "@OR" | "@XOR" |

For noncommutative functions, the conventional operand ordering is used. For example, in the case of division, the result is the value of operand1 divided by the value of operand2.

+,−,/,*—These perform the obvious arithmetic operations on two operands, which must be integer. The result is integer. Divide truncates toward zero, and its result is undefined if operand2 is zero.

@MAX,@MIN—These functions perform an arithmetic comparison between two operands, which must be integer. They return an integer which is the greater, or lesser, of the two operands.

@MOD—This takes two integer operands and returns the integer value operand1 modulo operand2. The result is undefined if either operand is negative, or if operand2 is zero.

<,>,=,#—These are relational operators for integer values. The operator '#' tests inequality. They return TRUE or FALSE.

@AND,@OR,@XOR—These are logical operations on the bit string representations of the values of the two operands or on the logical values TRUE or FALSE. If the operands are bit strings, a bit string is returned; if they are logical values, then TRUE or FALSE is returned.

5.5 Data manipulation operations

polish-expr → operand1 "," operand2 "," operand 3 "," "@EXT"

@EXT—This function extracts a bit string. The operands must be non-negative integers. Operand1 is the value from which the bit string is to be extracted. Operand2 and operand3 are the integer values of the starting and ending bit positions relative to the right end of operand1. The value is returned right-justified with binary zero fill. The least significant bit is numbered zero.

polish-expr → operand1 "," operand2 ","
      operand3 "," operand4 "," "@INS"

@INS—This function inserts a bit string. The operands must be non-negative integers. The value of operand2 is inserted inside operand1. Operand3 and operand4 are the integer values of starting and ending bit positions relative to the right end of the value of operand1. The value of operand2 is treated as a bit string and replaces the value of operand1 between these starting and ending bit positions, inclusive. The value of the function is the resultant packed bit string. Truncation or binary zero fill is on the left. The least significant bit is numbered zero.

5.6 Other operations

polish-expr → value "," condition ","
      errornum "," "@ERR"

value → expression

condition → expression

errornum → expression

@ERR—If condition is TRUE, then an error message is generated, with errornum becoming the error number. This function returns 'value.'

e.g., to emit external #3 into one byte and generate error #25 on overflow:

    LR(X3,X3,FF,>,25,@ERR,1).

conditional-expr → condition "," "@IF" ","
      expression1 "," "@ELSE" ","
      expression2 "," "@END"

condition → expression

@IF—If the value of condition is TRUE, then expression1 is evaluated and its value and type become the value and type of the function; expression2 is not evaluated. If the value of 'condition' is FALSE, then expression1 is not evaluated; expression2 is evaluated and its value and type become the value and type of the function.

6. Variables

Some internal variables of MUFOM processes (e.g., load pointer or symbol dictionary items) shall be manipulated according to operations expressed in the object module. Such variables are called MUFOM variables and their symbolic names may appear in expressions.

The internal variables of MUFOM are identified by a name with the following syntax:

MUFOM-variable → nonhexletter hexnumber?

The nonhexletter gives the class of the variable. If several variables of the same class exist, a hexnumber is required. If this hexnumber refers to the current section number, it may be omitted.

Except for the X-variable, the variables can appear in the left part of an AS-command (see Section 11).

6.1 G-variable (execution starting address)

G-variable → "G"

The G-variable contains the address of the first instruction to be executed. This value is to be loaded into the program counter to run the program. The implementer shall define the results of not assigning to a G-variable, or assigning to it more than once.

6.2 I-variables (external definition—symbol values)

I-variable → "I" hexnumber

The I-variable is assigned a value which is to be made available to other modules for the purpose of linkage edition. That value is also available in the module in which it is defined by reference to the I-variable. The value is associated with the external definition specified in the corresponding NI-command (see Section 10.1). The effect of more than one assignment to an I-variable is undefined.

6.3 L-variables (low limit)

L-variable → "L" section-number?

section-number → hexnumber

A section is loaded within a contiguous region of the target memory. The bounds of a section are given by its lowest address (L-variable) and its size (S-variable). The L-variable contains the value of the low address for the section specified by the section-number. There shall not be an assignment to an L-variable in a relocatable MUFOM section.

6.4 N-variables (name)

N-variable → "N" hexnumber

The N-variables are used for type checking in the TY-command (see Section 10.5). An N-variable refers to the name of a user's variable and is defined by the NN-command (see Section 10.3).

6.5 P-variables (load pointer)

P-variable → "P" section-number?

section-number → hexnumber

The P-variable of the section specified by section-number contains the address of the target memory location where the next element of binary information is to be loaded. The P-variable is automatically incremented whenever a new element is loaded. It may also be modified using an AS-command (see Section 11).

The initial value of the P-variable is equal to the value of the L-variable (low limit) for that section, which is the starting load address.

6.6 R-variables (relocation reference)

R-variable → "R" section-number?

section-number → hexnumber

The R-variable is a reference point within a relocatable section. Addresses within the section may be specified relative to the R-variable. The initial value of the R-variable is equal to the value of the L-variable for that section.

When the linkage editor joins several sections into one, it may generate assignments to the R-variable of the resulting section in such a way that the relocation offsets remain unchanged. Addresses which are to be relocated will in general use, as relocation points, the R-variable of the section.

6.7 S-variables (section size)

S-variable → "S" section-number?

section-number → hexnumber

313

Proposed Standard

IEEE P695

Preliminary
Subject to Revision

There is one S-variable for each section in an object module. The S-variable contains the size (in target machine MAUs) of the section given by section-number. The effect of assigning to any S-variable more than once is undefined. The L-variable and S-variable of an absolute section give bounds to that section. Relocatable sections shall be relocated outside such bounded regions.

6.8 W-variables (working register)

W-variable → "W" hexnumber

No special meaning is attached to these variables—in different parts of the same module, a W-variable may be used for different purposes (e.g., to store a value temporarily).

6.9 X-variables (external symbol reference)

X-variable → "X" hexnumber

The X-variables correspond to external references. They are mapped onto the I-variables of other modules. When an NX-command is encountered, it is compared with external definitions given by NI-commands (see Section 10.1). If an external definition is found, the external reference is resolved by setting the value of the X-variable to the value of the corresponding I-variable.

By definition, X-variables cannot be the left part of an AS-command. They occur mainly as parameters for relocation operations. The implementer shall specify the action of the loader if it should encounter an X-variable.

7. Module-level commands

7.1 MB (module begin) command

MB-command → "MB" target-machine-configuration
                ("," module-name)? "."

target-machine-configuration → identifier

module-name → char-string

e.g., MBI8080,07MONITOR.

The MB-command shall be the first command of an object module. The target-machine-configuration may define the target-machine's name, CPU type, and operating system. The module-name should appear in the load map.

7.2 ME (module end) command

ME-command → "ME."

The ME-command shall be the last command in an object module. It defines the end of the module.

7.3 DT (date and time of creation) command

DT-command → "DT" digit* "."

To specify the date and time of creation of the output of a process, the date and time record may be used. The first part is the year (4 digits), followed by month, day, hour, minute, second (each 2 digits), and the fraction of a second (any number of digits). Only the more significant portions of the date and time need be given; for example, on a machine that has only a date:

DT19810723.

This form approximates the standards ANSI X3.43-1977 and ISO 3307-1975. The absence of a period before the fraction of seconds is forced by the MUFOM convention of terminating a command by a period.

7.4 AD (address descriptor) command

AD-command → "AD" bits-per-MAU
                ("," MAUs-per-address
                ("," order)?)? "."

bits-per-MAU → hexnumber

MAUs-per-address → hexnumber

order → "L" | "M"

e.g., AD8,2,L. CO,05 8080.
      AD24,1. CO,05 7094.

(See Section 8.1 for a description of the "CO" command.)

In order to facilitate the use of machine-independent processes, the AD-command is used to specify address formats, the maximum size of an address, and the number of bits in a minimum addressable unit (MAU). The AD-command overrides implementer-defined default values.

Bits-per-MAU specifies the number of bits in a MAU.

MAUs-per-address specifies the maximum number of MAUs in an address to be relocated. If the MAUs-per-address is omitted, it is assumed to be one. A standard relocator or loader need not accept any module for which the product of bits-per-MAU and MAUs-per-address in the AD-command exceeds (decimal) 64.

The order field of the AD-command need only be specified when the maximum address size exceeds one MAU and the order is other than the default value M.

M specifies that the most significant MAU occupies the lowest address in the target machine; L specifies that the least significant MAU occupies the lowest address in the target machine.

An implementer-defined order code may specify another possible ordering. The AD-command has no effect on the linker.

8. Comments and checksum

8.1 Comments

MUFOM is an intermediate language which is usually not seen by the user. But even if object modules are not intended to be read or directly modified, comments may be useful in some cases.

For example, a process may generate a load map describing the overall structure of a module (which can be complex if it is the result of multiple linkage editions). To facilitate comprehension, MUFOM comments may be copied into the load map.

Comments may also be used to record the name of the source file to which the module corresponds, to insert a flag indicating if the compilation was successful, etc.

CO-command → "CO" comment-level? ","
           comment-text "."

comment-level → hexnumber

comment-text → char-string

e.g., CO3,1AI/O CONTROLLER (15 JUNE 81).

The comment-text in a CO-command may be used by a process to pass information to the user. The comment-level may be used by the process to select or exclude the comment from transmission or output. The interpretation of the comment-level shall be implementer-defined. A process may discard a CO-command or it may copy the CO-command, changing only the comment-level, if desired.

8.2 CS (checksum) command

CS-command → "CS" checksum? "."

checksum → hexdigit hexdigit

The checksum is formed by the unsigned binary adding of the binary values of successive ASCII characters (control characters are not added) together (modulo 128). The last byte to be added is the 'S' of the CS-command. The checksum should agree with (be equal to) the integer value of hexdigit hexdigit above. The running checksum is reset to zero both at the start of a module and after encountering the period terminating a CS-command. A simple "CS." resets the running checksum to zero without checking it. Checksum commands may be inserted anywhere any other command might be expected.

9. Sectioning

An object module can be divided into one or more sections. A section is a separately controlled region of the

program. It has a type, which globally influences the actions performed in accordance with the commands that it contains.

Within the same module, a section is identified by a "section number." A section is introduced (or resumed) by an SB-command containing its number, and it is terminated (or suspended) by a new SB-command with a different section number or by an ME-command.

9.1 SB (section begin) command

SB-command → "SB" section-number "."

section-number → hexnumber

e.g., SB5.

The implementer shall specify the maximum possible section-number. All section numbers between zero and the maximum (inclusive) shall be valid.

Until an SB-command is encountered, the section number is zero.

9.2 ST (section type) command

ST-command → "ST" section-number (","
           section-type)*
           ("," section-name)? "."

section-number → hexnumber

section-type → identifier

section-name → char-string

Examples of section types:

ST0,R,U,04SUBR.   CO,0D code section.
ST1,S.   CO,0D unnamed data.
ST23,E,03COM.   CO,0D named common.
ST1F,M.   CO,0D blank common.
ST4,Z,S.   CO,12 data in zero page.

In an ST-command, section-type defines the type of the section identified by section-number. If present, section-name gives a symbolic name to that section.

A section can be absolute or relocatable. A section is absolute when its loading addresses are absolute (known at assembly or compile time). A section is relocatable when its loading addresses are relative to a relocation base whose value is initially not known.

Relocatable sections may be individually loaded into separate storage areas. However, in some cases, the loading addresses of sections shall be related. During the loading process, the user may have full control of the storage layout if the loader allows: for example, by using overlay directives. Except in special cases (e.g., overlays), MUFOM allows interdependency between sections of different modules. Thus, during the linkage edition, the module structure is built to correspond to the structure of the source programs.

For the linkage editor, it is possible to express three mutually exclusive kinds of relations among sections:

- Several sections are to be joined into a single one.
- Several sections are to be overlapped.
- Sections are not to coexist.

As these sections usually appear in different object modules, the relationship is established according to their types and symbolic names.

MUFOM categorizes sections in four ways. These provide the relocator with the information needed to lay out sections appropriately. The codes and/or categories may be extended for target machines where the standard is not sufficient. It may be meaningful to specify more, or less, than one attribute from each category. Some combinations of attributes are not meaningful.

Access. This attribute controls how the relocator groups sections together and lays them out in memory.

Writable (RAM, code W). This is the default in an ST-command if no access attribute is specified.

Read only (ROM, code R).

Execute only (code X).

Zero page (code Z).

Abs (code A). There shall be an assignment to the L-variable.

Named. This property is derived from the presence of the name.

Overlap. This attribute controls what to do with two sections if they have the same name and access attribute. (Two unnamed sections are said to have the same name if they have the same access attribute.)

Equal (code E). Error if lengths differ.

Max (code M). Use largest length encountered (e.g., blank common).

Unique (code U). Names should be unique (e.g., code).

Cumulative (code C). Concatenate sections together. The resulting section shall be aligned in such a way as to preserve the alignments of its components (see Section 9.3).

Separate (code S). No connection between sections. Multiple sections can have the same name, and the relocator may allocate them at unrelated places in memory.

When to allocate.

Now (code N). This is the normal case. This is the default if none is specified.

Postpone (code P). Relocator must allocate after all 'now' sections, thereby providing a way of getting "the last address allocated."

In an object module, if the ST-command is present, it may precede the corresponding SB-command. If no ST-command is given for a section, its type is absolute (A).

9.3 SA (section alignment) command

SA-command → "SA" section-number "," MAU-
         boundary? ("," page-size) ? "."

MAU-boundary → expression

page-size → expression

Examples:

Start section 1 on a 2-MAU boundary:

SA1,2.

Force section 2 to reside in a 256-MAU page:

SA2,,100.

When a section is required to start on a boundary which is some integral multiple of more than one MAU, the SA-command is used.

If page size is supplied, the section may not be allocated across a page boundary.

10. Symbolic name and type declaration

Some symbolic names which appear in source programs must be retained in the object modules for further processing (e.g., linkage edition). In MUFOM, each symbol is declared by a separate command. Such commands begin with the character "N" followed by a letter which determines the class of that name. These commands are employed in the resolution of external references and in the specification of attributes associated with names.

10.1 NI (name of internal symbol) command

NI-command → "N" I-variable "," ext-def-name "."

I-variable → "I" hexnumber

ext-def-name → char-string

e.g., NIA,04SINE.

An NI-command shall be provided for each symbol which is defined in the current module and which may be referenced from another module. This is called external definition. It indicates that in the current module the I-variable (see Section 6.2) is associated with the external definition of ext-def-name. The effect of more than one NI-command in the same linkage edition with the same ext-def-name is undefined. An NI-command shall always come before all occurrences of its corresponding I-variable.

If the module produced by the linkage editor may be linked in a further step, the NI-commands are retained unless the implementer gives an option to the linkage editor to suppress them (see Section 13).

10.2 NX (name of external symbol) command

NX-command → "N" X-variable "," ext-ref-name "."

X-variable → "X" hexnumber

ext-ref-name → char-string

e.g., NX11,04SINE.

An NX-command shall be provided for each external symbol which is referenced in the current module. It indicates that in the current module the X-variable (see Section 6.9) is associated with the external reference of ext-ref-name. An NX-command shall always precede any occurrences of its corresponding X-variable.

Since the module produced by the linkage editor may be linked in a further step, the NX-commands which correspond to unresolved references are retained.

10.3 NN (name) command

NN-command → "N" N-variable "," name "."

N-variable → "N" hexnumber

name → char-string

An NN-command shall be provided for each symbol which is defined in the current module and which may not be referenced from any other module (i.e., is local to the module). It may be passed to a symbolic debugger, or it may provide symbols for the type table. It indicates that in the current module the corresponding N-variable (see Section 6.4) is associated with the local definition of name. The effect of more than one NN-command in the same module with the same name is undefined. An NN-command shall always come before all occurrences of its corresponding N-variable.

10.4 AT (attributes) command

AT-command → "AT" variable "," type-table-entry ("," lex-level ("," hexnumber)*)? "."

variable → I-variable | N-variable | X-variable

type-table-entry → hexnumber

lex-level → hexnumber

The AT-command is used to define attributes of a symbol such as type or debugging information. The name and value (i.e., load address) attributes are defined by other commands. The type-table-entry identifies an entry in the type table which defines the type for this symbol. The lex-level may be used to show the scope in block-structured language modules; additional hexnumbers are implementer-defined. Normally the AT-command designates I-, N-, or X-variables. In the last case, type checking is performed, and the type-table-entry for each X-variable must be compatible with the type-table-entry for the corresponding I-variable (see the TY-command below).

10.5 TY (type) command

TY-command → "TY" type-table-entry ("," parameter) + "."

type-table-entry → hexnumber

parameter → hexnumber | N-variable | "T" type-table-entry

The TY-command specifies an entry in the type table. The type-table-entry is an access number that is used in this module to refer to this entry. The remainder of the command specifies a list of type parameters. A hexnumber parameter is a literal; an N-variable refers to the character string that is the name of that variable; and a T-number refers recursively to another entry in the type table.

Type compatibility is established between two entries if the strings represent identical type trees: that is, they have the same number of parameters of the same form; the numeric parameters are respectively equal; the N-variable entries refer to variables with the same names; and the type tree references refer to compatible type table entries.

August 1983

Proposed Standard

IEEE P695

Preliminary
Subject to Revision

'Don't care' types are defined with entries of zero: a numeric parameter of zero is considered equal to any numeric parameter; N0 is considered to be the same name as any other N-variable; and T0 is considered to be compatible with any type.

Example—in the following table, types T3 and T4 are compatible:

```
T1,13,N0,88.
T2,13,N8,0.
T3,44,T7,T1.
T4,44,T0,T2.
```

11. AS (assignment) command

AS-command → "AS" MUFOM-variable ","
            expression "."

e.g., ASP,A00.
     ASI7,R,8C, + .

The value of expression is assigned to the variable.

12. Loading commands

The most important part of an object module is formed by the internal representation of instructions, addresses, and data as translated from the source program. Due to the sequential use of memory addresses, it is possible to isolate "blocks" where the information is destined to be loaded into contiguous locations. If all the information is completely known, as is the case for absolute loading, each block represents an exact image (encoded in the MUFOM representation) of a memory region after the loading. In such a case, the block may be specified by one or more successive LD-commands. Otherwise the information may be divided between LD and LR commands, which are successively loaded in the order processed.

12.1 LD (load) command

LD-command → "LD" load-constant + "."

load-constant → hexdigit +

e.g., LD1D7F1D8033C63006A144A144A16010415A
     2B2A3D2D403C3E.

The load-constant is a value which is loaded into one or more MAUs. The load-constant shall be a fixed number of digits with the most significant first. The number of digits shall be defined by the implementer. Only processes which are specific to a particular target machine (e.g., code generators, loaders) are required to encode or decode load constants; the linker and relocator do not use or modify the LD-commands, but only copy them.

12.2 IR (initialize relocation base) command

IR-command → "IR" relocation-letter ","
            relocation-base
            ("," number-of-bits)? "."

relocation-letter → nonhexletter

relocation-base → expression

number-of-bits → expression

e.g., IRQ,X4,10.
     IRG,R3,45, – ,8.
     IRT,XA,3.

The IR-command initializes a relocation base (designated by the relocation-letter) for use in the LR (load-relocate) command. The relocation-base is evaluated by the relocator at the time the IR command is encountered and used to offset each address that designates this base in all subsequent LR-commands, until another IR command reinitializes this base.

The number-of-bits associates an address field size with this relocation base, for all subsequent references. This size shall not exceed the product of MAUs-per-address and bits-per-MAU as specified in the AD-command (see Section 7.4). If number-of-bits is not specified, it is equal to that product.

12.3 LR (load relocate) command

LR-command → "LR" load-item + "."

load-item → relocation-letter offset "," | load-constant |
           "(" load-value ("," number-of-MAUs)?
           ")"

relocation-letter → nonhexletter

offset → hexnumber

load-value → expression

number-of-MAUs → expression

e.g., LR0000HB2,0001(P,10, + ,2).

The LR-command is a compact notation for loading and for relocating information. Three different kinds of load-item may coexist in the command:

A load-constant is absolute (unrelocated) code that is to be loaded into as many MAUs as are required, in the same form as the LD-command (0000 and 0001 in the example above).

An offset preceded by relocation-letter (HB2 above) is added to the designated relocation base, which will have been specified by its most recent IR-command (see Section 12.2). As many MAUs are loaded as are required to contain the number of bits specified in the IR-command.

A parenthesized expression permits arbitrary relocation expressions (load-values). The number-of-MAUs, if omitted, is assumed to be the MAUs-per-address specified in the AD-command (see Section 7.4). The specified or default number of MAUs is loaded with the value of the expression, right-justified (i.e., the most significant bits are discarded or filled out with binary zeros, as appropriate). In the example above, the last load item is sixteen plus the location counter P, filling 2 MAUs.

If, in the example above, it is assumed that P is initially hex 0123, and relocation base H has been initialized with a value of hex 1A and a field width of 5 bits, and a MAU is defined as 16 bits wide, then the result of that LR command is the following bit pattern (shown in hex):

0000 00AC 0001 0000 0136

The first MAU results from the load constant 0000. The second MAU results from the relocation-letter H with offset B2 (note the sum of 1A + B2 has the carry-out of the fifth bit suppressed). The third MAU results from the load constant 0001. The fourth and fifth MAUs result from the expression in parentheses (note that P has incremented to 0126 at the point of evaluation).

12.4 RE (replicate) command

RE-command → "RE" expression ".".

e.g., REA.LR0000.
RE64.LR(7F800000,P, + ,4).

The RE-command evaluates the expression to determine the number of times the immediately following LR-command is to be replicated (see Section 12.3). The maximum length of the LR-command portion to be processed by the RE-command is implementation-dependent, but it shall be at least 64 characters.

13. Linkage edition

This section contains commands which refer only to linkage edition. They give additional control over the actions of the linkage editor. The actions of these commands may further depend on options available with the linkage editor. For example, the option to retain NI-commands (see Section 10.1) might be overridden by a user option given to the linkage editor.

13.1 RI (retain internal symbol) command

RI-command → "R" I-variable ("," level-number)? ".".

I-variable → "I" hexnumber

level-number → hex-number

This command indicates that the symbolic information previously defined by an NI-command (with the same I-variable) is to be retained in the object modules produced by any subsequent processing. The optional level number may be used to specify under what circumstances the symbol is to be retained.

13.2 WX (weak external symbol) command

WX-command → "W" X-variable
               ("," default-value)? ".".

X-variable → "X" hexnumber

default-value → expression

This command indicates that the external symbol specified by a previous NX-command (with the same X-variable) is to be flagged as a weak external.

In the case that the external reference is unsatisfied, the evaluated expression is the value of the X-variable.

14. Libraries

These commands refer specifically to the problem of loading routines which are contained in libraries. They are meant to give suitable defaults and to overcome the problem of two or more routines with the same name being present in separate libraries.

14.1 LI (specify default library search list) command

LI-command → "LI" char-string ("," char-string)* ".".

This command specifies the default order in which libraries are to be searched to resolve unsatisfied external references. Char-string identifies a library, and the search is made over the libraries specified by these char-strings in left-to-right order. LI overrides any previous LI-command within the same module.

14.2 LX (library external) command

LX-command → "L" X-variable ("," char-string) + ".".

The LX-command specifies the library or libraries from which the individual external reference corresponding to the X-variable is to be satisfied.

319

Proposed Standard
IEEE P695

Preliminary
Subject to Revision

15. MUFOM kernel

The following features shall be supported by a minimally conforming implementation.

Expressions:

Operators: +, −, @NEG
(Implied stack at least 2 values deep)

Variables:

G, I, L, P, R, S, X (only W, N missing)

Commands:

MB
ME
SB
ST (without N or P attributes)
SA
NI, NX
LR, IR (without options)
AS

16. Binary format

The MUFOM format is specified for media portability. An optional binary format may be implemented for internal use where file space or I/O time is critical. An implementation of the binary format shall provide bidirectional translation between it and the character form. See Appendix B for an example of a binary encoding.

Appendix A—Collected syntax

This appendix is not a part of P695/D3.1 and is for information only.

variable → letter (letter | digit)*

digit → "0" | "1" | "2" | "3" | "4" | "5" | "6" | "7" | "8" | "9"

hexletter → "A" | "B" | "C" | "D" | "E" | "F"

hexdigit → digit | hexletter

hexnumber → hexdigit +

nonhexletter → "G" | "H" | "I" | "J" | "K" | "L" | "M" | "N" | "O" | "P" | "Q" | "R" | "S" | "T" | "U" | "V" | "W" | "X" | "Y" | "Z"

letter → hexletter | nonhexletter

alphanum → letter | digit

identifier → letter alphanum*

character → any ASCII graphic character

char-string-length → hexdigit hexdigit

char-string → char-string-length character*

MUFOM-variable → nonhexletter hexnumber?

expression → hexnumber | MUFOM-variable | polish-expr | conditional-expr

polish-expr → (operand ",")* function

operand → expression

function → "@" identifier | operator

operator → "+" | "−" | "/" | "*" | "<" | ">" | "=" | "#"

polish-expr → "@F"

polish-expr → "@T"

polish-expr → operand "," monad-f

monad-f → "@ABS" | "@NEG" | "@NOT" | "@ISDEF"

polish-expr → operand1 "," operand 2 "," dyad-f

dyad-f → "+" | "−" | "/" | "*" | "@MAX" | "@MIN" | "@MOD" | "<" | ">" | "=" | "#" "@AND" | "@OR" | "@XOR" |

polish-expr → operand1 "," operand2 "," operand3 "," "@EXT"

polish-expr → operand1 "," operand2 "," operand3 "," operand4 "," "@INS"

polish-expr → value "," condition "," errornum "," "@ERR"

value → expression

condition → expression

errornum → expression

conditional-expr → condition "," "@IF" "," expression1 "," "@ELSE" "," expression2 "," "@END"

condition → expression

MUFOM-variable → nonhexletter hexnumber?

G-variable → "G"

I-variable → "I" hexnumber

L-variable → "L" section-number?

section-number → hexnumber

N-variable → "N" hexnumber

P-variable → "P" section-number?

section-number → hexnumber

R-variable → "R" section-number?

section-number → hexnumber

S-variable → "S" section-number?

section-number → hexnumber

W-variable → "W" hexnumber

X-variable → "X" hexnumber

MB-command → "MB" target-machine-configuration
("," module-name)? "."

target-machine-configuration → identifier

module-name → char-string

ME-command → "ME."

DT-command → "DT" digit* "."

AD-command → "AD" bits-per-MAU
("," MAUs-per-address
("," order)?)? "."

bits-per-MAU → hexnumber

MAUs-per-address → hexnumber

order → "L" | "M"

CO-command → "CO" comment-level? ","
comment-text "."

comment-level → hexnumber

comment-text → char-string

CS-command → "CS" checksum? "."

checksum → hexdigit hexdigit

SB-command → "SB" section-number "."

section-number → hexnumber

ST-command → "ST" section-number ("," section-
type)* ("," section-name)? "."

section-number → hexnumber

section-type → identifier

section-name → char-string

SA-command → "SA" section-number
"," MAU-boundary?
("," page-size)? "."

MAU-boundary → expression

page-size → expression

NI-command → "N" I-variable ","
ext-def-name "."

I-variable → "I" hexnumber

ext-def-name → char-string

NX-command → "N" X-variable "," ext-ref-name "."

X-variable → "X" hexnumber

ext-ref-name → char-string

NN-command → "N" N-variable "," name "."

N-variable → "N" hexnumber

name → char-string

AT-command → "AT" variable "," type-table-entry
("," lex-level ("," hexnumber)*)? "."

variable → I-variable | N-variable | X-variable

type-table-entry → hexnumber

lex level → hexnumber

TY-command → "TY" type-table-entry
("," parameter)+ "."

type-table-entry → hexnumber

parameter → hexnumber | N-variable |
"T" type-table-entry

AS-command → "AS" MUFOM-variable ","
expression "."

LD-command → "LD" load-constant+ "."

load-constant → hexdigit+

IR-command → "IR" relocation-letter ","
relocation-base
("," number-of-bits)? "."

relocation-letter → nonhexletter

relocation-base → expression

number-of-bits → expression

LR-command → "LR" load-item+ "."

321

load-item → relocation-letter offset "," | load-constant | "(" load-value ("," number-of-MAUs)? ")"

relocation-letter → nonhexletter

offset → hexnumber

load-value → expression

number-of-MAUs → expression

RE-command → "RE" expression "."

RI-command → "R" I-variable ("," level-number)? "."

I-variable → "I" hexnumber

level-number → hex-number

WX-command → "W" X-variable ("," default-value)? "."

X-variable → "X" hexnumber

default-value → expression

LI-command → "LI" char-string ("," char-string)* "."

LX-command → "L" X-variable ("," char-string) + "."

111xxxxx	Standard command names (see list)
xxxxxxxx	Checksum—modulo 256***

*If small hexnumbers is optional and left out, hexnumber omitted symbol must be used.

**Can be arbitrary length in the character form.

***This checksum value will in general differ from the checksum value for the character form (see Section 15.1 above).

Appendix B—Suggested binary encoding

This appendix is not a part of P695/D3.1 and is for information only.

A simple interference matrix of the syntactical forms in MUFOM shows that there is no place where there is a choice between character-string, small-hexnumber, load-constant, or identifier. Thus the same internal representation may be used for the first byte of all four of these without danger of ambiguity. All other syntactic forms defined in this standard can be uniquely encoded in 128 or fewer codes, leaving the remaining 128 codes to identify the first byte of the four.

The following encoding, while not intended to be definitive, shows how all the standard commands of this document may be encoded with gaps to add implementation-defined enhancements:

0nnnnnnn CCC . . . C	Character string, to 127 bytes
0xxxxxxx	Small (hex) number, 0 to 127*
0nnnnnnn BBB . . . B	Load constant, to 127 bytes**
0nnnnnnn CCC . . . C	Identifier, to 127 bytes**
10000000	Hex number omitted
1000nnnn BBB . . . B	Hex number, 0 to 8 bytes
1001xxxx	Implementer-defined functions
101xxxxx	Standard functions (see list)
110xxxxx (0nnnnnnn)	Standard variables and identifiers (see list)

Encodings for standard command names, functions, and identifiers:

#	FUNCTION	IDENTIFIERS AND VARIABLES	COMMANDS
0	@F		MB
1	@T	A	ME
2	@ABS	B	AS
3	@NEG	C	IR
4	@NOT	D	LR
5	+	E	SB
6	−	F	ST
7	/	G	SA
8	*	H	NI
9	@MAX	I	NX
10	@MIN	J	CO
11	@MOD	K	DT
12	<	L	AD
13	>	M	LD
14	=	N	CS (with sum)
15	#	O	CS.
16	@AND	P	NN
17	@OR	Q	AT
18	@XOR	R	TY
19	@EXT	S	RI
20	@INS	T	WX
21	@ERR	U	LI
22	@IF	V	LX
23	@ELSE	W	RE
24	@END	X	
25	@ISDEF	Y	
26		Z	
27			
28			
29			
30	(		
31	)		

August 1983

Proposed Standard

IEEE P695

Preliminary
Subject to Revision

Appendix C—Command and variable usage by processes

This appendix is not a part of P695/D3.1 and is for information only.

This appendix lists the MUFOM commands and variables against the conceptual processes.

This is a list of the conceptual processes, what they act upon, and what they produce. An implementation may also provide for "directives" into any or all processes. An implementation is likely to combine some of the conceptual processes into a single process.

INPUT/OUTPUT   CONCEPTUAL PROCESS

Several modules

  Linkage editor (the process that combines several relocatable modules, resolving the externals)

Several sections

  Relocator (the process that assigns an absolute starting address for each module)

Single "section"

  Expression evaluator (the process that evaluates all expressions in the MUFOM commands)

Absolute section

  Loader (the process that brings the binary information into memory)

Memory filled

UTILITY MATRIX

Codes:

U   Used by the process.

. . . Sent on (if present); i.e., ignored by process.

C   Possibly created by process (an implementation may create others, too).

M   Modified and then sent on.

UC   (Used and created) is a stronger transformation than M—the outgoing item may bear no relationship to the incoming item in contents and/or position.

Commands & variables	Linkage editor	Relo-cator	Expr. Eval.	Loader	
Meta:					
MB, ME	. UC				(required)
DT	. . . . . . C				
CO	. . C . . . C . . . C				
CS	. UC . . . UC . . UC . . U				
Descriptive:					
AD	. . . . . . U . . . U . . . U				
SB, ST	. UC . . . U				
SA	. . U . . . U				
NI,NX,RI, WX,LI,LX	. . U				
NN, AT, TY	. UC . . . . U				(on past loader)
Binary info:					
LD	. . . . U				
LR, IR	. . M . . . M . . M . . . U				
RE	. . . . M . . . U				(excluding LR part)
Active:					
AS	. UC . . . UC . MU . . U				(see variables)
Variables:					
P	. . . . . . C . . . U . . . . U				
R	. . . . . . M . . . U				
W	. . . . U				
L	. . . . . . U				
S	. UC . . . U				(required*)
G	. . . . U . . . U				
I, X	. .U				
N	. .C . . . . U				(on past loader)
Operators:					
@NEG, @INS	. . . . . . C . . . UC . . U				
others	. . . . . . C . . . U				
binary info	. . . . C . . U				(into memory)

*If the relocator does not textually substitute values for S-variables, then they need to be propagated to the expression evaluator.

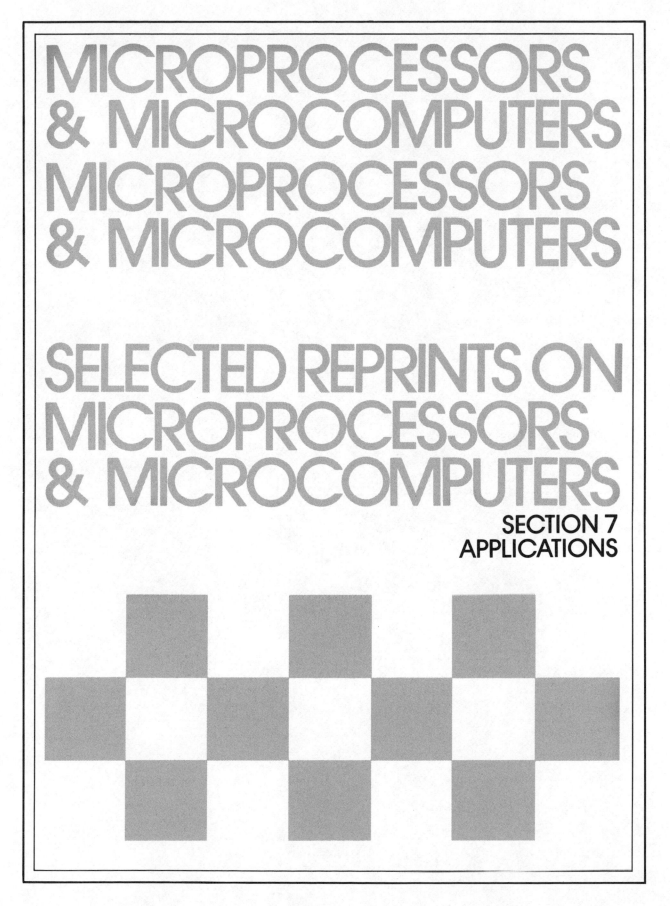

MICROPROCESSORS & MICROCOMPUTERS

MICROPROCESSORS & MICROCOMPUTERS

SELECTED REPRINTS ON MICROPROCESSORS & MICROCOMPUTERS

**SECTION 7
APPLICATIONS**

The replacement of a hydraulic control system with a microcomputer adds flexibility,

reliability, and safety to the operation of a parachute-drop ride.

A Microcomputer-Based Controller for an Amusement Park Ride

Victor P. Nelson

Auburn University

Hugh L. Fellows, Jr.

Thrill, Incorporated

In many applications requiring reliable, real-time control systems, mechanical and/or hydraulic techniques are used to implement the various control functions. While such systems are indeed reliable and are fairly well understood, they tend to be extremely bulky, complex, and expensive. In addition, they have very little flexibility beyond the basic functions for which they were designed. Essentially, each feature included in the controller requires a dedicated set of hardware in the design. Minor design modifications or parameter adjustments may result in the necessity to remachine parts, to completely rebuild subsystems, or to add new ones. Once the controller is in the field, valve settings and other controls may have to be continuously adjusted to maintain the controller within its specifications as parts age, weather conditions change, and so on.

Low-cost microprocessors are an attractive alternative to the above approach to real-time controller design. In addition to obvious size and cost benefits, microprocessors bring flexibility to the controller by allowing functions to be added or altered through software changes, often with little or no effect on the system hardware. Since the performance of a microprocessor is essentially independent of its age and other operating conditions, field adjustments are virtually eliminated and consistent day-to-day operation is ensured. One potential shortcoming is that the reliability of microprocessors and other electrical components in hazardous environments is unknown (as compared to the reliability of their mechanical and hydraulic counterparts). Controller designers, however, can compensate for this fact by carefully integrating safety features with the basic control functions in the software and hardware of the system to provide reliability and fault tolerance.

Figure 1.

327

EHO214-7/84/0000/0327$01.00©1981 IEEE

The Ripcord, a transportable, parachute-drop amusement ride (shown in Figure 1), is an example of an application in which a mechanical/hydraulic control system has been replaced with a small microcomputer. The ride, designed and constructed by Thrill, Inc., of Dothan, Alabama, consists of a seat, connected to a parachute, which is elevated to a height of about 83 feet and then "dropped" to simulate free-fall. This "free-fall" is actually a carefully regulated descent, designed to provide a thrilling ride while ensuring maximum safety. The number of necessary functions and safety features, as well as size and cost considerations, led to the decision to base the controller on a microcomputer. Because Ripcord is repeatedly dismantled, transported, and then reassembled, the compactness of a microcomputer-based controller is an obvious advantage over the mechanical/hydraulic system.

Ride operation and control

The basic components of the microcomputer-controlled Ripcord are illustrated in Figure 2. The seat and parachute are raised by a 7½-hp gearmotor, lowered by a 3¾-hp gearmotor, and stopped by an electric brake. The brake can be applied either by the controller or, independently, by a limit switch, which the ride encounters during its descent at a height of about 11 feet. Speed adjust-

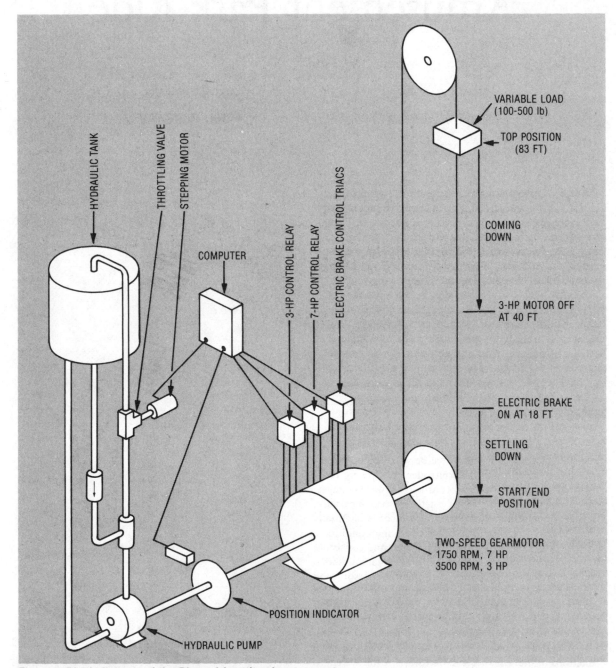

Figure 2. Block diagram of the Ripcord functional components.

IEEE MICRO

ments are made via a stepping-motor-positioned throttling valve. A number of devices measuring ride speed, position, and safety parameters provide logical inputs to the controller.

The controller microcomputer, diagrammed in Figure 3, is the Intel MCS-85 minimum system configuration,* consisting of the 8085 (CPU), 8755 (EPROM and I/O), and the 8156 (RAM, timer, and I/O). The controller is optically isolated from all external lines for lightning protection.

The normal operation of the ride consists of the following six stages:

Ascent. The rider and seat are pulled to the apex of the ride by the "up" motor, with the electric brake released

*MCS-85 User's Manual, Intel Corp., 3065 Bowers Ave., Santa Clara, CA 95051, Sept. 1978.

and the throttling valve completely in, at a synchronous speed of about six feet per second.

Pause. At the apex, the motor is de-energized and, when the ride has slowed to a stop, the brake is applied. While the brake is on, the throttling valve is partially opened to prepare for descent.

Acceleration. The brake is released and the "down" motor is energized to accelerate the rider and seat to a speed of about 13 feet per second downward, simulating free-fall. The throttling valve is used as necessary to maintain the acceleration at the rate of gravity, while preventing excessive overshoot or undershoot of the final target speed.

Descent. The throttling valve keeps the speed constant until the ride descends to a height of about 40 feet.

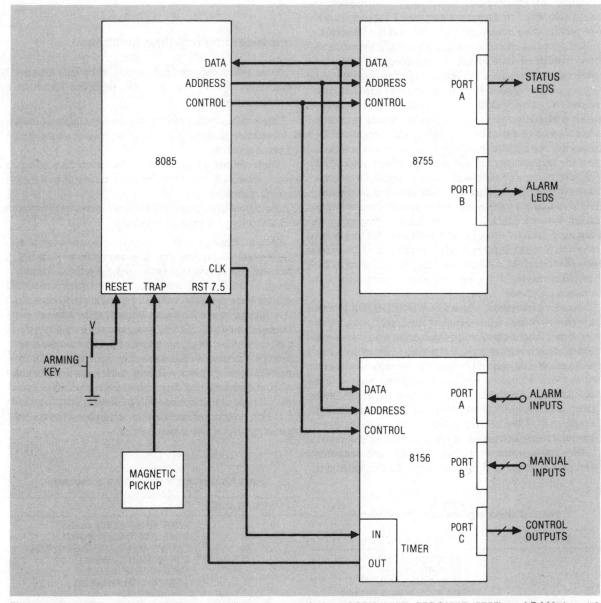

Figure 3. The MCS-85 minimum system configuration consisting of CPU (8085), EPROM/IO (8755), and RAM/timer/IO (8156).

329

Deceleration. The "down" motor is de-energized and the throttling valve operated to decelerate the ride linearly between 40 feet and 11 feet to a final speed of about one foot per second.

Settling. The brake is applied for one second at 11 feet by both the computer and the limit switch (independently) to stop the ride. The brake is then released to allow the ride to settle slowly back to the ground. Then the controller is reinitialized for the next ride.

All control signals for these functions (listed in Table 1) are supplied by the CPU via the parallel I/O lines of the 8156, and, similarly, all inputs to the computer (Table 2) are applied to the 8156. These inputs include both alarm monitors and manual operator controls. One additional input, a key-operated "arming/reset" switch, operates the 8085's RESET line. This switch must be used not only to initialize the ride at start-up, but also to reinitialize it after the detection of any error condition, ensuring that the ride cannot be operated following an abnormality until a manager (with the key) has inspected it.

In the original version of the Ripcord, a hydraulic system, illustrated in Figure 4, provided the speed and deceleration controls. As shown, a piston moved up and down in a hydraulic cylinder as the ride moved up and down. Thus, the position of the piston was the only indication of vertical position for the ride. Speed control was maintained by a deceleration valve, which regulated flow through the hydraulic pump. This valve was positioned by the cam action of the ride-positioned piston. The piston, moving upward with the ride, opened the deceleration valve by engaging the roller attached to the valve, thus allowing a maximum rate of acceleration as the ride started down from the top. As the ride descended, the piston gradually disengaged from the roller and caused the valve to close accordingly, resulting in the deceleration of the ride. Combinations of relays and limit switches provided the various on/off controls for the motors and brake.

As can be imagined, there was little flexibility in this controller scheme. All settings of the deceleration valve were dependent on piston position only, and thus were controlled only by the vertical position of the ride. There was no other ride-speed indication, nor any way to make minor speed adjustments in the different phases of the ride. Alarm indications were few, and the frequent setting up and taking down of the ride often resulted in the disruption of fixed valve settings, making the ride stray from its designed ranges of speed and other parameters.

The development of the control microcomputer brought a number of improvements to the original de-

sign. First, speed can be accurately measured and minor adjustments made at any point in the descent of the ride because the throttling valve can be positioned directly by the computer via the stepping motor. Second, the computer can accurately determine the ride's vertical position, eliminating the need for all but one limit switch, which checks the computer's computation. The computer determines when to trigger each of the various control actions, guided by its knowledge of the overall state of the ride, including vertical position, ride speed, and other parameters. Thus, the control signals are functions of *all* ride parameters, not simply a single value. Third, the control scheme, implemented in software rather than hardware, can be more elaborate. Finally, the reduction of equipment complexity is enormous. The original control system occupied two boxes of $7' \times 4' \times 1'$, and its elaborate system of pressurized-air and hydraulic-fluid piping was a "plumber's nightmare." The new controller occupies a single $4' \times 3' \times \frac{1}{2}'$ box.

Implementing real-time functions

In real-time control applications, the various external events and system functions can be divided into three general categories:

Time-critical (TC) events require immediate attention at some precise instant in time, which may or may not be known a priori.

Time-limited (TL) events require attention within some interval of time, but the exact timing within the interval is unimportant.

Non-time-dependent (NTD) functions can be executed with virtually no time constraints.

When defining a real-time application, one must carefully evaluate the time-dependence category of each system event to ensure that each will be given the proper attention. The actual methods used to implement and schedule these control functions depend on three factors: the number of events in each category, their order of occurrence, and the degree of concurrency in the system, i.e., the number of events which could simultaneously require the attention of the controller. In the case of concurrent events, priority relations between them should also be determined and considered in the scheduling process. The actual implementation of event scheduling can be either program-controlled or interrupt-driven, depending on the above requirements.

Table 1.
Control signals provided by the computer.

8156 BIT NUMBER	CONTROL FUNCTION
C_0	7-HP MOTOR $\overline{\text{ON}}$/OFF
C_1	3-HP MOTOR $\overline{\text{ON}}$/OFF
C_2	ELECTRIC BRAKE ON/$\overline{\text{OFF}}$
C_3	EMERGENCY POWER INTERRUPT
C_4	STEPPER MOTOR IN (PULSED)
C_5	STEPPER MOTOR OUT (PULSED)

Table 2.
Input signals monitored by the computer.

8156 BIT NUMBER	
A_1	CABLE HIGH-TENSION ALARM
A_2	CABLE LOW-TENSION ALARM
A_3	LOW HYDRAULIC PRESSURE ALARM
A_7	STOP BUTTON (MANUAL)
B_0, B_1	PAUSE-LENGTH SELECT
B_2	START BUTTON (MANUAL)
B_3	LIMIT SWITCH
B_4, B_5	TEST BUTTONS (MANUAL)
B_7	BRAKE RELEASE BUTTON (MANUAL)

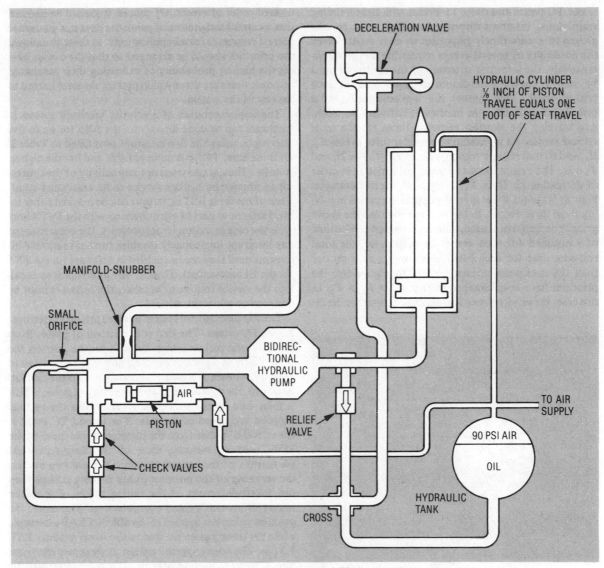

Figure 4. The speed and deceleration controller of the original Ripcord control system.

Program-controlled scheduling is used for NTD events and for those TL events having very loose timing restrictions. The scheduling may consist of simply executing functions in a round-robin fashion or, if timing restrictions warrant, monitoring "status" indicators to determine when to initiate events. As an example, consider the main loop of the Ripcord control program, listed in Figure 5. In this loop, the CPU cycles the individual control subroutines, the transition from one to the other normally occurring at specific vertical position values or nominal speed values. Hence, within each subroutine, the controller continuously monitors these parameters for the first occurrence of their checkpoint values, at which time it terminates the current control function and moves to the next.

In contrast, static-alarm checking routines (for low hydraulic pressure, abnormal cable tension, etc.) are basically NTD functions in that they can be completely asynchronous to the other system functions, the only restriction being that each alarm must be monitored often enough to ensure the safety of the ride. The routines can be executed whenever it is convenient, without the controller's having to check for an initiation time, because they are embedded within the loops of the control subroutines listed in Figure 5. This assumes, of course, that each subroutine loop is executed often enough to maintain the desired alarm check frequency.

```
MAIN:  LXI   SP,900H     ; INITIALIZE THE STACK POINTER
       CALL  COLD        ; INITIALIZE THE SYSTEM
LOOP:  CALL  OPERATOR    ; WAIT FOR START BUTTON
       CALL  ASCEND      ; UP MOTOR ON FOR ASCENT
       CALL  PAUSE       ; UP MOTOR OFF, BRAKE ON AT TOP
       CALL  ACCEL       ; BRAKE OFF, DOWN MOTOR ON
       CALL  REGULATE    ; HOLD CONSTANT SPEED
       CALL  DECEL       ; DOWN MOTOR OFF TO SLOW RIDE
       CALL  SETTLE      ; SLOW DESCENT TO GROUND
       JMP   LOOP        ; NEXT RIDE IF NO ERRORS
```

Figure 5. The main loop of the Ripcord control program (stored at RCM address 0).

331

For TC events and those TL events with tighter timing restrictions, interrupt-driven scheduling must be employed to ensure timely responses to each event. Given the possibility of several events requesting service simultaneously, the interrupt structure of the controller must be used to ensure a maximum response time for each critical event. This implies the implementation of a priority scheme either in hardware, software, or both, guaranteeing the shortest response times for the most critical events. As an example, consider three events E_1, E_2, and E_3 that require response times $T_1 = t$, $T_2 = 2t$, and $T_3 = 3t$. The events should be given priorities P_i in order of decreasing T_i. Thus, $P_1 > P_2 > P_3$ for this example. Figures 6(a)-6(c) show several possible scenarios involving these three events. In the first two figures, the above priority assignment is used, with an interrupt service time of t assumed for each event. In both cases, the total response time for each event either meets or is shorter than the maximum allowed value. In Figure 6(c) the priorities have been changed so that $P_2 > P_1 > P_3$. In this case, the service time of E_1 exceeds its limit for the in-

dicated order of events. Of course, it should be realized that a careful assignment of priorities does not guarantee correct responses for all applications. In these situations, the priorities should be arranged so that the events having the highest probability of exceeding their maximum response times are those which present the least hazard to the rest of the system.

The implementation of a priority interrupt system in hardware can be done directly on the 8085 for up to five interrupts, using the five interrupt pins listed in Table 3. Of these lines, TRAP is nonmaskable and has the highest priority. Thus, it can interrupt any activity of the processor to provide immediate service to its associated event. Each of the three RST interrupts can be masked either individually or as part of a group along with the INTR line. As is the case in most microprocessors, the occurrence of any interrupt immediately disables further maskable interrupts until they are re-enabled in software (in the 8085 via the EI instruction). Thus, if one interrupt is to break into the service routine of another, the software must be designed to allow this action.

The Ripcord control system has two primary interrupt-driven TC events. The first is the arrival of pulses from the magnetic pickup which "rides" on the gear on the drive shaft, as shown in Figure 2 and in greater detail in Figure 7. At each 3/8 inch of vertical travel of the ride (up or down), the pickup generates an electrical pulse, which is then used by the processor to determine the vertical position and speed of the ride. The second TC event is the arrival of pulses from the programmable timer of the 8156, used to measure each of the time-dependent parameters of the control system. Of these two events, the servicing of the position pulses is more critical than the acknowledgment of the timing pulses, due to the nature of the ride's speed computations. Therefore, the position pulses are applied to the 8085's TRAP interrupt, while the timer pulses are sent to the lower-priority RST 7.5 pin. The edge-triggered nature of these two interrupt pins allows the leading edge of each pulse to trigger the interrupts, providing a degree of consistency.

The computation of ride speed uses information from both interrupt sources. If speed is equal to distance/time, and if the linear distance between successive position-pulse interrupts is constant, then the time between successive interrupts can itself be used as a measure of the speed of the ride (inversely proportional). Note that, in an application such as this in which time and memory space are at a premium, all parameters should be stored and manipulated in as convenient a form as possible. Thus, an actual computation of the speed of the ride is unnecessary so long as the processor can determine how

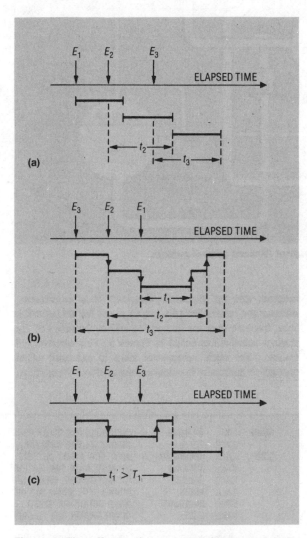

Figure 6. The effects of proper and improper priority assignments: (a) a sequence of appropriate responses for $P_1 > P_2 > P_3$, (b) another sequence of proper responses for $P_1 > P_2 > P_3$, and (c) a sequence of responses for $P_1 > P_2 > P_3$ that is an improper response to event E_1.

Table 3.
Intel 8085 interrupt request input lines
(*MCS-85 User's Manual*, Intel Corp.).

INTERRUPT PIN	TRIGGER CHARACTERISTICS	PRIORITY
TRAP	RISING EDGE/HIGH-LEVEL	1
RST 7.5	RISING EDGE	2
RST 6.5	HIGH-LEVEL	3
RST 5.5	HIGH-LEVEL	4
INTR	HIGH-LEVEL	5

the speed compares with expected values. The speed measurement is made by the position-pulse service routine, which stops the timer, measures the time T_{rem} remaining in the count register, and then resets it. The total time elapsed since the previous interrupt is then computed by

$$T_{total} = (T_{clk} - T_{rem}) + T_{clk}*N_{int} \qquad (1)$$

where T_{clk} is the clock period and N_{int} is the number of timer interrupts that have occurred since the previous position-pulse interrupt. To minimize the effects of noise and possible missed pulses, T_{total} is averaged over several successive intervals (corresponding to about two inches of ride travel). This prevents the controller from attempting to initiate drastic corrective actions for single out-of-range measurements.

The selection of the value of T_{clk} is important in systems for which several events are to be timed by the same clock. Two approaches to this selection can be taken. One is to make T_{clk} large, and then measure each parameter by reading the timer buffer as described for the speed computation above. The second approach is to make T_{clk} small enough for all event times to be expressed as an integral number of periods, i.e., by $T_{clk}*N_{int}$. The approach to be used depends on the minimum and maximum expected event times in the system and the required precision for each measurement. Table 4 lists some of the major events in the Ripcord system with their corresponding expected/desired times. The shortest event is the sending of pulses to the stepper motor, requiring a minimum period of 1.67 msec. The majority of the remaining measurements are long enough to be measured as an integral number of these intervals, and so this value was selected for T_{clk}. Also, the other events do not require significant timing accuracy. Speed computations are the exception, and are computed as described above to maintain their accuracy.

Although not in themselves TC events, several auxiliary system functions are performed as part of the position-pulse and timer-interrupt service routines. For example, the stepping motor, if it is to be operated, must be pulsed at a rate no greater than 600 pulses per second, which is the selected timer-interrupt frequency. Thus, within the timer service routine, a check is made to determine if the stepper currently requires manipulation; if so, one pulse will be generated at this time.

In the position-pulse service routine, in addition to speed computation, checks are made for nominal and abnormal speeds, and emergency and corrective actions are taken as required. The vertical ride position is also updated at this time. In terms of the total number of position pulses N_p received, the vertical position V_p is given by

$$V_p = P*(\text{\tiny{1/8}} \text{ inch}) \qquad (2)$$

where

$$P = \begin{cases} N_p & ; N_p \le N_{top} \\ 2*N_{top} - N_p & ; N_p > N_{top} \end{cases}$$

and N_{top} represents the height at the top of the ride. Note that the multiplication in Equation 2 is not actually performed, since P itself is a sufficient measure of height.

System software design

The Ripcord control functions were designed in a top-down fashion and then implemented in a bottom-up manner to provide a modular system that could be efficiently modified and maintained. The system software consists of four main modules, as illustrated in Figure 8. The two interrupt-driven functions discussed earlier operate as foreground events, while the main control program runs in the background. The occurrence of any serious error condition will result in the replacement of the main control program by an emergency descent procedure in the background. A map of the program memory (in EPROM), showing the amount of code associated with each module, is given in Figure 9.

As described earlier, the main program loop consists of the six basic ride stages, listed in Figure 5. The transitions between stages are controlled by the vertical position, VP, and ride speed, SP, values generated by the position-pulse interrupt routine. As an example, the flowchart of the ASCENT subroutine is given in Figure 10. Once the ascent has begun, the main loop of the subroutine continuously monitors the static alarms, which are available at the 8156 inputs, and the value of VP. When $VP \ge N_{top}$, the "up" motor is de-energized and the ride is allowed to coast to a stop, detected by watching SP for a value close to zero. At this time, the brake is

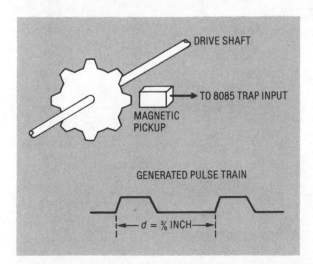

Figure 7. The magnetic pickup, riding on a gear on the drive shaft, generates a pulse as each tooth of the gear passes under it.

Table 4.
Sample timing requirements for several events in the Ripcord control system.

SYSTEM EVENT	REQUIRED TIMING
PULSES TO STEPPING MOTOR	$t \ge 1.67$ MSEC
PULSES TO POWER-HOLD CIRCUIT	$t \le 2.00$ MSEC
PAUSE AT TOP OF RIDE	0.5 SEC $< t <$ 3 SEC
DELAY FOR MOTOR/BRAKE TRANSIENTS	$t = 7$ MSEC
SPEED COMPUTATIONS	2 MSEC $< t <$ 10 SEC
DELAY FOR ASCENT TO COME UP TO SPEED	$t = 0.5$ SEC

applied to provide a smooth stop and the routine is exited. (An earlier version applied the brake immediately at $VP = N_{top}$, making the ride more interesting, but displeasing the safety inspectors.) The remaining control subroutines operate in a similar manner, with the exception of the acceleration routine, which terminates on either a terminal VP value or a terminal SP value, whichever is reached first.

The most critical part of the control program is the regulation of the downward speed. The ride must simulate free-fall to provide a reasonable degree of excitement and yet must be carefully regulated for safety. This is accomplished by *pulling*, rather than dropping, the ride downward. The speed is forced to conform to the position-versus-speed curve of Figure 11, with the throttling valve used as necessary to make minor speed corrections in each phase of the descent. The correct speed value at each vertical position is determined either by computation or by table lookup, depending on the stage of the descent.

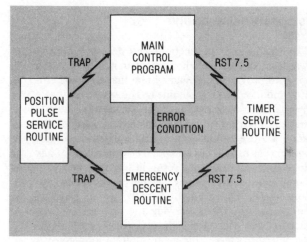

Figure 8. The four main software modules of the Ripcord control system.

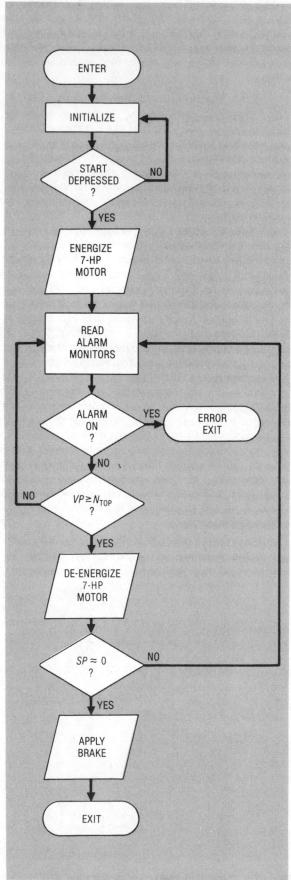

MAIN LOOP: 739 BYTES
    CALLING LOOP: 000-020
    SUBROUTINES: 065-326

TIMER SERVICE ROUTINE: 210 BYTES
    CALLING SEQUENCE: 03C-064
    TIMER SERVICE: 327-390
    STEPPER CONTROL: 692-6D0

POSITION-PULSE SERVICE ROUTINE: 424 BYTES
    CALLING SEQUENCE: 024-03B
    SPEED COMPUTATIONS: 43B-562
    POSITION UPDATE: 6D1-728

EMERGENCY PROCEDURES: 380 BYTES
    DIAGNOSTICS: 391-3E7, 629-691
    EMERGENCY STOP: 563-628

CONSTANT STORAGE AND
MISCELLANEOUS PROCEDURES: 380 BYTES

UNUSED: 3 BYTES

Figure 9. Memory map of the Ripcord control program (all addresses are in hexadecimal).

Figure 10. Flowchart of the ascent stage of the ride.

During the acceleration stage, the "down" motor is energized to increase speed to roughly 13 ft/sec, the acceleration of gravity, to produce the free-fall sensation. Similarly, during deceleration, the motor is de-energized and the speed reduced linearly to one ft/sec so that the brake can be applied. In each case, the variation in weights of the riders makes the throttling valve necessary to keep the speed on the curve. The correct speed value, SP_{cor} is computed as a function of VP along the linear portions of the curve by

$$SP_{cor} = SP_{init} + (SP_{end} - SP_{init}) \left(\frac{VP - VP_{init}}{VP_{end} - VP_{init}} \right) \quad (3)$$

where SP_{init}, SP_{end}, VP_{init}, and VP_{end} are initial and final speed and position values, respectively. Since the interrupt routines actually generate time measurements rather than speeds, Equation 3 can be modified to give the time T_{cor} corresponding to SP_{cor}:

$$T_{cor} = K_1/(VP - K_2) \quad (4)$$

where K_1 and K_2 are constants. For example, in the linear deceleration part of the curve, $VP_{init} = 1288$ counts (35.5 feet), $VP_{end} = 417$ counts (11.5 feet), $SP_{init} = 13.23$ feet per second, and $SP_{end} =$ one foot per second. From Equation 3, we get

$$SP_{cor} = 0.014VP - 4.86 \quad (5)$$

Now, since each count is 3/8 inch, we have $SP_{cor} = 0.031 ft/T_{cor}$. Thus Equation 5 can be rewritten in the form of Equation 4:

$$T_{cor} = 2.23/(VP - 347) \quad (6)$$

Note that the numerator of Equation 6 must be scaled to allow it to be used in integer form by the 8085. The computation of T_{cor} thus requires one subtraction and one division for each value, computed after each position pulse. Ordinarily, the division might pose a problem due to its execution time, which must fit between interrupts. In this case, however, repeated subtraction can be used, since the division time is conveniently proportional to T_{cor}. Thus as T_{cor} increases, so does the interval between successive position pulses, leaving ample time for the computations.

In the acceleration phase, a piecewise linear approximation of the curve was made to allow the use of the above procedure. Along the remainder of the curve, T_{cor} is a constant.

Safety features

The overall safety of the ride was perhaps the biggest concern during the design phase. The built-in safety features include the monitoring of static-alarm conditions such as abnormal cable tension, abnormal hydraulic pressure, and the depression of the manual stop button, as well as of a number of dynamic conditions, such as ride speed. In addition, the correct operation of most of the system components is continuously verified, including the magnetic pickup, the timer, and even the CPU itself. An abnormality in any of these conditions results in the following set of reactions by the controller:

(1) The error is flagged and, depending on its severity, the ride is either allowed to continue to completion or sent into the emergency descent routine.
(2) The emergency descent routine executes a sequence of operations designed to get the ride slowly, but safely, back to the ground. It begins by killing the "down" motor, and then uses the brake (applied by de-energizing it) and the "up" motor, if needed, to control the downward ride speed. If these devices are not effective, then the power to the CPU is removed.
(3) Once the ride is on the ground, the CPU is placed into an endless loop to prevent it from being reused. This prevents the operator from restarting the ride until a service person rearms the controller by resetting the CPU with a special key.

The operational status of the magnetic pickup is monitored in three ways. If the time between two successive position pulses exceeds the value corresponding to a minimum speed, it is assumed that the pickup has failed and will not be supplying further pulses. Similarly, if pulses continue to arrive after the apex of the ride has been reached, a pickup failure is assumed. The third test consists of marking the value of VP when the limit switch (set at 11 feet) is "seen" on the upward trip, and then comparing that value to the value of VP when the switch is encountered on the way down. A significant disagreement between these two values is flagged as a pickup failure and the ride is disarmed.

Although no specific tests of the timer are made, any abnormality on its part will show up as a speed out-of-bounds error, when it is used in the speed computations, and will thus be trapped in that manner, forcing the controller into the emergency descent routine. The final diagnostic test involves the CPU itself. Once the system has been turned on initially, power to the CPU is applied

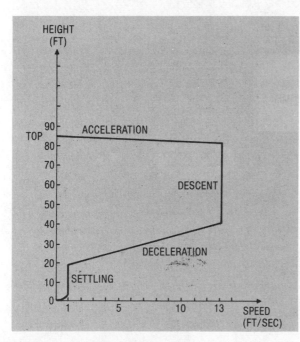

Figure 11. Vertical-speed-versus-height curve for the downward trip.

and held via a retriggerable one-shot multivibrator, illustrated in Figure 12. In order to remain powered, the CPU must retrigger the one-shot within its two-msec time-out period by means of a pulse applied to its input. The pulse is applied in software within the two interrupt service routines, one of which should be entered at least every $T_{clk} = 1.67$ msec. If the CPU fails, it is assumed unable to provide regular pulses at the correct frequency, and thus the one-shot times out and removes the power from the processor. All ride states and error conditions are recorded on LEDs in the ride control box for monitoring and diagnosis, simplifying servicing after an error condition.

The microcomputer-based real-time controller for the Ripcord has proved to be a compact, flexible, and reliable system. Minor operational changes were easily made in software, while many safety features and diagnostic procedures were added at relatively little extra cost, compared to the cost of equivalent mechanical components or electrical circuits. Thus, all anticipated malfunctions are well covered for continuous fail-safe

operation. The success of the Ripcord controller should lead to the use of similar microcomputer-based control systems for other complex amusement rides and other real-time applications with comparable timing and reliability requirements. ∎

Hugh Fellows received his BS degree in aerospace engineering from Auburn University in 1967. After a short period with Thiokol Chemical Company, he returned to earn his MS in December of 1968. Since then, he has worked in aerospace propulsion with Martin Marietta Construction Engineering at Walt Disney World and has designed and built amusement equipment for his own company. Currently, he is a consulting engineer in Dothan, Alabama.

Victor P. Nelson's biographical sketch appears on page 6. His address is Department of Electrical Engineering, Auburn University, AL 36849.

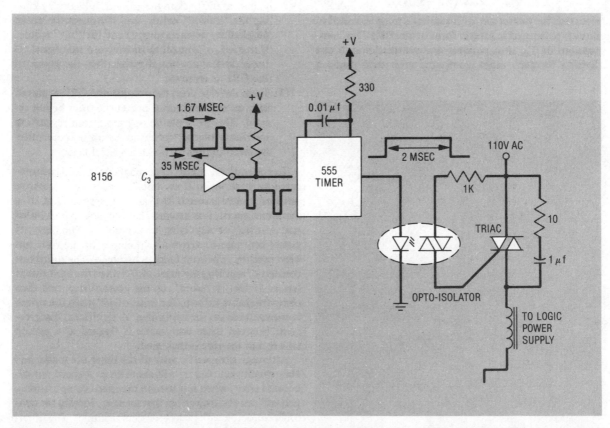

Figure 12. Power maintenance circuit used to de-energize the controller if the CPU becomes unable to generate a regular pulse train.

Implemented on a single-chip microcomputer, this digital signal generator can provide

low-distortion waveforms of precise frequency in the low-frequency audio spectrum.

A Digital Signal Generator

Tracy S. Kinsel and John H. Wuorinen

Bell Telephone Laboratories

The digital signal generator described here has general application where low-distortion waveforms of precise frequency in the low-frequency audio spectrum are required. Several authors[1-3] have previously described, in basic terms, digital signal generators that use SSI and MSI components. The implementation featured in this article uses a microcomputer and has several new and interesting features.

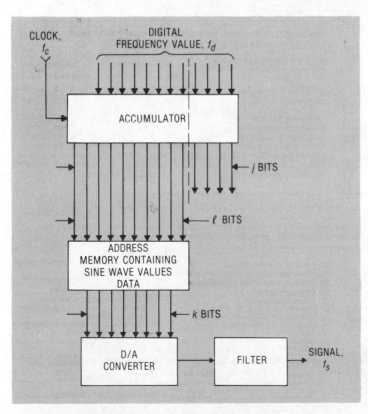

Figure 1. Illustration of the digital signal generation algorithm.

Algorithm

The basis of the algorithm is the synthesis of a sampled sine wave by means of a table look-up followed by a D/A converter. The output of the converter is smoothed by a filter.

The sampled sine wave signal is given by

$$\sin(2\Pi f_s n\Delta t + \theta)$$

where Δt is the time interval between sample generations, n is the index number of the sample, f_s is the frequency of the sine wave to be generated, and θ is an arbitrary phase. The argument of the sine wave is an arithmetic series of the type $n \cdot a + b$, where a and b are constants. An accumulator with a modulus of 2Π (as shown in Figure 1) can be used to generate such a series.

A digital value f_d, which establishes the output sine wave frequency f_s, is repeatedly added to the accumulator at a clock rate of $f_c (= \vee \Delta t)$. The value f_d is given by

$$f_d = \text{INT}\ (2^j\ \frac{f_s}{f_c}\ +\ \frac{1}{2}\ ) \qquad (1)$$

where INT is the truncation operation and j is the number of bits in the accumulator. Essentially, this equation calculates the fraction f_s/f_c (which must be < 1), shifts the binary point j places to the right, and then rounds to the nearest binary integer. For example, the following would generate a 1000-Hz sine wave using an 18-bit accumulator with a Δt of 30 μsec.

$$
\begin{aligned}
f_d &= \text{INT}(2^{18}\text{x}1000\text{x}30\text{x}10^{-6} + .5)_{10}\\
&= \text{INT}(7864.3 + .5)_{10}\\
&= \text{INT}(7864.8)_{10}\\
&= 7864_{10}\\
&= 1\text{EB}8_{16}
\end{aligned}
$$

337

The accumulator in Figure 1 is used to generate a pointer, which is in turn used to scan a table of sine wave values. Scanning the table solely with integer value steps limits the number of output frequencies; fractional step sizes greatly enlarge the variety of output frequencies.

The arrangement in Figure 1 allows the generation of a scanning pointer that is based on a fractional step size given by f_d. The dashed line marks the location of the binary point within f_d. The memory pointer is obtained by using only the ℓ most significant output bits of the accumulator. This is the equivalent of performing a truncation operation on the full value of the pointer. (See the sidebar below for examples.) Although an actual truncation operation is simpler, it adds more distortion to the signal. A more accurate operation would involve some kind of interpolation between the table values.

After the table look-up, the sine wave values are output to a D/A converter, which generates the sampled waveform. A low-pass filter is used to smooth the signal.

The number of possible output signal frequencies is 2^{j-1}, and the spacing between them is $f_c/2^j$. Thus the algorithm can be used to generate a sine wave with a frequency arbitrarily close to a desired value by using an accumulator of sufficient size.

Basic design rules. The basic design rules [1-3] of this type of generator are as follows. The number of bits, k, required in the D/A converter is determined by the quantization noise of the sampling process. The signal-to-noise ratio at the output of the converter is given by $20 \log_{10}(2^k) \simeq 6k$ dB. Once k is chosen, the size of the sine wave table in memory (for a complete period) need be no

---

Table scanning using a fractional step size

A fractional-valued step size as input to the accumulator can increase the number of possible output frequencies. The simplest way to use the output of the accumulator is to drop the fractional part and use the integer part as a memory pointer. For example, part (a) of the figure shows the case of a table scan using $f_d = 4.2$ as input to the accumulator. The top line shows the contents of the accumulator after each cycle, and the middle line shows the size of the interval between accessed table locations after truncation of the value of the accumulator. The example shows that the table is scanned in steps of four followed by an oc-

casional step of five. The latter occurs when the fractional part of the accumulator carries over to the integer part. For the general case, the table is scanned with steps of size Δ and $\Delta + 1$, where $\Delta = \mathrm{INT}(f_d)$.

The larger steps of $\Delta + 1$ can occur with a frequency lower than the signal frequency, as demonstrated by (b)—a case of $f_d = 4.1$.

These larger steps can occur many times in each cycle of the waveform, as demonstrated by (c)—a case of $f_d = 4.4$. Increasing the number of steps of $\Delta + 1$ in each period of the waveform raises the frequency of the signal.

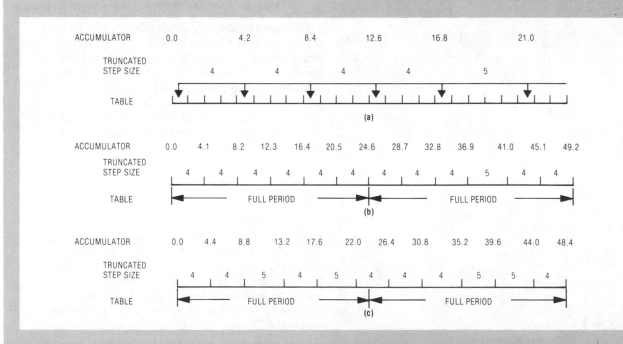

Numerical examples demonstrate table scanning that uses fractional step sizes followed by truncation. Figure (a) demonstrates the appearance of an occasional large step; in the example, it is equal to five. Figure (b) illustrates the case where the large step occurs less frequently than a signal period. Figure (c) illustrates the case where the large step occurs more frequently than a signal period.

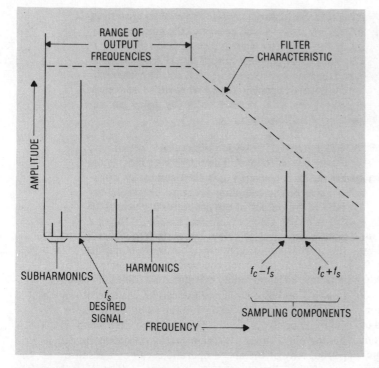

Figure 2. Output spectrum for sine wave generation.

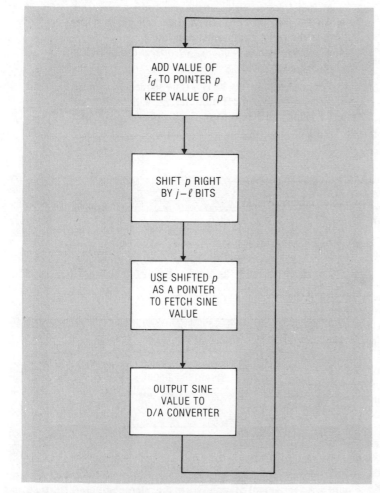

Figure 3. General flowchart of the algorithm.

larger than $2^{k+2}=2^{\ell}$. The number of bits in the accumulator, j, is determined by the fineness of the frequency variation required, as given above.

Signal spectrum. This algorithm, as indicated earlier, introduces additional distortion to the signal. Figure 2 shows a generalized output spectrum including f_s, the desired signal at the fundamental frequency. There are, in addition, the following distortion components.

- *Subharmonics:* These appear when the larger truncated step size occurs with a period longer than the signal period, as in case (b) of the sidebar.
- *Harmonics:* These appear when the larger truncated step size occurs with a period shorter than the signal period, as in case (c) of the sidebar. They are also generated by use of a waveform table with finite resolution.
- *Sampling components:* For an ideal square-step D/A converter, these appear at $nf_c \pm f_s$, where n is an integer. These last components can be reduced by a low-pass filter with the ideal characteristics shown in Figure 2.

The case of sine wave generation can be generalized to arbitrary waveform generation by storing appropriate data in the table. The waveform cannot be completely arbitrary, since undersampling of the signal waveform can occur at high frequencies (large step sizes).

Figure 3 is a general flowchart of the algorithm. The frequency of executing the loop gives the value of f_c.

Hardware implementation

There are cost and flexibility advantages in using a microprocessor in the construction of such a signal generator. This strategy allows one or more accumulators to be implemented by software to generate composite waveforms. An arrangement with an Intel 8049 single-chip microcomputer[4] and an external D/A converter is shown in Figure 4; other microprocessors could also be used.

For a fixed waveform, the waveform values can be stored in the program memory of the device. For the general case, a variable waveform can be loaded into RAM memory, which is accessed by the microcomputer.

The limitations imposed by the 8049 architecture restrict the look-up table to 256 entries. For microprocessors with larger memory pointers, this limitation might not exist.

For the rest of the discussion, assume that a sine wave output is desired. Assume also that the distortion requirements on the waveform dictate the use of an eight-bit D/A converter. As pointed out above, this implies that a full-period sine wave table contains 1024 values and that a quarter-period table (which we will use) contains 256 values. For the frequency precision required by our application, an 18-bit accumulator is adequate.

The accumulator is implemented, as shown in Figure 5, in three eight-bit-wide registers: Reg 2, Reg 3, and Reg 4. Reg 2 is the least significant. Frequency input f_d is stored in Reg 5 and Reg 6 and added to the accumulator

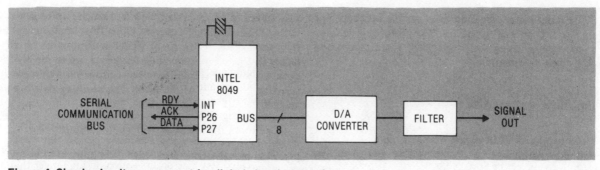

Figure 4. Simple circuit arrangement for digital signal generation.

registers with a triple-precision addition algorithm. Great economy in program execution time is achieved by aligning the register boundaries as shown in Figure 5. This arrangement avoids the time-consuming shift operation shown in Figure 3.

The two most significant bits of the accumulator, those containing the quadrant information, are stored in Reg 4. They will be used to construct the full period from a quarter-period table stored in memory. For the moment, we shall ignore the upper six bits of this register. Hence, only 18 bits of the 24 are used.

The middle register (Reg 3) contains the truncated address pointer, used to access the quarter-period sine wave table stored on page three of the program memory. Sine wave data are acquired through the 8049 instruction MOVP3 A,@A. Before the instruction is executed, the microprocessor eight-bit accumulator—not to be confused with the 18-bit wide accumulator—is loaded with the address pointer from Reg 3. After the instruction is executed, the microprocessor accumulator contains the sine wave data. The two quadrant bits of the 18-bit accumulator are tested to determine which part of the sine wave is to be generated. The four quadrants are generated by complementing the microprocessor accumulator before and/or after the MOVP3 instruction. Complementing the microprocessor accumulator *before* reserves the direction in which the pointer scans the table; complementing it *after* generates the lower half of the sine wave. These operations result in a smooth joining of the quadrants at the boundaries and eliminate discontinuities.

Appendix I is a program that accomplishes the above. The NOP instructions balance the execution time of the four quadrants. The sampling period is determined by the execution time of the program loop. For the Intel 8049 with an 11-MHz crystal executing PROGRAM 0, it is 30 μsec.

Two different sine waves can be generated simultaneously by implementing two 18-bit accumulators in the two register banks. The digital sine values can be output to separate D/A converters for generating two independent signals. Alternatively, arithmetic operations can be performed on the values before they are output to a single D/A converter, which then generates a complex waveform. For example, sums, differences, or products of two sine waves can be performed by the arithmetic unit in the microprocessor. The last operation is general-

ly slow, resulting in a low sampling frequency—unless the microprocessor contains a hardware multiplier.

The signal frequency can be changed at any time by putting a different value, calculated by equation (1), into Reg 5 and Reg 6. The phase can be changed at any time by putting a new value into the 18-bit accumulator. On-off modulation of the signal can be performed by putting out 0 to the D/A converter to produce the off period. Any of the above operations can be a result of any of the following.

- *Timing* (using the on-chip programmable timer).
- *Counting cycles* of the waveform (the upper six bits of Reg 4 count cycles of the generator waveform).
- An *external stimulus* (new data can be provided over the serial communication lines).
- A *predetermined sequence of operations* stored in the on-chip RAM.

An example of the above is a tone sequence or music generator that uses on-off modulation, with each "on" interval being a different tone. Such a program is shown in Appendix II.

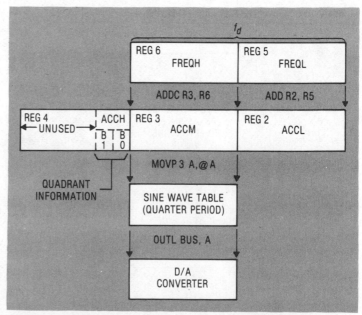

Figure 5. Arrangement of registers in the microcomputer. The instructions shown between the blocks are used in the program.

The serial communication lines use the interrupt line and two I/O lines of the device. The protocol is handled in software by using two flags: RDY (data ready) and ACK (data accepted).

Experimental results

The arrangement in Figure 4 was set up with an Intel 8748 microcomputer, a programmable device in the same family as the 8049. Clock frequency was six MHz, and the D/A converter was the Analog Devices AD7530. The filter was implemented by a laser-trimmed, hybrid integrated circuit[5] configured as an active RC biquadratic, low-pass filter section, with a transfer function given by

$$T(s) = \frac{2.35171 \times 10^8}{s^2 + 2.0315 \times 10^4 s + 2.37185 \times 10^8}$$

where s is the complex frequency variable. This simple and economical filter, packaged in a 16-pin DIP, allows

Table 1.
Experimental results obtained
from the digital signal generator.

DIGITAL INPUT WORD (R6, R5)	CALCULATED FREQUENCY	MEASURED FREQUENCY (Hz)	TOTAL HARMONIC DISTORTION (dB)
0800 Hex	142.045	142.095	-55.3
1000	284.091	284.188	-54.4
1004	284.368	284.460	-51.8
1500	372.869	373.000	-52.9
1504	373.147	373.273	-51.0
2000	568.182	568.380	-52.9
2700	692.472	692.735	-51.4
2704	692.749	692.960	-50.2
6018	1706.210	1706.520	-45.2

sine waves to be generated with frequencies up to one-tenth of the sampling frequency. Other filter implementations can allow the range of signal generation to be a larger fraction of the sampling frequency, up to the Nyquist limit of 0.5. Total harmonic distortion was measured at the output of the filter. The resulting data are given in Table 1.

In general, distortion increases with increasing frequency because fewer signal samples occur per sine wave period at higher frequencies. Also there appears to be an increase in distortion due to the setting of the less significant bits in the digital input word. As pointed out earlier, this is caused by the nature of the algorithm.

Application to the Call Progress System

The Call Progress System[6] is used in a telephone central office to generate the tones that signal the customer, such as the dial tone and the busy tone. International applications demand a high degree of flexibility. The data for a specific set of tones needed for the country of application are stored in EPROM. When the system is initialized, this EPROM is read by a microprocessor and the data are transmitted over the serial communication lines to all the tone generators.

The specific tone generator is shown in Figure 6. For continuous single-frequency tones, the upper frequency limit is 3.3 kHz. A high on RESTART restarts the signal at the beginning of the modulation sequence. This feature is needed for synchronization of several tones. The amplitude of the signal is set by putting a DC value generated by a second, latched converter into the reference port of the first multiplying D/A converter. A similar arrangement could generate a product or amplitude-modulated waveform. ■

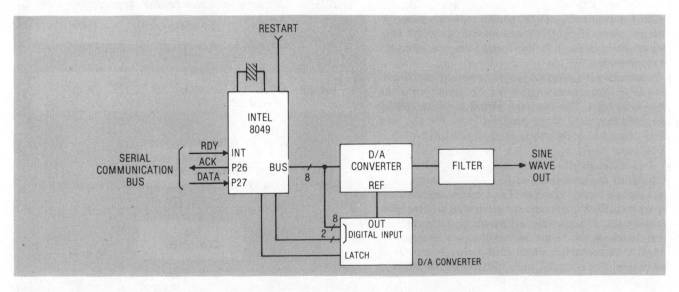

Figure 6. Circuit arrangement for digital signal generation for application in the Call Progress System.

Appendix I: Assembly listing for a program that generates a single continuous sine wave

Before the program is executed, the 16-bit value of f_d should be placed in on-chip RAM with the low byte at location PERTAB + 4 and the high byte at PERTAB + 5.

```
ISIS-II MCS-48/UPI-41 MACRO ASSEMBLER, V2.0


LOC  OBJ       SEQ        SOURCE STATEMENT

               8 ;- - - - - - - - - - - - - - - - - - - - - - - - - - -
               9 ;
              10 ;        P R O G R A M     0
              11 ;
              12 ;        GENERATES A CONTINUOUS SINGLE FREQUENCY TONE
              13 ;
              14 ;- - - - - - - - - - - - - - - - - - - - - - - - - - -
              15 ;
              16 ;
              17 ;
              18 ;        INPUTS:
              19 ;        PERTAB+4- FREQ1L, LOW BYTE OF FD
              20 ;        PERTAB+5- FREQ1H, HIGH BYTE OF FD
              21 ;
              22 ;
0100 D5       23 PROG0:   SEL     RB1
0101 35       24          DIS     TCNTI
0102 B824     25          MOV     R0, #PERTAB+4
0104 F0       26          MOV     A, @R0    ; GET FREQ1L
0105 AD       27          MOV     R5, A     ; PUT IN REG 5
0106 18       28          INC     R0
0107 F0       29          MOV     A, @R0    ; GET FREQ1H
0108 AE       30          MOV     R6, A     ; PUT IN REG 6
0109 27       31          CLR     A         ; INITIALIZE ACC
010A AA       32          MOV     R2, A     ; INITIALIZE 18 BIT ACCUMULATOR
010B AB       33          MOV     R3, A
010C AC       34          MOV     R4, A
010D AF       35          MOV     R7, A     ; FOR LATER USE
010E 05       36          EN      I         ; ENABLE INTERRUPT TO RECEIVE DAT
010F 97       37          CLR     C         ; TRIPLE PRECISION ADDITION
0110 FA       38 LOOP0:   MOV     A, R2     ; LEAST SIGNIFICANT BYTE
0111 6D       39          ADD     A, R5
0112 AA       40          MOV     R2, A
0113 FB       41          MOV     A, R3     ; MIDDLE SIGNIFICANT BYTE
0114 7E       42          ADDC    A, R6
0115 AB       43          MOV     R3, A
0116 FC       44          MOV     A, R4     ; MOST SIGNIFICANT BYTE
0117 7F       45          ADDC    A, R7     ; FASTER THAN "ADDC    A, #0"
0118 AC       46          MOV     R4, A
              47 ;
              48 ;        F I R S T   Q U A D R A N T
              49 ;
0119 322B     50          JB1     NSIN0     ; TEST FOR SIGN
011B 1224     51 PSIN0:   JB0     PDWN0     ; POSITIVE, TEST QUADRANT
011D FB       52          MOV     A, R3     ; POSITIVE, SCAN UP TABLE
011E 00       53          NOP               ; FILLER FOR EQUALIZING QUADRANTS
011F E3       54          MOVP3   A, @A     ; FETCH SINE VALUE
0120 00       55          NOP               ; FILLER
0121 02       56          OUTL    BUS, A    ; OUTPUT TO D/A
0122 2410     57          JMP     LOOP0
              58 ;
```

November 1981

```
                              59 ;          S E C O N D   Q U A D R A N T
                              60 ;
0124 FB                       61 PDWN0:  MOV     A, R3      ; POSITIVE, SCAN DOWN TABLE
0125 37                       62         CPL     A          ; ADJUST POINTER
0126 E3                       63         MOVP3   A, @A      ; FETCH SINE VALUE
0127 00                       64         NOP                ; FILLER
0128 02                       65         OUTL    BUS, A     ; OUTPUT TO D/A
0129 2410                     66         JMP     LOOP0
                              67 ;
                              68 ;          T H I R D   Q U A D R A N T
                              69 ;
012B 1234                     70 NSIN0:  JB0     NDWN0      ; NEGATIVE, TEST QUADRANT
012D FB                       71         MOV     A, R3      ; NEGATIVE, SCAN UP TABLE
012E 00                       72         NOP                ; FILLER
012F E3                       73         MOVP3   A, @A      ; FETCH SINE VALUE
0130 37                       74         CPL     A          ; ADJUST VALUE
0131 02                       75         OUTL    BUS, A     ; OUTPUT TO D/A
0132 2410                     76         JMP     LOOP0
                              77 ;
                              78 ;          F O U R T H   Q U A D R A N T
                              79 ;
0134 FB                       80 NDWN0:  MOV     A, R3      ; NEGATIVE, SCAN DOWN TABLE
0135 37                       81         CPL     A          ; ADJUST POINTER
0136 E3                       82         MOVP3   A, @A      ; FETCH SINE VALUE
0137 37                       83         CPL     A          ; ADJUST VALUE
0138 02                       84         OUTL    BUS, A     ; OUTPUT TO D/A
0139 2410                     85         JMP     LOOP0
                              86 ;
                              87 ;
                              88 ;
                              89 ;
                              90 ;
```

Appendix II: Assembly listing for a program that generates a tone sequence or a music generator

An appropriate low-frequency clock into pin T1 of the 8049 is required. Before the program is executed, the on-chip RAM should be loaded with the following values:

- PERTAB + 5: Number of tones or off-intervals in the sequence, which is repeated indefinitely.
- PERTAB + 6: Duration of the first interval. If the least significant bit is 1, the interval generates a tone; if it is 0, the interval is silent.
- PERTAB + 7: Low byte of f_d for the first interval.
- PERTAB + 8: High byte of f_d for the first interval.
- PERTAB + 9: Duration of the second interval.
- PERTAB + 10: Low byte of f_d for the second interval.
- etc., to limit of space available in RAM.

For off-interval, omit value of f_d.

```
ISIS-II MCS-48/UPI-41 MACRO ASSEMBLER,  V2. 0


LOC  OBJ        SEQ          SOURCE STATEMENT

                 94 ;
                 95 ;- - - - - - - - - - - - - - - - - - - - - - - - - - - -
                 96 ;          P R O G R A M   1
                 97 ;
                 98 ;        GENERATES A SEQUENCED TONE
                 99 ;
                100 ;- - - - - - - - - - - - - - - - - - - - - - - - - - - -
                101 ;
                102 ;
                103 ;        INPUTS:
```

```
                    104 ;           PERTAB+5- NUMBER OF INTERVALS
                    105 ;           PERTAB+6- DURATION OF INTERVAL 1
                    106 ;                 LSB = 0, CADENCE OFF
                    107 ;                 LSB = 1, CADENCE ON
                    108 ;             FREQUENCY OF INTERVAL 1
                    109 ;           PERTAB+7- FREQ1L; FD, LOW BYTE
                    110 ;           PERTAB+8- FREQ1H; FD, HIGH BYTE
                    111 ;           PERTAB+9- DURATION OF INTERVAL 2
                    112 ;             FREQUENCY OF INTERVAL 2
                    113 ;           PERTAB+10- FREQ2L
                    114 ;           ETC.
                    115 ;
                    116 ;           R E G I S T E R   A S S I G N M E N T
                    117 ;           RB1: REG0=POINTER TO PERTAB
                    118 ;                REG1=INTERVAL COUNTER
                    119 ;
                    120 ;
                    121 ;
                    122 ;           FOR OFF INTERVAL OMIT FREQL AND FREQH.
                    123 ;
                    124 ;
0100 35             125 PROG1:  DIS     TCNTI
0101 05             126         EN      I          ;ENABLE INTERRUPT TO RECEIVE DAT
0102 D5             127         SEL     RB1
0103 45             128 STRT4:  STRT    CNT        ;START EVENT COUNTER
0104 B825           129         MOV     R0,#PERTAB+5    ;NUMBER OF INTERVALS
0106 F0             130         MOV     A,@R0
0107 A9             131         MOV     R1,A       ;STORE IN R1, INTERVAL COUNTER
0108 19             132         INC     R1
0109 E90D           133 CADSL4: DJNZ    R1,$+4     ;FINISHED ALL INTERVALS?
010B 2403           134         JMP     STRT4      ;YES
010D 18             135         INC     R0         ;NO
010E F0             136         MOV     A,@R0      ;FETCH DURATION OF INTERVAL
010F 121B           137         JB0     CADON4     ;ON INTERVAL
0111 53FE           138 CADOF4: ANL     A,#0FEH    ;MASK OFF LSB
0113 62             139         MOV     T,A        ;LOAD EVENT COUNTER
0114 2380           140         MOV     A,#80H
0116 02             141         OUTL    BUS,A      ;OUTPUT 0 TO D/A
0117 1609           142         JTF     CADSL4     ;COUNTER OVERFLOW
0119 2417           143         JMP     $-2
011B 53FE           144 CADON4: ANL     A,#0FEH    ;MASK OFF LSB
011D 62             145         MOV     T,A        ;LOAD EVENT COUNTER
011E 18             146         INC     R0
011F F0             147         MOV     A,@R0      ;FETCH FREQL FOR THIS INTERVAL
0120 AD             148         MOV     R5,A
0121 18             149         INC     R0
0122 F0             150         MOV     A,@R0      ;FETCH FREQH FOR THIS INTERVAL
0123 AE             151         MOV     R6,A
0124 27             152         CLR     A
0125 AA             153         MOV     R2,A       ;INITIALIZE 18 BIT ACCUMULATOR
0126 AB             154         MOV     R3,A
0127 AC             155         MOV     R4,A
0128 AF             156         MOV     R7,A       ;FOR USE LATER
0129 97             157         CLR     C
012A FA             158 LOOP4:  MOV     A,R2       ;TRIPLE PRECISION ADD
012B 6D             159         ADD     A,R5
012C AA             160         MOV     R2,A
012D FB             161         MOV     A,R3
012E 7E             162         ADDC    A,R6
012F AB             163         MOV     R3,A
0130 FC             164         MOV     A,R4
0131 7F             165         ADDC    A,R7       ;FASTER THAN "ADDC    A,#0"
0132 AC             166         MOV     R4,A
                    167 ;
```

```
                                168 ;          F I R S T    Q U A D R A N T
                                169 ;
0133 3249                       170            JB1      NSIN41   ; TEST FOR SIGN
0135 1240                       171 PSIN41:    JB0      PDWN41   ; POSITIVE, TEST QUADRANT
0137 FB                         172            MOV      A, R3    ; POSITIVE, SCAN UP TABLE
0138 00                         173            NOP
0139 E3                         174            MOVP3    A, @A    ; FETCH SINE VALUE
013A 00                         175            NOP
013B 02                         176            OUTL     BUS, A   ; OUTPUT
013C 1609                       177            JTF      CADSL4
013E 242A                       178            JMP      LOOP4
                                179 ;
                                180 ;          S E C O N D    Q U A D R A N T
                                181 ;
0140 FB                         182 PDWN41:    MOV      A, R3    ; POSITIVE, SCAN DOWN TABLE
0141 37                         183            CPL      A
0142 E3                         184            MOVP3    A, @A
0143 00                         185            NOP
0144 02                         186            OUTL     BUS, A
0145 1609                       187            JTF      CADSL4
0147 242A                       188            JMP      LOOP4
                                189 ;
                                190 ;          T H I R D    Q U A D R A N T
                                191 ;
0149 1254                       192 NSIN41:    JB0      NDWN41   ; NEGATIVE, TEST QUADRANT
014B FB                         193            MOV      A, R3
014C 00                         194            NOP
014D E3                         195            MOVP3    A, @A
014E 37                         196            CPL      A
014F 02                         197            OUTL     BUS, A
0150 1609                       198            JTF      CADSL4
0152 242A                       199            JMP      LOOP4
                                200 ;
                                201 ;          F O U R T H    Q U A D R A N T
                                202 ;
0154 FB                         203 NDWN41:    MOV      A, R3    ; NEGATIVE, SCAN DOWN TABLE
0155 37                         204            CPL      A
0156 E3                         205            MOVP3    A, @A
0157 37                         206            CPL      A
0158 02                         207            OUTL     BUS, A
0159 1609                       208            JTF      CADSL4
015B 242A                       209            JMP      LOOP4
                                210 ;
                                211 ;
                                212 ;
                                213 ;
                                214 ;
                                215 ;
```

Acknowledgments

We wish to thank D. E. Combs for supplying the experimental data in Table 1 and for many helpful comments. We also wish to express our appreciation for helpful discussions with T. M. Burford, J. Plany, and H. Rubin and our indebtedness to K. B. Coulthart for his assistance.

References

1. J. Tierney, "Digital Frequency Synthesizers," Chap. V in *Frequency Synthesis: Techniques and Applications*, J. Gorski-Popiel, ed., IEEE Press, New York, 1975.

2. J. Gorski-Popiel, *Frequency Synthesis: Techniques and Applications*, IEEE Press, New York, 1975, pp. 39-44.

3. J. Tierney, C. M. Rader, and B. Gold, "A Digital Frequency Synthesizer," *IEEE Trans. Audio Electroacoust.*, Vol. AU-19, 1971, p. 43.

4. *MCS-48 Family of Single Chip Microcomputers—User's Manual,* Intel Corp., Santa Clara, Calif., Apr. 1979.

5. W. Worobey and J. Rutkiewicz, "Tantalum Thin-Film RC Circuit Technology for a Universal Active Filter," *IEEE Trans. Parts, Hybrids, Packag.,* Vol. PHP-12, 1976, p. 276.

6. J. H. Wuorinen and T. S. Kinsel, "Call Progress System for Provision of Calling Tones and Ringing Power," *Intelec,* 1979, p. 466.

Tracy S. Kinsel joined the staff of Bell Telephone Laboratories at Murray Hill, New Jersey, in 1963. Presently, he is a supervisor in the common subsystems laboratory at Bell Laboratories at Whippany, New Jersey, where he is involved with the development of digital magnetic tape recording subsystems. He has also worked in optical communications, optical testing of photolithographic masks, test systems for microprocessor devices, and general microprocessor applications.

Kinsel received the AB degree in 1952 and the MS degree in physics in 1955 from the University of Chicago. He received a PhD degree in physics from Rutgers University in 1963. He is a member of the American Physical Society.

John H. Wuorinen, Jr., has headed the Memory and Call Progress System department at the Bell Laboratories in Whippany, New Jersey, since 1974. He joined Bell Labs in 1962; he has held positions of responsibility at the Murray Hill and Columbus facilities in addition to his post at Whippany. From 1956 to 1962, he was an instructor of electrical engineering at Columbia University. His professional interests include computer and transistor theory, silicon and magnetic integrated circuits, memory systems, and electronic subsystems for use in electronic telephone switching offices.

Wuorinen received a BA from Columbia College in 1953, BS and MS degrees from Columbia Engineering School in 1954 and 1956, respectively, and a PhD from the Columbia Graduate Faculties in 1963. He is a member of the IEEE, Sigma Xi, Phi Beta Kappa, Eta Kappa Nu, and Tau Beta Pi.

The authors' address is Bell Telephone Laboratories, Whippany, NJ 07981.

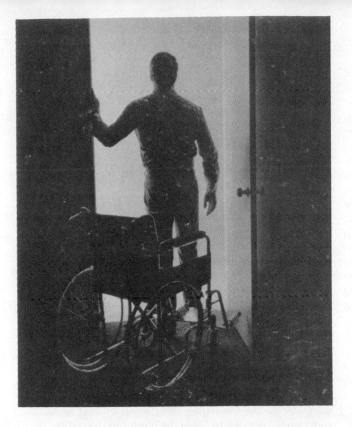

Reprinted from *Computer*, June 1982, pages 33-45. Copyright © 1982 by The Institute of Electrical and Electronics Engineers, Inc.

Because this workstation's device drivers are integrated into its resident CP/M operating system, it can run any CP/M-compatible program and produce output in synthesized speech or braille.

An Integrated Workstation for the Visually Handicapped

Clifford P. Grossner,

T. Radhakrishnan, and

Andy Pospiech

Concordia University

It is estimated that at least ten percent of the world's population suffer from some sort of physical handicap.[1] In many cases the handicapped tend to stay in their houses or in institutions because of communication barriers and a lack of mobility. A handicapped person tries to compensate for his lost faculty by relying more heavily on one or more of his remaining faculties. For example, a blind person develops his hearing and touch as replacements for sight, and a hearing-impaired person substitutes vision for hearing. A quadriplegic has no use of his arms or legs but generally possesses sight, hearing, and speech, which he can use effectively. Similarly, a person affected by cerebral palsy loses nearly all muscular control, but retains the ability to see and hear. In most cases handicapped people are anxious to be employed in some occupation. If suitable opportunities and aids are created, handicapped people are perfectly able to cope with the responsibilities of a full-time career.[1,2]

A person usually interacts with a computer by means of a keyboard and CRT screen, along with a printer for hard-copy output. However, a handicapped person may find it difficult or impossible to use a keyboard or CRT screen, or both. It is possible, although not easy, to design alternate input or output devices that can be used by a handicapped individual.[3,4,5,6] For instance, advances in electronic technology have now made it possible to add speech output to computer-based workstations.[7]

Once a handicapped person has access to a workstation, his ability to integrate into the regular work force is greatly increased. Any document available in machine-readable form will be accessible to the handicapped person without any need for its translation. The handicapped person can also use the workstation to prepare documents that are readable by anyone. Thus, the handicapped individual can overcome most of his communication problems by using a workstation. In addi-

347

tion, being knowledgeable about computer-based workstations can in itself create new avenues for employment.

Here we are concerned with the design and development of an integrated workstation intended for the visually handicapped. Among this group are those who are partially blind as well as those who are totally blind. In some cases, a partially blind person can read letters that are magnified sufficiently. Such magnification can be achieved on a CRT screen through suitably written computer programs. We shall refer to this process as large-print vision. The workstation we describe is targeted mainly to totally blind persons but can also support programs written for large-print vision. It can be used for purposes such as reading documents available in machine-readable form, writing programs, and word processing, or as a tool for communicating with sighted or other unsighted users. In this workstation, both voice and braille output are integrated into one system. This integration makes the workstation less cumbersome for the blind to use.

Communication needs of the blind

A fundamental need of every visually handicapped person is communication with the outside world. He needs to communicate with sighted persons as well as with other visually handicapped persons, and, if he is a programmer or one who works with a terminal, he needs to communicate with a computer.[8]

Speech and writing are the two most commonly used modes of communication in our daily activities and they differ from each other in many respects. Speech is omnipresent—it can be simultaneously heard by many people. Speech leaves the listener's hands free to do other things.[9] However, although speech can be stored by recording on a magnetic medium, it is not amenable to the random accessing of different segments of the stored information. A written document, on the other hand, can be read and reread and assimilated at a much faster rate. If a blind person has not lost the ability to speak or hear, his speech channel is open to support two-way communications. However, he is still at a disadvantage if he has to rely *only* on speech.

A blind person is usually trained to read documents written in braille. Although he cannot write by hand as a sighted person does, he can learn to use the keyboard of a typewriter or computer to prepare typewritten documents. But he also needs to be able to *read* documents whether they are typed by him to communicate with others or vice versa. Reading machines for the blind do exist, but they are too expensive for an average individual to buy.[10]

Consider communications between a blind person and his home computer. For a sighted person, a keyboard is a viable device for man-to-machine communication. However, a keyboard that is well-designed for the use of a sighted person, such as that of the IBM Personal Computer,[11] may not necessarily be optimal for a blind person. In the case of machine-to-man communications, the standard CRT screen is of no use to a totally blind person. However, recent technological advances have now made it cost-effective to add speech and braille output capabilities to computers.[12] But work still needs to be done to integrate these capabilities into a single computer system.

The needs of a blind person who is a programmer will be greater than those of one who is not. For example, a blind programmer will need specialized text editors and program debuggers designed specifically for the convenience of the blind.

Written communication among blind persons is possible through the use of braille. But large texts and long program listings in braille are too bulky to easily store and handle. As a result, randomly accessing information in braille is difficult. If computers are used by both the writer and reader of documents, however, diskettes or cassettes can be substituted for brailled paper, thus alleviating the size and random-access problems.

Most sighted persons cannot read documents written in braille. Similarly, blind persons cannot read hand- or typewritten documents. This communication gap needs to be closed if the blind are to be integrated with the sighted in cooperative endeavors. A good compromise is to store documents in machine-readable form and let a computer do the translation of information that needs to be communicated between the blind and the sighted. Consider a blind programmer communicating with a sighted programmer. It is natural to expect that the information exchanged between them will be in a machine-readable form. In addition to exchanging texts and programs, they will need to communicate representations such as block diagrams and flow charts to one another.

A workstation intended for a blind programmer should enable him to use any program written for or by a sighted programmer.

If we propose that all written communications with the blind should take place through machine-readable documents, then both the senders and receivers of such documents will require workstations which can be used to read and write those documents. One of the major goals in the design of any workstation is the development of a "user-friendly" man-machine interface. For a blind person, this interface will have to include additional input/output devices such as braille displays and printers and speech synthesizers. And for a blind programmer, compatibility between his programs and those of his sighted colleagues will have to be maintained. After his workstation has been augmented with additional I/O devices, the blind programmer should be able to use any program written for or by sighted programmers. Because a blind person will rely more heavily on a computer for communications than a sighted person, the question of system portability will be more important to him. Finally, the cost of the workstation should not be significantly more than that of one designed for sighted people.

348

Commercially available systems

If all written communication with the blind can take place through machine-readable documents, the use of a personal computer becomes an interesting alternative. The computer can be equipped with speech and braille output devices along with software drivers which perform the translations required to present information on those devices. The main subsystems and components that are required for a workstation of this kind are as follows:

• A generalized text-to-speech conversion system such as the Votrax Type 'N Talk[13] or the Intex Talker.[14] The software driver of the workstation sends a copy of the text displayed on the CRT to such text-to-speech systems, which in turn produce the spoken equivalent of the text. Most of the commercially available low-cost text-to-speech conversion systems[13,14] use a phoneme-based LSI speech synthesizer chip like the SC-01[15] and a resident microcomputer that receives ASCII text and converts it into phonemes acceptable to the speech synthesizer.

• A braille display device which displays a selected line of text.[16] This is a tactile-mode substitute for the visual-mode display provided by the CRT screen. Due to technical constraints, most of the commercial devices of this kind display a maximum of 20 characters at a time. Such a device is usually controlled by a microcomputer resident in the display unit. Devices designed to translate information stored on cassettes into braille are presently marketed by Triformation,[17] Telesensory,[18] and Papenmeier[19] as stand-alone units under the names of Microbrailler, Versabraille, and Braillex, respectively.

• A personal computer with the necessary memory, mass storage, I/O ports, and facilities for program development.

• Software drivers to connect speech and braille output devices to the personal computer and to route the information appearing on the screen to the appropriate channel. In addition to drivers, a text editor specially designed to meet the characteristics of these output channels and the needs of a blind person is needed. Such an editor should enable a blind person to examine a program or data file.[20]

With present technology it is possible for a blind person to buy the generalized text-to-speech conversion system, the braille display device, and the personal computer off the shelf and interconnect them himself. Software utilities for editing or transferring a file between Versabraille and an Apple microcomputer are sold by some software vendors.[21] However, even these commercially available software packages require some sort of customizing.

In the fall of 1982 we taught an introductory programming course for the blind at Concordia University in Montreal. For the students in this course we bought a Type 'N Talk, Versabraille, and IBM Personal Computer from three different vendors and interconnected them to form a workstation. The interconnection of these subsystems and the integration of the required software drivers were not trivial tasks. While the drivers themselves were not complex, their insertion into a pre-existing operating system posed several problems. One major stumbling block was the small amount of detailed information provided with most commercially available operating systems. Therefore, integration required the systems analyst to have a fair amount of prior knowledge of, and experience with, the operating system used. Certainly such interconnection and integration tasks are beyond the abilities of most end users.

The systems discussed above were designed to operate as independent entities. Hence, combining them in the

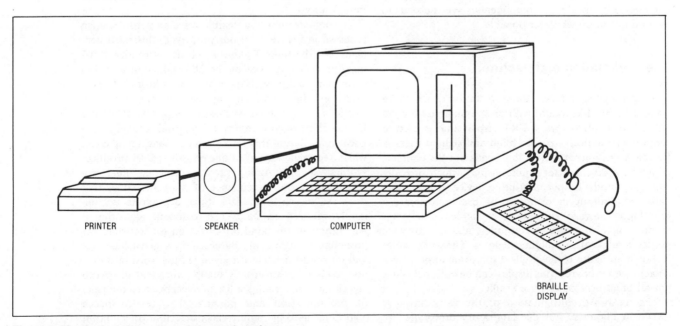

Figure 1. Physical configuration of the workstation.

PRINTER   SPEAKER   COMPUTER   BRAILLE DISPLAY

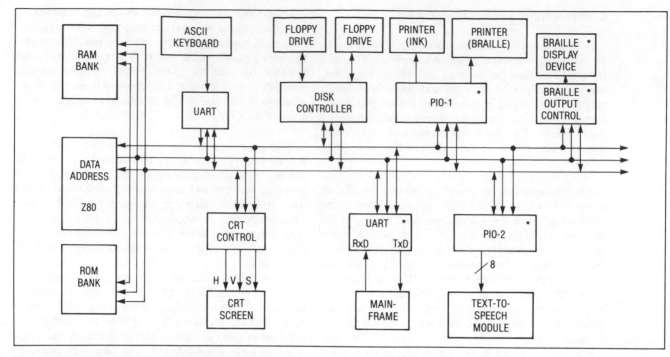

Figure 2. Hardware configuration of the workstation.

manner just described resulted in duplication of hardware and higher costs. For example, the Versabraille unit contains a cassette drive for information storage and is controlled by its own microprocessor. It operates as a stand-alone system, outputting or storing on cassettes information entered in braille. It can communicate with other computers. Since we were interested only in the braille display, much of the capacity of this unit was not utilized. A less costly approach would have been to use a braille display system specially designed to interface with a microcomputer.

We were faced with two constraints. We needed to keep the cost of the workstation down and integrate commercially available components. We needed to avoid duplication wherever possible.

The workstation architecture

As seen by the end user, the workstation consists of a standard ASCII keyboard with programmable function and cursor-control keys, a CRT display that is used to support interactions between blind and sighted users, a flexible voice output system that reads out the contents of a file, a 20-character braille display which provides soft-copy braille output, a printing device that provides hard-copy output in character or braille formats, a minifloppy storage subsystem, a modem for communicating with a remote computer, and the software needed to make use of all these devices. The workstation is shown in Figure 1; the braille display unit appears as a detachable keyboard. This display can be optional, since not all blind persons can use braille.

The hardware configuration of the workstation is shown in Figure 2. For our laboratory prototype, we used a Heathkit H-88 computer. We added certain hard-

ware modules, which are indicated with asterisks in the figure. The H-88 is based on the Z80 microprocessor and CP/M operating system. The microprocessor performs the central processing and integrates the different peripheral devices through the diskette-based operating system. The RAM space is used both for user program development and data manipulation. One floppy disk drive is provided in the standard configuration; a second can be added. Two ports available from PIO-1 are used to control the regular character printer and a braille embosser. When high-quality hard-copy braille is not required, inexpensive braille output can be obtained on a regular dot-matrix printer that has had some minor modifications.[22]

The organization of a flexible voice output subsystem is shown in Figure 3. In our prototype, this subsystem comprises the Intex Talker, which uses a resident 6502 microprocessor to control speech production and perform handshaking with the workstation host processor. Many existing voice output systems are based on Votrax's SC-01 speech synthesizer chip. The SC-01 is a CMOS chip which contains an electronic model of the vocal tract. Using this internal model and input codes which represent various phonemes, the SC-01 produces synthesized voice. An input text is translated under program control into a sequence of phoneme codes that drive the speech synthesizer. Such a program is commonly referred to as a text-to-speech algorithm.[23] Algorithms of this kind are based on general rules for pronouncing strings of characters in a given language and on rules for parsing a given textual word into pronounceable substrings. Usually, the text-to-speech algorithm also contains a list of exceptions to the rules of pronunciation and parsing. The text-to-speech algorithms used in commercially available voice output systems are considered proprietary.

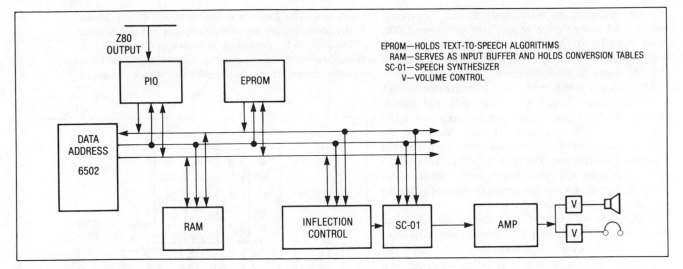

EPROM—HOLDS TEXT-TO-SPEECH ALGORITHMS
RAM—SERVES AS INPUT BUFFER AND HOLDS CONVERSION TABLES
SC-01—SPEECH SYNTHESIZER
V—VOLUME CONTROL

Figure 3. The speech module (based on the Intex Talker).

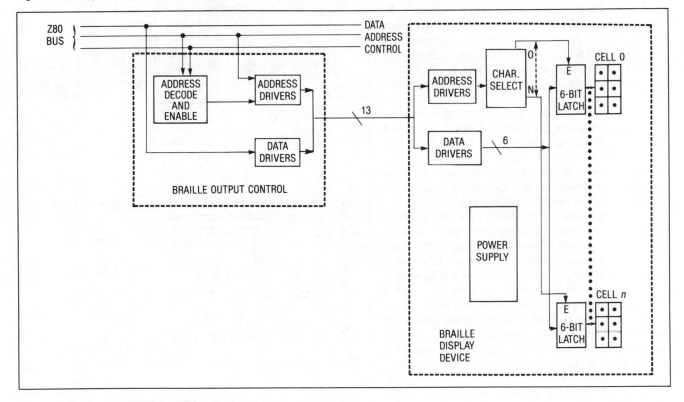

Figure 4. The braille display module.

The text-to-speech algorithm of the hardware unit shown in Figure 3 is contained in the EPROM and is executed by the 6502 microprocessor. The RAM is used to store the input text and the translated phoneme codes. The programmable inflection-control component, which improves the quality of the synthesized speech, forms an additional input to the speech synthesizer chip. Rules that govern the control of inflection and other speech parameters are generally built into the text-to-speech algorithm. The Intex Talker is a complete voice output system with its own software; it can operate as a stand-alone unit. It is included as a part of our workstation and is connected to the Z80 microprocessor

through PIO-2 (see Figure 2). It is quite possible to absorb the functions of the 6502 contained in the Intex Talker into the host computer of the workstation. However, we found that the direct use of an inexpensive off-the-shelf subsystem made the system more cost-effective—constructing our own version of the Intex Talker would have been too expensive for a low-volume application such as ours.

Another module shown in Figure 2 is the braille display device. Although a braille display is available as a part of so-called "paperless" braille units,[17,18,19] no off-the-shelf braille display system designed to interface directly to a host microcomputer is as yet available.

Furthermore, paperless braille units, unlike voice output systems, are quite expensive and cost well over $6000. After considering these points, we designed our own braille display system for our workstation. Details of this system are shown in Figure 4.

The system is interfaced to the Z80 processor through a braille output control unit. The data and control registers of the braille display unit are parts of the I/O space of the Z80 processor. Their selection is accomplished by decoding a certain number of the most significant address bits. The least significant address bits are used to select individual braille cells. The data lines of the Z80 processor are connected to the braille display unit through standard line drivers.

Each braille cell of the display unit comprises six dot positions arranged in a matrix of three rows and two columns. Our prototype design includes 20 cells and it can easily be extended by adding more cells. Associated with each cell there is a six-bit braille cell latch, or BCL, which stores the bit (dot) patterns of the character to be displayed on that cell. Each BCL has a unique address in the I/O address space of the Z80 microprocessor—by writing into that I/O address through the braille control unit, the Z80 can store a character code in a BCL.

The mechanical part of the display system is responsible for converting the electronic bit patterns in the various BCLs into a tactile form. Each dot of a braille cell is associated with a pin controlled by a solenoid. In a 20-character display system there are 120 (6 × 20) dots or solenoids. In order to reduce the cost of the prototype, we decided to use commercially available solenoids as opposed to any specialized designs. We selected 0.5-inch diameter tubular solenoids.

In a typical braille cell produced by standard braille embossers, the distance between two dots in either a horizontal or vertical direction is 0.1 inch. The intercharacter or intercell distance from center to center is 0.25 inch. It is a mechanical design problem to arrange the 0.5-inch diameter solenoids so they can drive a braille cell of this size. In our design, the solenoids are laid out as shown in Figure 5a. A motion translation mechanism (Figure 5b) is employed to produce a braille display cell of the required size. As shown in Figure 5b, the plungers are attached to the push rods by a sleeve. This sleeve is also used to let the plunger, and hence the push rod, fall only by a distance equal to D when the solenoid is de-energized. The dotted lines in Figure 5a indicate the position of the push rods under the surface of the top plate. The overall dimensions of the 20-character display are about 4 × 11 × 3 inches.

The solenoids we used each have a coil resistance of 50 ohms and, when operating at continuous duty, draw about 240 milliamperes of current from a 12-volt supply. In the worst case all 120 dots may be raised, drawing a large amount of current from the power supply. One of our design goals was to minimize the demands on the power supply unit. This can be accomplished by reducing the drive current required by each solenoid, by adding external resistance in series. Another way to reduce the average power consumption is to use pulsed instead of steady DC driving. For optimum performance, we also had to choose the appropriate pulse duration (duty

cycle) and pulse frequency. However, the design details of the power supply are outside the scope of this article.

The solenoid drive circuit is shown in Figure 6. The diode shown in this figure is usually called a freewheeling diode. The resistances R1 and R2 are chosen to

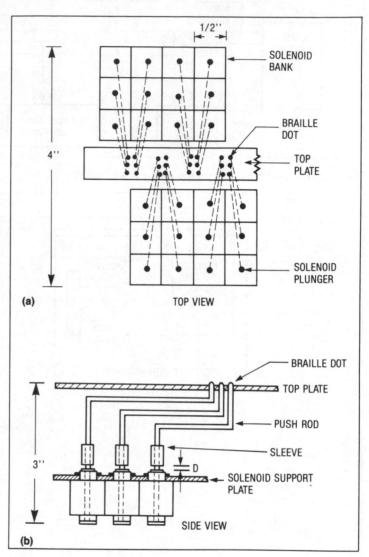

(a)   TOP VIEW

(b)   SIDE VIEW

Figure 5. The solenoid arrangement in the braille display—top view, showing four braille cells (a), and side view (b).

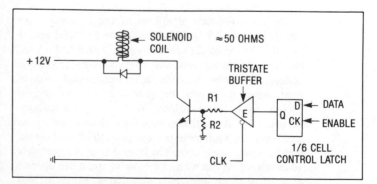

Figure 6. The solenoid drive circuit.

bias the transistor. The flip-flop shown is one of the six flip-flops contained in a braille cell latch. Data are latched into a BCL by the Z80 processor when the enable signal is given by the cell-select logic of the braille display. The clock signal applied to the enable pin of the tristate buffer determines the duty cycle and frequency of the pulsed drive.

We had to satisfy a number of physical constraints in the design of our braille display. Each braille character had to be big enough to be sensed by a finger tip. The space between each character had to be optimum—just big enough to permit characters to be distinguished from one another but small enough to keep the amount of hand travel required to read a sequence of characters to a minimum. This of course required the drive mechanism for each cell to be as small as possible. In addition, we made the unit detachable so that a user could hold it in his lap and read a long document. This required the weight of the braille display unit to be as low as possible. We also minimized the power consumption and heat dissipation of the unit, which in turn contributed to its low cost and small size.

Software structure

The workstation described here can be called an integrated workstation because it contributes to the notion of integration at different levels. At one level we aim at the integration of sighted programmers or office workers with their visually handicapped counterparts. Consider a scenario, such as an automated office, in which each worker is assigned a workstation and the different workstations are interconnected through a local-area network. Communications between the sighted and the blind can take place in such a network through machine-readable documents. The sighted and the blind can even communicate with each other without a network by exchanging diskettes. Here, the compatibility of documents and computer programs exchanged between these two groups is important. As another level of integration consider the different applications of a workstation. An end user can use a workstation for developing programs or reading documents stored on diskettes, or even for communicating with others over a communications network.

At the operating system level of the workstation there is yet another kind of integration. Device drivers for speech and braille output devices are integrated into the BIOS—basic input/output system—of the resident operating system and therefore are accessible to any program that makes use of the BIOS.

The software components of the workstation (Figure 7) are organized into three levels. At Level 0 are the various device drivers. File management functions, command interpreters, and error handlers are placed in

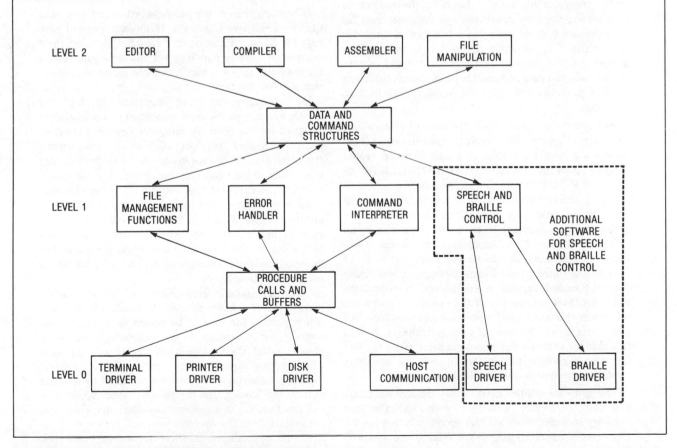

Figure 7. Structure of the microcomputer operating system.

Level 1. System-oriented operations such as editing, compiling, assembling, and file manipulations form Level 2. The software modules enclosed by the dotted lines have been developed by us as add-on modifications to the CP/M operating system.

The device drivers are hardware-dependent and usually include very primitive routines that perform simple functions such as reading or writing single characters to a terminal. A set of such routines are normally required to control each peripheral of the workstation. These routines are also responsible for any code translation or system initialization. At the system support level (Level 1) are software modules which perform basic "housekeeping" functions. An example of this is the file management system, which maintains all the files on a diskette and allows other programs to access the files by name rather than by track and sector numbers. The programs at Level 2 are the most complex and for the most part define all the functions available to the end user. File manipulation programs, for example, allow the user to delete files, copy files from one diskette to another, or initialize new diskettes.

The software components of the operating system are arranged into the levels described above according to how they interact with each other. Each level depends on the levels below it to provide a set of coherent and useful functions to the end user. The utility, or Level 2, programs depend heavily on the Level 0 and Level 1 programs. Consequently, any changes made at these lower levels will directly affect the operations of these utilities. Utility programs interact with Level 1 software modules through specific data structures. For instance, most file management systems maintain a file-control block for each active file. Similarly, Level 1 software modules activate various routines at Level 0 by means of procedure calls and pass parameters via machine registers, a method generally employed for low-level information exchange.

At Level 0 we included two new device drivers which control the speech and braille output devices. These drivers are invoked whenever a call is made by the CP/M operating system to its CONSOLE-IN or CONSOLE-OUT drivers. When information is sent to the CRT screen through CONSOLE-OUT, our additional driver sends this information to the braille and speech devices according to the format specified by an I/O control byte. This I/O control byte stores details about user-selected device-control functions such as speech rate, fundamental frequency or pitch, and braille "font" (Grade I, regular, or computer). Every time the CONSOLE-IN routine of CP/M receives a character, our driver checks to see if a function key was depressed and updates the I/O control byte accordingly. It is in this manner that the function keys are interpreted and the user is given dynamic control over the operating modes of the speech and braille output devices.

The software utilities used by the visually handicapped can be divided into two categories. The first category includes those utilities specifically written for the visually handicapped, like a talking text editor.[20] Such software takes into consideration the special characteristics of output devices such as speech synthesizers and the special needs of the handicapped. The second category comprises utilities that were written for sighted users but which are also used by the handicapped. Such software usually employs a CRT display as its output device. In our workstation, the visual display can be automatically augmented by the speech and braille displays for programs in this category. This is a direct result of our integration of new device drivers into the resident operating system.

A visually handicapped user can control the workstation's speech and braille output by means of the following function-key assignments, which will be recognized by the command interpreter:

- Key F0: Turn ON or OFF speech output (toggle).
- Key F1: SPEAK or SPELL mode (toggle). In SPEAK mode the computer speaks out the display word by word, and in SPELL mode character by character.
- Key F2: CONTINUOUS or STEP mode (toggle). In CONTINUOUS mode the computer speaks out the text in one stretch, whereas in STEP mode each unit (word or character) is spoken only after the user presses a GO FORWARD (cursor right key) or GO BACKWARD (cursor left key) button. Pressing the space bar repeats the cursor character and does not advance the cursor.
- Key F3: Change type of braille to be generated—Grade I, regular, or computer.
- Key F4: Turn ON or OFF braille output (toggle).

In teaching the visually handicapped to edit files using speech output, we found the facilities associated with keys F0, F1, and F2 to be very valuable. By using these features, a visually handicapped student could scan a file at a speed suited to him in order to locate and correct errors in his programs.

Human engineering is an important aspect of any design, and it is all the more important in a workstation designed for the blind. A computer keyboard contains many specialized keys in addition to the normal character keys of a typewriter. A blind person may know how to type but may not feel comfortable with nonstandard keys. He may spend a lot of time locating them (which he does by comparing their positions to the positions of standard keys he knows well). In order to assist beginners in this endeavor, we placed braille codes on the key tops of commonly used keys. We found that this increased the confidence of the beginning student in using the keyboard.

Other human-engineered features of our workstation include the detachable lightweight braille display unit, which permits the user to be seated in a comfortable position while reading long documents, and headphones, which the visually handicapped user can wear when working around others. The "disk in use" light on the floppy disk drives has been augmented by a tactile output—by sensing this the visually handicapped user can avoid unloading a diskette from the drive when he is not supposed to. The operator's manual for the workstation will be available in three forms—in braille, on audiocassette, and as machine-readable files.

Our workstation integrates certain desirable features for the visually handicapped such as outputs in speech, braille, and print. Print and braille are available in both hard- and soft-copy form. Since device drivers for these speech and braille output devices are integrated into the resident operating system, any utility not originally designed for the blind can run on the workstation and produce speech or braille output. The workstation can be used by the sighted as well as by the blind. It can support communication between the sighted and the blind or between one blind person and another by employing machine-readable diskette-based files and network interconnections.

By using off-the-shelf components for our computer and speech-output modules and by designing our own braille display unit, we constructed a prototype unit of the workstation. It is now being field-tested by blind programmers enrolled in our course, "Introduction to Computers and Computing for the Physically Handicapped." We believe that our workstation is much more versatile than the paperless braille units presently available in the market. ■

Acknowledgments

The financial assistance provided by the Natural Sciences and Engineering Research Council of Canada and by the Teaching Development Grant Program of Concordia University is gratefully acknowledged.

References

1. W. Myers, "Personal Computers Aid the Handicapped," *IEEE Micro,* Vol. 2, No. 1, Feb. 1982, pp. 26-40.

2. S.G. Ryan and D.N. Bedi, "Toward Computer Literacy for Visually Impaired Students," *J. Visual Impairment and Blindness,* Vol. 72, Oct. 1978, pp. 302-306.

3. S. Ciarcia, "Mind Over Matter, Add Biofeedback to Your Computer," *Byte,* June 1979, pp. 49-56.

4. R.E. Savoie, J.S. Brugler, and J.C. Bliss, "Development of a Hand-Held Talking Calculator for the Blind," *AFIPS Conf. Proc.,* Vol. 45, 1976 NCC, pp. 221-225.

5. D.W. Seymour, "Record Means and Method of Making Same," U.S. Patent No. 3,132,962, June 1962.

6. G.P. Carbonneau, "Braille Communication Terminal," US Patent No. 3,880,269, Apr. 1975.

7. A.L. Robinson, "Communicating with Computers by Voice," *IEEE Trans. Professional Communication,* Vol. PC-22, No. 3, Sept. 1979, pp. 159-165.

8. H.D. Toong and A. Gupta, "Personal Computers," *Scientific American,* Vol. 247, No. 6, Dec. 1982, pp. 86-107.

9. R.S. Nickerson and K.N. Stevens, "Approaches to the Study of the Relationship Between Intelligibility and Physical Properties of Speech," Tech. Report, Nat'l Tech. Institute for the Deaf, Rochester, NY, June 1979, pp. 20-23.

10. R.C. Kurzweil, "Kurzweil Reading Machine for the Blind" (user's manual), Kurzweil Computer Products, Cambridge, MA.

11. *IBM Personal Computer User's Manual,* International Business Machines Corp., Boca Raton, FL, 1980.

12. S. Hiratsuka and H. Arai, "Line Printer for the Raised Dot Language of Braille Characters," US Patent No. 4,183,683, Jan. 15, 1980.

13. *Type 'N Talk User's Manual,* Votrax Corp., Troy, MI, 1981.

14. *Intex Talker User's Manual,* Intex Micro Systems Corp., Troy, MI, 1982.

15. *SC-01 Speech Synthesizer Data Sheet,* Votrax Corp., Troy, MI, 1981.

16. D.V. Charlesworth, "Braille Tape Reader," US Patent No. 3,886,020, Feb. 1975.

17. *Microbrailler User's Manual,* Triformation Systems, Stuart, FL, 1981.

18. *The Versabraille System User's Manual,* Telesensory Systems, Palo Alto, CA, 1981.

19. *Braillex User's Manual,* Papenmeier Corp., Upperco, MD, 1982.

20. T. Radhakrishnan and A. Madras, "A Voice-based Editor for Programming in Basic," Tech. Report, Dept. of Computer Science, Concordia University, Montreal, 1983.

21. D. Holladay, "Connecting a Versabraille Paperless Brailler to an Apple II Computer" (internal report), Raised Dot Computing, 1982. (Available from the company at 310 S. 7th St., Lewisburg, PA 17837.)

22. A. Fant, Jr., "Braille Writing in Pascal," *Byte,* Vol. 7, No. 9, Sept. 1982, pp. 250-268.

23. J. Allen, "Synthesis of Speech from Unrestricted Text," *Proc. IEEE,* Vol. 64, No. 4, Apr. 1976, pp. 433-442.

Clifford P. Grossner is a systems analyst in the Department of Computer Science at Concordia University, Montreal. His areas of interest include microcomputer system design and applications, design of microprogrammed bit-slice CPUs, and microcomputer interconnection networks for parallel processing. Grossner obtained his B.Comp.Sc and M.Comp.Sc degrees from Concordia University in 1980 and 1982, respectively. He is a member of the IEEE Computer Society.

Thiruvengadam Radhakrishnan is an associate professor of computer science at Concordia University. He obtained his BE, with honors, from Madras University in 1966 and his M.Tech and PhD degrees from the Indian Institute of Technology at Kanpur, India. His interests include microprocessor-based systems, local-area networks, computer applications to the handicapped, and man-machine communications in database applications.

Andy Pospiech was an undergraduate student and research assistant at Concordia University. Among his interests are microcomputer system design and applications and microcomputer network design. He obtained his B.Comp.Sc from Concordia University in April 1983.

The authors' address is Dept. of Computer Science, Concordia University, Montreal, Quebec H3G 1M8, Canada.

Reprinted from *IEEE Micro,* October 1983, pages 5-15. Copyright © 1983 by The Institute of Electrical and Electronics Engineers, Inc.

By adding this IEEE 796 module to his workstation or personal computer,

a user can put "electronic envelopes" around his e-mail messages.

A Microprocessor-based Cryptoprocessor

Christian Müller-Schloer

Siemens AG

Computer communication systems, local-area networks, interconnected local-area networks, and electronic mail systems are playing an increasingly important role in office automation, telecommunications, and factory automation. A prerequisite for extensive usage of these services, with full or partial replacement of conventional paper mail by an electronic medium, is security. It must be possible to guarantee the secrecy of a message so that only the addressee is able to read it (i.e., it must be possible to provide the equivalent of a paper envelope). Furthermore, the receiver of a message wants to verify that the indicated and the real sender are one and the same (i.e., there must be a provision for electronic signatures and signature verification).[1]

Recent advances have made the technology of cryptography a viable candidate for solving these problems. The DES—Data Encryption Standard[2]—as well as public-key systems[3,4] have been discussed extensively. In this article I describe an experimental secure communication system and its implementation with a special module—the cryptoprocessor (CP). I present the overall system structure and user interface and provide an overview of cryptography and a review of the design considerations. I describe the software interface to the main component, the cryptoprocessor, and its data structure, hardware, software, and performance.

Application environment of the cryptoprocessor

In order to clarify what the requirements of a secure communication system are, I describe in the following

paragraphs the functionality of a secure electronic mail system from a user's point of view. Such a system should offer the same functionality as today's paper mail system. It must be convenient to use and should not require users to have any knowledge of the underlying security mechanisms. The basic functions are

- secrecy and
- authentication (electronic signatures).

In addition to conventional electronic mail functions like editing, searching, storing, retrieving, and printing, a secure electronic mail system has the following:

- *Sign in/sign out:* Since we allow any subscriber to use any station in the network (thereby assuring full user mobility), a specific period of time must be defined during which a station is dedicated exclusively to one user. This period begins with *sign in* and ends with *sign out.* The user is required to supply his secret password for authentication.
- *Store protected/retrieve protected:* With *store protected,* files of any kind, generally letters or documents, can be stored on a mass storage device in encrypted form so that even physical reading does not help an intruder understand the contents. A *retrieve protected* operation automatically results in the retrieval of the properly decrypted file if the user has signed in under the same password as he used when he stored the file. No explicit key input is required.
- *Sign letter/verify signature:* An electronic signature

356

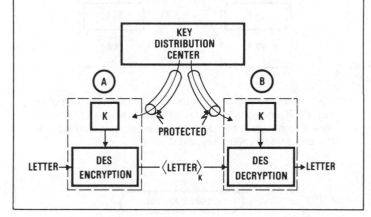
• *High-level functions:* As in the paper mail system, high-level security functions such as registered mail,[11] notarized documents, and multiple-signature documents (e.g., forms) can be implemented. These functions generally require a network structure with trusted authorities.[5]

In order to simplify the implementation of the above-mentioned features (or similar ones), an extension of the operating system of the station by a well-defined set of instructions is desirable. The technology used to implement these features is cryptography. In the next section we will review the basic properties of cryptographic systems.

Cryptography and design considerations

The term cryptography, which generally means the science of enciphering and deciphering data, is used here to refer to the method of encoding and decoding data. Encryption and decryption are controlled by "keys." "Key" refers to a parameter used to control a computer algorithm which transforms a given set of data into a new set of data which bears no obvious resemblance to the original one. In a classical single-key system (see discussion at left), the same key, K, is used for encryption and decryption. Therefore, anyone who can read a message can also modify it. The most widely used single-key system is DES, the Data Encryption Standard.[2]

Single-key systems like the DES are fast, inexpensive, and simple to use. DES chips are available from a number of manufacturers. However, DES keys have to be distributed to all potential communication partners; this presents a major problem in large networks. Another disadvantage is that single-key systems provide no means to realize true electronic signatures.

Two-key systems, and in particular public-key cryptosystems (e.g., RSA, the Rivest-Shamir-Adleman system[4]—see discussion at right), can solve some of these structural problems. Provided that certain precautions are taken,[5,6] no key predistribution is required since all public keys can be read from a public read-only file.[7] Electronic signatures can be implemented in a very elegant way. The main disadvantage of public-key cryptosystems, however, is their low speed.

However, the structural advantages of a public-key system can be combined with the speed and usability of DES, providing the best of both worlds. Such a system is known as a *hybrid system.*[8] (See "How does a hybrid system work?" on page 8.) Such a design makes sense, since for the transmission of a typical secret *and* signed two-page letter, two RSA encryptions and 250 DES encryptions are necessary.

For the realization of a cryptographic hybrid system, a number of design considerations are of importance. The key generation, although time consuming, must be done on the user's site in order to avoid transmission of secret keys over the network. Encryption and decryption must be executed on an end-to-end basis so that no messages are exposed in cleartext during transmission. Both of these requirements call for cryptographic processing in the ter-

is attached to a letter in such a way that the whole document cannot be modified by anyone except the sender. This is the equivalent of a written signature. The *verify signature* operation checks the validity of the electronic signature. The necessary key management is handled automatically.

• *Sign/verify with time stamp:* A signature is attached to the letter together with an indication of date and time. Neither the letter nor the time stamp can be manipulated after they have been signed. This operation is typically carried out by a trusted authority (an "electronic notary public").

• *Send/receive secret letter:* Sender and receiver addresses have to be supplied by the sender. Key management and secrecy encryption are handled by the system. No key predistribution is necessary. A *receive secret letter* operation results in a properly decrypted message if the user trying to read it has signed in under the password of the intended receiver. There is no need to restrict the transfer of encrypted files. Therefore, files can be received by the proper addressee anywhere in the network.

• *Open/close secret two-way channel:* For simultaneous communication between two stations, a virtual channel is established with *open secret two-way channel.* All messages sent over this channel are encrypted in a user-transparent way. *Close secret two-way channel* erases all information concerning this channel.

• *Housekeeping:* The system housekeeping routine handles the generation and distribution of keys basically without user intervention. In the case of a possible security leak, the user can request a new set of keys or even a new password. He can be sure that after *sign out* no sensitive information is left in the station (unless the station has been tampered with).

How does a two-key system work?

A key generation algorithm produces, starting from a random number, two keys: KEY1 and KEY2.

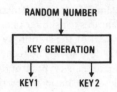

Given limited time, it is not possible to derive KEY1 from KEY2, or KEY2 from KEY1. KEY1 and KEY2 are closely related, however.

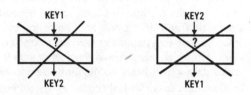

Plaintext *en*crypted with KEY1 cannot be *de*crypted with KEY1. For decryption, KEY2 has to be used.

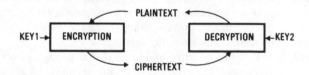

KEY1 and KEY2 are interchangeable with respect to encryption and decryption.

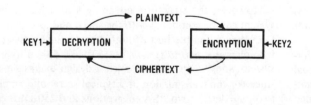

How does a public-key system work?

Given a two-key system, each user generates two keys: KEY1 and KEY2. He declares one of them, say KEY1, public (public key PK) and makes it accessible to everybody. He keeps the other one, KEY2, secret (secret key SK).

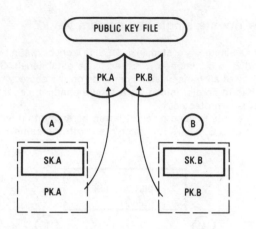

If A wants to *send a secret letter* to B, then A gets B's public key, PK.B, encrypts the letter with PK.B, and sends it to B. Now B and only B can decrypt the letter, since only B has the proper decryption key, SK.B.

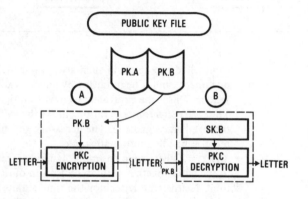

If A wants to *sign a letter,* he encrypts it with his own secret key, SK.A. Note that this letter now is not secret! If B wants to verify that A has signed the letter, then he gets A's public key, PK.A, and uses it for decryption. If he gets a meaningful result, then A must have signed the letter.

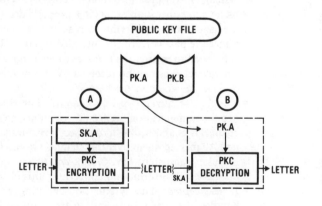

If a letter must be signed *and* secret, then *both* of the above two steps must be applied.

How does a hybrid system work?

Encryptions and decryptions with a public-key system are slow. But such a system can be combined with a single-key system (e.g., DES) to save time without giving up the public-key system's functional advantages.

To send a secret letter, user A generates a DES key K at random and applies a DES encryption with K to his letter. For a two-page letter, about 250 DES encryptions (seven bytes/encryption) are necessary. Then the public-key method is used to protect K. Only one of the slow public-key encryptions has to be carried out! The recipient B uses the public-key method to obtain K, and a DES decryption with K to retrieve the letter.

A similar scheme is used for signed letters.

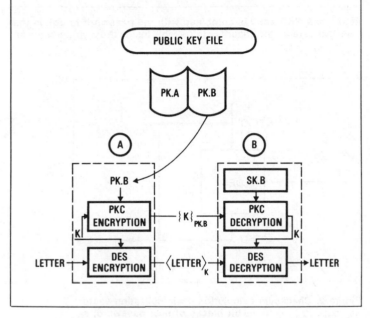

minal or personal workstation. Because of the extensive number crunching needed for RSA, some sort of dedicated hardware is desirable. We have chosen to implement this hardware in the form of a coprocessor called the cryptoprocessor (CP). The CP has a fixed security-related instruction set which serves as an extension to the host operating system and which, if properly protected, cannot be modified by an intruder. Thus, the designer retains control over the behavior of the security system. Physical manipulation (tampering) must also be prevented. This protection is easier to provide if the security-related hardware and software are contained in one physical device (module). The CP should also be inexpensive and applicable in a variety of systems. Therefore, we implemented it as an IEEE-796-compatible (Multibus) single-board computer.

The design of a secure network

In order to understand some of the CP's features, it is necessary to first understand the design of a secure network (i.e., a secure electronic mail system). We describe one solution below. It is, however, not the only implementation that is possible with the CP.

From the key management point of view, all stations are equivalent. Therefore, a station must be dedicated dynamically to a specific user during the time he is performing sensitive work. This state is entered with a *sign in* operation and terminated with *sign out*. At *sign in* time the station receives all user-specific information needed to perform its crypto-related tasks from the public-key file, PKF. The PKF entry contains the following data for every user (see Figure 1):

- Name, address.
- Public-key data, PKD, consisting of the user's public key, PK, and the RSA modulus n.[4]
- Secret-key data, SKD, consisting of the user's secret key, SK, and the numbers p and q, where $p \cdot q = n$. p, q, and n are used for the different encryption and decryption steps. The security of the RSA algorithm is based on the fact that it is impossible to determine p and q from n in a reasonable time if n is sufficiently large. SKD is encrypted with the key, K_{loc}.
- A codeword.[7]

Note that the PKF entries are accessible by everybody. Therefore they do not contain any information that is useful by itself. Only by combination with a user password can the cryptoprocessor (or anybody else) derive secret information. The password does not need to be stored anywhere. Ideally it should be memorized by its owner.

At *sign in* time the user supplies his password, PW, to the cryptoprocessor, where it is "hashed" into a checksum, CS:

$$CS = HASH\ (PW).$$

HASH is a DES-based hashing function[9,10] and is shown in Figure 2.

From CS and the codeword, CW, the local key, K_{loc}, is derived:

$$K_{loc} = CS \oplus CW,$$

where $\oplus$ stands for the EXOR function and K_{loc} is used to obtain the secret-key data, SKD (see again Figure 1).

Now the user is "signed in"; i.e., the security status table, SST, contains all the data in cleartext that are necessary for cryptographic processing. The *sign out* operation performed at the end of a session deletes these sensitive data.

The public-key file, PKF, is administered by a trusted central authority, CA, which sends the information to any station on demand. All the CA has to guarantee is that the PKF can be read only and not modified. The PKF entry is generated when the user is enrolled; it can be signed by the CA.[7] Figure 3 shows a secure network comprising user stations, the nonsecure communications system, and the CA.

Functionality of the cryptoprocessor

The CP processes security-related tasks sent from the host. Its instruction set enables an application programmer to implement all user-level services without understanding the details of cryptography. All CP services are strictly local; i.e., the CP does not communicate with the outside world by itself. For example, the information from the public-key file must be obtained by the host and supplied to the CP with the call.

The CP accepts three groups of instructions—housekeeping commands, key management commands, and cryptocommands.

Housekeeping

- *SignIn*. The host supplies the PKF entry of the present user along with his password. The security status table (see discussion below) is filled and the SignIn state is entered.
- *CheckSignIn*. Checks whether a user is presently signed in.
- *SignOut*. All sensitive user-specific information is deleted from the CP's local memory.
- *GiveCPStatus*. Gives the CP's present status (e.g., key generation, self testing).
- *Selftest*. Starts a self-test routine and sends the results back to the host.

Key management

- *GenDESKey*. A DES key is generated at random, stored in the security status table under KT, and returned to the host encrypted under a public key supplied with the call.
- *GiveNewKeyPair*. Upon input of a password, PW, a new K_{loc} is generated at random and used to encrypt new secret-key data, SKD, obtained from the key stack (see discussion below) along with the corresponding public-key data, PKD. A checksum, CS, is hashed from PW and EXORed with K_{loc} to give the new codeword, CW. The values for CW, PKD, and $<SKD> K_{loc}$ are returned.
- *LoadDESKeyLoc*. The content of KT from the security status table is loaded so that it can be used as the DES key for the next DES encryption/decryption call.
- *LoadDESKey*. A supplied DES key, encrypted under PK, is decrypted with SK, entered into KT in the security status table, and loaded so that it can be used as the DES key for the next DES encryption call.
- *GenRandomNo*. Generates a random number and returns it.

Cryptocommands

- *EncrW/OwnPK*. Encrypts with PK, the public key from the SST.
- *EncrW/OwnSK*. Encrypts with SK, the secret key from the SST.
- *EncrW/SupplPK*. Encrypts with supplied public key.

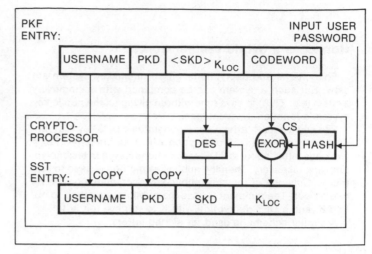

Figure 1. A PKF entry is combined with the password to obtain the cleartext data for the security status table inside the cryptoprocessor.

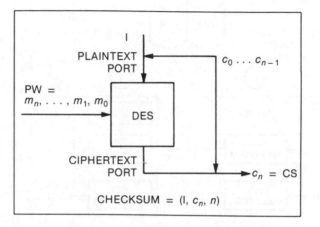

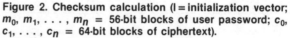

Figure 2. Checksum calculation (I = initialization vector; m_0, m_1, . . . , m_n = 56-bit blocks of user password; c_0, c_1, . . . , c_n = 64-bit blocks of ciphertext).

- *EncrW/DESKey*. Expects that a DES key has been previously loaded. Encrypts with that key.
- *DecrW/DESKey*. Expects that a DES key has been previously loaded. Decrypts with that key.
- *Hash*. Performs a DES hash and returns the checksum.

Data structure

The CP uses local RAM memory for storage of variables and certain other security-related data. For security reasons, this memory must be inaccessible from the outside world. Therefore, the shared memory used for communication between the host and the CP is physically separated from the local RAM. In our case, host memory is used for communication.

As described in the previous sections, a secret user password and user-specific information from the public-key file are supplied to the CP at SignIn time. This information is used by the CP to derive cleartext keys

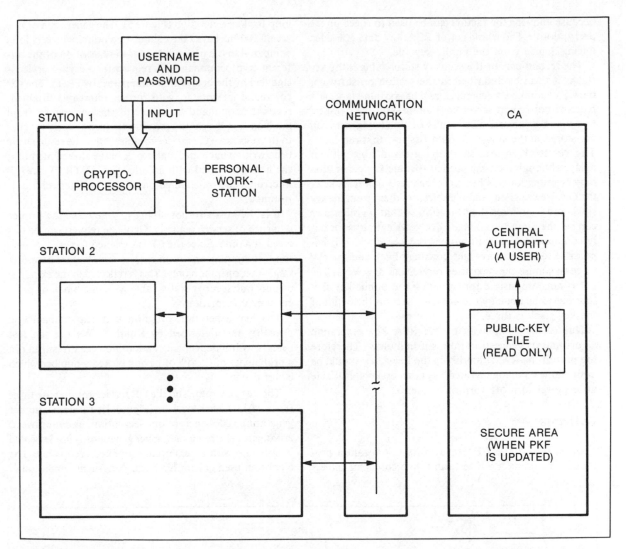

Figure 3. Schematic diagram of a secure network comprising workstations, a nonsecure communication system, and a central authority.

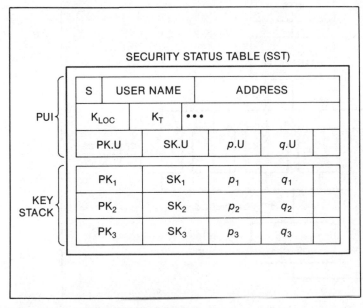

SECURITY STATUS TABLE (SST)

S	USER NAME		ADDRESS	
K_{LOC}		K_T	•••	
PK.U		SK.U	p.U	q.U
PK_1		SK_1	p_1	q_1
PK_2		SK_2	p_2	q_2
PK_3		SK_3	p_3	q_3

PUI { (first three rows)

KEY STACK { (last three rows)

Figure 4. The security status table.

needed for execution of most of the CP commands. Information about keys is organized in a data structure called the SST—security status table (Figure 4).

The SST consists of two parts: the PUI (for present user information) and the key stack. The PUI contains a variable, S, indicating whether a user is presently signed in and the name and address of this user. K_{loc} is a local DES key calculated from the password and codeword, CW; it can be loaded for DES encryption/decryption with the LoadDESKeyLoc command. K_{loc} is used, for example, to protect locally stored files or the secret-key data, SKD, in the public-key file. K_T is a temporary DES key generated and entered into the SST with the GenDESKey command, and loaded for encryption/decryption with the LoadDESKeyTemp command. K_T is used, for example, for encryption of secret letters or for communication via a protected two-way channel. PK.U and SK.U are the public and the secret RSA keys, respectively, of the user, U, presently signed in; p.U and q.U are the corresponding factors of n.U, the modulus needed for RSA encryption/decryption. The owner of a set of key data stores the factors p.U and q.U rather than the product n.U itself

IEEE MICRO

because knowing the factors can be used to speed up the decryption.[12] The whole set of RSA key data is loaded during SignIn from the public-key file.

The second part of the security status table is the key stack. As will be described in the section on software, the CP continuously generates, as a background task, new pairs of public and secret keys along with their respective p and q factors. The results of this key generation are stored in the key stack on a first-in, first-out basis. The key stack ensures that keys are available without delay, although the time needed for one key generation may be rather long. When a user requests new RSA keys, the GiveNewKeyPair command fetches them from the key stack and overwrites their location so that no other user can get the same keys. Since GiveNewKeyPair is the only command which manipulates the key stack, it is impossible to inspect keys and put them back and thereby to compromise the next user requesting new keys. The CP is not responsible for updating the public-key file; that has to be done by the host. At present the depth of the key stack is three.

Due to the complexity of the RSA key generation algorithm, its generation rate is usually low. Therefore the part of the RAM that holds the key stack should be nonvolatile so that generated keys can be kept available after power turn-off/turn-on sequences.

Software

Upon restart the CP executes its initialization procedure, including a self test, and then enters an endless loop for key generation (Figure 5). The generation of one set of 300-bit keys takes about one hour, which is long compared to the time needed for the execution of the different cryptocommands. A request for a cryptoservice is signaled by the host with an interrupt (INTR.1). The CP command interpreter, with further interrupts disabled, reads the command and some of the parameters from mailbox B in the shared memory (Figure 6) and branches to the respective CP service routine. After the results have been written back into mailbox A in the shared memory, the host is notified with an interrupt (INTR.2), the CP interrupts are re-enabled, and the key generation is resumed.

It is the host's responsibility to guarantee the proper sequence of service requests. Only one request can be serviced at a time. Since the CP is designed for use in a personal computing environment, its architecture supports single-user operation only. This is reflected in the existence of only one security status table with one block of present user information.

The key generation program uses the probabilistic primality test described by Knuth.[13] We use ten test rounds with independent random numbers, resulting in a probability of $(1/4)^{10}$ of having picked a number which is not prime.

The key generator and the CP service routine use three types of low-level services (Figure 7): random number generation, DES encryption/decryption, and multiword arithmetic. The random number generator is implemented in software with an externally supplied seed value. The algorithm used in Knuth's linear congruential method.[14]

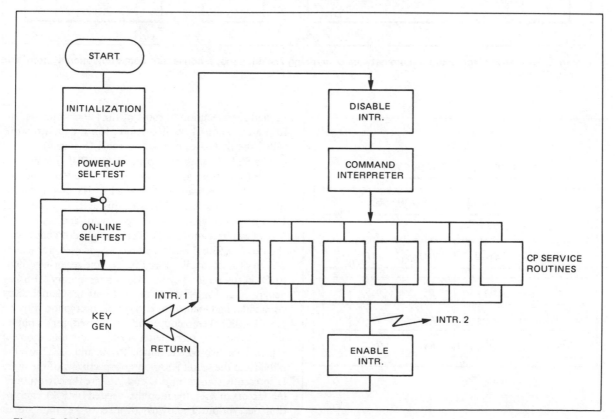

Figure 5. Software structure of the cryptoprocessor.

October 1983

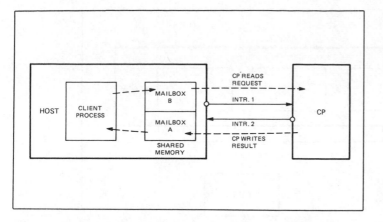

Figure 6. Communication between the host and the cryptoprocessor.

Replacing the manual seed value input with a hardware random number generator is desirable. If this is done, however, it is crucial that the hardware be on the CP board and be protected from physical manipulation. DES encryption/decryption is performed by a Western Digital WD2001 cryptochip.

The most critical portion is multiword arithmetic (MWA), since it is the basis for the time-consuming RSA-related operations on words of arbitrary length (multiwords). The MWA can be compiled with a word length of any integral multiple of 16 bits. The subroutines of MWA comprise shift left, shift right, multi-word compare, addition, subtraction, multiplication, modular multiplication, modular division, and modular exponentiation. To support key generation, procedures to calculate the Jacobi symbol and to find relative primes and random primes are provided. Modular exponentiation corresponds to RSA encryption and decryption operations and is performed by repeated squaring and multiplication.[4]

The subroutine with the longest overall run time (i.e., individual run time times the number of subroutine calls) is modular division (DIVMOD). It is the bottleneck of modular multiplication and modular exponentiation and, hence, of RSA encryption/decryption. DIVMOD has been repeatedly optimized. The algorithm is implemented by repeated shifting and subtractions. All programs of the MWA have been written in 8086 assembly language. The key generation program and the CP service routines have been written in Pascal and PL/M 86.

Hardware

The cryptoprocessor is realized as a single-board computer based on the Intel 8086 microprocessor. Its clock rate is 5 MHz, but a faster 8-MHz version is also available. The board is IEEE-796-bus-compatible. The program resides in an 8K-byte ROM. The RAM which holds the security status table and buffers for cleartext and ciphertext is also 8K bytes in size. The part of the RAM containing the key stack should be replaced by an E^2ROM.

The memory is not dual-ported; hence, access only from the on-board 8086 is allowed. An 8259A programmable interrupt controller receives the interrupts from the host and starts the interrupt service routine (command interpreter). Interrupts originating from the CP are initiated by the 8086 CPU via an output port. The encryption rate of the Western Digital WD2001 DES chip is 1.3M bits per second if clocked with 2 MHz (excluding software overhead).

The RSA key generation, encryption, and decryption are done entirely in software. Although a special RSA chip will eventually be available,[15] simpler hardware is sufficient to speed up the RSA algorithms adequately. Figure 8 gives an overview of the CP hardware.

Performance

Our discussion of the performance of the CP concentrates on the bottleneck, the RSA algorithm, since no other performance problems are encountered. As long as special hardware is not yet implemented, key generation and encryption/decryption have to be performed in software. Key generation is not a major problem since it can run in the background without high speed requirements. For the generation of one pair of 320-bit keys, our 8086 system takes about one hour. Since usually only a few users share a terminal and since they typically request new keys only once every half-year or year, a key generation rate of 24 keys per day seems quite sufficient.

Software encryption rates, on the other hand, are a problem. Here one has to trade off carefully between short encryption times and long system breaking times. System breaking times is the time needed for an intruder to find a secret key. Breaking the RSA system can be based on factoring the modulus $n.U$. The fastest known factoring algorithm[4] has a run time on the order of

$$\exp\left((\ln n)\cdot(\ln(\ln n)) \right),$$

where n is the number to be factored—in our case, $n.U$. Figure 9 shows measured software encryption times for an 8086 versus system breaking times according to the above formula. One microsecond per operation was assumed. A conversion from Pascal to assembly language (ASSEMBLY1) resulted in a considerable speed improvement. The fine tuning of some basic routines produced an additional speed-up by a factor of 2. These measurements were made on the 5-MHz cryptoprocessor. Curve fitting resulted in a formula for the encryption time t as follows:

$$t = 0.1 \cdot WDS^{2.65} \text{ sec,}$$

where WDS = key length in 16-bit words. Encryptions with the 8-MHz 8086 are about 38 percent faster than with the 5-MHz system.

A system with a key length of 18 words (288 bits) provides a medium degree of security—it has an estimated breaking time of $1.3 \cdot 10^8$ seconds (= 4.2 years). For this case, the two encryptions needed for a secret and signed letter take about four minutes at 8 MHz. This is accep-

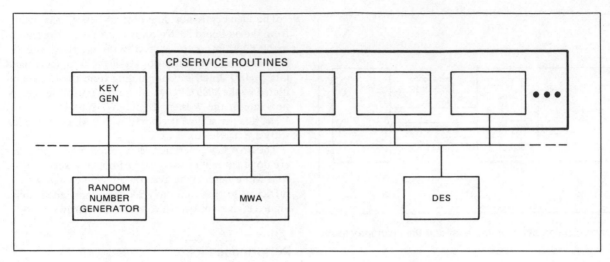

Figure 7. CP service routines and low-level services.

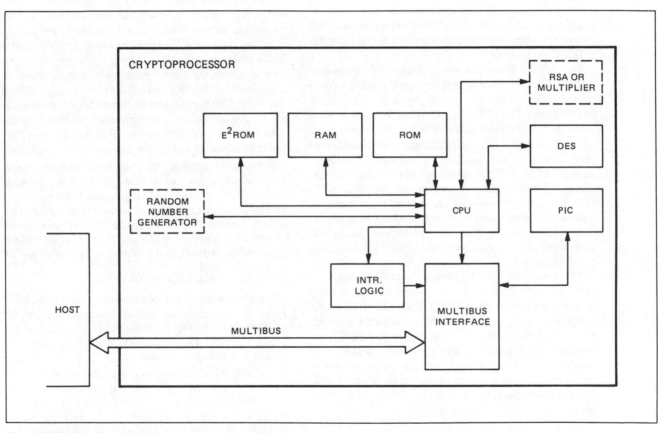

Figure 8. Hardware organization of the cryptoprocessor.

table in an electronic mail system if letters are processed off line. With the addition of special hardware (e.g., a 16 × 16 multiplier), it should be possible to improve the times by an order of magnitude. This means that the processing of a letter should take 150 seconds with 512-bit keys. The factoring time of $2 \cdot 10^6$ years should contain an adequate security margin unless a dramatically improved factoring algorithm is found.

Although the encryption rate of the RSA chip (0.43 seconds per encryption or 1200 bits per second, with 512-bit keys[15]) may not be sufficient for high-volume on-line encryption, it is very satisfactory in a hybrid system. Even a less complex chip that performs only modular exponentiation would be adequate.

Security considerations

The overall security of our system depends on two assumptions:

364

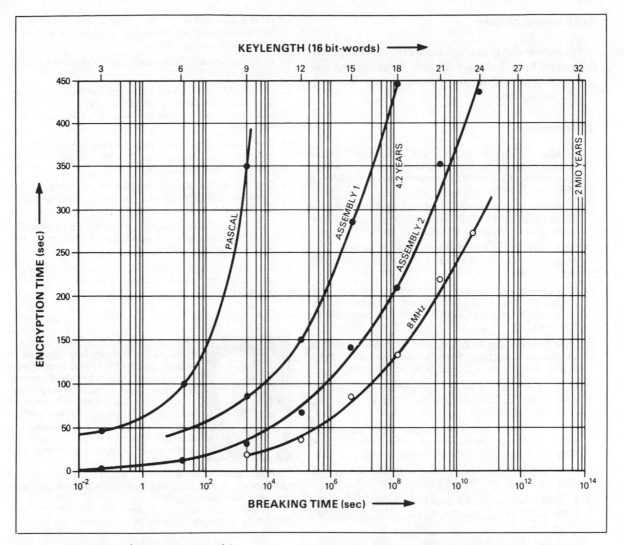

KEYLENGTH (16 bit-words)

BREAKING TIME (sec)

Figure 9. Measured (●) and calculated (○) encryption times vs. estimated system breaking times for different versions of the cryptoprocessor. The performances of PASCAL, ASSEMBLY1, and ASSEMBLY2 were measured on the 5-MHz 8086-based CP. The curve farthest to the right shows the speed-up of ASSEMBLY2 that would result from using the 8-MHz 8086-based CP.

- The DES and RSA algorithms are cryptographically strong. At present there exist no indications of weaknesses in either one. The recently reported breaking of the knapsack algorithm by Adi Shamir should not influence the security of the RSA scheme, since it is based on a different one-way function. However, if the RSA system proves to be weak, a different public-key algorithm can be "plugged in" to the cryptoprocessor. If the DES key length proves to be too short, a triple encryption[16] can be employed.
- The workstation and the cryptoprocessor are secure. Measures like unique identification and encapsulation of the CP are employed, possibly in conjunction with direct password input to the CP, to prevent breaches in security.

Cryptographic techniques put certain constraints on the design of secure communication networks. One of these is the requirement that cryptographic processing

take place as close as possible to the user, i.e., in his terminal or personal computer. Because of the complexity of the algorithms involved, expecially those employed in public-key cryptosystems, a dedicated cryptomodule is desirable. The cryptoprocessor described in this article provides a fixed high-level instruction set to the host-computer application programmer without requiring him to have in-depth crypto-related knowledge. It is a hybrid system—it uses the Data Encryption Standard as well as the RSA public-key system.

An experimental realization of the cryptoprocessor based on an IEEE-796-bus-compatible 8086 single-board computer showed the feasibility of the concept, at least for medium-security applications with an RSA key length of around 300 bits. With special hardware (a fast multiplier of an RSA chip), even faster high-security systems should be possible. ∎

365

Acknowledgments

The author wishes to thank Felix Bretschneider, Mary Ervin, and Mike Rottinger for their programming support and Neal Wagner and Patrick Fasang for many helpful suggestions.

References

1. H. Lagger, C. Müller-Schloer, and H. Unterberger, "Security Aspects of Computer-Controlled Communication Systems" (in German), *Elektronische Rechenanlagen,* Vol. 22, No. 6, 1980, pp. 276-280.

2. "Data Encryption Standard," Federal Information Processing Standard (FIPS) Publication No. 46, National Bureau of Standards, Washington, DC, Jan. 1977.

3. M.E. Hellman, "The Mathematics of Public-Key Cryptography," *Scientific American,* Vol. 241, No. 2, Aug. 1979, pp. 146-157.

4. R. L. Rivest, A. Shamir, and L. Adleman, "A Method for Obtaining Digital Signatures and Public-Key Cryptosystems," *Comm. ACM,* Vol. 21, No. 2, Feb. 1978, pp. 120-126.

5. R.M. Needham and M.D. Schroeder, "Using Encryption for Authentication in Large Networks of Computers," *Comm. ACM,* Vol. 21, No. 12, Dec. 1978, pp. 993-999.

6. G. J. Popek and C. S. Kline, "Encryption and Secure Computer Networks," *Computing Surveys,* Vol. 11, No. 4, Dec. 1979, pp. 331-356.

7. C. Müller-Schloer and N. R. Wagner, "The Implementation of a Cryptography-based Secure Office System," *AFIPS Conf. Proc.,* Vol. 51, 1982 NCC, pp. 487-492.

8. B. G. Kolata, "New Codes Coming into Use," *Science,* Vol. 208, May 1980, pp. 694-695.

9. C. Müller-Schloer, "DES-generated Checksums for Electronic Signatures," *Cryptologia,* Vol. 7, No. 3, July 1983, pp. 257-273.

10. D. W. Davies and W. L. Price, "The Application of Digital Signatures Based on Public-Key Cryptosystems," *Proc. ICCC 1980,* Atlanta, GA.

11. C. Müller-Schloer, "Registered Mail," US Patent Application No. VPA 81 E 8223.

12. M. O. Rabin, "Digitalized Signatures and Public-Key Functions as Intractable as Factorization," tech. report, Laboratory for Computer Science, MIT, Cambridge, MA, Jan. 1979.

13. D. E. Knuth, *The Art of Computer Programming—Vol. 2, Seminumerical Algorithms,* 2nd ed., Addison-Wesley, Reading, MA, 1981, p. 379.

14. D. E. Knuth, *The Art of Computer Programming—Vol. 2, Seminumerical Algorithms,* 2nd ed., Addison-Wesley, Reading, MA, 1981, pp. 9-24.

15. R. L. Rivest, "A Description of a Single-Chip Implementation of the RSA Cipher," *Lambda* (now *VLSI Design*), Vol. 1, No. 3, 4th qtr. 1980, pp. 14-18.

16. R. C. Merkle and M. E. Hellman, "On the Security of Multiple Encryption," *Comm. ACM,* Vol. 24, No. 7, July 1981, pp. 465-467.

Christian Müller-Schloer leads a custom IC group at the Siemens Research Labs in Munich. From 1980 to 1982 he worked at the Siemens Research Labs in Princeton, New Jersey, on the design of secure communication systems. From 1977, when he joined Siemens, to 1980 he was involved in the development of CAD systems and electronic communication systems for office automation and electronic mail applications.

Müller-Schloer received an MSEE from the Technical University, Munich, in 1975 and a PhD in semiconductor physics from the same institution in 1977.

Müller-Schloer's address is Siemens AG, ZTI SYS 222, Otto Hahn Ring 6, 8000 Munich 83, West Germany.

366